HISTORY OF THE SECOND WORLD WAR

UNITED KINGDOM MILITARY SERIES

Edited by SIR JAMES BUTLER

The authors of the Military Histories have been given full access to official documents. They and the editor are alone responsible for the statements made and the views expressed.

THE MEDITERRANEAN AND MIDDLE EAST

VOLUME III

(September 1941 to September 1942)

British Fortunes reach their Lowest Ebb

BY

MAJOR-GENERAL I. S. O. PLAYFAIR
C.B., D.S.O., M.C.

WITH
CAPTAIN F. C. FLYNN, R.N.
BRIGADIER C. J. C. MOLONY
GROUP CAPTAIN T. P. GLEAVE, C.B.E.

This edition of The Mediterranean and Middle East: Volume III
first published in 2004
by The Naval & Military Press Ltd

Published by
The Naval & Military Press Ltd
Unit 10 Ridgewood Industrial Park,
Uckfield, East Sussex,
TN22 5QE England
Tel: +44 (0) 1825 749494
Fax: +44 (0) 1825 765701
www.naval-military-press.com

The Mediterranean and Middle East: Volume III first published in 1960.
© Crown copyright. Reprinted with the permission of
the Controller of HMSO and Queen's Printer for Scotland.

In reprinting in facsimile from the original, any imperfections are inevitably reproduced and the quality may fall short of modern type and cartographic standards.

Printed and bound by Antony Rowe Ltd, Eastbourne

CONTENTS

Page

INTRODUCTION xv

CHAPTER I. THE GROWTH OF THE 'CRUSADER' PLAN

Reorganization of the Army 1
The plan in outline 5
The administrative implications 9
The Royal Air Force's preparations 12
The enemy picture 19
The situation at Tobruk 22
The armoured forces compared 26

CHAPTER II. THE WINTER BATTLE, 1941, ('CRUSADER')—I

The conditions 33
The first encounters (18th and 19th November) . . 38
The *D.A.K.* moves east (20th November) . . . 41
Sidi Rezegh and the sortie from Tobruk (21st–23rd November) 44
Rommel's dash for the frontier (24th November) . . 53
The *D.A.K.* on the frontier (25th–27th November) . . 56
The fighting south-east of Tobruk (25th–26th November) and return of the *D.A.K.* 61
Sidi Rezegh, El Duda, Belhamed (28th November–1st December) 64
The stage reached by 1st December 66

CHAPTER III. THE WINTER BATTLE—II

The fighting at Bir el Gubi and the relief of Tobruk. . 73
The enemy's stand at Gazala (1st–16th December 1941) . 81
The pursuit to Benghazi (16th–24th December) . . 84
The fighting round Agedabia 88
The air situation at the end of the year 92
The reduction of the frontier defences (16th December–17th January) 94
Some aspects of 'Crusader' in retrospect . . . 96

Page

CHAPTER IV. THE STRUGGLE FOR SEA COMMUNICATIONS (NOVEMBER–DECEMBER 1941)

Force K's successes against Axis shipping 103
Loss of the *Ark Royal* and the *Barham* 108
The night encounter off Cape Bon 109
The First Battle of Sirte and the disaster to Force K . . 110
The *Queen Elizabeth* and the *Valiant* damaged by human torpedoes 115
The Mediterranean Fleet at the close of 1941 117

CHAPTER V. THE SITUATION AFTER THE ENTRY OF JAPAN INTO THE WAR

The exploitation of 'Crusader' 119
Diversions and withdrawals from the Middle East . . 122
The command in Persia and Iraq 128
The political crisis in Egypt 130
The German view 131

CHAPTER VI. RETREAT TO GAZALA

The position in Western Cyrenaica 135
The enemy's intentions 139
The advance begins 140
1st Armoured Division avoids the net 143
The move on Benghazi 149
Withdrawal from the Jebel 151
Some disquieting thoughts 152

CHAPTER VII. MALTA CONVOYS AND THE SECOND BATTLE OF SIRTE

Malta convoys in January 1942 155
The enemy's 'Battleship convoys' 158
The February convoy fails 159
Conditions in Malta in January and February . . 161
The March convoy and the Second Battle of Sirte . . 163
Air and submarine operations 173
Axis designs on Malta 174

CHAPTER VIII. MALTA'S GREATEST TRIAL (APRIL–MAY 1942)

Admiral Cunningham departs 177
April: climax of the German attack 178
May: the raids slacken, but Malta has been neutralized . 184
Axis plans and preparations 193

Page

CHAPTER IX. THE LULL IN THE DESERT (FEBRUARY–MAY 1942)
The question of a new offensive 197
The R.A.F. and its problems 205
The Army's dispositions and plans. 213
The enemy's intentions 219

CHAPTER X. THE BATTLE OF GAZALA (26TH MAY–15TH JUNE)
The enemy's advance is stopped (26th–29th May) . . 223
The enemy tears open a gap at Sidi Muftah (30th May–1st June) 228
The Cauldron disaster (5th–6th June) 231
The loss of Bir Hacheim (10th June) 235
The defeat of the British armour (11th–13th June). . 239
The problem of Tobruk (15th–16th June) 245
The withdrawal from the Gazala position (14th–15th June) 249

CHAPTER XI. THE BATTLE OF GAZALA (CONTD.): THE LOSS OF TOBRUK
The problems of the 8th Army and the Desert Air Force . 253
The Tobruk defences 260
General Rommel's plan 265
The defensive battle 267
Events leading to the surrender 271
Conclusion. 273

CHAPTER XII. THE RETREAT TO EL ALAMEIN
The change in Axis strategy 277
The decision not to stand on the frontier 279
The delaying action of the Desert Air Force . . . 281
General Auchinleck takes command 284
The fighting of 26th and 27th June 287
The 10th Corps left in the lurch 293
Back to El Alamein 295

CHAPTER XIII. MALTA AND THE WAR AT SEA (JUNE–SEPTEMBER 1942)
The Malta convoys in June—'Harpoon'. 299
'Vigorous'. 307
The Navy leaves Alexandria. 315
The August convoy to Malta—'Pedestal' 316
The battle of supplies 323

Page

CHAPTER XIV. THE FIGHTING IN THE EL ALAMEIN LINE

The El Alamein line 331
Outline of the July fighting 334
The part played by the Desert Air Force 335
The enemy's situation 338
Rommel's advance is held (1st–4th July) 340
The British attack at Tell el Eisa (10th–14th July) . . 345
'First Ruweisat' (14th–17th July) 347
'Second Ruweisat' (El Mreir) (21st–22nd July) . . 353
The last British attack—at Miteirya (26th July) . . 357

CHAPTER XV. THE MOMENTOUS DECISIONS OF JULY AND AUGUST 1942

The shape of future strategy 361
Changes in Command 367
Growing strength 371
American organization in the Middle East . . . 373
The Persia and Iraq Command 375
Changes in the Axis Command 377

CHAPTER XVI. AUGUST 1942 AND THE BATTLE OF ALAM EL HALFA

Air operations 379
The enemy's intentions 381
The defence plan 384
The battle 385

CONCLUSION 392

CHRONOLOGY OF MAIN EVENTS FROM SEPTEMBER 1941 TO SEPTEMBER 1942 394

INDEX 461

APPENDICES

Page

APPENDIX 1. Principal Commanders and Staff Officers in the Mediterranean and Middle East 401

APPENDIX 2. Principal Italian and German Commanders and Staff Officers 407

APPENDIX 3. Strength of the opposing Fleets 409

APPENDIX 4. Distribution of the Army 412

APPENDIX 5. Distribution of the Royal Air Force . . 414

APPENDIX 6. A note on the Persia and Iraq Command . 424

APPENDIX 7. A note on artillery weapons 427

APPENDIX 8. A note on tanks, armour, and anti-tank guns. 434

APPENDIX 9. Some particulars of British and enemy aircraft 445

APPENDIX 10. Arrivals of reinforcement aircraft. . . . 458

APPENDIX 11. Operational code names 460

MAPS AND DIAGRAMS

Facing page

1. The Mediterranean and Middle East Theatre of War . xvii
2. The Western Desert, November 1941 1

'Crusader'—the opening moves, 18th–21st November

3. 18th Nov. Dispositions after the British advance . . 37
4. 19th Nov. Capture of Sidi Rezegh airfield . . . 37
5. 20th Nov. Moves of the *D.A.K.* 37
6. 21st Nov. Break out from Tobruk 37

'Crusader'—Sidi Rezegh and the frontier

7. 21st Nov. The German armour hurries north . . 45
8. 22nd Nov. Loss of Sidi Rezegh airfield . . . 45
9. 23rd Nov. Destruction of 5th South African Brigade . 45
10. 24–26th Nov. Rommel's dash to the frontier . . 45

'Crusader'—Renewed fighting round Sidi Rezegh

11. 27th–28th Nov. Return of the Panzer Divisions . . 63
12. 29th Nov. Attack on El Duda and loss of Pt 175 . . 63
13. 30th Nov.–1st Dec. Sidi Rezegh and Belhamed . . 63
14. 4th–5th Dec. Bir el Gubi and Tobruk . . . 63

15. Attempt to turn the Gazala position 81
16. The pursuit by 13th Corps 83
17. Operations at Halfaya and Bardia 93
18. Action off Cape Bon, night of 12/13th December . . 109
19. Fleet movements, 16th–18th December 111
20. Attack by Human Torpedoes at Alexandria . . *page* 116
21. The enemy's advance to Benghazi, January 1942 . *facing* 135
22. Fleet movements, 21st–23rd March 1942 . . . 163
23. Action in the Gulf of Sirte, 22nd March 165
24. Malta, showing airfields in April 1942 177
25. Gazala: dispositions at dawn 27th May 1942 . . . 215
26. Rommel concentrates in the Cauldron 225
27. British plan of attack on the Cauldron 225
28. The decisive armoured actions of 12th–13th June . . 225

Facing page

29. Tobruk, 20th June 1942 261
30. The Delta and Western Desert of Egypt, summer 1942 . 281
31. Matruh, 26th–27th June 283
32. Convoy to Malta: operation 'Harpoon', 14th–15th June. 301
33. Operation 'Harpoon': action on 15th June . . . 301
34. Operation 'Vigorous', 14th–16th June 309
35. Convoy to Malta: operation 'Pedestal', 11th–13th August 317
36. The end of Rommel's advance: El Alamein, 2nd July . 331
37. 'First Ruweisat', 14th–15th July 347
38. 'Second Ruweisat' (El Mreir), 21st July 347
39. Alam el Halfa: Rommel's plan of attack on 30th August . 379
40. Persia and Iraq 425

PHOTOGRAPHS

Most of the photographs are Crown Copyright and are reproduced by courtesy of the Imperial War Museum and the Ministries concerned.

Meeting of 'All the Talents' at Cairo, August 1942 *Frontispiece*

1. The loss of H.M.S. *Ark Royal*, November 1941
2. British cruisers at the Second Battle of Sirte
3. H.M.S. *Breconshire*, hit and disabled
4. The *Pampas* bombed in harbour, Malta
5. Albacores over Malta
6. The bombing of Floriana, Malta, April 1942
7. R.A.F. attack on a German airfield
8. Benghazi harbour, January 1942

following page 100

9. The Infantry tank Matilda
10. The Valentine, used first as an 'I' tank and later as a cruiser
11. American light tank, General Stuart
12. American medium tank, General Grant
13. British cruiser tank, Crusader
14. A British tank transporter
15. German Pzkw III Special with long 5-cm gun and spaced armour
16. Pzkw III with short 5-cm gun
17. Pzkw IV with short 7·5-cm gun
18. Pzkw IV Special with long 7·5-cm gun
19. German half-tracked infantry carrier
20. Italian M 13/40 medium tank
21. British 2-pdr anti-tank gun portée
22. 25-pdr field guns
23. 6-pdr anti-tank gun
24. 40-mm Bofors, the British light A.A. gun
25. German 5-cm *Pak* 38 anti-tank gun
26. The 8·8-cm *Flak* 36 on its trailer
27. British 4·5-inch gun
28. British 3·7-inch heavy A.A. gun
29. The Bishop self-propelled gun
30. Humber armoured car
31. Italian 75/18 self-propelled gun
32. Bren carriers

following page 244

33. German A.A. gunners in action against the R.A.F.
34. The end of a Ju. 87 (Stuka) . . . .
35. Bostons taking off from a desert airfield . .
36. Flight of Hurricanes over the desert . .
37. Operation 'Pedestal': H.M.S. *Victorious*, *Indomitable* and *Eagle* . . . .
38. H.M.S. *Indomitable* hit, 12th August 1942 . .
39. Operation 'Pedestal': the damaged *Ohio* being nursed into harbour . . . . . .
40. The *Ohio* in the Grand Harbour, Malta, August 1942 . . . .

following page 324

INTRODUCTION

THE first of this series of six volumes covered the opening stages of the war in the Mediterranean and Middle East, where by early in 1941 the British had scored great successes over the Italians at sea, in East Africa, and in the Western Desert. Germany then came to the help of her ally, and our second volume told how the British were bundled out of Greece and Crete and lost nearly all their gains in the Western Desert. But they still held their vital bases—Gibraltar, Malta and Egypt—and in the autumn of 1941 they were able, with strength growing, morale high, and resolution unweakened by past shocks and setbacks, to try once more to drive the Axis forces from the Western Desert. With this offensive the present volume opens.

In our first volume we pointed out the need to take constant account of the weapons and equipment which were developing so rapidly under the stimulus of war. The period covered by the present volume saw many innovations, some of the most important being those which bore upon the perpetual struggle between tanks and the various means of countering them—armour, guns and mines. Stages in this struggle are summed up in the text from time to time, and relevant details are given in Appendices 7 and 8. In 1941 and early 1942 the British had a great deal of leeway to make up in arms and equipment. Their shortcomings of 1939 had been made worse by the appalling losses in France in 1940, and the resulting plight forced them to keep on manufacturing many obsolescent weapons—because it was these weapons or nothing until the plant to make new types could be set up. The Germans, on the other hand, in settling the basic design of much of their armament by pre-war research and practical trials, had allowed for developments; after the campaign in France, for example, they were able to make improvements to their tanks with little delay and without interfering with production.

It should therefore cause no surprise to read in the present volume that the British armoured forces in the Middle East were still handicapped in several ways. Before the (American) Grant tank and the 6-pdr anti-tank gun came upon the scene tank crews were conscious of being continually at a disadvantage, and felt that the British equipment was partly to blame. For instance, their tanks easily caught fire—the Crusader was the worst offender—a horrible fact upon which the enemy remarked. The British crews deserve admiration for their steadfastness in this bad period, coming up again and again to endure punishment and to strive to return it.

At this point it is right to recall once more that, important as the material factors were, the usefulness of weapons and all the other aids to success in battle lay in the hands of the men who served and tended them. This thought might well stand as a headline to every page of this book, as a reminder of the men whose conduct was of such outstanding importance in this tale of thronging events, but has in the main to be taken for granted. It may be recalled, too, that the purpose of the 'campaign volumes' of this History is to provide a broad survey of events from an inter-Service point of view. A volume which covers a whole crowded year of struggle by sea, land, and air must leave out a great deal, and to the usual difficulty of deciding what to discard is added the problem of keeping a fair balance. Our aim has been to tell a story which will show the essential unity of the war in this theatre and the dependence of the Services on one another. Above all, in following the fighting in the Western Desert it must be remembered that the British were able to fight there at all, or indeed anywhere in the Mediterranean and Middle East, only because the sea communications with their sources of supply were kept open.

By 1942 the pressure on space becomes intense and the accounts of the Army's operations tend to deal more and more with the principal actors and the larger formations, and to exclude—to our great regret—many exciting adventures of units and detachments. A great deal of hard, devoted, and often gallant work by the supporting arms and ancillary services must also be taken for granted.

The same is true of the air forces, with the added difficulty that the results of their operations over the land cannot be expressed in terms of ground won or lost. Their activities were diverse: protecting bases and lines of communication, attacking those of the enemy several hundred miles away, attacking the opposing air forces, intervening directly in the land fighting, and so on. The results can best be judged over a period, for the air's influence on the land battle was cumulative. In this theatre it is rarely possible to be sure of the result of any particular attack, but when evidence has come to light we give it. Our method in general is to describe the effort expended on a particular mission in terms of the number of sorties flown over a period. We often set out the figures as so many aircraft every 24 hours, a scale which is reasonably easy to picture. We hope in this way to give the reader a yardstick with which to measure the steady growth of the British air effort and to compare the intensity of attacks on the more important targets. We possess fairly complete records of the *Luftwaffe's* day by day losses in aircraft from all causes, and less complete, though useful, details of those of the Italians.

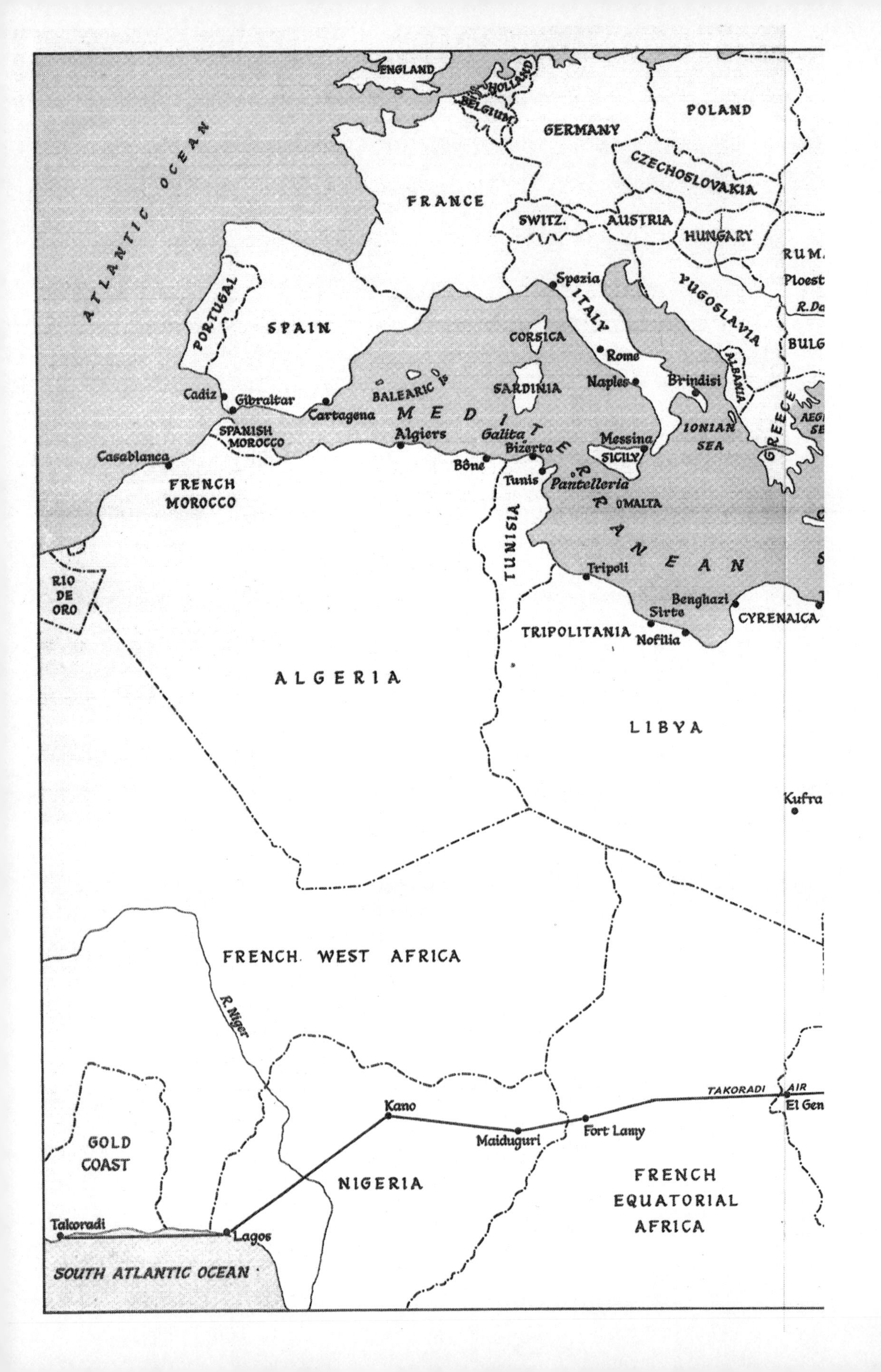

ENGLAND
HOLLAND
BELGIUM
POLAND
GERMANY
CZECHOSLOVAKIA
ATLANTIC OCEAN
FRANCE
SWITZ.
AUSTRIA
HUNGARY
PORTUGAL
SPAIN
Spezia
ITALY
YUGOSLAVIA
CORSICA
Rome
ALBANIA
SARDINIA
Naples
Brindisi
BALEARIC IS
Cadiz
Gibraltar
Cartagena
MEDITERRANEAN
SPANISH MOROCCO
Algiers
Galita
Bizerta
Messina
IONIAN SEA
GREECE
Casablanca
Bône
Tunis
SICILY
Pantelleria
FRENCH MOROCCO
MALTA
TUNISIA
RIO DE ORO
Tripoli
Benghazi
Sirte
CYRENAICA
TRIPOLITANIA
Nofilia
ALGERIA
LIBYA
Kufra
FRENCH WEST AFRICA
R. Niger
TAKORADI AIR
Kano
Maiduguri
Fort Lamy
GOLD COAST
NIGERIA
FRENCH EQUATORIAL AFRICA
Takoradi
Lagos
SOUTH ATLANTIC OCEAN

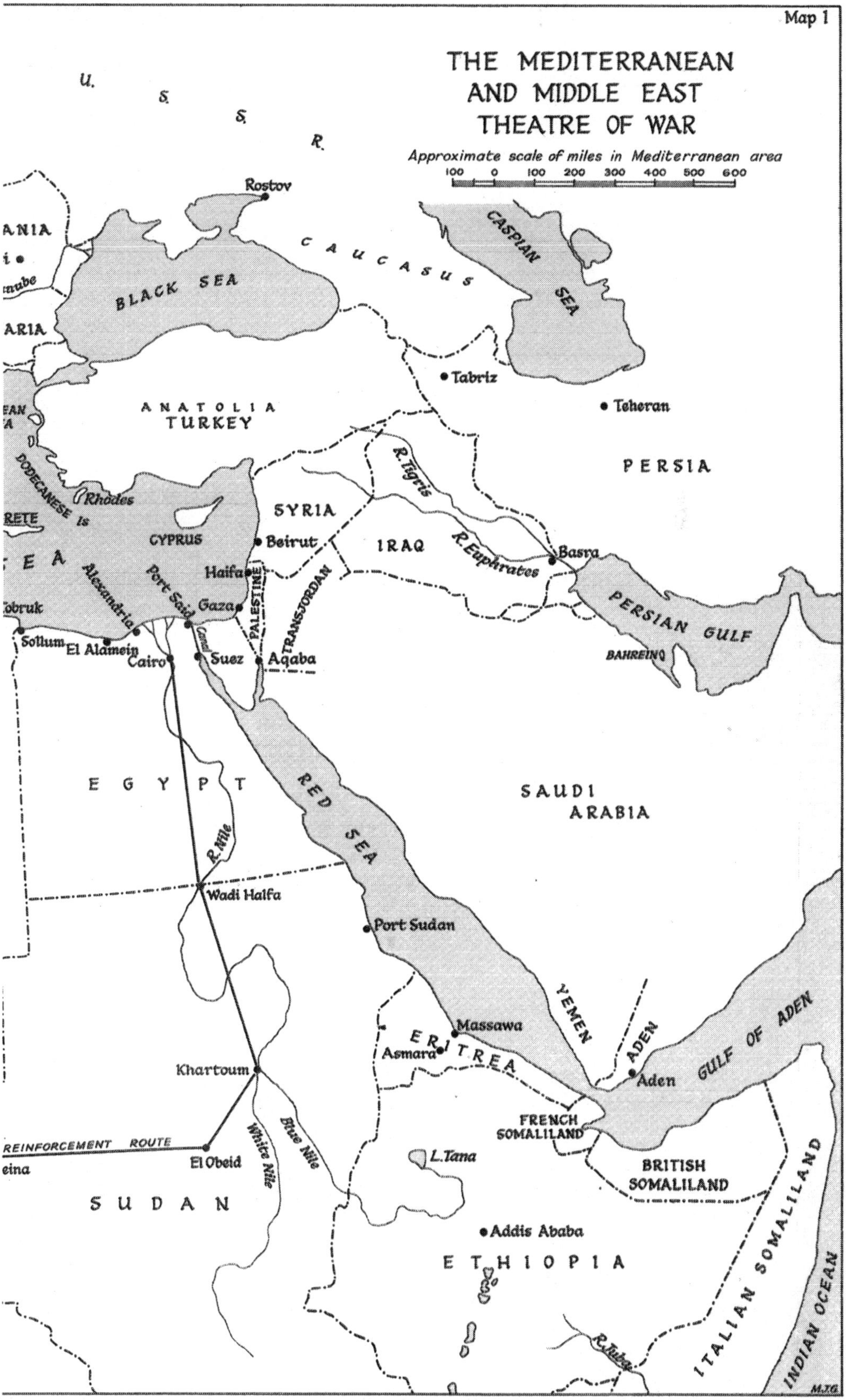

Map 1

THE MEDITERRANEAN AND MIDDLE EAST THEATRE OF WAR

Approximate scale of miles in Mediterranean area

100 0 100 200 300 400 500 600

U. S. S. R.

Rostov

BLACK SEA

CAUCASUS

CASPIAN SEA

Tabriz

Teheran

ANATOLIA
TURKEY

PERSIA

R. Tigris

R. Euphrates

Basra

SYRIA

IRAQ

Beirut

Haifa

PALESTINE

TRANSJORDAN

Gaza

CYPRUS

Rhodes

DODECANESE Is

Alexandria

Port Said

Canal

Suez

Aqaba

Tobruk

Sollum

El Alamein

Cairo

PERSIAN GULF

BAHREIN

EGYPT

R. Nile

RED SEA

SAUDI ARABIA

Wadi Halfa

Port Sudan

YEMEN

ADEN

Aden

GULF OF ADEN

Massawa

Asmara

ERITREA

Khartoum

FRENCH SOMALILAND

BRITISH SOMALILAND

REINFORCEMENT ROUTE

El Obeid

White Nile

Blue Nile

L. Tana

SUDAN

Addis Ababa

ETHIOPIA

ITALIAN SOMALILAND

R. Juba

INDIAN OCEAN

M.J.G.

A word is needed about Orders of Battle. That of the Mediterranean Fleet (App. 3) presents no difficulty. The forces controlled by the Royal Air Force, Middle East Command, varied but slightly over quite long periods, and we have given in App. 5 the Order of Battle of all the Middle East air forces in November 1941, and of the Western Desert Air Force in May 1942 (at the beginning of the fighting at Gazala) and in September 1942 (during the battle of Alam el Halfa). In the case of the Army, however, there were a great many units that one would like to mention, but they were frequently being changed about or temporarily re-grouped. For this reason alone a comprehensive Order of Battle would be unmanageable and a selective one misleading. We therefore show in App. 4 the outline distribution of the Army in October 1941 and again in May 1942, and either in the text or in a footnote we give the actual composition of formations whenever it seems necessary.

Most of the photographs reproduced in the two previous volumes were chosen to illustrate conditions on different fronts. But after the summer of 1941 the fighting on land is confined to the Western Desert, so we have now been able to make room for illustrations of some of the most important weapons and equipment used by both sides in 1941 and 1942.

We have been helped in our work by many persons with first-hand knowledge who have been good enough to read our drafts. We have had the benefit of comments by the Official Historian of Australia, Mr. Gavin Long; of New Zealand, the late Sir Howard Kippenberger and Brigadier M. C. Fairbrother; of the Union of South Africa, Mr. J. A. I. Agar-Hamilton; also by Dr. Kent R. Greenfield and Brig.-General Paul M. Robinett of the Office of the Chief of Military History, Washington, D.C. We have had much help from the Heads of the Historical Branches, Commander P. K. Kemp, Brigadier H. B. Latham and Mr. J. C. Nerney, and from the Archivists, Librarians, and Keepers of the various records and photographs in the Cabinet Office, the Ministries, and the Imperial War Museum, and their staffs. We have had the use of narratives compiled by Brigadier G. F. Ellenberger, Lieut.-Colonel G. R. Johnson, Lieut.-Colonel M. E. S. Laws, and Squadron Leader G. T. Johns. Others who have helped us particularly with this volume are Commanders G. A. Titterton and L. J. Pitcairn-Jones, Brigadier W. P. Pessell and Squadron Leader W. M. Mills. On German and Italian documents we have been helped by Mr. B. M. Melland and Commander M. G. Saunders, and in particular by Mrs. J. M. Hamilton and Squadron Leader L. A. Jackets; also by Dr. G. W. S. Friedrichsen, who has handled for us the German material in the United States. All but a few of the maps have been drawn by Mr. M. J. Godliman and Mr. D. K. Purle, of the Cabinet Office Mapping Section, under the direction of Colonel

T. M. M. Penney. General research has been done by Mrs. G. F. Oakley, Miss Jean Burt, and Miss D. F. Butler, and secretarial work and the typing of drafts by Miss D. G. Plant. To all these, and to the Editor for his unfailing support and advice, we wish to express our gratitude.

I. S. O. P.
F. C. F.
C. J. C. M.
T. P. G.

'An army is of little value in the field unless there are wise counsels at home.'

CICERO: *De Officiis*

'Excellent as our tactical achievements were in all theatres of war, there was not that solid strategic foundation which would have directed our tactical skill into the right channels.'

ROMMEL: *Krieg ohne Hass*

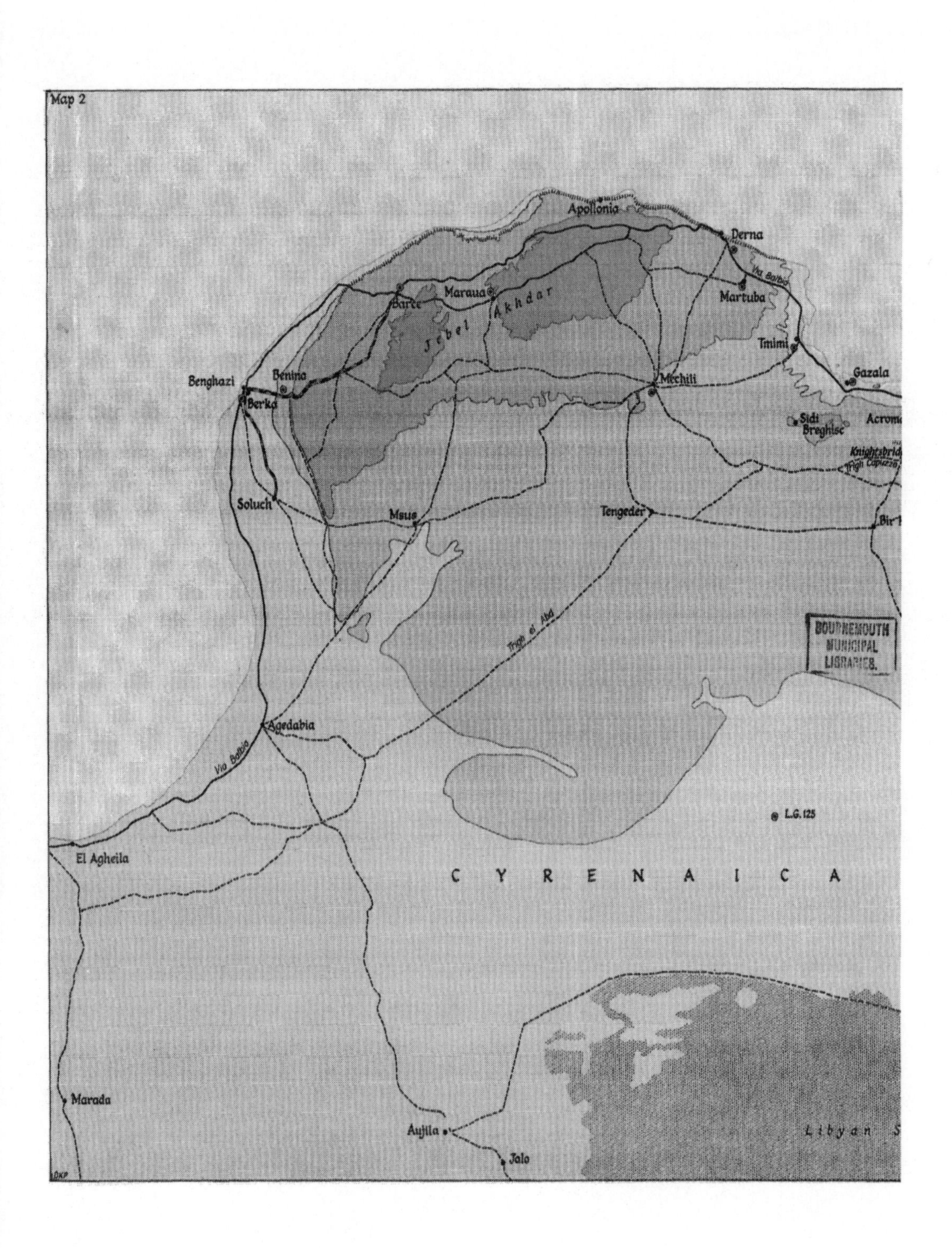

BOURNEMOUTH MUNICIPAL LIBRARIES.

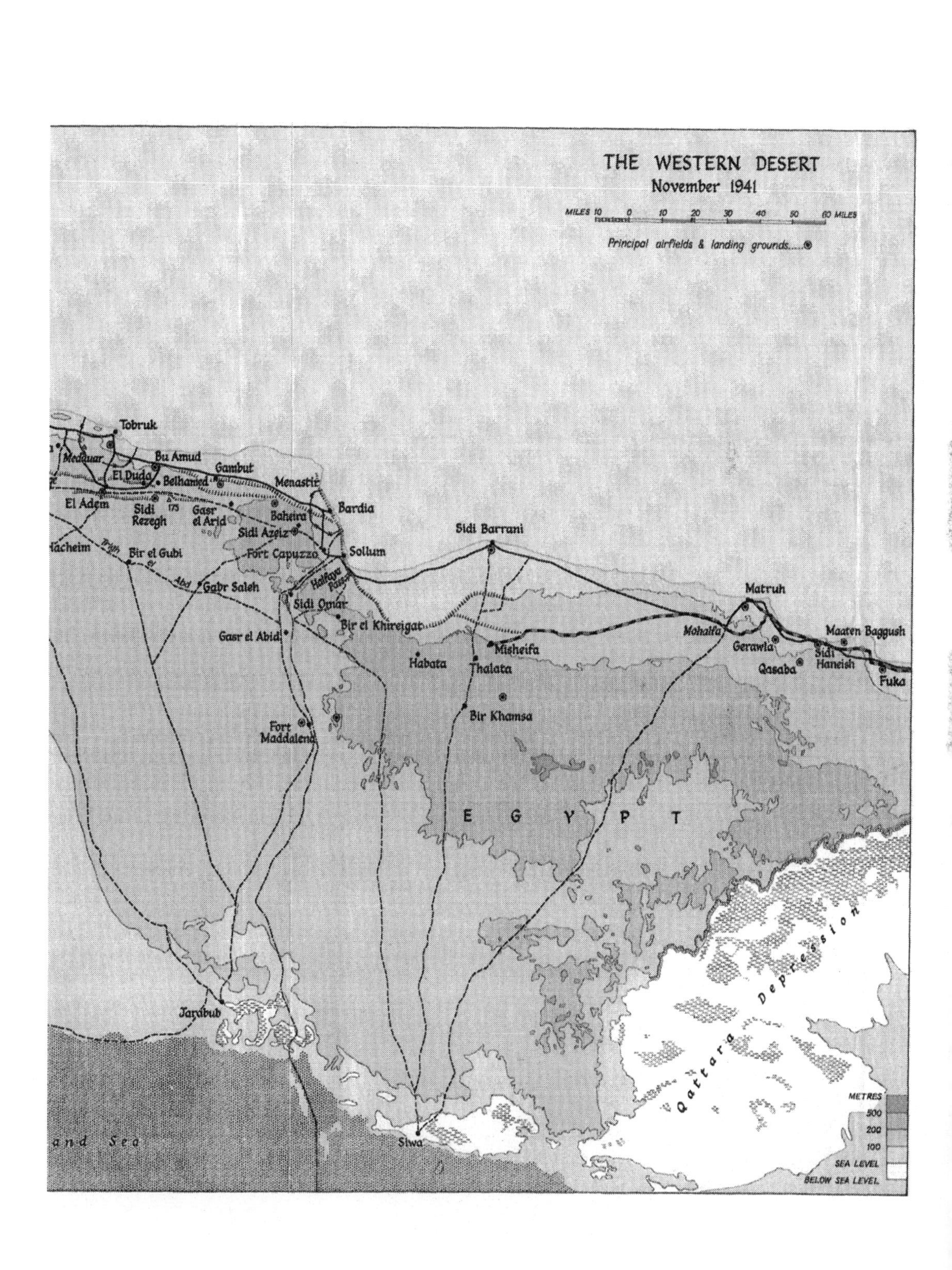
THE WESTERN DESERT
November 1941
MILES 10 0 10 20 30 40 50 60 MILES
Principal airfields & landing grounds
Tobruk
Medauar
Bu Amud
El Duda
Belhamed
Gambut
Menastir
El Adem
Sidi Rezegh
Gasr el Arid
Baheira
Bardia
Sidi Azeiz
Bir el Gubi
Fort Capuzzo
Sollum
Sidi Barrani
Gabr Saleh
Halfaya Pass
Sidi Omar
Bir el Khireigat
Gasr el Abid
Habata
Thalata
Misheifa
Matruh
Mohalfa
Gerawla
Qasaba
Maaten Baggush
Sidi Haneish
Fuka
Bir Khamsa
Fort Maddalena
E G Y P T
Qattara Depression
Jarabub
Siwa
METRES
500
200
100
SEA LEVEL
BELOW SEA LEVEL

CHAPTER I

THE GROWTH OF THE 'CRUSADER' PLAN

See Map 2

THE loss of Greece and Crete and the successful end of the main campaign in Italian East Africa had, by the summer of 1941, narrowed the possible theatres of major land operations down to two—one to the north of Egypt and one to the west. The Army had become largely concentrated in Egypt and Palestine and, after the defeat of the Vichy French, in Syria also. The growth of his forces made it clear to General Auchinleck that future operations were likely to be carried out by more than one Corps, so he decided to form an Army Headquarters, backed by a 'Base and Line of Communication Area', on each front.

Accordingly, General Sir Maitland Wilson was given command of a new 9th Army in the north, and Palestine and Transjordan became a 'Base and L. of C. Area.' In the west the 8th Army was formed under General Sir Alan Cunningham, who had left East Africa at the end of August. 'H.Q. British Troops in Egypt' became a 'Base and L. of C. Area' and remained responsible for the anti-aircraft defence and internal security of Egypt. The choice of the most suitable officers as Army Commanders was obviously an important question, on which opinions were exchanged with London. The Prime Minister thought that General Wilson ought to take command in the Western Desert, but General Auchinleck, who was deeply impressed by the importance of the northern front, was satisfied that he had made the right choices and was allowed to have his way.

The creation of Headquarters 8th Army was the signal for many changes. Western Desert Force became 13th Corps once more, and on 18th September Lieut.-General A. R. Godwin-Austen (from the 12th African Division) succeeded Lieut.-General Sir Noel Beresford-Peirse who left to take command in the Sudan. A new Corps, later numbered the 30th, which was intended to control the armoured forces, was forming under Lieut.-General V. V. Pope, who had until recently been Director of Armoured Fighting Vehicles at the War Office. The Headquarters of this Corps began to mobilize in Egypt at the beginning of October, with officers found largely from the remains of the ill-fated 2nd Armoured Division. On 5th October General Pope and his senior staff officers, Brigadiers Russell and Unwin, were killed in an air accident. Major-General C. W. M. Norrie, commander of the 1st Armoured Division, who was already in the Middle East, was then chosen to command the 30th Corps. By 21st October the Corps Headquarters had moved into the desert and begun to function. A third Corps Headquarters, the 10th, under Lieut.-General W. G. Holmes, arrived from England early in August and was made responsible for preparing a defensive position at El Alamein. Before long most of his officers and men were taken for the new 8th Army, and General Holmes with a much reduced staff was sent to Syria to join the 9th Army. Responsibility for the El Alamein position then passed to the Egypt Base Area.

The 6th (British) Division was in Syria, very incomplete but gradually being built up. The 50th (British) Division, which had been a bone of contention between General Wavell and the Prime Minister,[1] had arrived from the United Kingdom and was sent by General Auchinleck to work on the defences of Cyprus. This island had gained in importance now that there was a threat of attack through Turkey, but the Prime Minister strongly disagreed with this use of the newly arrived British division, partly because the threat to Cyprus could not be regarded as imminent, and partly because the United Kingdom, while providing a very reasonable share of the total forces in the Middle East, was not noticeably well represented by numbers of complete formations in the field. The 50th Division stayed in Cyprus until October, when it was relieved by the 5th Indian Division which had been in Iraq. The relief was carried out during the first eight days of November by ten destroyers and the fast minelayer *Abdiel*. The 50th Division then came under command of the 9th Army.

The Australian and New Zealand troops were already thoroughly familiar with life in the Western Desert, Palestine and Syria, and both contingents had accumulated a number of 'overheads' peculiar to themselves. Two South African Divisions now arrived, also backed by a large number of non-divisional units. There were many differences between the British and South African systems of administration, and many matters of importance to the South Africans lay outside the province of G.H.Q. Middle East. Field-Marshal Smuts therefore decided to form a separate administrative headquarters for South African troops, and towards the end of September Major-General F. H. Theron was appointed 'General Officer, Administration, Union Defence Force, Middle East'.

The pressure on General Auchinleck to hasten the start of the offensive in Cyrenaica—to be known as 'Crusader'—has already been referred to.[2] Briefly the argument was that German preoccupation

---

[1] Volume II, p. 225.
[2] Volume II, Chapter XIII.

with Russia afforded a lull, and if we did not use it to improve our position in the Western Desert the opportunity might never recur. Nevertheless the Defence Committee agreed that the first aim should be to recapture the whole of Cyrenaica, and in General Auchinleck's opinion, with which Air Marshal Tedder agreed, it was no use starting to do this with inadequate means. It would only postpone still further the date on which an offensive could be launched with a fair prospect of success. General Auchinleck admitted that risks must be run, and he was ready to run them if they were 'reasonably justified'.

Mr. Churchill, on the other hand, has expressed the view that the enemy should have been engaged continuously by the growing British forces, and compelled to use up the resources which were so difficult to replace. By waiting until everything was ready General Auchinleck was likely to find the enemy stronger, and if the war in Russia should prosper there might even be more German troops to deal with. He has recorded his conviction that 'General Auchinleck's four and a half months' delay in engaging the enemy was alike a mistake and a misfortune'.[1]

What would have happened if the offensive had started much sooner can only be guessed, but in the light of the facts regarding the state of the British organization, equipment, and training, it is difficult to avoid the conclusion that the growing British assets would have been used up piecemeal, and that a state of stalemate might have been reached. It will be of interest to keep the two opposing conceptions in mind while studying the elaborate preparations that were made for 'Crusader' and the protracted fighting that ultimately took place.

It is easy to understand that the many scattered campaigns which General Wavell had been obliged to fight with incomplete forces had greatly disorganized the Army. The repeated milking of units and formations to fit out one expedition after another had naturally had widespread effects. Brigades and divisional units had become separated from their divisions, and battalions from their brigades. The armoured formations had almost ceased to exist. To restore coherence and make proper training possible General Auchinleck was faced with the need for much reorganization, which had of course to be carried out without relaxing vigilance on the western frontier or too far depleting the forces ready to defend Egypt. The relief of the Australian troops in Tobruk, referred to later in this chapter, was an added complication.

Fortunately the means of re-equipping were no longer desperately short. From July 1941 onwards the results of the opening of the Red Sea to American shipping and the flow of munitions from the United States, the United Kingdom, and the Dominions, as their production

[1] Winston S. Churchill: *The Second World War* Volume III (1950) pp. 357-8 and 364.

got into its stride, began to be seen. By the end of October there had arrived some 300 British cruiser tanks, 300 American Stuart light tanks, 170 'I' tanks, 34,000 lorries, 600 field guns, 80 heavy and 160 light anti-aircraft guns, 200 anti-tank guns, and 900 mortars, to name only a few items. Yet these consignments, large as they were, were not large enough to replace all the losses and wastage that had occurred and allow any considerable reserves to be built up.

Of all the pressing tasks none was of greater importance than that of reorganizing the armoured forces. This problem was referred to in the previous volume in connexion with the decision of the Defence Committee to send out one of the armoured brigades—the 22nd—of the 1st Armoured Division from the United Kingdom as quickly as possible. It was to be followed by the rest of the Division early in 1942. Even after the arrival of the 22nd Armoured Brigade General Auchinleck would still not have the two armoured divisions which he regarded as the very least required for the recapture of the whole of Cyrenaica, but he was ready to try with what he would have. His policy was to rebuild the 7th Armoured Division by equipping the 7th Armoured Brigade with various types of British cruiser tanks, and the 4th Armoured Brigade with American Stuarts, known to the Americans as M3 light tanks but used by the British as cruisers. The 22nd Armoured Brigade would bring from England its cruisers of the latest type. The available infantry tanks were to be used to equip two brigades, designated Army Tank Brigades.

General Auchinleck had insisted, in spite of protests from home, that the number of tanks in reserve must be high; fifty per cent, he thought, would not be too liberal. His armoured force was below the strength he thought necessary, and if the armoured units were to keep up their fighting value they must have their losses replaced quickly. The only way of doing this was to hold an ample reserve, seeing that a new tank took many weeks to come from England and longer still from the United States, and ocean-going convoys were few and far between. As regards damaged tanks, there was still a lack of towing vehicles and transporters, the distances from front to base were vast, and the rail communications primitive by European standards. There was no engineering industry to speak of in the Middle East, and there was no repair equipment other than what the army had brought with it. Moreover, the Ordnance Workshops were short of experienced tank mechanics. For these and many other reasons it took about three months for a damaged tank to rejoin its unit. The scale of reserves was therefore almost as important as the initial equipment.

The flow of tanks to Egypt, however, enabled the process of re-equipping to keep very nearly to the programme. The 1st Army Tank Brigade was equipped early in September, and the 4th Armoured

Brigade by the end of the month, but at the end of October the 7th Armoured Brigade was still short of some of its tanks. In mid-September the 32nd Army Tank Brigade was formed in Tobruk as a mixed force of cruisers and 'I' tanks. Finally, the 22nd Armoured Brigade did not begin to disembark until 4th October, when it was discovered that all its tanks required a special modification which trebled the time normally spent by new arrivals in the base workshops; the task was not completed until 25th October. It is not surprising that this incident led to a searching enquiry in Whitehall, for the Middle East had given warning of this particular weakness in the Crusader tank.

By 25th October, then, there were three armoured brigades equipped, but not fully or even uniformly trained. Training is a matter which it is very easy to take for granted—especially from a distance—but the fact is that armoured warfare makes big demands on the skill of the tank crews in driving, navigation, gunnery, intercommunication, rapid recognition of many types of vehicle, and running repairs. That they should have confidence in their tanks is very necessary. Apart from all this the handling of units and formations together and in co-operation with the other arms requires practice. Commanders could not be expected to get good results in battle if they had not mastered the technique of command and control in training conditions. It was realized that the British standard of training in 'Battleaxe' had been much too low, and General Auchinleck was determined that in the urge to start at the earliest moment he would not be pushed into another 'Battleaxe'. By the end of October the last armoured brigade to be ready, the 22nd, had still had no training as a brigade in the totally unfamiliar desert conditions. The 4th Armoured Brigade, with its new Stuarts, had had a setback owing to the wear on the tracks during the journey forward from railhead. Training had to stop while British and American experts anxiously experimented. It was found that the tracks (the sole pads of which were of rubber) wore quickly to an extent which seemed to threaten collapse, but that the process then halted and the tracks remained perfectly serviceable. Before long the reliability of the Stuart made it very popular with the crews.

General Auchinleck had decided that, in keeping with the agreed aim of capturing the whole of Cyrenaica, the immediate object would be to destroy the enemy's armoured forces. On this basis he instructed General Cunningham early in September to study two broad plans: one for an advance from Jarabub through Jalo to cut the enemy's supply line, perhaps near Benghazi, the other for a main thrust towards Tobruk, with feint attacks in the south. General Auchinleck estimated that the British forces could be ready by early November, and he was anxious that the offensive should begin no later.

The information about the enemy was briefly as follows. Apart from a few Italian formations in Tripolitania all the Axis forces were in Cyrenaica. In the Egyptian frontier area between Sollum and Sidi Omar there were an Italian division and some German troops. Between Bardia and Tobruk there were two German armoured divisions, while around Tobruk were three Italian divisions and some German infantry. An Italian mobile corps of three divisions (one armoured, two motorized) was thought to be forming in the Jebel Akhdar area. These dispositions were unlikely to change unless the enemy tried again to capture Tobruk or to advance eastwards from the Egyptian frontier. As regards the Axis supply situation it was estimated that by 1st November there would be enough supplies at hand for three months' land and one month's air operations. The relative British and enemy strengths in November would probably be: in tanks, as 6 to 4; in aircraft, as 2 to 3—an estimate which was soon to be changed, as will be seen presently.[1]

General Cunningham was not attracted by the idea of advancing on Benghazi from the south, unless the enemy had first shown signs of withdrawing. The advance might well induce no move on the enemy's part, because his stocks in the forward area would make him independent of Benghazi for some time. In this event it would be necessary to attack him, and both time and surprise would have been lost. A force advancing against Benghazi would need armour and air support, as would any forces operating in the frontier area. Instead of keeping these all-important arms concentrated they would therefore have to be divided. Moreover the Benghazi force would meet increasingly heavy air attacks and its line of communication would be long and vulnerable. On the other hand a move by British armour towards Tobruk would be likely to draw the enemy's armoured divisions into battle, because they could not stand by and allow Tobruk to be relieved. This view was accepted by the three Commanders-in-Chief on 3rd October.

General Cunningham's idea was to cross the undefended frontier between Sidi Omar and Fort Maddalena. The main body of the British armoured forces would move north-west with the object of engaging the hostile armour near Tobruk, after which the siege would be raised in conjunction with a sortie by the garrison. Meanwhile another Force would contain and envelop the enemy's frontier defences and would then clear up the area between Bardia and Tobruk. Later still it would reduce any pockets of enemy which remained in the frontier area. Between the two Forces there would at first be a Centre Force, of an armoured brigade group, whose task would be

[1] Mere numbers of tanks gave only a very incomplete comparison—see p. 26ff.

to prevent interference by the enemy's armour with the flank and rear of the main advance. General Auchinleck weighed every conceivable course open to Rommel and concluded that he would probably concentrate his armour somewhere south of Fort Capuzzo and strike at the flank of Cunningham's force advancing towards Tobruk.

In the final plan the idea of an independent Centre Force was discarded. Instead, the 30th Corps, in which would be all three armoured brigades, was given the tasks of destroying the enemy's armoured forces and preventing them from attacking the left flank of the 13th Corps, the formation that was to operate in the frontier area.

It is of interest to consider how the main task of destroying the enemy's armoured forces was to be carried out. The chief opponents, the two German Panzer divisions, seemed to be lying separated, but within supporting distance of each other, near Gambut and to the west. As a first step the British armour was to move a day's march to a central position near Gabr Saleh, some thirty miles west of Sidi Omar. From here it could move towards Tobruk or towards Bardia according to how the enemy reacted. General Cunningham hoped that General Rommel would show his hand by the end of the first day; if he did not, he kept for himself the critical decision as to which way the British armour should move next. To waste no time the Army Commander intended to move with General Norrie's 30th Corps Headquarters.

It should be noted that the break-out from Tobruk was not to begin until the 30th Corps had defeated the enemy's armoured forces or otherwise prevented them from interfering. The intention was then to capture the two ridges at Sidi Rezegh and El Duda between which ran the enemy's main line of communication. The 30th Corps would capture the former and the garrison of Tobruk the latter. General Norrie was to decide when the sortie should begin, and from that moment the garrison of Tobruk would come under his command.

In the 13th Corps two brigades of 4th Indian Division were to contain the enemy in the frontier position and cover the 8th Army's forward bases and railhead. On the first day of the offensive the third brigade was to move out to Sidi Omar and secure the flank of the gap through which the main advance was to pass. When General Cunningham gave the word—which was expected to be when the enemy's armour had been firmly engaged—the New Zealand Division was to move northwards round Sidi Omar and get in rear of the enemy's positions on the frontier. If instead of standing firm on the frontier the enemy attempted to withdraw, 13th Corps was to cut him off, or, if that failed, pursue vigorously.

General Norrie felt about his part in the plan that the move to Gabr Saleh might not cause the enemy to do anything on the first day. He thought that if this were so he should advance on the second day to the area El Adem–Sidi Rezegh for which the enemy would be bound to fight in order to maintain intact the line of communication of all his forces east of Tobruk. However the arrival towards the end of October of the Ariete Division in the neighbourhood of Bir Hacheim confirmed General Cunningham in his view that the British armoured force should be prepared either to give battle from its central position, or to move in any direction (to Sidi Rezegh for example) that he might choose as a result of the latest information.

General Norrie disliked also the task of protecting the left flank of 13th Corps as he wished to be able to use all his armoured brigades in the main task of destroying the enemy's armour. General Cunningham and General Godwin-Austen however thought that though 13th Corps unaided could withstand one of the German armoured divisions it would need help if it were attacked by both. Godwin-Austen therefore wanted to have control of the 4th Armoured Brigade Group to protect the left flank of his Corps. General Cunningham ruled that the 4th Armoured Brigade Group was to remain under the command of Norrie, who would be responsible for protecting the flank of the 13th Corps.

There were plans, too, for subsidiary operations. The Oasis Force was to move on Jalo, and give protection to a landing ground (called L.G. 125) to be made a hundred miles north-west of Jarabub from which the Air Force was to make attacks on the coastal area south of Benghazi. The Oasis Force was itself to harass the enemy as opportunity offered, and it was to help to give the impression that a major move was being made from the south. To add to this deception a bogus concentration was staged at Jarabub, of camps, dumps, and dummy tanks, and an appropriate volume of spurious wireless traffic was maintained. These and other devices helped to divert attention from the real preparations, which, of course, depended for their secrecy largely upon the success of the Air Force in preventing reconnaissance by hostile aircraft.

Since the capture of Kufra in April 1941 the Long Range Desert Group had grown to two squadrons, each of three patrols, having received reinforcements of Royal Northumberland Fusiliers, Argyll and Sutherland Highlanders and Southern Rhodesians, and from the 1st Cavalry Division. Among other welcome additions were a 4·5-inch howitzer and a light tank; best of all, the Group managed (by private enterprise) to acquire two Waco aircraft. Colonel Bagnold was recalled to Cairo in August to advise on long-range matters, and command of the Group passed to Lieut.-Colonel Prendergast, who himself piloted one of the aircraft.

In July the Group began to reconnoitre the distant desert in order to learn about tracks, water, and sites for landing grounds, a task which took the Patrols well into Tripolitania. In September the Group came under the orders of the 8th Army and set an unobtrusive watch on the coast road to the west of El Agheila, where it observed the traffic in the enemy's extreme back area and collected some useful information. In October it was given its tasks for 'Crusader'; these were to report on the 'going' and on enemy movements in certain areas, to send in tactical reports, and to harass small bodies of the enemy.

Meanwhile on the frontier the British screen was gradually being strengthened. During August the protective detachments had been found by 7th Support Group and 22nd Guards Brigade. Early in September Major-General Messervy, commanding 4th Indian Division, took command of all troops in the forward area, and his own Indian Brigades—5th, 7th and 11th—gradually joined the division. So important was it that the administrative preparations, shortly to be described, should not be apparent to the enemy that it is of interest to know that late in August General Rommel's suspicions were aroused by the supposed discovery of certain supply dumps, one of which was only fifteen miles from the frontier, at Bir el Khireigat. An elaborate raid was devised by the 21st Panzer Division, and fighter and dive-bomber aircraft were specially brought up to Gambut to support it. The moon would not be suitable until 14th September, but by then it had been found that the dump was a disused one. The object was then changed to the destruction of the British forces located just east of Bir el Khireigat. At this time the British screen of the 7th Support Group (Brigadier J. C. Campbell) had orders not to become involved; they fought a skilful and successful action, and the raid achieved nothing. The German columns were caught refuelling by Nos. 12 and 24 Squadrons S.A.A.F. escorted by fighters, and Gambut airfield was also attacked by bombers and fighters. The Germans lost 56 men, and 9 aircraft were destroyed or damaged. Five of their tanks were abandoned, and the German records show that the number of fit tanks in 21st Panzer Division dropped from 110 on 11th September to 43 on the 20th. The number crept up again, but not until 12th November was it as high as it had been before this raid took place. The British losses were fifteen men, one armoured car, and seven aircraft. The importance of the incident lay in the fact that the impression of imminent action by the British was dispelled, and no further attempt was made to probe the British screen which from now onwards had more and more to conceal.

It has been seen that the broad plan for 'Crusader' required large forces to cross the Egyptian frontier, which was no less than 130 miles from the existing railhead, and then to advance to a battle area another 50 to 80 miles ahead. The main thrust was to be made by the highly mobile 30th Corps and was expected to entail much manoeuvring for, and fighting, an armoured battle in a part of the desert which was away from any roads and almost waterless. Large quantities of fuel, ammunition, water, and supplies would have to be carried forward over vast distances. As the plan did not include the early capture of Halfaya, Sollum, and Bardia, there was no prospect of establishing supply lines by sea or by the coastal road until the siege of Tobruk was raised. It was obvious that the administrative preparations would have to be very thorough, and it was soon apparent that the railhead would have to be pushed as far west as possible, and that large stocks of supplies of all kinds would have to be built up.

In May 1941 General Wavell had ordered the extension of the railway, on which work had been suspended, to begin again, but lack of material, plant and transport hampered its progress. By September, the 10th New Zealand Railway Construction Company, with various Pioneer and Labour units, had laid the track up the escarpment to Mohalfa, twenty miles from Matruh. At the end of the month the 13th New Zealand Railway Construction Company joined in the task and the rate of track-laying rose to two miles a day. By 15th November a railhead was opened at Misheifa, which had been selected as the point which must be reached before the offensive began. A dummy railhead was built also. This race with time could scarcely have been closer.

The 8th Army's administrative plan was broadly as follows. Three Forward Bases were chosen; one near Sidi Barrani for the troops in the coastal sector; one near Thalata (just west of Misheifa railhead) for 30th Corps and most of 13th Corps; and one on the frontier near Jarabub for the Oasis Force. The minimum quantity of stores and supplies required to support full-scale operations for the first week was nearly 32,000 tons, of which 25,000 were wanted at Thalata. It was hoped that at the end of the week Tobruk would be relieved and would soon become usable as a sea-head. It will be seen that this hope was not fulfilled. West of the Forward Bases, and fed from them, were to be a number of Field Maintenance Centres (F.M.C.), organizations derived from the novel though less elaborate Field Supply Depots which had been worked by the supply and transport services in the first desert campaign. The F.M.C. consisted, in addition to a Field Supply Depot, of a Field Ammunition Depot, a Water Issue Section, and dumps of engineer, medical, and ordnance stores. Prisoners' cages, field post offices, salvage dumps, and units to deal with stragglers and men in transit were added as required. For the whole F.M.C. there was a commander and a small staff to supervise the lay-out, dispersion, and camouflage, and control the movements of convoys and the labour and transport. Four F.M.Cs were provided for 30th Corps and two for 13th Corps. They were a great success and became a permanent feature of 8th Army's administrative system.

The supply of water was, as usual, an immense problem. A detailed survey made in August of all drinkable sources west of the Matruh-Siwa road showed that not only was there nothing like enough water, but also that there was not enough transport to carry the balance forward from Matruh, which was the point to which the pipeline from Alexandria was being extended from El Daba. This meant that the piped supply had to be greatly increased and the pipeline extended as far west as possible, which entailed the laying of some 160 miles of piping and the building of seven pumping stations and nine reservoirs. Many difficulties arose from competing demands for transport and machinery, and on 11th October a serious mishap occurred during an air attack on Fuka. The new pumps were damaged, and nearly all the water which had been accumulated to fill the pipes and reservoirs west of Fuka was lost. Every available water-carrying train was used, and the water-carrier *Petrella* plied continuously between Alexandria and Matruh; even so the filling process took four weeks and the piped water reached the Misheifa area on 13th November. The whole project took eight weeks and another race with time was won. Water could now be pumped 270 miles from Alexandria, but strictness in its use could not be relaxed. Indeed, besides being rationed in quantity (¾ gallon a man daily), water was now treated literally as a 'ration', being issued for the number shown on a unit's ration indent and having to be accounted for.

The immensity of the dumping programme is well illustrated by the fact that at one time the transport engaged upon it was consuming 180,000 gallons of petrol a day. It is small wonder that the administrative staff looked forward anxiously to the punctual opening of Tobruk. The main supply line could then be transferred to the sea, and for this purpose the Inshore Squadron would sail convoys from Alexandria, the first being sailed to arrive three days after the relief of the fortress, by which time it was hoped to have fighter protection over the harbour. The aim was to deliver 400 tons of cased petrol, 100 tons of bulk petrol, and 600 tons of stores daily. As the advance continued, Naval parties were to be ready to enter Derna and Benghazi on the heels of the Army, clear the harbours of obstructions and mines, and prepare for the arrival at these ports of 200 and 600 tons a day respectively. Arrangements were also to be made for removing casualties and prisoners by sea from all three places. To meet one of the most serious deficiencies two motor launches and eighteen lighters were to be carried in the Infantry Landing Ship H.M.S. *Glenroy*. In the meantime the normal supplies for the garrison of Tobruk would continue to be run in, and up to 600 tons of water would be delivered daily at Matruh until the Army reached the wells of the Jebel district, which it was hoped would not take more than a fortnight.

So anxious was General Auchinleck to start the offensive early in

November, and so great was the pressure from home, that a word is necessary about the reasons for some very unwelcome postponements. Early in October it was clear that the transport would not have finished the dumping programme and be ready for active operations before 11th November. This fact, coupled with the late arrival of 22nd Armoured Brigade, caused the date to be fixed as 11th November, which, although disappointing, would at least give 30th Corps Headquarters a little more time to shake down. Then came the discovery that the 22nd Armoured Brigade's tanks required attention in workshops, and the date had to be changed to 15th November. Early in November another delay occurred. The role of 1st South African Division required it to be very mobile, but difficulties over providing its full scale of transport interfered with its training and General Brink asked for six extra days—or a minimum of three. The request was sound, but the urge to start was great. The Middle East Defence Committee[1] examined all possible courses and decided to grant three extra days. This brought the date to 18th November.

The growth of the air forces in the Middle East in the autumn of 1941 was described in Volume II of this history. To co-operate with the Army in the Desert, No. 204 Group had grown into the Western Desert Air Force, which, under the command of Air Vice-Marshal A. Coningham, a New Zealander, came to be welded into a large and flexible force with a strong family feeling and *esprit de corps*. It was composed at first of:

Short-range fighters	8 squadrons
Long-range fighters	1 squadron
Medium bombers	6 squadrons
Tactical reconnaissance (formerly Army Co-operation)	1 squadron*

* With the creation of the Western Desert Air Force for the specific purpose of co-operating with the Army the term 'Army Co-operation Squadron' will be replaced by 'Tactical Reconnaissance Squadron'.

and was to be helped from time to time by the Wellingtons of No. 205 Group, a squadron of Fleet Air Arm bombers, some general reconnaissance aircraft, and one or more transport squadrons.

Everything possible was done to build up the strength of the force with pilots, aircraft and aircrews taken from other stations in the Middle East. The number of aircraft in the 'initial equipment' of each squadron was raised from sixteen to eighteen, and seven more were held in immediate reserve. In order to keep up this strength by a flow of aircraft, an Aircraft Replacement Pool, to hold seven days' replacements, was formed at Wadi Natrun into which aircraft were fed from

[1] i.e. The Minister of State and the three Commanders-in-Chief.

the Maintenance Units. Farther forward were other Pools holding two days' replacements. This system was the outcome of Air Marshal Tedder's drive to improve maintenance and repair, and of his policy of not forming more squadrons than he could keep fully manned and equipped. During the four weeks from the middle of October no fewer than 232 replacement aircraft were fed into the front-line squadrons. The flow of aircraft from Takoradi, through Malta, and by sea round the Cape was by now large enough to allow substantial reserves to be built up—a position which was not matched by corresponding reserves of pilots and trained crews.

In order to be able to pursue the enemy the Desert Air Force would have to be mobile, and its control organization able to leap-frog forward—part functioning and part moving; the two existing wing headquarters were used alternately in this way. (Later a fighter group with duplicate control centres was formed.) It was also necessary for the squadrons themselves to be able to throw off advanced parties.[1] All this was largely a matter of having the necessary transport, and, although the bare necessities were in fact met, the lack of suitable types of vehicles was felt throughout 'Crusader'. The second need was for landing-grounds so sited that squadrons could keep a moving land battle within range. The fighters would advance by short bounds to rapidly made landing grounds, and the bombers, capable of longer strides, would follow and take over suitable sites vacated by the fighters. The need for dispersion meant that more landing grounds than usual would be needed; their construction and protection were the responsibility of the Army.

Early in November the hitherto large fighter wings were split into several flying wings of two squadrons each, the intention being that each flying wing should occupy a separate landing-ground. Three of these landing-grounds, each linked by land-line to its main parent wing headquarters, formed a 'fighter airfield area', the whole being covered by the same air and ground defence and warning systems.

As with the Army, certain aspects of training required urgent attention. In particular the dilution of the fighter squadrons and their long employment on defensive tasks had made it necessary to raise the standard of their training. Under the supervision of the recently joined Senior Air Staff Officer to the Desert Air Force, Air Commodore B. E. Embry, the latest tactics, which had been tried and proved at home, were strenuously practised.

The study that had been made of army/air co-operation, after the unsuccessful operation 'Battleaxe' in June, had resulted in the crea-

[1] Each squadron's maintenance staff was in fact divided into three parties. The A (Advanced) party was simply a refuelling team for moving to advanced or new landing-grounds. The B (Rear) party carried out day-to-day maintenance at the operational landing-ground. A third party (C) remained at the base airfield, where the squadron's workshops were situated.

tion of a joint 'Air Support Control' at the headquarters of each corps and armoured division for passing information rapidly, and for directing aircraft on to targets reported by the troops or by other aircraft.[1] This decentralization was intended to give quick results, but it was recognized that the provision of direct support ought not to be allowed to jeopardize possession of air superiority, and that all the available bombers might be needed on occasions to act against a single target. For these reasons the A.O.C. Desert Air Force decided, with the full agreement of the Commander of the 8th Army, to retain ultimate control of all air support himself and to place his advanced headquarters in close contact with the Army Commander. This meant limiting the functions of the Air Support Controls to passing messages received from reconnaissance aircraft and the troops and to making requests for action to the A.O.C. These requests were passed simultaneously to the wings concerned, so that there should be no delay in acting upon the A.O.C's decision.

These, briefly, were the steps taken to ensure that the Desert Air Force would retain its flexibility and support the land operations in the most effective way. There was naturally a good deal of speculation as to the relative strengths of the air forces on both sides. Indeed the New Zealand Government, with memories of Greece and Crete, asked to be assured that their troops would have adequate air support in the coming fight. The estimates of the probable Axis strength made in the Middle East differed considerably from the Air Ministry's calculations, one reason being that the Axis air forces were greatly scattered, and the extent to which they could reinforce Cyrenaica from other areas—including Russia—was doubtful. (It will be remembered that this was one of the unknown quantities of the Italian position in 1940; it was now complicated by the presence of the *Luftwaffe*.)

The Vice-Chief of the Air Staff flew to Cairo to try to resolve the differences, and on 20th October general agreement was reached that the Germans and Italians would together have about 385 serviceable aircraft in Cyrenaica. The British would have 528. Farther afield, in Crete and the Aegean, the enemy would have about 72 serviceable aircraft of all types (excluding short-range fighters) while the British would have 48 heavy and medium bombers fit to operate from Malta. The figures for the enemy were based on the assumption that he could not afford to hold any aircraft back in reserve; the British figures, on the other hand, were for aircraft actually in the squadrons, and did not take into account the reserves, which amounted to half as many again. The low estimate of the military value of the Italians was an important factor, offset to some extent by certain advantages possessed by the German Me. 109F over any British fighters. After an exhaustive

[1] The system is explained in Volume II.

study the Prime Minister was able to assure the New Zealand Government of his conviction that our army would enjoy the benefits of air superiority.

These estimates were not far wide of the mark. The British took the field with upwards of 650 aircraft (including the heavy bombers in Egypt) with over 550 serviceable, in addition to 74 at Malta of which 66 were serviceable. In Cyrenaica the Axis had a total of 536 aircraft, of which only 342 were serviceable. Thus in the Desert we certainly had numerical superiority, but the enemy had a potential reserve of a further 750 serviceable aircraft of suitable types (excluding a large number of transport aircraft) in Tripolitania, Sicily, Sardinia, Greece and Crete, apart from those in the Italian Metropolitan Air Force and the Navy. The participation of any of these in 'Crusader' depended, however, largely upon the results of British activities by sea and air against the fuel supplies to North Africa. Shortage of fuel on the spot did in fact make any considerable reinforcement of Cyrenaica impracticable until the second month of the offensive. The Prime Minister's assurance to the New Zealand Government was therefore justified.

From the middle of October onwards the activities of the air forces in Egypt and Malta were closely related to the 'Crusader' plan; indeed, their part in the operation may be said to have begun on that date—nearly five weeks before the Army's D day. Broadly, their tasks were to try to meet all the many demands of the army and air force for reconnaissance; to interfere with the enemy's supply system by land and sea, so as to handicap him in the coming land battle; and to attack his air force in Cyrenaica with the aim of gaining air superiority. All this without disclosing too much of the British intentions.

The first of these tasks taxed the available resources to the utmost, because both Services were eager for information of all kinds about the enemy. The newly formed Strategical Reconnaissance Unit covered places as far apart as Siwa and Benghazi, the Photographic Reconnaissance Unit took photographs of selected points, and the Survey Flight, also newly formed, worked with the 8th Army to provide special photographs for mapping purposes.

As regards the enemy's supply system, the principle was to attack it at vital points from the ports of loading all the way to depots in the forward area. The method was first to interfere mainly with the rearward points of the system and then deal with the stocks that had been accumulated nearer to the front. For this purpose the Wellingtons of No. 38 Squadron's detachment at Malta attacked Tripoli and the main ports of loading. Naples was attacked on twelve nights by a total of 96 Wellingtons, and on one occasion an oil depot was hit and an enormous fire started which included the railway station and the surrounding buildings. At Brindisi one attack by 21 Wellingtons was particularly successful, and many transportation targets were hit. Tripoli was visited on eight nights by a total of 58 Wellingtons, and, as at Naples, some of the new 4,000 lb. bombs were used against the port and railway installations. The story of the attacks on Axis shipping, culminating in a very successful month in September, when six ships were sunk by aircraft and four by submarines, was told in the previous volume. During October seven ships were sunk on the Italy/North Africa run, two by submarines, five by aircraft; about 20 per cent of the total cargo carried during the month, including fuel, was lost in this way.

The Wellington squadrons of No. 205 Group, based in Egypt, had as their principal target the port of Benghazi, for the simple reason that, apart from a few small ports used by coastal shipping, all the enemy's supplies had to be landed at either Tripoli or Benghazi and the use of Benghazi saved a very long haul by road from Tripoli. Accordingly the Wellingtons kept up a steadily increasing effort, and during the first week of November dropped nearly 200 tons of high-explosive and incendiaries in and around the harbour area. The night attacks were supplemented during the day-time by Marylands of the South African Air Force, and the dislocation caused by these day and night attacks is reflected in the frequent references in enemy documents to the need for more anti-aircraft defence at Benghazi.

Gradually the main weight of the air attack was shifted to points farther east: petrol, store and ammunition dumps, workshops and concentrations of transport. To give some idea of the intensity, from 4th to 13th November the depots and shops at Derna were attacked by a total of 50 Wellingtons and 26 Blenheims by night and by 11 Marylands by day, or an average of about 9 aircraft every 24 hours. The skilled navigation of the Fleet Air Arm Albacores was of particular value in dropping flares accurately over targets for the Blenheims to attack.[1]

During this phase of the air operations only a modest effort was made against the enemy's forward landing-grounds. In the last fortnight of October 68 sorties were flown against them, and another 72 during the following week. It was hoped that daylight attacks on landing-grounds would induce the enemy to give battle, but only on three occasions did this happen, and German records show only one Me. 109 damaged for the loss of three Hurricanes. In fact this was a disappointing phase as regards coat-trailing, for which the cloudy weather was no doubt partly responsible, but it left the British fighters freer to use their guns against road transport and other ground targets.

[1] In their slow-flying aircraft with its good all-round vision of the ground the Albacore crews became adept in navigation over the Desert at night. They became the 'pathfinders' who located and illuminated targets for air attack, for which purpose their own bombloads were adjusted to make room for as many flares as possible. Because of their skilled navigation at night the Albacores came also to be used for night reconnaissance.

Meanwhile aircraft based at Malta were attending to airfields in Sicily and Tripolitania. Castel Benito, the main airfield of Tripoli, was heavily attacked on two successive nights by a total of 39 Wellingtons, and photographs showed 16 aircraft destroyed or damaged.

On 13th November a new phase began, designed to exert the greatest possible pressure on the enemy's air force and to cover the concentration of the 8th Army and the Desert Air Force. During this phase the low cloud grew steadily worse, and hampered reconnaissance severely. Nevertheless the enemy's bomber and air transport landing grounds at Benina, Derna, Barce and Berka, and dive-bomber base at Tmimi were attacked by day, as also were Martuba and the main German fighter base at Gazala, as well as landing-grounds at Gambut and Baheira from which these fighters operated. By night the Wellingtons added their main weight (while continuing to attack the enemy's supply system from Benghazi forward) as did the Albacores of the Fleet Air Arm. Meanwhile there were frequent fighter sweeps over the enemy's forward area, but they caused no particular reaction by the Axis fighters.

The bogus activities at Jarabub, described on page 8, did however succeed in arousing the enemy's interest. This led to a brisk fight on 15th November in which one Blenheim was lost, five others and two Hurricanes were damaged, and some petrol and transport were destroyed. The German records show their losses to have been three Me. 110s, one Ju. 88 and one Me. 109 destroyed, and one Ju. 88 damaged—a satisfactory balance-sheet and good evidence of the success of this diversion. Elsewhere during the past few weeks the *Luftwaffe* had persisted in its daily attacks on Tobruk, as a preliminary to its capture. Suez was visited on five nights, otherwise only Fuka—a medium bomber base—received particular attention. Generally speaking, except for Tobruk, the enemy's air attacks were scattered and on a small scale.

A bold attempt to destroy Axis aircraft on their own airfields ended in a sad failure. The Special Air Service Brigade (later to be called the 1st S.A.S. Regiment) had been formed in the Middle East to raid and destroy equipment behind the enemy's lines, for which purpose they had been trained to reach their targets by land, sea, or air. On the night of 16th November one detachment of their parachute troops took off in three Bombays for Gazala, and another in two Bombays for Tmimi, to do as much damage as they could at these airfields. Driving rain and low cloud made navigation terribly difficult and only one aircraft dropped its troops in the right place. Conditions on the ground were likewise appalling, for the deluges of rain had turned dust into bog, and, to make matters worse, several men were injured on landing. The operation had to be called off: some of the party escaped and others were killed or taken prisoner.

But the rain which proved fatal to this particular enterprise had its good results also, for the British landing grounds were much less affected than the enemy's, and on the eve of 'Crusader' the Axis air force was mostly bogged down—just when it might have noticed that a large move was afoot. As it was, there had been nothing to indicate that the enemy was aware, or even suspicious, of what was going on behind the British lines.

The total British effort during the five weeks of preliminary air operations from 14th October to 17th November amounted to nearly 3,000 sorties, including Malta's bombers, but excluding anti-shipping operations. This may be pictured as about 80 aircraft of all kinds every 24 hours. At least 22 German aircraft are known to have been destroyed and a further 13 damaged, and the Italian losses are thought to have been heavier. Considering all that the British had been doing, and the distances, the bad weather, and the fact that they had been continually on the offensive, their own losses (including Malta's) of 59 bombers and 26 fighters from all causes were remarkably low.

By 17th November Air Vice-Marshal Coningham's force had been built up to:

Short-range fighters	14 squadrons (including one naval squadron)
Long-range fighters	2 squadrons
Medium bombers	8 squadrons (for a short time 9)
Tactical reconnaissance	3 squadrons
Survey reconnaissance	1 flight
Strategical reconnaissance	1 flight

Of these, six squadrons and two flights were South African, two squadrons were Australian, one squadron was Rhodesian and one Free French. Help was also given by heavy bombers and photographic reconnaissance aircraft, and indirectly by other fighter squadrons in the Middle East. Detachments placed under Coningham's operational control from time to time included general reconnaissance, transport and additional Fleet Air Arm aircraft. The flying units which he controlled, or which were available to him, at the beginning of 'Crusader', together with their roles and the types of aircraft employed, are given in Appendix 5. Particulars of the performance of types of aircraft generally are given in Appendix 9.

Air Marshal Tedder was able to report on the evening of 17th November to the Chief of the Air Staff in London 'Squadrons are at full strength, aircraft and crews, with reserve aircraft, and whole force is on its toes.' It would have been no exaggeration to add that it had already trodden pretty hard upon the enemy's. His supply system had been battered, his air forces had been repeatedly shot up at their bases, his troop dispositions had been thoroughly reconnoitred, and

British aircraft had roamed at will over his territory. When the land battle began it was intended to persist with the three main duties of maintaining air superiority, interfering with the enemy's supply system, and carrying out as much reconnaissance as possible. There was this important addition, that so far as was compatible with preventing the enemy's air forces from intervening in the battle, every available aircraft was to be directed to meeting the demands of the land fighting.

Thus there had not only been no appreciable interference with the preparations for 'Crusader', but there was good reason to hope that the Army's advance would come as a surprise and would be given such a scale of air support as it had never enjoyed before.

As with the R.A.F., the Navy's part in 'Crusader' had long since begun and the toll of Axis merchant ships supplying North Africa had been mounting. These losses had already affected General Rommel's plans, and it will be seen in Chapter IV that they were to reach their peak in November. During the opening stage of the land battle the Navy's tasks were to take the usual form: support by gunfire, raids along the coast, and supply of many of the essential needs of the Army and R.A.F. In addition there were to be movements of the main Fleet designed to divert enemy aircraft from the land battle. Between 16th and 19th November the Mediterranean Fleet—without the customary co-operation of the whole of No. 201 Group, part of which would be supporting the land battle—and Forces H and K with some merchant ships were to simulate the passage of a convoy from Gibraltar through the Mediterranean, and on the 22nd a dummy convoy was to sail from Malta as if for a landing near Tripoli. In addition patrols were to be maintained along the coast to interfere with traffic between Greece and Derna and with small craft carrying supplies to the enemy's forward area.

The German 'Armoured Group Africa', with General Rommel in command and General Gause as Chief of Staff, was formed at the end of July 1941. The chain of command of the Axis forces, down to divisions, then became as shown on page 20.

The 21st Corps comprised the troops investing Tobruk; the Savona Division was holding the Egyptian frontier, supported by German troops of the newly arrived *Afrika* Division; the Italian Mobile Corps was situated well to the west of Tobruk, and was not under General Rommel's command.

By the beginning of September the Italian and German High Commands had agreed that possession of the port of Tobruk was an

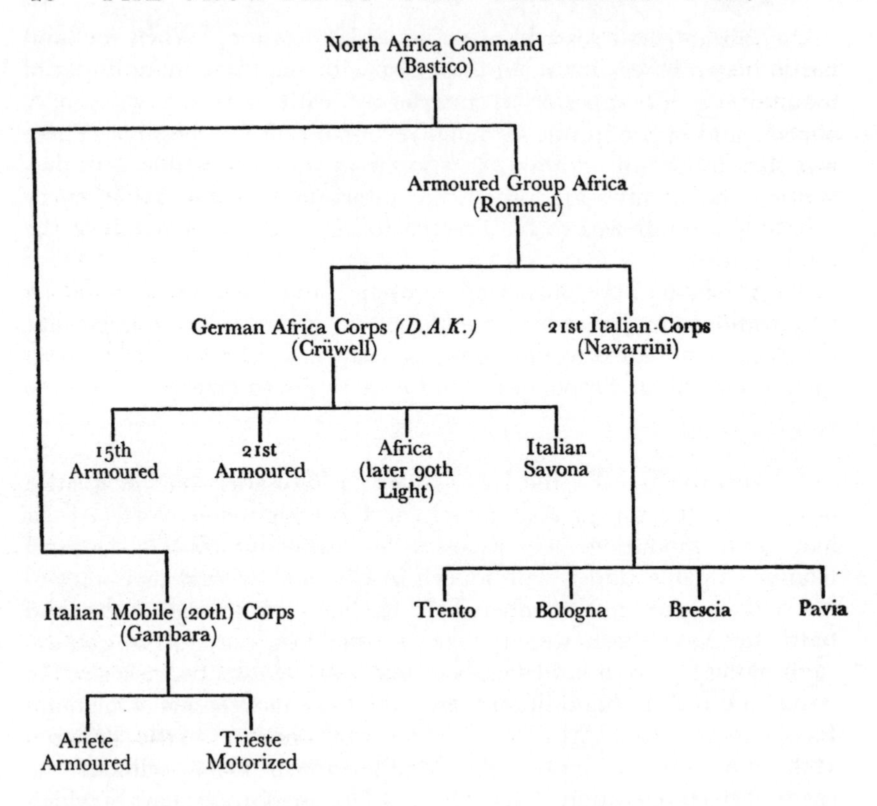

essential preliminary to an advance into Egypt. It was hoped to attack Tobruk early in November, but the losses at sea rose alarmingly during September and General Rommel said that if the supply situation did not improve he would be unable to attack at all. *Fliegerkorps X* was at once ordered to protect shipping to Benghazi and Derna in preference to making attacks on ships and bases in Egypt, but an appeal by the German Admiralty for more aircraft to enable escorts to be given to the Tripoli convoys was refused because of the over-riding importance of the Russian front.

The German *OKW* had noticed the steady increase in the British forces in the Middle East, and early in October concluded that they would probably be used first to relieve Tobruk and would then be transferred to the Caucasus region. Their estimate of British strength was fairly accurate, but the completeness of the British equipment was greatly exaggerated. The Italians, who were less interested in the Caucasus, thought that a more likely British object would be to secure the whole of Libya, which would partly offset the Axis successes in Russia. They estimated the British air strength as double that of the Axis.

On 20th October the Italian *Comando Supremo* warned General Bastico of a possible British offensive, but both he and General Rommel thought that this could not be imminent. In any case Rommel was intending to attack Tobruk in about the third week of November and was satisfied that the Axis mobile reserves could deal with any British action taken before then or even while Tobruk was being attacked.

For a long time Hitler had been trying to persuade Mussolini to allow German naval and air officers and specialists to take a more active part in the Mediterranean war, and not be confined to liaison duties. At the end of October he decided to make a strong bid for German domination. The Headquarters of *Luftflotte* 2, together with *Fliegerkorps II* (General Loerzer), were to be withdrawn from the Russian front and put under the command of Field-Marshal Albert Kesselring, who was to become Commander-in-Chief South (*Oberbefehlshaber Süd*) with the task of establishing naval and air superiority in the zone between Italy and North Africa. For this purpose he was to paralyse Malta and disrupt east-west traffic through the Mediterranean. He was also to co-operate with the Axis forces in North Africa. He would be subordinate to the Duce and was to have a mixed German and Italian staff. He was to command *Fliegerkorps II* and *X* and could issue directives to the German and Italian naval forces allotted to him; General Rommel was not to come under his orders, but would remain responsible to General Bastico. The Italians did not welcome the appointment of Kesselring but were given no choice, and had to accept the situation.

During the opening stages of 'Crusader' the senior German Air Force commander in the Mediterranean area was General Geisler, commanding *Fliegerkorps X*, with his headquarters in Greece. The commander in North Africa, *Fliegerführer Afrika*, was still General Fröhlich, who was responsible to General Geisler. The Italian air force in Libya consisted of the 5th *Squadra*, command of which was taken over from General Aimone-Cat by General Marchesi on 6th November. A liaison staff, known as *Italuft*, had been set up in Rome in 1940 and became responsible for co-ordinating the action of *Fliegerkorps X*, and through it that of *Fliegerführer Afrika*, and the 5th *Squadra*.

General Rommel flew to Rome on 14th November for a conference on transport and supply. After discussing the proposed attack on Tobruk, Cavallero wrote to Bastico telling him to launch it as soon as he could with the strongest possible forces. On the night of the 17th/18th Rommel was in Athens on his way back from Rome when a daring attempt was made to paralyse his Command by a blow at the brain centre. A party of No. 11 (Scottish) Commando was put ashore from the submarines *Torbay* and *Talisman* near Apollonia with the idea of attacking the house in which it was (wrongly) thought that General

Rommel was living. Overcoming many difficulties the party reached their objective and a hand to hand fight ensued. Lieut.-Colonel G. C. T. Keyes, son of Admiral of the Fleet Sir Roger Keyes, was killed; for his gallant conduct in the raid he was posthumously awarded the Victoria Cross.[1]

The insistence of the Germans and Italian High Commands upon the need to capture Tobruk is a measure of the importance of this key port, and great credit is due to Major-General L. J. Morshead, the 9th Australian Division and the attached troops for their spirited defence. Since the failure of the enemy's attack in May 1941 life in Tobruk had settled down to a round of minor enterprises. Strong patrols from each forward battalion were out almost nightly, observing, listening, and reconnoitring, and when a likely quarry was detected it was attacked. The garrison soon became, and remained, virtual masters of no-man's-land. Large sorties could not be made without an increase of the garrison, which General Auchinleck could not agree to. Nevertheless the 20th Australian Infantry Brigade made a series of night attacks to improve the position in the Ras el Medauar salient, and the 24th Australian Infantry Brigade later tried unsuccessfully to retake the shoulders of the salient. Thereafter the smaller operations of an aggressive defence were the rule.

The enemy's main activity on land was to encircle the place with a minefield covered by field works. His artillery was active and his air attacks frequent, being made chiefly against the harbour and the administrative areas. It was estimated that the anti-aircraft artillery engaged nearly 500 aircraft every month from July to October, and although the attacks did surprisingly little damage, they added to the general strain on the troops, who had the feeling of being very few for the large area to be held. Life was monotonous, training was strenuous; almost the only amenity was bathing. But the food was on the whole good, the medical arrangements were certainly good, the sick rate was low, and morale stayed high, although weariness became evident as time went on.

The enemy, as has been seen, had decided that it was useless to attack again until his artillery, in particular, was considerably stronger. This governed the earliest date by which an assault could be mounted, and before this happened the garrison was able to play its part in 'Crusader', and, without waiting to be attacked, itself break out

---

[1] The enemy, too, had had the idea of landing raiding parties from submarines. Two nights earlier fifteen men of the *Lehrregiment Brandenburg z.b.V.*800 (a unit trained specially for demolition raids, with detachments on every front) were put ashore by *U*.331 near El Daba in order to cut the coastal railway. They were all captured without doing any damage.

through the investing lines. But this honour did not fall to the 9th Australian Division, for reasons to be described.

On 18th July General Blamey proposed to General Auchinleck that the Australian troops in Tobruk should be relieved, and the Australian Government made a simultaneous approach to the War Cabinet. The Syrian campaign was over and there was a strong desire for all Australians in the Middle East to be united in one command. Moreover the long period in the front line had had its effect on the physical condition of the troops, whose fighting value, it was thought, must have declined.

General Auchinleck was instructed by the War Office to give full and sympathetic consideration to the views of the Australian Government. When the first Australian contingent was being raised it had been accepted by both governments that Australian troops should serve as one force, and General Auchinleck replied agreeing in principle to the new proposal. Plans were worked out to make use of the moonless periods in August and in the two following months, the danger from air attack being too great for a movement of this size to be made at any other times, or in other than fast warships. The first stage was put into effect by the relief in August of the 18th Australian Infantry Brigade and the 18th Cavalry (Indian Army) by the 1st Polish Carpathian Brigade.

At the end of August Mr. Fadden succeeded Mr. Menzies as Prime Minister of Australia, and prompted by General Blamey brought up the matter again. He had received no assurance when the reliefs would be complete and all the Australian forces united. He said that it was a vital national question, and that there would be grave repercussions if a catastrophe should occur to the Tobruk garrison through their decline in health and their consequent inability to withstand a determined attack. Mr. Churchill naturally did not wish the supply of Tobruk or any pending operations to be hampered by the relief, and he asked General Auchinleck, if this would be the result, to give him the facts to put to the Australian Government.

General Auchinleck replied on 10th September, at which time he was hoping to begin 'Crusader' in the first week of November. The first stage of the relief in August had shown that the naval risks were considerable, for nearly every ship had been attacked by aircraft. To go on with the relief would add to the burden on the destroyers at the expense of other naval operations. Five squadrons of fighters had been locked up in escort duties, and even these were not really enough. The risks of carrying men during any but the moonless periods were too great, and the last of the possible periods, 16th to 26th October, coincided with the time when the maximum effort ought to be concentrated on gaining air superiority for 'Crusader'. It would also leave very little time for completing the arrangements for the sortie by the Tobruk garrison. He stated that the power of endurance of the troops at Tobruk was noticeably reduced, but that their health and morale were very good. He made some alternative suggestions for strengthening the garrison, and reported that the Naval and Air Commanders-in-Chief and the Minister of State agreed with him that to attempt any further relief of the Tobruk garrison, however desirable it might be on political grounds, was not a justifiable military operation and would definitely prejudice the success of 'Crusader'.

The matter was earnestly discussed by Mr. Churchill and Mr. Fadden by telegram, but the Australian Government could not give way, and on 15th September the Chiefs of Staff ordered the relief to be carried out. General Auchinleck was distressed by the whole affair and felt that he did not possess the confidence of the Australian Government. Mr. Churchill, however, assured him that he and the Chiefs of Staff had full confidence in his military judgment. As time went on it appeared to General Auchinleck that although the last stage of the relief would not interfere with the postponed start of 'Crusader' there would be advantages in deferring it. On 13th October Mr. Churchill put this to Mr. Curtin, who had in turn succeeded Mr. Fadden, but the new Australian Government could not grant the request and the three Services had to make the best of it.

Needless to say it was the work of the Inshore Squadron and the auxiliary craft and naval shore parties that had made the defence of Tobruk possible at all. The Inshore Squadron had assumed its name, and most of the little ships of which it was formed were first assembled, at the time of the British offensive in December 1940. Its main activities then took two forms—supporting the Army by gunfire, and landing some of its essential requirements, especially fresh water and petrol. When the siege of Tobruk began in April 1941 the main task of the Inshore Squadron became to work the only line of supply possible—by sea.

The running in of supplies became a fine art. Ships had to find their way through the boom on a dark night and berth in a harbour strewn with wrecks. The base parties had to secure the ships and lighters, discharge the stores and get the ships away again—all without lights and in less than an hour. Ships of many types were used in this service. The regulars were destroyers, sloops, gunboats, minesweepers and, later, fast minelayers; there were also small merchant vessels, landing craft, tugs, and even captured sailing ships, mostly commissioned by the Royal Navy. Australian and South African warships played a prominent part.[1]

---

[1] Some of these ships did not belong to the Inshore Squadron, but were drawn from the Fleet as required. As part of the 'Crusader' plan the small ships were reorganized into two groups—one still known as the Inshore Squadron and the other as the Western Desert Escort Force.

It was a hazardous and wearing task. Losses came principally from air attack but also from mines. As the efficient anti-aircraft defence caused the air attacks on Tobruk to decrease, so those against ships on passage became more severe. When fighter protection was available the ships were routed close inshore, but it was not unusual for a whole squadron of escorting fighters to be outnumbered by the enemy. For the passage of a slow tanker four or more fighter squadrons were not too much. The most dangerous times were dawn, dusk, and in moonlight.

It is easy to see what an added burden the relief of Tobruk threw on the Inshore Squadron. For the first stage—the relief of 18th Australian Infantry Brigade by the 1st Polish Carpathian Brigade between 19th and 29th August—the nightly convoys consisted usually of two destroyers and one fast minelayer (*Abdiel* or *Latona*) carrying troops, and a third destroyer laden with stores. Cruiser escorts were provided to give extra anti-aircraft protection. 6,116 troops and 1,297 tons of stores were landed and 5,040 troops were taken off. The Army had no casualties but the cruiser *Phoebe* and the destroyer *Nizam* were both damaged by air attack.

Between 19th and 27th September the 16th Infantry Brigade Group of 70th Division, as 6th (British) Division was now called, Headquarters 32nd Army Tank Brigade, and the 4th Royal Tank Regiment —6,308 men in all—were brought in, and the 24th Australian Infantry Brigade Group of 5,989 men taken out. Over 2,000 tons of stores were landed, and no ships were lost. For the third stage of the relief, between 12th and 25th October, the remainder of 70th Division was brought in and nearly all the Australians taken off. During this period the ships plying to and from Tobruk were less lucky. The destroyer *Hero* was damaged by a bomb, the gunboat *Gnat* had her bows blown off, and the petrol carrier *Pass of Balmaha* and the storeship *Samos* were sunk by a submarine. Worst of all, the valuable fast minelayer *Latona* was sunk by air attack. On this occasion she was carrying stores and ammunition; 23 officers and men of the Royal Navy and 14 soldiers were killed or wounded. Her loss, and the increasing weight of the attacks, convinced Admiral Cunningham that it was too risky to continue. Consequently 2/13th Australian Battalion, two companies of the 2/15th, and some men of divisional headquarters were left behind. So ended an undertaking to which the Commanders-in-Chief, and Admiral Cunningham in particular, had been strongly opposed, but which, in the event, caused no delay to the start of 'Crusader'. Command of the fortress passed to Major-General R. M. Scobie, commander of the 70th Division.

The achievement of the Navy and Merchant Service during the whole period of the siege—11th April to 10th December 1941—is baldly given by the following figures:

Men taken out of Tobruk (including wounded and prisoners)	47,280
Men carried in	34,113
Stores carried in	*tons* 33,946
Warships and merchant ships lost	34
,, ,, ,, ,, damaged	33

During the six and a half months from April to October the casualties in the garrison were

	Killed	Wounded	Missing	Total
Australian	744	1,974	476	3,194
British	88	406	15	509
Indian	1	25	—	26
Polish	22	82	3	107
Total	855	2,487	494	3,836

'Crusader', or—as it is sometimes called—the Winter Battle, was fought over a vast area by the largest concentration of armoured vehicles that had yet been used in the Western Desert. Each side had, in addition, a number of unarmoured formations, but it was thought that the armoured forces were dominant and that the battle would be won or lost according to what happened to them. The vital question of training has already been referred to, and it is necessary also to take account of some of the material factors which affected the relative strength of the armoured forces from time to time.

Generalization about the tanks themselves is apt to be misleading. The introduction of a new or modified model did not mean the immediate disappearance of the older tanks; consequently there were often several different models in use together. Particulars of the tanks which were present during the period of this volume are given in Appendix 8, together with a short explanation of some of the technical aspects of the ding-dong struggle between guns and armour.[1] A few of the most important features at the time of 'Crusader' deserve mention here.

The German tanks were of pre-war design, and the earlier models had been thoroughly tested in training and in battle in Poland and in France. In Libya there were three main types, Pzkw II, III, and IV,

[1] A similar appendix, covering the spring and summer of 1941, will be found in Volume II.

all mechanically reliable. The Pzkw II was lightly armed and armoured and of little fighting value, but was useful for reconnaissance. The Pzkw IV was a support tank, armed with a low-velocity 7·5-cm gun effective with high explosive shell against unarmoured troops and capable of damaging tanks at long range. The Pzkw III was the war-horse of the tank *v.* tank battle in the Desert. It mounted a short 5-cm. gun firing a 4½-lb. armour-piercing shell. Against homogeneous (i.e. not face-hardened) armour, such as the British used, its penetration was much the same as that of the solid shot of its opposite number —the British 2-pdr—though a shell, even if it did not penetrate, was capable of doing quite serious damage. In addition, like the German anti-tank guns of the time, the Pzkw III carried a small proportion of light armour-piercing shot, known to the British as 'arrowhead'. This had very good penetration at short range, and might almost be called 'anti-Matilda' ammunition—so impressed had the Germans been by the thick frontal armour of the Matilda tanks captured in France.

In November 1941 the basic armour on the Pzkw III and IV was not very different in thickness from that on the British cruisers, but in the more vulnerable places it was face-hardened, while the British armour was not. Moreover, many Pzkw IIIs—the exact number is uncertain—were strengthened in front with additional face-hardened plates. Trials were later to show that if small projectiles, such as the 2-pdr shot, were not to shatter ineffectively against the extra plates they must be protected by a cap. No capped ammunition was available for the British 2-pdr.

The Italians had a light tank of no account and a rather slow medium tank—the M13/40—armed with a 47-mm. gun. The mechanical design and construction of this tank were sound, but it was too lightly armoured and the plates tended to crack when hit.

There was no German or Italian counterpart to the British 'I' tanks, whose role was to co-operate closely with the infantry. The Matilda was a genuine 'I' tank, but the Valentine, which gradually replaced it, had been designed as a cruiser, and was faster and less heavily armoured than the Matilda.[1] In November 1941 the 'I' tanks in the Middle East were not employed with the armoured divisions, so that, valuable though they were, they cannot at this stage be included without reservation in the balance-sheet of the armoured forces.

The early British-made cruisers were by now suffering from what General Norrie described as 'general debility'. The latest arrival, the Crusader, was reasonably fast and handy, but had certain weaknesses

---

[1] In the Middle East the Valentine came to be used both as an 'I' tank and as a cruiser: e.g. the 8th Armoured Division, which arrived in the Middle East in July 1942, consisted almost entirely of Valentines.

which in the desert led to far too many mechanical breakdowns, resulting often in total loss.[1] All British tanks were armed with the 2-pdr gun.[2] The American Stuarts filled a serious gap in Allied cruiser tank production and though they were really light tanks they were very welcome in the Middle East. They had a good turn of speed and were mechanically reliable, and their 37-mm. gun (using capped ammunition) was slightly better than the 2-pdr, but the fighting compartment was inconvenient and the radius of action without refuelling was so small as to be a tactical handicap. The table on page 30 shows how the various tanks were allotted to brigades.

It is important to remember that the opposing tank was not the tank's sole enemy. The anti-tank mine was already having an effect upon tactics, and before long its influence was to become very great indeed. Both sides were to lay minefields in profusion. Before 'Crusader' began they were already in being at Tobruk, and along the frontier defences which stretched from Sidi Omar to Halfaya and Sollum.

A feature of the German tactics in 'Battleaxe' in June 1941 had been the effective use of anti-tank guns; in particular, the 8·8-cm. dual-purpose (anti-tank and anti-aircraft) gun had done great execution among British tanks.[3] During 'Crusader' it is highly probable that most of the damage to British tanks was done by the 5-cm. anti-tank gun (Pak 38) which worked in close co-operation with the German armour. This gun was longer, and had better penetration, than the 5-cm. tank gun mounted in the Pzkw III or the British 2-pdr. There were also various Italian anti-tank guns, of which the most numerous was the 47-mm. At this time all the larger anti-tank guns in the frontier defences were Italian, except for twenty-three German 8·8-cms—which were doubtless positioned where it was expected that Matildas might be used. Nearly all the anti-tank guns in the force investing Tobruk were Italian. The Germans kept their ninety-six 5-cm. Pak 38s and the remaining twelve 8·8-cms with the *D.A.K.*, together with a number of the older 3·7-cm. anti-tank guns. The British 2-pdr anti-tank gun was the same as the gun mounted in their

[1] To avoid confusion, the British Crusader tank (also known as A 15 or Cruiser Mark VI) is printed without quotation-marks, whereas the battle is referred to as 'Crusader'.

[2] Except for a few close-support tanks; see table on page 440.

[3] The German 8·8-cm. gun, though manned by the *Luftwaffe*, had been brought to North Africa primarily as an anti-tank weapon. For this role it had the advantages over the British 3·7-inch A.A. gun of a shield, an excellent telescopic sight, and later of a type of trailer that enabled it to come rapidly into action and so take part in comparatively open fighting. The primary role of the British 3·7-inch guns was definitely anti-aircraft, and most of them were deployed in accordance with a plan agreed between the three Services at points vulnerable to air attack all over the Middle East—such as depots, ports, the Canal, airfields and advanced landing-grounds. But these guns, too, if fitted with a suitable sight, could engage ground targets, including tanks. In April 1942 about sixty were so fitted, and a few were in action in an anti-tank role during part of the battle of Gazala.

tanks, and, like it, suffered from having no capped ammunition. Until the 2-pdr was replaced by the 6-pdr in 1942 great reliance had to be placed on the 25-pdr field gun, which became the best weapon against enemy tanks, often to the detriment of its normal tactical role.

At this time a British armoured division was designed to contain two armoured brigades each of three armoured regiments each of about fifty tanks. The artillery and motor-borne infantry were grouped in a Support Group. If, therefore, infantry were needed to work with an armoured brigade, they were provided either by the Support Group or by another (unarmoured) division. Apart from the two armoured brigades in the sole British armoured division there was one armoured brigade which had some supporting arms of its own and was known as the 4th Armoured Brigade Group. It was sometimes under command of 30th Corps and sometimes of 7th Armoured Division.

The Germans had two armoured divisions, 15th and 21st. Each contained one tank regiment of two battalions; one reconnaissance unit, which included an armoured car company; one machine-gun battalion; one *Panzerjäger* or 'tank-hunting' (i.e. anti-tank) unit; one engineer battalion; and one artillery regiment of three batteries. At this time, however, one battery of 21st Panzer Division had been lent to the *Afrika* Division for the attack on Tobruk. Each armoured division had also a lorried infantry regiment of two battalions, but the 21st had been further milked of one of its two, which was now at Halfaya holding part of the frontier defences. The *Afrika* Division (soon to be renamed 90th Light) consisted almost entirely of infantry, of which it had seven battalions.[1] The Italian Ariete Armoured Division contained three battalions of tanks, a motorized Bersaglieri regiment, artillery, engineers, etc.

Thus the Germans and Italians together had, in their armoured divisions, seven battalions with about 390 tanks in all, including the the German Pzkw IIs but excluding the Italian light tanks. The British 8th Army had nine battalions (or regiments), with nearly 500 tanks of cruiser class. In addition, there were three battalions of 'I' tanks in the 8th Army and a mixed force of 'I' tanks, light tanks, and cruisers in the Tobruk garrison.

The distribution of tanks by types was as follows:[2]

---

[1] The infantry regiments of German armoured and light divisions were at this time styled *Schützen Regimenter*, of which the British equivalent was lorried or motorized infantry. The necessary vehicles were borne on the establishment of the regiments, which, unlike other infantry, came within the province of the Director of Mobile Troops. In July 1942 the lorried infantry regiments were renamed *Panzer Grenadier* regiments.

[2] The figures are not all the same in the unit, brigade, division, corps, and army diaries; nor is it always clear whether tanks in the Light Repair Sections and Advanced Workshops are included. The figures given are compiled mainly from Units' own records.

BRITISH

30th Corps

Type	HQ 30 Corps	HQ 7 Armd Div	4 Armd Bde	7 Armd Bde	22 Armd Bde	Total
Early cruisers various	..	6	..	26	..	32
Cruisers A13	..	..	..	62	..	62[1]
Cruisers A15 (Crusaders)	..	2	..	53	155	210
Stuarts LM 3	8	..	165	..	..	173
Total	8	8	165	141	155	477

13th Corps

1st Army Tank Brigade — 3 cruisers and 132 'I' tanks (about half Matilda, half Valentine)

In Tobruk

32nd Army Tank Brigade — 32 assorted cruisers
25 light tanks
69 'I' tanks (Matilda)

GERMAN AND ITALIAN

Type	15 Pz Div	21 Pz Div	Ariete Div	Total
Pzkw II	38	32	..	70
Pzkw III	75	64	..	139
Pzkw IV	20	15	..	35
M 13/40	..	..	146	146
Total	133	111	146	390

52 Italian light tanks were with the Ariete Division, and 110 were distributed among the other Italian (non-armoured) divisions.

There was a striking difference in the tank reserves. The Germans appear to have had almost none, and their first substantial reinforcements arrived late in December. The British had a few Stuarts in

[1] Mere numbers do not always give a true picture. For instance, sixteen of the A 13s joined 2nd R.T.R. from workshops at the last minute; they were reported unfit for operations, but had to be taken into action.

reserve in the forward area, and a large number of assorted tanks undergoing repair or essential modification in workshops—92 cruisers (mostly new Crusaders), 90 new Stuarts, and 77 'I' tanks. Convoy WS 12 was already at sea bringing 124 Crusaders, 60 Stuarts, and 52 'I' tanks, all except the last named being part of the 1st Armoured Division. No more convoys were expected before the end of January.

By the middle of November, then, the situation was that the British, with more tanks and aircraft than had ever been assembled in the Western Desert before, were about to launch a major offensive, and General Rommel was about to make his long-delayed attack on Tobruk. It was touch-and-go which side would be ready first; in the event it was the British, who, moreover, had been successful in concealing their intentions. Rommel was expecting them to do something to divert his attention from Tobruk, but had no wish to play their game by allowing it to be diverted. He was therefore in no mind to respond quickly to the first British moves, whatever they might be. But, as has been seen, the development of the British plan was to depend largely on the enemy's reactions. Because of these curious circumstances a special interest lies in seeing how far the commanders on both sides were hindered or helped by their expectations of what was going to happen.

CHAPTER II

THE WINTER BATTLE, 1941 ('CRUSADER')–I

See Map 2

'CRUSADER' was a British victory, in that Tobruk was relieved, the enemy was driven from Cyrenaica with heavy losses, and all the Axis troops holding positions on the Egyptian frontier were destroyed or captured. This all took longer than expected, however, and in doing it the British exhausted themselves.

The region Sollum-Fort Maddalena-Bir el Gubi-Tobruk, where the first fortnight's fighting took place, is a corner of the Western Desert larger than Norfolk and Suffolk.[1] Except near the coast the surface is generally hard, flat, and open, so that desert-worthy vehicles can roam almost anywhere except after heavy rain. Along an imaginary line from Bardia to El Adem the ground breaks up into undulations, with the ridges running east and west; the northern faces are usually the steeper, forming escarpments passable by vehicles at only occasional places. A few miles farther north runs the coast road—the Italian *Via Balbia*—and the ground then tumbles in a tangle of wadis to the sea.

The ridges or escarpments lie roughly in two rows, one wholly to the north of the Trigh Capuzzo and one partly north and partly south of it. Towards El Adem the Trigh runs between the two, as also does the Tobruk by-pass road. This road was built by the enemy to take the place of that portion of the *Via Balbia* denied to them by our occupation of Tobruk. Twelve miles east of El Adem, that is just opposite Sidi Rezegh, the by-pass road turns north and passes between minor hill-features at El Duda on the west and Belhamed on the east.[2] The area Sidi Rezegh-El Duda-Belhamed, which was obviously a sensitive spot on the enemy's communications, was the scene of some of the heaviest fighting of all.

'Crusader' was a complicated battle, and in order that its essential features shall stand out clearly the dispositions and movements on Maps 3 to 16 have been drawn as simply as possible. But to form a

[1] For a general description of the Western Desert see Volume I, pp. 115-7.

[2] An alternative spelling is Ed Duda. The usual practice is to keep the 'l' of the definite article ('al' or 'el') even though it is assimilated in pronunciation to one of the letters t, th, d, dh, r, z, s, sh, l, or n. Thus El Regima is pronounced Er Regima: El Nbeidat, En Nbeidat; El Duda, Ed Duda; and so on.

true picture of the scene it is necessary to bear in mind a few facts.

First, the enormous number of vehicles. By now the 8th Army was almost entirely motorized, that is to say nearly all the men and equipment were carried in some sort of mechanical transport—armoured car, tank, towing vehicle, tracked Bren carrier, special vehicle, or truck. Some men fought in their vehicles, some on foot. In a 'motorized' battalion the transport was permanently allotted, but in others only the 'specialists' (signallers, mortar platoons, etc.) had permanent transport, and extra lorries from the transport pool were needed to lift all the other men if the battalion had to move any distance quickly. Broadly speaking, all the units of 30th Corps were motorized, while some of 13th Corps were not. As for the enemy, in their three armoured divisions (15th, 21st and Ariete) and their one motorized division (Trieste) everyone was carried. In the incomplete German *Afrika* Division none of the infantry was as yet lorry-borne.[1] The other Italian divisions had not enough transport to make them mobile. Altogether there may have been anything up to thirty thousand vehicles moving about in the region between Tobruk and the Egyptian frontier.

To avoid attention from the air it was usual for vehicles to move widely dispersed, whether they were lifting troops or delivering ammunition, petrol, water or food, or were returning to refill either empty or carrying casualties, prisoners or salvage. The Germans dispersed their vehicles less widely than the British, but neither side moved in the compact columns and blobs shown in the history books, except at night or when it was necessary to concentrate for some tactical purpose. The usual pattern by day was one of diffuse swarms or long strings of widely separated vehicles trying to avoid bunching or looking in any way conspicuous. When they halted for the night for rest, maintenance, or replenishment they would normally close up into a more compact formation—called a leaguer—for better control and defence.

So much movement in extended formation made great demands upon the skill and self-reliance of drivers and crews, especially during the time when each side was burrowing far behind the other's 'front'. Then, even in the back areas, every move, and sometimes every halt, became an adventure. Friend and foe would suddenly meet, stray vehicles would be pounced upon, headquarters would be overrun, and leaguers would be shot up. A breakdown could be serious, for apart from the danger of being lost there was always the chance that the next vehicle to appear would be hostile. Rommel himself was very nearly captured, and many other important persons had narrow

---

[1] The title "155th Lorried Infantry Regiment' in the *Afrika* Division is misleading. The headquarters was that of a Lorried Infantry Regiment, but the battalions (all belonging to different regiments) of which the 155th Regiment was made up were not provided with lorries.

escapes. But the freedom of movement in the desert also gave experienced and mobile troops a good deal of security because they could easily dodge trouble.

It is easy to imagine what complex patterns these mechanical armies got themselves into. Not even from the air could they be completely sorted out. The battlefield was large and much of it almost featureless, so that the exact position of anything seen was often difficult to describe. After the first two wet days the weather gradually improved, but even so an aircraft flying low—as it often had to—had only a small field of view, while the prevalent low cloud and whipped-up sand made visibility from a greater height very uncertain. Moreover, the numbers of aircraft on each side specifically devoted to tactical reconnaissance were quite small; the British, for instance, started the battle with three squadrons in which the pilots were specially trained in such duties. Their reports were supplemented, of course, by what the fighter and bomber pilots saw, but the broad result was that although a great deal was observed and accurately reported of the enemy's moves and dispositions the plots on the map did not always represent the whole story and sometimes made little sense.

Another of the difficulties of the Air Force in helping the Army was that the 'bomb-line', or line beyond which anything seen might be attacked, was not easy to define in practice, for instead of there being a clearly defined front the forces of the two sides were often biting each other's flanks or tail. Aircraft were rarely able to join in a swaying fight between the armoured forces, and even on the fringe of such a fight they could not always tell friend from foe. The Army was loath to paint large distinguishing marks on its vehicles, though it was later forced to follow the enemy's lead in this respect. Difficult as it was to distinguish troops from the air it was not always easy to do so from the ground either. One vehicle at a distance or at an angle is much like another, especially when the silhouettes are broken by festoons of sandbags, kit, and spares, and to make matters worse each side made great use of vehicles captured from the other.[1] The British armoured car regiments, however, were good at recognition and their reports were generally accurate.

There was another important aspect of the struggle to gain information. During battle a commander wants to have timely and accurate information not only of the position of the enemy's troops, but also of their condition. The first news about the enemy's losses usually came from the unit that had caused them, and for some time this would

[1] The importance of early recognition is well brought out in one of 21st Panzer Division's reports on its battle experiences: 'Tank recognition is the basis of all tank defence measures. In fighting heavily armoured vehicles the correct moment to open fire, the point of aim, and the choice of ammunition differ with each type of vehicle'.

be all the higher commanders had to go upon. The Germans often seemed to have recovered in a remarkable way, and it is now clear that the first estimates of the numbers of their tanks destroyed were usually far too high. Indeed, the total would have accounted for the two Panzer regiments several times over, and this would only have been possible if the Germans had received constant and considerable reinforcements of tanks, whereas in fact they received hardly any. It is only fair to say that the enemy also suffered from exaggerated reports.

Yet another factor tended to thicken the fog of battle at this time. Even at night, when there would often be a pause, it was not always possible for the higher headquarters to get accurate and up-to-the-minute information of the state or even the position of their own troops. This was because the great extent of the battlefield and the speed of movement compelled at all levels a wide use of wireless communication (in addition to other methods) and this was much less reliable than it later became.[1] Not only had pre-war economy hindered the development of the Army's signal equipment (partly no doubt because the Army could carry out its peace time duties with less dependence upon wireless than could the other Services) but the size of the requirement in desert warfare had been underestimated. More channels were required for operational and administrative control in highly mobile desert warfare than elsewhere, and there were not enough wireless sets. Nor, with the exception of the short-range sets for tank-to-tank and intra-unit communications, did the wireless equipment possess the necessary range, and there was much trouble from fading, particularly in the hours of darkness. The pre-war medium-range sets had proved quite unsuitable for the desert, and pending the production of a satisfactory type, a medley of equipment, procured from various sources, had to be employed as a makeshift. Again, there was difficulty in finding the means and the time to charge the batteries of short-range sets under battle conditions. This was a particularly thorny problem for tanks, which used the tank-engine for charging, because it was found that the time spent on the move (i.e. with the engine running) was less than had been expected; the batteries had therefore to be charged frequently by some external means. At this time there was a serious shortage of charging plant, and the expenditure of spare batteries was consequently enormous.

The net result was that in 1941 there were liable to be interruptions to wireless communications at critical times, especially on the longer links; indeed, Army Headquarters was on occasions out of telegraphic

---

[1] The system known as 'J', whereby the wireless transmissions of forward headquarters were intercepted at Army and Corps headquarters and passed to the operations staffs, had not yet been developed.

"CRUSADER"
The opening moves:
18th-21st November
1941

LEGEND

British troops are shown in red,
German in blue and Italian in green.

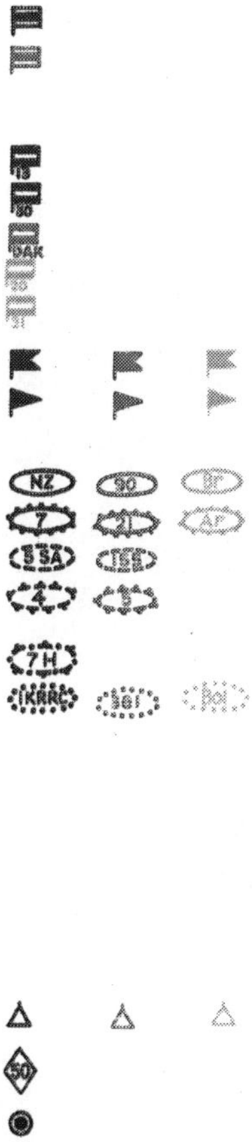

Headquarters of Armies

8th (Cunningham)
Panzergruppe Afrika (Rommel)

Headquarters of Corps

13th (Godwin-Austen)
30th (Norrie)
D.A.K. (Crüwell)
20th (Gambara)
21st (Navarrini)

Headquarters of Divisions
Headquarters of Brigades (or equivalent)

NZ 90 Br Divisions
7 21 Ar Armoured Divisions
5 SA 155 Brigades (or equivalent)
4 5 Armoured Brigades and Panzer Regiments
7 H Armoured (British) Regiments
KRRC 361 Bol Other units and detachments

Italian Divisions

Ar = Ariete
Tre = Trieste } 20th Corps

Bol = Bologna
Br = Brescia
Pa = Pavia
Trn = Trento } 21st Corps

Sa = Savona

Recce. Patrols
50 Field Maintenance Centres
Airfields and landing grounds

Map 3

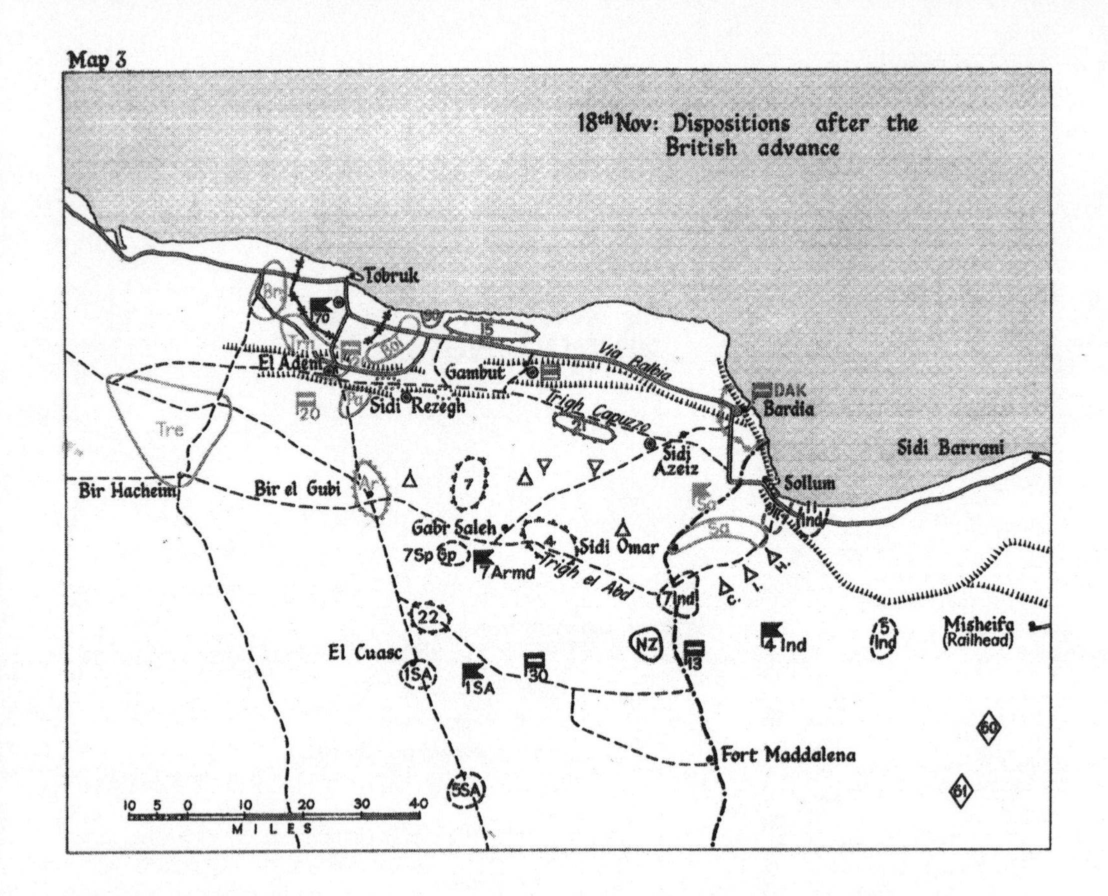
18th Nov: Dispositions after the British advance
Tobruk
70
Bol
15
90
Tre
El Adem
Gambut
Via Balbia
DAK
Bardia
20
Sidi Rezegh
Trigh Capuzzo
Sidi Azeiz
Sidi Barrani
Bir Hacheim
Bir el Gubi
Ar
7
Sollum
Sa
11 Ind
Gabr Saleh
Sidi Omar
7Sp Gp
7Armd
Trigh el Abd
7Ind
22
El Cuasc
1SA
30
NZ
13
4 Ind
5 Ind
Misheifa (Railhead)
Fort Maddalena
5SA
60
61
10 5 0 10 20 30 40
MILES

Map 5

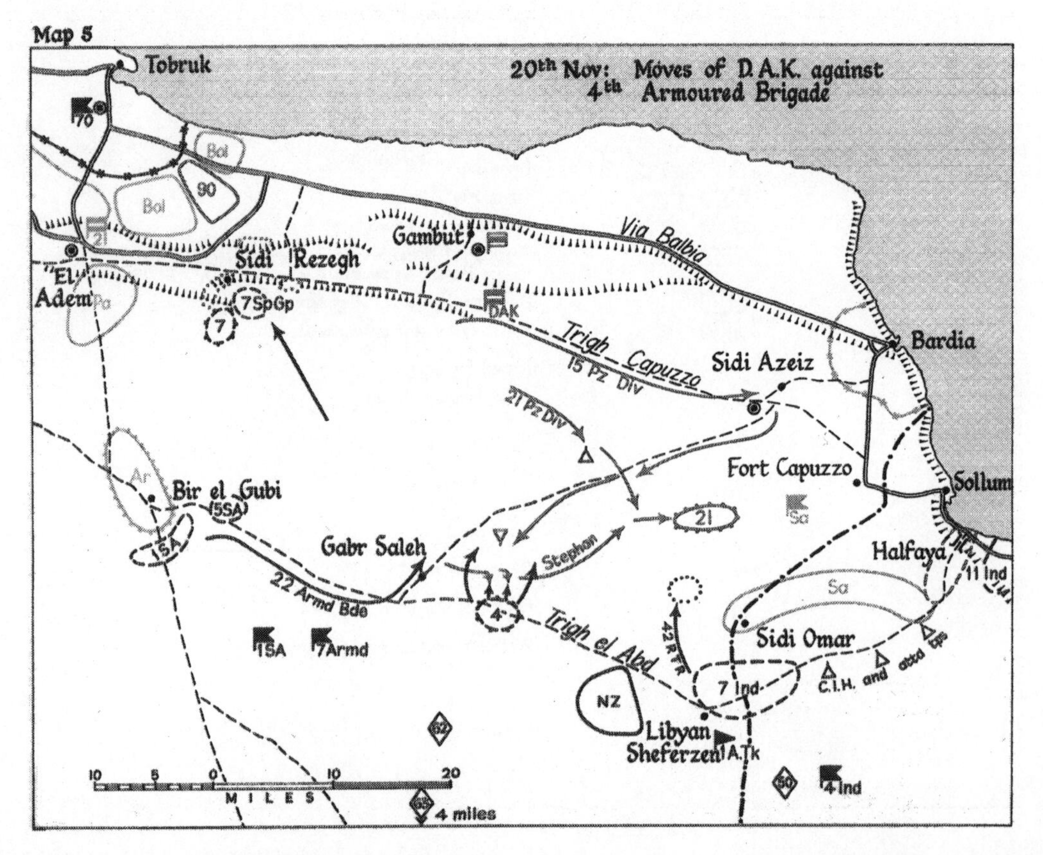
20th Nov: Moves of D.A.K. against 4th Armoured Brigade
Tobruk
70
Bol
90
21
El Adem
Pa
Sidi Rezegh
7SpGp
7
Gambut
Via Balbia
DAK
Trigh Capuzzo
15 Pz Div
Sidi Azeiz
Bardia
21 Pz Div
Fort Capuzzo
Sollum
Sa
Ar
Bir el Gubi
5SA
1SA
21
Gabr Saleh
Stephan
Halfaya
11 Ind
22 Armd Bde
4
Trigh el Abd
42 RTR
Sidi Omar
C.I.H. and attd tps
7 Ind
NZ
Libyan
Sheferzen
A.Tk
7Armd
62
50
4 Ind
4 miles
10 5 0 10 20
MILES

Map 4

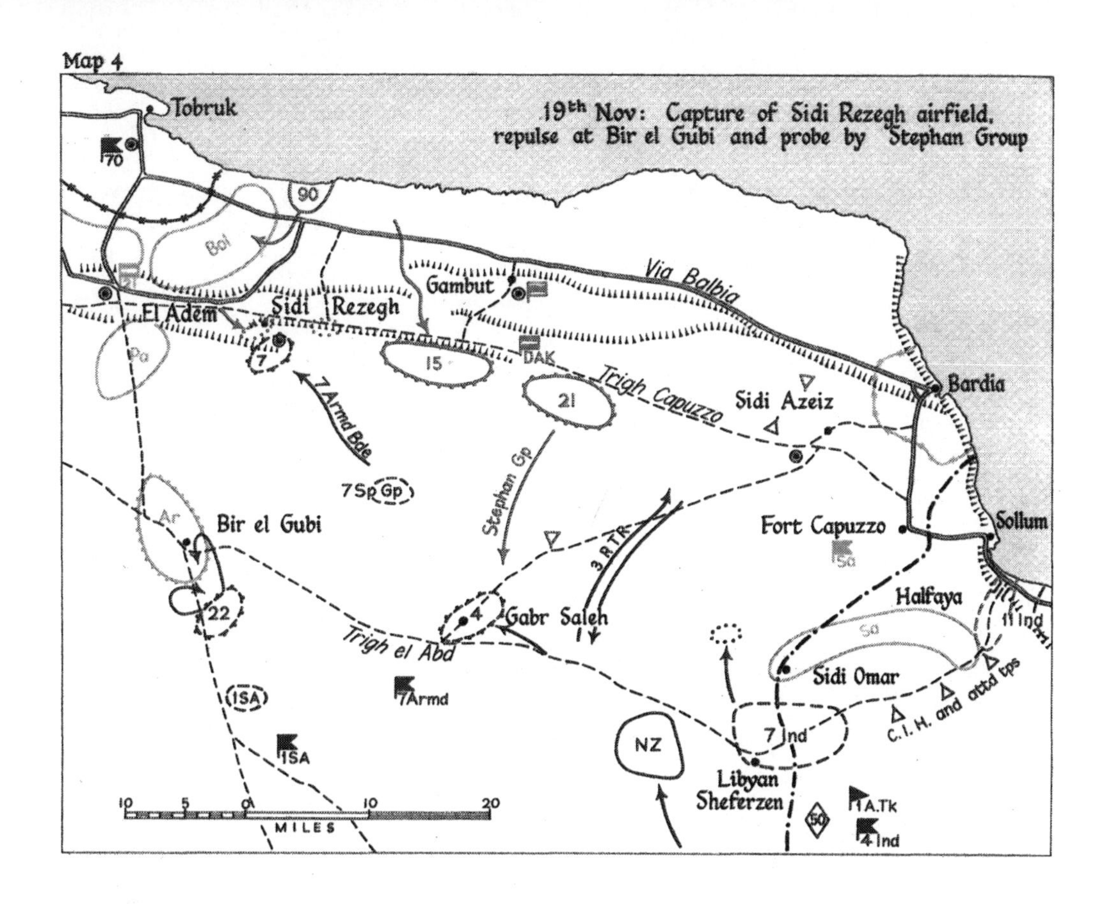

19th Nov: Capture of Sidi Rezegh airfield, repulse at Bir el Gubi and probe by Stephan Group
Tobruk
70
90
Bol
El Adem
Sidi Rezegh
Gambut
Via Balbia
Pa
7
15
DAK
7 Armd Bde
21
Trigh Capuzzo
Sidi Azeiz
Bardia
Stephan Gp
7 Sp Gp
Ar
Bir el Gubi
3 RTR
Fort Capuzzo
Sollum
Sa
Halfaya
22
4
Gabr Saleh
Trigh el Abd
Sa
11 Ind
Sidi Omar
C.I.H. and attd tps
1SA
7 Armd
7 Ind
NZ
1SA
Libyan Sheferzen
1 A.Tk
50
4 Ind
MILES
10 5 0 10 20

Map 6

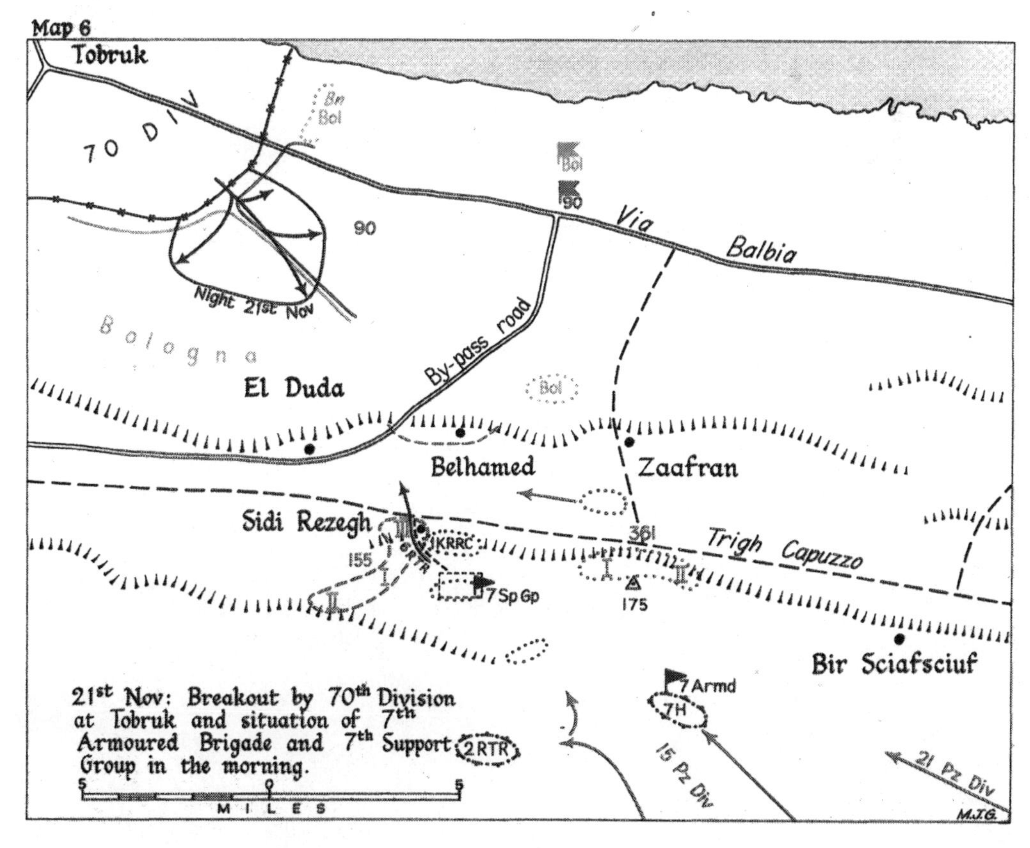

Tobruk
Bn Bol
70 DIV
Bol
90
90
Via Balbia
Night 21st Nov
Bologna
By-pass road
Bol
El Duda
Belhamed
Zaafran
Sidi Rezegh
KRRC
361
Trigh Capuzzo
155
6 RTR
7 Sp Gp
175
Bir Sciafsciuf
7 Armd
7H
21st Nov: Breakout by 70th Division at Tobruk and situation of 7th Armoured Brigade and 7th Support Group in the morning.
2 RTR
15 Pz Div
21 Pz Div
MILES
5 0 5
M.J.G.

and telephonic touch with one or both Corps.[1] Thus there were frequently serious delays between the issue of an order and its receipt by all the units which were required to act on it. A further difficulty arose from ciphering delays, aggravated by a shortage of cipher staffs. Attempts were made to evade the need for ciphering by such dodges as 'veiled' conversations, but the enemy's records show that he gathered much information from these rather ingenuous attempts. The German diaries disclose that they also had their troubles, for there are many references to the failure of wireless communications at crucial moments.

The foregoing remarks will perhaps explain some of the differences in this particular battle between what is now understood to have happened and what the commanders on both sides believed to be happening.

The main forces under General Cunningham's command and their initial tasks in the plan already outlined were as follows:

30th Corps (Lieut.-General C. W. M. Norrie)

To advance north-west, find and destroy the enemy's armour, and protect the left flank of the 13th Corps:

7th Armoured Division (Major-General W. H. E. Gott)—
7th and 22nd Armoured Brigades.
4th Armoured Brigade Group (Brigadier A. H. Gatehouse).

To protect the communications of the 7th Armoured Division on the west and south-west; later to capture the Sidi Rezegh ridge:

1st South African Division (Major-General G. L. Brink)—
1st and 5th South African Infantry Brigades.

To protect the communications, supply dumps and landing-grounds in 30th Corps' area:

22nd Guards Brigade (Brigadier J. C. O. Marriott).

13th Corps (Lieut.-General A. R. Godwin-Austen)

To pin down and cut off the enemy's troops on the Egyptian frontier; later to advance west:

New Zealand Division (Major-General B. C. Freyberg)—
4th, 5th and 6th New Zealand Infantry Brigades.
4th Indian Division (Major-General F. W. Messervy)—
5th, 7th and 11th Indian Infantry Brigades.
1st Army Tank Brigade (Brigadier H. R. B. Watkins).

---

[1] In the text 'telephone conversation' sometimes, for brevity's sake, covers 'conversation on the key', a method by which an operator tapped out in Morse a dictated message and wrote down the answer. The method could be slow and exasperating.

Tobruk Garrison (Major-General R. M. Scobie)[1]

To make a sortie when ordered:

70th Division—14th, 16th and 23rd Infantry Brigades.
Polish Carpathian Infantry Brigade Group (Major-General S. Kopanski).
32nd Army Tank Brigade (Brigadier A. C. Willison).

Oasis Force (Brigadier D. W. Reid)[2]

To secure Jarabub, advance to protect landing-ground 125, *and seize Jalo:*
29th Indian Infantry Brigade Group.
6th South African Armoured Car Regiment.

Army Reserve
2nd South African Division (Major-General I. P. de Villiers)—3rd, 4th and 6th South African Infantry Brigades.

On 16th November the Mediterranean Fleet from Alexandria, Force H from Gibraltar, and Force K from Malta, together with some merchant ships, began the series of movements to simulate the passage of a convoy from Gibraltar through the Mediterranean, with the object of attracting the attention of the enemy, and of his air forces in particular.

At midnight on 17th November the concentration of the 8th Army and Desert Air Force was complete. The night, as usual at this time of year, was bitterly cold. Good driving, wide dispersion, the use of simple camouflage, strict wireless discipline, the low cloud, and the success of the Royal Air Force in hampering the enemy's reconnaissance had all helped to conceal the British intentions and had led General Rommel to conclude—in spite of Italian misgivings—that the only action to be expected would be some sort of counter to his own attack on Tobruk. What is more, he calculated that anything the British might do would be too late. He was therefore content to rely upon the armoured cars of Reconnaissance Units 3 and 33 to give warning of any British movements. Accordingly on 18th November only these units lay in the path of the British 30th Corps.

See Map 3

At dawn the 30th Corps began to cross the frontier, and by evening had approximately reached its objectives for the day.[3] The 13th Corps

---

[1] Also commanded 70th Division.

[2] Also commanded 29th Indian Infantry Brigade.

[3] Mechanical breakdowns had reduced the number of runner tanks to 119 in the 7th Armoured Brigade and 136 in the 22nd. The figure for 4th Armoured Brigade is not recorded, but it is known that there were very few breakdowns among the Stuart tanks.

had closed up to the enemy's frontier positions.[1] Though the weather, by continuing to ground the Axis air forces, had favoured the British, visibility from the air was poor. On the ground nothing had been seen of the enemy except their reconnaissance troops, so there was nothing to guide General Cunningham in deciding what to do next. He had taken the first step by moving his own armour one day's march to a central and threatening position, and had intended the next step to be the sequel to some move of the enemy's, but as yet the enemy had not moved.

At the enemy's headquarters opinion was in fact divided. General Crüwell, commanding the *D.A.K.*, was inclined to see in the British moves the start of an offensive. Rommel, however, who had just arrived back from Rome, believed them to indicate no more than a reconnaissance in force, and made no changes in his dispositions. The 15th Panzer Division remained assembled between Tobruk and Gambut, ready to take part in the coming attack on Tobruk. The 21st Panzer Division lay some twenty miles to the west of Sidi Azeiz in a convenient position for supporting the frontier garrisons. The Ariete Division was at Bir el Gubi, covering the desert flank. Headquarters *D.A.K.* was due to leave Bardia for Gambut next day—a further preliminary to the attack on Tobruk.

Thus we now know that Rommel did not intend to react, even on the next day, in the way that the British commanders hoped. They were eager for him to do something which would help them to judge where and when the great armoured battle might be fought. They were therefore in the odd position of possessing the initiative, and, because the enemy did not act, of being uncertain how to use it. General Gott's orders for the 7th Armoured Division early on 19th November reflect this state of mind. The task was to secure Bir el Gubi and later Sidi Rezegh. The 4th Armoured Brigade was to remain where it was to protect the right flank of the Division and the left flank of 13th Corps. The 7th Armoured Brigade was to reconnoitre towards Sidi Rezegh and to secure an area on the escarpment if an opportunity occurred. The 22nd Armoured Brigade was to reconnoitre towards Bir el Gubi and to secure ground in that area as opportunity offered. The Support Group was to be ready to act with either the 7th or 22nd Armoured Brigades.

See Map 4

The 22nd Armoured Brigade (Brigadier J. Scott-Cockburn), of three newly arrived Yeomanry regiments armed with the latest Crusader tanks, was nearing Bir el Gubi when General Gott arrived and—

[1] Between the sea and the New Zealand Division were 11th Indian Infantry Brigade, Central India Horse, and 7th Indian Infantry Brigade.

according to its own diary—ordered it to attack.[1] He may have felt that it would be unwise to leave the Ariete Division unmolested on his left flank, and may have thought that there was a chance of doing some damage to it at little cost. He may have wished to give the 22nd Armoured Brigade some battle experience before they met the Germans, but without becoming heavily committed. Anyhow, the Brigade attacked, perhaps rather impetuously, with the support of only one 25-pdr battery, and after driving in the covering troops came under strong fire from the Italian prepared positions. At length it broke off the action having lost 25 of its 136 tanks. 34 Italian tanks were destroyed and 15 were damaged, and 12 Italian guns were lost.[2]

Meanwhile the 7th Armoured Brigade (Brigadier G. M. O. Davy), advancing north, had seen no enemy, and towards one o'clock was ordered to seize a position east of Sidi Rezegh.[3] It moved fast and surprised Sidi Rezegh airfield, capturing 19 Italian aircraft. There it remained, to the alarm of those troops of the 90th Light (*Afrika*) Division deployed along the escarpment which lay north of the airfield, who had at the moment very few anti-tank guns.

The morning's reports strengthened General Crüwell's view that a British offensive was developing. Rommel, however, would have none of it, though he yielded to the extent of allowing 15th Panzer Division to be moved south-west of Gambut, whence it could reconnoitre, and agreed that 21st Panzer Division should send a battle group to support its armoured cars which were being chased towards Sidi Azeiz by the King's Dragoon Guards. The Stephan group was accordingly formed of 5th Panzer Regiment, probably with 80 to 90 tanks and some field and anti-aircraft guns. This set off towards Gabr Saleh and ran headlong into the 4th Armoured Brigade Group (Brigadier A. H. Gatehouse) just before 4 p.m.[4] The fight was evenly matched in numbers of tanks for one British armoured regiment (3rd Royal Tank Regiment) had been sent off to support the armoured cars in the direction of Sidi Azeiz. It was recalled, but did not rejoin its brigade before dark, by which time Colonel Stephan had disengaged. The British had 23 Stuart tanks put out of action, and the Germans recorded 2 of theirs destroyed and 6 damaged.

---

[1] 22nd Armoured Brigade: 2nd Royal Gloucestershire Hussars, 3rd and 4th County of London Yeomanry, 'C' Battery R.H.A., one troop 102nd (Northumberland Hussars) Anti-Tank Regiment R.H.A.

[2] It has been suggested by some who were present that the Ariete Division was met in unexpected strength at Bir el Gubi. Its composition was accurately known, however, and a document issued by 7th Armoured Division on 15th November shows that the Ariete Division was thought to have moved forward to the Bir el Gubi area.

[3] 7th Armoured Brigade: 7th Queen's Own Hussars, 2nd and 6th Royal Tank Regiment, 4th Regiment R.H.A. (less one battery), one troop 102nd (Northumberland Hussars) Anti-Tank Regiment R.H.A.

[4] 4th Armoured Brigade Group: 8th King's Royal Irish Hussars, 3rd and 5th Royal Tank Regiment, 2nd Regiment R.H.A., 102nd (Northumberland Hussars) Anti-Tank Regiment R.H.A. (less one battery), 2nd Scots Guards.

While the 30th Corps was fighting these widely separated and indecisive engagements, the 13th Corps was having an uneventful day. The 7th Indian Infantry Brigade lapped round the Omars, and the New Zealand Division moved a few miles forward. During the previous night the cruisers *Naiad* and *Euryalus* had bombarded the Halfaya defences.

The enemy's air force was still largely grounded, though the weather had improved enough for Beaufighters to attack the Stuka base at Tmimi, and Wellingtons were able to continue their night attacks on grounded aircraft at Derna, Gazala, Martuba and Tmimi. During the day tactical reconnaissance aircraft of No. 451 Squadron R.A.A.F. saw many enemy tanks and vehicles between Gambut and Fort Capuzzo, which were then attacked by almost the full strength of the two medium bomber wings. The inference from enemy movements observed during the day was that the general trend was westward.

Apart from this the day had again given General Cunningham little to go upon, but there had been some success in the north and he decided to exploit it. He therefore ordered the 7th Support Group to join the 7th Armoured Brigade at Sidi Rezegh; the 1st South African Division to move up close to Bir el Gubi and hold one brigade ready to move to Sidi Rezegh in the afternoon; the 22nd Armoured Brigade to operate north of Bir el Gubi; and the 4th Armoured Brigade to remain at Gabr Saleh.

The evening of 19th November found General Rommel still preoccupied with Tobruk. It now seemed that the British were trying to prevent his attack or even to raise the siege. He therefore ordered General Crüwell to destroy them before they could interfere. Crüwell decided to use both his armoured divisions against the British columns in turn, and chose as the first victim a force which had been reported to have advanced north-east almost to Sidi Azeiz.[1] In this belief he ordered the 15th Panzer Division to move east, while the 21st made for Sidi Omar to prevent the enemy escaping southwards. The frontier garrison would bar the way to the east. A typical German plan for encirclement.

See Map 5

Early on 20th November General Cunningham left General Norrie's headquarters and returned to his own. Here reports of the move of Headquarters *D.A.K.* from Bardia towards Tobruk, and other westerly trends of movement, had given the impression that the enemy might be trying to slip away. General Gott was now at Sidi

[1] The move of 3rd Royal Tank Regiment in support of the King's Dragoon Guards' armoured cars earlier in the day almost certainly gave rise to this report.

Rezegh. It seemed to him that the enemy here were weak, and at about 10 a.m. he suggested to General Norrie that the Support Group should be able to gain touch with the 70th Division if General Scobie were ordered to make his sortie on the morning of 21st November. Norrie was attracted by this suggestion, although it meant a radical change from the previous intention of defeating the enemy's armour first. It will be referred to again presently.

Meanwhile General Crüwell's two Panzer Divisions were slowly moving east, and some hours went by before he realized that there was nothing in front of him except some armoured cars. Mid-way between Sidi Omar and Sidi Azeiz the 21st Panzer Division halted, out of fuel and short of ammunition. Crüwell asked Rommel's permission to advance with the 15th Panzer Division on Gabr Saleh, but was told to do this early next day, using both divisions. In spite of this Crüwell sent 15th Panzer Division ahead with orders to gain contact, and told the 21st to join it by a night march. The German armour was reacting as General Auchinleck had foretold.

Some of the German messages which arranged all this were intercepted. As a result the 8th Army warned General Norrie at 11 a.m. on 20th November that the two Panzer Divisions had joined forces and would attack the 4th Armoured Brigade at noon. Norrie at once gave orders for the 22nd Armoured Brigade to be recalled from Bir el Gubi, twenty-five miles away, their task of masking the Ariete Division to be taken over by the 1st South African Division. There is little doubt that the British Commanders now considered that the armoured battle, which had been such a feature of their plans, was imminent. What is more, it may be inferred that they were confident of the outcome, although at best the four German tank battalions would be faced by six British, because the 7th Armoured Brigade was 'off the board'. If this confidence did not exist, it is difficult to explain the decision now taken about the sortie from Tobruk. For at about 4 p.m. General Cunningham approved Gott's suggestion, put to him by Norrie, who then ordered the 70th Division to make its sortie at dawn on 21st November. One of the South African brigades was to reach Sidi Rezegh by 7 a.m., to co-operate with the Support Group, and the other was 'to mask the Italians at Bir el Gubi'. This was a change from the original plan in which the whole 1st South African Division was to co-operate with the sortie from Tobruk *after* the enemy's armour had been decisively engaged.

Just as this decision was being taken the 15th Panzer Division, with 135 tanks,[1] gained contact with the 4th Armoured Brigade—later than had been expected. Even so, the 22nd Armoured Brigade did not arrive from Bir el Gubi in time to play an effective part, and the

[1] 38 Pzkw II, 76 Pzkw III, 21 Pzkw IV, The full strength of a Panzer Regiment was 135.

battle was indecisive. Twenty-six British tanks were lost or damaged; the German records do not establish their losses for that day, though the British thought they had damaged about thirty.[1]

Just before 5 p.m. the 5th South African Infantry Brigade (Brigadier B. F. Armstrong) began to move towards Sidi Rezegh. At dusk it halted, with General Gott's approval, because General Brink did not consider the troops sufficiently desert-wise to make the move in the dark. At 8 p.m. Gott gave his orders for the operations next day, which aimed at securing the airfield and making ground towards El Duda. He was not in signal touch with Tobruk, where General Scobie was preparing to carry out his well-rehearsed plan for capturing two main and several subsidiary localities between the south-east corner of the perimeter and El Duda, thus creating a defended 'corridor' leading into Tobruk. The principal attacks were to be made by tanks and infantry in close co-operation, of the 32nd Army Tank Brigade (Brigadier A. C. Willison), the 14th Infantry Brigade (Brigadier B. H. Chappel) and the 16th Infantry Brigade (Brigadier C. E. N. Lomax).[2]

By 20th November the enemy's airfields had dried sufficiently for his aircraft to take off and try to hinder the British movements and gain some much needed information. This led to some minor encounters in the air. The Beaufighters again attacked Tmimi, and the Germans record a loss of eight aircraft in the day. On the ground a westerly trend of movement was still apparent, and the medium bombers were sent to interfere with it by attacking transport on the Tobruk by-pass road. An attempt by other medium bombers to help the 4th Armoured Brigade in its fight near Gabr Saleh did not succeed owing to the difficulty of telling friend from foe, and the pilots had the mortification of returning to base with their bombs. It was on the 20th that the fighter-bomber made its first appearance in the Desert, the Hurricanes of No. 80 Squadron R.A.F. having been adapted to carry eight 40-lb. bombs each. This was an important step in the development of what proved to be a formidable weapon for supporting the Army. After dark on the 20th aircraft dropped flares and spotted for the cruisers *Ajax*, *Neptune* and *Hobart*, which bombarded groups of vehicles in an area some three miles south-west of Bardia.

---

[1] It is almost impossible to deduce from the German records how many tanks were destroyed or damaged in any particular action. The numbers of fit tanks present with each of the Panzer Regiments are known from day to day, but in the absence of figures for tanks which returned to their units after being repaired, the losses cannot be deduced by subtraction. Occasionally, however, the German diaries record specific losses. Much the same is true of the British.

[2] The 32nd Army Tank Brigade consisted of C Squadron King's Dragoon Guards, 1st and 4th Royal Tank Regiment, D Squadron 7th Royal Tank Regiment. From the 14th Infantry Brigade were the 2nd York and Lancaster Regiment and the 2nd Black Watch, and from the 16th Infantry Brigade the 2nd King's Own. The artillery consisted of the 1st, 104th, 107th Regiments R.H.A. and the 144th Field Regiment R.A.; the engineer detachments were from the 2nd and 54th Field Companies R.E.

The Panzer Army Group's Battle Report for 20th November shows that the events of the day had at last made it clear that the British were not merely fighting a spoiling battle but had launched a major offensive. In reaching this conclusion the Germans had been helped, so they said, by a British broadcast from Cairo which announced that the object of the large and well-equipped 8th Army was to destroy the Axis forces in North Africa and make contact with the Free French. General Rommel now knew what his problem was, and viewed with some concern the prospect of a long struggle for which his resources were none too plentiful. He decided, however, to hold his frontier positions, maintain the siege of Tobruk for as long as possible, and try to defeat the British forces in detail. Believing the 4th Armoured Brigade to have been disposed of already, he ordered General Crüwell to move the whole *D.A.K.* from Gabr Saleh towards Sidi Rezegh and destroy the British force there next day.

See Map 6

The fighting about Tobruk and Sidi Rezegh which began on 21st November, and lasted with few pauses for three days, was the fiercest yet seen in the desert. Round Sidi Rezegh airfield in particular the action was unbelievably confused, and the rapid changes in the situation, the smoke and the dust, the sudden appearances of tanks first from one direction and then from another, made great demands on the junior leaders. They certainly did not fail, as the many stories of individual gallantry prove. No fewer than four Victoria Crosses were won: by 2nd Lieutenant G. Ward Gunn, Royal Horse Artillery; by Rifleman J. Beeley, The King's Royal Rifle Corps; by Captain P. J. Gardner, The Royal Tank Regiment; and by Brigadier J. C. Campbell, Commander of the 7th Support Group. The magnificent example of 'Jock' Campbell, R.H.A., became a Desert legend. He was already known as an outstanding leader of enterprise and daring; at Sidi Rezegh his conduct was an inspiration.

During the night 20th/21st November the 70th Division carried out the intricate preliminaries of its sortie with speed and secrecy. Gaps through the wire and minefields were made and marked, and four bridges (with a spare for each) were laid over the anti-tank ditch. Tanks, guns, and infantry moved into position for the break-out, as did some armoured cars, the crews of which, each helped by a sapper, were to lift mines. The break-out (with diversions by the Polish and 23rd Infantry Brigades elsewhere) began at dawn on 21st November.

For co-operation from the south General Gott and Brigadier Davy had made the following plan. At a suitable time on the 21st the 7th Armoured Brigade and the Support Group, both under Brigadier Davy's command, were to attack northwards from Sidi Rezegh air-

"CRUSADER"
The first battle for Sidi Rezegh and Rommel's dash to the frontier 21st-26th November 1941

LEGEND

British troops are shown in red,
German in blue and Italian in green.

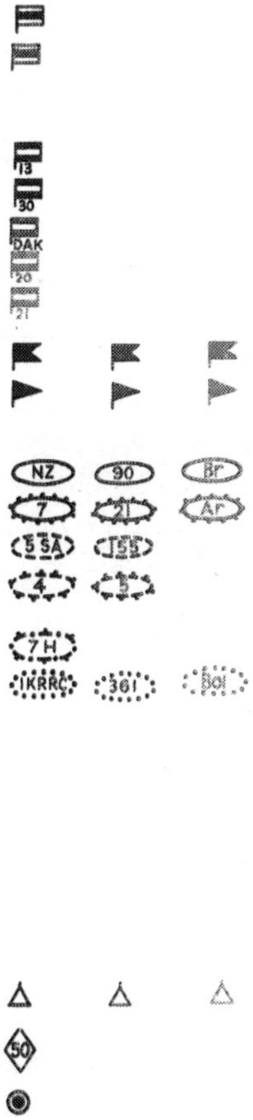

Headquarters of Armies

8th (Cunningham)
Panzergruppe Afrika (Rommel)

Headquarters of Corps

13th (Godwin-Austen)
30th (Norrie)
D.A.K. (Crüwell)
20th (Gambara)
21st (Navarrini)

Headquarters of Divisions
Headquarters of Brigades (or equivalent)

NZ 90 Br — Divisions
7 21 Ar — Armoured Divisions
5 SA 15 — Brigades (or equivalent)
4 5 — Armoured Brigades and Panzer Regiments
7H — Armoured (British) Regiments
1KRRC 361 Bol — Other units and detachments

Italian Divisions

Ar = Ariete, Tre = Trieste — 20th Corps

Bol = Bologna, Br = Brescia, Pa = Pavia, Trn = Trento — 21st Corps

Sa = Savona

Recce. Patrols
50 — Field Maintenance Centres
Airfields and landing grounds

Map 7

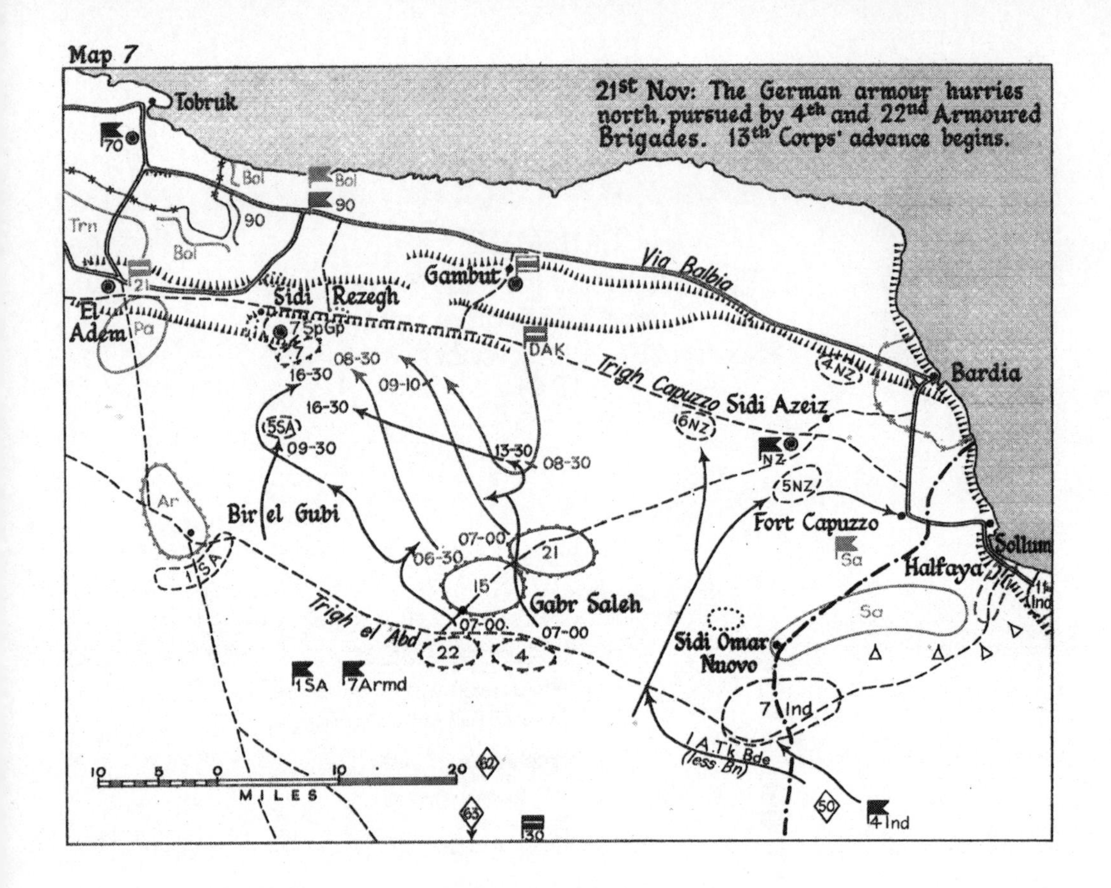
21st Nov: The German armour hurries north, pursued by 4th and 22nd Armoured Brigades. 13th Corps' advance begins.
Tobruk
70
Bol
90
Trn
21
El Adem
Pa
Sidi Rezegh
7 Sp Gp
Gambut
Via Balbia
DAK
Trigh Capuzzo
4NZ
Bardia
Sidi Azeiz
6NZ
NZ
5NZ
Fort Capuzzo
Sollum
Sa
Halfaya
Ind
5SA
Ar
Bir el Gubi
1SA
15
Gabr Saleh
Trigh el Abd
22
4
1SA
7Armd
Sidi Omar Nuovo
7 Ind
1 A.Tk Bde (less Bn)
50
4 Ind
60
63
130
MILES
08-30
09-10
16-30
09-30
13-30
07-00
06-30

Map 9

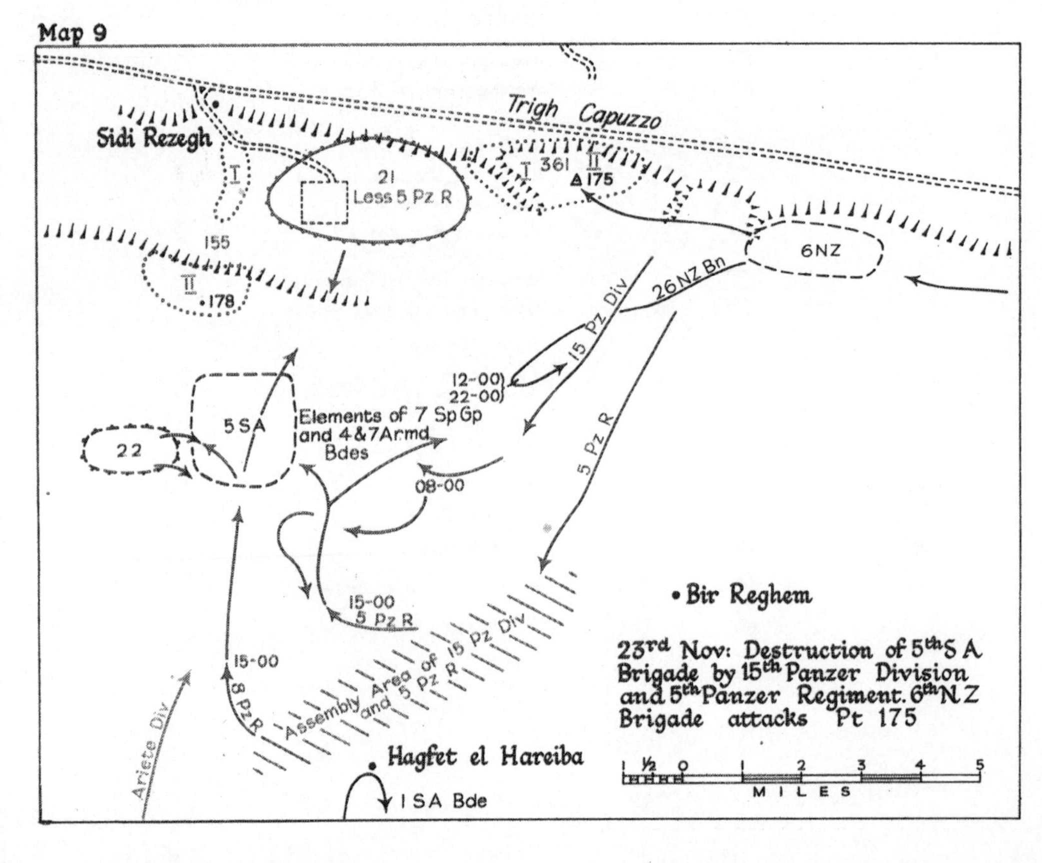
Trigh Capuzzo
Sidi Rezegh
21
Less 5 Pz R
361
175
155
178
6NZ
26 NZ Bn
15 Pz Div
12-00
22-00
5 SA
Elements of 7 Sp Gp and 4 & 7 Armd Bdes
22
08-00
5 Pz R
15-00
5 Pz R
Assembly Area of 15 Pz Div and 5 Pz R
15-00
8 Pz R
Ariete Div
Bir Reghem
23rd Nov: Destruction of 5th S A Brigade by 15th Panzer Division and 5th Panzer Regiment. 6th N Z Brigade attacks Pt 175
Hagfet el Hareiba
1 SA Bde
MILES

Map 8

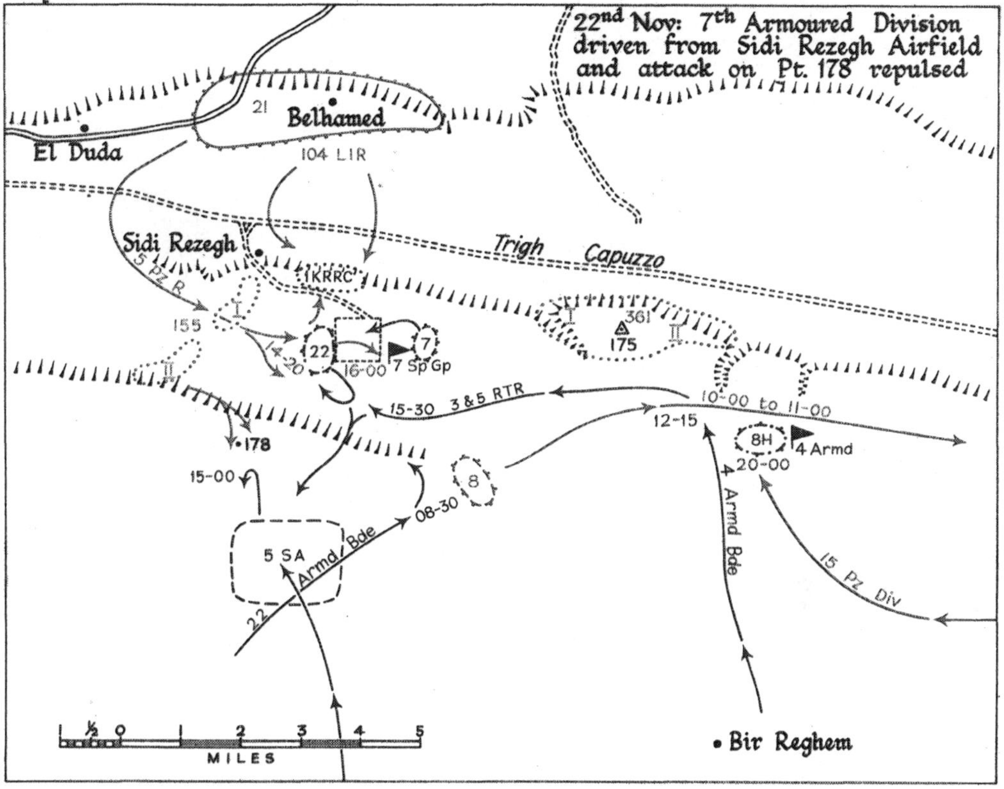

22nd Nov: 7th Armoured Division driven from Sidi Rezegh Airfield and attack on Pt. 178 repulsed

El Duda
Belhamed
21
104 LIR
Sidi Rezegh
5 Pz R
Trigh Capuzzo
1 KRRC
155
I
II
22
7
16-00
7 Sp Gp
14-20
361
175
15-30 3 & 5 RTR
10-00 to 11-00
12-15
8H
4 Armd
20-00
178
15-00
8
08-30
5 SA
22 Armd Bde
4 Armd Bde
15 Pz Div
Bir Reghem
½ 0 1 2 3 4 5
MILES

Map 10

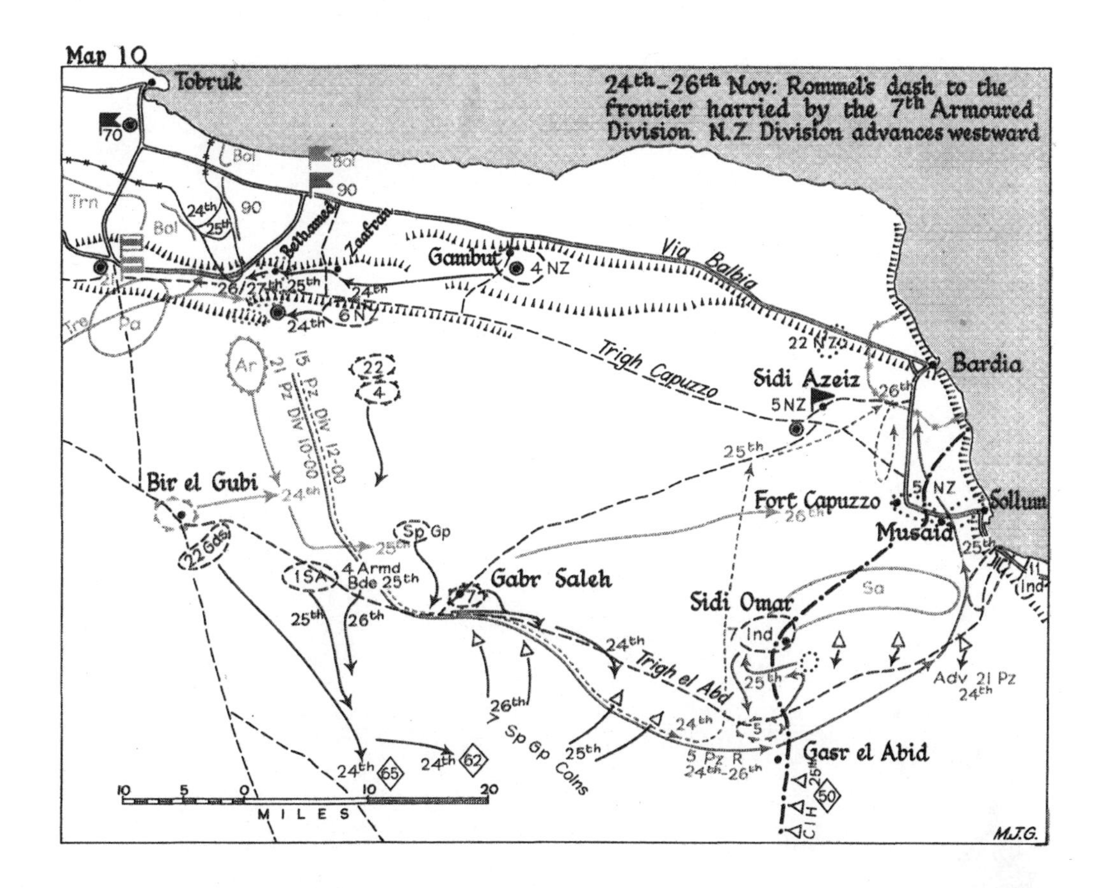

field to secure part of the ridge overlooking the Trigh Capuzzo.[1] The right of the attack was given to the 1st K.R.R.C., and the left to the 6th R.T.R. followed by one company of the 2nd Rifle Brigade. The remaining troops had covering and reserve roles, and artillery support was to be given by the 3rd and 4th Regiments, R.H.A., and the 60th Field Regiment, R.A. When the objective had been gained the 6th R.T.R. was to move down past Sidi Rezegh with a view to joining hands with the forces from Tobruk at El Duda.

At about 8 a.m., half an hour before the attack was to begin, enemy tanks were reported approaching from the south-east. (These were the 15th and 21st Panzer Divisions, which had been making their best speed from Gabr Saleh.) It was past the time for the sortie from Tobruk to have begun, so Brigadier Davy could not alter his plan for co-operation. Placing Brigadier Campbell in command of the northern attack he turned with the 7th Hussars and the 2nd R.T.R. to engage the German armour. The heavy fighting thus begun lasted until late in the afternoon.

The northward attack partially succeeded; the 1st K.R.R.C. and the Rifle Brigade's company gained and held their objectives, but the 6th R.T.R. in crossing the Trigh Capuzzo lost three-quarters of its tanks, mainly to guns on the opposite ridge. In the south the 7th Hussars and 2nd R.T.R. fought many close engagements, into which as the day went on guns of the Horse and Field Artillery, the survivors of the 6th R.T.R., and the remainder of the 2nd Rifle Brigade were drawn. Casualties were heavy and included four commanding officers. At the end only 28 tanks were fit to fight. But the enemy had been held off and the ground deemed vital was still in British hands.

See also Map 7

During the morning the 4th and 22nd Armoured Brigades had been ordered to follow and engage the 15th and 21st Panzer Divisions but they had been delayed for one reason or another—refuelling, boggy ground and the enemy's skilful rearguards—so that the jaws of the British armour did not close on the Panzer Divisions, as everyone had been hoping they would.

The sortie from Tobruk was opposed partly by Germans, and not entirely by Italians as had been expected. The enemy were well dug in behind wire and mines. They resisted stubbornly and brought down intense artillery and machine-gun fire. The fighting probably reached its height at the defended locality known as 'Tiger', which fell to the 1st and 4th Royal Tank Regiment and 2nd Black Watch.

[1] 7th Support Group: 1st Battalion The King's Royal Rifle Corps, 2nd Battalion The Rifle Brigade, 3rd Regiment R.H.A. (anti-tank), 60th Field Regiment R.A., one battery 51st Field Regiment R.A.

By the afternoon 70th Division had won a salient nearly 4,000 yards deep and about as broad. 550 German and 527 Italian prisoners had been taken. General Scobie had intended to continue his thrust in the afternoon towards El Duda, but decided not to do so when he heard that he would get no help from the 7th Armoured Division and because of strong counter attacks. The 5th South African Brigade had halted on General Gott's orders clear of the mêlée.

The situation was now so extraordinary that a brief summary will not be out of place. Over the twenty or so miles of country from the front of the Tobruk sortie to the open desert south-east of Sidi Rezegh airfield the forces of both sides were sandwiched like the layers of a Neapolitan ice. In turn, starting from the north, there were (a) the troops of the 70th Division who had broken out, opposed by (b) German and Italian troops facing north and west; (c) a layer of Axis troops facing south, opposing (d) part of the 7th Support Group north of Sidi Rezegh airfield; the rest of 7th Support Group and 7th Armoured Brigade facing south to oppose (e) the bulk of *D.A.K.* heading north, pursued by (f) the 4th and 22nd Armoured Brigades. To complete the picture there were troops of the 361st *Afrika* Regiment on Pt 175 to the east of Sidi Rezegh airfield, and the whole of the 155th Regiment to the west. A complicated situation indeed, which, if suggested as the setting of a training exercise, must have been rejected for the reason that in real life these things simply could not happen.

At the Headquarters of 30th Corps and 8th Army the impressions formed during the day were favourable. General Norrie interpreted the move of the German armoured divisions towards Sidi Rezegh as a withdrawal, and hoped that the 4th and 22nd Armoured Brigades would catch them in flank and rear. He therefore suggested that the Army Commander might consider unleashing the 13th Corps. General Cunningham agreed and ordered Godwin-Austen to advance 'as he pleased' but without taking undue risks. By evening the New Zealand Brigade Groups had reached the positions shown on Map 7: one brigade, which had been directed on Tobruk, had begun to advance along the Trigh Capuzzo; the other two were carrying out their tasks of getting behind the enemy in the Bardia-Sollum area, after ships of the 7th Cruiser Squadron had bombarded groups of vehicles (thought to be tanks) reported from the air. The 4th Indian Division was preparing to attack Sidi Omar Nuovo.

The impression of a hard but prospering battle at Sidi Rezegh grew during the day. One report estimated that 170 German tanks had been damaged; another suggested that 60 were surrounded south-east of Sidi Rezegh. 209 British tanks remained fit to fight, and General Gott intended to clear up the situation at Sidi Rezegh next day with a view to attacking again toward El Duda.

The day's fighting left General Crüwell in a cautious mood. The successful sortie from Tobruk, the failure to defeat Brigadier Davy's force near Sidi Rezegh, and a general over-estimate of the British strength made him feel that his armour was in danger of being surrounded. He decided to move the *D.A.K.* eastwards to the Gambut area during the night and thus regain some liberty of manoeuvre. Rommel on the other hand knew little of the situation at Sidi Rezegh and was worried by the sortie from Tobruk. At 9.30 p.m. he ordered Crüwell to hold on in the Belhamed-Sidi Rezegh area; 155th Infantry Regiment and the *Afrika* Regiment were placed under his command and the armour was to stand by to counter-attack. Crüwell then tried to compromise. He sent the 15th Panzer Division east towards Gambut and the 21st Panzer Division to Belhamed. These moves were carried out during the night although some tanks, for want of fuel, were still south of Pt 175 at dawn on the 22nd.

See Map 8

Next morning, 22nd November, desultory fighting took place around Sidi Rezegh airfield. The 5th South African Infantry Brigade began to move northwards at 10.30 a.m. and General Gott ordered them to capture part of the southern escarpment about Pt 178. The attack was made at 3 p.m. and failed, the leading battalion—3rd Transvaal Scottish—being pinned down by fire and suffering 117 casualties. The Brigade withdrew at dark and took up a defensive position about two miles to the south-east of Pt 178. Meanwhile General Crüwell, anxious to regain the initiative, and seeing his opportunity, had decided to attack the British forces in the airfield area in the afternoon. The 21st Panzer Division was given the task; the 5th Panzer Regiment (with 57 tanks) was to advance from the west over the ground held by the 155th Regiment, while the 104th Lorried Infantry Regiment attacked from the north.

The German attack was met by the 7th and 22nd Armoured Brigades (with 107 tanks in all) and the greatly weakened Support Group. The 4th Armoured Brigade (with about 100) had been following some stragglers from 15th Panzer Division and had reached a position five miles to the east. General Gott recalled it, but it arrived to find the battlefield drenched in smoke and dust and the situation so obscure that it was unable to intervene effectively. Meanwhile the 15th Panzer Division, from about eighteen miles to the east, had been ordered to make a wide encircling move and join the battle from the south-west. The struggle around the airfield raged on, and a large part of the Support Group was overrun and driven off. Many tanks had been knocked out, and Gott decided to fall back at dark on to the 5th South African Infantry Brigade. The 4th Armoured Brigade would be on the east flank and the 22nd on the west.

This disengagement succeeded, but a stroke of misfortune followed. A call for support from the 21st Panzer Division had caused the 15th Panzer Division to abandon its encircling move and march to the sound of the guns. Its new course led straight through the area where part of the 4th Armoured Brigade was leaguering, and shortly after dusk the Germans literally crashed over Brigade Headquarters and the 8th Hussars. The enemy claimed to have captured 267 prisoners and about 50 tanks: certainly the Brigade was dispersed, and communication and control were not restored until the morning of 24th November. Apart from this disaster, the day's fighting had reduced the 7th Armoured Brigade from 28 fit tanks to 10, and the 22nd Armoured Brigade from 79 to 34. The Germans had retaken the vital ground and still had 173 tanks fit to fight.

Elsewhere, however, during 22nd November British operations had gone well. The 70th Division improved its position in the Tobruk salient, but because of the obscure situation at Sidi Rezegh General Norrie ordered General Scobie not to press his sortie. The New Zealanders took Fort Capuzzo and Musaid, cut the Bardia water pipe and all the enemy's telegraph and telephone lines, and blocked the Bardia-Tobruk road. Two battalions of the 7th Indian Infantry Brigade (Brigadier H. R. Briggs), supported by 42nd Royal Tank Regiment and one squadron 44th Royal Tank Regiment, captured Sidi Omar Nuovo and the greater part of Libyan Omar.[1] This sharp action was very costly in tanks, of which 37, mostly Matildas, were put out of action by anti-tank guns and mines.

During the day General Cunningham had become convinced that the fighting would become more and more an affair of infantry. He waited until midnight for reports from the battlefield of Sidi Rezegh. Then, as they did not come, he gave orders for the New Zealand Division to move on Tobruk, and the Commander of 13th Corps directed that it was also to continue to contain the Bardia-Capuzzo area with minimum strength. The 30th Corps was to maintain its object of defeating the enemy's armour and was to be ready to help the New Zealand Division should it be attacked by tanks. The true state of all the British armour was not yet known at Corps or Army Headquarters, nor even at 7th Armoured Division. The much depleted 7th Armoured Brigade was to hold on south of Sidi Rezegh airfield.

That same evening General Rommel was considering what he could

---

[1] 7th Indian Infantry Brigade Group: 1st Battalion Royal Sussex Regiment, 4/11th Sikh Regiment, 4/16th Punjab Regiment, 25th Field Regiment R.A., 65th (Norfolk Yeomanry) Anti-Tank Regiment R.A. In support were also 7th Medium Regiment R.A., 1st Field Regiment R.A., 42nd Royal Tank Regiment.

do to help the hard pressed Sidi Omar-Sollum front.[1] Air reconnaissance had shown that there were still strong British forces about, and as these represented a threat to the encirclement of Tobruk they must first be destroyed. He therefore ordered General Crüwell to attack with his whole Corps towards Bir el Gubi, whence the Ariete Division was to advance to meet it. The British were to be crushed between the two. Crüwell altered this plan by ordering 15th Panzer Division and 5th Panzer Regiment (from the 21st Panzer Division) to join forces with the Ariete Division. The whole armoured force was then to attack north, acting as a giant hammer, the anvil being formed by the rest of 21st Panzer Division (that is, the division less its armour). It is noticeable that the Germans were constantly trying to get a grip of vital ground with their infantry and supporting arms, and use the positions thus secured as a pivot of manoeuvre for their armour. To this end they made full use of the mobility of their lorry-borne infantry.

Very early on 23rd November General Cunningham visited General Godwin-Austen and modified his orders. The 13th Corps was now to take control of 'the infantry operation against Tobruk' from a time on the 24th to be decided between the two Corps Commanders. The 13th Corps would take the 70th Division under command and probably both South African Brigades also. The task of the 30th Corps remained much as before. It was not until now that the true state of the British armour began to be suspected at advanced Army Headquarters: the 4th Armoured Brigade was said to have four tanks, and the 22nd fifty. Of the 7th nothing was known. Moreover, it was soon evident that the enemy was attacking again.

See Map 9

In fact General Crüwell had not waited for the 5th Panzer Regiment, which was late, and hurried the 15th Panzer Division off to meet the Ariete Division. On the way it cut through the 7th Support Group and scattered its vehicles. Then, swinging west, it smashed into the halted transport of the 5th South African Brigade, where it did a good deal of damage but received some sharp buffets in return. Shortly after noon it met the Ariete to the north-east of Bir el Gubi. Here they were joined by the 5th Panzer Regiment, but there were various delays and Crüwell's hammer-blow began an hour late at 3 p.m. His plan was to launch the 150 tanks at the South African position and follow them closely with his lorried infantry. The South

---

[1] Early on 23rd November Rommel telegraphed to Rome pointing out the urgent need to unite all the Axis forces in the theatre of operations under a single commander. This was an obviously sensible request, especially as the Ariete Division had been fighting on the 19th. Mussolini replied at once placing Gambara's 20th Corps under Rommel's orders. Rommel himself was to remain subject to Bastico's general direction.

Africans, having had time to prepare for this onslaught, gave it a hot reception; in particular the German accounts make much of the intense artillery fire. The 22nd Armoured Brigade did its best to relieve the pressure but the odds were too great. By nightfall the defence had been overcome. The 5th South African Brigade had 3,394 casualties—mostly prisoners—and ceased to exist as a fighting formation. The 22nd Armoured Brigade lost one third of its thirty-four tanks. The Germans did not escape lightly: at least sixty (and possibly seventy) tanks were destroyed or damaged and although their human casualties were imprecisely recorded the loss in officers and non-commissioned officers was very high. It was not long, however, before Rommel was hounding *D.A.K.* on to further exertions, and it speaks very highly for their efficiency that they were able to respond so quickly. Before recounting their fresh adventures it will be convenient to summarize the positions on the various fronts and then consider the situation from General Cunningham's point of view.

At 30th Corps General Norrie decided that he must withdraw the 7th Armoured Division to reorganize, and bring in the 1st South African Brigade (Brigadier D. H. Pienaar) to guard the western flank. His present supposed total of 75 tanks would increase by repairs and from reserves, and he still hoped to be able to attack again. The policy of the 13th Corps was to contain and harass the enemy in the frontier area in the hope that his supplies would run out. The 7th Indian Infantry Brigade therefore continued to clear Libyan Omar, while the 5th New Zealand Brigade (Brigadier J. Hargest) captured Sollum barracks. The rest of the New Zealand Division was advancing towards Tobruk; the 4th Brigade (Brigadier L. M. Inglis) occupied Gambut and the 6th (Brigadier H. E. Barrowclough), by a happy mistake in navigation, ran upon and dispersed the main headquarters of the *D.A.K.* near Gasr el Arid. This brigade was hastened on by General Norrie, under whose command it had been placed: it climbed the escarpment and making good speed westwards captured part of Pt 175 from the 361st Infantry Regiment, with the help of one squadron of Valentine tanks of the 8th Royal Tank Regiment. The casualties were heavy—over 400 in all.

Away to the south the Oasis Force (Brigadier D. W. Reid) had all this time been advancing through the desert westwards towards Aujila. Landing-ground 125 was established nearly midway between Jarabub and Agedabia and from it two fighter squadrons supported the further advance.[1] The force suffered much from German and Italian bombing, but pressed on with determination and took Aujila on 22nd November and Jalo, with over 600 Italians, on the 24th. The consumption of petrol had been higher than expected, owing to

[1] No. 33 (long-range Hurricanes) and No. 113 (Blenheim fighters).

the heavy going, and very little was found at Jalo. Brigadier Reid was consequently restricted to sending out light reconnaissances over the ground towards Agedabia with a view to operating against the coastal road later. The force remained at Jalo with little petrol and on half rations until 20th December.

During the three days' fighting at Sidi Rezegh the tactical reconnaissance squadrons, helped by the Bostons of the South African Air Force, had been making strenuous efforts to keep the Corps Commanders informed of events on the ground. The enemy's air forces had shown increased activity, and had had the advantage of working from bases nearer to Sidi Rezegh than were the British advanced landing grounds at Fort Maddalena. The Germans suddenly resorted, rather unexpectedly, to fighter sweeps, which led to some encounters. One of these, on the 22nd, ended in the loss by No. 3 Squadron R.A.A.F. and No. 112 Squadron R.A.F. of seven Tomahawks for a recorded loss of only three Me. 109s, but the enemy then gave up fighter sweeps and contented himself with trying to pick off stragglers and unescorted bombers, which suggests that he did not want any more fighting of this sort. Whatever the reason, this enabled Air Vice-Marshal Coningham to divert more and more fighters to the low-level attack of ground targets, especially vehicles, which was to become such a feature of desert warfare. During these three days the fighters flew as many as 715 sorties.

Meanwhile the British medium bombers attacked vehicles on the fringe of the battle; on the 21st at Bir Hacheim, on the next two days at Bir el Gubi and on the road between Acroma and El Adem. On one of these tasks a force of six Blenheims of No. 45 Squadron was caught by German fighters, and four were lost; after this the day-bombers were given close fighter escorts.

The attempts by the day-bombers to provide direct support proved disappointing. Many of them were kept 'at call' awaiting the opportunity to deal quickly with some worth-while target chosen by the army, but the call seldom came. As the supply of petrol was causing some anxiety (three days' estimated requirement having been used in one day) the day-bombers' activities might have been curtailed in any case, but the experience showed that there was much room for improvement in the system of integrating the work of the medium bombers with that of the army in a complicated battle of this type.

Beyond the battle area the Wellingtons from Malta and Egypt by night, and the Beaufighters by day, kept up the pressure against the enemy's airfields in Western Cyrenaica from which bomber and Stuka forces were operating. At sea the Navy had carried out its planned diversions, but their effect on the distribution of enemy aircraft or on the movements of shipping is not known.

We must now turn to Army Headquarters. By the evening of 22nd November General Cunningham had become worried by the rate at which British tanks were being lost, and on the 23rd his anxiety increased. Reports that morning caused him to think that he had about 44 tanks fit to fight, and that the enemy had about 120. It seemed clear that he no longer had the superiority in armour on which the whole plan was based, and this was such a serious matter that he asked the Commander-in-Chief to fly from Cairo to hear a first-hand report. General Auchinleck arrived late in the afternoon, and General Cunningham told him that because of the losses of cruiser and Stuart tanks the enemy was probably superior in fast types. They would therefore be able to attack the British infantry without interference from the British armour. They might even be able to cut off the British formations in the Sidi Rezegh area, and if this happened there would be practically nothing in reserve with which to stop a hostile advance into Egypt. He wished the Commander-in-Chief to decide whether he was to break off the battle and adopt a defensive attitude or continue the offensive. He pointed out that the second course might result in there being no fast tanks left at all.

There can be no doubt that General Cunningham was right to put matters squarely before the Commander-in-Chief. He had every reason to be alarmed at the British losses and his fear that the enemy would try to invade Egypt was, as will be seen, not far wide of the mark. But General Auchinleck never wavered. He shouldered the responsibility and told Cunningham to continue the offensive, confirming this decision in a Directive of which a part reads: 'You will therefore continue to attack the enemy relentlessly using all your resources even to the last tank. Your main object will be as always to destroy the enemy tank forces. Your ultimate object remains the conquest of Cyrenaica and then to advance on Tripoli . . .'

General Cunningham thereupon issued fresh orders. General Godwin-Austen's 13th Corps was to be responsible from midnight 23rd/24th for all operations against the enemy investing Tobruk. Under his command would come the 70th Division and all infantry north of a line east and west through Sidi Azeiz. His task was to capture Sidi Rezegh and El Duda 'at all costs' and to exploit westward. The 11th Indian Infantry Brigade was to be relieved on the lines of communication by a brigade of the 2nd South African Division and would come under 13th Corps. The 5th Indian Infantry Brigade was also to be released from guard duties on the line of communication and would rejoin its division. The 30th Corps was to reorganize, but was to be ready to protect 1st South African Brigade and the New Zealand Division from attack by tanks.

See Map 10

The next four days, 24th to 27th November, saw this remarkable battle take a new turn. After a short lull, fighting broke out again to the south-east of Tobruk, but of a quite different character from that of the preceding few days. Its outcome had an important effect on the other operations about to be described, but these operations will, for the sake of clarity, be dealt with as a continuous story before the scene shifts back again to the neighbourhood of Sidi Rezegh.

The hard pounding of 23rd November left not only the British but also the *D.A.K.* in some confusion. General Crüwell had been out of touch with Rommel all day and not until 6 a.m. on the 24th did the two meet. By that time Crüwell felt able to report that he had destroyed most of the 7th Armoured Division and the 1st South African Division, though parts of both had escaped to the south. He suggested that he should pursue them and finish them off, but Rommel would have none of this and told Crüwell that he intended to move with the whole of *D.A.K.* straight to Sidi Omar and take the pressure off his frontier troops. The Ariete and Trieste Divisions would also move east. A small force under General Böttcher would be left to prevent the New Zealanders from gaining touch with the Tobruk garrison.[1]

Whether this was a good decision is an interesting point. There can be no doubt that the moment had come to exploit the success gained around Sidi Rezegh; the question was how to do it. Crüwell, on the one hand, saw a chance of wiping out the British armoured force altogether, and the effect of this on any subsequent operations would be very great. He was strongly against leaving the present battlefield without reaping what he regarded as the full fruits of his victory. It has already been seen that Rommel, on the other hand, had been eager for an opportunity to go to the help of his frontier troops. He had not tried to do so before because he was determined not to let the British raise the siege of Tobruk. But when Crüwell made his report on the morning of 24th November it must have seemed to Rommel that although the British armour could not be written off it could be disregarded for the time being. The enemy must be off his balance, which meant that the moment for bold action had come. General Rommel may have thought of previous occasions on which the British had shown themselves very sensitive to roaming armoured forces—at Mechili in April and in 'Battleaxe' in June. The sudden appearance of tanks so far to the east of the recent armoured battles ought certainly to embarrass them; it might even lead to a general withdrawal. The great thing was to strike at once. Waving aside General Crüwell and his remonstrances, Rommel set off to lead in person an adventure after his own heart.

---

[1] The Böttcher Group consisted of: one battalion of 361st Infantry Regiment; two battalions of 155th Lorried [sic] Infantry Regiment; 900th Engineer Battalion; and elements of the Army artillery. See also page 34n.

Meanwhile at Headquarters 8th Army there was renewed confidence in spite of the disaster to the 5th South African Brigade. The latest calculations of the enemy's strength suggested that most of his effort had been spent and that he could have few tanks left. Early air reconnaissance saw no signs of a fresh advance. During the morning General Cunningham visited Norrie at Gott's headquarters to the south-west of Gabr Saleh. Little seems to have been known of the situation, except that a front of sorts was being formed from about seven miles south of Pt 175 to midway between Bir el Gubi and Gabr Saleh. The 4th and 22nd Armoured Brigades were at the northern end of this front.

At 10 a.m. the 21st Panzer Division, with Rommel and the 5th Panzer Regiment in the lead, set off southwards from near Sidi Rezegh to gain the Trigh el Abd and follow it to the frontier.[1] At noon the 15th Panzer Division started in the same direction.[2] Although this advance happened to pass out of snapping distance of most of the 7th Armoured Division's remaining teeth, it swept before it many units and stragglers belonging to the British tail. The advanced and rear headquarters of the 30th Corps were caught up in the flurry and some of the staff were captured together with a quantity of water, petrol, and other stores. As might be expected, rumour spread rapidly among the vehicles, many of which were unarmed and most of which were already streaming east on their legitimate business. Acted on by rumour a stream of this sort tends to swell and gain speed. This one was no exception. Some lorries had never travelled so fast before. To use the current slang, there was a good deal of 'flap'.

Meanwhile the 22nd Armoured Brigade was joined by the 4th to help in the task of covering the left flank of the New Zealand Division, and for some time these brigades remained more or less where they were. The 7th Support Group and the very weak 7th Armoured Brigade, however, were able to make bites at the northern flank of the moving German columns, and the artillery with the 1st South African Brigade engaged such targets as they could identify. These clashes and scuffles delayed the 5th Panzer Regiment, but Rommel and portions of the 21st Panzer Division reached the frontier near Gasr el Abid at about 4 p.m. having covered some sixty miles in six hours.

It is interesting to see what was known of all this. General Cunningham left the 7th Armoured Division just before noon because General Norrie feared that the German advance might overrun the landing-strip on which his aircraft was waiting. (In fact the aircraft was shelled while taking off.) At 1.45 p.m. he flew to Sidi Azeiz, to see General

[1] 5th Panzer Regiment had 45 fit tanks (11 Pzkw II, 28 Pzkw III, 6 Pzkw IV).

[2] 8th Panzer Regiment (15th Division) had 61 fit tanks (18 Pzkw II, 36 Pzkw III, 7 Pzkw IV).

Godwin-Austen. At 2.15 p.m. a report from 30th Corps reached Advanced Army Headquarters that enemy tanks and transport were moving south-east near Gabr Saleh but were a nuisance only. Just before 4 p.m. hostile tanks were reported approaching the frontier and half an hour later General Cunningham, returning in his aircraft, saw columns advancing along the Trigh el Abd. Defensive measures were ordered, but everyone was in the dark as to what was happening.

It was a difficult day for the Royal Air Force. The tactical reconnaissance squadrons had been working from landing-grounds at Gabr Saleh and Sidi Azeiz, and eight of the fighter squadrons from those near Fort Maddalena—not far from the frontier. Because the Army could not guarantee to protect them, and because the situation was so obscure, Air Vice-Marshal Coningham reluctantly decided to withdraw temporarily to landing-grounds farther east. This was a complicated move, which had to be made at short notice, and led to some dangerous congestion. That night there were as many as 175 aircraft standing wing-tip to wing-tip on one landing-ground, but the enemy was evidently unaware of this unusual target. The day's uncertainty had tended to lessen the opposition by air to the movements of the *D.A.K.*, but the British fighters made several attacks, in which they were severely handicapped by the difficulty of telling friend from foe, made worse by the enemy's use of quantities of captured British vehicles. The day-bombers attacked transport in the vicinity of Bir el Gubi, El Adem, and Acroma, though most of them remained 'on call' by the Army and were not given many targets.

At 5 p.m. Rommel met Crüwell at Gasr el Abid and announced his plan for the next day, which was to surround and destroy all the British forces on the Egyptian frontier. Briefly, the 21st Panzer Division was to cross the frontier, turn, and attack west. The 15th was to strike north astride the frontier. The Ariete and Trieste Divisions would advance eastwards towards Fort Capuzzo.[1] The 33rd Reconnaissance Unit was to make for Habata and raid the British supply line. Rommel had already sent on towards the Halfaya Pass Major-General von Ravenstein and any units of his 21st Panzer Division that had arrived, but the 5th Panzer Regiment was too late to follow and spent the night at Gasr el Abid. The 15th Panzer Division was still fifteen miles west of the frontier. The Ariete Division was only a few miles east of Bir el Gubi.

General Crüwell disliked this plan, and his dislike grew with its unfolding. For one thing, the administrative difficulties of this sudden swoop by the whole *D.A.K.* were very great; for another, the piecemeal arrival of the units in the race to the frontier led in many cases to their receiving two sets of orders—one from General Rommel and

[1] No such orders seem to have been given to the Trieste Division, which actually moved on 24th November from Bir Hacheim to the El Adem area.

one from General Crüwell. It will be seen that for much of the time the *D.A.K.* was in considerable confusion. (Incidentally, both Rommel and Crüwell lost their way during the first night and narrowly escaped capture.) It was unfortunate that during this confusion the British tactical reconnaissance squadrons were to be very much handicapped by having to withdraw a long way from the scene. Their chances of getting much-needed information were consequently reduced, and their close links with both Corps Headquarters temporarily broken.

General Auchinleck, still at Headquarters 8th Army, was able to discuss the situation with General Cunningham. It seemed that a few enemy tanks, supported by infantry and artillery, were making for railhead at Misheifa. It was decided that the operations of the 13th Corps at Tobruk were to continue; the 4th Indian Division was to stand fast; the 5th Indian Infantry Brigade was to move and cover the railhead; a force of tanks was to be organized from reserves; the 2nd South African Division was to be warned; and any disorganized units were to be collected as they reached the frontier.

Meanwhile General Norrie had taken steps to protect the valuable No. 62 Field Maintenance Centre, which seemed to be a likely objective for enemy raiding parties. The 22nd Guards Brigade moved there during the day; the 4th Armoured Brigade, which had chased and scattered an enemy supply column, leaguered about sixteen miles to the north, and the Support Group and 7th Armoured Brigade arrived during the night.

The plot of movements on the frontier on 25th and 26th November resembled the scurrying of ants. Neither side had much idea of what was happening—the Germans because they had little help from their air forces, the British because their ground and air observers could get no continuous picture of the scene but only scattered, if numerous, sightings of hostile columns, which seemed to be here, there, and everywhere. It will be best to summarize events from the enemy's point of view for the reason that he held the initiative.[1]

Early on 25th November Rommel told Crüwell that the Ariete Division had not arrived and that the plan was changed. The 15th Panzer Division was therefore to attack eastwards between Sidi Omar and Sidi Azeiz, and the 21st westwards from the direction of Halfaya

[1] An example of the twists of fortune which took place at this time is provided by the experience of No. 50 Field Maintenance Centre, situated a few miles from the frontier to the south of Sidi Omar. This served the 13th Corps, whose rear headquarters were not far away. Early on 25th November a hostile column drove right into the Centre and captured or scattered most of the staff. Yet by the afternoon the area was clear of enemy and the day's maintenance convoys were unloading as usual. Little damage had been done to the stocks and the enemy found hardly any of the well-dispersed petrol; even the prisoners' cage with its 900 occupants was intact.

Pass (as before). A small mixed column was to be held at Rommel's disposal for capturing Jarabub, 120 miles to the south.

Crüwell accordingly sent off the 5th Panzer Regiment to rejoin von Ravenstein, but Rommel—impatient perhaps of delays—intercepted it and ordered it to advance northwards instead. It was checked and turned back after a hot duel in the open to the north-east of Sidi Omar with the 1st Field Regiment R.A. who, with the utmost steadiness, let the tanks approach within 800 yards before opening fire. Five guns were knocked out and the Regiment had 66 casualties in the course of this exemplary action. In the afternoon the 5th Panzer Regiment again tried to advance, this time farther to the west (in full view, incidentally, of General Messervy's headquarters). Again it ran into severe artillery fire and again withdrew.[1] The regiment's records show a loss of 18 tanks that day. By night it was still south of Sidi Omar with 25 fit tanks.

Meanwhile the 15th Panzer Division had got itself (with its 53 tanks) strung out between Sidi Omar and Sidi Azeiz and was in supply difficulties, while, in the absence of his Panzer Regiment, von Ravenstein and the rest of his division had remained near the Halfaya Pass. To conclude this record of a bad day the intended thrust to Habata was a fiasco, for the 33rd Reconnaissance Unit, short of many of its scout cars, was delayed for want of ammunition and was repeatedly attacked by the Royal Air Force, lost about twenty vehicles, and never started on its raid at all. On this day the full power of the British day-bomber force was used against the enemy columns which were astride the frontier or had crossed it. The attacks on the 33rd Reconnaissance Unit cannot be separated from the general onslaught, but they were probably the work of Blenheims of Nos. 11, 14, 45 and 84 Squadrons R.A.F., the Lorraine Squadron, and Marylands of Nos. 12 and 21 Squadrons S.A.A.F.

An entry in the *D.A.K's* diary for 25th November reads: 'Continuous heavy raids in the Sidi Omar area. Heavy losses among our troops. Where are the German fighters?' Part of the answer is that since the 4th New Zealand Brigade had reached Gambut the German fighters were deprived of the use of the landing-grounds there. They were thus faced with the same difficulty in reaching the frontier as the British fighters had experienced when the land battle was at Sidi Rezegh and the fighter airfields were in the neighbourhood of Fort Maddalena.

General Rommel's troubles were not confined to the frontier area. The Ariete Division had bumped into the 1st South African Brigade west of Gabr Saleh, and had wasted the whole day before disengaging

---

[1] The second advance was met by the artillery in the area of the 7th Indian Infantry Brigade, namely: 25th Field Regiment R.A., the 6-inch howitzers of the 68th Medium Regiment R.A., a Battery of the 2nd South African Anti-Tank Regiment, and a troop of the 57th Light Anti-Aircraft Battery R.A.

and moving off to the north-east. Worse still, a message was received at 4.30 p.m. from Lieut.-Colonel Westphal, the Operations Officer at *Panzer Gruppe* headquarters at El Adem, timed 9.45 a.m., reporting that the Böttcher Group was being attacked near Belhamed and was in difficulties. Another message towards midnight, however, was more reassuring: all was quiet.

Next morning, 26th November, Rommel visited Crüwell, who firmly believed that the *D.A.K.* ought to return to Tobruk at once. Rommel, however, wished first to defeat the enemy on the Sollum front and do it quickly. But the 15th Panzer Division, under orders to attack towards Fort Capuzzo, was still short of ammunition, fuel, and water, and had to go to Bardia to refill. On the way it encountered some New Zealanders at Sidi Azeiz, and Crüwell came to the conclusion that this indicated that a British force was advancing towards Tobruk, a view which was strengthened by the receipt of a new message from Westphal reporting that the Böttcher Group was again being attacked. Crüwell, with his mind always on Tobruk, decided that the New Zealanders at Sidi Azeiz must be attacked, and that he would use the bulk of 15th Panzer Division when it was ready. He sent the 115th Lorried Infantry Regiment to clean up the area Capuzzo-Sollum and himself went south to organize an attack on Sidi Omar with the 5th Panzer Regiment and the 3rd Reconnaissance Unit. This could not be made for want of fuel. The attack by the 115th Lorried Infantry Regiment was not made either, for Rommel himself called it off just as it was beginning. The force for raiding Jarabub never started, and indeed was never fully assembled.

There seems to have been no contact with von Ravenstein since the previous day, and he may well have been growing restive. Anyway, for some reason which is not clear, he launched the rest of his division towards Fort Capuzzo from the east, broke through the 28th (Maori) Battalion and reached Bardia at midnight. By this time the Ariete, making slow progress, was about fifteen miles west of Fort Capuzzo.

As the evening wore on General Rommel realized that the situation at Tobruk required the speedy intervention of the *D.A.K.*, and late that night gave orders for the 21st Panzer Division (less its detachment at Sidi Omar) to move towards El Adem next morning. Still hoping to snatch something from the wreck of his plans he ordered the 15th Panzer Division to clear up the situation at Sollum, after which it too was to make for El Adem. Later in the night he tried to save time by launching this Division in the dark, but before it was ready—it does not seem to have hurried—he cancelled the order and told it to start at once for Tobruk. There was some confusion with von Ravenstein's Group of the 21st Panzer Division, but eventually, leaving the

115th Lorried Infantry Regiment to demonstrate, the Division got under way. At Sidi Azeiz it attacked and eventually overran the headquarters of the 5th New Zealand Brigade and captured some welcome supplies.[1] It then continued to head for Tobruk, followed in the afternoon by the 115th Lorried Infantry Regiment. Meanwhile von Ravenstein's force had started west from Bardia only to be held up by a battalion group of the 5th New Zealand Brigade at Menastir and was forced to move down to the Trigh Capuzzo.[2]

In the Sidi Omar sector the 5th Panzer Regiment and 3rd Reconnaissance Unit filled up with captured British petrol and attacked in the afternoon with the object of retaking the ground captured by the 4th Indian Division. They received two sets of orders, got into difficulties with the minefield, and made 'a very half-hearted attack'—in the words of the 4th Indian Division's diary. In the afternoon *D.A.K.* called the action off. After a difficult night march the force caught up the 15th Panzer Division and found enough fuel in captured British vehicles to continue its move westwards.

So ended General Rommel's spectacular stroke. Without compelling the British to alter their plans it had caused some temporary embarrassment and local confusion. It failed completely in its purpose of relieving the frontier troops. The Germans lost at least thirty of their hundred tanks, while the British armour was given a chance to refit—a chance of which good use was made. As for dislocating the British supply lines, there is no evidence that this was anything but a subsidiary object, and neither of the two intended raids even started. In the Tobruk area the British, taking no notice of the fracas on the frontier, proceeded to do just what Rommel had previously been at such pains to prevent. In short, it is hard to avoid the conclusion that if Rommel had behaved on this occasion more like *le bon général ordinaire*, and less like the impulsive leader who was accustomed to see his exploits succeed provided they were bold enough, matters might have turned out much worse for the British. The enemy's frontier garrisons deserve sympathy, for not only had they not been rescued but much of their accumulated stocks had been used up by their would-be rescuers.

What must command admiration, however, is the discipline, skill and general efficiency of the *D.A.K.*—and not least the mechanical reliability of its tanks—which enabled it to take on this ambitious adventure so soon after three days of strenuous manoeuvring and fighting. At the end it was weakened—indeed, the 21st Panzer

[1] See Map 11. With H.Q. 5th N.Z. Brigade were small detachments of field, anti-tank, and anti-aircraft artillery, one infantry company, a few machine-guns, and various transport.

[2] The force blocking the main road from Bardia consisted of 22nd N.Z. Battalion with one machine-gun company, small detachments of field, anti-tank, and anti-aircraft artillery, and transport.

Division was limping badly and was of little use for a long time—but the 15th Panzer Division was by no means at the limit of its endurance.

The difficulties and uncertainties of the past few eventful days had made great demands on the Desert Air Force, which responded by making a tremendous effort. It has been seen that the *D.A.K.* was withdrawn from the frontier on account of the fighting near Tobruk, which is shortly to be described in some detail. But although there had thus been two land fronts, fifty miles apart, the air was all one to the Desert Air Force, whose squadrons had ranged from the frontier to Tobruk, striking at the enemy's columns whenever and wherever they could be identified, and providing air cover for the British troops over a large area. For example, on 25th November, while the day-bombers were attacking the enemy around Sidi Omar, a fighter wing of twenty-three Tomahawks was sweeping over El Duda and Belhamed. Here it met a force estimated at from sixty to eighty German and Italian aircraft which was evidently carrying out some planned operation with dive-bombers, bombers, escorts, top cover, and all. In the ensuing fight, which took place in full view of the troops, eight enemy aircraft were shot down for the loss of two Tomahawks. Thus the enemy's air forces were far from negligible, and the fact that they had not much effect on the ground operations is a striking tribute to the Desert Air Force and its vigorous handling.

With the object of weakening the enemy still further and of interfering with his flow of supplies, Wellingtons from Egypt attacked Benina and Berka airfields and the port of Benghazi, while others from Malta attacked Naples and targets at Sirte and other places along the coastal road. Particular attention was paid to the arrival at Derna airfield of transport aircraft thought to be bringing fuel and other cargoes from Greece.

On 26th November the weight of the British day-bombers was shifted from Sidi Omar to the Tobruk area, and all the fighters were again working from the Fort Maddalena landing-grounds. The air force was thus ready for the next phase.

On 25th November General Auchinleck flew back to Cairo and that evening took a decision on a matter which had been occupying his mind. He had been satisfied with General Cunningham's conduct of the battle and with the steps taken to carry out the instructions that he had himself given after he had come forward at General Cunningham's request. He had nevertheless formed the opinion that Cunningham was thinking in terms of defence rather than of offence and he (Auchinleck) had therefore lost confidence in the Army Commander's ability to press to the bitter end the offensive he had been ordered to continue. The decision to remove General Cunningham from his command was an extremely painful one to take, but General Auchinleck was convinced that it was right. It was of course vitally necessary to install the new Army Commander at once. There was no time for a newcomer to get into the Commander-in-Chief's mind or to learn the conditions and study the plan. He must be steeped in all this already, and must have character, energy and enthusiasm. General Auchinleck therefore decided to appoint his own Deputy Chief of the General Staff, Major-General N. M. Ritchie, who took over command of the 8th Army next day. General Cunningham, though he could not bring himself to agree with the Commander-in-Chief's reasons, took the heavy and unexpected blow with complete loyalty and selflessness.

See Map 10

It is now time to describe the events which forced General Rommel to withdraw from the frontier.

While the *D.A.K.* was moving south-east on 24th November the New Zealand Division (less the 5th New Zealand Infantry Brigade left behind in the area Bardia-Sollum-Sidi Azeiz) and the 1st Army Tank Brigade (less one regiment) with 86 'I' tanks were on their way towards Tobruk.[1] The 6th New Zealand Infantry Brigade had reached Pt 175 on the previous day and the 4th was advancing west of Gambut.

Early on 25th November the 4th New Zealand Infantry Brigade reached Zaafran unopposed, while the 6th made ground to the west along the escarpment, up to and including Sidi Rezegh airfield. General Godwin-Austen's orders were that the New Zealand Division was to capture Belhamed, Sidi Rezegh and El Duda, after which the 70th Division would break out and join them. General Freyberg accordingly ordered a night attack in which his 4th Brigade was to take Belhamed and the 6th Sidi Rezegh and El Duda. At 9 p.m. the attack began. Most of the Belhamed feature was taken against stout opposition, but dawn found the 6th Brigade somewhat disorganised and holding on precariously about Sidi Rezegh having been unable to press on towards El Duda.

On 26th November there was much confused fighting in the New Zealand sectors. At noon General Scobie, hearing that the attacks had been held up, decided to take El Duda himself. By about 3 o'clock this had been done by the 32nd Army Tank Brigade with the 1st Essex Regiment and a machine-gun company of the Royal Northumberland Fusiliers under Brigadier Willison's command. For great gallantry in a duel between the tanks and some enemy guns Captain

[1] 8th Royal Tank Regiment with 49 Valentines, and the 44th Royal Tank Regiment with 37 Matildas.

J. J. B. Jackman of the Royal Northumberland Fusiliers was awarded the Victoria Cross.

That night the 6th New Zealand Infantry Brigade made another attack on Sidi Rezegh and this time succeeded, but with considerable loss. At the same time a detachment from Belhamed consisting of the 19th New Zealand Battalion and a squadron of the 44th Royal Tank Regiment moved across to El Duda and came under command of Brigadier Willison. With Belhamed, El Duda, and Sidi Rezegh all lost it is no wonder that General Crüwell was anxious about his communications.

As often happens in war, however, the trials were not all on one side. In the disorganization which attended the *D.A.K's* rush for the frontier it had not been possible for regular convoys to reach the New Zealand Division and its supplies were running low. General Godwin-Austen realized that this Division, short of its third brigade, could do no more than hold its ground, and that the 70th Division could do no more than hold Tobruk and the 'corridor'. In response to his request for another infantry brigade General Ritchie allotted him the 1st South African Infantry Brigade which was to move to a rendezvous, chosen by him, under control of the 30th Corps. Intercepted signals now showed that the *D.A.K.* and the Ariete Division were about to return. Only the Royal Air Force and the 7th Armoured Division could do anything to prevent the New Zealanders being attacked from behind. As luck would have it the weather on 27th November was bad, and air operations were much restricted.

See also Map 11

After three gruelling days the morning of 24th November had found the 7th Armoured Division licking its wounds, but it was soon required to guard 6th New Zealand Brigade's southern flank, attack the speeding German columns, and move to the protection of No. 62 Field Maintenance Centre. The heavy casualties of the last three days had necessitated a good deal of reorganization, and the 7th Armoured Brigade was withdrawn to Egypt after sending considerable reinforcements of tanks and crews to the other two brigades. There was much recovery, salvage, and maintenance to be done and many new crews to be absorbed. The Support Group, also much weakened, broke up into small raiding columns to prey on the rear of the enemy in the area of the frontier and to find and harass the Ariete Division.

On the morning of 27th November these columns were out as usual and the armoured cars of the King's Dragoon Guards were watching the Trigh Capuzzo. Shortly after noon they reported a column approaching Gasr el Arid. General Gott ordered the 22nd Armoured Brigade to head it off and the 4th Armoured Brigade to attack its

"CRUSADER"
Renewed fighting around Sidi Rezegh
27th November - 1st December
1941

LEGEND

British troops are shown in red,
German in blue and Italian in green.

Headquarters of Armies

8th (Cunningham)
Panzergruppe Afrika (Rommel)

Headquarters of Corps

13th (Godwin-Austen)
30th (Norrie)
D.A.K. (Crüwell)
20th (Gambara)
21st (Navarrini)

Headquarters of Divisions
Headquarters of Brigades (or equivalent)

NZ 90 Br Divisions
7 21 Ar Armoured Divisions
5 SA 15 S Brigades (or equivalent)
4 5 Armoured Brigades and Panzer Regiments
7H Armoured (British) Regiments
1KRRC 361 Bol Other units and detachments

Italian Divisions

Ar = Ariete
Tre = Trieste
} 20th Corps

Bol = Bologna
Br = Brescia
Pa = Pavia
Trn = Trento
} 21st Corps

Sa = Savona

Recce. Patrols

50 Field Maintenance Centres

Airfields and landing grounds

Map 11

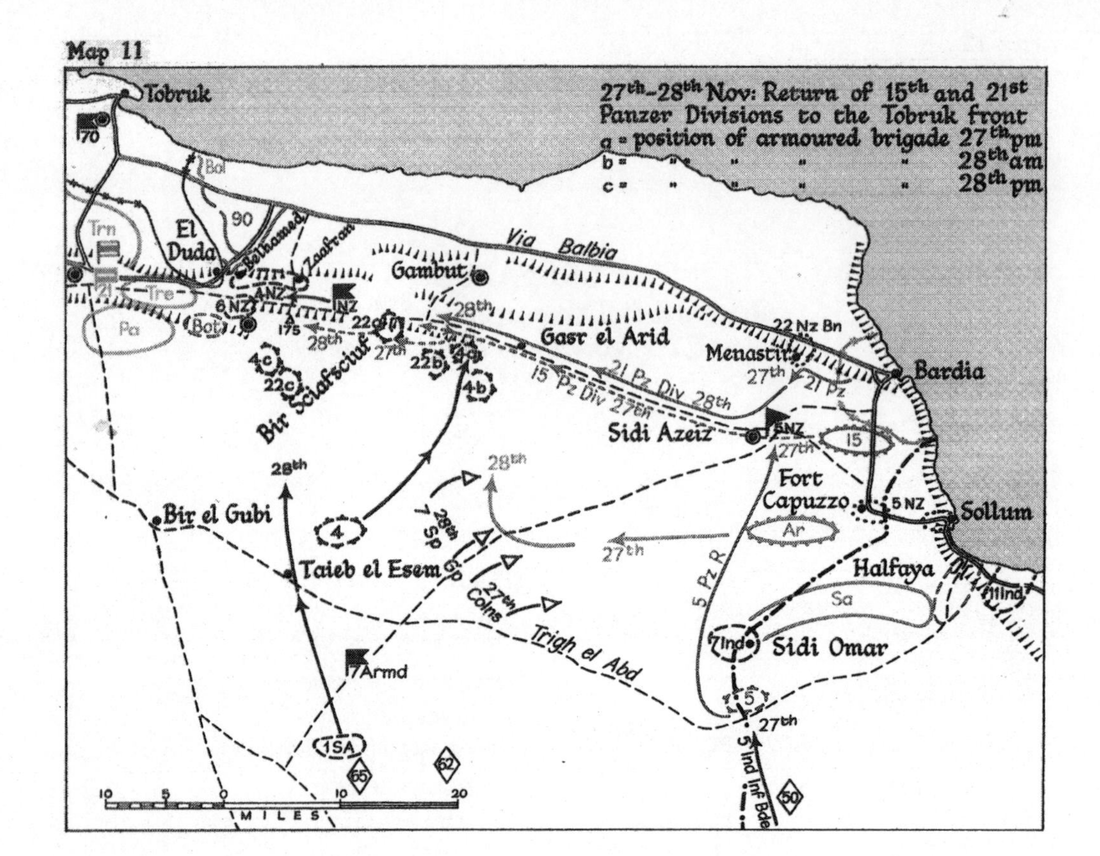

27th-28th Nov: Return of 15th and 21st Panzer Divisions to the Tobruk front
a = position of armoured brigade 27th pm
b = " " " " 28th am
c = " " " " 28th pm
Tobruk
70
Bol
90
Trn
El Duda
Belhamed
Zaafran
Via Balbia
Gambut
Tre
Pa
4NZ
6NZ
NZ
Bol
175
22a
28th
4c
22c
27th
22b
4a
4b
Bir Sciafsciuf
Gasr el Arid
22 Nz Bn
Menastir
Bardia
21 Pz Div 28th
15 Pz Div 27th
21 Pz
5NZ
Sidi Azeiz
15
Fort Capuzzo
5 NZ
Sollum
Ar
27th
Halfaya
Sa
11Ind
5 Pz R
7Ind
Sidi Omar
5
5 Ind Inf Bde
50
Bir el Gubi
28th
4
7 Sp
Taieb el Esem
Gp
27th Colns
Trigh el Abd
7Armd
1SA
65
62
MILES

Map 13

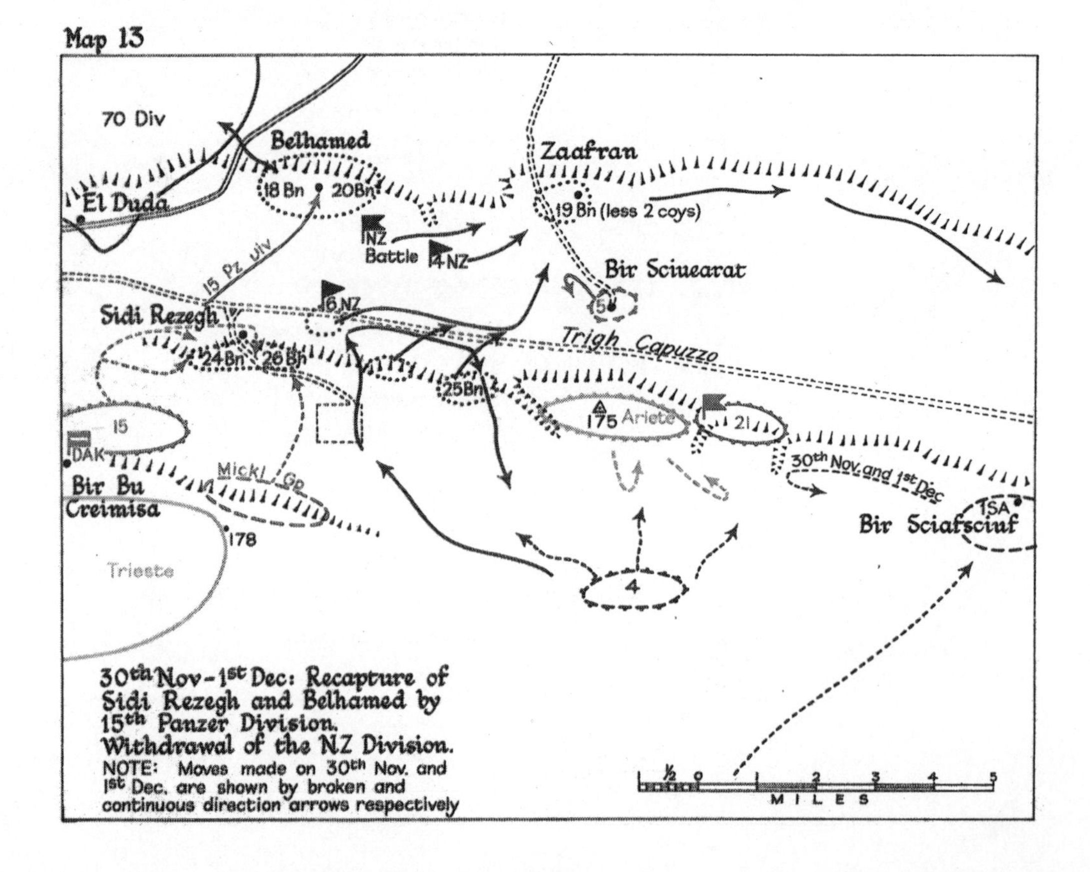

70 Div
Belhamed
Zaafran
El Duda
18 Bn
20Bn
19 Bn (less 2 coys)
NZ Battle
4NZ
Bir Sciuearat
15 Pz Div
Sidi Rezegh
6NZ
5
24Bn
26Bn
Trigh Capuzzo
25Bn
175 Ariete
21
15
DAK
Bir Bu Creimisa
Mickl Gp
178
Trieste
30th Nov. and 1st Dec
1SA
Bir Sciafsciuf
4
30th Nov-1st Dec: Recapture of Sidi Rezegh and Belhamed by 15th Panzer Division.
Withdrawal of the NZ Division.
NOTE: Moves made on 30th Nov. and 1st Dec. are shown by broken and continuous direction arrows respectively
MILES

Map 12

29th Nov: 15th Panzer Division attacks El Duda. Ariete Division takes Pt 175

Map 14

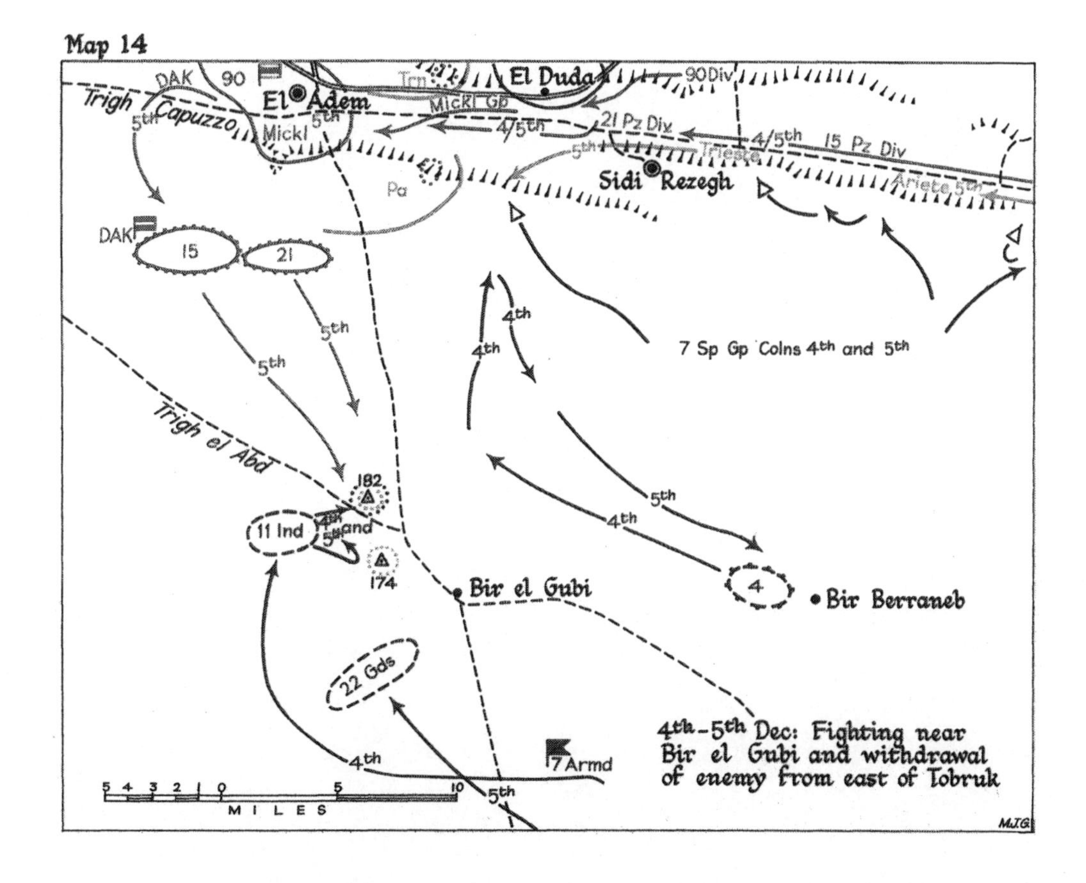

4th–5th Dec: Fighting near Bir el Gubi and withdrawal of enemy from east of Tobruk

flank.[1] This was done, though their messages show that the movements of the two armoured brigades were not well co-ordinated. The enemy column was the 15th Panzer Division, which reacted vigorously, shaking out quickly into battle formation with its field artillery and anti-tank guns supporting its tanks—a good example of efficient battle-drill. Medium bombers of the R.A.F. made several attacks, the results of which were difficult to observe in the bad weather, but the King's Dragoon Guards reported having seen some effective bombing. Fighting went on until dark, by which time both sides had suffered appreciable losses, though the enemy was evidently less disorganized than would appear from the British reports. He had, however, been roughly handled, and the German accounts speak highly—as they so often do—of the British artillery fire.[2] At all events, the British armour withdrew a few miles south to leaguer, and early next morning the armoured cars reported an enemy force in position above the escarpment near Bir Sciafsciuf. An extract from the diary of the 15th Panzer Division shows what had happened. 'The divisional commander [General Neumann-Silkow] decided to push on during the night in order to gain a favourable point on the escarpment by daybreak from which to continue his advance. After about 12 km the division reached the area south of Sciafsciuf and secured the pass up the escarpment. The division then took up an all round defensive position.' At 6.45 p.m. the previous evening General Ritchie had signalled to the 30th Corps that it was of the utmost importance to prevent the enemy escaping westwards south of the Sidi Rezegh escarpment, and General Gott gave orders to this effect as soon as he heard of the armoured cars' report. The Support Group was to continue to harass the Ariete Division and prevent it from joining the armoured battle.

During the morning of 28th November there was only scrappy fighting. More columns were reported coming up the Trigh Capuzzo, but the Air Force could do little to hinder them as it was a day of 'ten-tenths' cloud. Not until the afternoon did the 15th Panzer Division again move west, by which time the British Armoured Brigades had been given the additional task of protecting the 1st South African Infantry Brigade which was to be moved up to the help of the New Zealanders. 15th Panzer Division (with 43 tanks) then moved along the escarpment towards Sidi Rezegh airfield. On the way it overran a group of New Zealand Dressing Stations which was in a wadi to the east of Pt 175, capturing a thousand patients and all the staff. (In

[1] The 4th Armoured Brigade started the day with 77 tanks; 22nd Armoured Brigade with 45; 15th Panzer Division with 50. The 21st Panzer Division had only 24, and the Ariete Division probably about 100.

[2] With 4th Armoured Brigade were two batteries 2nd Regiment R.H.A. and 102nd (N.H.) Anti-Tank Regiment R.H.A. (less one battery). With 22nd Armoured Brigade were C Battery 4th Regiment R.H.A. and D Battery 102nd (N.H.) Anti-Tank Regiment R.H.A.

this battle without fronts or flanks many other medical units had similar experiences. Nearly all continued to work, taking in wounded from both sides and treating them under terribly difficult conditions.) In the absence of the 21st Panzer Division, whose troubles on the frontier and at Bardia had greatly delayed it, the commander of the 15th Panzer Division was most anxious that the Ariete Division should move up on his southern flank. This is what the Support Group was trying to prevent.[1]

The attempt to bring the 1st South African Infantry Brigade rapidly to the help of the New Zealanders did not succeed. At about 2.30 p.m. on 28th November General Norrie told Brigadier Pienaar to move north from Taieb el Esem and secure the area Pt 175—Sidi Rezegh which was in 13th Corps' area. After the Brigade had covered about eleven miles there was a muddle—which cannot be explained—between the two Corps about a message, and it halted for the night about the same distance from the objective. Later that night the headquarters of the 13th Corps and rear H.Q. of the New Zealand Division moved into Tobruk, though General Freyberg himself remained outside with a small staff.

See Map 12

General Rommel, with his forces once more within striking distance of the vital triangle Belhamed-Sidi Rezegh-El Duda, was determined that Tobruk should not be relieved. His idea was for General Crüwell to form up north of Belhamed and strike west and south-west. Crüwell submitted that his present dispositions and the lie of the ground (particularly the escarpments) favoured a converging attack, and spent the day reconnoitring and making preparations. At 8 p.m. on 28th November he issued his orders. The 21st Panzer Division was to take Belhamed from the east, supported by a bombardment by 90th Light Division. The 15th Panzer Division was to attack El Duda from the south-west and the Ariete Division was to hold the ring on the south. At about 9 p.m. a message came from Rommel laying down a different object, namely, to prevent the enemy escaping into Tobruk. Crüwell decided that it was too late to alter his orders, and let them stand. Early next morning he met his divisional commanders, but General von Ravenstein was missing from the meeting as he had driven into 21st New Zealand Battalion's position at Pt 175 and been made prisoner. General Böttcher succeeded him in command of 21st Panzer Division, and Colonel Mickl took over the Böttcher Group.

---

[1] The Support Group had now only one motor battalion, the second having gone back to refit. The 25-pdrs were reduced in numbers as follows: 4th Regiment R.H.A. (less C Battery) from 16 guns to 12; 60th Field Regiment R.A. from 24 to 14; 203rd Field Battery R.A. from 12 to 7.

Early on 29th November the 15th Panzer Division began to move westwards, passed south of Sidi Rezegh, descended the escarpment where it was easy, and turned at about noon to attack El Duda from the west. The 21st Panzer Division, on the other hand, was slow in moving on Belhamed and by dusk had not even reached its start line at Zaafran. The Ariete was gradually approaching from the south-east.

The British armour was occupied in protecting the 1st South African Infantry Brigade, which had been told by General Norrie to move north as soon as its reconnaissance elements had gained touch with the New Zealanders.[1] While carrying out this task both Armoured Brigades became engaged with the Ariete Division, other parts of which were being harassed by the columns of the Support Group farther to the east. Early in the afternoon the Armoured Brigades were told to do everything they could to interfere with the expected attacks on the New Zealand Division, and their artillery, together with that of the South African Brigade, came into action with this object.

Late in the afternoon, however, some Italian tanks of the Ariete Division managed to reach the neighbourhood of Pt 175, and owing apparently to an error in identification they were allowed to penetrate into the position which they thereupon captured—a sad sequel to the 6th New Zealand Infantry Brigade's previous successes in this locality. It was also an unhappy ending to a day which had started well for the New Zealand Division, for shortly after dawn a large convoy of over 250 lorries had arrived with food, ammunition and water. It will have been obvious that the fluid character of the operations must have made the work of the supply echelons very difficult, and great credit is due to them for the way they carried out their unending task. This particular convoy was a little out of the ordinary. It assembled near Fort Maddalena and took on most of its loads at No. 62 Field Maintenance Centre. From there it was led for forty miles by a New Zealander, Brigadier G. H. Clifton, the Chief Engineer of the 30th Corps. Escorted by South African armoured cars and by a detachment of Stuart tanks on their way to join the 4th Armoured Brigade the convoy made its hazardous way through the night to the east of Pt 175, bumped down the escarpment, and reached its destination westward along the Trigh Capuzzo—a fine achievement by the R.A.S.C. drivers.

At El Duda there had been heavy fighting all through the afternoon of the 29th. The 15th Panzer Division's attack from the west came in at about 2 p.m. and by 6.30 p.m. it had taken the western end of the position. The 1st Essex Regiment, which had lost the best part of two companies, clung to the ground it still held, while the 2/13th Australian Battalion and the 1st R.H.A. beat off attempts by the enemy infantry to infiltrate elsewhere. The 104th and 107th Regiments

[1] The 4th Armoured Brigade started the day with 60 tanks and the 22nd with 24.

R.H.A. supported the defence. Soon after 1.30 a.m. two companies of Australians and eleven 'I' tanks of the 4th Royal Tank Regiment counter-attacked in the moonlight and regained all the lost ground. It is interesting to learn from the diary of the *D.A.K.* that the 8th Panzer Regiment (of 15th Panzer Division) was intended to win El Duda back again, but a wrongly decoded signal caused the Regiment to be withdrawn towards El Adem.

General Ritchie was convinced of the need to send the 1st South African Infantry Brigade to the help of the New Zealanders; again General Norrie tried to do so and again he failed. Early in the afternoon of 29th November one South African armoured car (of a patrol of three) succeeded in reaching General Freyberg and formed a wireless link by which an order was sent to Brigadier Pienaar to move up to Pt 175. Shortly after 5 p.m. Pt 175 was lost by the New Zealanders and this information was passed on to Pienaar. At 6.25 p.m. 30th Corps placed Brigadier Pienaar under command of the New Zealand Division and told him that General Ritchie was most anxious that he should link up with it that night. A little later General Freyberg again told Brigadier Pienaar to push on to Pt 175. Wireless communication then broke down and Pienaar did not feel the situation clear enough to justify him in going on with his move. Some of the messages sent by Army, Corps, and Divisional headquarters are evidence of a strong desire to help the New Zealanders while ensuring that the 1st South African Brigade should not suffer the same sort of fate as the 5th had suffered six days before, but they added to the general uncertainty instead of clearing it up. At the time the situation must have seemed very confused; it was perhaps not realized that 15th Panzer Division had all passed to the west of Sidi Rezegh, nor that 21st Panzer Division was in very poor shape indeed. It had in fact only twenty tanks, and was submitting what the *D.A.K.* diary calls 'alarmist reports' as it struggled to make for Zaafran, with its flank and rear on the Trigh Capuzzo being harassed by light British columns and attacked by the medium bombers. If all this had been known the 7th Armoured Division might have concentrated on the task of holding off the Ariete Division until the South Africans could reach Pt 175.

See Map 13

Early on 30th November the enemy deduced from his air reports that fresh British forces were collecting to the south. General Rommel decided that his immediate purpose must be to defeat the New Zealand Division before these forces could smash the ring which was being drawn round it. The plan was for the Ariete Division to make ground westward from Pt 175 while the Mickl Group captured Sidi Rezegh; the 15th Panzer Division, whose armoured regiment's false move to

El Adem had been stopped, was to support the Mickl Group and then advance on Belhamed while the 90th Light Division came south to meet it. The 21st Panzer Division had still the task of advancing westward through Zaafran, but was making very heavy weather and could not be counted on to add much pressure.

It was afternoon before all this could be arranged and the morning passed to the accompaniment of greatly increased artillery fire. The attack on Sidi Rezegh began at about 3 p.m. Of the four battalions of the 6th New Zealand Infantry Brigade two were below and two were slightly over 200 strong, and for more than three hours the 24th and 26th New Zealand Battalions, on whom the main weight fell, resisted before being overrun at dusk. The Germans claimed 600 prisoners and several guns.

As the 7th Armoured Division was apparently unable to counter the moves of the German armour, General Freyberg, feeling hard pressed, asked General Godwin-Austen if he might send what remained of the 6th New Zealand Infantry Brigade into Tobruk. This request was refused on the ground that the South Africans were to recapture Pt 175 during the night, and then go on to Sidi Rezegh, and that armoured help had been asked for early next morning. Unfortunately, these hopes were not to be fulfilled.

During 30th November the 1st South African Infantry Brigade led by General Norrie in person had moved slowly north-east to Bir Sciafsciuf, covered by the 4th Armoured Brigade which had now absorbed all the remaining tanks of the 22nd Armoured Brigade. The intention was to capture Pt 175 from the east. The advance towards this point began in the evening, but there were many delays and by dawn on the 1st December the South African Brigade was still more than a mile from its objective and unable to make further progress. In the course of several brushes the Ariete Division had 19 light and medium tanks destroyed or damaged.

Before he knew of this General Godwin-Austen had sent, early on 1st December, a signal to the Army Commander about future policy. If the attempt to retake Pt 175 failed, and if the British armour could not prevent the constant attacks by the enemy's armour, it might be necessary to decide whether to withdraw the 13th Corps into Tobruk, as much more fighting might weaken the Corps to the point of endangering its ability to hold the place.[1] General Ritchie, who was intent upon resuming the offensive at the earliest possible moment, flew to headquarters 13th Corps to explain his ideas for the future. Meanwhile the New Zealand Division had taken another severe blow.

On the morning of 1st December, as soon as 15th Panzer Division was ready, the next stage of the enemy's attempt to drive the New

---

[1] The 13th Corps had become responsible for operations at Tobruk from midnight 23rd/24th November. See page 52.

Zealand Division away from the vicinity of the Tobruk perimeter began with a heavy attack on the escarpment at Belhamed. This was gallantly opposed by the 4th New Zealand Brigade, but it succeeded and the 20th Battalion was overrun. General Freyberg's Division was thus cut in two.

Shortly after 8 a.m. the enemy appeared to be preparing to turn against Brigadier Barrowclough's 6th New Zealand Brigade from the west and north-west, and at this moment some British tanks were seen approaching from the south. The accounts of what followed, as recorded by commanders on the spot, are in many respects contradictory, but certain facts can be established. The British tanks belonged to the 4th Armoured Brigade, which was moving to the help of the New Zealanders with orders to 'counter attack the enemy's tanks at all costs'. Its two leading regiments, 5th R.T.R. and 8th Hussars, reached the exposed positions north of Sidi Rezegh occupied by the remains of the 6th New Zealand Brigade, and at about 9 a.m. Lieut.-Colonel H. D. Drew, commanding 5th R.T.R., reported to Brigadier Barrowclough in order to learn the situation and make a plan. Only preliminary action had been taken when a message was received over the radio-telephone from Headquarters 4th Armoured Brigade transmitting an order from General Gott for the New Zealanders to retire. The commanders of the tank regiments thereupon made preparations to cover this retirement, which they understood would be made southward—that is in the direction from which they themselves had come. The whole airfield area and the escarpment above it were now under heavy artillery fire from the Germans on the west and the Ariete Division on Pt 175. Instead of withdrawing south (as Colonel Drew and Brigadier Gatehouse had expected) the New Zealanders made off towards their own divisional axis. In this way what was left of the New Zealand Division became concentrated about Zaafran. By 2 p.m. General Freyberg came to the conclusion that his sole practicable course was to withdraw altogether and refit. The only superior commander with whom he was in signal touch was General Norrie, who took upon himself to agree—a decision which General Ritchie later approved.

During the whole of this phase of the fighting near Tobruk the weather was none too good for flying. Nevertheless the reconnaissance aircraft, working at high pressure, produced much valuable information. The land fighting was now concentrated into a comparatively small area, and the main day-bomber effort was applied to helping the New Zealand and 70th Divisions by attacking vehicles of all kinds in the El Adem area. On the 30th the weather improved and many targets were seen between El Adem and Sidi Rezegh, the result, no doubt, of the move of the Trieste Division and the deployment of its artillery in support of the Mickl Group. Day-bombers had now to be escorted by fighters, and in fact about half the total fighter sorties—which in these four days totalled 1,029—were used in this way, the remainder being devoted to offensive sweeps and ground attacks in the main battle area. The Beaufighters continued to make low-flying attacks on airfields.

During the night of 1st December the New Zealand Division successfully disengaged from the scene of its successes and failures, and made its way east from Zaafran, then south across the Trigh Capuzzo and from there right back to the Egyptian frontier. General Norrie, who witnessed the early stage of the withdrawal, wrote 'I was much impressed by the discipline of the N.Z. troops in spite of the very rough time they had had . . .' The ten remaining fit tanks of the 1st Army Tank Brigade, which had supported the New Zealanders so stoutly in the week's fighting, withdrew also. Certain New Zealand units, including the 19th and part of the 20th Battalion, joined the Tobruk garrison. The 1st South African Brigade went back to Taieb el Esem.

General Godwin-Austen on the afternoon of 1st December had still been in some doubt whether to hold on to El Duda, as this might stretch the 70th Division somewhat riskily. A message from Lieut.-Colonel J. S. Nichols, of the 1st Essex Regiment, commanding at El Duda, settled the matter: the defences, he said, were growing stronger every hour, and he felt confident of resisting attack from any direction. General Scobie replied 'Well done, I admire your spirit,' and the decision to hold on was taken.

Back on the frontier the 7th Indian Infantry Brigade had finally cleared Libyan Omar, and a re-assembled 5th New Zealand Infantry Brigade was bottling up Bardia. To free these troops for General Ritchie's next phase the 2nd South African Division was moving forward to take over the frontier area from 4th Indian Division.

On 30th November General Bastico, whom Rommel was not in the habit of consulting, came forward to El Adem to discuss the situation. Rommel explained that the battle had become one of attrition, and the outlook, he said, was grave. Both sides had lost heavily and this was particularly serious for the Axis because their losses could not speedily be made good. The British on the other hand were bringing up fresh troops. Both Commanders sent urgent requests to Rome for men and material of all kinds, particularly tanks, armoured cars, medium artillery, signal equipment, and desert-worthy vehicles. They must have realized, however, that the present battle would have to be fought with what they already had, except for the few men and stores that could be hurried over by transport aircraft. It seems that what they really wanted was to force an approach to the French for permission to use the Tunisian ports, especially Bizerta, so as to expose the convoys to a much smaller risk of attack, and thus enable forces to be collected for the effective defence of Tripolitania. Mussolini took up this question once again with Hitler, pointing out that in November only 40,000 of the required 120,000 tons of stores and supplies had been shipped to North Africa and that the rate of dispatch was falling.[1] General von Rintelen added that in his view a regular schedule of troop shipments could not be resumed unless *Luftflotte* 2 succeeded in keeping Malta in check.

Meanwhile occasional small freighters, mostly carrying fuel or ammunition, were reaching Benghazi, where the Royal Air Force were trying to make it as difficult as possible to unload and clear their cargoes. An especially determined effort was made on the four nights from 28th November to 1st December, for which purpose the Wellingtons of No. 205 Group in Egypt were reinforced by others from Malta and eighty sorties were flown, carrying a high proportion of 4,000-lb. bombs.[2] It is difficult to assess the damage caused by this and other attacks, for though the results were thought to be satisfactory with hits on the quays and on ships at anchor, the port of Benghazi seems to have continued to cope with the small number of ships arriving. As will be seen, a few very important cargoes arrived later in December and were successfully cleared.

'Crusader' was a long way from being over, but an important stage had been reached: the British were able to introduce fresh troops and the enemy was not. This shows how wise General Auchinleck had been in insisting that the pressure must be kept up, and how right General Ritchie now was in seeking to renew the offensive. These decisions required some courage to make. The British had rightly judged that the enemy could not afford to lose the ground around Sidi Rezegh, and now, after a gruelling fortnight and sadly heavy losses, all the vital ground except El Duda was still in enemy hands. Tobruk had been open to the outside world for a short time, and was now sealed off again with an enlarged perimeter. The great armoured clash on which the British had pinned their hopes had never come off: instead there had been a number of separate actions in which the British armour usually found itself at a disadvantage. Either it was without much of its artillery—and the value of the 25-pdr against tanks had been amply proved—or one or both of its motor battalions, or else one at least of its armoured brigades was out of the hunt for one reason or another, usually in order to protect some other formation. When to these handicaps are added the inherent weaknesses, such as the short effective range of the British tank and anti-tank guns, the

---

[1] M. A. Bragadin: *Che ha fatto la Marina?* (Milan 1950, 2nd ed.) p. 259, where the figure 29,843 tons is given for arrivals in North Africa.

[2] This happened to coincide with the successful operations against ships at sea by Force K and R.A.F. Blenheims described on pages 105-6.

proneness of the cruisers to mechanical breakdown, and the short radius of action of the Stuarts, it is easy to see how much the tenacity, skill and courage of the troops had to make up for. The Germans, on the other hand, were adept at committing their forces to battle in a sound tactical manner, thereby giving them the best possible chance of success, and the action of the various arms was closely related. A glaring exception was the piecemeal use of the 21st Panzer Division on the frontier from 25th to 27th November, but it is unlikely that this would have happened if General Crüwell had been given a clear task and left to carry it out.

British superiority in the air made the failure to make full use of the day-bombers all the more disappointing. Since the start of 'Crusader' these aircraft had spent much of their time at the call of the Army, waiting for the ideal target and no doubt allowing many good ones to escape. Their chances of intervening in a swaying fight must have been very small, even if friend could have been distinguished from foe, and it is hardly surprising that there were many complaints of their bombs falling among their own troops. Similar complaints appear in the diaries of German units and there is also a record of a meeting at which Rommel asked the Commander of *Fliegerkorps X* to give him a liaison officer competent to order up fighters and bombers if speedy intervention were needed; the request was refused on the ground that it would be against the best use of the air force as a whole. The interesting point is that, contrary to an impression widely held at the time, the enemy in North Africa did not have a highly organized and efficient system of army/air co-operation; the British had at least laid the foundations of a system and were bent on making it work although they had not yet overcome all the difficulties.

The broad impressions left by the first fortnight of 'Crusader' are that the British airmen and the better trained of the troops had shown themselves in morale and skill to be at least a match for the Germans. The Army had still much to learn about the use of large armoured forces and especially about the art of combining the various resources on the battlefield. There was room for improvement, too, as regards the help that the Army and Air Force could give one another.

CHAPTER III

THE WINTER BATTLE–II

GENERAL RITCHIE'S plan for renewing the offensive was as follows. He believed, quite correctly, that the enemy were hard pressed, and he wished to give them no breathing-space. He decided that as a first step the 30th Corps should seize El Adem, a vital centre of communications to the enemy—as vital as the Belhamed-El Duda area in which the German armour now seemed to be settling down behind a strong screen of anti-tank weapons. Mobile columns were to raid the enemy's supply lines between Tmimi and Acroma. The 30th Corps was to have command of the 7th Armoured Division, the 22nd Guards Brigade, the 1st South African Brigade, and the whole of the 4th Indian Division as soon as it could be relieved by the 2nd South African Division; until then only the 11th Indian Infantry Brigade would be available. General Ritchie wished the 13th Corps to hold the ground it had won in the new Tobruk salient, but left Godwin-Austen free to withdraw to the old perimeter if he thought it necessary. Back on the frontier the 2nd South African Division was to prevent the enemy from sending supplies westward from Bardia and would mop up the Axis positions as opportunity offered. The 5th New Zealand Infantry Brigade would remain under command of the 2nd South African Division, and the rest of the New Zealand Division was to refit at Maaten Baggush.

On 1st December, the day these orders were issued, General Auchinleck arrived at 8th Army Headquarters to be at hand if needed. He stayed for ten days, but left the conduct of operations entirely to General Ritchie. His own main care was to set in train the move of reinforcements for the Desert front. The 1st Armoured Division, which had sailed from England at the end of September, had begun to disembark at Suez during the second half of November[1]. The 12th Lancers (armoured cars) and the divisional artillery were ordered to join the 8th Army as soon as possible, and the 2nd Armoured Brigade (60 Stuart and 106 Crusader tanks) was to undergo intensive desert training. The Royal Dragoons (armoured cars) were to be sent forward from Syria and the newly formed 38th Indian Infantry Brigade from Egypt. From Cyprus was to come the 150th Infantry

[1] The 22nd Armoured Brigade, which had come out in an earlier convoy, belonged to this Division.

Brigade and from Palestine the 50th Divisional Reconnaissance Battalion;[1] these were both ordered to Maaten Baggush to be in general reserve.

When General Godwin-Austen reported that the 13th Corps could not only hold the Tobruk salient but could also attack, General Ritchie became more than ever anxious to begin his new phase quickly. But he did not want any half measures, and decided to leave the timing to General Norrie, who had most to arrange. Norrie at first proposed to attack on 3rd December, but soon felt the need of a few more days.

No one was more anxious than Air Vice-Marshal Coningham for the new phase to begin, for the unexpectedly slow progress of 'Crusader' had caused many difficulties for the Air Force. The plan had been for the fighters to 'hop' in turn to Fort Maddalena, Gambut, and Gazala, reaching Barce and Maraua by the beginning of the second week. The day-bombers, taking longer strides, would move from Bir Khamsa to Gambut and on to Barce and Maraua in the path of the advancing fighters. As it turned out, the fighters had to operate from Fort Maddalena and the day-bombers from bases well to the east of the frontier for much longer than had been expected. In particular the course of the fighting seriously delayed the initial 'hop' to the Gambut area, so that the fighters could not move forward and the day-bombers could not be refuelled nearer to their targets. Only out of sheer necessity had the tactical reconnaissance squadrons moved forward to be near their Corps Headquarters.

General Rommel had deduced from signals intercepted on 1st December that he was unlikely to be attacked before the 3rd, and his anxiety about his frontier garrisons led him once more to make a move in their direction. The tanks of both Panzer Divisions were immobilized for badly needed repairs and maintenance, and the reason for making what could only be a rather tentative move without them is not entirely clear. Overruling Crüwell's protests against what looked like a feeble repetition of a previous mistake, Rommel ordered columns to go along the coast road and the Trigh Capuzzo to reconnoitre and disperse any enemy forces met. Each column was to consist of roughly an infantry battalion, an anti-tank company and some guns. The 20th Corps would move along the Trigh Capuzzo and guard the southern flank. The weather had deteriorated again on 2nd December, and the conditions were bad enough to ground most of the aircraft on both sides. On the 3rd they were still bad, but a little better, and both German columns were seen from the air. The northern one was ambushed ten miles from Bardia by the 5th New

[1] 4th Battalion Royal Northumberland Fusiliers had become 50th Battalion of the newly formed Reconnaissance Corps.

Zealand Infantry Brigade and almost annihilated. The southern column collided with a small force from 4th Indian Division, was heavily shelled, attacked by Blenheims and Hurricane fighter-bombers, and withdrew. In spite of these setbacks the Germans intended to try again next day, and also to retake El Duda, which in British hands was no doubt being a nuisance by blocking the Tobruk by-pass road.

It is always possible that Rommel's real reason for despatching these two columns was to mislead his enemy. This view is unsupported by contemporary evidence—which is not surprising—but the move had some such effect, for Ritchie gave orders that the 4th Armoured Brigade was to be placed where it could intervene, and this prevented it from being quickly available for the coming action near Bir el Gubi.

See Map 14

General Norrie meanwhile had not been idle. Reconnaissance had discovered an enemy position about six miles north-west of Bir el Gubi and he decided that it must be captured before the advance on El Adem could begin. General Gott gave the task on 3rd December to the 11th Indian Infantry Brigade (Brigadier A. Anderson) supported by sixteen 'I' tanks of the 8th Royal Tank Regiment, the 7th Medium Regiment R.A., part of the 51st Field Regiment R.A. and a battery of the 73rd Anti-Tank Regiment R.A. The operation was carried out with exemplary speed. From his position on 3rd December thirty miles east of Bir el Gubi Brigadier Anderson could only form an outline plan, which was certainly a bold one—to make an unreconnoitred night march of over twenty miles and attack from the west such of the enemy as daylight should disclose to be in front of him. To the credit of the Brigade and its supporting arms the night march was successfully accomplished, the attack made, and part of the objective taken. Renewed attacks on 5th December did not succeed and meanwhile the enemy had reacted to the threat.

On the morning of 4th December the Germans attacked El Duda and were repulsed. By noon General Rommel felt he could not disregard the happenings at Bir el Gubi, because an outflanking move from this quarter would be dangerous. He broke off the action at El Duda, recalled the columns heading for Bardia and Sidi Azeiz, and decided to send both Panzer Divisions and the Ariete and Trieste Divisions to the southern flank. This meant weakening himself so much in front of Tobruk that he would have to withdraw from the eastern face, and during the night the process of thinning out began. On 5th December he intended to use all his mobile troops to deal with the British at Bir el Gubi and then sweep on into the rearward area of the 30th Corps, but this plan did not come off. The Ariete Division, harried by columns of the 7th Support Group, never arrived and the

Trieste Division does not seem to have left its assembly area on the southern escarpment. The 8th Panzer Regiment and some lorried infantry overran part of the 11th Indian Infantry Brigade, but did not pass on any farther.

The danger from the south caused the enemy's air force to make great efforts to interfere with the movements of the British troops about Bir el Gubi. Large formations of escorted dive-bombers made frequent attacks, causing casualties and damaging vehicles. Many of these attacks were intercepted and broken up by the British fighters, and as the days passed the numbers of dive-bombers fell until only fighters were usually encountered. The rising rate of losses in these engagements caused some anxiety, however, and pointed to the need for a fighter (such as the Spitfire V) to combat the Me. 109F whose rate of climb and speed made it superior to any British single-engined fighter in the Middle East. Apart from this a general increase in the numbers of German and Italian fighters was becoming evident.

Conversely, the southerly move of the Axis mobile forces and the large volume of traffic passing El Adem presented many targets to the British medium bombers and Hurricane fighter-bombers, and by night the Wellingtons and Fleet Air Arm Albacores kept up the pressure by attacking transport along the road from El Adem through Acroma to Gazala. The need now arose for more day-bombers, since the flow of Marylands had ceased and the Baltimores were behind schedule. Accordingly the Bostons of No. 24 Squadron S.A.A.F., hitherto employed on tactical reconnaissance, joined the day-bomber force. To harass still further the retreating enemy the junction of the Tobruk by-pass road with the Tobruk-Gazala road was bombarded on several nights by the gunboat *Aphis* with the help of flares dropped by the Fleet Air Arm.

The evening of 5th December had found the higher commanders on both sides in some perplexity. Generals Rommel and Bastico, it will be remembered, had appealed urgently to Rome for reinforcements of all kinds. The answer was brought on 4th December by Colonel Montezemolo, head of the Operations Branch of *Comando Supremo*, his unwelcome news being that British naval and air activity in the Mediterranean was preventing anything being sent save small quantities of fuel, food, and medical stores.[1] Nothing better was to be expected until the end of December, when the operations of the *Luftwaffe* from Sicily might enable regular convoys to be run. General Rommel thereupon painted a depressing picture of what might happen. He expected the British to outflank him from the south and he might have to withdraw to Tripolitania. He would hope to extricate most of the immobile (chiefly Italian) infantry, but much material would be lost. The frontier garrisons were almost out of supplies and

[1] The relevant naval and air operations are described in the following chapter.

would have to retire into Bardia, whence they might have to be withdrawn by sea and air.

It had been General Norrie's intention to advance towards El Adem on 6th December, and in order to make the whole of the 4th Indian Division available he decided that the 22nd Guards Brigade should relieve the 11th Indian Infantry Brigade west of Bir el Gubi early on 6th December, and that it should clear up the situation there while the main advance went on. By dawn on the 6th, however, Norrie had become less hopeful, and felt that it was necessary to use the 4th Indian Division in the Bir el Gubi area and at the same time reconnoitre widely to discover the enemy's new dispositions. The 8th Army's intelligence staff were inclined to think that the enemy was about to withdraw, and while not himself convinced of this General Ritchie urged Norrie to avoid Bir el Gubi and apply pressure in a northwesterly direction. That afternoon the *D.A.K.* tried to advance on Bir el Gubi but the plan miscarried because of unwonted muddles between the two Panzer Divisions, and the more familiar failure of the Italians to arrive at the right place at the right time. In the end, towards evening of 6th December, the 15th Panzer Division clashed with the Guards Brigade, was heavily bombed and shelled, lost several tanks and accomplished nothing. Its commander, Major-General Neumann-Silkow, was mortally wounded.

Early next morning General Rommel went forward to see things for himself. He found Crüwell anxious about the British concentration in the south. The British were superior on the ground and in the air, and the condition of the Axis troops was growing worse. Petrol and ammunition were becoming dangerously scarce. Then and there Rommel decided to call off any further attacks and to make a fighting withdrawal to the Gazala position. This was the defensive position chosen in May 1941 after the Axis attacks on Tobruk had failed and when their policy was to hold Western Cyrenaica regardless of who held Sollum, Bardia, or even Tobruk. To this end a position was constructed on the eastern edge of the Jebel Akhdar with its left at Gazala and its right thrown well back into the desert. Work was begun at once and good progress had been made by June. Now, six months later, the defences were not in good order, but they were better than nothing. Four Italian divisions were to occupy them; the Italian mobile corps was to be on the southern flank, and wider still, echeloned back, the *D.A.K.*

Very early on 7th December General Norrie was told to begin his advance during the day as soon as the situation seemed favourable. He was to communicate his intentions to General Godwin-Austen, who was eagerly waiting to make a move towards El Adem from El Duda. The 13th Corps and 2nd South African Division were ordered to clear the enemy from the country between Tobruk and Bardia north of the Trigh Capuzzo, especially from airfields and landing-grounds—which were badly needed for the move forward of the air forces.

The enemy's delaying tactics on the 30th Corps' front were so successful, however, that no progress was made that day, and General Gott even began to think that the enemy was being reinforced. General Norrie decided that the moment to advance had not come, and informed General Ritchie who correctly judged the true position to be that Rommel was hitting out to cover an imminent withdrawal. Ritchie would therefore have liked 30th Corps to strike, but as it was at least occupying the attention of the hostile armour he did not insist, and merely told Norrie to keep up the pressure and to by-pass the enemy where possible. Godwin-Austen, on the other hand, was to begin his operations.

Accordingly that night two battalions of the 23rd Infantry Brigade (Brigadier C. H. V. Cox) and a few tanks broke out of the western face of the El Duda salient and advanced almost as far as the Tobruk-El Adem road. Early next morning, 8th December, it became clear that the enemy was retiring from the neighbourhood of Bir el Gubi and General Norrie directed the 7th Armoured Division to advance to the track junction (later to become famous as Knightsbridge) about twelve miles south of Acroma. The 4th Indian Division was to move northwards to the escarpment which runs west from El Adem towards Knightsbridge, and then extend its right to join hands with the 13th Corps. From the rate of progress it seems that the enemy's delaying tactics must have been effective, for nowhere was the withdrawal much interfered with.

By 10th December the Brescia and Trento Divisions had withdrawn from their positions opposite the western half of the Tobruk perimeter. Thus the siege of Tobruk—which had begun on 11th April—came to an end after eight months. It had been hoped that its relief would occur within a week of the start of 'Crusader', and the fact that it took three weeks threw a great strain on the cross-country transport and caused immense quantities of petrol to be consumed in carrying supplies anything up to 120 miles from railhead. It was realized that the arrival of the first bulk-loaded ships at a newly opened port does not solve all the problems of supply, for not until some retail stocks are built up can day-to-day demands be met. Some stocks had been built up at Tobruk, but the course of the fighting in and around the corridor had led to much of them being used up. It was obvious that the land link forward from railhead would still be wanted for some time and this pointed to the need for clearing the coast road past Halfaya, Sollum and Bardia, so as to open a shorter and better route.

An important result of the relief of Tobruk was to make the group of landing-grounds Tobruk, El Adem, Sidi Rezegh and Bu Amud available for the British fighters, and on 11th December Headquarters No. 262 Fighter Wing arrived to take control of the fighters of Nos. 262 and 258 Wings on these landing-grounds. This meant that fighter escorts would be able to reach well beyond Bir el Gubi and El Adem, which they could not do when the fighters were forced to remain back at Fort Maddalena instead of moving to Gambut as intended. There had in fact been considerable losses in operations by day-bombers unescorted by fighters, and even the Hurricane fighter-bombers had suffered in this way; cloud cover could sometimes be used, but in those conditions the targets were often obscured. Another important result of the move to the new landing-grounds was that fighter cover could be provided over Tobruk and ships could unload in daylight.

All this time the Wellingtons and other aircraft from Malta were steadily attacking Tripoli, the Italian ports of departure, and various targets in Sicily and on the Italian mainland.

It is not surprising that in view of their troubles over sea convoys at this time the Germans and Italians should have made great use of their numerous transport aircraft for carrying essential stores to North Africa. The Italians flew from Italy and Sicily, and ferried loads (in particular, of ammunition) forward from Tripoli, and now a steady German traffic began between Maleme, in Crete, and Derna. In an attempt to counter this move, in which Whitehall showed great interest, the Wellingtons from Egypt attacked Maleme while Marylands, Blenheims and Beaufighters were pressed into service as intruders against the transport aircraft in flight. Painted green and black, and flying very low over the sea, the Ju. 52s were not easy to attack, and only the Beaufighters were really suitable for the task. But there were too few of these to interfere seriously with the traffic, which continued virtually unhindered.

In the enemy's High Command the suggestion that the whole of Cyrenaica might have to be given up had caused a great stir. After receiving Colonel Montezemolo's report *Comando Supremo* sent instructions to General Bastico on 7th December agreeing that it was necessary to give up the siege of Tobruk. But although freedom of action was left to Bastico, they thought that an attempt should be made to defend Cyrenaica in order to retain Benghazi, and that a retreat into Tripolitania was a last resort. In either case it was imperative to hold Agedabia strongly and to recapture Jalo, in order to prevent a wide British outflanking manoeuvre and keep secure the lines of communication with Tripoli. Next day Bastico met Rommel, who began an ill-tempered conference by enlarging upon the shortcomings of Italian troops and of General Gambara. General Bastico took offence at these remarks, but agreement was reached eventually to occupy the

Gazala position and to send part of the 90th Light Division and some Italian artillery to hold Agedabia. The same evening *Comando Supremo*, in agreement with *OKH*, ordered that Bardia and the frontier positions were still to be held and that they were to be supplied by air and sea; how this was to be done was not stated.

On 9th December General Bastico issued a directive on policy for the immediate future. This confirmed the steps that General Rommel was already taking and met his wishes by placing all the land forces in Cyrenaica under his command.[1] Next day Gambara resumed his duties as Chief of Staff to Bastico, and was replaced at 20th Corps by General Piazzoni, the commander of the Trieste Division. That night the 90th Light Division began to move to Agedabia, and lost its commander, Major-General Sümmermann, who was killed during an air attack. This was an incident in the persistent harrying by the Royal Air Force from which the Axis forces had been suffering for some time. Shortage of fuel was hampering the action of their own air and land forces, especially the armour, which made it very doubtful whether they would be able to counter the attempts which the British were certain to make to outflank the Gazala position from the south. Indeed General Rommel thought that he might soon have to retire again.

When *Comando Supremo* heard this they issued another directive to Bastico in which the decision to defend or abandon Cyrenaica was left '*al comandante in sito*'—which it seems was intended to refer to Rommel, to whose notice Bastico, in the Duce's name, was to bring certain points before the decision was taken. These were the heavy British losses and the fact that they seemed unable to pursue, the time they would take to stage the outflanking of Agedabia, the disorganization [sic] caused by General Cunningham's replacement, and the effect that Japan's entry into the war might be expected to have upon the British plans.[2] Again, it was hoped that reinforcements would reach Libya by the end of December; meanwhile *Luftwaffe* units were already arriving in Sicily and would do much to improve the position in the Mediterranean. General Bastico took this directive to mean that it was he who was responsible for deciding what to do, and sent a slightly modified version to Rommel on 12th December, adding that Cyrenaica was to be resolutely defended at Gazala, and that there was to be no question of further withdrawal. Rommel replied that as the air forces could not be counted on to prevent a British outflanking manoeuvre it would not be possible to hold the Gazala position for long.

---

[1] This gave him the Headquarters of the Italian 10th Corps (General Gioda) and a few miscellaneous units.

[2] The consequences of the entry of Japan into the war are discussed in Chapter V.

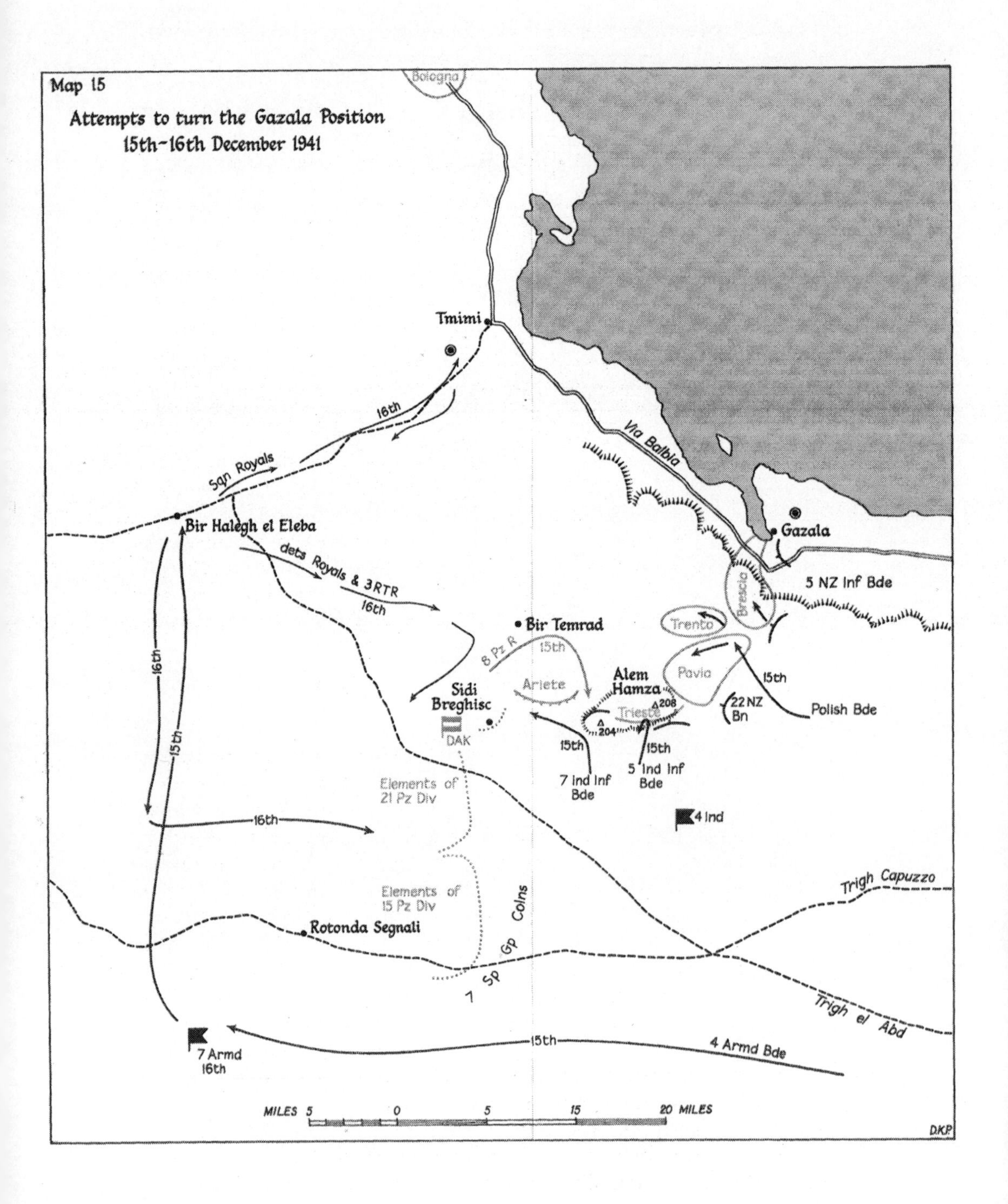
Map 15
Attempts to turn the Gazala Position
15th–16th December 1941
Bologna
Tmimi
Via Balbia
Gazala
16th
Sqn Royals
Bir Halegh el Eleba
dets Royals & 3RTR
16th
Bir Temrad
8 Pz R
15th
Ariete
Sidi
Breghisc
DAK
Alem
Hamza
208
204
Trieste
Trento
Pavia
Brescia
5 NZ Inf Bde
15th
22 NZ
Bn
Polish Bde
15th
15th
7 Ind Inf
Bde
5 Ind Inf
Bde
4 Ind
16th
15th
16th
Elements of
21 Pz Div
Elements of
15 Pz Div
7 Sp Gp Colns
Rotonda Segnali
Trigh Capuzzo
Trigh el Abd
15th
4 Armd Bde
7 Armd
16th
MILES 5 0 5 15 20 MILES
DKP

On 9th December General Ritchie gave orders for an adjustment of the chain of command, of which he had given warning two days earlier. This was that the 13th Corps would control the operations to drive the enemy out of Cyrenaica while the 30th Corps took charge of the reduction of the enemy's positions on the Egyptian frontier. Among his reasons were that a single commander would be able to control all the troops that could be maintained west of Tobruk, and as Tobruk would be the supply base, and the 13th Corps was already there, General Godwin-Austen was well placed to take command with the least delay. What mattered most was to give the enemy no respite, and Ritchie set aside General Norrie's prompt suggestion that Headquarters 30th Corps was the better fitted to conduct mobile operations —having indeed been formed for that very purpose. (As against this, there was only one armoured division, which now had only one armoured brigade.) An additional reason was that General Auchinleck was contemplating withdrawing the 30th Corps into G.H.Q. reserve as an insurance against a possible threat to the northern front. On 11th December the 13th Corps took over the 7th Armoured Division and the 4th Indian Division, and next day the 30th Corps left for the frontier area. General Ritchie announced also his intention of taking the 22nd Guards Brigade under his direct command and sending it as soon as possible by the desert route to capture Benghazi and prevent the enemy escaping to Tripolitania.

See Map 15

The extent of the enemy's position at Gazala was fairly accurately known. It ran in a bold curve from the coast to the Alem Hamza ridge about twelve miles inland, south of which there were no recognizable defences. By 13th December the British had closed up, and the enemy's attitude suggested that he was going to make a stand. General Godwin-Austen therefore hoped to force a decisive battle. His plan was briefly for the 5th New Zealand Brigade (which had been brought up from the frontier) to pin the enemy east of Gazala, while the Polish Brigade (from Tobruk) on its left swung north to cut the coast road west of Gazala. The 4th Indian Division was to attack westward from Alem Hamza while the 7th Support Group dealt with any enemy south of Sidi Breghisc. The 4th Armoured Brigade was to make a wide flanking movement, passing south of Rotonda Segnali to Bir Halegh el Eleba from where it would operate against the rear of the enemy in the area Bir Temrad-Sidi Breghisc. The Brigade was to reach Bir Halegh el Eleba not later than 11 a.m. on 15th December. The enemy was thought to have about fifty tanks, and Godwin-Austen impressed upon General Gott how important it was to destroy these. In his belief the

4th Armoured Brigade with its 90 Stuart tanks had a rare opportunity in its grasp.[1]

On 15th December the 13th Corps began its attack. Near the coast the New Zealanders made some progress and took several hundred Italian prisoners, as did the Polish Brigade (Major-General S. Kopanski), which was nevertheless unable to work round to the west of Gazala. Both brigades of the 4th Indian Division had a hard day. The 1st Battalion The Buffs, of the 5th Indian Infantry Brigade (Brigadier D. Russell), had already made ground to Pt 204, three miles west of Alem Hamza, and the plan was for the rest of the Brigade to take Alem Hamza from the south while on the left the 7th Indian Infantry Brigade captured Sidi Breghisc. Both attacks failed. In the afternoon, after a heavy shelling, the 8th Panzer Regiment and 2nd Machine-Gun Battalion counter-attacked Pt 204 and after a fierce action lasting an hour and a half overran the Buffs and their attached troops, who lost altogether over a thousand men, many of whom were taken prisoner.[2] On the other hand the 8th Panzer Regiment—the hard core of the enemy's armour—appears to have lost 9 (or possibly 12) of the 23 tanks with which it started the day. All these actions, disappointing though they were, did at least mean that the enemy was thoroughly occupied, and General Godwin-Austen had great hopes of the effect which the arrival of the 4th Armoured Brigade in the enemy's back area would have. As it happened it had hardly any.

The Brigade had to cover nearly seventy miles to reach Bir Halegh el Eleba, where it was due at 11 a.m. Over bad going—and on this day some of the going was very bad indeed, entailing much running in low gear—this was beyond the limit of the Stuart tanks. By loading them with spare petrol and by 'topping up' on the way the Brigade managed to reach its destination at 3 p.m. That evening General Gott realized that the petrol vehicles of 'B' Echelon, which had themselves been late in replenishing, would not reach the Brigade that day. Rather than risk the tanks being caught with very little petrol so far behind the front, he authorized Brigadier Gatehouse to move south next morning to meet the petrol vehicles. He signalled to 13th Corps that the Brigade would not be able to operate until the early afternoon of 16th December. To this Godwin-Austen replied that it was to attack as soon as possible the enemy opposing the 4th Indian Division, which was to hold fast until this attack was made. The 7th Armoured Division was also to send a column to cut the coast road at Tmimi.

---

[1] German records credit 15th Panzer Division with 23 fit tanks, and 21st Panzer Division with 19. The number with the Ariete Division at this time is not known.

[2] The mixed force included: one squadron 4th Royal Tank Regiment, 31st Field Regiment R.A., one troop 73rd Anti-Tank Regiment R.A.

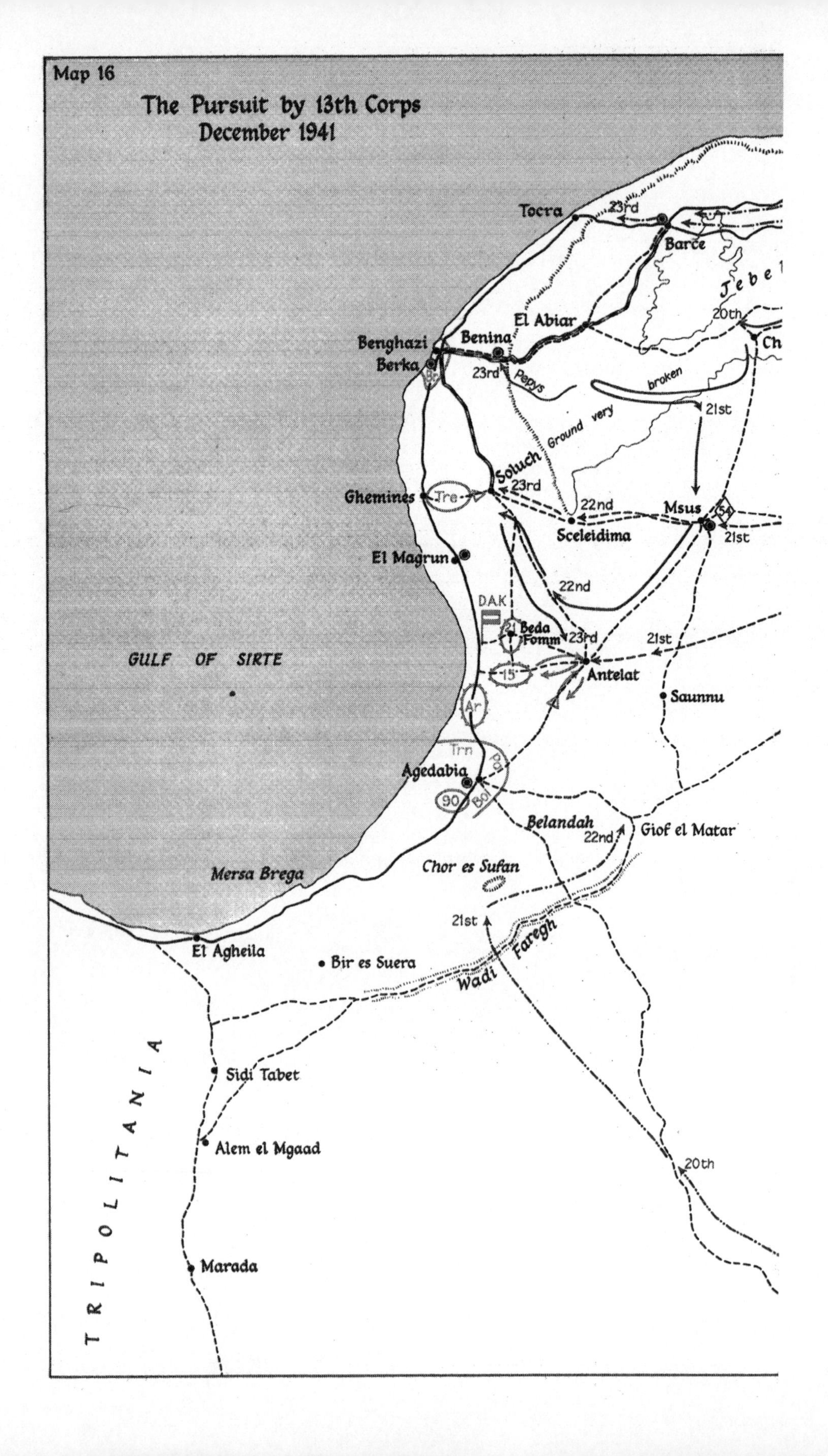

Map 16
The Pursuit by 13th Corps
December 1941
Tocra
23rd
Barce
Jebel
20th
El Abiar
Benghazi
Benina
Berka
23rd
Pepys
broken
Ground very
21st
Soluch
23rd
Ghemines
Tre
22nd
Msus
Sceleidima
21st
El Magrun
22nd
DAK
Beda
Fomm
23rd
21st
GULF OF SIRTE
Antelat
15
Saunnu
Ar
Trn
Agedabia
90
Bol
Belandah
22nd
Giof el Matar
Chor es Sufan
Mersa Brega
21st
Wadi Faregh
El Agheila
Bir es Suera
TRIPOLITANIA
Sidi Tabet
Alem el Mgaad
20th
Marada

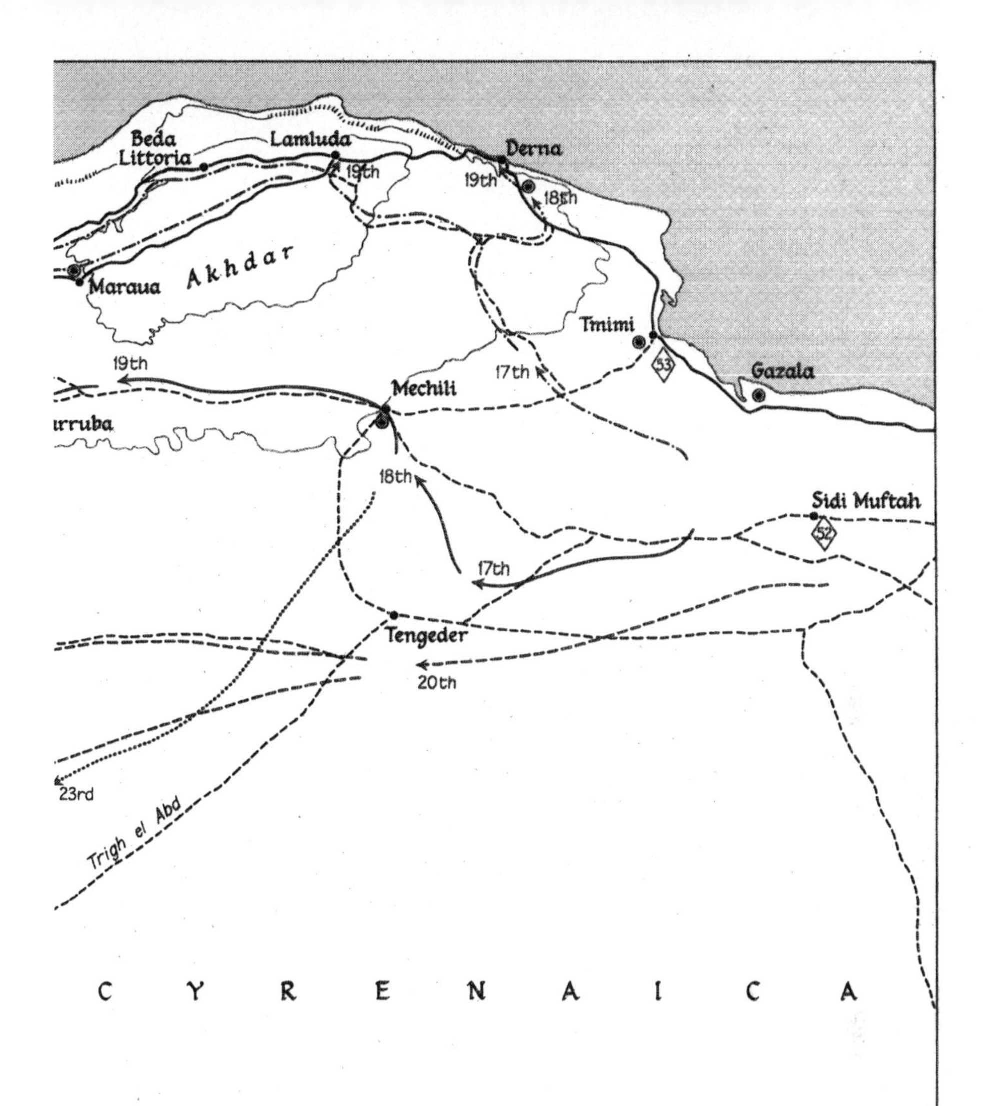
Beda
Littoria
Lamluda
Derna
19th
18th
Maraua
Akhdar
Tmimi
53
Gazala
19th
17th
Mechili
rruba
18th
Sidi Muftah
52
17th
Tengeder
20th
23rd
Trigh el Abd
C Y R E N A I C A

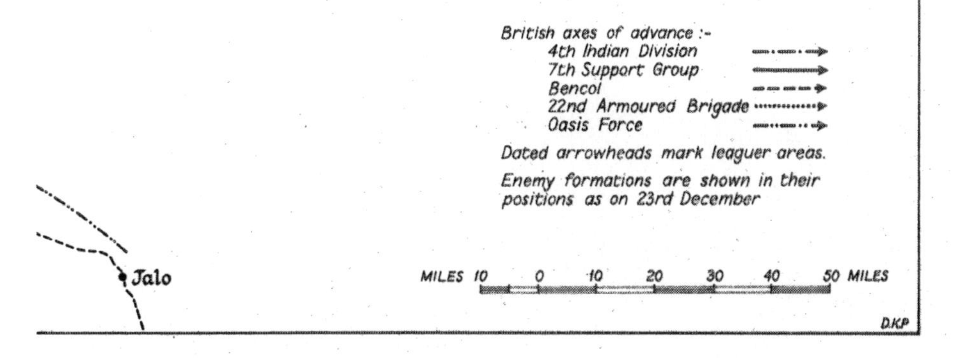
British axes of advance :-
4th Indian Division
7th Support Group
Bencol
22nd Armoured Brigade
Oasis Force
Dated arrowheads mark leaguer areas.
Enemy formations are shown in their positions as on 23rd December
Jalo
MILES 10 0 10 20 30 40 50 MILES
D.K.P

But on 16th December, in spite of General Godwin-Austen's hopes, there was no decisive action. The small column sent to Tmimi shot up a few vehicles and captured a handful of prisoners before it withdrew for want of petrol—an enterprise which does not seem to have worried the enemy although his main line of retreat ran through Tmimi. At 7 a.m. the 4th Armoured Brigade set off south to meet its petrol and supplies. After replenishing it seems to have moved shortly after noon to a point south of Sidi Breghisc where it exchanged fire with some hostile guns. A small detachment sent to Bir Temrad had some indecisive skirmishing. General Godwin-Austen, seeing what he thought was a great opportunity slipping away, continued to urge Gott to cut the enemy's line of retreat. By evening the enemy showed clear signs of preparing to withdraw. The 4th Armoured Brigade was unable to interfere, and during the night the enemy broke away.

If the British armour could not interfere with this orderly disengagement and withdrawal, what of the air force? It has been mentioned that the British day-bombers had been unable to apply their full weight against targets west of a line Bir el Gubi-El Adem because they could not be given fighter escorts from the Fort Maddalena landing-grounds. This meant that while the enemy was moving back to take up his new dispositions at Gazala he could not be heavily attacked by day from the air. This handicap was not likely to recur because of strenuous efforts to prepare fighter landing-grounds well forward, only a few miles east of Gazala, in readiness for the next stage.

As soon as the fighters began to operate from around Tobruk the whole of the enemy's new deployment area could have been attacked by escorted day-bombers. Unfortunately, during the four days from 13th to 16th December, when the enemy was halted in the Gazala position, the Army seems to have been unable for one reason or another to give the Air Force any worth-while targets. The weather was not particularly good; indeed the 15th was a day of gales, rain, and sandstorms. Another reason seems to have been that General Godwin-Austen's plan for biting off the northern part of the enemy's front and for encircling the remainder—he also had it in mind to send columns to raid the coast road—made it difficult to choose a 'bomb-line', or line beyond which anything seen could be attacked from the air, without danger to the British troops. There was still the old problem of identification and there seems to have been a feeling that if the enemy did begin to withdraw the fact would become apparent and some marvellous targets for air attack would appear. The result was, as Air Vice-Marshal Coningham reported sadly, that for nearly three days the enemy's troops in the comparatively small area south-west of Gazala had not one bomb dropped on them.

See Map 16

In the enemy's High Command the disagreements had continued. On 13th December General Rommel reported to *OKH* that he would probably be compelled to withdraw during the night 14th/15th to Derna and Mechili. General Bastico received this news by liaison officer and at once asked *Comando Supremo* whether the final decision was to be his or Rommel's. His own opinion was that the Gazala line could be held. He seems to have become suspicious of Rommel and to have formed the idea that if a crisis occurred the Germans would retire and leave the less mobile Italians to fend for themselves. Next day a compromise was arranged—to hold on for the moment but to prepare to withdraw to Derna and Mechili.

On 15th December Rommel got news of the move of the 4th Armoured Brigade, heading as he thought for Mechili. This convinced him that he would have to withdraw from the Gazala position during the night 16th/17th. General Cavallero, accompanied by Field-Marshal Kesselring, flew from Rome to try to resolve the differences with Bastico, and on the morning of the 16th he put to him the argument that events outside the Mediterranean (he was no doubt thinking of the Far East) might influence the campaign and that one object should therefore be to gain time. Tripolitania was to be defended at all costs but large reinforcements could not be counted upon. When Cavallero visited Rommel that afternoon he learned that he had already taken his own decision to withdraw from Gazala and that the movement had begun; the 21st Corps was directed through Tmimi on Derna, and the 20th Corps and *D.A.K.* on Mechili. Rommel's intention was to concentrate finally about El Agheila and Marada. Cavallero was content to point out that the defence of Tripolitania was the main object, but that Cyrenaica must only be given up gradually in order to save equipment and stores.

Next morning, 17th December, there was yet another meeting and this time Rommel said that he meant to hold on at Derna and Mechili as long as he could, but that if the British advanced to Mechili, or south of it, it would be necessary to retreat from Cyrenaica leaving only rearguards behind. Cavallero agreed in general terms. That afternoon a German air report reached Rommel that British columns (in fact the 7th Support Group) were advancing towards Tengeder, and he informed Cavallero that this made a further withdrawal essential. Cavallero, who doubted the correctness of the air report, later sent the liaison officer with an urgent request for delay on the ground that the Italian troops were exhausted and short of transport. Rommel replied that there was not a moment to lose, and that he intended to leave nothing save a mobile rearguard east of a line Beda Littoria-Maraua. He suggested that the Italian Command would perform a most valuable service if they retired to Tripoli and organized the reinforcements. He then ordered General Crüwell to move south of Benghazi and be ready to operate towards Agedabia. The Italian Corps were to make for Benghazi. When Cavallero heard of these orders he set off with Bastico and Gambara to protest to Rommel. The meeting was stormy, but there was nothing for it but to confirm Rommel's decision.

While General Rommel was determined to get back with all speed to Agedabia and El Agheila, and hand to the British the drag of a rapidly lengthening line of communication, General Ritchie had thought it likely that the enemy would fight delaying actions as far back as Derna and Mechili. Accordingly the 4th Indian Division was directed on Lamluda and the 7th Armoured Division on Mechili, while a strong column was to slip round the southern flank and harry the enemy as far to the west as possible. The 22nd Guards Brigade Group (or 'Bencol'), commanded by Brigadier J. C. O. Marriott, under the direct control of 8th Army, was to cross the desert farther south still and make all speed for Benghazi, which it was to seize and hold. But the units of 'Bencol' had first to be assembled from other tasks, and many of their worn out vehicles replaced. Not until 20th December could the force be ready. On the 18th Ritchie realized that the enemy did not mean to stand at Derna and Mechili, and he thereupon changed the role of 'Bencol' from capturing Benghazi to preventing the enemy escaping southward from it. The strong harassing column which 7th Armoured Division had been ordered to send westward was cancelled, and General Gott was directed by General Godwin-Austen to press on to Benina and Benghazi. Next day 'Bencol' was ordered to pass south of Tengeder, and send one detachment to secure the landing-ground at Msus and another through Sceleidima towards Ghemines; the main body was to advance to the south-west of Antelat—a large number of tasks for such a small force if it should meet with any strong opposition.[1]

By this time—19th December—the 7th Indian Infantry Brigade had reached Derna, where it parted with most of its transport to sustain the advance across the desert. Reconnaissance troops and the 5th Indian Infantry Brigade pushed on as best they could, delayed by bad weather and by demolished roads and tracks. The Support Group of the 7th Armoured Division reached Charruba on the 20th and made touch with rearguards of the Trieste and Ariete Divisions. The weather and going were very bad and there was trouble over petrol. Next day the enemy had disappeared, the going became worse, and there were again doubts whether petrol would arrive. General Gott decided to send a small column (named 'Pepys') at once to the important Benina

[1] The main units of 'Bencol' were: 11th Hussars (armoured cars); one squadron of the 2nd Royal Gloucestershire Hussars (fourteen Stuart tanks); 51st Field Regiment R.A.; 3rd Coldstream Guards; 2nd Scots Guards.

airfield, and to send the rest of the Support Group across the better going towards Msus and Antelat on the 22nd December. By the evening of 21st December 'Bencol', which had made good speed, had one squadron of the 11th Hussars near Sceleidima and one near Antelat, the Coldstream Guards fifteen miles east of Antelat, and the Scots Guards near Msus.

At this time the enemy's divisions, which had also been having their troubles from weather, bad going, and shortage of petrol, apart from being much harassed from the air, were situated as follows. The 15th Panzer was at Beda Fomm and the 21st Panzer at Ghemines; the Ariete, Trieste and Pavia were near El Abiar; the Trento and Brescia near Barce and Tocra; and the 90th Light and the Bologna were at Agedabia. General Rommel's plan was for the mobile troops to hold off the British advance from the east long enough to enable the Italian infantry to escape to the south.

When the idea of sending a column across the desert to Benghazi was first thought of, it was proposed to attach an air component of five or six squadrons. But by the time 'Bencol' was ready to start the landing-ground at Mechili had become available for the fighters, which made the provision of a special air component unnecessary. During the advance through Cyrenaica Nos. 208 and 237 (Rhodesian) Tactical Reconnaissance Squadrons, operating at first from Tmimi, were responsible for most of the information about the enemy's movements. In view of the large area to be covered, however, some of the long-range Hurricanes of No. 33 Squadron were used to extend the range of reconnaissance, and other fighters engaged on offensive sweeps were also given reconnaissance tasks. As early as 18th December a considerable force of fighters had been established at Gazala and, in spite of the Army's great difficulty in finding transport for lifting petrol forward, the fighters were operating from Mechili on the 20th and from Msus on the 23rd. Shortly afterwards No. 262 Wing established an advanced headquarters at Msus to control the fighter operations.

When the enemy had begun to retreat from Gazala the British day-bombers were moving forward to landing-grounds at Gambut, Sidi Rezegh and Bu Amud. The 8th Army chose a bomb-line a long way ahead, and attacks were at once made on the retreating columns, especially where the main road winds up and down the coastal escarpment near Derna, where traffic was likely to pile up. Later these attacks were lifted on to the two roads running west from Lamluda. Meanwhile the route from Mechili to Charruba was harassed, until the main road north and south of Benghazi became in turn the principal object of attack. The Wellingtons and Albacores carried the attacks on into the night, but it is doubtful whether the targets they could find were worth the effort. The scale of all these operations was not as heavy as had been hoped, and ideas of turning the retreat into a rout were not realized. The enemy's diaries make frequent mention of the harassing effect of the British air attacks, but there is no doubt that the retreat as a whole was delayed very little—indeed the speed with which it was conducted is evidence of this. Nevertheless it was plain for all to see that the losses of vehicles and equipment from air attacks had been heavy.

The fact is that the day-bombers were passing through a difficult time. The weather was bad, which made it harder than ever to distinguish friend from foe. (Not that the enemy was free from this trouble, for on several occasions Stukas are known to have dive-bombed their own troops.) There was a shortage of transport for moving fuel and supplies from Tobruk and from railhead, and also for bringing forward bombs and other heavy stores from previously occupied airfields. The day-bombers had certainly not been given many good targets in direct support of the Army, but that did not mean that they had been idle, and the prolonged operations in desert conditions had greatly reduced the number of aircraft fit to fly. Bostons were having much engine trouble and the flow of Marylands (which the Bostons were replacing) had ceased, so that Nos. 12 and 21 Squadrons S.A.A.F. had to be put together to form one squadron. Blenheims were beginning to leave for the Far East. In short, the enemy's retreat came at a time when the British were at full stretch in the air as well as on the ground.

This made it all the harder to maintain a just proportion between attacks on the enemy's troops and on his air force. The latter, though shaken and struggling, could not be disregarded, and the more it was smothered the more would the Royal Air Force be easing the task of the British troops. The German and Italian Air Forces were now being forced back and their airfields were becoming congested. This was the moment to attack them. On 17th December Air Vice-Marshal Coningham began to deal systematically with the principal airfields, by night as well as by day, particularly Benina, Maraua, Berka and Barce. Large numbers of aircraft were eventually found abandoned on these airfields—at Benina, for instance, there were sixty-four of which all but two were German.

Further heavy air attacks were made on Benghazi harbour on 17th December and succeeding nights, stimulated by reports that a convoy was expected there. German records show that in fact the 4,700-ton merchant ship *Ankara* of No. 52 Convoy arrived at Benghazi on the 19th, the rest of the convoy having made for Tripoli. The *Ankara's* cargo included twenty-two tanks, which were safely received by the 8th Panzer Regiment a few days later.[1] In the circumstances the un-

[1] The *Monginevro* of the same convoy reached Tripoli on 19th December. Part of her cargo consisted of 23 tanks, which were also sent to the 8th Panzer Regiment. About half the arrivals at each port were Pzkw IIIs. The *Carlo del Greco* carrying 23 tanks, and the *Fabio Filzi* with a further 22, had both been sunk on 13th December.

loading and clearing of this ship's cargo must have been a creditable performance, though it is hard to say how bad the state of the harbour was before the enemy carried out the deliberate demolitions which 'Pepys' Column saw and heard from Benina on the 23rd. Certainly when the King's Dragoon Guards and 'Pepys' Column entered the town on the 24th—not long after the Brescia Division's rearguard had moved out—they found the town and port in chaos and the harbour encumbered with wrecks.

On 21st December General Ritchie, much impressed by reports of an accumulation of fighter aircraft on El Magrun airfield, ordered 'Bencol' to turn and threaten it—if possible, that night. He then took the obvious step of placing 'Bencol' under 13th Corps, whereupon General Godwin-Austen ordered it to complete its operation at El Magrun and to secure in turn Agedabia and El Agheila and to patrol towards Marada. The 7th Armoured Division—in effect the Support Group—was to harass the enemy retreating by the coast road. These tasks are evidence of the strong desire for bold action, but in view of what is now known of the enemy's dispositions they had very little chance of succeeding. However, 'Bencol' was to be reinforced by the 12th Lancers (armoured cars) and by the 3rd Royal Tank Regiment (Stuart tanks). The relief of the 7th Armoured Division by the newly arrived 1st Armoured Division was now in progress, and the reconstituted 22nd Armoured Brigade, with 80 cruisers and 30 Stuarts, had already relieved the 4th Armoured Brigade (less the 3rd Royal Tank Regiment) at Mechili.[1]

Little progress was made on 22nd December. The 22nd Armoured Brigade prepared to set off from Mechili towards Saunnu. The 7th Support Group reached a point about fifteen miles south of Sceleidima. 'Bencol' did its best to do everything at once. The detachment heading for El Magrun was held up at Sceleidima and the 12th Lancers were held up farther north. A company of the Coldstream Guards with a few field and anti-tank guns was sent towards Beda Fomm and another company towards Agedabia. Early next morning part of the 15th Panzer Division near Beda Fomm saw its opportunity and attacked the small column of the Coldstream Guards and drove it, with the 3rd Royal Tank Regiment which had come up in support, east of Antelat. Later, on the appearance of the Support Group, which had been recalled from its previous task, the German force withdrew. Meanwhile the Italian infantry divisions, except the Brescia, slipped away down the coast road. For some time Ritchie and Godwin-Austen did not realize what had happened, but believed that the bulk of the

[1] 3rd and 4th County of London Yeomanry had Crusader tanks, and the 2nd Royal Gloucestershire Hussars had Stuarts.

Italians were still near Benghazi and that 'Bencol' was successfully engaging the remains of the enemy's armour. Orders for the 24th were that the 7th Support Group was to clear up between Benghazi and Antelat; 'Bencol' (with 3rd Royal Tank Regiment) was to seize Agedabia; and the 22nd Armoured Brigade was to advance on the southern flank and encircle the enemy. Brigadier Reid's Oasis Force, which had reached Giof el Matar from Jalo on 22nd December, was to cut the coast road as far south of Agedabia as it could.

Little came of these orders. On 24th December the Support Group failed to intercept the enemy withdrawing along the road from Benghazi; 'Bencol' moved a few miles towards Agedabia; the 22nd Armoured Brigade reached Saunnu and ran out of petrol for twenty-four hours. By the evening the Brescia Division, the last to leave Benghazi, had joined the 20th Corps and the *D.A.K.* in the neighbourhood of Agedabia. Rommel's intention of making a clean break away from Gazala and concentrating as soon as possible at Agedabia had succeeded.

The Oasis Force had sent out a number of small columns to harass enemy transport on the coast road north and south of Agedabia. Further enterprises behind the enemy's lines were carried out by a detachment of the Special Air Service Brigade, and by three Patrols of the Long Range Desert Group which had joined Brigadier Reid at Jalo. Between them they raided Tamet landing-ground twice and Agedabia airfield once in the second half of December, claiming on each occasion to have destroyed from twenty to thirty Italian aircraft.[1]

Christmas Day was spent in gaining contact with the enemy's new positions. By the next evening it seemed likely that the enemy would hold on until turned out, and as his units were now very weak, and the Italians in particular very tired, it might be that the opportunity still existed to deal a telling blow. General Godwin-Austen accordingly arranged for the 22nd Guards Brigade to attack during the night 26th/27th and for the 22nd Armoured Brigade to operate on the southern flank next morning. The 22nd Guards Brigade was spread out over a wide area, and what actually happened was that one battalion made a hastily prepared and difficult night advance in the rain, and followed it with an unsuccessful attack. On the flank the armour had some indecisive skirmishing. This disappointing result did not deter Godwin-Austen from trying to press on with all speed, and a renewal of the attack was ordered for 28th December.

---

[1] In F. Manzetti: *Seconda Offensiva Britannica in Africa Settentrionale* (Italian Official History) (Rome 1949) pp. 128, 136, two of these raids are mentioned; eleven aircraft are stated to have been destroyed at Tamet and 'about fifteen' at Agedabia. Tamet lies thirty miles west of Sirte.

It had always been the intention to use Tobruk as an advanced base as soon as possible, and it has already been seen that certain reserve stocks had been built up there. The replacement of the Australians had used shipping space which would otherwise have been available, and subsequently the course of the fighting had resulted in the stocks being much depleted. When it became necessary to supply forces west of Tobruk the first difficulty was the lack of certain items and the next was a shortage of transport needed to carry forward supplies over ever-growing distances. The Royal Navy had relieved the worst of the initial shortages, of ammunition in particular, by special shipments towards the end of November, and naval parties had begun on 26th November to restore the port to full working order. The plan to carry lighters to Tobruk in the Infantry Landing Ship *Glenroy* broke down, for on the 23rd November the *Glenroy* was torpedoed by an Italian Savoia 79 and reached Alexandria with difficulty. Fortunately there were a few lighters already at Tobruk, and three tank landing craft and some Jaffa lighters arrived with the first regular convoy on 2nd December so that unloading could proceed. After 13th December, when the Royal Air Force was able to provide fighter cover over Tobruk, Admiral Cunningham allowed ships to arrive in daylight.

The essential work of the little ships in running a supply line to Tobruk and beyond was hampered by exceptionally bad weather and by attacks from the air and from a growing number of German U-boats. In November and December H.M.A.S. *Parramatta*, H.M.S. *Salvia*, *Chantala* and *Chakdina* and the merchant ships *Shuntien*, *Warszawa* and *Volo* were sunk, and H.M.S. *Flamingo* and *Glenroy* and the water carrier *Myriel* were damaged. During the same period H.M.S. *Farndale* sank the submarine *Caracciolo*, H.M.S. *Hotspur* and *Hasty* sank the *U.79*, and H.M.S. *Kipling* sank the *U.75*. In mid-December the composition of the Western Desert Escort Force was changed when the 10th Corvette Group (H.M.S. *Peony*, *Salvia* and *Hyacinth*) replaced the 25th (South African) Anti-submarine Group (H.M.S.A.S. *Falk*, *Flo*, *Cocker*, and *Thorgrim*).

There were too few warships to meet all the demands, and the strain on them was severe. Besides protecting the convoys for supplying the Army's advance, escorts had to be provided for the vital oil traffic between Haifa and Alexandria and for convoys to and fro between Alexandria, Port Said, Cyprus and the Levant ports. In all some 55 anti-submarine vessels were required and Admiral Cunningham had 45 serviceable on the average, including the Fleet destroyers. In appealing for more he told the Admiralty he could 'by no means guarantee the security of the Army's supply to Tripoli should we reach there'.

From the opening of 'Crusader' on 18th November until 25th

December some 18,000 tons, of which more than half was petrol and aviation spirit, had arrived at Tobruk. By the end of December the port was handling 600 tons a day and the rate was rising, but even so this did not cover the current needs and at the same time allow for reserves to be built up fast enough. Consequently it was still necessary to run large convoys of lorries across the desert from railhead at Misheifa; this tied up vehicles which were badly wanted farther west and used a lot of petrol. It was soon clear that there could be no question of pursuing the enemy with a strong force; all the available transport would have to be used to maintain a comparatively small one. Field Maintenance Centres were opened in succession at Sidi Muftah (south of Gazala) on 15th December, near Tmimi on the 18th, and at Msus on the 24th. The last of these, stocked by convoys from Tobruk, supplied all the troops south of Benghazi. The worst shortage was of petrol, for only enough for the barest needs of 13th Corps was reaching Tobruk, and a great deal was being wasted by the appalling leakage from the flimsy 4-gallon tins: it was estimated that a convoy sometimes lost as much as 40 per cent. The decision by 8th Army that the roads through the hilly Jebel country were not to be used for maintenance convoys, because of the demolitions and the danger from air attack, added to the difficulties, for the bad going in the desert was made worse by frequent sand-storms and an unusual amount of rain. On 26th December there was no petrol at all in the F.M.C. at Msus, and on the 28th only 32,000 gallons arrived in response to a demand for 60,000. There were difficulties over other stores also, for Headquarters 8th Army was now controlling the contents of convoys to Msus, and the state of the wireless communications was such that the 8th Army did not always know what was most urgently required.

General Crüwell, whose armoured force was situated to the south of Agedabia, had noticed on 27th December that there was a wide gap between the British 22nd Armoured Brigade at Chor es Sufan and the 22nd Guards Brigade north of Agedabia. General Rommel agreed with his suggestion to defeat the British armour in detail and the result was a clash on 28th December between the two Panzer Divisions, with about sixty tanks of which forty-four were Pzkw IIIs and IVs, and the 22nd Armoured Brigade with ninety tanks, of which thirty-five were Stuarts and the remainder Crusaders.[1] The result was a notable success for the Germans, who drove the 22nd Armoured Brigade south across the Wadi Faregh with the loss of 37 tanks—many,

[1]On 28th and again on 30th December the 22nd Armoured Brigade had under command the 2nd Regiment R.H.A. (two batteries each of eight 25-pdrs); the 102nd (N.H.) Anti-Tank Regiment R.H.A. (three batteries each of twelve 2-pdrs); the 122nd Anti-Aircraft Battery R.A.; 9th Battalion, The Rifle Brigade.

it is said, through mechanical breakdown. Seven German tanks were destroyed.

This success did not alter General Rommel's intention to withdraw to El Agheila—to which Mussolini had now agreed—but he decided to give battle at Agedabia for a little longer in order to gain time for his infantry to rest and reorganize, and in the hope of damaging the British sufficiently to prevent them following up. On 30th December the *D.A.K.* again attacked the 22nd Armoured Brigade, which by this time had been drawn in to Belandah. Once again the Germans won the day, and twenty-three out of sixty-two British tanks were destroyed or damaged; again the Germans recorded the total loss of seven of their own. The 22nd Armoured Brigade, whose remaining tanks were nearly all Stuarts, was then withdrawn to refit.

General Ritchie could now do no more than try to gather a sufficient force to turn the enemy out of his positions at Agedabia, but for reasons which are discussed in Chapter VI he could not do this at once. General Rommel, for his part, believed that the *D.A.K's* recent successes had for the time being removed the danger to his right flank, and expected a few days' breathing space. Finding it difficult to reorganize and supply his troops in their present positions he decided to retire to El Agheila and there use the respite he had won to recruit his strength. The movement began on 1st January, and although some thinning-out was noticed by patrols and much traffic was seen, the British were not convinced until the 5th that a withdrawal was taking place, nor could they have interfered seriously with it even if they had known. The weather then grew worse and the enemy's rearguards left Agedabia on 6th January under cover of a day-long sandstorm. Small British columns followed, and within a week they had discovered that the enemy was holding a series of defended localities from Mersa Brega on the coast towards Bir es Suera, with their desert flank drawn back to Sidi Tabet and Alem el Mgaad. Part of this front was protected by impassable salt marshes and the rest was mainly soft sand dotted with 'camel humps', over which the going was said to be as bad as anywhere in the desert.

In the air both sides were feeling the strain of prolonged operations, bad weather, and all the maintenance troubles which, severe at any time in the desert, were made much worse by the constant change of airfields. The intensity of bombing had fallen off greatly; the Germans made occasional raids with escorted Stukas, and the British day-bombers, whose difficulties have already been referred to, also made attacks from time to time in connexion with the fighting round Agedabia. The German records mention in particular a very successful attack by ten British aircraft on 29th December, which caused

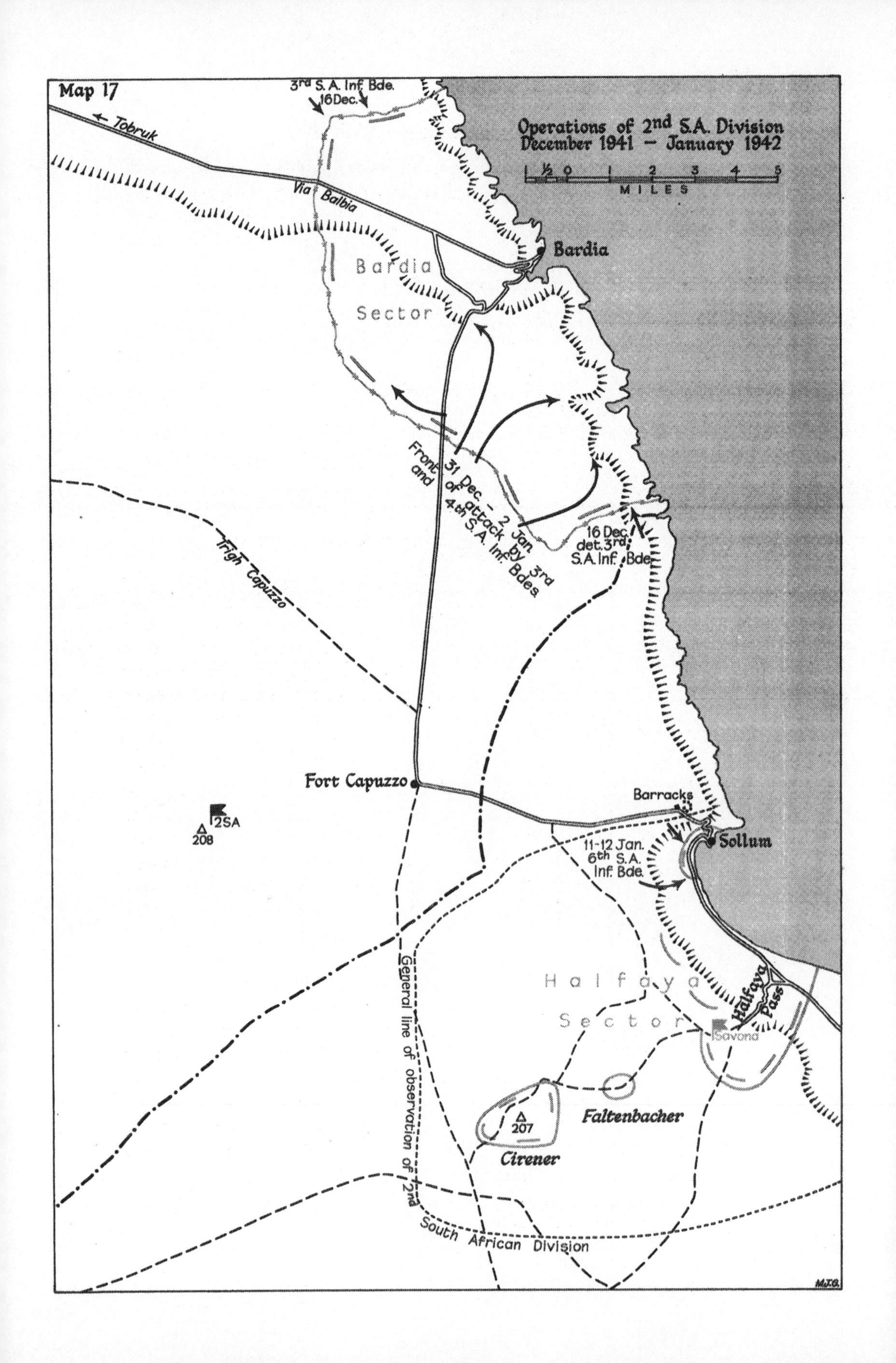

Map 17
Operations of 2nd S.A. Division
December 1941 – January 1942
MILES
3rd S.A. Inf. Bde. 16 Dec.
← Tobruk
Via Balbia
Bardia
Bardia Sector
Front of attack by 3rd and 4th S.A. Inf. Bdes. 31 Dec. – 2 Jan.
16 Dec. det. 3rd S.A. Inf. Bde.
Trigh Capuzzo
Fort Capuzzo
Barracks
Sollum
11-12 Jan. 6th S.A. Inf. Bde.
2SA
208
Halfaya Sector
Halfaya Pass
Savona
207
Faltenbacher
Cirener
General line of observation of 2nd South African Division

over forty casualties. Of the eight day-bomber squadrons two were refitting and two were under orders for the Far East.[1] Two were being used on the reduction of the Halfaya defences—to be described presently—leaving only two, No. 11 Squadron and No. 21 Squadron S.A.A.F., to support the operations around Mersa Brega.

The conditions on land meant that much depended upon the tactical reconnaissance squadrons for information of the enemy, and, as usual, these were worked very hard. Fighters on both sides were active in patrolling and in attacking vehicles on the roads and desert tracks, and the long-range Hurricanes of No. 33 Squadron and the Beaufighters of No. 272 Squadron again carried their attacks and extended the range of reconnaissance into the enemy's back area. In general the British had a large measure of air superiority although the enemy managed on occasions to operate in considerable strength; on 28th December, for example, they sent up—according to their own records—over a hundred aircraft.

The Me. 109F was still a cause of anxiety, but on New Year's Day the new Kittyhawks of No. 3 Squadron R.A.A.F. had their first combat near Antelat with a large mixed force. The Germans recorded no losses on that day, but this new fighter, better armed and with greater speed and rate of climb than the Tomahawk, was very welcome, even though it had not the all-round performance of the Me. 109F. Another newcomer was a Liberator, which on 11th January dropped a large load of 500-lb. bombs on Tripoli, more as an experiment than as a normal operational flight. With the introduction into the Royal Air Force of a new category of heavy bombers (Liberator, Lancaster, Halifax, Stirling), the Wellingtons were reclassified as 'medium' and the Blenheims, Marylands, Bostons and Baltimores as 'light' bombers, and will be so referred to hereafter. Yet another first appearance was that of the Italian C.R.42 biplane fighter in the role of fighter-bomber: an up-to-date use of a fighter as a direct support aircraft, but a very out-of-date aircraft (comparable with the Gladiator) to adapt for the purpose.

The scale of the Axis air effort in North Africa at the turn of the year was limited principally by maintenance, and the chief interest of both the Italians and Germans lay in neutralizing Malta in order to ease the passage of their badly needed supplies. Conversely, the British did all they could to interfere by surface, submarine, and air attacks on enemy shipping at sea and by air attacks on the ports. From Malta the Wellingtons continued to attack Tripoli, and the Blenheims joined in and also attacked some of the minor landing places on the shores of the Gulf of Sirte which reconnaissance had

[1] The two squadrons (Nos. 45 and 84) under orders for the Far East were able to take part in the reduction of Bardia before they left the desert—see page 96.

shown to be used by coastal shipping. Wellingtons from Egypt continued the attacks on these targets by night, refuelling at El Adem. The German air transport traffic, bringing petrol from Crete to Derna, and the measures taken to interrupt it, have already been referred to. After Cyrenaica was lost the transport aircraft began to concentrate at airfields in Sicily, and on 4th January large numbers were seen at Castel Vetrano where they were attacked by a force of Blenheims from Malta; seventy-five aircraft were found parked wing-tip to wing-tip and the airfield was left a smoking ruin. That night the Wellingtons rekindled the flames. The Italians recorded that many aircraft were lost in these attacks.

As the heavy German air offensive against Malta took effect, the supply situation of the Axis forces in North Africa began to improve. Italian air activity, for example, which had sunk very low, showed signs of reviving directly after nearly 2,300 tons of aviation fuel arrived in Tripoli on 5th January[1]. The further consequences of the renewed flow of supplies to Tripolitania are considered in Chapter VI.

See Map 17

Early in December the difficulty of maintaining land and air forces in Western Cyrenaica had pointed to the need for clearing the enemy from the Egyptian frontier, thus opening the way for an extension of the railway to Fort Capuzzo—seventy miles in advance of the present railhead at Misheifa. This would not only halve the mileage run by lorry convoys to Tobruk but would enable them to use the Trigh Capuzzo and Via Balbia, both of which had comparatively good surfaces, although the former was only a track. Indeed, the capture of the enemy's frontier positions which blocked the way was essential if the momentum of the advance in Western Cyrenaica was to be restored and the pursuit carried on into Tripolitania. It was from this point of view that Air Vice-Marshal Coningham agreed to use the four squadrons of No. 270 Bomber Wing at Gambut to co-operate with General Norrie's 30th Corps, a decision which drew a telegram of surprise from the Air Ministry, but which, in the light of all the facts, was undoubtedly sound.

When General Norrie was given control of these operations he had under his command the 2nd South African Division (Major-General I. P. de Villiers), the 1st Army Tank Brigade, and the 1st South African Division whose 2nd Brigade was in reserve at Buq Buq while the 5th was refitting at Matruh. A few days previously the enemy had given up some minor localities but continued to hold two separate sectors: the Bardia Sector, within the original perimeter, and the

---

[1] The arrival of this convoy is described on page 158.

Halfaya Sector, comprising the localities of Halfaya Pass, 'Faltenbacher', 'Cirener' and Lower Sollum. At Bardia were about 2,200 Germans mostly of the administrative services, and 6,600 Italian troops and a few guns, all under the German Major-General Artur Schmitt. In the Halfaya Sector (Major-General Fedele De Giorgis) were some 4,200 Italians of the Savona Division and 2,100 Germans under Major Bach of the 104th Lorried Infantry Regiment. Supplies were scarce, because the *D.A.K.* had helped itself during its expedition to the frontier towards the end of November, and only small quantities could be brought in by aircraft, submarine, and motor ferry barge.[1] Nevertheless the garrisons were ordered to hold out because the Axis High Command believed (rightly) that they were doing valuable service by blocking the coast road, and they were after all locking up more than a division of British troops. On 19th December General Rommel reported to Rome that the garrisons could not be supplied indefinitely and were too badly equipped to resist a heavy attack. He repeated his previous suggestion that they should be withdrawn to Crete in Italian warships, but *Comando Supremo* again insisted that they must hold out, and *OKW* agreed.

The 2nd South African Division was not yet fully equipped and its state of training was still elementary. Since 5th December it had acted as cat to the frontier mouse and had also successfully cleared up enemy detachments and installations between Tobruk and Bardia. In addition, General Ritchie had asked General de Villiers to try to mop up the frontier garrisons, but with the least possible loss. General de Villiers decided to attack the north-western front of Bardia with the 3rd South African Brigade (Brigadier C. E. Borain) on 16th December, but the enemy's strength and morale were found to be higher than was expected and the task proved to be beyond the power of a single brigade. General de Villiers wisely broke off the operations after two days' fighting and then, under General Norrie, began to prepare a much heavier attack.

On this occasion General de Villiers decided to use his whole division, and was allotted the 8th and 44th Royal Tank Regiments of the 1st Army Tank Brigade (Brigadier H. R. B. Watkins) with Valentine and Matilda tanks; the New Zealand Divisional Cavalry Regiment with light tanks and Bren carriers; the 67th and 68th Medium Regiments R.A. and the 211th Medium Battery R.A.; the 7th Field Regiment S.A.A. and the 1st Carpathian (Polish) Field Regiment.

[1] Four motor ferry barges (*Marinefährprahm* or *MFP*) had come from Germany in sections and were assembled at Palermo. They sailed for Africa on 23rd November and one was lost in a storm between Tripoli and Benghazi. The others were loaded with military stores and reached Bardia on 17th, 18th and 21st December. One was retained at Bardia for supplying Sollum and for possible evacuation tasks, but was shelled by a battery of the 5th Field Regiment S.A.A. on 24th December, beached and destroyed. On 27th December, the German Admiral in Italy issued an order that *MFPs* were no longer to be used for the supply of harbours in Cyrenaica.

No. 270 Wing R.A.F. (Nos. 14, 45, 84, and Lorraine Squadrons) carried out preliminary bombing and No. 451 Squadron R.A.A.F. did the tactical and artillery reconnaissance. They were helped by the weakness of the enemy's anti-aircraft fire and by the fact that none of his fighters in North Africa could reach the area, while the weather was too bad for any intervention from Crete.

Supported by the fire of the cruiser *Ajax* and the gunboat *Aphis*, and by intense bombing from the air, the attack began on the southern front on 31st December, and was driven home by the 3rd and 4th South African Brigades (the 4th—Brigadier A. A. Hayton) in spite of the worsening weather. On 2nd January General Schmitt surrendered, with Rommel's approval. The British casualties were 139 killed and 295 wounded, and 1,171 British prisoners of war were released from captivity.

It was soon the turn of the Halfaya Sector. For some days a policy of close investment, bombardment, and propaganda was followed in an attempt to avoid the casualties of an attack. Only two squadrons—No. 14 R.A.F. and the Lorraine (both with Blenheims)—were available, as Nos. 45 and 84 had been withdrawn for despatch to the Far East. This had no result, so on 11th January the 6th South African Brigade (Brigadier F. Cooper) attacked Lower Sollum, which surrendered next day, and the enemy's last access to the sea was cut off. A careful plan was made for reducing the remaining localities but it was not needed. Hungry, thirsty, bombed, shelled and short of ammunition the enemy could endure no more. On the 17th General De Giorgis and Major Bach surrendered.

Thus the British had succeeded in their object of clearing Cyrenaica of the enemy, though not by means of a rapid stroke, as had been planned, but only after a long and costly struggle which consumed so many of their resources that by the time they reached the western end of Cyrenaica their blow was spent. It had been realized that the difficulties of supply would increase enormously in Western Cyrenaica, and it was for this reason, wrote General Auchinleck in his Despatch, that he had been anxious to destroy the enemy as far east as possible.

In a sense the Winter Battle was not yet over, for before January was out history had repeated itself and Rommel was driving the British out of Western Cyrenaica very much as he had done in the previous April. Before describing this reverse it will be necessary to deal with some immensely important events which had been taking place in November and December 1941—notably the struggle for the vital sea communications in the Mediterranean and the entry of Japan and the U.S.A. into the war. The high-water mark of the British offensive is nevertheless a suitable point at which to consider briefly some of the hard facts and outstanding features of this first big clash in the desert between two well equipped modern forces.

The casualties were approximately as follows. They have been rounded off because the dates for which the figures are available do not quite correspond. However they cover all the serious fighting of November, December and the first half of January.

Total Forces		Killed	Wounded	Missing	Total Casual-ties	Percentage of Total Force
German	65,000	1,100	3,400	10,100	14,600	22½
Italian	54,000	1,200	2,700	19,800	23,700	43
Total Axis	119,000	2,300	6,100	29,900*	38,300	32
British	118,000	2,900	7,300	7,500	17,700	15

* Of these, 13,800 were taken prisoner at Bardia and Halfaya.

It is interesting to compare the parts played by the high commanders on the two sides. General Auchinleck had, with the Naval and Air Commanders-in-Chief, laid down the policy for the British offensive and he had approved the plan, into which he had gone very thoroughly before entrusting it to the Army Commander to execute. When a crisis arose over the heavy losses of the British armour Auchinleck came forward and gave the courageous decision to continue the offensive. Thereafter he spent days at a time close to Army Headquarters, not interfering with General Ritchie but ensuring that his own advice and support were available if they were wanted. All important operational matters were discussed between the two. It may be wondered whether, in these circumstances, there could have been much distinction between 'advice' and 'orders'. Besides all this the Commander-in-Chief continued to deal with the many problems which concerned the Middle East as a whole.

General Bastico, the Commander-in-Chief of the Axis Armed Forces in North Africa, was in a somewhat uneasy position. He had in General Rommel a commander of great experience and proved ability who was in his element in the desert, where his ideas on the handling of armoured forces had full play. Rommel was ready to accept any amount of responsibility; in fact his self-reliance made him impatient of interference from behind and he did not hesitate to short-circuit General Bastico by communicating with Rome or Berlin if it suited him. In practice Bastico's control over Rommel was what

Rommel chose to accept. While things went well he was left to himself, but after the relief of Tobruk he was constantly being called to conferences and meetings at which Bastico tried to establish his authority, and there were times when Rommel was openly critical of the back-seat drivers. His severest trial came when his many counsellors—among whom was Kesselring—pressed him to stand and seek a decision at Gazala, or at the worst to retire slowly step by step. They loaded him with reasons against drawing right back to the frontier of Tripolitania, but Rommel, in close touch with the tactical situation, was adamant. The British were slow, but they would press doggedly on and he would not be able to stop them. A retreat was therefore inevitable, and could only succeed if it took place before the British could interfere seriously. If General Rommel had weakened on this decision there is little doubt that the Axis forces would have been destroyed and the whole course of the war in the Desert changed. He deserves great credit for seeing the issue clearly and for refusing to be shaken from his decision.

In the air the systems of command on the two sides differed in several respects. The German air force in Cyrenaica was a detachment of *Fliegerkorps X*, whose commander, General Geisler, had his headquarters in Greece and had been mainly concerned with the maritime air war. With the arrival of the headquarters of *Luftflotte* 2 in November 1941 his immediate superior became Field-Marshal Kesselring, who gave him the additional task of helping to neutralize Malta. The *Fliegerführer Afrika*, Major-General Fröhlich, had been responsible to Geisler, but now came directly under Kesselring, though he was still in the unenviable position of having to satisfy the demands of General Rommel without being under his command, and without being his equal in rank. To complete the picture, Rommel was not in any way subordinate to Kesselring. The Italian air forces were separate, and co-operated by a system of liaison.

The British Air Officer Commanding-in-Chief, Air Marshal Tedder, had allotted every possible squadron to the Desert Air Force, whose commander, Air Vice-Marshal Coningham, controlled all the air operations directly connected with 'Crusader'. Coningham lived and moved with the commander of the 8th Army, and together they were responsible for carrying out the plan approved by the Commanders-in-Chief in Cairo. This was the basis of all the subsequent successful co-operation between the two Services.

The action taken by the Royal Air Force in the weeks before 'Crusader' undoubtedly won a large measure of air superiority, which contributed greatly to the surprise achieved by the offensive when it came. It resulted also in the air attacks on the troops being comparatively light, and those units which were well dispersed had few losses. (Indeed it was often said that our dispersion was overdone; certainly the Germans habitually used closer formations.) It had been realized that a state of air superiority, once reached, might not last for long, and the main object of placing all the British air forces under an Air Officer in close touch with Army Headquarters was to ensure that he could concentrate all his resources to meet the principal need of the moment—which might well be to resume the fight for air superiority. But no battles go quite as expected, and as 'Crusader' swayed between Sidi Rezegh and the Egyptian frontier it was evident that even if the air situation in general is favourable it may be locally and temporarily unfavourable. And as the front moved westward and our blows grew weaker, the enemy was able to hit back from his more stable bases. For this among other reasons a time was soon to come when air superiority in Western Cyrenaica hung in the balance; indeed, for a short period it was to pass to the enemy.

None of this alters the fact that during 'Crusader' the Army enjoyed the best air support it had ever had, and the diaries show how appreciative it was. From 18th November to 20th January the Germans in Libya lost, according to their own records, at least 232 aircraft from all causes and the Italians at least 100. The totals must in fact have been higher, for on the airfields and landing-grounds from Gambut to Benina no fewer than 228 German and as many Italian aircraft were found abandoned in various states of disrepair, apart from many others scattered about in the desert or discarded in scrap heaps. It was the first time the Luftwaffe had been bundled off its airfields, and at Benina in particular, which had been a centre of organization and supply, there was much of interest to be learned from the records and equipment. The British losses in aircraft in the Desert during the same period were about 300, the total number of sorties (including those of Malta's bombers on tasks other than shipping strikes) having been nearly 12,000, which means an average of more than 190 sorties a day over the nine weeks.

A great deal of equipment was lost by the land forces of both sides, especially by the Italians, who had not the transport to move it. The recorded data for tanks do not allow of exact statements under the headings of those destroyed, damaged, or broken down. They do, however, point to the broad conclusion that the British lost in combat, destroyed and damaged, far more than the Germans and had many more mechanical breakdowns. The course of the fighting made it often possible for the Germans to recover their damaged tanks immediately after a combat, but the eventual advance by the British meant that a large proportion of their tank casualties were recovered also. In this connexion the figures for tanks of the 7th Armoured Division handled by the recovery and repair units show what an important part these organizations played:

Date	Battle casualties and breakdowns*	Initial recoveries*	Number repaired*	Number under repair
23 Nov	about 200	—	—	—
29 Nov	about 300	187	72	46
6 Dec	450	338	138	64
12 Dec	526	456	231	50
1 Jan	about 600	—	—	—

*denotes cumulative totals.

In addition to the above numbers there were just over 200 casualties to British 'I' tanks.

The probable figure for German losses is 220 and for Italian about 120. These figures do not include tanks returned to their units after being damaged and repaired, of which there must have been a great many in the case of the Germans.

Although 'Crusader' achieved a large measure of success, and caused the enemy heavy losses, there were many disquieting features. The British tank crews felt handicapped by being armed with nothing more powerful than the 2-pdr gun. The latest cruisers were far too prone to mechanical breakdown. The Stuarts were faster and much more reliable, which had quickly made them popular with the crews, but their vulnerability and short radius of action, added to the weakness of their gun, had seriously limited their value. The lack of a more powerful anti-tank gun than the 2-pdr was widely felt, and had it not been for the 25-pdr field artillery weapon the anti-tank position would have been serious indeed. And in the air the Me. 109F was superior in performance to any British fighter in the Middle East.

It must not be supposed, however, that shortcomings in equipment were solely to blame for the failure of 'Crusader' to gain a more decisive success. The British showed that they had much to learn about the handling of large land forces. This was not altogether surprising, because in peace nothing existed (except on paper) larger than a division—and that usually in skeleton, so that higher training was largely a matter of make-believe. Since 1940 the pace of events in the Middle East had hurried formations into action almost as soon as they were created. A great deal had therefore to be learned the hard and costly way—in battle.

The fundamental failing of the British at this time was the habit of fighting at a disadvantage owing to not having concentrated their strength at the decisive place. The German report on the battle emphasizes the point and attributes the British failure to achieve final success to 'this fundamental tactical mistake'. As has been seen,

1. The loss of H.M.S. *Ark Royal*, 14th November 1941: the destroyer *Legion* going alongside.

2. The Second Battle of Sirte. Laying smoke to cover the convoy: H.M.S. *Cleopatra* (flag) seen from H.M.S. *Euryalus*.

3. The *Breconshire* on her last run, lying hit and disabled: the cruiser *Penelope* passes a line to try to tow her into harbour.

4. The *Pampas* reached Malta but was heavily bombed in harbour: the smoke is from her burning oil fuel.

5. Albacores of the Fleet Air Arm over Malta; showing the many stone walls which cover the island.

6. Malta: the bombing of Floriana on 24th April 1942.

7. German photograph taken during a R.A.F. attack, probably on El Adem airfield.

8. Benghazi harbour, January 1942, after repeated bombing by the R.A.F.

General Crüwell was quick to take advantage of it on several occasions. Unfortunately the lesson had not been fully learned, and the story of the fighting in the early summer of 1942 will be found to contain some further examples—with disastrous consequences. During 'Crusader' the neglect of such a well-established principle seems to have been largely due to a feeling that tanks were required to counter tanks, with the result that part of the British armour was often given the role of protecting some unarmoured formation.

The British must nevertheless be given credit for having made a bold, imaginative plan. It was felt that any kind of repetition of the 'Battleaxe' plan (which began with an attack on the frontier defences) was to be avoided as smacking too much of the obvious, although this is not in itself a sufficient reason for discarding such a course. A wide sweep and a deep penetration by a highly mobile force was decided upon, and a piece of ground at Sidi Rezegh was chosen as the provisional objective. This was judged to be of such importance to the enemy that he would be obliged to try to regain it. So far so good, but the corollary was surely twofold; first, to occupy the Sidi Rezegh area 'fustest with the most men'[1] and prepare to defend it strongly; and second, to dispose the 30th Corps so that it could deal decisively with the expected incursion by the enemy's armour, and not merely fend it off. Instead of making sure of these aims, or even one of them, the British were ready for neither. They did not take a firm hold of the vital ground, nor did they succeed in concentrating a superior force against the enemy's armour, which reacted in the way that General Auchinleck had foreseen.[2]

It may be wondered how the enemy, who were so short of transport, were able to keep themselves supplied during this prolonged struggle. The answer is that their problem was unlike the one that faced the British, whose plan necessitated a very long line of communication across the open desert, where the wear and tear and the consumption of petrol were enormous. Most of the hard fighting took place within reach of the enemy's depots—such as Gambut, Acroma, and Gazala—which had been stocked during the preceding months and were close to the well surfaced roads. On the few occasions when the Axis troops operated at a distance from these depots they were soon in trouble. They would have been in still greater trouble had they not captured a large amount of British transport.

As time went by, many of these depots were captured, and at others the stocks were depleted by the severity of the fighting. Consequently the enemy grew increasingly anxious about the arrival of fresh supplies

---

[1] This epitome of the art of war is attributed to the Confederate cavalry leader General Nathan Forrest. It is sometimes quoted as 'to git thar fustest with the mostest'.

[2] See page 7.

by sea—especially of fuel and ammunition. The air attacks on the ports of loading and on Tripoli, Benghazi, Derna and the smaller off-loading places in the Gulf of Sirte have already been referred to. It remains to describe the efforts of the Royal Navy and Royal Air Force to damage the remaining link in the chain by sinking as many ships on passage to North Africa as possible. The whole struggle was essentially one, and the successes and setbacks at sea belong as much to the 'Crusader' story as does the fighting in Cyrenaica itself.

CHAPTER IV

THE STRUGGLE FOR SEA COMMUNICATIONS
(November – December 1941)

THE increasing success during the summer and early autumn of 1941 of the efforts of British submarines and aircraft to interrupt Axis communications with North Africa has been related in the previous volume.[1] Viewed through the enemy's eyes the losses, damage, and delays which had taken place were serious indeed. The British, however, had not been satisfied with the results so far as they could estimate them. The time taken to prepare 'Crusader' made it possible that, unless General Rommel's preparations were considerably interfered with, he would take the initiative and attack Tobruk. Even if he did not, the success of 'Crusader' might depend to a great extent upon the maintenance of a virtual blockade of the enemy-held coastline of North Africa. For these reasons a surface striking force (Force K) had been formed towards the end of October, with some sacrifice by the Home Fleet and Force H, and sent to Malta to reinforce the submarines and aircraft. The sailings of Italian convoys had already been reduced because of the heavy losses in previous months. The presence of Force K caused still further delays, and, as will be seen, thanks to its activities in November the sailings of the enemy's more important convoys became operations in which a large part of the Italian Fleet took part. This made further inroads into the limited supplies of oil fuel allotted to Italy by the Germans.

Force K, consisting of the cruisers *Aurora* (Captain W. G. Agnew) and *Penelope* and the destroyers *Lance* and *Lively*, had its first success early in November. During the afternoon of the 8th, a Maryland of No. 69 Squadron R.A.F. returned to Malta and reported having sighted a convoy of six merchant vessels and four destroyers on an easterly course forty miles east of Cape Spartivento in Calabria. At 5.30 p.m. Force K left Malta to intercept this convoy, and at 12.40 a.m. next morning was fortunate enough to sight it close to the position forecast. The weather was ideal and Captain Agnew was able to make his approach unobserved, with the enemy silhouetted against a rising moon. As Force K closed the range a second group of ships was sighted

[1] Volume II, Chapter XIV.

about six miles away to the north-west. This group appeared to consist of two large vessels—thought to be merchant ships—and two destroyers. Force K held its course towards the rear of the convoy first sighted and the *Aurora* and *Penelope* opened fire simultaneously on two escorting destroyers at a range of about three miles. Three salvoes were fired at *Aurora's* target, the *Fulmine*, and she was left sinking. Until then the enemy seems to have been unaware of the presence of Force K. Led by the *Aurora* up the starboard side of the convoy the four British warships shifted fire from one merchant ship to another as each blew up or burst into flames. As the Italian destroyers appeared from time to time through the smoke made by the burning vessels they were immediately, though fleetingly, engaged. Some torpedo tracks were sighted, but no British ships were hit. The enemy convoy made no attempt to scatter; indeed to Captain Agnew it seemed almost as if the merchant ships were awaiting their turn to be destroyed. By 1.30 a.m. all the ships of the convoy not already sunk or blown up were burning furiously. What appeared to be the remaining two destroyers of the escort escaped under a smoke screen. After a careful search for any ships which were not sinking, Force K set course at twenty-five knots for Malta, as it was most desirable to be within range of fighter cover by dawn. Shortly after the Hurricane escort had arrived Italian torpedo-bombers escorted by fighters made four attacks, but came under heavy fire from the ships and did not press their attacks home. At 1 p.m. Force K entered harbour.

The enemy convoy, known as the '*Duisburg*' convoy, had sailed for Tripoli through the Straits of Messina. It had consisted of seven merchant ships, totalling 40,000 tons, which were all sunk. Of the six escorting destroyers, one, the *Fulmine*, had been sunk by Force K, and a second, the *Libeccio*, damaged in the same encounter, had been sunk later in the day by the submarine *Upholder*, which had been an interested spectator of the moonlit engagement. The group sighted to the north-west immediately before fire was opened had consisted of a covering force of the two 8-inch cruisers, *Trieste* and *Trento*, and four destroyers. This force had been patrolling some 1,500 yards to starboard of the convoy, because it was thought that this was the most probable direction from which an attack might come. It maintained a higher speed, and periodically reversed its course; when Force K opened fire it happened to be at the northernmost point of its beat. Its subsequent movements to come to the help of its convoy appear to have been neither speedy nor well judged. Be that as it may, a British force of two 6-inch cruisers and two destroyers completely destroyed a convoy escorted and supported by two 8-inch cruisers and ten destroyers in little over half an hour, without suffering either casualties or damage. The possession of radar by the British cruisers helped in getting early hits on the frequently changing targets, and without it the engagement would have taken longer but there seems no reason to doubt that the result would have been much the same.

The destruction of this large convoy was a severe blow to the Axis forces in Cyrenaica. Small quantities of supplies continued to arrive in ships sailing singly, or in pairs, sometimes unescorted. Transport by submarine was increased, and some petrol was carried in by surface warships. Meanwhile the Italians were preparing a large operation, to include the passage of four convoys with powerful naval and air protection. These convoys sailed from their various assembly ports on the evening of 20th November, two days after 'Crusader' had begun. Those from Taranto and Navarino—three ships in all—and a cruiser from Brindisi, carrying petrol, arrived safely at Benghazi. The more important convoys from Naples, of four large ships and their protecting warships, were quickly reported by aircraft and submarines and repeatedly attacked during daylight and after dark on the 21st. The 8-inch cruiser *Trieste* was torpedoed by the submarine *Utmost* and the 6-inch cruiser *Duca Degli Abruzzi* by a Swordfish of No. 830 Squadron, Fleet Air Arm. Both ships reached Messina with difficulty. Having been robbed of such an important part of their escort, it was decided that the convoys could no longer be exposed to the risk of attack by Force K, and they were ordered to turn back.

While, as the Italians believed, British attention was still focused on this large operation, the Italian Admiralty again sailed several small convoys on various routes, but when British warships were reported in the Central Mediterranean some of these convoys were diverted and some were ordered to return. One of them, bound from Piraeus to Benghazi, consisting of the German merchant ships *Maritza* and *Procida* escorted by two torpedo boats, failed to receive any such orders. On 24th November this convoy was intercepted by Force K, and both merchant ships, with cargoes which included petrol, motor transport and bombs, were sunk by H.M.S. *Penelope*. The two Italian torpedo boats put up a gallant defence, until it was obvious that both merchant vessels would certainly be sunk; they then escaped in a heavy squall of rain. Of the various supply ships which the enemy had sailed for African ports on this occasion, one reached Benghazi and one Tripoli.

As a result of these losses it was expected—correctly, as it turned out—that the Italians might reduce the frequency of their convoys, and that they would certainly increase the protection of any which sailed. Towards the end of November Force B, comprising the cruisers *Ajax* (flag of Rear-Admiral H. B. Rawlings) and *Neptune* and two destroyers, was sent to Malta to strengthen Force K and provide a force which could operate separately if occasion arose. On 29th November a further attempt was made by the enemy to run through a number of small convoys on separate routes, and two forces comprising in all one battleship, four cruisers and nine destroyers put to sea in support. But this operation was an even greater failure than the previous one. On 29th and 30th November Blenheims of No. 18 Squadron from Malta sank the Italian merchant ship *Capo Faro* and damaged two others, the *Volturno* and *Iseo*. Early on the morning of 1st December, while Force B was sweeping to the northward in search of Italian warships which had been reported in the vicinity, Force K sank the Italian auxiliary cruiser *Adriatico*, carrying ammunition, artillery and supplies. Force K, acting on further reports from aircraft, then steamed westward at high speed for nearly 400 miles and at 6 o'clock that evening completed the destruction of the Italian tanker *Iridio Mantovani* carrying 9,000 tons of petrol, benzine, and gasoline, and blew up her escort—the destroyer *Da Mosto*. The *Mantovani* had been badly damaged the same afternoon by four Blenheims of No. 107 Squadron R.A.F. and was down by the stern when the *Aurora* opened fire. Of the Axis supply ships sailed on this occasion only one survived to reach Benghazi on 2nd December.

Up to the end of June 1941 the German and Italian reinforcements and supplies to North Africa had not been seriously curtailed as the result of sinkings or damage to ships. If military operations had been hampered by shortages it was mainly because of delays between the ports of disembarkation and the front, or because the total quantities shipped were not enough. Since July, however, the losses at sea had mounted steadily, and in November, according to the Italian official naval historian, 62 per cent of the stores embarked in Italy were lost.[1] The loss of aviation and motor spirit was particularly severe, and during November only 2,500 tons had arrived. It was in order to find a way out of this desperate situation that the Italians made another attempt to persuade the Germans to obtain the use of Bizerta and the communications through Tunisia, either by agreement or force. Hitler, however, had no wish to make concessions to France in return for these advantages, and the attempt came to nothing.

The two following tables show the results of British attacks on the Axis line of supply to North Africa during November and December 1941. The figures for December are included here for convenience; the story of the principal convoy operations in that month will be related presently.

In these two months the enemy's shipping losses from all causes in the whole Mediterranean amounted to 30 ships of over 500 tons and some 20 smaller vessels, totalling in all about 115,000 tons.

---

[1] M. A. Bragadin: *Che ha fatto la Marina?* p. 259.

Number and tonnage of Italian and German merchant ships of over 500 tons engaged in carrying supplies to North Africa sunk at sea or at the ports of loading or unloading

Month	By surface warships	By submarine	By aircraft	From other causes	Total
November	9 — 44,539	1 — 5,996	3 — 5,691	1 — 2,826	14 — 59,052
December	2 — 12,516*	5 — 25,006	1 — 1,235		8 — 38,757
Total	11 — 57,055	6 — 31,002	4 — 6,926	1 — 2,826	22 — 97,809

* Includes the tanker *Iridio Mantovani* of 10,540 tons.

Cargoes disembarked in North Africa and percentage lost on passage[1]

Month	Type	Cargo disembarked in North Africa (tons)	Percentage lost on the way
November	General military cargo and fuel	30,000	62
December	General military cargo and fuel	39,000	18

[1] Op. cit: pp. 259, 278.

The corresponding tables for the previous five months appear on page 281 of Volume II. They show that from 1st July to 31st October 1941 twenty per cent of all cargo was lost on the way, and that on the average 72,000 tons reached North Africa every month. This tonnage was not enough to satisfy requirements, yet during November and December the figure was roughly halved and the percentage lost was more than doubled. In November the quantity loaded in Italy had been well up to the previous monthly average, but the losses at sea—mainly caused by Force K—were very heavy. In December the losses at sea were much lighter, but for fear of Force K much less had been sent. Most of the 39,000 tons which arrived in December was carried in a special 'battleship convoy'.

Sinkings by British submarines in the whole Mediterranean during these two months had stayed at about the average of the previous few months. Aircraft made 200 anti-shipping sorties during November and December, but did not keep up their previous average of sinkings because of extremely bad weather, the increasing severity of the attacks on Malta's airfields, and the claims of the 'Crusader' battle.

By early December the Axis prospects had begun to improve. Some German submarines had already arrived, and others were on their way; ten were under orders to operate in the Eastern Mediterranean and no fewer than fifteen to the east and west of the Straits of Gibraltar. Field-Marshal Kesselring had arrived in Rome on 28th November and *Fliegerkorps II* was now arriving in Sicily. The Mediterranean Fleet was passing through a period of severe losses, which, coupled with the particularly bad weather in the Central Mediterranean, caused the pendulum to swing back in favour of the Axis in a surprisingly short time.

The arrival of the German submarines was as disastrous for the British as that of Force K had been for the Italians. On 10th November Force H had left Gibraltar on an aircraft ferrying trip. On the 12th, thirty-seven Hurricanes were flown off the *Ark Royal* and thirty-four of them, accompanied by seven Blenheims from Gibraltar, arrived safely at Malta. On the afternoon of the 13th, as Force H was returning to Gibraltar, the *Ark Royal* was attacked by the German submarine *U.81* and struck by a torpedo under the bridge on the starboard side. She took a list of twelve degrees within a few minutes and all the electrical power failed. The starboard engines were out of action and a number of bulkheads were strained and leaking. In half an hour the list had increased to eighteen degrees and was partially corrected by counter-flooding, but it was thought advisable to take off all officers and men not required to salve the ship. By 9 p.m. two tugs from Gibraltar had taken her in tow, and an hour later steam had been raised again. The chances seemed good, when, unhappily, at 2.15 on the morning of the 14th, fire broke out in the port boiler room. Steam pressure was lost again and with it all power for pumping. Although a destroyer came alongside for the second time to supply electrical power, the pumps could no longer keep down the rising water. By 4.30 the list had increased to thirty-five degrees and it was decided to abandon ship. She sank shortly after 6 a.m., only twenty-five miles from Gibraltar. The fire in the port boiler room had been caused by the list bringing about flooding in the funnel uptake, so that the flaming gases from the relit boilers were unable to escape. But for this misfortune this fine ship, which had so often been sunk by Dr. Goebbels, would probably have been saved.

It had been hoped that during this operation the Italians' attention would be focused on Force H. The opportunity had been taken to try to run two unescorted merchant vessels with supplies to Malta, using the same stratagems as the *Empire Guillemot* had used in August.

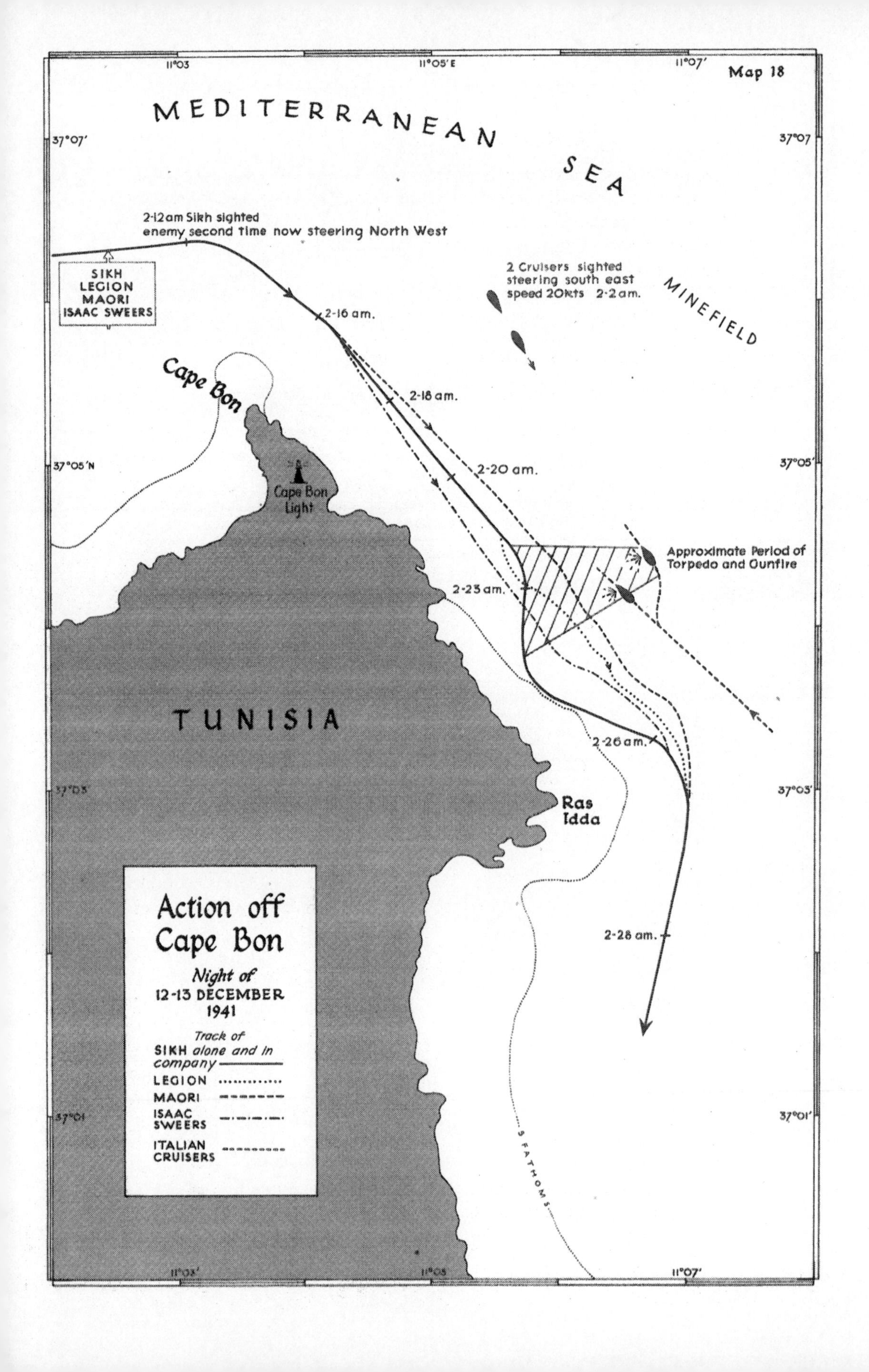

Map 18
11°03
11°05′E
11°07′
37°07′
37°05′N
37°03′
37°01′
MEDITERRANEAN SEA
2-12 am Sikh sighted enemy second time now steering North West
SIKH
LEGION
MAORI
ISAAC SWEERS
2 Cruisers sighted steering south east speed 20kts 2-2 am.
MINEFIELD
2-16 am.
2-18 am.
2-20 am.
2-23 am.
2-26 am.
2-28 am.
Cape Bon
Cape Bon Light
Approximate Period of Torpedo and Gunfire
TUNISIA
Ras Idda
5 FATHOMS
Action off Cape Bon
Night of 12-13 DECEMBER 1941
Track of
SIKH alone and in company
LEGION
MAORI
ISAAC SWEERS
ITALIAN CRUISERS

Their disguise was evidently penetrated, and the two ships, the *Empire Pelican* and *Empire Defender*, were sunk between Galita Island and the Tunisian coast on successive days—14th and 15th November—by Italian torpedo-bombers. The sailing of other ships similarly disguised was then cancelled.

Happily the sinking of the *Ark Royal* had been attended with the loss of only one life, but Force K's success on 24th November had a disastrous sequel in which many lives were lost. With a view to supporting Force K and the other light forces which had been dispatched from Alexandria to join in the search for enemy convoys, Admiral Cunningham had taken the battlefleet to sea. At about 4.30 p.m. on the 25th the *Barham* was hit by three torpedoes fired by the German submarine *U.331* which, with great skill and daring, had passed undetected through the screen of protecting destroyers. After firing, *U.331* momentarily lost trim. She was sighted on the surface about 150 yards on the port bow of the *Valiant* which was next astern of the *Barham*, but the *Valiant* was under helm and could not reverse her swing in time to ram the submarine, nor could she depress her guns sufficiently to hit her. *U.331* regained control and succeeded in diving. Within three minutes the *Barham* had listed heavily to port and continued to heel over until she was on her beam ends. About a minute after reaching this position she blew up with a tremendous explosion. When the smoke and steam had cleared away she had vanished. 56 officers—including Captain G. C. Cooke—and 806 ratings were lost; 450 survivors including Vice-Admiral Pridham-Wippell were picked up. The subsequent hunt for the submarine was unsuccessful.

See Map 18

It has already been mentioned that to overcome the crisis in their supplies to North Africa the Italians were using warships to transport fuel and munitions. On the night of 12th December the cruisers *Barbiano* and *Giussano* sailed from Palermo for Tripoli with a cargo of cased petrol. At about 2 o'clock next morning, just after passing Cape Bon, the commander of this force, Vice-Admiral Toscano, decided to reverse course temporarily as he believed his ships had been reported from the air. With so dangerous a cargo he particularly wished to evade the air striking force which he had no doubt would be dispatched from Malta. He knew that British destroyers had been sighted sixty miles east of Algiers at 3 p.m., but he estimated that they would not yet be near. In fact these destroyers, the *Sikh* (Commander G. H. Stokes), *Maori*, and *Legion*, and the Dutch destroyer *Isaac Sweers*, all reinforcements for the Mediterranean Fleet, were approaching Cape Bon from the westward at thirty knots. Commander Stokes had received a report of the Italian cruisers and had increased speed in the hope of intercepting them. At two minutes past 2 o'clock the British force sighted flashing lights ahead and the outlines of two ships steaming south, disappearing behind Cape Bon. On rounding the cape the *Sikh* had a clear view of the enemy, who were now somewhat unexpectedly steaming north. Commander Stokes led his ships close in under the high land, where he hoped to remain unobserved, fired torpedoes at the first cruiser and engaged the second with gunfire at a range of 1,000 yards. The enemy was completely surprised. Two torpedoes from the *Sikh* hit the leader and caused her to burst into flames forward and aft. The second enemy ship fired one salvo which fell on the land. Almost immediately she was struck by a torpedo from the *Legion*. Gunfire and further torpedoes from the four destroyers soon smothered both the Italian cruisers and left them ablaze and sinking. A torpedo boat, the *Cigno*, which had accompanied the Italian cruisers, was engaged in passing by each of the Allied destroyers but escaped destruction. To the Italians the whole affair was yet another unpleasant reminder of the Royal Navy's training and equipment for night action.

See Map 19

While this successful encounter was taking place off Cape Bon, reports were reaching Admiral Cunningham of enemy movements in the Ionian Sea. He deduced (correctly) that convoys were departing for North Africa, and sent the 15th Cruiser Squadron (*Naiad*, *Euryalus* and *Galatea*), now commanded by Rear-Admiral P. L. Vian, to intercept them. Admiral Vian, with his flag in the *Naiad*, was to have joined the cruisers and destroyers from Malta, but on 14th December it became clear that the Italians were returning to harbour and the British ships were recalled. The Italians had in fact been misled by clever use of wireless traffic and believed that British battleships were at sea. Short though this excursion had been, the submarines on both sides had seized their opportunities. South of the Straits of Messina H.M.S. *Urge* had torpedoed the battleship *Vittorio Veneto*, putting her out of action for several months. A few hours later, at midnight on the 14th, as the returning 15th Cruiser Squadron was about to enter the swept channel outside Alexandria, the *Galatea* was hit by two torpedoes from *U.557* and sank with heavy loss of life.

At 10 p.m. on the 15th Admiral Vian left Alexandria again. With his remaining two cruisers, the anti-aircraft cruiser *Carlisle*, and eight destroyers, he was escorting the supply ship H.M.S. *Breconshire* carrying oil fuel to Malta, where the high-speed operations of Forces B and K had run the stocks very low. It was intended that most of Admiral Vian's ships should turn back to Alexandria after nightfall on the 16th, and that four destroyers should continue with the *Breconshire*

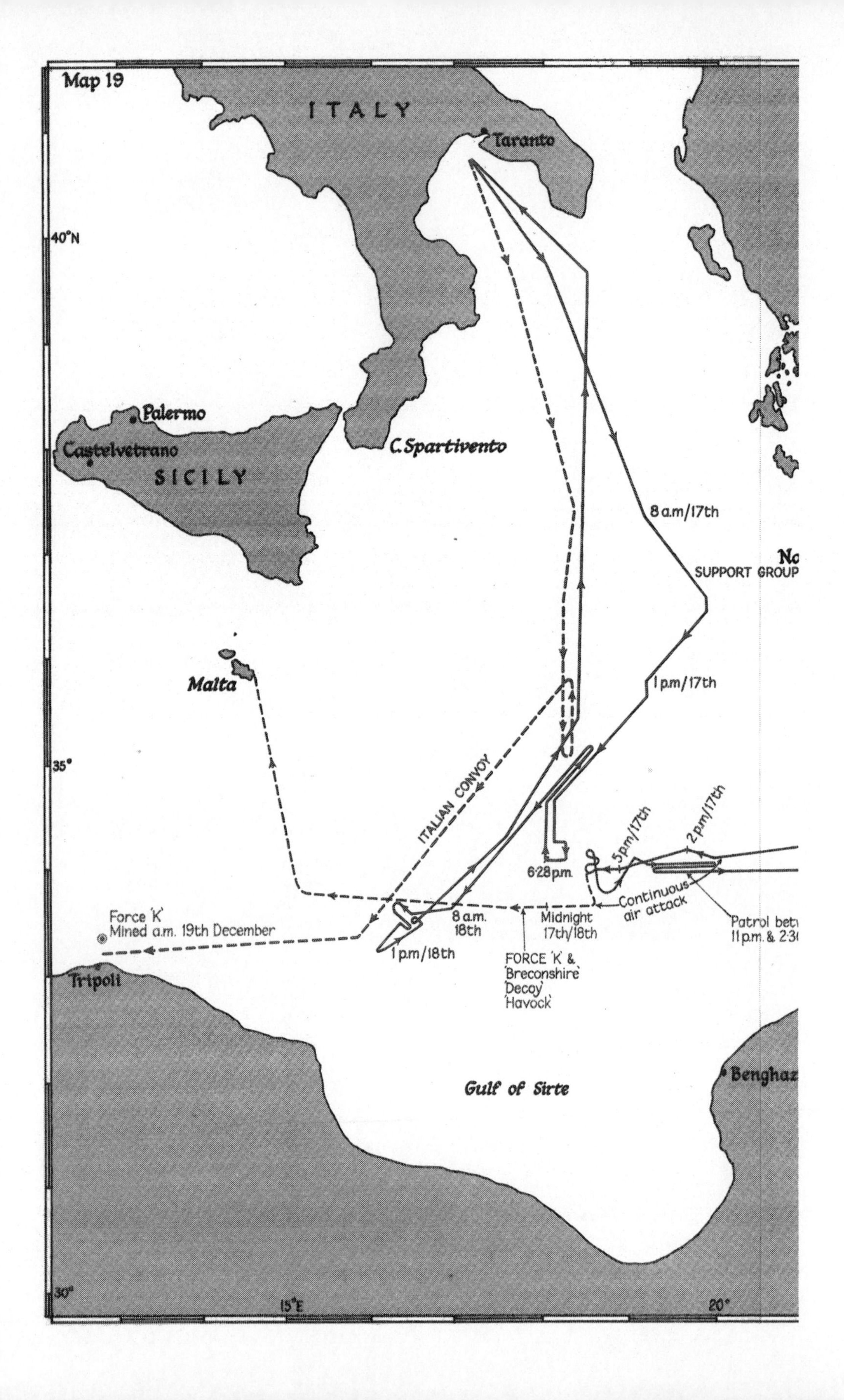

Map 19
ITALY
Taranto
40°N
Palermo
Castelvetrano
SICILY
C. Spartivento
8 a.m/17th
SUPPORT GROUP
Malta
1 p.m/17th
35°
ITALIAN CONVOY
5 p.m/17th
2 p.m/17th
6·28 p.m.
Continuous air attack
Force 'K' Mined a.m. 19th December
8 a.m. 18th
Midnight 17th/18th
1 p.m/18th
FORCE 'K' & 'Breconshire' 'Decoy' 'Havock'
Tripoli
Gulf of Sirte
30°
15°E
20°

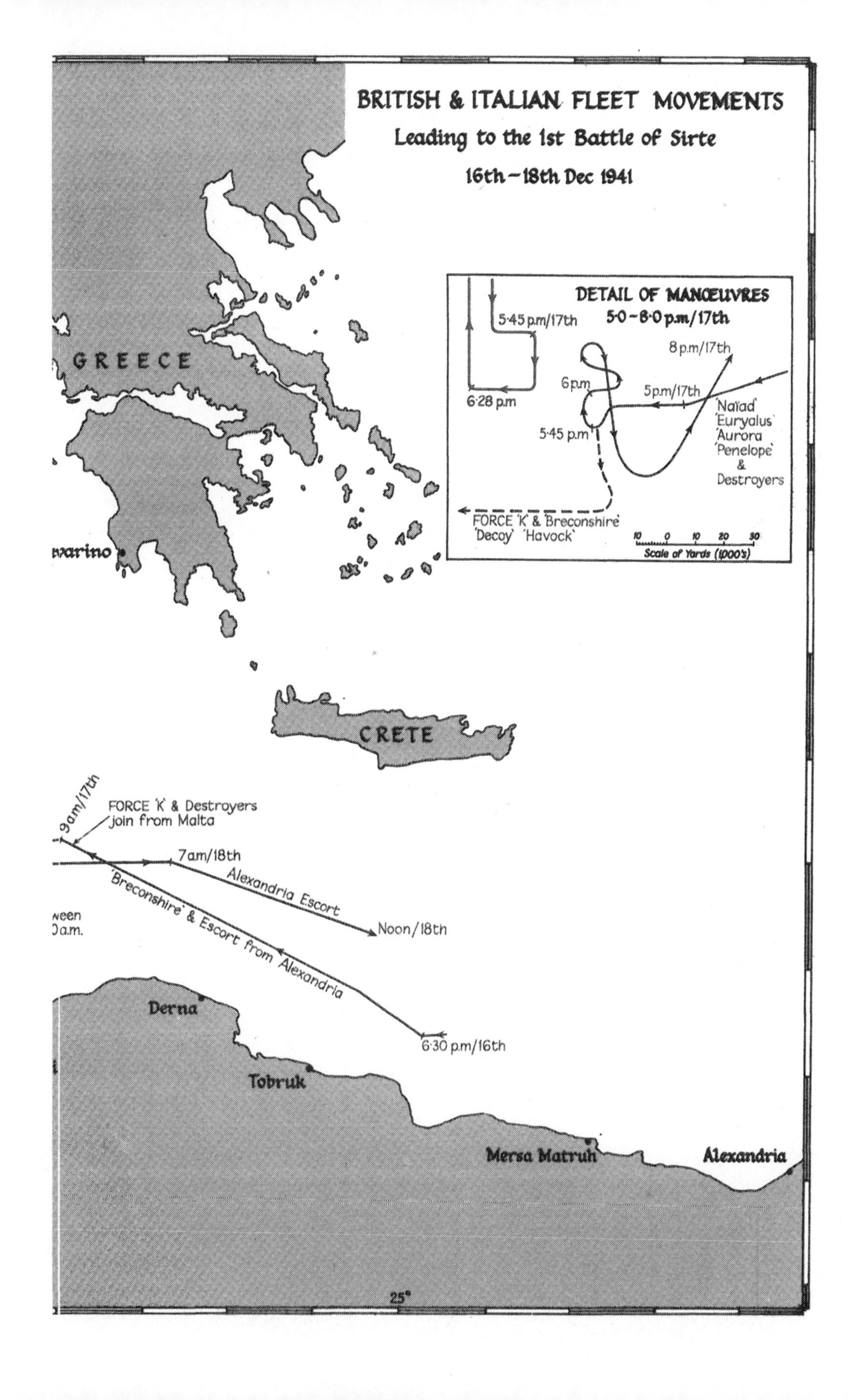

BRITISH & ITALIAN FLEET MOVEMENTS
Leading to the 1st Battle of Sirte
16th – 18th Dec 1941
DETAIL OF MANŒUVRES
5·0 – 8·0 p.m/17th
5·45 p.m/17th
6·28 p.m
8 p.m/17th
6 p.m
5 p.m/17th
5·45 p.m
'Naïad'
'Euryalus'
'Aurora'
'Penelope'
&
Destroyers
FORCE 'K' & 'Breconshire'
'Decoy' 'Havock'
10 0 10 20 30
Scale of Yards (1000's)
GREECE
varino
CRETE
9am/17th
FORCE 'K' & Destroyers
join from Malta
7am/18th
Alexandria Escort
Noon/18th
'Breconshire' & Escort from Alexandria
ween
0a.m.
6·30 p.m/16th
Derna
Tobruk
Mersa Matruh
Alexandria
25°

until relieved by an escort from Malta early on the 17th. The operation was already in progress when news was received that the Italian Fleet was also at sea again, covering a convoy for Tripoli. Admiral Cunningham decided that the British operation should continue, and hoped that the *Breconshire* would pass clear across the enemy's line of advance by nightfall on the 17th December. She could then continue to Malta with a small escort and Admiral Vian's main force would be released for attacking the enemy convoy by night. For the time being Vian was ordered to remain with the *Breconshire*, sending back only the *Carlisle*, which was, in the new circumstances, too slow. The Vice-Admiral, Malta, was requested to send all available ships to join Admiral Vian and to arrange for the maximum air reconnaissance.

It had been possible to provide fighter cover for the *Breconshire* only during the first day out from Alexandria. This had prevented the enemy from shadowing continuously, but the force was sighted and reported. The British aircraft available for reconnaissance were very few. For the *Breconshire* to evade the enemy and for Admiral Vian to reach a position from which to launch a night attack on the heavily escorted Italian convoy, the information about the enemy's movements would need to be very good. As will be seen, it was not good enough.

Force K (*Aurora*, *Penelope*, *Lance* and *Lively*) and Commander Stokes's four destroyers joined Admiral Vian at 8 o'clock on the morning of the 17th. The cruiser *Neptune* and two more destroyers were to leave Malta that evening to reinforce him still further. At Alexandria, 500 miles away, Admiral Cunningham had been unable to take his remaining two battleships to sea in support because—not for the first time—he had no destroyers left to screen them. His feelings may be imagined.

Meanwhile on the afternoon of the 16th an Italian convoy of three ships for Tripoli and a second of one ship for Benghazi had left Taranto. They were closely escorted by the battleship *Duilio*, three 6-inch cruisers and eleven destroyers, and were covered to the eastward (as this was thought to be the most likely direction from which surface attack might come) by the battleships *Littorio*, *Doria*, and *Giulio Cesare*, two 8-inch cruisers, and ten destroyers. The whole formidable force was under the command of the Italian Commander-in-Chief, Admiral Angelo Iachino, flying his flag in the *Littorio*.[1]

Admiral Iachino had news of the departure of Admiral Vian's force from Alexandria, and on the morning of the 17th he received his first air sighting report. This was shortly before 10.30, and placed the British ships some 160 miles south and slightly east of his own position. He decided to stand on and keep within supporting distance of his convoy. At 11 a.m. the *Littorio* Group increased speed to 22 knots and

[1] This was the operation of which Count Ciano wrote in his Diary: 'All the ships and all the Admirals at sea. May God help us!'

altered course to south-west. At 11.48 speed was further increased to 24 knots, which was the *Doria's* maximum. The *Breconshire* was mistaken for a battleship by German and Italian reconnaissance aircraft and continued to be reported as such throughout the day. This mistake caused the Italians to assume that the British were at sea for the special purpose of attacking the Italian convoy.

By 2 p.m. on the 17th Admiral Vian had received two reconnaissance reports, from which he was aware of an enemy force, containing at least three battleships, some 120 miles to the northward of him steering south at slow speed. Judging this information to be incomplete, as it 'left powerful enemy units unaccounted for', he made an alteration of course to the southward and held on under frequent air attacks, waiting for more information. Three further reports received during the afternoon appeared to show that none of the Italian force was likely to be within sixty miles of the British by nightfall. At about 5.30, however, two floatplanes, of types usually carried by warships, made their appearance and were accompanied by five torpedo-bombers which hung about without attacking. This, coupled with the dropping of signal flares by the shadowing aircraft, gave Admiral Vian the impression of a set-piece, and suggested that the enemy's surface forces must be somewhere near. Ten minutes later, just before sunset, masts were sighted to the north-west of the *Naiad*. The enemy appeared to be in five columns with heavy ships in the centre, consisting of two *Cavour* class battleships and some 8-inch cruisers. At a range of some seventeen miles the enemy opened fire in what was to become known as the First Battle of Sirte.

Admiral Vian immediately detached the *Breconshire* with two destroyers to the southward, while, with his four cruisers and the ten destroyers now remaining, he turned towards the enemy. It was not his intention to offer battle under conditions so vastly favourable to the Italians, but he hoped under cover of smoke to divert attention from the *Breconshire* until darkness fell. Only if diversionary movements and gunfire failed did he intend to launch a torpedo attack. Shortly before dark he detached Force K to reinforce the *Breconshire's* escort.

By dark Admiral Vian had lost touch, not only with the enemy, who he believed had turned north, but temporarily with most of his own ships. This he described as 'a disadvantage of diversionary tactics.' Admiral Cunningham had ordered him not to seek out the enemy battleships by night, but to go for the Benghazi part of the convoy. Between 11 p.m. and 2.30 a.m. he therefore patrolled with his now reunited force across the enemy's line of approach to Benghazi. At 2.30, in obedience to a signal from Admiral Cunningham, course was set for the return voyage to Alexandria. Meanwhile the *Breconshire* was making towards Malta, now escorted by Force K as well as by the two destroyers originally detached. Early on the 18th these were joined by the *Neptune* and a further two destroyers, and the whole force arrived at Malta at 3 p.m.

Admiral Iachino's information from the air had also not been entirely satisfactory. Having learnt of Admiral Vian's alteration to the southward, he too had thought it unlikely that action could be joined before nightfall, and out of respect for the night-fighting efficiency of the British he was considering whether to reverse course for part of the night when the bursts of the British anti-aircraft shells repelling the air attacks at 5.30 p.m. were seen in the sky due east. Admiral Iachino promptly turned towards these shell bursts and at 5.40 sighted the British ships to the south-east. Fire was opened by the Italian heavy ships but they had difficulty in distinguishing their targets against the rapidly darkening eastern sky. The Italian destroyers were ordered out to counter what appeared to be an attack by the British flotillas and shortly after 6 o'clock Admiral Iachino withdrew his battleships to the westward from the menace of torpedoes in the uncertain light. By 6.30 all the Italian forces were steering north and contact with the British had been lost. Shortly after 10 p.m. Iachino decided to steer almost directly for Tripoli, and turned the convoy, its escort, and his own covering force to this course. Expecting night attacks from the British light forces he disposed his warships to protect the convoy and maintained a patrol with his covering force some thirty miles to the south-east. About sixty miles further to the south-east Admiral Vian was maintaining his own patrol, and neither Admiral was aware of the other's movements.

Next day, 18th December, the Italian Fleet cruised some 200 miles to the south-east of Malta, covering the convoy as it approached Tripoli. The ship (the *Ankara*) for Benghazi was detached during the afternoon and the other three merchantmen steamed separately westward along the African coast, escorted each by two destroyers. By evening all other Italian warships were on their way back to their bases.

Having fuelled at Malta, where they had arrived with the *Breconshire*, the cruisers *Neptune*, *Aurora*, *Penelope* and four destroyers sailed again at nightfall on the 18th in the hope of intercepting the Italian convoy which, it was believed, might still not have entered Tripoli. Air reconnaissance and air attack were much handicapped by stormy weather and poor visibility. At Malta it was raining hard, clouds were very low, and the runways had been heavily bombed. A Wellington had reported the enemy as split up and covering a large area to the east of Tripoli. A striking force of Swordfish failed to find these targets but four Albacores attacked and damaged one of the convoy—the *Napoli*—with torpedoes. In the hope of delaying the convoy until the British warships arrived Wellingtons bombed Tripoli and laid mines off the entrance, with the result that the Italian merchantmen anchored for the night ten miles east of the port, in the shelter of their minefields.

The British ships, commanded by Captain R. C. O'Conor in the *Neptune*, made for a position near Tripoli at maximum speed into a heavy sea, but did not receive the air reports concerning the enemy convoy. It is probable that Captain O'Conor intended to turn and sweep eastward from this position. Half an hour after midnight on the 19th, his ships, having reduced speed after crossing the 100-fathom line, were about seventeen miles to the north-eastward of Tripoli, when a mine detonated in the *Neptune's* starboard paravane. It did little damage, but as she was going astern the *Neptune* ran into another mine which wrecked her propellers and steering gear. The ships astern sheered off to starboard and port to clear the minefield, but the *Aurora* and *Penelope* also ran into mines. The *Aurora*, though badly damaged, was able to steer for Malta at sixteen knots escorted by two destroyers. The *Penelope*, only slightly damaged, stood by the helpless *Neptune* ready to take her in tow when she drifted clear of the minefield. At 1 a.m. the *Neptune*, drifting to port, exploded a third mine. The destroyer *Kandahar* entered the minefield in an attempt to take the *Neptune* in tow, but also struck a mine which blew her stern off. As nothing could be done to reach either the *Neptune* or *Kandahar*, Captain A. D. Nicholl of the *Penelope* was obliged to leave the scene with the remaining destroyer and return to Malta. At 4 a.m. another mine exploded under the *Neptune* and she turned over and sank. Early next morning the destroyer *Jaguar*, ably helped by an A.S.V. Wellington, found the *Kandahar* and rescued all but ninety-one of her company.[1] The sea was too rough for the *Jaguar* to go alongside and the *Kandahar's* crew had to swim across. The *Kandahar* was then sunk with a torpedo. From the *Neptune* there was only one survivor, a leading seaman, who was picked up five days later, on Christmas Eve, by an Italian torpedo boat. The minefield which had caused this disaster had been laid in the previous June, but had not come to the knowledge of the British.

Once again, and not for the last time, British and Italian convoy operations had coincided. H.M.S. *Breconshire* had been safely passed through to Malta, but the Italians had also achieved what they had set out to do. What was more serious, they had probably gained considerable confidence as a result. For a whole day a large part of the Italian Fleet had been operating within 200 miles of Malta without being seriously attacked, and the enemy was now aware that the British surface force at Malta was eliminated, at any rate for the time being.

---

[1] 'A.S.V.' means that the aircraft was fitted with a radar device for detecting the presence of surface vessels from the air.

See Map 20

While this disaster to the Malta force was taking place off Tripoli, another was in the making inside Alexandria harbour. As a result of information received from the Admiralty the Commander-in-Chief had issued a warning on the 18th that an attack by human torpedoes might be expected and, among other special precautions, torpedo baffles had been laid on each side of the two battleships. At 3.25 on the morning of 19th December, two Italians dressed in rubber overalls were picked up from the buoy to which the *Valiant* was moored. Interrogated, the two prisoners disclosed nothing. It was presumed they had already placed explosives under the ship. It was made clear to them that they would be involved in anything which happened to the *Valiant*, and they were placed in custody low down near the bottom of the ship. At 5.47 there was an explosion under the stern of the tanker *Sagona*, which damaged her seriously and also the destroyer *Jervis* berthed alongside. At 5.50 one of the *Valiant's* prisoners asked to speak to the Captain and warned him that his ship would soon blow up. A quarter of an hour later there was an explosion under the *Valiant's* foremost turrets and after another four minutes a third explosion under one of the *Queen Elizabeth's* boiler rooms. As a result of precautions there were only eight casualties, but both battleships were heavily flooded and put out of action for many months.

This, the outstanding success of the Italian Tenth Light Flotilla during the war, was achieved with human torpedoes, three of which had been transported by the submarine *Scirè* to a position about 1½ miles north of the eastern harbour of Alexandria. Here they were launched, giving them a distance of about five miles to cover to reach the entrance to the Fleet anchorage. All three had the good fortune to arrive off this entrance while the boom gate was open to admit some destroyers, and they slipped through. Although severely shaken by depth charges dropped by patrol craft, they then selected their targets and found no great difficulty in passing over the protecting nets round the battleships. In the case of the *Valiant* it was not easy to secure the charge to her bilge keels, and after great exertions the whole apparatus was eventually dumped on the sea-bed some fifteen feet below the ship's bottom. In the attack on the *Queen Elizabeth* the explosive head was slung from her bilge keels in the manner intended. Of the six Italians responsible for these extraordinarily brave and arduous attacks, two were picked up by the *Valiant* as already related. The other four were captured ashore during the next two days, having failed to reach the submarine *Zaffiro* which had been sent to pick them up off Rosetta.

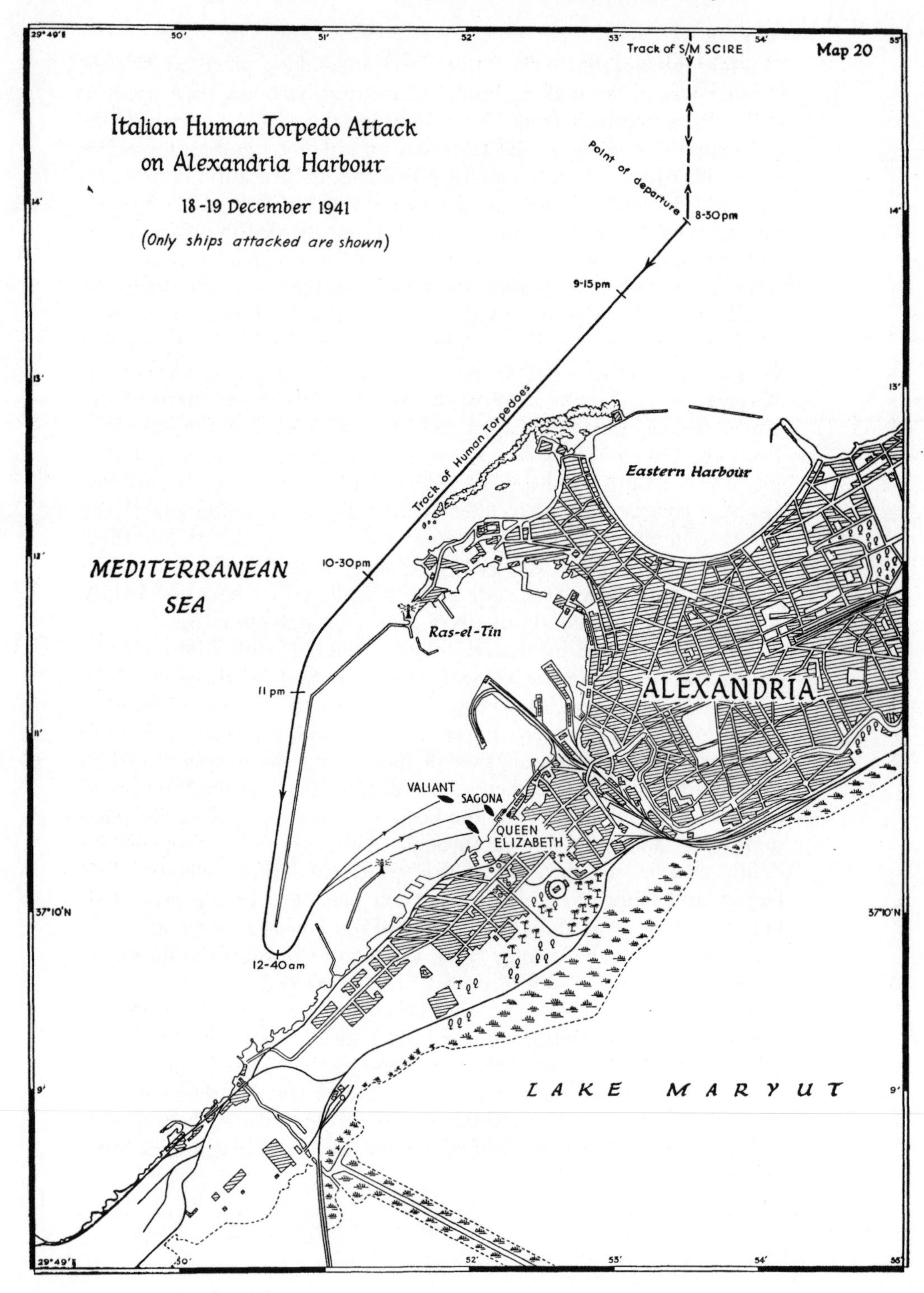

Map 20
Italian Human Torpedo Attack on Alexandria Harbour
18-19 December 1941
(Only ships attacked are shown)
Track of S/M SCIRE
Point of departure
8-30 pm
9-15 pm
10-30 pm
11 pm
12-40 am
Track of Human Torpedoes
Eastern Harbour
MEDITERRANEAN SEA
Ras-el-Tin
ALEXANDRIA
VALIANT
SAGONA
QUEEN ELIZABETH
LAKE MARYUT
29°49'E
50'
51'
52'
53'
54'
55'
14'
13'
12'
11'
37°10'N
9'

Admiral Cunningham had now even fewer serviceable ships than he had had in June, after the heavy losses which accompanied the fall of Crete. A demand at the end of October for the release of two destroyers to join the Eastern Fleet brought the total he had had to part with for this reason up to six. He had pointed out that this would leave him with only ten destroyers in a reliable condition, and this at a time when the impending offensive in Cyrenaica would, if successful, result in a need for more of these ships to maintain the army by the longer coastal route.

The Admiralty had been able to help, partly at the expense of the North Atlantic and partly by replacing some of Admiral Somerville's destroyers with a smaller type. The destroyers under Commander Stokes, which so distinguished themselves off Cape Bon, were the first of these reinforcements to arrive. Four more reached Alexandria at the end of December in company with the cruiser *Dido*, whose damage sustained off Crete had now been repaired. Other destroyers of the smaller 'Hunt' class were on the way.[1]

There were, however, no battleships or carriers with which to replace the *Ark Royal*, *Barham*, *Queen Elizabeth*, and *Valiant*. The cruiser *Hobart* returned to Australia and several sloops were withdrawn for service in the Indian Ocean or Australian waters. At Gibraltar Force H now comprised one battleship, the *Malaya*, one small carrier, the *Argus*, one cruiser, the *Hermione*, and a few destroyers. It was a seriously reduced Fleet that had to keep Malta supplied, support the Army's advance—perhaps as far as Tripoli—and continue to intercept the enemy's convoys. At Alexandria the only fighting ships with heavier armaments than a destroyer were Admiral Vian's three light cruisers—*Naiad*, *Dido* and *Euryalus*. The hard core of the Fleet had been lost at the moment when the possession of the airfields in Cyrenaica would have made it possible to cover operations in the Central Mediterranean with shore-based fighters. The Italians, on the other hand, had now four battleships fit for service, and had had some reason for gaining confidence. And although they might not know for certain that Admiral Cunningham no longer had any battleships, this information could not be kept from them for long.

It was fortunate indeed that the Italian submarines, in spite of their numbers, were achieving so little. Their only direct success in 1941 had been the sinking of the cruiser *Bonaventure*, although the *Scirè*'s part in the attacks by human torpedoes at Alexandria and Gibraltar must not be forgotten. During the year the Italians had lost ten submarines within the Mediterranean. The German submarines, on the other hand, in their first two months in the Mediterranean had sunk

---

[1] 'Hunt' class—small escort destroyers of 1,000 tons displacement, built during the war and named after packs of hounds.

one aircraft carrier, one battleship, and one cruiser. Six German submarines had been sunk, but the numbers were growing and by the end of December there were twenty-one inside the Mediterranean. While a reduction of the number operating in the Atlantic was very welcome, it meant that the submarines in the Mediterranean could now be a greater nuisance to the Inshore Squadron and to the supply ships plying along the North African coast as well as to the Fleet as a whole. Worse still, the *Luftwaffe's* renewed attacks on Malta were becoming heavier and more frequent, and the number of German aircraft in Sicily was known to be increasing.

The outlook at sea, therefore, at the end of 1941 could hardly be called encouraging.

CHAPTER V

THE SITUATION AFTER THE ENTRY OF JAPAN INTO THE WAR

THE Commanders-in-Chief in the Middle East had always intended to follow up 'Crusader' by driving the enemy out of the whole of Libya. When, in the previous winter, the Italians had been defeated and Cyrenaica overrun, the British Government had felt obliged to send a force to oppose the Germans in Greece and discard the possibility of advancing to Tripoli. But by the early autumn of 1941 General Auchinleck was beginning to consider plans for a pursuit through Tripolitania—operation 'Acrobat'—which was to follow a successful 'Crusader'.

The advantages of occupying Tripoli would be considerable. There would be an immense gain in prestige; convoys to Malta from the east would be far less vulnerable; bases for launching expeditions against Sicily or Italy would be gained; and the French in North Africa might perhaps be encouraged to join the British. The last point was important because it would be extremely difficult for the Axis forces, once they had lost Tripoli, to stage a return to Africa provided they were not allowed to set foot in Tunisia. It would be one thing for the British to maintain a small garrison at Tripoli to prevent the Axis regaining a footing in Libya, but quite another for them to be opposed by a force properly established in Tunisia.

General Auchinleck informed the Minister of State on 9th September that he attached great importance to capturing Tripoli. So long as enemy forces remained in Libya the back door to Egypt would be only partially closed. This would handicap any future offensive plans, and be a real danger if a German attack from the north should throw the British on the defensive. The Chiefs of Staff were asked to say what further action was contemplated in the event of Tripoli being captured. They, too, were determined to gain every possible advantage from a successful 'Crusader' and 'Acrobat', and suggested, among other plans, one to capture Sicily by an expedition which would sail from the United Kingdom. The Defence Committee approved this suggestion and passed it to the Commanders-in-Chief in the Middle East, who received it with no enthusiasm.[1] They felt that the best

[1] The organization in London for the conduct of the war is referred to in Volume I of this History, p. 191n. For a fuller treatment see J. R. M. Butler: *Grand Strategy*, Volume II (1957) chapter XI.

action for new forces from the United Kingdom would be to occupy Bizerta, and suggested that there might be ways of eliciting an invitation from the French. They felt that this was more important than capturing Sicily, which would create a very difficult maintenance problem. Their view was accepted in London and it was decided, instead, to make ready to respond to any request for help that might come from General Weygand in North Africa. To this end an expedition—'Gymnast'—was to be prepared which would land at various ports, the most easterly being Algiers.

After the Armistice in June 1940 General Weygand had become Minister of National Defence in Marshal Pétain's Government. Early in October of that year he was appointed to the new post of Delegate General of the Government in North Africa. In this capacity he was charged with co-ordinating political and economic action, but he was also to be Commander-in-Chief of the land and air forces in North Africa and of the naval forces allotted to the defence of its coasts. For a year General Weygand strove to achieve French unity, to build up confidence, to prepare the armed forces for any emergency, and to balk the Axis Armistice Commissions in every possible way. As the Delegate of the French Government and a loyal supporter of Marshal Pétain he could hardly be expected to have any sympathy with the Free French Movement, but as an implacable enemy of the Germans he naturally came into conflict with those who saw collaboration with Germany as the best prospect for France. While there was no positive reason for expecting him to call upon the British for help, it was hoped that he might do so if 'Acrobat' were successful or if the Germans made demands upon him for military facilities in North Africa—at Bizerta, for example. Even then it was not at all certain that he would be satisfied with the help that the British could offer. The project went ahead, nevertheless; the Prime Minister had been impressed by information from the British Ambassador in Washington that President Roosevelt was interested in the idea of sending a large American force to Casablanca, if General Weygand should make a request to the United States for assistance.

The Commanders-in-Chief in the Middle East had expressed their liking for some such project, but pointed out that they would be unable to make any contribution to it except possibly by naval action. The Prime Minister then explained operation 'Gymnast' and said that, regardless of whether the Germans made demands upon the French, the moment success in 'Crusader' became apparent he would appeal to President Roosevelt to put pressure on General Weygand and he himself would offer the aid prepared. This was on 18th November. The next day came word of General Weygand's dismissal from his post and of his recall to France.

The only effect of this mishap upon the Prime Minister's resolve was to make him decide to address his offer, when the time came, to the Vichy Government instead of to General Weygand. On 23rd November he reminded General Auchinleck that he was waiting for the moment to appeal to President Roosevelt and to tell the Vichy Government that it was now or never. He ended: 'I hope the moment may come within the next week'. As has been seen, however, 'Crusader' was having a hard passage and was not going as quickly as had been hoped.

Having had time to examine the 'Gymnast' plan the Commanders-in-Chief commented upon it on 28th November. The objective, they thought, should be Tunisia, in order to keep open the Sicilian Channel. The occupation of Morocco or Algeria would be of little value. The port of disembarkation should not be too far to the west; it should be Philippeville, Bône, Bizerta, or Tunis. They admitted that this would expose 'Gymnast' to air attack, but they suggested that the support of our air forces from Malta and the enemy's other preoccupations would lessen it. The Chiefs of Staff did not answer this proposal; their next step was to appoint General Sir Harold Alexander to the command of 'Gymnast'. If the French invited us the initial force would consist of three fighter squadrons flown in from Malta and Gibraltar, for which the ground crews and two anti-aircraft regiments would go by sea. (These troops did in fact sail on 8th December, but their destination was changed a few days later and they went round the Cape with convoy W.S.14, of which more will be heard presently.) The main force of 'Gymnast' was to be roughly two divisions and one armoured division, which could leave the United Kingdom from twenty-three to thirty-two days after the decision to collect the shipping had been taken.

On the night of 7th/8th December 1941 the Japanese landed on the coast of Malaya. A little more than an hour later they attacked the American base at Pearl Harbour. On 8th December the United Kingdom and the United States of America declared war on Japan, and on 11th December Germany and Italy followed suit with declarations of war upon the United States.

Thus the Japanese action had the tremendous result of forcing the United States into war with Germany and Italy. But this did not alter the fact that the attack on Pearl Harbour and the landing in Malaya caused the British and Americans to become directly committed to fighting in a vast maritime theatre of war thousands of miles from the Mediterranean. Many vital problems arose from this inescapable fact. In the middle of December Mr. Churchill went to Washington with a strong staff of advisers to discuss them.[1] It did not take the British

[1] Field-Marshal Sir John Dill, who had recently been succeeded as C.I.G.S. by General Sir Alan Brooke, remained in Washington to become Head of the British Joint Staff Mission.

and American Chiefs of Staff long to agree upon a broad policy for the conduct of the war in which their countries were now Allies: this was, to defeat Germany first.

As far as Mediterranean planning was concerned the Americans at once began to study the problem of landing an expedition in North Africa under the code-name of 'Super Gymnast'. The basic assumption was that there would be enough French co-operation to ensure that no more than slight unco-ordinated opposition would be met, and that the ports and railways would be worked by the French for the benefit of the Allies. The primary object would be to secure French Morocco as a base from which control might be extended over all North Africa and later into Europe. The operation would be under American command and the planning would be done at Washington. The provisional date would be 25th May 1942.

By the end of January the British Chiefs of Staff were feeling doubtful about their own share of the plan. All the available shipping was fully occupied in movements to the Middle East and Far East. The British forces were stretched to the limit. 'Gymnast' had been conceived in the hope that we should be invited into North Africa, which now seemed most unlikely. Yet without French help the operation would be quite impracticable. On 1st February the Prime Minister agreed that preparations should cease, and on 12th March the Chiefs of Staff informed Washington that in their view no operations of the 'Gymnast' type could take place before the autumn. A few days later the United States Chiefs of Staff agreed, and the matter was dropped. But not for good, for the Allied landings on the coasts of Morocco and Algeria, which took place in the following November, were, in effect, 'Super Gymnast' brought up to date.

Before Mr. Churchill and his advisers had gone to Washington in December a decision had been reached on the immediate British policy. Everything possible was to be sent to the Far East, but no units or equipment already in the Middle East or Iraq were to be withdrawn. A number of units on the way, however, were to be diverted, either to Bombay or to Singapore. Thus, in convoy W.S. 12Z, due at Durban on Christmas Eve, the following units intended for Iraq were diverted: one complete anti-tank regiment and the men of a second; one heavy and one light anti-aircraft regiment; Headquarters No. 267 Wing and four fighter squadrons, with fifty-one Hurricane IIs and twenty-four pilots. Eighty pilots en route for Takoradi and five Hurricanes for Basra were also to be diverted, and eight more Hurricanes were to be sent out from the United Kingdom to bring the Wing up to strength. From convoy W.S. 14, due at Durban on 9th January, the following were to be diverted: the heavy and light anti-aircraft regiments that had been originally intended for the first flight of 'Gymnast', and ground staffs and limited equipment of Headquarters No. 266 Wing with three fighter squadrons, but no aircraft. Forty Hurricanes were to be lifted from Takoradi and taken by sea to Bombay to provide the first instalment of aircraft for this Wing. As an exception to the general policy of no removals from the Middle East, General Auchinleck was ordered to despatch fifty light tanks to India—no great loss.

Much more unwelcome was the decision to divert the 18th Division, then rounding the Cape. The Prime Minister explained this to General Auchinleck by pointing to the improved prospects of the 'Crusader' battle and the pronounced Russian successes which had relieved the immediate anxieties about the Caucasus and the south Caspian area. The Chiefs of Staff supplemented this by saying that General Auchinleck could use the 50th Division, now in Iraq, in any way he wished. On the other hand, the 17th Indian Division, in India, could no longer be regarded as earmarked for Iraq, and the Commander-in-Chief, India, was free to use it as he wished. As a further exception to the 'no withdrawals' policy came an order to despatch immediately the four anti-aircraft batteries of the Mobile Naval Base Defence Organization.

Orders for the withdrawal of Royal Air Force units soon followed. As soon as 'Crusader' was finished the Middle East was to prepare six bomber squadrons, one Air Stores Park and one Repair and Salvage Unit for despatch to Bombay. Meanwhile, in response to a request from the Chief of the Air Staff on 9th December, six Blenheim IVs had left for Singapore on the 12th and six more on the 14th. On 18th December the Chiefs of Staff told the Commanders-in-Chief of their anxiety about Burma and asked that one of the Blenheim squadrons should be sent immediately provided that neither 'Crusader' nor 'Acrobat' would be affected. The first six aircraft of No. 113 Squadron left on 30th December; three other squadrons, Nos. 45, 84, and 211, left during January and February.

On 10th December, only a few hours before the loss of the *Prince of Wales* and *Repulse* off the coast of Malaya, the First Sea Lord, weighing the redispositions necessary as the result of Japan's entry into the war, had asked Admiral Cunningham and Admiral Somerville what would be the result of withdrawing all capital ships and carriers from either or both of their commands. The main points of their replies were as follows. The removal of the battleship from Force H would tend to encourage the Italian Fleet to concentrate eastwards. There would be little effect at the Western end of the Mediterranean, except that preparations for special operations, such as escorting convoys, would be difficult to conceal, and the enemy would have time to take counter measures. In the Eastern Mediterranean the removal of all the capital ships would be equivalent to depriving ourselves of the ultimate means of cutting off the enemy's supplies to Africa and of running convoys to Malta from the east. But if the army gained a firm hold on Cyrenaica and its airfields, and if ample air forces could be based there and at Malta—under Admiral Cunningham's control—it should be possible to supply the army and maintain Malta. The ability to keep up the pressure on the enemy's supply lines would, however, be seriously affected. Apart from this, the Italians would gain in morale and might venture into the Eastern Mediterranean, especially by sorties from the Aegean. The political effect on Turkey and Egypt must be expected to be very bad. Nevertheless, if the air forces were very considerably increased, the withdrawal of all the capital ships could be accepted as a gamble.

The gamble was, however, forced upon Admiral Cunningham and the Admiralty in a very unwelcome form. Disaster befell Force K and was quickly followed by the Italian attack at Alexandria in which the two remaining British battleships were badly damaged. On 24th December the Admiralty informed Admiral Cunningham that he could expect no replacements; all available carriers and battleships would almost certainly be wanted in the Far East. There were hopes of providing some of the air reinforcements for which he had pressed, but, in many instances, not for a long time.

Withdrawals of smaller ships from the Middle East were briefly referred to in the previous chapter. Besides the cruiser *Hobart* the sloop *Yarra* was to return to Australia; the sloops *Sutlej* and *Jumna* and the minesweepers *Lismore* and *Bathurst*, from the Red Sea to the East Indies; the sloops *Indus*, *Hindustan* and *Falmouth*, from the Persian Gulf to the East Indies. Two submarines were to leave the Mediterranean about the New Year.

The Commanders-in-Chief and the Minister of State—in other words, the Middle East Defence Committee—naturally gave much thought to the probable effects of all these changes, and cabled their views on 18th December to the Prime Minister. Their main preoccupation was with the northern flank. They regarded the defence of Persia, Iraq, Syria and Egypt as one problem, and for the northern flank they had counted upon having seven divisions by the next spring. It looked as if they would have only three. The diversion of so many anti-aircraft batteries further aggravated a situation about which they were already anxious. The contemplated diversion of expected air reinforcements was also serious, and might make it impossible to meet the commitment to send twenty-four squadrons to Turkey;[1] moreover, it might seriously affect the security of our sea communications in the

[1] It had been agreed at the Anglo-Turkish talks in September 1941 that if Turkey were attacked the British would send certain forces to her help; the number of squadrons was raised from 20 to 24 in October.

Mediterranean and the task of interrupting the enemy's. The Commander-in-Chief, Mediterranean, emphasized this aspect when he suggested that the criterion in deciding on the moves of air forces should be to leave enough of them to control the Central Mediterranean despite the absence of British battleships. He thought that if success were not gained against the enemy's heavy ships within the next three months the enemy would obtain control of the Mediterranean and would be able to attack Malta and to reinforce Tripoli at will.

On 24th December the Chiefs of Staff asked each Commander-in-Chief to send home a representative, well versed in 'Acrobat', to explain the implications of the diversions and withdrawals. Two days later the Prime Minister addressed 'a hard request' to General Auchinleck; he was to part at once with a force of at least a hundred American tanks. In addition, a consignment of Hurricanes for No. 266 Wing was to be picked up and ferried away to the Far East by H.M.S. *Indomitable*. It was still the intention not to remove anything that would prevent 'Acrobat', and it was hoped to reinforce the Middle East with some Fulmars. General Auchinleck replied that he could spare 110 American Stuart tanks manned by 7th Armoured Brigade; it would be complete with headquarters, signals, workshop and recovery unit and would contain two armoured regiments, one 25-pdr battery, and one anti-tank battery—all just back from the Libyan frontier. He also offered to send an Australian infantry brigade group, provided that it could be replaced before April, and a quantity of small arms and anti-tank rifles.

To reach London ahead of their representatives, the Commanders-in-Chief cabled their hopes and fears about the war. They assumed that the ultimate object was to defeat Germany by a land offensive against her territory, and that the attitude towards Japan would be defensive. Bases in the Middle East, including Malta, must be securely held. They reminded the Chiefs of Staff that the Mediterranean theatre offered good opportunities for offensive action, but it would be essential to occupy Tunisia first. It was already possible to deploy American air forces in the Middle East, and they could be used there to great advantage.

The Chiefs of Staff sent a telegram on the Government's reinforcement policy on 1st January 1942, by which date it had been agreed by the British and American Governments that their primary object was the defeat of Germany. The British policy was to divert to the Far East no more resources than would be necessary for holding the Japanese. Subject to this, 'Crusader' was to be exploited to the greatest extent possible. The army reinforcements were given in detail. Six divisions, one light tank squadron and one armoured brigade were considered necessary for the Far East. These would come from the

Middle East or from reinforcements intended for the Middle East. In addition to the two divisions already mentioned—the 18th (British) and the 17th Indian—the following were to go: the Australian Corps of two divisions (6th and 7th) and two divisions from Iraq or India.

This drew from the Commanders-in-Chief the comment that none of these moves would affect 'Crusader', and the Middle East representatives confirmed in London that they would not affect 'Acrobat' either. But the situation on the Turkish or northern front would be greatly altered. Hitherto the Middle East had been aiming at being ready to meet an attack from the north by April 1942, a date which was perhaps unnecessarily early in view of the German reverses in Russia. The Commanders-in-Chief now requested a decision on the date by which they ought to be ready, and further asked that the resources diverted to the Far East should be replaced at least one month before this date. One of the most serious shortages was of anti-aircraft artillery; Iraq and Persia had virtually no anti-aircraft protection at all and the rest of the Middle East was a long way short of its requirements. In spite of this, the Australian Corps was to take with it one heavy and two light anti-aircraft regiments; forty guns held as a pool for use in Turkey were to go; and one heavy and one light anti-aircraft regiment in convoy W.S. 15, due at Durban in the middle of February, were to be diverted.

On 17th January General Auchinleck began to suspect that he might lose his one remaining Australian division, the 9th, and expressed to the C.I.G.S. his hope that its withdrawal would be strongly resisted, because the situation would be precarious if the enemy were to attack from the north before all the divisions withdrawn had been replaced by divisions complete with their equipment and transport. The British estimate of German capabilities by this time had become more definite. It was calculated that Germany's most probable course in 1942 would be to resume a full-scale offensive against Russia, which might bring her into contact with British forces in Persia not earlier than mid-August. This action would not preclude the reinforcement of General Rommel on a sufficient scale and in time to oppose 'Acrobat' effectively. (It will be seen in the next chapter that important reinforcements were in fact arriving.) If the Germans decided not to resume their offensive in Russia, but to attack Turkey instead, they might be in a position to reach the northern frontier of Syria by the end of May at the earliest. It was this possibility that caused General Auchinleck anxiety, because there was no prospect of his forces in Syria and Iraq being made up to the strength he considered necessary. Indeed, a month later he was told that the 70th Division was to go to Ceylon and Burma—it went in March—and that he was also to part with the 9th Australian Division, and possibly another division from Iraq.

This news, together with the parallel reduction in air forces, and following a reverse in Cyrenaica—to be described in the next chapter—seemed to General Auchinleck to be extremely serious. The Commanders-in-Chief and the Minister of State sent their considered views three days later. They recalled their requirements, which had been accepted by the Chiefs of Staff, and pointed out that the forces remaining after these withdrawals had taken place would be insufficient to maintain the Middle East position in face of an attack from the north. 'We are, in fact, relying on this attack not taking place.' The effect on Turkey of these withdrawals could not fail to be grave. None of the countries in the Middle East could be regarded as stable, and any signs of weakening by further withdrawals would encourage disaffection. The forces remaining might therefore be required to preserve order, and, at the same time, defend the western approaches to Egypt. The whole situation might change for the worse unless we could interfere effectively with enemy reinforcement to Libya. The Commanders-in-Chief concluded that it was vital to reinforce the Middle East, for although they hoped to be able to hold the present positions in Libya for some months, and possibly even to gain ground, they could do no more than cause some delay to an enemy advancing through Iraq and Syria towards the Persian Gulf and Suez Canal.

In the event, General Auchinleck's worst anxieties were relieved by the action of President Roosevelt. One United States division was sailing for Australia early in March. Just as it was leaving the Prime Minister asked President Roosevelt if he would offer to send two more United States divisions, one to New Zealand and one to Australia. This would make it possible to leave the New Zealand Division and the 9th Australian Division in the Middle East and economize shipping. The President readily consented, and New Zealand gladly accepted the offer. The Australian Government took longer to reach a decision, and not until a month later did they express themselves prepared to agree, in view of the shipping difficulties, to postpone the return of their 9th Division to Australia. The President further agreed to a request by Mr. Churchill for American shipping to carry two British divisions from the United Kingdom to the Middle East or India as the situation might require. Three British divisions, interspersed with drafts and details, were already scheduled to sail from the United Kingdom in British ships in the next five convoys. This meant that five British divisions in all would leave the United Kingdom in the period March to July. This was most welcome news to General Auchinleck, who telegraphed to say that it should help to ease his situation considerably.

H.M.S. *Indomitable* returned to Port Sudan on 23rd February after ferrying the forty-eight Hurricanes to the Far East. The Prime Minister had decided that she should make another trip with Hurricanes and on the 27th she left Port Sudan with sixty. Fifty of these were to make up the equipment of the squadrons in convoy W.S. 14 already on their way to Singapore. The remaining ten, together with twenty-six other Hurricanes which left the Middle East to fly to India, were for Nos. 30 and 261 Fighter Squadrons, and it was in this way that these two units also came to be withdrawn from the Middle East. In all, the Middle East parted with four complete Blenheim squadrons, two complete Hurricane squadrons and, in addition, twelve Blenheim IV aircraft. Besides these, seven complete fighter squadrons, which were originally intended for the Middle East, were diverted en route.

During the rebellion in Iraq in May 1941 the command of the land forces in Iraq had passed to the Commander-in-Chief, Middle East, mainly because effective support for northern Iraq could be sent only from Palestine and because air operations in Iraq were controlled by the Air Officer Commanding-in-Chief, Middle East. The command of the land forces had reverted to India at the end of June, though the Chiefs of Staff intended that the whole area should come under the Middle East again if the Germans looked like moving through southern Caucasia into Persia and northern Iraq. The Chiefs of Staff recognized the advantages of leaving India responsible for the troops in Iraq, the bulk of whom were Indian, but they naturally wished to avoid making a change of command at the last minute. As the threat did not seem to be imminent, they had decided to await the outcome of 'Crusader' before saddling General Auchinleck with this additional burden.

On 12th December they came to the conclusion that the change ought to be made. The threat from the north was still not imminent; in fact the Russian winter had begun, the German attack had everywhere exhausted itself, and the Russians had been able to gain local successes north and south of Moscow and in the Ukraine. 'Crusader' was well on the way to driving the enemy out of Cyrenaica. But the Japanese attack on Thailand and Malaya, and the consequent threat to Burma (which had been placed under General Wavell's command), was a new factor in the problem; in a message to General Wavell the Prime Minister expressed the opinion that he 'must now look East'. Even so, Wavell opposed the transfer of command in Iraq and Persia to Auchinleck, reiterating the arguments which had caused its previous deferment. General Auchinleck, on the other hand, was strongly in favour of it, because it would make, he thought, for speedier planning and would enable the operational and administrative aspects to be more closely related. The Minister of State supported the suggestion, adding that the problem of concerting supplies, and later perhaps even operations, with the Americans, would be greatly lightened if they had only one Command to deal with. On hearing these views the Defence Committee agreed with the Chiefs of Staff that the transfer of command should take place as soon as possible. On 12th January 1942 General Auchinleck took over. The title of Lieut.-General E. P. Quinan's force, hitherto known as 'British Troops in Iraq', was changed to the Tenth Army.

A Treaty of Alliance was signed at Teheran on 29th January between the United Kingdom, the Soviet Union, and Persia, by which the Allies undertook to defend Persia from aggression by Germany or any other power. Persia, in return, undertook to co-operate in every way possible, especially by facilitating the use of the railways, roads, rivers, airfields, ports, pipelines and signal installations. The assistance of Persian armed forces was to be limited to the maintenance of internal security in Persia.

In the latter half of February 1942 there were some changes in His Majesty's Government. Mr. Oliver Lyttelton, the Minister of State in the Middle East, left to become Minister of Production. There had been no mention of a successor, and the Commanders-in-Chief thought it right to put forward their views on the importance of the post, based on their experience of the seven months during which it had existed.

They regarded the Minister of State as a link with His Majesty's Government which was indispensable to the successful prosecution of the war in the Middle East. His guidance and advice on military policy from the political and governmental point of view had been invaluable. He had been able to relieve the Commanders-in-Chief of innumerable political and economic problems connected with Persia, Iraq, Syria, Palestine, Egypt, the Sudan, North and East Africa, and the Arab world generally—apart from helping them in their dealings with the Americans and with numerous Allies. They could not cope with all this work and at the same time exercise their primary functions as Commanders-in-Chief. Moreover, the office of the Minister of State had become a focus for the co-ordination of the views of the Services and of the other authorities in the Middle East; this made it easy to concert action and was to the general advantage.

In short, they were convinced of the need to have in the Middle East a member of the War Cabinet who possessed the confidence of the Government at home. He should be served by an adequate staff, qualified to deal with the many and varied political, financial, economic, and propaganda problems which were constantly arising.

Mr. Lyttelton left the Middle East at the end of February 1942. Three weeks later Mr. R. G. Casey, Australian Minister in Washington, was appointed to succeed him and was made a member of the British War Cabinet. He did not arrive until 5th May, and in the meanwhile Sir Walter Monckton acted as Minister of State.

The internal situation in Egypt had been calm for so long that it is easy to forget how important it was for the British that conditions in the main base area should be stable. Towards the end of 1941 there was a political crisis. The war had undoubtedly brought many difficulties for the Egyptian Government. There had been some bombing, but not much; the cost of living was rising; and there were many Egyptians who disliked the military occupation of their country. As against this, the occupation could hardly be called oppressive; for one thing, vast sums were passing into the pockets of the people in wages and by the spending of the pay of the British troops. The big problem of what to do with the cotton crop, on the sale of which Egypt largely relied for her prosperity, was solved by the British Government, who undertook to buy it all—as they had done in 1940. The stipulation that less land was to be planted with cotton and more with food crops had been only partially observed, and the shortage of food was one of the Egyptian Government's major anxieties.

Towards the end of 1941 the prestige and authority of Hussein Sirry's Cabinet had greatly declined. The Wafd party, who were not represented in the Government, were busy proclaiming that the British had infringed the Anglo-Egyptian Treaty and were destroying the independence and economy of the country. Late in December the Minister of Finance was forced to resign on charges of corruption and nepotism: this produced a bitter squabble between the Liberals and Saadists as to which party should provide his successor. The Wafd now began to make the Egyptian Prime Minister the target of their attacks rather than the British, and, as he was also being subjected to a Palace offensive directed by Aly Maher Pasha, his position went from bad to worse. On 1st February, after a dispute with the King on a technicality, he was forced to resign. It was quite clear to the British Ambassador that the only acceptable solution would be the return of the Wafdists to power. Strong pressure was put upon the King to agree. Finally he did so, and Nahas Pasha became Prime Minister. He at once adopted an attitude of co-operation with Great Britain, and maintained it loyally and courageously through the dark days that followed. His openly declared sympathy with the British cause put a stop to most of the overt anti-British agitation. A general election took place in March and was boycotted by the opposition, leaving the Wafd in undisputed power.

The Tripartite Pact of 27th September 1940 between Germany, Italy and Japan was ostensibly a defensive treaty by which the parties agreed to give support if any of them should be attacked by a Power not at present engaged in the war in Europe or in China. It was directed primarily against America, but also against possible British activities in the Far East. It did not oblige Japan or Italy to declare war on Russia when Germany attacked her.

When the German plans for '*Barbarossa*' were almost complete Hitler decided to encourage the Japanese to act in the Far East in such a way as to focus American interest on the Pacific and tie down strong British forces. It was expected that favourable conditions would be created by '*Barbarossa*', but the Japanese were not to be told about it.

For their part the Japanese were not anxious to be involved in war with the United States—certainly not until they had reached some form of agreement with Russia. The Japanese Foreign Minister, Matsuoka, visited Moscow and Berlin in the spring of 1941 and Ribbentrop did all he could, short of disclosing the German intentions, to prevent the Japanese reaching a private agreement with Moscow. In this he failed, for on 13th April Matsuoka concluded a Pact of Neutrality, thus securing the Japanese rear without German assistance.

No sooner had the Germans attacked Russia than Hitler began to press Japan to declare war on Russia also. The Japanese Government however decided to adhere to its programme of gradual expansion and military preparation, as it had not given up all hope of reaching a peaceful settlement with America. The stages in the deterioration of the situation in the Pacific area are described in another volume of these histories.[1] It is enough here to mention that the Japanese showed no intention of attacking Russia; on the contrary, their attention was being focused increasingly on the Pacific and South China Sea.

The terms of the Tripartite Pact did not oblige Germany or Italy to support Japan if she were the aggressor. Accordingly, while negotiations were still going on in Washington, the Japanese tried to find out what help they might expect if, after all, America entered the war. The Far East and Middle East were too widely separated to allow of direct co-operation, and the Japanese suggested that the best form of mutual support would be to undertake not to make a separate armistice or peace. To this Ribbentrop replied that this would be taken for granted in Berlin.

On 3rd December the Japanese Ambassadors in Berlin and Rome informed the two Governments that the negotiations in Washington had broken down, and requested that Germany and Italy should undertake to declare war on the United States. To this they received cautious replies.

[1] S. Woodburn Kirby: *The War against Japan*, Volume I.

The early Japanese successes came at a time when the fortunes of the Axis powers had taken a turn for the worse. Rommel had been driven out of Cyrenaica, and the Russians had recaptured Rostov. Farther north, fighting was halted by the unexpectedly early onslaught of cold weather; the advance on Moscow came to a standstill, and the final offensive, planned for early December, never took place. The Russians, who were better able to cope with the winter conditions, now exerted their full strength and the Germans were soon retreating at several points. Moscow was saved and the self-confidence of the German Army badly shaken. Differences of opinion in the High Command, which had been simmering for some time, came to a head on 19th December with the dismissal of Field-Marshal von Brauchitsch, and Hitler assumed the additional responsibility of commanding the Army.

Against this darkening background it is not surprising that the attack on Pearl Harbour was hailed with admiration and delight. On 14th December *OKW* issued a memorandum reviewing the whole situation in the light of the entry of Japan and the United States into the war. Emphasis was laid on the disruptive effect that Japan's action would have on Allied planning. Japanese naval strength and the attacks by land on British and American bases would probably force a change of policy. Would the Allies concentrate first upon defeating Germany and Italy, and abandon for the time being the objectives under Japanese attack? Or would they deplete their forces in the Atlantic and Mediterranean and concentrate upon defeating Japan? Or would they try to hold everywhere and wait for American armaments production to get into its stride?

To these questions the memorandum could find no answer; it therefore examined at length the most unfavourable course for the Axis, namely the first, and came to the conclusion that neither side could contemplate a decisive attack for at least a year. The first consideration for the Germans must be to bring the Russian campaign to a successful conclusion. The Allied aim would probably be to set up assembly-bases in West Africa and Morocco, in the Middle East, and in the United Kingdom, with the idea of subsequently operating in areas within reach of these bases. These areas could not be divined yet, and might be anywhere from the Caucasus to Norway. However, the assembly of forces would take so long and would require so much shipping that wherever the Allies intended to use them their preparations would become known to the Germans in time for effective counter-measures to be taken. This comforting conclusion earned the marginal comment on one copy 'It is to be hoped so'.

To sum up: the entry of Japan into the war found the British in the Middle East in firm possession of their vital bases, in no immediate danger of being attacked from the north, and well on the way to regaining the whole of Cyrenaica; indeed, they had high hopes of pressing on as far as Tripoli. During the next few weeks many Army and Air Force units were removed from the Middle East to go to India or the Far East, and others, on the way out, were diverted there; and a number of ships of the Royal Australian and Royal Indian Navies were sent back to their home waters. Yet the Commanders-in-Chief were satisfied that none of these transfers would affect 'Crusader', nor were they likely to affect 'Acrobat'. Far more serious were the naval losses that had been sustained in December which left the Mediterranean Fleet without a battleship or carrier, and reduced Force H to one battleship and one small carrier.

This was the situation when history repeated itself and General Rommel regained the initiative on land.

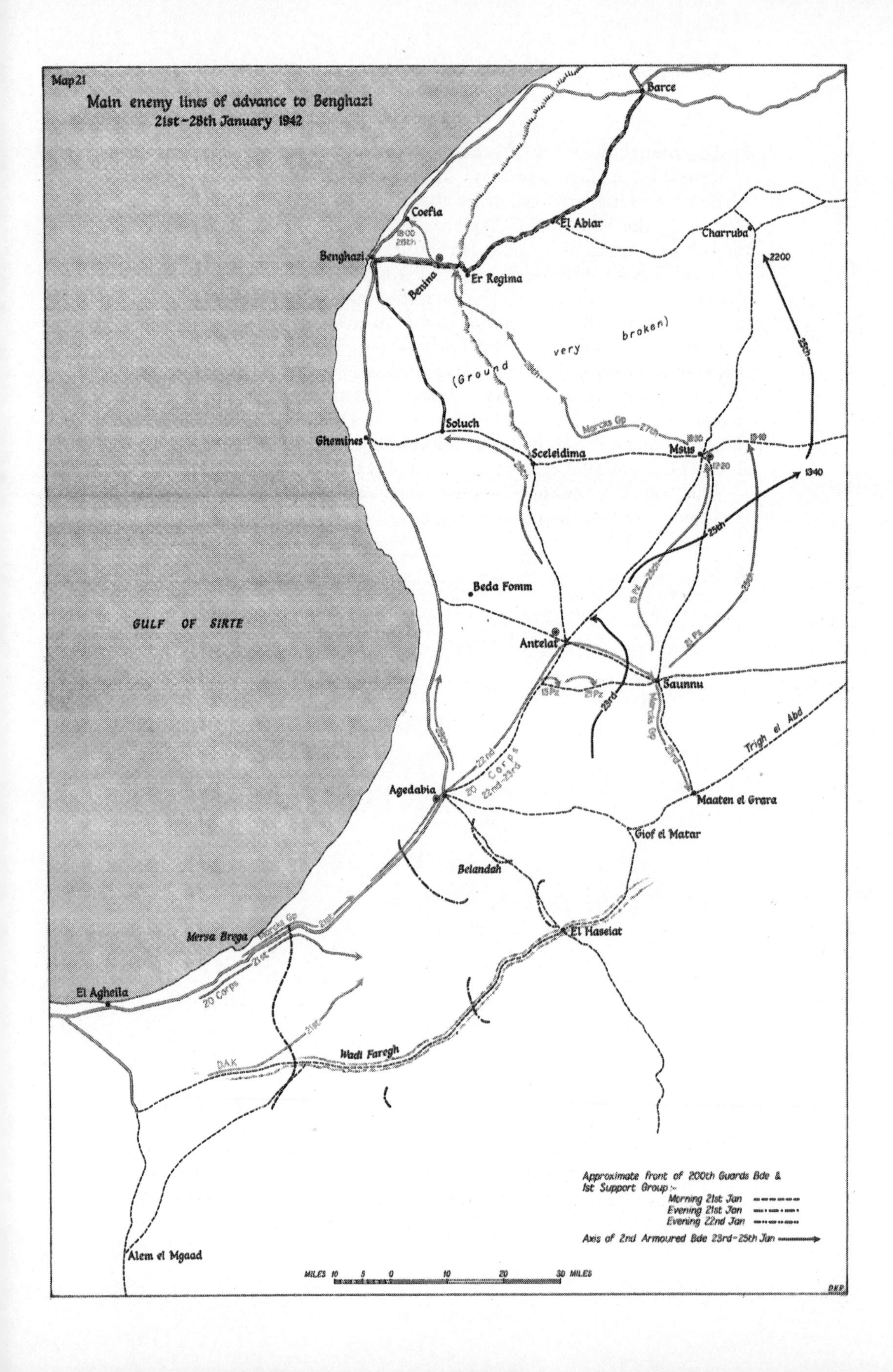
Map 21
Main enemy lines of advance to Benghazi
21st–28th January 1942
Barce
Coefia
El Abiar
Charruba
Benghazi
Benina
Er Regima
2200
(Ground very broken)
Soluch
Ghemines
Sceleidima
Msus
Marcks Gp
27th
1340
25th
Beda Fomm
GULF OF SIRTE
Antelat
Saunnu
15 Pz
21 Pz
23rd
Trigh el Abd
20 Corps
22nd–23rd
Agedabia
Maaten el Grara
Giof el Matar
Belandah
El Haseiat
Mersa Brega
El Agheila
Wadi Faregh
D.A.K.
Approximate front of 200th Guards Bde &
Ist Support Group:–
Morning 21st Jan
Evening 21st Jan
Evening 22nd Jan
Axis of 2nd Armoured Bde 23rd–25th Jan
Alem el Mgaad
MILES 10 5 0 10 20 30 MILES
DKP

CHAPTER VI

RETREAT TO GAZALA

See Maps 2 and 21

THE middle of January 1942 found the British and Axis forces in loose contact in the difficult country near the bend of the Gulf of Sirte. General Auchinleck had always intended to chase the retreating enemy into Tripolitania, and had caused plans to be made for doing so. By the end of December, however, it was evident that the British could not keep up the momentum of their advance even against slight opposition; moreover, the unsuccessful tank actions of 28th and 30th December showed that the German armour, although weak in numbers, was still full of fight. Clearly, if the British were to advance any farther they would first have to build up an adequate force and, equally important, accumulate the supplies to support it. General Godwin-Austen was given these tasks, and used as a basis a plan for attacking the enemy frontally with one infantry brigade while the greater part of an armoured division passed round the desert flank; simultaneously another infantry brigade was to land from the sea in the enemy's rear.

As usual, administrative problems were dominant. It has already been seen how the failure to defeat the enemy quickly in November led to great difficulties in nourishing the battle, and these difficulties grew more serious as the front moved westward. By the first week in January the position was briefly as follows. To supply the 13th Corps and its attached troops, and to provide the Royal Air Force with those commodities and services for which the Army was responsible, required some 1,400 tons a day. The average daily amounts received at Tobruk by sea and by lorry convoys from the railhead at Misheifa together came to 1,150 tons. Far from there being any surplus for building up reserve stocks, without which there could be no advance, there was thus a shortfall of some 250 tons on daily needs alone. An obvious remedy was to increase the port capacity at Tobruk, stock Derna wholly by sea, and restore Benghazi to working order. The transport at present locked up in convoys from Misheifa could then be used to deliver from these ports.

When Benghazi was first captured in February 1941 little use could be made of the port, mainly on account of its inadequate air defences. The experiences of 1942 were to be depressingly similar, though for different reasons. This time the harbour, which was strewn with wrecks, had been devastated, and there were gaps in the wall through which the sea could break. (*See Photo* 8). As early as 25th December 1941—the day after the last enemy troops left—Axis aircraft began to lay magnetic mines. The Naval port party was quickly at work, and four minesweepers arrived on the 29th, followed a week later by Army Dock and Port Operating Companies. The first convoy of three merchant ships arrived on 7th January, followed by the administrative units needed to staff the Advanced Base. The almost incessant westerly gales, the lack of tugs, and the fact that a wreck still prevented deep-draught ships passing the entrance, made the rate of discharge very uncertain.

The fact is that the administrative resources of the 8th Army were now stretched to the limit. The troops were still living 'hard', and it was possible to improve only slightly the monotonous battle-ration which they had been eating for seven weeks. The over-riding need for certain commodities, especially petrol and lubricants, often shut out such desirable things as bacon, oatmeal, cigarettes and rum. No reserve stocks could be built up, the sea routes were precarious, and the consumption and waste of petrol by transport on the long desert journeys were appalling. Taking one thing with another, there can have been little hope of beginning offensive operations before the end of February. As it turned out, this was not soon enough.

The intention to relieve the 7th Armoured Division by the 1st Armoured Division has already been mentioned, and it has been related how the 22nd Armoured Brigade replaced the 4th before the start of the move across the desert from Mechili. The 1st Armoured Division had had an unlucky year. It had had a short experience of fighting in France in 1940, was reorganized after Dunkirk, and by February 1941 contained, with a few exceptions, the units which it later took to the Middle East. By April 1941 it possessed a strange assortment of tanks, from which almost all the latest cruisers were then withdrawn in order to make up the 'Tiger' convoy for the Middle East. By early July good progress was being made with re-equipping the Division, when the Chiefs of Staff decided once more to remove the latest cruisers for modification preparatory to sending them to the Middle East. Shortly afterwards the further decision was taken to send the 22nd Armoured Brigade, which accordingly sailed in August, made up with most of the available Crusader tanks. The rest of the Division sailed during the second half of September, before it could be completely equipped with modern cruisers. The effect of all these changes upon training was of course deplorable.

The exploits of the 22nd Armoured Brigade in 'Crusader' are already familiar. The main body of the Division began to arrive in Egypt during the second half of November. During December it moved forward, but not as a whole. It came under the 13th Corps on 3rd

January 1942, and Major-General Messervy took temporary command in place of Major-General Lumsden, who had been wounded in an air attack, and Major-General Tuker took over command of the 4th Indian Division from General Messervy. Just previously to this the 22nd Armoured Brigade had suffered the reverses near Agedabia which have already been described, and had to be withdrawn to Tobruk to refit. Thus it befell that, as in April 1941, the British armoured division on guard at the gateway to Cyrenaica had had very little training as a division and lacked half its armour. Its one armoured brigade—the 2nd—not only had no petrol with which to continue its training but suffered from another handicap. It had been thought in December that a first need would be for a strong armoured brigade group well forward. The 2nd Armoured Brigade had therefore been given 1st Battalion The Rifle Brigade, 11th (H.A.C.) Regiment R.H.A. and 76th Anti-Tank Regiment R.A., from the 1st Support Group. These units had trained with the Brigade on the long march up from Matruh, but now, in consequence of the decision that the 1st Support Group should relieve the 7th, they reverted to the 1st Support Group and were replaced by units new to the 2nd Armoured Brigade and its ways.

General Auchinleck and his senior Commanders were agreed, however, that it would be almost impossible for the enemy to take the offensive for a long time; the evidence concerning the German and Italian losses, their lack of reinforcements, and their supply difficulties, all pointed to this conclusion. But if the unexpected should happen, and if the enemy could not be immediately stopped, it was intended that the 13th Corps should fight on the line Agedabia-El Haseiat. General Messervy's tasks were accordingly, first, to harass the enemy with mobile columns while the British offensive was being prepared, and second, to be ready for a defensive battle. To the latter end he had delaying positions reconnoitred, but his suggestion that the 4th Indian Division should move forward to Agedabia and the 2nd Armoured Brigade to Giof el Matar was not agreed to, because the supplying of so many troops so far forward would have seriously delayed the preparations for the intended offensive. This was the reason given at the time, but the fact is that the administrative machine could not have maintained these additional troops so far forward. Consequently the 4th Indian Division continued to have one infantry brigade group at Benghazi and one at Barce. (The third was refitting at Tobruk). The only troops within a hundred miles of the enemy were those of the incomplete 1st Armoured Division, the 22nd (now re-numbered 200th) Guards Brigade, and part of Oasis Force, which was being broken up.

On the thirty miles of front from Mersa Brega to the Wadi Faregh were the 200th Guards Brigade (Brigadier J. C. O. Marriott) on the right,[1] and the 1st Support Group (Brigadier C. M. Vallentin) on the left.[2] Each of these formations was divided into small columns of infantry and artillery for carrying out the division's primary role of harassing the enemy. As the Guards Brigade had only enough artillery for four columns, which required in all the infantry of one battalion, the second battalion was stationed back at Agedabia. There was no third battalion in this brigade. On the left, the 1st Support Group was of comparable strength but was new to its surroundings, having only relieved the 7th Support Group on 19th January. It had some appallingly hummocky ground to work over, which had tried the skill of the most experienced desert drivers; General Messervy described it as the only large area he knew over which tracked vehicles were faster than wheeled. To make matters worse for the 1st Support Group a number of their vehicles turned out to be not fully desertworthy and there was much trouble with burst tyres and lack of spare parts. Even the three armoured car regiments that had been patrolling on that front had had so many vehicles damaged that all except one squadron had been withdrawn to refit.

Under command of the Support Group was a composite squadron of twenty-four Stuart tanks, apart from which there were no tanks forward of Antelat, where the 2nd Armoured Brigade Group (Brigadier R. Briggs) was assembled to carry out some desert training.[3] The three regiments of this Brigade had each about twenty-six cruiser tanks and eighteen Stuarts, having lost in all twenty cruisers from mechanical breakdown during the move forward from Egypt.[4]

Air Vice-Marshal Coningham's chief concern was to prepare to support the advance into Tripolitania. His estimate of the squadrons required for the purpose was ten single-engine and one twin-engine fighter, four day-bomber and two tactical reconnaissance squadrons, and, in addition, various other reconnaissance aircraft and air transports, together with the radar, maintenance, administrative and

---

[1] 200th Guards Brigade Group: 3rd Battalion Coldstream Guards; 2nd Battalion Scots Guards; B Squadron 11th Hussars; 1st and 51st Field Regiments R.A. (each of two batteries); 27/28th Medium Battery R.A.; C and D Batteries 73rd Anti-Tank Regiment R.A.; 6th Battery 2nd Anti-Tank Regiment S.A.A.; 6th and 197th Light Anti-Aircraft Batteries R.A.; 1st Field Squadron R.E.

[2] 1st Support Group: Composite Squadron 3rd and 4th County of London Yeomanry; 11th (H.A.C.) Regiment R.H.A.; 20th Battery 7th Field Regiment S.A.A.; 76th Anti-Tank Regiment R.A.; 260th Battery 65th Anti-Tank Regiment R.A.; 43rd and 44th Light Anti-Aircraft Batteries R.A.; Detachment 7th Field Squadron R.E.; 2nd Battalion The King's Royal Rifle Corps; 1st Battalion The Rifle Brigade.

[3] 2nd Armoured Brigade Group: The Queen's Bays; 9th Queen's Royal Lancers; 10th Royal Hussars; 2nd Regiment R.H.A.; 8th Field Regiment R.A. (two batteries); 7th Field Regiment S.A.A. (less 20th Battery); 102nd (N.H.) Anti-Tank Regiment R.H.A.; 2nd Anti-Tank Regiment S.A.A. (less 6th Battery); Detachment 7th Field Squadron R.E.; 9th Battalion The Rifle Brigade.

[4] The tanks were brought by rail to Matruh, and thereafter moved forward on their own tracks, a distance to Antelat of some 450 miles.

armoured car units for essential ground duties. To free his headquarters of the task of administering those squadrons and units that would remain in Cyrenaica, No. 211 Group, hitherto a nucleus headquarters, was brought in and assumed the appropriate local responsibilities. By 20th January the main units of the Desert Air Force were disposed as follows. Nine single-engine fighter squadrons were at Antelat, and four were divided between Benina, Derna, El Adem and Tobruk protecting the ports and shipping. The Beaufighters were at Gerawla. The day-bomber force consisted of only two squadrons at Gambut and Bu Amud, instead of the requisite four, one having been withdrawn for re-equipping and one transferred to Syria. The forward radar units were at Benghazi, Derna and Tobruk, while Air Vice-Marshal Coningham's headquarters, with Air Commodore G. R. Beamish now as Senior Air Staff Officer, were at Tmimi.

It was indeed true that the enemy had reached his selected defensive position at Mersa Brega considerably exhausted, and the deduction that he was in no fit state to start an offensive was a fair one. On 5th January, however, a convoy reached Tripoli bringing, among other badly needed items, 54 tanks, their crews, and a consignment of fuel. By 10th January General Rommel felt sure that the British were awaiting reinforcements and that there was hope of a valuable breathing space. But at a staff conference held on 12th January his senior intelligence officer, Major F. W. von Mellenthin, predicted that for the next fortnight the Axis forces would be slightly stronger than the British immediately opposed to them. Thereafter the British would grow stronger: even now, if they were to concentrate their forces, they should be able to bite off a part of the Axis position. He therefore thought it dangerous to continue on the defensive. Colonel Westphal, the head of the Operations Section, then suggested that their dispersion and local weakness made the British susceptible to a spoiling attack in the Agedabia area—not that any success could be exploited, owing to the scarcity of German troops and supplies. General Rommel did not jump at the idea, but finally agreed. It was to be a dead secret and the preparations were to be explained, plausibly enough, as measures to meet an imminent British attack.[1]

On 14th January the equipment recently unloaded at Tripoli began to reach the front. The next day wireless messages were intercepted which suggested that the British were in administrative difficulties and not completely ready for action. On the 17th more equipment

[1] On 22nd January General Rommel's command was renamed '*Panzerarmee Afrika*'. It consisted of the following divisions, all greatly below strength and short of much of their equipment. *D.A.K.*: 15th Panzer, 21st Panzer. 90th Light. 10th Corps: Bologna, Brescia. 20th Corps: Ariete (armoured), Trieste (motorized). 21st Corps: Pavia, Trento, Sabratha. Total strength, about 12,500 Germans and 25,000 Italians.

arrived from Tripoli, and the German strength in tanks rose to 84 and the Italian to 89. On the 18th General Rommel issued his orders for an attack on the 21st. The *D.A.K.* would advance on the south, with its right on the Wadi Faregh; the (Italian) 20th Corps in the centre; and a special Group under Colonel Marcks on the left, along and to the north of the coastal road.[1] The Marcks Group would later be directed either towards Agedabia or to the south-east, according to how things went. A simple and modest plan.

The comparative quiet of the past few weeks had enabled the enemy to regain some of his strength in the air. By the third week of January there were 515 German and Italian aircraft in Tripolitania, of which 300 were serviceable. On the British side the Desert Air Force was still very much stretched and was suffering from many shortages; of its 445 aircraft about 280 were immediately available for operations. The weather, which had distinctly favoured the British on the eve of 'Crusader', now helped the enemy, whose preliminary movements were obscured by sand-storms. On the night 20th/21st there were also heavy squalls of rain, which might be thought to have affected both sides alike but for the fact that the worst conditions of all were at Antelat, where the airfield was turned into what an eyewitness described as 'a chocolate blancmange'. To avoid the risk of all the aircraft being caught on the ground, four squadrons of fighters were with great difficulty flown off early on 21st January to Msus and one squadron to Gazala. At these airfields the conditions were much better, but a great deal of range was thereby sacrificed. This explains the German claim that the British 'scarcely put in an appearance' in the air on that day. Nevertheless, an aircraft of No. 208 Squadron did report large concentrations of vehicles around Mersa Brega and some distance inland.

The enemy's advance began soon after 8 a.m. on 21st January. The weak British columns fell back by their pre-arranged routes, inflicting as much damage as they could. On the left the Support Group was soon in trouble on account of the bad going, the frequent dive-bombing, and general inexperience of desert tactics. During the day sixteen field guns were lost, some from enemy action and some because the tractors became ditched in the soft sand; many other vehicles were lost in the same way. The enemy had his difficulties too, and even the veteran 15th Panzer Division, advancing just north of the Wadi Faregh, became partially stuck in the dunes. By nightfall the whole enemy's front had advanced roughly ten or twelve miles, and the

---

[1] The Marcks Group consisted of two lorried infantry battalions drawn from 21st Panzer and 90th Light Divisions, with a mixture of German and Italian artillery.

Germans recorded that the British Guards Brigade and Support Group had, by withdrawing, escaped destruction.

To General Messervy it was evident that the enemy had probed forward on a wide front, but the information at the end of the day suggested that the chief danger would be where the Guards Brigade and the Support Group joined. He therefore ordered the former to remain south of Agedabia and the latter to prolong the left flank to near El Haseiat; the 2nd Armoured Brigade (Brigadier R. Briggs) was to advance to Giof el Matar and be ready to attack the enemy's flank if he broke through.

But General Rommel had no particular designs on the British centre, and he ordered the advance to continue as far as Agedabia on 22nd January. Starting very early the Marcks Group set off along the main road, was delayed but not stopped by the guns of the Guards Brigade's columns, and reached Agedabia by 11 a.m. Rommel at once saw his chance. He met General Crüwell and announced his plan, which was to spread a net from Agedabia to Antelat and on to Saunnu. The 2nd Machine-Gun Battalion would make for Antelat, the Marcks Group for Saunnu, and the *D.A.K.* and 20th Corps, in that order, would deploy between the Marcks Group and Agedabia. All would then turn south-east against the trapped British and drive them away from their lines of supply. The day was to be spent in getting into position.

Realizing that some of the enemy were slipping past his right flank, General Messervy ordered the Guards Brigade to block the main road. But Brigadier Marriott had sent the 2nd Scots Guards back towards Antelat because they had no supporting arms, and his columns were outpaced. The enemy had therefore no great difficulty in reaching his positions on 'the net'. The destination of the 2nd Armoured Brigade was changed from Giof el Matar to a point about twelve miles north of it, where it arrived by the evening.[1] By then the 200th Guards Brigade (less the 2nd Scots Guards) and the 1st Support Group were roughly on the line Agedabia-El Haseiat.

General Godwin-Austen, whose advanced headquarters had moved from Antelat to Msus, was anxious lest the enemy should do just what they were in fact doing. Realizing the danger to the supplies at Msus, on which the Armoured Division depended, he ordered General Messervy to block the tracks leading to Msus from Agedabia and Saunnu. Suspecting also an approaching threat to the whole of Western Cyrenaica he told the 4th Indian Division to hold up any enemy on the coast road and, as a precaution, to be prepared to cover an evacuation of Benghazi. The 7th Indian Infantry Brigade accordingly moved out about twelve miles south of Benghazi.

[1] A detachment of 2nd Regiment R.H.A., 102nd (N.H.) Anti-Tank Regiment R.H.A., and 9th Rifle Brigade was left with orders to block the Antelat-Agedabia track. Owing to lack of petrol it could not even reach Antelat.

As on the previous day the German and Italian Air Forces were very active, and flew nearly 500 sorties in the two days. Antelat airfield was still in a shocking state, and on the morning of the 22nd the remaining fighters began to fly off to Msus. At about 1 p.m. the danger to the airfield caused 13th Corps to tell the Officer Commanding No. 262 Wing to leave Antelat. It was as well that most of the fighters had already gone, for each aircraft had to be manhandled to a short narrow strip of barely serviceable ground. The airfield came under shell-fire as the last aircraft took off, and the remaining maintenance parties were rescued by Nos. 1 and 2 Armoured Car Companies, R.A.F. Blenheims and long-range Hurricanes now began to take a hand in attacking columns reported by aircraft on tactical reconnaissance, and that night some of the Wellingtons from Sidi Barrani set out to try to hinder enemy reinforcements which might be coming from Tripolitania.

During the afternoon of the 22nd General Ritchie returned from a visit to Cairo, where he had been working on the coming advance into Tripolitania. In his view Rommel was probably trying to gain elbow-room east of the El Agheila defile, meaning to make a counter-offensive when he was strong enough. Before then the Axis could maintain nothing more than strong reconnaissance forces east of Agedabia and El Haseiat. Ritchie was therefore undismayed. As a first step he intended to give the 4th Indian Division enough transport to enable it to act within supporting distance of the Armoured Division. He believed that the enemy was holding back most of his tanks well to the south-west of Agedabia, and was confident that there would be a 'God-sent opportunity to hit him really hard when he puts out his neck as it seems possible that he may be already doing'.

This was a robust reading of the situation, but not an accurate one. If any neck had been stuck out it was a British neck, which the enemy was now menacing with strong forces. In spite of the object-lesson provided by the reverse which had befallen General Wavell's army the year before, the British dispositions had again been such as to invite attack without possessing the necessary strength to meet it. Many people wondered why the British High Command had not turned the earlier experiences to better account.

On the strategic level powerful interests were at work. Events in Russia and the Far East, and the possibility of an Allied landing in French Morocco, all made it very desirable to exploit 'Crusader' by advancing into Tripolitania as soon as possible—operation 'Acrobat'. But a pause for building up the 8th Army's resources was clearly essential, and General Auchinleck had to decide which of two courses would be the quicker: to maintain active contact with the enemy about El Agheila and accept the risk of the British light forces in that area being driven back, or, alternatively, to yield some 150 miles of desert and develop his strength in the neighbourhood of, say, Msus and Benghazi—this course being simply a withdrawal '*pour mieux sauter*'. General Auchinleck judged, very nearly rightly, that Rommel was unlikely for some time to be able to mount an offensive in strength after the hammering he had received during 'Crusader', and decided that the policy must be to keep up such pressure as was possible rather than break away altogether. The risk of a reconnaissance in force by the enemy must be accepted. General Ritchie, knowing his Commander-in-Chief's wishes, was not the man to act otherwise than with energy and enthusiasm in giving effect to them, but as Dr. Cruttwell has so happily put it in commenting on the Mesopotamian Campaign of 1915 'too often the capacity to advance is identified with the desirability of advancing.'[1] As has been seen the capacity of the 8th Army to advance was over-estimated; it could barely maintain itself where it was. Had not the enemy judged the situation very shrewdly in the middle of January, and after some hesitation taken the right action, the British bluff—for that is what it was—might have succeeded. As it happened, the British High Command took a chance which did not come off.

The basic idea of each side on 23rd January was simple enough: the British wanted to draw back the 1st Armoured Division and the enemy wanted to catch as much of it as possible in their net. The result was a number of separate encounters during the day, spread over a wide area.

At 4.45 a.m. General Godwin-Austen signalled to General Messervy that it was vital for him to be able to prevent the enemy advancing on Msus. The Germans were known to have reached not only Antelat but also Saunnu, where they would be a menace to the Armoured Division's tail. Messervy ordered Brigadier Briggs to send a regiment to clear up Saunnu—the Bays were sent—and with the rest of his brigade to get astride the Msus track to the north-east of Antelat. The Support Group and the Guards Brigade (less the 2nd Scots Guards, who were out of touch) were to join up north-east of Antelat by moving towards Saunnu or even farther east if necessary.

The two Panzer Divisions, according to their own reports, seem to have been under the impression that their main task was to block the retreating British, who, with their main line of supply cut, would naturally be expected to try to fight their way out. The information up to dark on the night before suggested that some of the British might try to break away along the Trigh El Abd, and this is probably why the Marcks Group was sent off early on the 23rd to Maaten el Grara. It left Saunnu at 5 a.m., with the result that the Bays arrived to find

[1] C. R. M. F. Cruttwell: *A History of the Great War 1914-18* (Oxford, 1934) p. 341.

the place clear. General Rommel intended the 21st Panzer Division to take the place of the Marcks Group at Saunnu, but there was a mistake in the transmission of the order and the Division did not move.

Ground haze hampered the air forces of both sides during the early part of the morning. A steady stream of enemy traffic was seen, however, moving along the coast road and between Agedabia and Antelat, and was attacked by the long-range Hurricanes of No. 33 Squadron. No Blenheims were available, as they were wanted for use against an Italian convoy at sea. Over the battle area the fighters from Msus worked hard to regain their ascendancy, and on this day the air attacks on the British troops began to wane. The need for information about the enemy's movements was so great that the practice now began of using some of the fighter squadrons to get it.

Realizing that the enemy was present in strength between Agedabia and Antelat, General Messervy ordered the 2nd Armoured Brigade to protect the western flank of the Division as it withdrew to the north of Antelat. At about 10 a.m. the leading regiment, the 9th Lancers, ran into the 21st Panzer Division and was ordered by Brigadier Briggs to pin the enemy while the 10th Hussars took the lead. This was done, and at about noon the 10th Hussars struck more enemy (also almost certainly of the 21st Panzer Division) and went into action. The 21st Panzer Division's call for help was received by the much stronger 15th Panzer Division, which lay just to the west. This Division had been ordered to reconnoitre towards Giof el Matar, and possibly for this reason felt unable to respond without the permission of *D.A.K.*, which it did not succeed in getting. (Perhaps the 21st Panzer Division had not got over its old habit of sending alarmist reports.)

Brigadier Briggs had now nothing in hand, and turned to join the Bays who had been recalled from Saunnu. He ordered the other two regiments to break away and follow, but the 10th Hussars were too closely engaged, and the 9th Lancers could not comply at once without uncovering the move northwards of Divisional Headquarters and various other units which all needed protection. This protection the two regiments gave.

Meanwhile General Rommel had set the two Panzer Divisions in motion, with the 21st directed on Saunnu. The 1st Support Group, moving north, collided with the 15th Panzer Division and was chased eastwards until nearly dusk. There was much confusion, but Brigadier Vallentin at length got his force in hand again a few miles south of Saunnu. The 9th Lancers reached Saunnu at about 5 p.m., almost at the same moment as the 21st Panzer Division. There was an immediate clash, and the 21st Field Battery, South African Artillery, in action at point blank range, was overrun, but not before it had knocked out several tanks. The 10th Hussars, who had had great difficulty in disengaging, were also caught up in the *D.A.K.'s* drive and their supporting artillery suffered heavily in fighting their guns to the last. In each of these actions the Artillery had upheld its best traditions.[1] Both sides leaguered on the field.[2]

After joining with the Bays the Headquarters of the 2nd Armoured Brigade had managed to reach the Msus track some seven miles from Antelat, but the whole brigade, much reduced in strength, was not reunited in this area until next morning. The Support Group also joined up, as did the 200th Guards Brigade which had been lucky enough to reach the north-east of Saunnu with no other incident than a brush with part of 15th Panzer Division.

During the day the 11th Indian Infantry Brigade left Tobruk for Barce. General Tuker intended this brigade to take over the close defence of Benghazi from 7th Indian Infantry Brigade, which would then move south to operate on the right flank of the Armoured Division. General Ritchie, who had visited 13th Corps during the morning, was still full of confidence and informed the Commander-in-Chief that the situation was well in hand and that he intended to defeat the isolated enemy columns which he felt were all that the enemy could maintain so far forward. His purpose was still to turn to the offensive on a big scale.

Meanwhile General Rommel was having troubles of a different nature. General Bastico had become alarmed because the limited spoiling attack, to which he had agreed, was turning into a full-blown offensive of which he strongly disapproved. He signalled his fears to *Comando Supremo*, and asked that General Rommel should be made to take a more realistic view. This brought Cavallero to Rommel's headquarters on 23rd January, accompanied by Field-Marshal Kesselring and bringing a directive from Mussolini. In this it was stated that there was no immediate prospect of sending supplies and reinforcements to Africa in the face of the present British naval and air opposition. A defensive line should be held from Mersa Brega to Marada, in advance of which the mobile troops might carry out strictly limited offensives. Appealed to by Cavallero to call off the present operations, Rommel replied that he meant to attack as long as he could, and that only Hitler could stop him because most of the fighting would be done

[1] Supporting the 10th Hussars was the 19th Field Battery, South African Artillery, and the guns of one of the columns of the 1st Support Group—a detachment of 11th (H.A.C.) Regiment, Royal Horse Artillery, and the 237th Anti-Tank Battery, Royal Artillery.

[2] At the end of 23rd January the 9th Lancers had 28 tanks and the 10th Hussars 8 in the Saunnu area. On this day the 21st Panzer Division recorded the loss of 10 of its 20 tanks and claims to have knocked out 23 British tanks and 10 guns. 15th Panzer Division's losses on this day are not ascertainable, but between 21st and 23rd January, both dates inclusive, their effective strength fell from 80 tanks to 61. They are known to have had a number of tanks in reserve, so their losses may well have been more than 19 in the three days.

by Germans. Rommel noted in his diary that after Kesselring had made some attempt to back up Cavallero the latter 'went off growling'.

The 24th January was something of an anti-climax. It seems that Rommel was imperfectly informed of the encounters of the previous day, and still had the idea of rounding up all the British in the area Saunnu-Maaten el Grara-Agedabia. The general move south-eastwards was therefore resumed, and much time and petrol was wasted before the 'pursuit' was called off, and the *D.A.K.* was ordered to get ready to move north next day.

The events of 23rd January had bred doubts in General Godwin-Austen's mind which he expressed in a signal to General Ritchie early on the 24th. He felt that no great damage had been done to the enemy, whose striking power we had underestimated; that an advance on the coast road could not be seriously resisted; and that the Armoured Division could not defend the Msus track and also protect the open eastern flank. He therefore asked for discretion to order a general withdrawal towards Mechili. To this Ritchie quickly replied that although the news was disquieting the enemy must be near his limit, and there might yet be a chance of attacking him. For this it was necessary to collect forces at Msus and south of Benghazi, because the enemy would not be strong enough to deal with a double threat. Therefore the 13th Corps must stand at Msus and cover Benghazi, giving ground for tactical reasons only. But he authorized Godwin-Austen to withdraw if necessary, and as a precaution he was to begin to clear administrative units from Benghazi and Msus and to prepare demolition plans. Godwin-Austen replied that he thought there was a grave danger of the 1st Armoured Division being too weak to hold the desert flank. He had ordered General Messervy to impose as much delay as possible without jeopardizing his force, but he was most anxious that a series of local withdrawals should not entangle him in a running fight, and he had given Messervy permission to withdraw to Mechili if in danger. That evening General Ritchie reported to the Commander-in-Chief the gist of the day's exchange of views, and pointed out that the preparations for withdrawal were an insurance policy. For the same reason he had ordered General Norrie to reconnoitre delaying positions in the area Gazala-Tobruk.

Air Vice-Marshal Coningham's reaction to these conflicting views was to prepare for the worst case, and to give orders for the withdrawal of all maintenance and heavy ground units, including radar. The main force of fighters would be kept fully mobile for rearguard action, moving first to Mechili and then, if necessary, successively to Gazala and Gambut. Two fighter squadrons would remain for the present at Benghazi, and would fall back on Martuba to join two other squadrons; all four would ultimately move to El Adem. The day-bombers would remain temporarily in the Tobruk area. All captured air force material would be destroyed, and arrangements would be made to destroy any fuel and unserviceable transport that could not be towed away.

The move of the fighters from Msus to Mechili meant that only limited action was possible on the 24th, but the enemy's activity was also much less. Only one formation was encountered, of which three Ju. 87s were destroyed without loss. Meanwhile Beaufighters of No. 272 Squadron struck at road transport in the neighbourhood of Nofilia, now deep in enemy territory. That evening the Air Officer Commanding-in-Chief, influenced no doubt by the feeling of frustration in Cairo, signalled that he was sending forward twelve cannon-fighter Blenheims with aircrews and maintenance parties to 'help stop this nonsense'.

On 25th January the whole of the *D.A.K.* struck northwards and drove the 1st Armoured Division towards Charruba where some supplies had been collected. The diary of 15th Panzer Division remarks that its armoured regiment 'broke into the enemy at a tearing speed and threw him into complete confusion'. Rommel stopped the chase at Msus because his fuel was running out, but he felt that he had hit the British hard enough to prevent them from resuming the offensive. The spoiling attack had in fact succeeded. A pause was essential, and gave him time to consider what to do next.

The events of the 25th had seemed to confirm General Godwin-Austen's views. That evening he used his discretionary powers and ordered the 4th Indian Division to withdraw from Benghazi, which was then cleared of all seaworthy ships, and the 1st Armoured Division to move to Mechili. But during the afternoon the Commander-in-Chief and Air Marshal Tedder had come forward to Ritchie's headquarters and together they came to the conclusion that the German thrust to Msus must have been the exploitation of an unexpected success, and that there was still time to repel it. At 8.30 p.m. General Ritchie gave orders which put a brake on 13th Corps' withdrawal, and just before midnight he cancelled it altogether, on the ground that the enemy must be in serious difficulties over his maintenance. The 4th Indian Division was to send columns against his lines of communication north-east of Agedabia; the 1st Armoured Division was to oppose any advance towards Charruba and protect the left flank of the 4th Indian Division between that place and El Abiar. 'The most offensive action is to be taken', wrote General Ritchie, 'together with greatest risks.'

Speaking to the Army Commander by radio-telephone General Godwin-Austen formally objected to the change of plan, mainly because he believed that the 1st Armoured Division could have scarcely more than forty tanks, and was unequal to its tasks. General Ritchie insisted, and took the 4th Indian Division under his own command. Godwin-Austen gave the necessary orders, but sent a personal message protesting against the new plan and the want of confidence in himself suggested by the refusal of his advice. General Ritchie soon found that the two divisional commanders also had their doubts. At noon on the 26th General Messervy reported that he had forty-one tanks fit to fight, and forty field guns, and followed this up by saying that he could do no more for the day than hold on at Charruba and patrol the track to El Abiar with armoured cars. Meanwhile General Tuker sent a message to 8th Army doubting if his new role was practicable, because his troops in hand amounted to one brigade and he could not expect much help from the Armoured Division. General Ritchie however was not to be diverted from his purpose, and plans to carry it out were pushed ahead.

During 26th January General Rommel, unable to do more for the present than 'take on supplies and salvage the extensive booty', made up his mind what to do next. He had intercepted enough wireless traffic to suggest that there were disagreements among the British commanders and that Benghazi might be given up. He decided not to continue his advance to the north-east for fear of exposing his supply lines to a stroke from Benghazi, but rather to go for Benghazi itself from an unlikely direction. He decided to send the Marcks Group and the 3rd and 33rd Reconnaissance Units to approach Benghazi across the notoriously difficult country from the south-east. They would then capture Benina and block the main road at Coefia to the north while the 20th Corps advanced by Sceleidima, Soluch and Ghemines, and the 90th Light Division moved up the main road from Beda Fomm. An essential part of the plan was that the *D.A.K.* was to manoeuvre so as to make the British expect the next thrust to be made towards Mechili. The attack would begin on 28th January. It was thus destined to forestall the 13th Corps' operations, which, after further disagreements and discussions on 27th January, were timed to begin on the 29th.

Meanwhile, on 25th January, the Desert Air Force was doing all it could to hamper the enemy's progress. Some of the fighters attacked ground targets, and the Beaufighters struck at enemy columns well in rear. The two day-bomber squadrons, which were attacking traffic between Antelat and Agedabia, were reinforced at night by forty Wellingtons, which carried on the attacks in depth as far as El Agheila. From Malta Air Vice-Marshal Lloyd gave what help he could with his limited resources in circumstances of great difficulty, as his airfields were being heavily attacked and were much affected by the wet weather. However, Tripoli was attacked by a small force of Wellingtons by night, and ports in Sicily by Blenheims during the day. Road traffic and rearward installations in Tripolitania between Tripoli and Sirte also received attention, though on a small scale.

On 26th January fierce sand-storms grounded the day-bombers and greatly hampered the fighters. Visibility was again very bad on the 27th, and the preliminary moves of the enemy's troops were concealed from the air, but, as luck would have it, the *D.A.K's* feint towards Mechili was seen and reported by two Tomahawks of No. 250 Squadron. That evening General Ritchie issued an order in which he referred to the enemy's thrusts towards Mechili and Benghazi, and stated that the first was probably the main effort. The 1st Armoured Division was to be directed against the rear of the force advancing east on Mechili, while the 4th Indian Division struck at the force advancing west on Benghazi. 'The enemy has divided his forces', wrote General Ritchie, 'and is weaker than we are in both areas. The keyword is offensive action everywhere.'

By noon on 28th January General Tuker reported a new threat in the form of two large columns which included 47 tanks approaching Sceleidima and Soluch from the south. (This was the Italian 20th Corps.) Tuker proposed to withdraw unless he could be given air support and the co-operation of the 1st Armoured Division. General Ritchie replied that the 1st Armoured Division could not help because it was operating towards Mechili. General Tuker then said that Benghazi should be evacuated at once, adding that he was not faced by Italians only, for he had positive identifications of troops of both the 21st Panzer and 90th Light Divisions.[1] Ritchie accepted this view, and Tuker then ordered the demolitions in Benghazi to be blown and told the 7th Indian Infantry Brigade Group (Brigadier H. R. Briggs) to withdraw that evening and to be north of Benghazi by first light on the 29th.

But the enemy was making the most of his initiative. That afternoon the 20th Corps overran a detachment of the Welch Regiment at Sceleidima and moved on to Soluch. The Marcks Group had managed to make its way across appalling country in the dark and in the rain. Just short of Er Regima they were joined by Rommel in person. The 3rd Reconnaissance Unit then began to feel its way towards Benghazi, while the 33rd scrambled across country to Coefia, where it arrived at 6 p.m. The main road here ran on a raised causeway with a deep ditch on each side, so that vehicles could not leave it. The enemy blocked the road just in time to catch the transport of the 7th Indian Infantry Brigade, and there was quickly a tangle of ditched and reversing lorries. The leading detachments of fighting troops were unable to dislodge the Germans. Brigadier Briggs already knew that there was little chance

[1] 90th Light Division was advancing up the coast road, and the 3rd Reconnaissance Unit, detached from 21st Panzer Division, was with Rommel. A lorried infantry battalion from each of these divisions was with the Marcks Group, which was following the Reconnaissance Units.

of breaking out to the east, and decided to try to dodge the enemy who were advancing from the south. Three columns, about 4,100 strong in all, accordingly set off during the night in the general direction of Soluch, Antelat and Saunnu—right across the enemy's busy back area. To reduce loads and save petrol a good deal of equipment had to be destroyed, but nearly all the arms and ammunition were brought away. It would have been too much to expect that the whole of this impudent move would pass unnoticed, but there were only a few encounters, during which some German and Italian prisoners were taken. The adventure ended with all the columns homing successfully either at Mechili or El Adem.

The Royal Air Force had been feeling the strain of operating in very bad weather and at the same time carrying out a step-by-step withdrawal. The enemy's air forces, for their part, were finding it hard to support such a sudden and unexpected advance, and by 28th January they were almost inactive. (Not until 5th February did the *Luftwaffe* establish itself on Benina airfield.) The principal air activities on the British side after the fall of Benghazi consisted of reconnaissance in depth over the desert, which established the fact that no wide movements were taking place, and over the Jebel country to keep a watch on the enemy following up. The fighters at this time were meeting practically no opposition, and they and the day-bombers made frequent attacks on columns on the roads, in the course of which many vehicles were destroyed or damaged. The Wellingtons of No. 205 Group continued their tactical work of attacking road transport in the Agedabia-El Agheila area, in which they were reinforced by the few available Liberators. Early in February the bad weather put a stop to night attacks of this sort.

The fact that Tripoli was now out of range of any aircraft based on Egypt (except the Liberators, whose employment was still experimental) gave added importance to the operations based on Malta. The Wellingtons from Malta attacked Tripoli, and to a lesser extent Naples, while the Blenheims were used against Tripoli and the Sicilian ports. While engaged on these tasks No. 21 Squadron R.A.F. lost seven aircraft and aircrews in three days. One Blenheim, while turning to correct an error in navigation, flew into the sea; three crashed into a hillside in cloud; and three were shot down into the sea within sight of Malta.

In the fortnight since the enemy's attack at Mersa Brega began, the Middle East air force (including Malta's bombers) had flown about 2,000 sorties on tasks other than shipping strikes. Nineteen German and at least as many Italian aircraft were destroyed, for a loss of 45 British aircraft, mostly in the Desert.

By 6th February the 8th Army had fallen back to the line Gazala-Bir Hacheim, back in fact to the very place where, only seven weeks before, General Rommel had broken away because he judged the tactical balance to be against him. The fighters were back again at El Adem and Gambut, and the day-bombers at Sidi Barrani and Maaten Baggush. The details of the withdrawal through the Jebel may be passed over. The enemy followed with only light forces, and, although there were some anxious moments, the 13th Corps was never in danger. Of greater interest are the changes in policy on both sides. General Ritchie had at first decided that the enemy, having secured Benghazi, would be unlikely to press the pursuit. As he intended to return to the offensive himself he wished to give up as little ground as he could. But on the morning of 30th January General Messervy reported that the 1st Armoured Division could not oppose more than 25 German medium tanks with any prospect of success. Ritchie thereupon agreed with Godwin-Austen's proposal to organize a defensive position at Gazala. General Tuker, whose division was still directly under Ritchie and was (less 7th Indian Infantry Brigade) retiring through the Jebel, suggested that there could be little profit and many dangers in trying to spin out the opposition. General Ritchie agreed and accepted a plan for withdrawing to the Gazala position by 4th February, but stipulated that mobile columns were to operate from Derna, Mechili and Tengeder for as long as possible. The withdrawal took place with little interference.

By 10 a.m. on 29th January General Rommel and his Group had occupied Benghazi, where they were joined that evening by the Ariete Division. There was not enough fuel left for a pursuit. Close on the heels of the event came permission (which may have caused some amusement) from Mussolini to occupy Benghazi with a small mobile force if the British withdrew. Two groups under Colonels Marcks and Geissler started to follow up as best they could, but were much delayed by road blocks, mines, and air attacks. At this stage Rommel had some difficulty in reconciling what he felt to be right with what Mussolini directed to be done. The Duce still regarded the area Jalo-Agedabia-Mersa Brega-Marada as the Axis defence zone, in front of which only mobile forces were to operate. But by 2nd February Rommel was considering whether to attack the British again, for they seemed to be exceptionally weak and demoralized. He decided, however, that he had not enough petrol. He told General Bastico that in order to hold [Western] Cyrenaica firmly it would be necessary to bring forward the infantry and the 20th Corps to the area Gazala-Tengeder.[1] This would have the advantage of providing a good jumping-off place for future

[1] The German reference is not to Western Cyrenaica, but to 'the whole of Cyrenaica'. The context, however, suggests that Western Cyrenaica is meant, and it may be mentioned that the Germans and Italians habitually referred to the north-eastern part of Cyrenaica between Bardia and Tobruk as Marmarica.

operations. Bastico replied on 4th February by sending a directive he had received from Mussolini three days before. Briefly, this stressed that it was very difficult to send supplies to Libya by sea because the stocks of oil fuel were nearly exhausted, and laid down once more that the chief task of the Axis forces was to defend Tripolitania and that this would govern their dispositions.

General Rommel was confident that the British could not attempt offensive operations for six or eight weeks. His own casualties in the past fortnight had been very light, but the time had come to make good the heavy losses incurred earlier during the 'Crusader' battle. He interpreted Mussolini's directive very broadly and decided to keep a small German and Italian mobile force well forward, backed by the rest of the *D.A.K.* and 90th Light Division in the Jebel; most of the 20th Corps and one division were to be near Benghazi; two divisions around Antelat; and two back at Mersa Brega and Marada.

On 2nd February, when the situation was clearly growing stable, General Godwin-Austen asked to be relieved from the command of the 13th Corps. He gave as his reasons that General Ritchie had shown a want of confidence in him, and that this had been remarked by his staff and subordinates, which made it impossible for him to continue in command. He referred to Ritchie's apparent disregard of his advice, to his having taken direct command of the 4th Indian Division, and to his having ordered certain reports from lower formations to be sent direct to the Army instead of through the Corps. General Auchinleck accepted Godwin-Austen's resignation, and this, in the circumstances, was understandable. The impression remains, however, that General Godwin-Austen's reading of the situation, unwelcome though it undoubtedly was, had at least been realistic.

On the enemy's side, too, the chain of command creaked from time to time, but the firm hand of General Rommel made up for its many weaknesses. He was not the Commander-in-Chief, it is true, but he was emphatically the man whose views mattered, for he did what he felt to be militarily right in spite of the frequent protests of his superior, General Bastico. And then, having made up his own mind on the policy, he had a habit of becoming a tactical leader, and, by taking command personally at the most important spot, ensuring that his ideas were carried out. This habit may have infuriated some of his subordinates and undoubtedly troubled his staff, but it must have been an inspiration to many. It certainly ensured that when drive was needed drive was forthcoming—and at once.

The British army casualties between 21st January and 6th February were about 1,390 officers and men killed, wounded, and missing.

Forty-two tanks were probably destroyed, and thirty others damaged or abandoned after breaking down. Forty field guns were lost.

The surprise, speed, and success of General Rommel's advance caused disappointment and concern not only to the Commanders-in-Chief but also in London. This unwelcome sequel to 'Crusader' seemed to have turned success into failure and to have spelt the ruin of 'Acrobat'. The defeat of the British armour was particularly disturbing.

The fundamental reason for the whole reverse has already been dealt with earlier in this chapter. At the time a number of post-mortem telegrams passed to and from London, and in one of them General Auchinleck made some sombre comments to the Prime Minister. He stressed once again the weakness of the 2-pdr gun and the unreliability of the British cruiser tank. He added that the tactical leadership of our armoured units was not good enough to offset the Germans' material advantages. He saw signs 'that personnel of the Royal Armoured Corps are in some instances losing confidence in their equipment'.

In fairness to the 1st Armoured Division it must be remembered that it had no experience of desert warfare. In General Messervy's opinion it was necessary to give newly arrived troops three months' training before they could with confidence be thrown into battle in the desert. That this was not an isolated view is shown by a signal from General Alexander (then Commander-in-Chief, Middle East) to the Prime Minister in October 1942, just before the Battle of El Alamein. '. . . New formations from the United Kingdom require much training under local conditions and much desert experience before they can pull their full weight in battle.' These views naturally prompt the thought: how did the enemy manage? The answer is probably twofold. First, that the basic German tactical training was more thorough, and secondly that their formations and units were not replaced by new ones, but received drafts of trained men. When, on 23rd January, during their first action, the 9th Lancers and 10th Hussars were successfully covering the withdrawal of the rest of the division, they were opposed by some of the most experienced leaders, tank crews, and anti-tank gunners in the desert—diluted, it is true, by recent arrivals, but nevertheless forming a hard core of knowledge and skill.

It is relevant here to turn to the *Panzerarmee Afrika's* report to Hitler on the fighting from 18th November to 6th February. Documents of this sort often contain tactful (and even artful) padding. They do not usually belittle the deeds of the enemy, and are often at pains to point out how stiff was the opposition and how heavy the odds in the enemy's favour. This report is no exception, but some of its references to the British were clearly not prompted entirely by self-praise. Thus:

> 'The assembly of all the forces for the autumn offensive was cleverly concealed (wireless deception was also used) and was favoured by the weather. The attack therefore came as a complete surprise. But although the British command showed skill and prudence in preparing the offensive they were less successful when it came to carrying it out. Disregarding the fundamental principle of employing all available forces at the most critical point, elements only of the 8th Army attacked on 18th and 19th November. Consequently the isolated formations were so severely knocked about that parts of them had to be withdrawn as unemployable while operations were still in progress. Never anywhere at any time during the fighting in Libya did the British High Command concentrate all its available forces at the decisive point. This fundamental tactical mistake was one of the reasons why the British offensive failed to achieve final success.'

And again:

> 'British troops fought well on the whole, though they never attained the same impetus as the Germans when attacking. Officers were courageous and self-sacrificing but rather timid if they had to act on their own initiative. N.C.Os were good throughout.'

And in conclusion:

> 'The military result was that the British 8th Army was so severely beaten that it was incapable of further large-scale operations for months afterwards.'

It would be truer to say that the 8th Army had over-reached itself and paid the penalty. But the estimate of the time needed to mount another offensive was not far wrong: the attempts to do so are described in Chapter IX, and it will be seen that the next British offensive, had it been allowed to take place, would not have begun before June.

CHAPTER VII

MALTA CONVOYS AND THE SECOND BATTLE OF SIRTE

IT has been seen again and again that the campaign on land was dominated by questions of supply. If the Axis powers could have prevented forces based on Malta from attacking their shipping, their losses would have been negligible. Conversely, to the British it was essential that Malta should remain in the fight; hence the immense importance of keeping the island supplied.

All the major operations of the Royal Navy in the Mediterranean in 1942 prior to the Anglo-American landings in November were concerned with taking convoys into Malta. The present chapter tells of these convoys between January and March. After March none was attempted until June, when convoys were sailed from Egypt and Gibraltar simultaneously.[1] The former had to turn back; the latter came through, but with heavy losses. In August a few ships of another Gibraltar convoy reached Malta, but thereafter the Home Fleet, from which most of the escorts came, was fully occupied with taking convoys to North Russia and preparing for the landing in Algeria. The next convoy to reach Malta came from Egypt, arriving on 20th November—the day the British again took Benghazi. Others arrived from Egypt in December. Altogether 61 supply ships sailed for Malta under escort during 1942: 32 arrived, 19 were lost on the way, and 10 had to turn back.[2] One aircraft-carrier, two cruisers, an anti-aircraft ship and nine destroyers were lost, and other warships seriously damaged in these operations. In addition, twenty small cargoes were carried in by submarines, and the fast minelayers *Welshman* and *Manxman* made six passages sailing alone. Some 370 fighter aircraft arrived also, flown off from carriers of the Royal Navy and from U.S.S. *Wasp*.

The last supply convoy to reach Malta during 1941 had come from Gibraltar in September. An attempt by two merchant vessels in November to make the passage from the west unescorted had ended in both being sunk. The *Breconshire* had arrived from Alexandria in mid-December, carrying little besides oil fuel. The Governor had not

[1] The June and August convoys are described in Chapter XIII.

[2] During 1941 thirty had arrived under escort out of a total of thirty-one sailed.

been fully informed of the contents of the September convoy so that the stocks which should all have been related to the most important item—flour—had become unbalanced. At the end of 1941 it was estimated that flour would last until May, coal to the end of March, benzine and kerosene until the end of April, and aviation spirit well into the summer. It was still the policy to build up stocks during the winter months, when the long nights reduced the risks to convoys from air and surface attack. But, as General Dobbie had pointed out, the building up of stocks competed for shipping space with the rising needs of the Royal Air Force for benzine, aviation spirit, and bombs. To meet all demands would require an unattainable number of supply ships; therefore if air operations of all kinds were to be sustained some risks would have to be taken with the stocks.

The September convoy to Malta had been sent from the Gibraltar end because the risk from air attack seemed less in the western basin. Force H had been strongly reinforced and the Italian Fleet had kept at a distance. But by January circumstances had changed. Ships could not be found either to reinforce Force H or to make good the severe losses suffered by the Mediterranean Fleet during the last two months of 1941. Nor had it been possible to offset these losses by greatly increasing the air reconnaissance and air striking forces. The Italian Fleet could thus challenge, in vastly superior strength, the passing of a convoy from either east or west. The risks from the air at and around Malta were common to both routes, but the capture of the airfields in the bulge of Cyrenaica made it possible by January for the Royal Air Force to give fighter cover to ships all the way from Alexandria to within range of the Malta fighters. This was a strong point in favour of the eastern route, and early in January it was decided to run one 30,000 ton convoy from Alexandria during the month. Thereafter the aim would be to run one of 45,000 tons every month.

But it was not only supply that was causing anxiety at Malta. Rumour, rather than definite intelligence, of Axis preparations to capture the island by sea and airborne assault was growing, and although the danger did not seem immediate it was thought necessary to increase the garrison still further, for the reinforcements sent in July had been absorbed in protecting the steadily growing airfields and aircraft dispersal areas. General Auchinleck was ordered by the Chiefs of Staff to send one light anti-aircraft regiment, one squadron of 'I' tanks, and two British battalions, in that order of priority.

Already in January, between the 5th and 8th of the month, one small convoy operation had taken place. H.M.S. *Glengyle,* whose speed and carrying capacity made her suitable to alternate with H.M.S. *Breconshire* (also a Glen Line ship) in supplying Malta with heavy and light oils, had been run in from Alexandria and the *Breconshire* brought out empty. Ships of comparable speed could not be found for the operation about to take place, and one infantry battalion had to be left behind for this reason. On 16th January four ships left Alexandria with the *Carlisle* and eight destroyers as escort. Early on the 17th one of the escort, the *Gurkha*, was torpedoed and sunk by the German submarine *U.133*. The Dutch destroyer *Isaac Sweers*, most ably handled, towed the *Gurkha* clear of burning oil and rescued all but nine of her company. During the forenoon of the 18th a covering force of three cruisers and three destroyers joined the convoy. One of the merchantmen, the *Thermopylae*, had trouble in steering and in maintaining her speed, and at noon Admiral Vian, who was in command of the operation, decided to send her into Benghazi escorted by the *Carlisle* and two destroyers. An hour later Force K—the cruiser *Penelope* and five destroyers—joined from Malta, and that evening, as there were no reports of enemy forces at sea, Admiral Vian turned his own warships back for Alexandria. There had been a number of attacks during the day, mostly by single aircraft, but they had all been driven off by gunfire from the ships and by Beaufighters of Nos. 252 and 272 Squadrons which had moved from base to base along the coast to keep in touch with the convoy. Next day the *Thermopylae*, which Admiral Cunningham had later ordered to steer for Alexandria, was not so fortunate. To avoid submarines she and her escort were keeping too far from the coast to be covered by single-engined fighters. Hit by bombs and set on fire, she had to be sunk, but most of her crew and army passengers were saved. On the afternoon of the 19th the remaining three merchantmen reached Malta escorted by Force K and with the island's fighters overhead. Particularly heavy German air attacks greeted their arrival and persisted over the next two days. But the supplies, amounting to 21,000 tons, were safely unloaded. Eight tanks and twenty Bofors guns and their crews, and two-thirds of one infantry battalion, had been brought in; ten tanks and sixteen Bofors had been lost in the *Thermopylae*. Nearly 2,000 men and a great deal of equipment awaited passage from Egypt.

This operation had shown the advantage of possessing the Benghazi airfields and the value of No. 201 Naval Co-operation Group R.A.F. (Air Vice-Marshal L. H. Slatter).[1] Although the forward airfields were not fully organized at the time, fighter cover had been most effective. In ascribing credit for this success, the work of Malta's aircraft must not be forgotten, and Admiral Cunningham recorded that for the first time since the war began the air reconnaissance had been really adequate and that a sense of security was felt throughout the whole operation. The Italian Fleet did not leave harbour, for it appears that reports of the British convoy were received too late.

This was to be the last convoy that Sir Wilbraham Ford would

[1] The circumstances in which this Group was set up are described in the previous volume.

welcome to Malta. On the day it arrived he handed over his duties as Vice-Admiral, Malta, to Vice-Admiral Sir Ralph Leatham, until recently Commander-in-Chief, East Indies Station. Admiral Ford had held the appointment with great distinction for five strenuous years. Four days earlier Rear-Admiral H. B. Rawlings also hauled down his flag. He had commanded the 7th Cruiser Squadron since May, and, including his previous appointment in the Battle Squadron, he had flown his flag in the Mediterranean since November 1940. No flag officer took his place, and the remaining cruisers were all included in Rear-Admiral Vian's command. In the absence of any aircraft carriers Rear-Admiral D. W. Boyd's appointment as Rear-Admiral, Air, also lapsed, and on 21st January he transferred his flag to H.M.S. *Indomitable* in the Indian Ocean.

Between 24th and 28th January the oil shuttle service between Alexandria and Malta was repeated. This time the *Breconshire* was passed in and the *Glengyle* and another empty ship, the *Rowallan Castle*, returned to Alexandria. It was fortunate that there was no damage from air attack, for the British were even then being driven off the west Cyrenaican airfields, and although cover was provided over the eastbound ships on the 27th, none could be given to the *Breconshire*.

The enemy's success with his heavily escorted convoy in December was described in Chapter IV. He followed this up with further 'battleship convoys', and in January some 66,000 tons of general supplies and fuel arrived in Libya, very little being lost on the way. Although this was below the monthly requirement it was a marked improvement on November and December. The bulk had been carried to Tripoli in two convoys, each of which happened to precede by a short interval one of the British shuttle services in and out of Malta. The first convoy, of six merchant ships, arrived on 5th January protected by no less than four battleships, six cruisers, and twenty-four destroyers and torpedo boats—in fact by the Italian Fleet. It was entirely unmolested. The German air force provided air cover and made sustained attacks on Malta's airfields, in which a number of aircraft were destroyed or damaged and the airfields rendered temporarily unusable. Between 30th December and 5th January well over 400 enemy aircraft were estimated to have raided the island, the attacks on the 4th being exceptionally heavy. The weather was bad, and although reconnaissance aircraft made several reports of the enemy's ships, the striking forces from Malta and Benghazi failed to find them. Force K could muster only one cruiser and three destroyers, and in any case a night attack was out of the question without information of the enemy's movements. British submarines were spread across the Gulf of Taranto to intercept the returning Italian Fleet, but also had no luck. Fifty-four tanks, nineteen armoured cars, forty-two guns and much ammunition, fuel and general stores were unloaded at Tripoli from this convoy, and arrived just in time to back up General Rommel's advance described in the previous chapter.

On 25th January, by which time Rommel was in full cry, the second of the enemy's January convoys arrived at Tripoli, again strongly escorted. This time it had been detected and during daylight and after dark on the 23rd frequent bombing and torpedo-bombing attacks were made on it by R.A.F. and F.A.A. aircraft from Malta and Benghazi and even from Fuka. The Italian official account states that shortly after 5.30 p.m. on the 23rd the Italian liner *Victoria* of 13,000 tons was torpedoed and disabled—presumably by a Beaufort of No. 39 Squadron R.A.F. which attacked at that time. At 6.40 p.m. the *Victoria* was torpedoed twice more, this time by Albacores of No. 826 Squadron F.A.A. from Berka, and sank half an hour later. Nearly 1,100 troops, of the 1,400 she was carrying, were picked up by Italian warships. The remaining four ships of the convoy received no serious damage.

By the end of January the Western Cyrenaican airfields were again in Axis hands, and the task of protecting Malta convoys became as difficult as it had been before 'Crusader'; more difficult in fact, because the Italian Fleet had gained confidence. But it was no less imperative to keep Malta supplied, and on 6th February Admiral Cunningham reported that he proposed to sail a convoy shortly. A few days later he warned the First Sea Lord that the serviceable fighters at Malta were so few that he doubted whether they could give effective cover to an incoming convoy. Nevertheless one would be sent.

This convoy, consisting of the *Clan Chattan*, *Clan Campbell* and *Rowallan Castle*, escorted by the *Carlisle* and eight destroyers, left Alexandria on the evening of the 12th. By sailing it in two sections to arrive off Tobruk by dusk it was hoped that the enemy might think that Tobruk was the destination. After passing Tobruk the united convoy was to follow a north-westerly route which would, by daylight, take it out of range of the dive-bombers based in Cyrenaica. No fighter cover could be given during the passage across the central basin; the escorting cruisers and destroyers would have to beat off air attacks unaided. From Malta would come the *Breconshire* and three other empty ships, escorted by Force K.

All went well until the evening of the 13th when the *Clan Campbell* was hit by a bomb which reduced her speed, and she was sent into Tobruk. Next morning Admiral Vian with three cruisers and eight destroyers joined the escort. During the afternoon aircraft attacked intermittently, singly or in groups. The *Clan Chattan*, hit early in the afternoon by a bomb, began to burn furiously and had to be abandoned, after destroyers had taken off her crew and Service passengers. The convoy, now reduced to the *Rowallan Castle*, continued on its course. Just before 2 p.m. Force K—the *Penelope* and six destroyers—was sighted with the empty merchantmen, and three-quarters of an hour later, while Beaufighters from Malta gave cover overhead, the warships exchanged their charges. At 3 p.m. the *Rowallan Castle*, now escorted by Force K, was 'near missed' during a heavy bombing attack and reported her engines disabled. Realizing that a long delay would probably expose her and her escort to attack by greatly superior forces next day, Admiral Cunningham signalled that unless there was a good chance of her making ten knots under tow she was to be sunk. At about 7.30 p.m. this was done and Force K reached Malta empty-handed at daylight on the 15th.

Meanwhile Admiral Vian, eastbound with the empty merchant ships, passed near and sank the burning *Clan Chattan*. When north of Tobruk the convoy came within range of British shore-based fighters, which drove off several attacks by Italian aircraft. Early on the 16th Admiral Vian arrived at Alexandria with the *Breconshire*, having sent the other three empty ships on to Port Said. That evening the damaged *Clan Campbell* reached Alexandria from Tobruk.

As expected, the enemy had not been content to contest these movements with aircraft alone. Four cruisers and ten destroyers from Taranto and Messina had sailed with orders to intercept the Malta-bound convoy. Early on 15th February submarine *P.36* reported some of these ships as they steamed south out of the Straits of Messina, and soon after noon a Maryland sighted them about eighty miles south-east of Malta. Unfortunately the Maryland was shot down and her news delayed until the crew were rescued four hours later. But for this delay the Italians might have paid heavily for their enterprise. As it was, four Albacores of No. 828 Squadron F.A.A. found the enemy ships early on the 16th a hundred miles east of Sicily homeward bound, but they scored no hits. A few hours later *P.36* fired torpedoes at a part of this force and seriously damaged the destroyer *Carabiniere*.

Thus it was that during January, when the bulge of Cyrenaica was in British hands, three out of four ships carrying general supplies, and the *Breconshire* and *Glengyle* carrying oil, had arrived at Malta and their cargoes had been safely discharged. In February, however, when the coveted airfields were again in Axis hands, the empty ships had been brought safely out but no supply ship of any kind had reached Malta. On the 18th, after the February convoy had failed, General Dobbie summed up the situation. Issues had been reduced to siege level and, with a few important exceptions, supplies would last until the end of

June. At least 15,000 tons would be needed each month to keep stocks at their present figure. It appeared that the difficulties of getting convoys through from the east would not lessen while the position in Cyrenaica remained as it was. He therefore urged that all other means of sending supplies, from the west as well as from the east, should be examined.

On 27th February the Chiefs of Staff gave their own views. Malta was so important as a staging post and as a base for attacking the enemy's communications that the most drastic steps were justifiable to sustain it. They were unable to supply Malta from the west. The chances of doing so from the east depended on making an advance in Cyrenaica. It must be the aim to make this advance before the April dark period, in order that a substantial convoy could then be passed in. Meanwhile stocks must be kept up to the existing level. They suggested a further attempt in March, which no consideration of risk to the ships involved should deter, and during its progress the operation should be regarded as the primary military commitment. As if to emphasize its importance a change was made in the position of the General Officer Commanding the Troops at Malta, Major-General D. M. W. Beak, V.C. Hitherto he had been responsible to the Governor, unlike his Naval and Air colleagues who were responsible to their respective Commanders-in-Chief. The G.O.C. was now to come under General Auchinleck. This change in no way affected the co-operation which existed at Malta, but the Chiefs of Staff no doubt thought that it would remove any possibility of a conflict of interests—more perhaps in Cairo than in Malta.

The Commanders-in-Chief were prepared to run convoys in March and April, but they expected that both would have to take place under the 'present conditions of risk', because an offensive on land launched before the April dark period would be likely to fail. They also pointed out that the reoccupation of Western Cyrenaica would not be the complete answer to the problem of supplying Malta, because incoming convoys would need fighter protection and the scale of possible air attack from Sicilian airfields was so heavy that this might not be possible. But, in addition to fighters, air striking forces must be ready in Cyrenaica, as well as in Malta, to offset the Italian preponderance in surface warships.

In Malta the most steadfast could have been excused for losing hope. Those best aware of what the ships and aircraft based at Malta were doing to Axis supplies during the autumn of 1941 had felt that the comparative calm in the sky was too good to last. And they were right, although the progress of 'Crusader' had seemed to indicate that Malta's isolation would soon be at an end. But in December German aircraft had reappeared. Air attacks at the beginning of January had been light, but they increased in weight during the month and the estimate of 669 tons of bombs dropped in January was slightly higher than the figure for the previous April—the peak month for 1941. Much damage was done in the dockyard and on the airfields. In February, the main weight of the ever-increasing attack was on the airfields, although the destroyer *Maori* was sunk by a bomb in the Grand Harbour. The toll of buildings destroyed and damaged rose steadily. The estimate of bombs dropped in February was 1,020 tons. The heaviest attacks had been made either during the passage of an Axis convoy to Africa or on the arrival of a British convoy at Malta. In the one case the island's striking force was hampered, and in the other the fighters had to be split to give protection both to the airfields and to the incoming convoy. Large numbers of soldiers joined the airmen and the Maltese in filling craters on the airfields, building and repairing protective pens, and extending the dispersal areas.

Communal feeding had been introduced at the end of 1941 and had been a great boon to many, particularly the homeless; it had also reduced the consumption of kerosene. The 'Victory Kitchens' grew in popularity and by the end of 1942 were supplying nearly 200,000 people with hot meals. But living conditions in February were getting worse, and after the failure of that month's convoy General Dobbie became increasingly anxious about the effect on the civil population. Sugar, an especially important item in the Maltese diet, had been cut again. The kerosene ration was being held at the reduced summer scale. Fodder, of which there was already too little, had been further reduced. Long distance and week-end bus services had been abolished. The weather was unusually depressing but seemed to interfere little with the enemy's bombing. There was a general feeling of isolation. The Maltese liked to see evidence in the skies that British fighters could hold their own: there had not been much of this evidence lately; such Hurricanes as were still serviceable—there were thirty-two on 6th March—were outnumbered and outclassed by the German Me. 109s. It was therefore heartening when, on 7th March, it was realized that not only had the air ferrying trips been resumed, but that the new arrivals were the famous Spitfires.

The last ferry trip from Gibraltar had been in November and had ended with the loss of the *Ark Royal*. Since then aircraft carriers had been in great demand for the Atlantic and Indian Oceans. The *Scharnhorst*, *Gneisenau* and *Prinz Eugen* at Brest had been showing signs of stirring; the *Tirpitz* was at Trondheim. But on 12th February the Brest ships made their spectacular return to Germany by way of the Straits of Dover, and Force H, which had been helping to cover convoy W.S.16 from the Clyde, was able to return to Gibraltar on the 23rd. On 10th January Rear-Admiral E. N. Syfret had taken over command

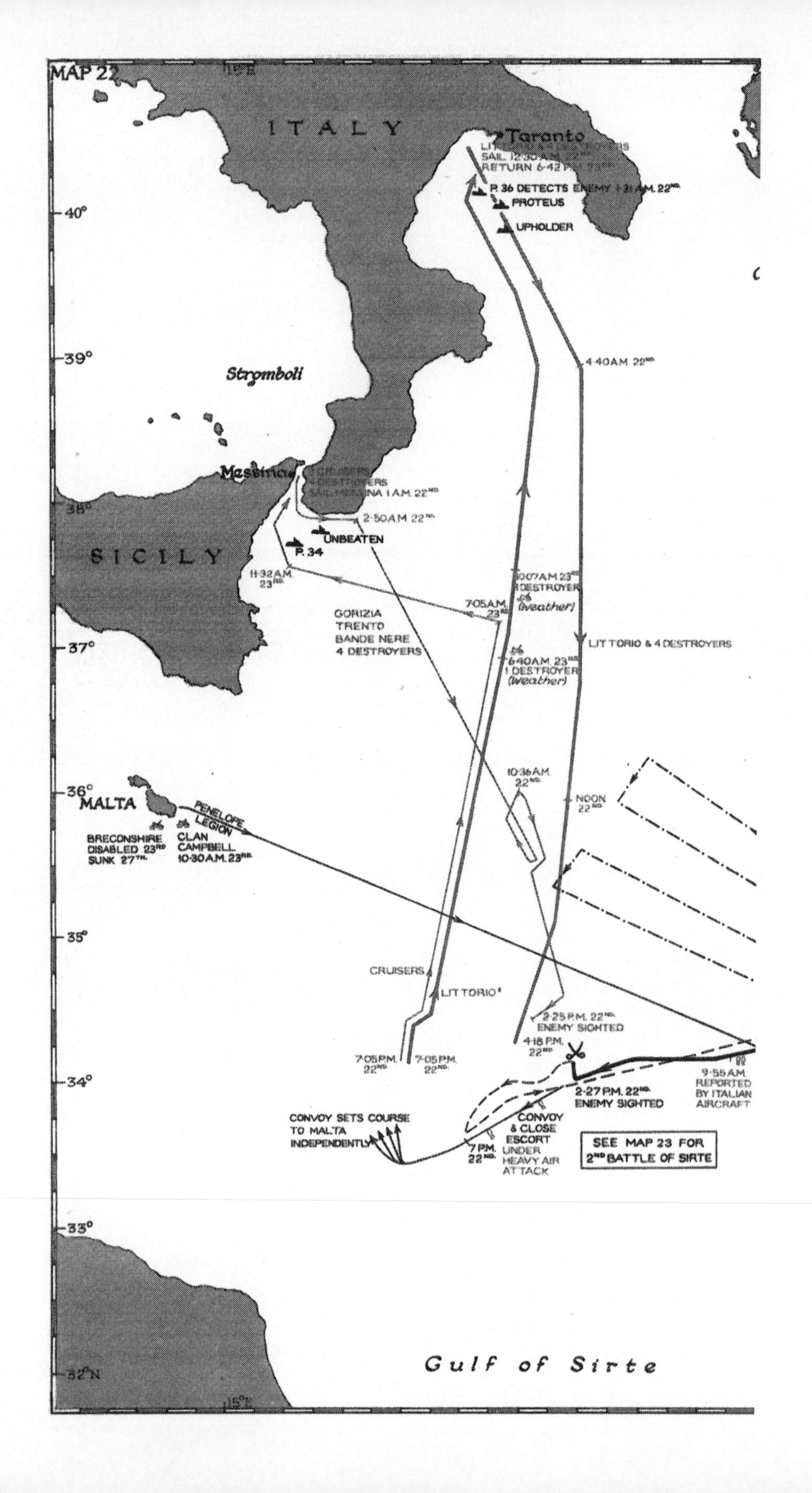
MAP 22
15°E
ITALY
Taranto
P. 36 DETECTS ENEMY 1·31 A.M. 22ND
PROTEUS
UPHOLDER
40°
39°
Stromboli
4·40 A.M. 22ND
Messina
2·50 A.M. 22ND
38°
UNBEATEN
P. 34
SICILY
11·32 A.M. 23RD
10·07 A.M. 23RD
1 DESTROYER
(weather)
7·05 A.M. 23RD
GORIZIA
TRENTO
BANDE NERE
4 DESTROYERS
37°
LITTORIO & 4 DESTROYERS
6·40 A.M. 23RD
1 DESTROYER
(weather)
10·36 A.M. 22ND
36°
MALTA
NOON 22ND
PENELOPE
LEGION
BRECONSHIRE
DISABLED 23RD
SUNK 27TH
CLAN
CAMPBELL
10·30 A.M. 23RD
35°
CRUISERS
LITTORIO
2·25 P.M. 22ND
ENEMY SIGHTED
4·18 P.M. 22ND
7·05 P.M. 22ND
7·05 P.M. 22ND
34°
9·55 A.M.
REPORTED
BY ITALIAN
AIRCRAFT
2·27 P.M. 22ND
ENEMY SIGHTED
CONVOY SETS COURSE
TO MALTA
INDEPENDENTLY
CONVOY
& CLOSE
ESCORT
UNDER
HEAVY AIR
ATTACK
7 P.M. 22ND
SEE MAP 23 FOR
2ND BATTLE OF SIRTE
33°
Gulf of Sirte
32°N
15°E

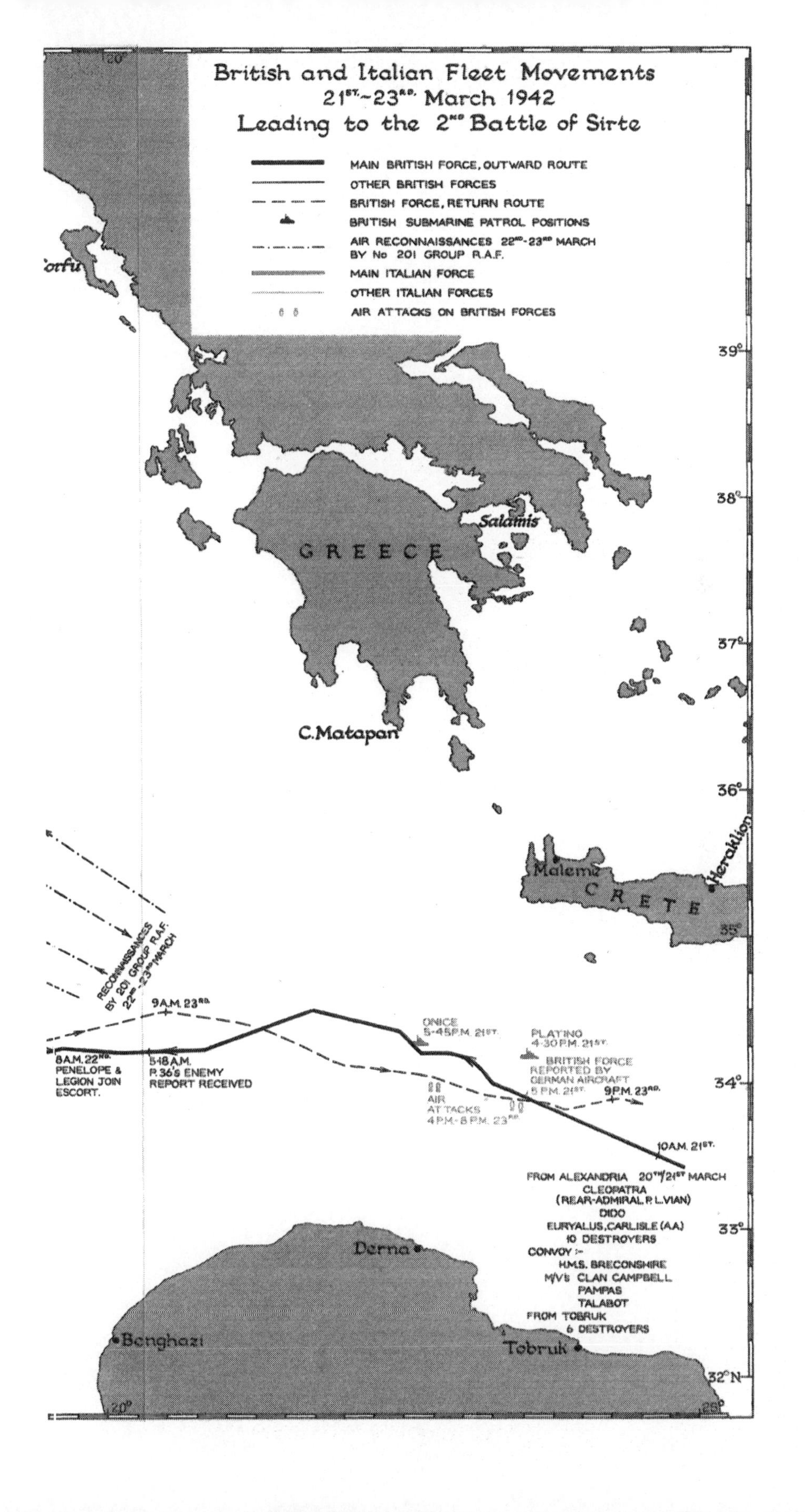
British and Italian Fleet Movements
21st-23rd March 1942
Leading to the 2nd Battle of Sirte
MAIN BRITISH FORCE, OUTWARD ROUTE
OTHER BRITISH FORCES
BRITISH FORCE, RETURN ROUTE
BRITISH SUBMARINE PATROL POSITIONS
AIR RECONNAISSANCES 22nd-23rd MARCH BY No 201 GROUP R.A.F.
MAIN ITALIAN FORCE
OTHER ITALIAN FORCES
AIR ATTACKS ON BRITISH FORCES
20°
Corfu
39°
38°
Salamis
GREECE
37°
C. Matapan
36°
Maleme
CRETE
Heraklion
35°
RECONNAISSANCES BY 201 GROUP R.A.F. 22nd-23rd MARCH
9 A.M. 23rd
8 A.M. 22nd PENELOPE & LEGION JOIN ESCORT.
5·48 A.M. P. 36's ENEMY REPORT RECEIVED
ONICE 5-45 P.M. 21st.
PLATINO 4-30 P.M. 21st.
BRITISH FORCE REPORTED BY GERMAN AIRCRAFT 5 P.M. 21st.
AIR ATTACKS 4 P.M.-8 P.M. 23rd
9 P.M. 23rd.
34°
10 A.M. 21st.
FROM ALEXANDRIA 20th/21st MARCH
CLEOPATRA
(REAR-ADMIRAL P. L. VIAN)
DIDO
EURYALUS, CARLISLE (AA)
10 DESTROYERS
CONVOY :-
H.M.S. BRECONSHIRE
M/V's CLAN CAMPBELL
PAMPAS
TALABOT
FROM TOBRUK
6 DESTROYERS
33°
Derna
Benghazi
Tobruk
32°N
20°
25°

of Force H from Vice-Admiral Sir James Somerville, who went to command a new fleet assembling in the Indian Ocean. On 6th March Admiral Syfret left Gibraltar in the battleship *Malaya*, with the *Eagle*, *Argus*, *Hermione* and nine destroyers in company. When H.M.S. *Eagle* was south-east of Majorca she flew off fifteen Spitfires all of which arrived safely at Malta. On 21st and again on 29th March similar operations took place, and sixteen more Spitfires were flown in. In the second trip the fly-off of five F.A.A. Albacores had to be cancelled because the weather at Malta was too bad for their arrival and delay in the western basin could not be accepted.

See Map 22

The enemy was still sending most of his supply ships in convoys heavily protected by warships and aircraft as he had done in December and January. During February and March 67,000 tons of supplies and 40,000 tons of fuel arrived in Libya, only 9 per cent having been lost on passage—almost all from submarine attack. The route lay east of Sicily and was, for much of the way, beyond the reach of the only torpedo-bombers then at Malta, which were in any case handicapped by the steadily increasing bombing of the airfields. One such convoy arrived at Tripoli on the 23rd February in spite of the aircraft sent to attack it and the submarines disposed on its track. A second convoy arrived on 10th March. On 9th March Beauforts of No. 39 Squadron claimed hits on an Italian cruiser, a destroyer and a large merchant vessel in a north-bound convoy. Later reports suggested that no serious damage had been done, but Admiral Cunningham decided that a search must be made, and sailed the 15th Cruiser Squadron and all the available destroyers from Alexandria early on 10th March. This would also afford an opportunity to fetch the cruiser *Cleopatra*, which had arrived at Malta from the United Kingdom in the middle of February. There were no signs of the damaged enemy ships, and none in fact had been damaged. The explosion of torpedoes at the end of their run had probably (and not for the first time) been mistaken for hits. When the *Cleopatra* and a destroyer were met next morning the whole force shaped course for Alexandria. Beaufighters gave good cover at extreme range and the enemy's air attacks did no damage. At about 8 p.m., however, Admiral Vian's flagship, the *Naiad*, was torpedoed by *U.565* and sank an hour later with the loss of eighty-two lives. Admiral Vian transferred his flag to the *Dido* for the remainder of the passage and then to the *Cleopatra*.

Very early on 15th March the *Dido*, *Euryalus* and six destroyers bombarded targets on the island of Rhodes. The enemy was known to be nervous about the Dodecanese islands and Crete, and it was hoped to draw off some of the German air force from attacking Malta. Preparations for the March convoy were now almost complete. A route midway between Crete and Cyrenaica would be used, but once past the bulge the ships would keep well to the south so as to increase the distance to be covered by any Italian surface forces which might attempt to intercept. Whatever the timing, one day without fighter cover could not be avoided. The best time to arrive at Malta was at dawn. The Army in Cyrenaica was to stage a threat to certain enemy airfields in order to draw off some of his aircraft. The Royal Air Force was to bomb airfields in Crete and Cyrenaica. Air reconnaissance would be flown from Egypt and Malta, and on the third day, when attack by surface ships was most probable, an air striking force would be at readiness. Three submarines were to patrol the approaches to Taranto and two south of the Straits of Messina. In a further attempt to distract the enemy's attention, Force H would be flying off aircraft for Malta.

On the morning of 20th March the convoy—the *Breconshire*, *Clan Campbell*, *Pampas* and a Norwegian, the *Talabot*—left Alexandria escorted by the anti-aircraft cruiser *Carlisle* and six destroyers. Rear-Admiral Vian followed that evening in the *Cleopatra*, with the *Dido*, *Euryalus* and four destroyers. These ships and a further six destroyers of the small Hunt class, which had been sent ahead on an anti-submarine sweep, were all in company with the convoy by the morning of the 21st and had reached the eastern end of the passage between Crete and Cyrenaica, where previous convoys had been heavily attacked from the air. Fighter cover was overhead.

Force K—the cruiser *Penelope* and the destroyer *Legion*—was to join from Malta next morning. The whole force would remain in company till dark on the 22nd. If there was no threat of attack by surface ships Admiral Vian was then to turn back for Alexandria with his four cruisers and ten Fleet destroyers (Force B), while Force K and the Hunts were to continue with the convoy and aim at reaching Malta at dawn on the 23rd. It was during daylight on the 22nd that Admiral Cunningham expected the Italian Fleet to intervene. If it did, Admiral Vian was to evade the enemy if possible until dark, when the convoy —dispersed if it seemed advisable—was to be sent on to Malta with the Hunt class destroyers, and the remaining warships were to attack the enemy. The convoy was to turn back only if it was evident that surface forces would intercept it during daylight to the east of longitude 18°E.

Early on the 22nd Force K joined at about 250 miles from Malta, in longitude 19° 30′E. The convoy was thus well on its way, having passed through the danger area between Crete and Cyrenaica without being attacked. Admiral Cunningham attributed this largely to the operations of the 8th Army, consisting of raids by columns of the 50th Division, the 1st South African Division, and the Free French Brigade.

Map 23

ACTION IN THE

22ND MARCH

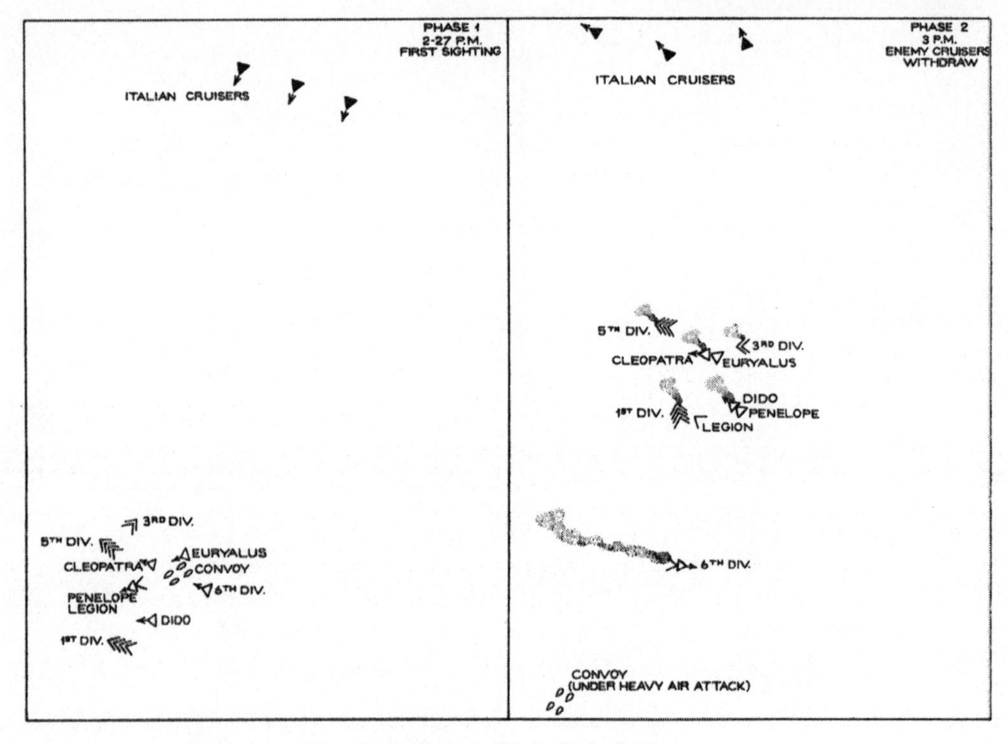

Scale in Sea Miles 0 1 2 3 4 5 6 7 8 9 10

1ST DIVISION JERVIS, KIPLING, KELVIN, KINGSTON.

2ND DIVISION DIDO, PENELOPE, LEGION (LEGION LATER JOINED 1ST DIV).

3RD DIVISION ZULU, HASTY.

SEA ROUGH

SUNSET 7-4 P.M.

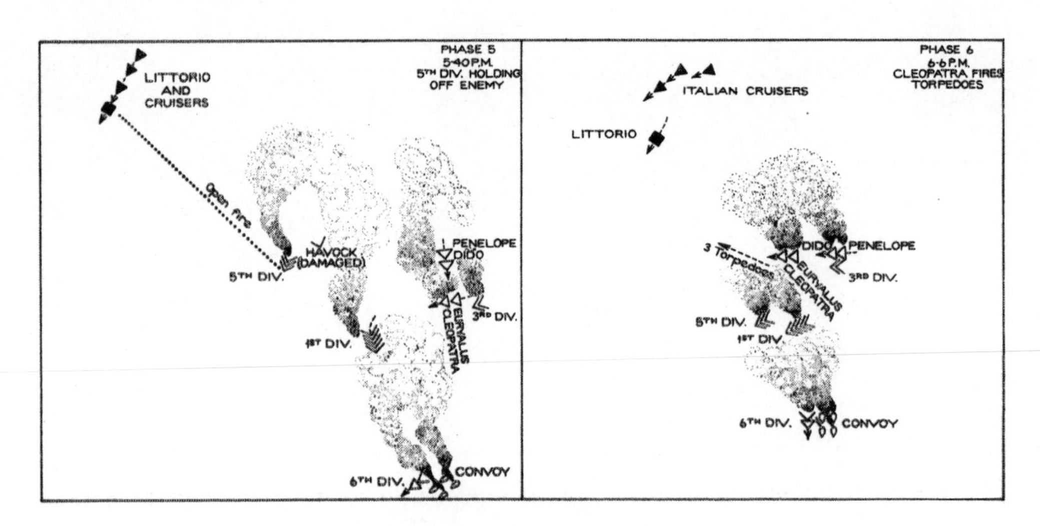

BETWEEN 2-27 AND 7 P.M. THE CONVOY MADE GOOD 238 DEGREES 48 SEA MILES.

AT 7 P.M. MALTA BORE 320 DEGREES, 183 MILES FROM THE CONVOY.

GULF OF SIRTE

1942

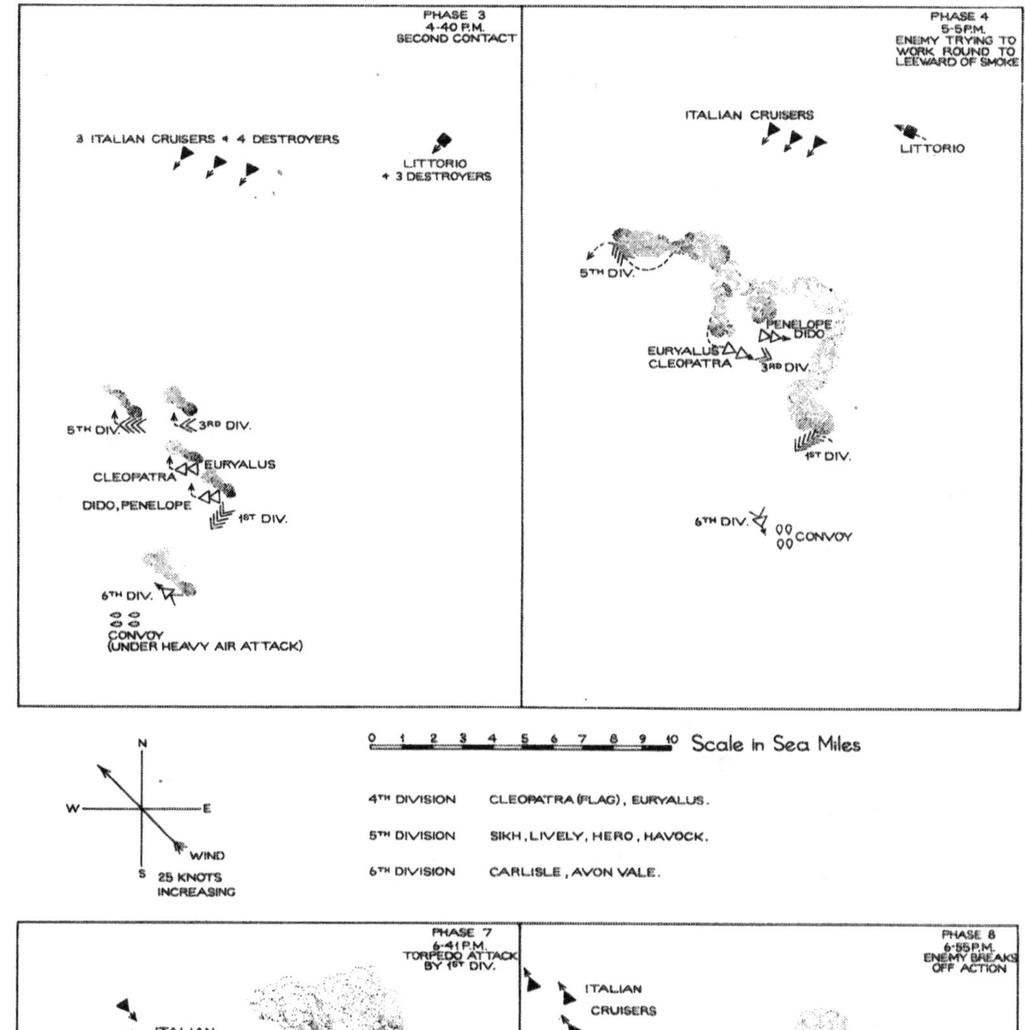

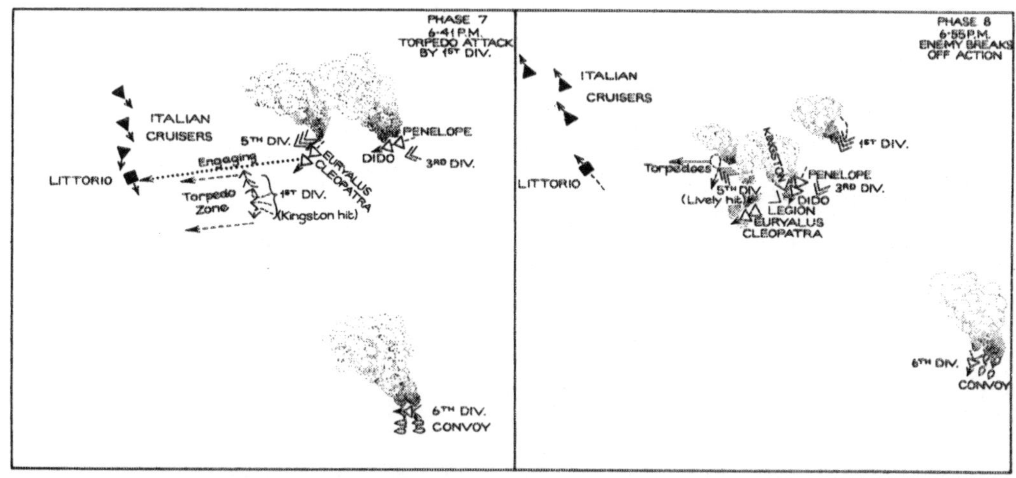

THE 5 HUNTS WHICH ACTED AS CLOSE ESCORT TO THE CONVOY ARE NOT SHOWN ON THESE MAPS.

THE ITALIAN DESTROYERS ARE NOT SHOWN. 3 WERE ATTACHED TO THE LITTORIO AND 4 TO THE CRUISERS.

These raids were made on 21st March, caused the enemy some 120 casualties, and drew the attention of his air forces from the sea, a result to which the Royal Air Force and Fleet Air Arm had also contributed by attacking the principal airfields in Cyrenaica from 18th March onwards. By the morning of the 22nd, however, Admiral Vian knew that he was unlikely to be left in peace much longer. German transport aircraft crossing from Cyrenaica to Crete had reported the convoy overnight, and soon after 5 a.m. a signal had been received from submarine *P.36* reporting heavy surface ships leaving Taranto about four hours earlier. This meant that air attacks must be expected at any moment and that the Italian Fleet might appear in the afternoon.

At 9 a.m. the last fighter patrol had to leave the convoy. Half an hour later the air attacks began, but during the forenoon they consisted only of a few long-range torpedo shots from Italian S.79s and were not dangerous—the gunfire of the entire force proving a big deterrent. Admiral Vian was determined that the convoy should go through, and at 12.30 assumed his dispositions for surface action. His ships were organized in six divisions:

1st Division	the destroyers *Jervis*, *Kipling*, *Kelvin* and *Kingston*.
2nd Division	the cruisers *Dido* and *Penelope* and the destroyer *Legion*.
3rd Division	the destroyers *Zulu* and *Hasty*.
4th Division	the cruisers *Cleopatra* (flag) and *Euryalus*.
5th Division	the destroyers *Sikh*, *Lively*, *Hero* and *Havock*.
6th Division	the anti-aircraft cruiser *Carlisle* and the Hunt class destroyer *Avon Vale*.

On the enemy's approach the ships of the first five divisions were to stand out from the convoy to act as a striking force, each division conforming generally to Admiral Vian's movements. The 6th Division was to lay smoke across the wake of the convoy, and the remaining five Hunts would form a close escort to protect the merchant ships, especially against air attack. If Admiral Vian decided against an immediate close engagement he had a special signal meaning 'carry out diversionary tactics, using smoke to cover the escape of the convoy', in which case the convoy was to turn away while the Divisions laid smoke at right angles to the bearing of the enemy, reversing course in time to attack with torpedoes as the enemy reached the smoke. The cruisers and some of the destroyers had previously practised these manœuvres.

See Map 23

Heavy bombing and bad weather had made air reconnaissance from Malta very difficult, and Admiral Vian's only report of the enemy's surface ships was that received from *P.36*. The first sign of their approach came at 1.30 p.m. when an aircraft dropped flares ahead of the convoy. Shortly after 2 o'clock the *Euryalus* reported smoke and at 2.27 she reported four ships to the north-east (Phase 1). These were two 8-inch cruisers, one 6-inch, and four destroyers, but at first there were thought to be three battleships.

The enemy had arrived a couple of hours sooner than expected. It was clear to Admiral Vian that he must drive them off before dark, for the ships of Force B could not be oiled at Malta and so could not afford to be entangled in operations at night far to the westward; nor could the convoy afford to continue for long off its proper course, when every hour's delay would increase the danger from the air next day. As soon as Admiral Vian received *Euryalus's* second report he made his special signal, and the ships of the striking force drew off to the northward while the convoy and its close escort turned away south-west. At 2.33 the striking force turned east to lay smoke, which the freshening south-east wind blew across the wake of the merchant ships. (*See Photo* 2).

The Italian ships, which had been standing towards the convoy in line abreast, now turned slowly through west to north-east and opened fire, while still out of range. At 2.42 they altered course right round to north-west, by which time Admiral Vian had recognized them as cruisers and had ordered his Divisions to steer towards them, leading the way with the *Cleopatra* and *Euryalus* (Phase 2). There were some brief exchanges of gunfire, but few of the British ships could see the enemy through the smoke. When the enemy drew off Admiral Vian signalled to Admiral Cunningham 'Enemy driven off', and steered to overtake the convoy. Meanwhile the convoy had been under heavy air attack from German Ju. 88s but had received no damage, thanks to skilful handling and to the steady shooting of the escort in the heavy sea. So much ammunition had been used, however, that Admiral Vian decided to send the 1st Division to reinforce the escort. Air attacks on the convoy continued until dark, fortunately without result; attacks on the striking force were comparatively light, the German aircraft having been ordered to concentrate on the merchant ships.

No sooner had the striking force overhauled the convoy than Italian ships came into sight again to the north-east. This time they were made out to be one *Littorio* class battleship, two 8-inch cruisers, one light cruiser, and four smaller ships. At 4.40 the striking force stood out again and laid smoke to bar the way.

There now ensued two and a half hours of sporadic fighting, during which four British light cruisers and eleven destroyers, with a total broadside of about 5,900 pounds, held off one of the most modern battleships, two heavy cruisers, one light cruiser, and seven destroyers, with a total broadside of about 24,000 pounds. The direction of the wind—south-east—was of great importance, for it meant that the British had the weather gauge, and their smoke screen, drifting north-westwards at over twenty miles an hour, soon covered a large area which the Italian ships were unwilling to approach for fear of torpedoes. They persistently tried to work round to westward of it—that is, to leeward—so that the smoke served to hold them off from the convoy and at the same time protected the British warships from their heavier opponents. Drenching spray and drifting smoke made gunnery very difficult for both sides, though the Italians had some help from aircraft which were free from any interference from British fighters. Admiral Vian's ships, manœuvring as they were at high speed, for much of the time in dense smoke and not always aware of the position and course of the other divisions, had some exciting moments—as exciting, perhaps, as any caused by the enemy. Fleeting glimpses made it difficult for Admiral Vian to account continuously for all the Italian ships which were thought to be present. Wishing to assure himself that none was slipping round to attack the convoy from to windward—which he thought would be the enemy's best course—he twice drove east to get a clearer view. The first time he got too far to the eastward, and the Italian ships to leeward were able to gain some ground on the convoy. Throughout the battle the 2nd and 3rd Divisions conformed closely to the movements of Admiral Vian's own 4th Division, while the 5th Division (Captain St. J. A. Micklethwait) acted as guard on the western flank in an exposed and at times unsupported position. Towards the end of the battle the 1st Division (Captain A. L. Poland) took over the 5th Division's role.

When Admiral Vian's striking force stood out again to the northward at 4.40 (Phase 3), the *Cleopatra* and *Euryalus*, and later the other two cruisers and the 5th Division, engaged three Italian cruisers at about ten miles and were themselves engaged by these cruisers and by the battleship, which was beyond their range. The *Cleopatra* was hit by a 6-inch shell and the *Euryalus* by 15-inch splinters. At 4.48 Admiral Vian turned west into his own smoke and ceased fire. The 5th Division, further to the west, soon got another fleeting view of the enemy and Captain Micklethwait tried to gain a favourable position for attacking with torpedoes. At 4.59 he opened gunfire on the three cruisers, now only five miles distant. Six minutes later the battleship also came in sight and he turned away to avoid punishment (Phase 4). For some twenty minutes the 5th Division stood to the southward, making smoke and watching the enemy ten miles off. At 5.20 a near miss from a 15-inch shell reduced the *Havock's* speed and she was detached. A few minutes later Captain Micklethwait, still bent on attacking with torpedoes, turned north with his three remaining destroyers, but conditions were unfavourable and he altered away again to keep between the enemy and the convoy.

Admiral Vian, manœuvring to hold his position with the 2nd, 3rd and 4th Divisions between the convoy and the enemy, fired at the flashes of the enemy's guns, or at ships dimly seen through the smoke. At 5.30 he made the first of his moves to get a clear view around the eastern limits of the smoke, but by 5.40 he was steering west again. He fired a few salvoes at the battleship, at extreme range, before disappearing into smoke of the 5th Division's making.

At 5.40 this Division also sighted the battleship again, this time to the north-west, only eight miles off and steering to the south at high speed (Phase 5). Captain Micklethwait opened fire on her from the *Sikh*, and the *Lively* and *Hero* also fired whenever they caught a glimpse of the target through their leader's smoke. Seas were sweeping over the three destroyers and they were moving heavily in the swell. The range was too great to see where their small shells were falling. The Italian battleship returned their fire, and at 5.48 the *Sikh* was straddled. She promptly fired two of her four torpedoes 'to avoid sinking with all torpedoes on board and in the hope of making the enemy turn away'.

So far Admiral Iachino had had to depend on reports from his aircraft for information of the convoy, and he pressed on in the hope of sighting it around the western limits of the smoke. (By 6 o'clock, had he known it, he was only ten and a half miles from the convoy, well within range and as close to it as he was ever to be.) Captain Micklethwait could see what was happening and tried to extend the smoke screen to the west while continuing his 'somewhat unequal contest' with the enemy.

Admiral Vian had been trying for fifteen minutes to cut his way through the smoke to get a view of the enemy. He well knew that the situation was critical, and at one minute before 6 o'clock he made a general signal to prepare to fire torpedoes under cover of smoke. Three minutes later his flagship got clear, sighted the battleship at six and a half miles, and opened gunfire (Phase 6). At six minutes past six the *Cleopatra* turned to port and fired three torpedoes. By the time the other ships were out of the smoke the Italian battleship had turned away into a smoke screen of her own, and the opportunity to fire torpedoes had passed. However, some relief had been given to the 5th Division, and Admiral Vian, still not happy about his eastern flank, turned in that direction again. By 6.17 he could see that all was clear to the north-east and he returned to support the 5th Division, which turned north to lay a fresh smoke screen.

Captain Poland, leading the 1st Division, now came on the scene. He had not joined the convoy's escort as he had been ordered to do, because reports that enemy ships were again in sight and a mutilated signal from Admiral Vian beginning 'Feint at . . .' made him decide to follow the convoy at a distance and lay smoke between it and the enemy. His first view of the enemy came at 5.45 when he saw gun flashes to the north-west through the smoke laid by the 5th Division, which he could see was under heavy fire from 15-inch guns. Shortly after 6 o'clock he received a signal from Captain Micklethwait that put the Italians only eight miles from the convoy and he altered course to north-west to close the enemy. At 6.34 he sighted the Italian battleship and promptly made a torpedo attack upon her, closing from six to three miles range in order to do so. Fortunately the fire from the enemy's battleship and cruisers, although heavy, was erratic. (The *Cleopatra* and *Euryalus* as well as the 1st Division were engaging them at the time.) At 6.41, just as the 1st Division turned to fire, a heavy shell hit the *Kingston* (Phase 7).[1] She managed, none the less, to fire three torpedoes before limping off, and the other ships of the Division fired twenty-two more. This was really the final exchange, for although Captain Micklethwait attempted another torpedo attack with his Division, the enemy, influenced perhaps by the 1st Division's attack, but more certainly by the approach of darkness, turned away at 6.50 and broke off the action (Phase 8).

In such an engagement it is not surprising that there were very few hits. The *Cleopatra* had been struck on the bridge by one 6-inch shell, and heavier shells had damaged the *Havock* and *Kingston*. The *Euryalus* and *Lively* had been struck by large splinters. Only one Italian ship was hit—at 6.51—and, as this was the battleship, the light British shell did only superficial damage. There had been no torpedo hits.

The Italians had received reports of the British convoy and its escorting warships early in the evening of 21st March from two submarines and from the German transport aircraft sighted by Admiral Vian. The battleship *Littorio* (flying the flag of the Italian Commander-in-Chief, Admiral Iachino) and four destroyers left Taranto on the 22nd, half an hour after midnight, and were joined at sea by the 8-inch cruisers *Gorizia* and *Trento*, the 6-inch cruiser *Bande Nere* and four destroyers from Messina. Two other destroyers which were delayed in leaving Taranto and one of the Littorio group which later developed a defect took no part in the subsequent engagement. Reinforcements of German and Italian aircraft, particularly torpedo-bombers, were sent from Sardinia to Sicily and from bases in the Aegean to Crete.

The first news of the British force on the 22nd was received just before 10 a.m. from a shore-based Italian aircraft, and Admiral Iachino adjusted his course to ensure early contact. He considered

[1] The British report states 15-inch, but the *Trento* claims an 8-inch hit at this moment.

circling round behind the British force from the east but decided in favour of a westerly approach, which he expected would result in making contact sooner and would bar the convoy's way to Malta, although it would mean surrendering the weather gauge. The task given to the cruiser force was to maintain contact with the enemy without fully engaging him, and to keep Iachino informed of his movements. This task, in the Admiral's opinion, was well carried out as far as the difficulties created by the smoke cloud permitted. The poor visibility and bad effect of the spray on the optical instruments combined to make the Italian gunfire ineffective, and in the hope of obtaining a lucky hit Admiral Iachino closed the range beyond the limits of safety from torpedo attack. His decision to break off the action on the approach of darkness was confirmed shortly after the turn to the north by a signal from Rome ordering this to be done. (A year had passed since the night action off Cape Matapan, but the Italian Fleet was still not equipped for using its bigger guns by night.) On the return passage to Taranto and Messina many of the Italian ships suffered serious damage from the heavy gale, and on the 23rd the destroyers *Sirocco* and *Lanciere* foundered.

As soon as the Italian ships had disappeared Admiral Vian, judging that they would be unlikely to return, collected his own ships and steered to close the convoy ten miles or so to the southward. At 7.40 p.m., in the growing darkness and before the convoy was in sight, he decided to shape course for Alexandria with Force B and to send the convoy to Malta in the manner previously arranged. Accordingly the *Penelope* and *Legion* parted company to overtake the convoy which had already been joined by the *Havock*. The *Kingston*, which like the *Havock* was too badly damaged to go back to Alexandria in the face of a rising gale, was also making to join the convoy. Captain C. A. G. Hutchison of the *Breconshire*, the convoy Commodore, had already dispersed the merchant ships for a given time on diverging courses, with a destroyer or two apiece as escort. Each ship was to make her best speed so as to reach Malta as early as possible next morning.

For the past four days the enemy had concentrated their air attacks on Malta's airfields, with the result that on 23rd March the defending Spitfires and Hurricanes could make only 42 sorties in all. Enemy aircraft appeared at first light, in spite of the thick weather, and the merchant ships had to run the gauntlet of attacks all the way to the Grand Harbour. Their escorts, desperately short of ammunition, fired only when the danger became immediate. The first ship to arrive was the *Talabot* at 9.15 a.m., over two hours late, closely followed by the *Pampas*. It was not easy for their exhausted crews to berth them in the high wind. As may be imagined they were given a tremendous welcome. They had had some narrow escapes, and two bombs had actually hit the *Pampas* without exploding.

The *Breconshire* had not been so lucky, for after surviving a score of attacks she was hit and disabled at 9.20 within eight miles of harbour. Her deep draught and the heavy sea made towing impossible, and she was anchored with three destroyers to protect her. At 10.30 the fourth ship, the *Clan Campbell*, with twenty miles to go, was hit by a bomb and quickly sank. The destroyer *Legion* was damaged by a near miss and had to be beached at Marsa Scirocco. Next day, the 24th March, the Hunt class destroyer *Southwold* struck a mine while standing by the *Breconshire*, and sank.

Admiral Vian, returning to the east, had had to reduce speed on account of the gale, and most of his destroyers had suffered damage from the sea though not from the air. At midday on 24th March Force B arrived at Alexandria 'honoured to receive the great demonstration' which took place.

Attempts to attack the homeward bound Italian ships failed. Beauforts of No. 39 Squadron R.A.F. from Egypt and Albacores of No. 828 Squadron F.A.A. from Malta had not found the enemy by dark on the 22nd, and were recalled. Heavy rain and high seas handicapped the submarines, although the *Upholder* had a fleeting glimpse of a battleship at which she fired unsuccessfully. There was, however, one success indirectly connected with the battle. On 1st April the submarine *Urge*, patrolling south-east of Stromboli, sank the cruiser *Bande Nere* which was going north to Spezia for repairs to damage received in the gale.

The enemy continued his attacks during daylight on the three surviving merchantmen and on the airfields at Malta. British fighters, greatly outnumbered, made 175 sorties on the 24th and over 300 on the 25th. At night the ground crews struggled to repair the damage done during the day. On the 25th, in spite of bad weather, the *Breconshire* was towed in to Marsa Scirocco where she sank on the 27th after further damage, having then suffered continual attacks for four days. Her service to Malta had far surpassed that of any other ship. Since April 1941 she had made six trips from Alexandria and one from Gibraltar. She had never had to turn back, and at Malta she had been twice damaged by air attacks. Even after she was sunk she performed a further service, for some hundreds of tons of oil fuel were pumped from her hull.

On the 26th the *Talabot* and *Pampas* were hit in their unloading berths. The *Talabot* had to be scuttled lest her cargo of ammunition should explode, and all but two of the *Pampas's* holds were flooded. On the same day the *Legion*, which had been towed into harbour from Marsa Scirocco, was sunk.

It was no use sailing any more convoys to Malta if the cargoes which arrived were then to be lost, and it was obvious that many more fighters were needed before another convoy could be received. Nor had the berthing of the ships been satisfactory, and it was decided that they should in future be berthed in shallow water or beached. Unloading was another trouble, for the stevedores had refused to work during 'red flag' periods of alert. On 31st March they were replaced on the half-sunken *Pampas* by men from the Services, who worked day and night regardless of air raids, though not so rapidly as the experienced stevedores could have done. Of the 26,000 tons loaded in Egypt, 1,052 were unloaded from the *Talabot* and 3,970 from the *Pampas*. Salvage contractors later produced a further 2,500 tons.

The Maltese had every reason to be disappointed by the outcome of the March convoy, and their feelings were fully shared by the men of the Royal Navy and Merchant Navy who had fought the convoy through and by the airmen who had striven so hard to protect it. In some respects the merchant ships and their anti-aircraft escort of Hunts had had a more arduous battle than the ships of Admiral Vian's striking force, yet it is upon the surface engagement that interest naturally centres. This Second Battle of Sirte was to become a classic example of successful action by an inferior fleet. By skill, boldness and bluff the British ships had prevented their much heavier opponents from coming within range of the convoy. Had the Italian heavy ships penetrated the smoke screen they would have surrendered some of their advantage in gun power and exposed themselves to torpedoes fired from the quicker manœuvring British ships. Admiral Vian was ready for this, but Admiral Iachino did not take the risk. He wished to bar the convoy's way to Malta and, for that reason among others, was not attracted by the idea of attacking from to windward. In the event, the Italian tactics did delay the convoy, which was consequently exposed to further attacks from the air next day before entering harbour. To this extent the Italian manœuvres succeeded.

It was now necessary to clear Malta of all surface ships except local defence vessels. Of the warships which had arrived with the convoy the *Carlisle* and four Hunts had sailed on the 25th for Alexandria, and four days later the *Aurora*, which had been refitting, sailed with the *Avon Vale* for Gibraltar. This left only the *Penelope*, which had been seriously damaged on the day the *Talabot* and *Pampas* were sunk, and four destroyers which had still to be made fit for sea. The submarines in harbour had to be widely dispersed, and by day remain submerged, which meant that the crews got little rest. One, the *P.39*, had been damaged beyond repair during bombing attacks on the 26th and others had been damaged, but less severely.

The local defence craft had been reinforced on 17th March by two motor launches from Gibraltar. During their passage through French territorial waters they had flown Italian colours, and although challenged several times by shore stations and by Italian aircraft they had not been fired on. A few days later two more motor launches on passage were attacked by aircraft, one being sunk and the other interned at Bône. Four submarines carrying petrol and kerosene had arrived at Malta during the month, two from Alexandria and two from Gibraltar.

During the first three months of 1942 the war against enemy shipping had not gone well. It has been related how the enemy had been sending most of his supplies to North Africa in battleship convoys; the sinkings on this all-important route had consequently fallen off and the quantity of cargo disembarked in North Africa had been steadily rising. The Royal Navy, after its heavy losses in capital ships at the end of 1941, was almost powerless to intervene. Since December a much reduced Force K had been able to take little offensive action, and after the March convoy it had ceased to exist. The Far East had continued to draw off ships: the fast minelayer *Abdiel*, three new Australian destroyers, and the Dutch destroyer *Isaac Sweers* had left the Mediterranean in January, and five more destroyers followed in February. By the end of March, weather damage and battle damage left Admiral Cunningham with only four cruisers and fifteen destroyers fit for service—indeed for a time his destroyers were reduced to six.

Admiral Cunningham had hoped that the great superiority in weight and numbers of ships which the Italian Fleet now possessed would have been offset by greatly increased British strength in the air. By the end of February No. 201 Naval Co-operation Group R.A.F. had indeed grown to sixteen R.A.F. and F.A.A. squadrons—three bomber, four torpedo-bomber, six reconnaissance and three fighter—and was giving cover to all naval operations within fighter range. But the loss of the airfields in the bulge of Cyrenaica in January was a serious blow which prevented the force repeating the highly successful work it had done in protecting the Malta convoys in January. As far as aircraft at Malta were concerned, they had had to contend with some very bad weather, with heavy bombing of their airfields, and with increasing enemy interference in the air. In spite of these handicaps, reconnaissance over enemy ports had become more regular and the figures for enemy ships sunk, though rather disappointing, had shown a considerable improvement on those for November and December. Bombers and torpedo-bombers had flown over 1,000 anti-shipping sorties during January, February and March. They had sunk five merchant ships and shared in the sinkings of three others, totalling in all 44,000 tons. In addition a number of ships had been damaged.

Submarines, which had been less affected than aircraft by bad weather and air attacks, had been doing better. During January, February and March they sank sixteen merchant ships (two of them shared) totalling 75,000 tons, and in addition to the cruiser *Bande Nere* they sank one German and five Italian submarines—a remarkable feat indeed for submarine versus submarine. Two other German submarines had been sunk, one by a mine and one by No. 230 Squadron R.A.F. In the same period four British submarines had been destroyed, two by mines, one by an Italian torpedo boat, and one by air attack in harbour at Malta.

In the course of these submarine patrols three Victoria Crosses had been won. The first two were awarded to Lieutenant P. S. W. Roberts and Petty Officer T. W. Gould, of H.M.S. *Thrasher*, for extricating, in conditions of great difficulty and danger, two unexploded bombs which had lodged in the hull casing. The third award was made to Commander A. C. C. Miers for a succession of deeds of skill and daring culminating in a search for four large troopships in Corfu Roads. They were unfortunately not there, but H.M.S. *Torbay* spent seventeen hours inside the Straits and torpedoed a 5,200-ton merchant ship before she withdrew.

The decision to send back the *Luftwaffe* to Sicily in order to renew the heavy attacks on Malta had been taken in October 1941.[1] By the middle of March 1942 the number of German bombers and fighters in Sicily was 335—almost the same as there had been a year before. But conditions at sea had changed in favour of the Axis Powers, who could reasonably expect that the shortages in Malta would make the air attacks harder to resist and harder to bear than in 1941.

Opinion had been divided for some time on whether Malta could be so badly hurt from the air as to be unable to recover the strength with which to make herself a serious nuisance again, or whether permanent results could be achieved only by capture. The advantages of seizing Malta would be very great, but to ensure that an assault would succeed it would be necessary to put a large force into training, and to assemble many aircraft, ships, and landing craft—largely at the expense of operations in North Africa. It was not worth taking all this trouble if Suez could be reached without it.

The first study of the capture of Malta had been made by the Germans in March 1941, but the invasion of Crete had intervened and the difficulties of this type of operation had become all too plain. However, in the summer of 1941 General Cavallero began to show

---

[1] See page 21.

interest, and further studies were produced by all and sundry, including even the Japanese! The Italians actually began in January 1942 to train for a sea- and air-borne attack, and on 8th March the Prince of Piedmont accepted the command of Army Group South, which was to be used for the assault. Admiral Raeder seems to have impressed Hitler with the importance of the Mediterranean sufficiently for him to order heavier air attacks on Malta, and by March Kesselring believed that he had almost withdrawn the island's sting by bombing, though he was apt to change his opinion according to the prospects of the desert battle. Thus at the end of March it was still undecided whether Malta would have to be captured or not, and the only practical step for the moment was to persist with the severe air attacks. The results of this policy are described in the next chapter.

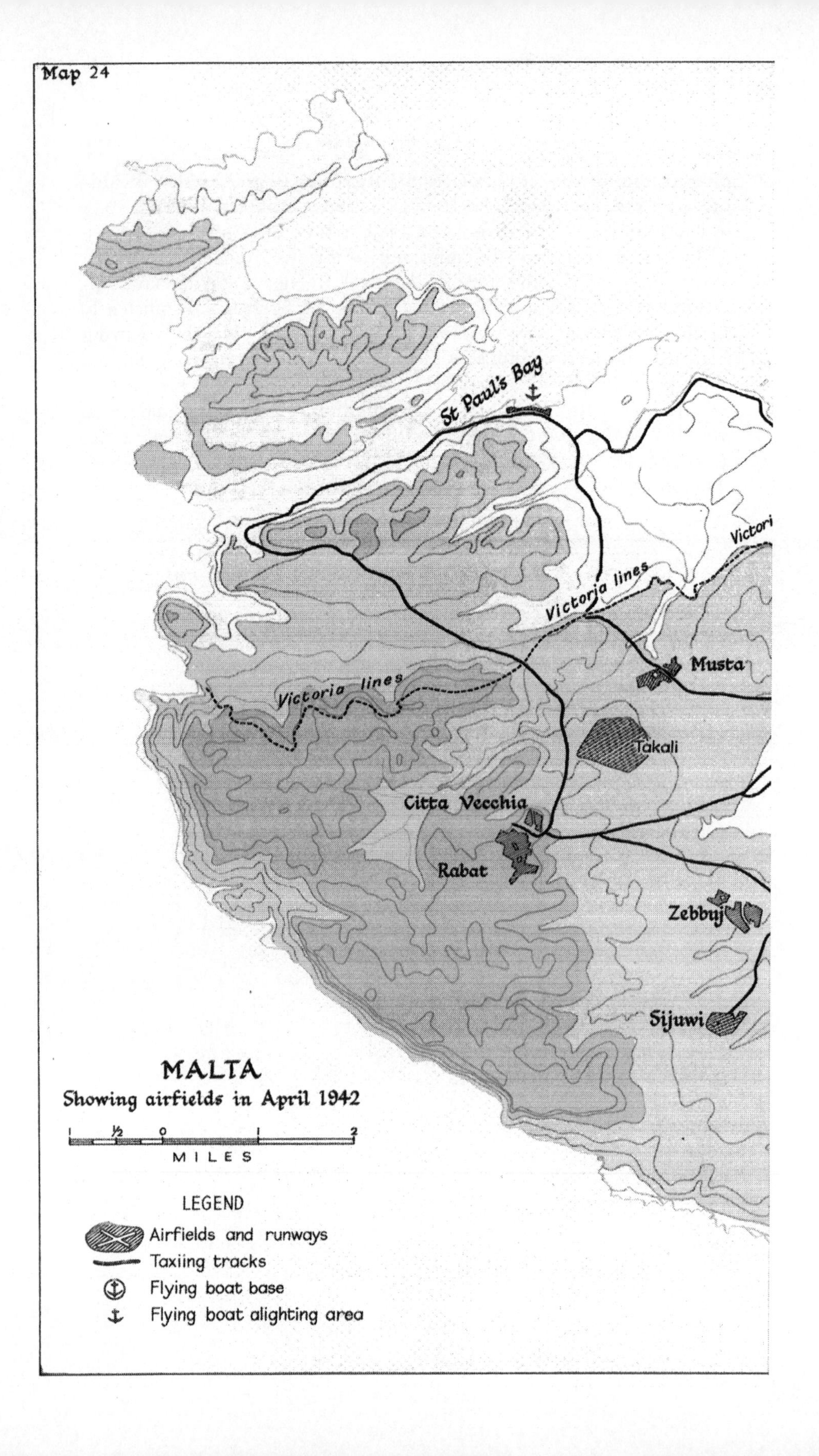

Map 24
St Paul's Bay
Victoria lines
Victoria lines
Victoria lines
Victori
Musta
Takali
Citta Vecchia
Rabat
Zebbuj
Sijuwi
MALTA
Showing airfields in April 1942
1 ½ 0 1 2
MILES
LEGEND
Airfields and runways
Taxiing tracks
Flying boat base
Flying boat alighting area

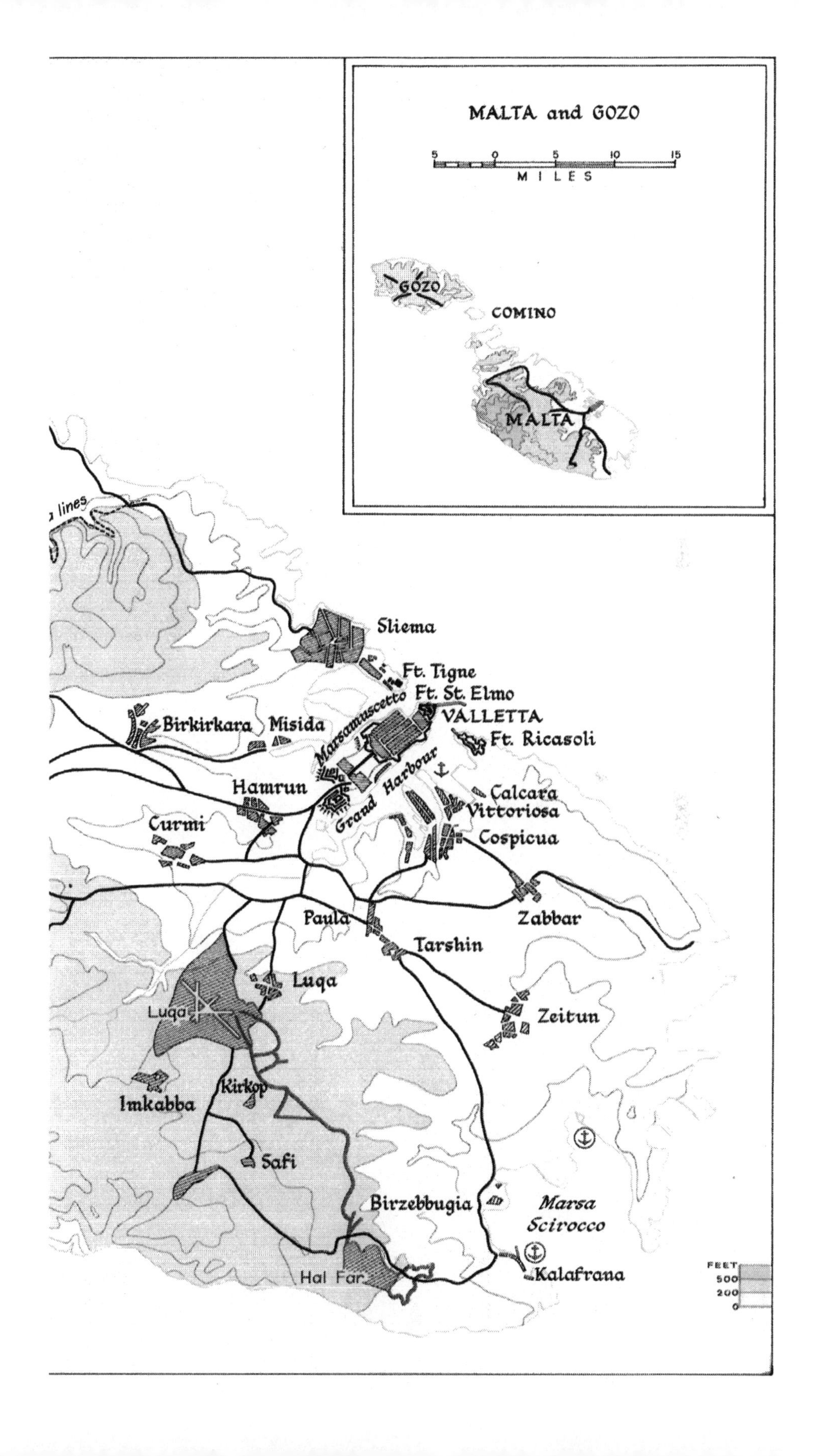

MALTA and GOZO
5
0
5
10
15
MILES
GOZO
COMINO
MALTA
Sliema
Ft. Tigne
Ft. St. Elmo
VALLETTA
Ft. Ricasoli
Birkirkara
Misida
Marsamuscetto
Grand Harbour
Hamrun
Calcara
Vittoriosa
Cospicua
Curmi
Paula
Zabbar
Tarshin
Luqa
Luqa
Zeitun
Kirkop
Imkabba
Safi
Birzebbugia
Marsa
Scirocco
Kalafrana
Hal Far
FEET
500
200
0

CHAPTER VIII

MALTA'S GREATEST TRIAL

(April – May 1942)

See Map 24

THE passage of the convoy to Malta at the end of March, which had brought about the second battle of Sirte, was the last important event in Admiral Cunningham's present tenure of the post of Commander-in-Chief, Mediterranean.[1] A Combined Chiefs of Staff's Committee had been set up in Washington, and on this he was wanted to represent the First Sea Lord. His achievements in the Mediterranean were known to the world, and no one had had so much experience of the latest conditions of fighting on and over the sea. Moreover, having been one of a triumvirate of Commanders-in-Chief in an intensely active theatre he was ideally fitted to advise on the combined operations which were clearly going to loom so large in the Allies' future plans. There was no sailor to whom the Americans would be likely to listen with greater respect at this early and vital stage in Anglo-American co-operation.

It goes without saying that to leave his Mediterranean Command caused Admiral Cunningham much distress, the more so because times were particularly hard. The sea, the handling of ships, and the training and command of men were what he loved; they appealed to him much more than the niceties of the conference table. Like many another great British sailor he had served much of his time with the Mediterranean Fleet; he had held important commands in it and for the past three years had been its Commander-in-Chief. After Italy entered the war—now nearly two crowded years ago—the issue at sea, as between ships, did not remain long in doubt. Nevertheless there were trials in plenty for all to bear, and especially for the Commander-in-Chief—the early loss of France as an ally, and all that this entailed, and, as time went on, the loss of many a fine ship and many fine officers and men. Fighters and gunfire had not always been able to counter the enemy's great preponderance in the air, and Admiral Cunningham had more than once been obliged to sacrifice his ships. Now, as he handed over command, the British still lacked air forces sufficiently strong and experienced to make up for the ships that had

[1] He became Commander-in-Chief, Mediterranean, again in 1943, by which time conditions were quite different.

been lost or withdrawn. On 1st April 1942 the Italian Fleet comprised 4 serviceable battleships, 9 cruisers, and 55 destroyers and torpedo boats, while the British Mediterranean Fleet had only 4 cruisers and 15 destroyers. At Gibraltar there remained fit for service only the small aircraft carrier *Argus* and two or three destroyers. There were 50 Italian and 20 German submarines in the Mediterranean, but the Allies had only 25. Based in Western Cyrenaica, Sicily, Greece, Crete, and the Dodecanese were some 290 German and 250 Italian bombers; in Eastern Cyrenaica, Egypt, and Malta were more than 400 British bombers, but over a large part of the Central and Eastern Basins the Mediterranean Fleet could be given no fighter cover. Thus the mastery that Admiral Cunningham had won was now in jeopardy.

Until the arrival of the new Commander-in-Chief, Admiral Sir Henry Harwood, the Mediterranean Command was taken over by Admiral Pridham-Wippell. Admiral Cunningham left by air on 3rd April, but he was ordered to keep his going secret from the enemy—so great was his prestige. And so, instead of saying goodbye to his officers and men in person, he could only leave behind messages of farewell and gratitude—one to the Fleet, one to the Merchant Navy and one to Malta. His message to Malta, so typical of him, stressed the island's offensive role against the enemy's shipping. It was the great success of this offensive, he wrote, which had led to the ceaseless battering of the fortress. In enduring this battering, which absorbed so much of the enemy's air effort, Malta was rendering yet another service to the Empire.

Instead of abating after the *Breconshire*, *Pampas*, and *Talabot* had been sunk with most of their cargoes still unloaded, the battering to which Admiral Cunningham had referred grew more violent. The 7th and 8th April were two of the worst days, on each of which the enemy made well over 250 sorties over the island. Between 24th March and 12th April over 2,000 sorties were made against the Grand Harbour, and the estimated weight of bombs dropped was 1,870 tons. The dockyard received the heaviest pounding of all, and work was virtually stopped except in the underground shops. To reduce congestion in the shelters, workers under eighteen were given leave with pay; some of the casual labour was discharged, and skilled tradesmen were lent to the other Services. Neither electric light nor power remained, except close to the underground generating station. Telephones were out of action most of the time, and for water the dockyard depended mainly on tanks refilled from barrels carried in hand carts. All the dry docks were damaged and soon only one was fit for use. In the dockyard and in the towns around the Grand Harbour it was difficult to keep a passage for even light traffic through the mounting rubble.

The other targets on which the enemy made concentrated attacks were the three airfields. Parties of soldiers and of Maltese civil labour, with a sprinkling of Royal Navy and Maltese Police, strove to clear away wreckage, fill craters, roll runways, and rebuild pens. This gave some relief to the understaffed ground crews of the Royal Air Force, and it kept the airfields open, so that fighters and the aircraft which arrived nightly on their way to Egypt and India were able to land and take off—though often at much hazard. Cables linking radar stations with control rooms and airfields were repeatedly cut, and fighters had often to be ordered into the air by light-signal fired from the nearest telephone terminal that was still working. By mid-April most of the 31 Spitfires which had arrived in March had been destroyed, and the Hurricanes of Nos. 185 and 229 Squadrons then bore the brunt of the air fighting. The bravery of the British pilots drew the admiration of the enemy, but in spite of all the hard work and ingenuity of the ground crews the number of serviceable fighters dwindled until there were only six, and sometimes even fewer.

There were long periods when the enemy's raids were met by gunfire alone, and during April the anti-aircraft gun positions, especially those round the airfields, were heavily and repeatedly attacked. It was indeed a strenuous time, for in this month there were 284 alerts—or more than nine a day, each often lasting several hours—during which the heavy guns fired 72,053 rounds and the light guns 88,176. Of the 35 German and 2 Italian aircraft recorded by the enemy as having been lost over Malta during April, 13 are shown as having fallen to the guns and 11 to the fighters. The concentration of guns was tremendous: over the most important parts of the island there was a density of at least 80 heavy guns, while the 144 light guns were deployed in an area nine miles by six.[1] As a precaution ammunition was rationed, but this never prevented a raid from being vigorously opposed and there was no real shortage. The anti-aircraft artillery comprised the 7th Light Anti-Aircraft Brigade and the 10th Heavy Anti-Aircraft Brigade.[2] The C.R.A. was Brigadier C. T. Beckett (later Major-General R.A. and Commandant, Anti-Aircraft Defences). The services of the Royal Malta Artillery were specially recognized by His Majesty the King who honoured the Regiment by becoming its Colonel-in-Chief.

It was related in the previous chapter that all surface warships fit

[1] The total number of heavy A.A. guns was 112. It had been laid down generally in 1939 that a density of 16 heavy A.A. guns over a vulnerable point of the greatest importance should be the aim.

[2] *7th Light Anti-Aircraft Brigade:* 32nd, 65th, 74th Light A.A. Regiments R.A.; 3rd Light A.A. Regiment R.M.A.; 4th Searchlight Regiment R.A./R.M.A.

10th Heavy Anti-Aircraft Brigade: 4th, 7th, 10th Heavy A.A. Regiments R.A.; 2nd, 11th Heavy A.A. Regiments R.M.A.

Unbrigaded Units: 225th Light A.A. Battery R.A.; 14th Heavy A.A. (Relief) Battery R.M.A.

to put to sea, other than local defence craft, had been sailed from Malta as soon as possible after the arrival of the convoy at the end of March. There remained the cruiser *Penelope*, badly damaged by near misses on the 26th, the destroyers *Havock* and *Kingston* damaged in Admiral Vian's battle, and the destroyer *Gallant* mined in January 1941 and still unrepaired. Of these only the *Penelope* was to survive. The *Havock* sailed for Gibraltar on 5th April but ran aground on the Tunisian coast when keeping close inshore to avoid minefields, and had to be destroyed by her company who were subsequently interned by the French.

The escape of the *Penelope* is a stirring instance of the will to win through. Damaged on 26th March, she was docked to be made seaworthy and quickly became the bull's-eye for many of the heaviest raids. Shipwrights and artificers of the ship's staff and five volunteer welders from the Royal Engineers joined the dockyard craftsmen in the race to complete her repairs before she should receive further and perhaps irreparable damage. On 4th April the caisson which closed the dock was damaged, the dock pump was put out of action, and *Penelope* herself was hit again. Water leaking through the damaged caisson stopped work on the ship's bottom, but the pump was mended and shipwrights standing in water up to their chests were able to begin work again. On the 5th many near misses made craters round the dock, and the decks were littered with blocks of masonry which interfered with the feeding of ammunition to the guns. During the next few days there were many more narrow escapes. Although her gun barrels had been renewed towards the end of March, the *Penelope* fired so much anti-aircraft ammunition that by 6th April her 4-inch guns were nearly worn out again; indeed, her Gunnery Officer was killed by a premature explosion at one of them. The ship's company were just about exhausted, and their ship was almost uninhabitable, but it was decided to make a final spurt to enable her to sail at nightfall on the 8th. The air attacks became fiercer than ever, and some hours before she was due to sail the 4-inch ammunition began to run out. Parties of soldiers and dockyard officials and men from other damaged ships helped to embark some last-minute supplies. In two weeks the *Penelope* had fired 6,500 rounds of 4-inch ammunition and 63,000 rounds of smaller calibre. In spite of the untiring efforts of the fighters and the anti-aircraft artillery, the *Penelope* felt that her own guns had saved her.

At 9.15 p.m. she passed the breakwater. Captain A. D. Nicholl, although wounded, was still in command. Bomb splinters had riddled her sides that morning, and the hundreds of holes plugged with wood made her look like a porcupine. At 27 knots her foremost mess decks became flooded and all possible top weight had to be jettisoned. Steering was very difficult, but Cape Bon was passed shortly before dawn next day. Along the coasts of Tunisia and Algeria there were frequent attacks by torpedo-bombers and by high- and low-level bombers. None, however, caused any more damage, although there were some near misses and again the 4-inch ammunition nearly ran out. On the afternoon of the 10th H.M.S. *Penelope* reached Gibraltar.

On 12th and 13th April Sir Walter Monckton (acting Minister of State) and Air Marshal Tedder visited Malta and reported to London what they had learned from the Governor, General Dobbie, and the members of the Malta Defence Committee. The salient points were as follows. The enemy was estimated to be operating some 160 fighters and 250 bombers from six airfields in Sicily, and could easily sustain 70 fighters in the air. He was making concentrated attacks probably because he was uncertain of the true strength of the defending fighters; this caused less dislocation than when the island was under warning for the whole day. But the British fighters had been worn down, and in order to conserve enough of them to cover the arrival of further Spitfires it had been necessary to allow many raids to take place unopposed in the air. Although Air Vice-Marshal Lloyd had been forced to send away the Blenheims and Wellingtons, he intended to call back eight Wellingtons to attack the enemy's airfields as soon as he had enough fighters 'to put up an umbrella'.[1]

The report went on to say that the enemy's object appeared to be to neutralize Malta, for there were no signs of impending invasion—just as well, because the garrison, with all its extraneous tasks (there were, for instance, 400 soldiers on each airfield), was in need of at least two months' training. The people of Malta were bearing up well, though they were suffering real hardship and were anxious about food. They knew what had happened to the last convoy, and the enemy's complete command of the air was plain for all to see. There was 34 days' supply of flour, apart from some stocks of wheat and maize which had to be milled, but the mills were all near the Grand Harbour and had been damaged. They were being brought into action again, but even if working at full capacity they could not keep pace with the daily requirements of flour and they might well be damaged again. It was vitally important to receive a convoy in May, but there must first be many more fighters and more ammunition. There were many other shortages. Only three out of ten tugs were serviceable, and the available berths had been reduced by sunken ships. There were only enough lighters to unload one ship at a time; more should be brought by the first convoy coming from the west, and minesweepers must come too. Finally, a tanker must come with black oil, and to reduce

[1] This he ultimately did, but the results only served to confirm past experience, namely, that bombing attacks on airfields by night were effective only if they were very heavy.

the risk from fire it should be discharged in Marsamuscetto rather than in the Grand Harbour. White oils should come in drums in the other merchant ships. Stocks of aviation spirit would last well into August.

This, for the most part, confirmed what was already well known. The Admiralty had informed Admiral Pridham-Wippell on 4th April that it would not be possible to run another convoy to Malta either from east or west until the island's fighters had been strongly reinforced. Steps were being taken, with American help, to fly in Spitfires about the third week in April. Of the British carriers now in the Atlantic and Home Commands the *Eagle* was in dock and would not be ready for a month, the *Victorious* could not take Spitfires in her lifts, and the *Argus* was altogether too small and too slow. The Prime Minister had therefore appealed to President Roosevelt: would he lend U.S.S. *Wasp*, a carrier recently attached to the Home Fleet? President Roosevelt at once agreed and on the 14th the *Wasp* (Captain J. W. Reeves, Jr) sailed from Greenock with 47 Spitfires, escorted by H.M.S. *Renown* (Commodore C. S. Daniel) and four British and two American destroyers. This force—Force W—entered the Mediterranean on the night 18th/19th and was joined by the cruisers *Charybdis* and *Cairo*. It should be explained that many of the ships of Force H had left Gibraltar on 1st April to take part in the operation to occupy Diego Suarez, the large land-locked anchorage in the north of Madagascar, and were not expected back until June. Meanwhile Force W was to take the place of Force H, under the direct command of the Flag Officer Commanding North Atlantic at Gibraltar. At 5.30 in the morning of 20th April the 47 Spitfires were flown off from forty-five miles north-east of Algiers. On this occasion there were no larger aircraft to act as leaders, but 46 landed safely at Malta. Force W was shadowed from time to time by aircraft which made no attack, and the *Wasp* passed westward through the Straits without declaring her presence by calling at Gibraltar.

Fliegerkorps II in Sicily learned from its radar of the flight of the Spitfires, and ninety minutes after the first one had landed the Germans began to make heavy attacks. Only a few of the new arrivals had been serviced and fuelled in readiness to take the air. During the next three days nearly 500 tons of bombs were dropped on Luqa and Takali airfields and on 23rd April General Dobbie reported that since the arrival of the new Spitfires 17 British fighters had been destroyed on the ground and 29 had been damaged. Many others had been lost in combat, and once again the serviceable fighters were reduced to six. This was indeed tragic: it strengthened the Commanders-in-Chief in their view that fighters alone could not gain enough air superiority at Malta for ships to be unloaded successfully. But without supplies the island could not live. The remedy was to smash the airfields in Sicily, and on 15th April the Commanders-in-Chief asked the Chiefs of Staff to send out a strong force of heavy bombers which could do this, and attack Tripoli and the Italian ports as well. At the end of the month the Governor made a similar request, but was told in reply that the provision of a force large enough to be effective was quite out of the question at the time. As Germany was now being heavily attacked from the United Kingdom, this naturally raises the whole issue of the strategic allocation of British bombers, which is outside the scope of this book.[1]

Meanwhile ideas and decisions about the next convoy were passing between London, Egypt, and Malta. It had been hoped to run one from each end of the Mediterranean in May, but on 18th April the Chiefs of Staff announced that no attempt would be made from the Gibraltar end. In the existing world-wide naval situation we could not afford to have capital ships or aircraft carriers damaged; these ships must not therefore be exposed to attack from the powerful air forces based in Sardinia and Sicily. Moreover, if the west-to-east convoy were dropped, reinforcements of heavy ships could reach the Indian Ocean at least three weeks sooner, and a May convoy to Northern Russia could be run.

General Dobbie naturally demurred. Too much, he thought, would now depend on the success of the convoy from Alexandria. The decision materially reduced Malta's chances of survival, not from any failure of morale or fighting efficiency but because it would be impossible to carry on without food and ammunition.

But worse was to follow. On 23rd April the Chiefs of Staff announced that in view of the general world situation and our immediate naval commitments outside the Mediterranean the Defence Committee had decided that no convoy could be run to Malta in May, either from west or east. They had already given their reasons for the former decision. Now the attempt from Alexandria had also to be postponed, because experience had shown that the Italian Fleet would challenge it in strength and it was unlikely that 'the providential escape of the March convoy, which was mainly due to weather,' would be repeated.[2] It would therefore be necessary to provide both capital ships and carriers in the escort, and these were not available. However, another big batch of Spitfires would be flown in, and anti-aircraft ammunition would be brought in by fast minelayer and possibly by submarine also. With this slight relief Malta must hold out until mid-June. Early in June the progress of General Auchinleck's offensive in the Desert

---

[1] See the forthcoming volume in this series by J. M. A. Gwyer: *Grand Strategy*, Volume III (June 1941–October 1942).

[2] In view of Admiral Vian's masterly use of the weather this could have been expressed more graciously.

would be known.[1] If he had captured Martuba or Benghazi the chances of getting a convoy through to Malta from the east without capital ship escort would be much greater. By then, too, it would be known how much of the German Air Force had been drawn away to South Russia. The situation in the Indian Ocean could be judged in the light of the capital ships now on their way: if it was favourable, Admiral Somerville could come through the Suez Canal with the three carriers and the *Warspite* to escort a convoy from Alexandria. It was hoped that this would consist of at least twelve 15-knot supply ships.

It is fitting here to recall the naval situation outside the Mediterranean when this decision was made. Losses from U-boats in the Atlantic were rising. (They reached their peak for the war in June.) Arctic convoys to Russia and Atlantic convoys were alike threatened by the presence in Norwegian waters of the *Tirpitz* and other powerful German warships. Some recent Russian convoys had been in trouble, and a backlog of cargoes was piling up on both sides of the Atlantic at a time when encouragement to Russia was paramount. It is true that the Home Fleet had just welcomed the arrival of a United States contingent, but H.M. ships thus released were urgently needed in the Indian Ocean where Admiral Somerville's Fleet was withdrawing from Ceylon to Kilindini to await reinforcements. The expedition to occupy Diego Suarez was just rounding the Cape of Good Hope. In the Far East the full extent of the Japanese intentions was still in doubt. There is no need to explain further why no convoys to Malta could be run in May 1942.

As April drew to a close the enemy had good reason for believing that he had dealt effectively with ships and dockyard, aircraft and airfields, and turned his attention more to Malta's camps, barracks, store depots and road centres. Hospitals, though clearly marked, were hit several times. But after 28th April there was a sudden falling off of German activity; instead, Italian bombers appeared more regularly, though only in small numbers. This marked the end of Malta's worst period. During April more than 9,500 sorties had been flown against the island, whereas Malta's had been reduced to 388, of which all but 30 were flown by her fighters. 20 of the 50 British aircraft lost were destroyed in the air, against a total for the enemy of 37. Over 6,700 tons of bombs were dropped, which is more than three times the figure for March. 3,000 of these fell in the dockyard area, and 2,600 on the airfields. (The estimated weight of bombs on Coventry on 14th November 1940 was 520 tons.) 11,450 buildings were destroyed or

[1] The controversy over the timing of the British offensive is related in the following chapter.

damaged which was more than twice as many as in the whole of 1941. 300 civilians were killed and 330 seriously injured; fortunately there were now good shelters for all, but some of the casualties were from delay-action bombs. Three destroyers, three submarines, three minesweepers, five tugs, a water carrier and the floating crane had been sunk in harbour, and other ships had been damaged.

The truth is that by this time Malta was almost neutralized. As a staging post for aircraft reinforcements it continued to work—indeed more aircraft passed through in March, April and May than in the previous three months. But as a base from which to strike at the enemy's shipping it could be discounted. As early as 3rd April the Admiralty suggested that the 10th Submarine Flotilla should move to Alexandria. Two boats had just been sunk and two damaged in harbour, and the remainder, when not on patrol, had to spend the daylight hours submerged. The proposal was opposed mainly because shipping to the west of Malta could not be attacked effectively from Alexandria, and for the time being the 10th Flotilla remained at Malta, the crews being relieved in harbour by the crews of submarines which had been sunk. On the 26th, however, it was agreed to withdraw the flotilla, and during the next two weeks this was done. The determining factor had been not bombs but mines, for the enemy had been using fast surface craft almost nightly to mine the approaches. Radar did not detect them and their engines could not be heard above the prevailing din. The few minesweepers which remained could not keep the channels adequately swept, and, as will be seen, this led to disaster.

The air striking force at Malta had become almost impotent. Reconnaissance aircraft were down to three. During April the Royal Air Force bombers made only twenty-two sorties. The Fleet Air Arm made eleven, and by the end of the month only two Albacores and two Swordfish remained.

April 1942 will be remembered in Malta as the time of the island's greatest trial, but also as the month in which the fortitude of the people was rewarded in a way that was almost unique.[1] On 15th April the following message was received from His Majesty the King: 'To honour her brave people I award the George Cross to the Island fortress of Malta to bear witness to a heroism and devotion that will long be famous in history.' This high honour was a sign that their sufferings were understood and was an encouragement to them in their resolve to bear whatever hardships might be yet to come. And further hardships were to come very soon.

---

[1] After the First World War Dunkirk was awarded the Distinguished Service Cross, and Verdun and Ypres the Military Cross.

Because there would be no convoy until June it was necessary to place the people on the lowest possible scale of rations. The issues of preserved meat, fats and sugar rations were already very small, and on 5th May the bread ration was cut by one quarter to 10½ ounces a day. This would eke out the stocks until the end of July, provided that all the wheat and maize could be milled, which depended on keeping the mills in action. This reduction of the bread ration was the sternest restrictive measure yet attempted by the Government of Malta. Coinciding as it did with a stoppage of 'pasta' and a shortage of potatoes caused by the partial failure of the winter crop, General Dobbie had fears of its effects on morale. As a slight compensation the price of bread was reduced.

Two days later the people received another shock. To the surprise of the Cabinet and Chiefs of Staff, Sir Walter Monckton had reported after his visit in April that the Governor, that most gallant Christian gentleman Sir William Dobbie, was worn out. Air Marshal Tedder had agreed with this view, which was also confirmed by Mr. Casey, who called at Malta early in May on his way out to Cairo to take up his appointment as Minister of State. General the Viscount Gort, V.C., who had been Governor of Gibraltar for the past twelve months, was chosen to succeed General Dobbie, and on 7th May he arrived. He was by the King's wish the bearer of the George Cross to the island. General Dobbie left the following day, carrying with him the devotion and admiration of the whole population, whom he had served and inspired through nearly two years of siege.

On 15th May a change was made in the Governor's status, and Lord Gort was appointed 'Supreme Commander of the Fighting Services and of the Civil Administration'. He had represented that this was necessary now that Malta was fighting for survival, and as there were no longer any striking forces based there the main reason for placing the Service Commanders under their respective Commanders-in-Chief in the Middle East no longer applied. It was an obviously wise step if invasion should be imminent.

And indeed it seemed to the Malta Defence Committee that invasion might be threatening. It was true that there had been a lull in the air attacks since 28th April, but several new airstrips had been observed in the Vale of Catania in Sicily, with railway sidings and sheds apparently under construction nearby. These might well be preparations for using gliders on a large scale. The lull might mean that aircraft were being reconditioned for an airborne invasion of Malta. With this local view the Chiefs of Staff did not agree. They said that they had no evidence of preparations for an invasion either by land, air or sea: on the contrary, they had reliable information that one German bomber and one fighter group had been withdrawn from Sicily and that more were to follow. This, in their opinion, was the cause of the lull. It will be referred to again later.

The promised big batch of Spitfires was now to arrive on 9th May. President Roosevelt had again agreed to the use of U.S.S. *Wasp*, and H.M.S. *Eagle* had completed her refit and was available also. The fast minelayer *Welshman*, carrying 340 tons of stores, mostly ammunition, was to arrive on the day after the new Spitfires, and these, it was hoped, would ensure her safe unloading. To avoid another disaster like that of 20th April, when the newly arrived fighters had been caught on the ground, everything possible was to be done before the Spitfires left the carriers to ensure that they would be able to go into action as soon as they had been refuelled. While awaiting their turn to land they were to orbit Takali airfield at a very low height, under the protection of the light A.A. guns. Men and materials for keeping the runways in repair were to be much increased. On landing, each aircraft would be met and directed by its own numbered runner to a self-contained dispersal pen, where it would be refuelled and serviced and have its long-range tank removed. So far as numbers permitted, a Malta pilot would then take over. In this manner it was hoped to cut down to about ten minutes the time before each Spitfire was ready to take off again. All ammunition restrictions were to be lifted during the arrival and servicing of the new aircraft and while the *Welshman* was in harbour.

Other measures to protect the *Welshman* would be the most intense anti-aircraft barrage yet fired, and, for the first time, a smoke screen over the harbour. The *Welshman* herself was bringing smoke containers to add to the generators already in position, which were manned by the 12th Field Regiment, R.A. To give the ship's company of the *Welshman* some rest while in harbour, working parties from each of the Services were ready to relieve them of the task of unloading the stores.

The *Wasp*, with her Spitfires, entered the Mediterranean during the night 7th/8th May and was joined by the *Eagle* who had embarked her aircraft at Gibraltar. Escorted once again by the *Renown* (Commodore C. S. Daniel), the cruiser *Charybdis* and British and American destroyers, the two carriers flew off 64 Spitfires between 6.30 and 7.30 in the morning of 9th May from a position about sixty miles north of Algiers. The enemy seems to have made no attempt to interfere, and by 15th May the *Wasp* was back at Scapa Flow, pleased by Mr. Churchill's congratulatory signal: 'Who said a *Wasp* couldn't sting twice?'

At Malta the arrival of the Spitfires was anxiously awaited. The first batch landed at 10.30 a.m. and by the time the enemy came over an hour later about half the new fighters were in the air again. There were still some anxious moments; but the 60 new arrivals soon gave a good account of themselves and the heavy bombing attacks expected at dusk did not come.[1] The reception arrangements had worked splendidly: some of the Spitfires were ready within six minutes of landing, and together they crowded in seventy-four sorties before the end of the day.

Meanwhile the *Welshman*, whose speed and accessible stowage made her very suitable for risking a dash with supplies to Malta, was drawing nearer. She had left Gibraltar early on 8th May disguised as a large French destroyer and had to pass within range of dive-bombers from Sardinia for a few hours of daylight on the 9th. She was examined twice by Ju. 88s, once by a Catalina from Gibraltar, and once by a French float-plane. As she approached Malta next morning she witnessed a brisk night action between minesweepers and enemy motor boats, and her paravanes cut two mines just before she passed the breakwater. By 6.45 a.m. unloading was in full swing and by 1.30 p.m. it was completed. Bombing attacks had begun in earnest at 10 a.m., and tons of masonry from six near misses were scattered over the ship, without doing any but superficial damage. The fighters and anti-aircraft guns continued their good work of the previous day, and for the loss of three Spitfires several enemy aircraft were destroyed and damaged. At 8.40 p.m., having been allowed to take 300 tons from Malta's precious stock of oil fuel, the *Welshman* sailed, loudly cheered from every vantage point round the Grand Harbour. Her return passage to Gibraltar was uneventful.

Local air superiority was now with the British, and was further assured by 17 more Spitfires flown in from the *Eagle* on 18th May, which made a total of 123 fresh Spitfires received in just over four weeks.[2] It is now known that the serviceable strength of *Fliegerkorps II* in Sicily fell during the last three weeks of May from 52 bombers to 42, from 88 fighters to 36, and from 14 reconnaissance aircraft to 13. The Germans and Italians together lost some 40 aircraft over Malta in May, against a British loss in combat of 25. Only six R.A.F. aircraft were destroyed on the ground, as against thirty in April.

The enemy's daylight attacks continued on a reduced scale, and his night attacks were more numerous but not very effective; several night raiders fell to the Beaufighters of No. 1435 Flight. The estimated weight of bombs dropped in May was 520 tons, a big reduction from the April figure, but as high as the peak month of 1941. A further 570 buildings had been hit—one twentieth of the number for April. Mine-laying had become as serious a matter as bombing: from the beginning of February fast German motor-boats laid nearly 600 mines and more than 400 anti-sweep devices in the approaches to Malta mostly in

[1] Of the original consignment of 64 Spitfires one crashed on taking off, one landed in Africa, one fell into the sea, and one crashed on landing at Malta.

[2] Six Albacores flown off from the *Eagle* had had to return to the carrier because of defects. This was the second time in two months that the Fleet Air Arm in Malta had been disappointed in their reinforcements.

April and May. As will be seen, certainly one British submarine, and possibly two, were lost on these minefields. During May a tug and a drifter were also sunk by mines and a motor launch was lost in action with enemy minelayers. The minefields were, of course, a serious danger to any convoy.

Malta was still in grave peril. The *Welshman* had eased the ammunition shortage, and three submarines had brought in small quantities of aviation spirit, kerosene, and ammunition. Yet all these stores, welcome though they were, did not alter the fact that if the June convoy failed Malta would fall without any further effort on the enemy's part. If this were to happen the enemy would be relieved of most of the danger to his own supply line; and not only would he be able to build up and sustain his forces in Cyrenaica but his air forces now in use against Malta would be free to attack British forces and base installations in Egypt. Thus the fall of Malta would be likely to have important and far-reaching effects.

Even the neutralization of Malta had gone a long way towards winning for the enemy—at least temporarily—the battle for supplies. The Italian Official Naval Historian records that ships supplying North Africa sailed in greater safety during April and the first half of May than at any other time in the war. Convoys could be routed within fifty miles of Malta, escorted by only one or two torpedo aircraft. The figures for cargo disembarked in North Africa are as follows:[1]

Cargo	Month 1942	
	April	May
General military cargo, other than fuel, tons	102,000	67,500
Fuel, tons	48,000	18,500
Total percentage lost	under 1	7

During April and May only 13 Italian and German merchant ships, totalling some 40,000 tons, and a few small coasting vessels were sunk in the whole of the Mediterranean. All these sinkings were the work of submarines, except for one ship of 6,800 tons which was shared with No. 221 Squadron R.A.F. With Malta neutralized, and the airfields of Western Cyrenaica in enemy hands, British aircraft could play only an occasional part in finding and attacking ships at sea; even so, the Royal Air Force flew about 750 anti-shipping sorties in April and May

[1] M. A. Bragadin: *Che ha fatto la Marina?* p. 279.

—an even higher average than that for the previous three months. Wellingtons had recently been fitted to carry torpedoes, and pilots were being trained in their use, but even Wellingtons could have little endurance left for searching for and attacking ships as far west as the longitude of Benghazi. On 14th April there was a particularly gallant attack on a convoy eighty-five miles south-east of Malta, in which five Beauforts and one Blenheim were lost, but no enemy ships were sunk. From Egypt the Royal Air Force bombers had also been hammering away at Benghazi, making 241 sorties in April and 230 in May, but in spite of this considerable effort the enemy's records show that the cargo landed at Benghazi rose steadily and that by the middle of May the unloading capacity reached 2,500 tons a day. Throughout May there was a big increase in the quantities shipped forward to Sirte and ports in Cyrenaica from Tripoli, which took some of the strain off General Rommel's land transport.

With this situation no doubt in mind, Admiral Harwood, who had arrived on 20th May, lost no time in repeating the request for long-range bombers made on 15th April by the three Commanders-in-Chief. In this they had been concerned primarily with the bombing of Sicilian airfields, which could no longer be done from Malta. Admiral Harwood wished for aircraft with sufficient endurance to search for, find, and shadow enemy convoys long enough to guide submarines on to them. Between 1st April and 13th May twenty-six convoys were known to have passed east of Malta: in every case submarines had been available at sea to intercept, but on only five occasions did reconnaissance aircraft direct them on to a target. British submarines had consequently been forced to operate off enemy ports, which were more dangerous and less fruitful hunting grounds than those which they would otherwise have chosen. To this the Admiralty replied on 27th July that there was no immediate prospect of providing the twelve Liberators that Admiral Harwood had in mind.

An attempt by destroyers from Alexandria to interfere with the Axis supply line met with disaster. On 10th May information was received of three merchant vessels escorted by three destroyers sailing from Taranto for North Africa. The destroyers *Jervis* (Captain A. L. Poland), *Jackal*, *Kipling* and *Lively* left Alexandria on the evening of the 10th in order to intercept this convoy about dawn on the 12th off Benghazi. The air striking force available consisted of five Beauforts, which could not reach the convoy except close to Benghazi in full daylight. The convoy would almost certainly be turned back if the British destroyers were seen by aircraft or submarines, and Captain Poland's force was therefore routed midway between Cyrenaica and Crete, although this was further for the protecting Beaufighters and out of range of single-engine fighters. As evasion was the policy, and as it was known that fighters on passage were detected and plotted by the enemy's radar, a standing patrol was not to be maintained over the destroyers during daylight on the 11th. Beaufighters were to be ready, however, to take off if enemy aircraft were sighted, and it was estimated that they could be over the destroyers before an attack could begin. Captain Poland was told that he was to abandon the operation if his force was sighted by the enemy during daylight on the 11th or if he was unable to reach a position some ninety miles north-west of Benghazi by 6 o'clock on the morning of the 12th.

Early in the afternoon of the 11th the destroyers were in fact sighted by an enemy aircraft. They turned back for Alexandria in accordance with their orders, and requested fighter cover. Shortly after 4.30 two Beaufighters of No. 272 Squadron arrived and established communication with the *Jervis* and *Lively*. Almost immediately the *Lively's* radar picked up an aircraft, but too late for the fighters to intercept eight Ju. 88s which, diving down to 3,000 feet, hit and 'near missed' the *Lively* with two salvoes. She sank in three minutes. Between 6 o'clock and 6.30 four Heinkels and nine Ju. 88s made further attacks, which though accurate, did no damage. The first Beaufighter patrol had to leave before the heaviest attack: four more arrived at about 6.45, and at first communication with two of them was reasonably good, but it was lost and not regained after one of them left for home at about 7.40. Just before 8 o'clock the *Jervis* detected a large group of aircraft approaching. Before the remaining fighters could reach a position to intercept, ten Ju. 88s, coming in with the setting sun almost directly behind them, dived to make a determined attack at 1,500 feet. The *Kipling* and *Jackal* were both hit, and the *Kipling* sank ten minutes later in a position some ninety miles north-west of Matruh. After dark the *Jervis* took the *Jackal* in tow, but an oil fire in one boiler room could not be controlled and shortly before 5 a.m. on the 12th the *Jervis* sank her with torpedoes. Escorted by other destroyers and Beaufighters the *Jervis* returned to Alexandria with survivors from the three sunken ships.

It had of course been realized that unusual risks were being run in this operation, particularly as any fighter cover off Benghazi would be at the extreme limit of its range. Fighter sweeps had been made over the enemy's forward areas in Cyrenaica, but these had not affected the issue as the German bombers had come from Greece or Crete. The preventive bombing of airfields had been discarded as impracticable, since there were fifteen of these in Cyrenaica, Greece, Crete and Rhodes, and only two squadrons of bombers in Egypt suitable for the task. It is now known that the Ju. 88s (which came from Heraklion) had just completed an anti-shipping course in Italy; certainly their bombing was exceptionally accurate and determined. The British destroyers' radar had been slow in detecting the enemy's approach and communication between the ships and the Beaufighters had not been satisfactory. These two failures undoubtedly tilted the scales in the enemy's favour.

No other operations of importance were carried out from Alexandria in May. Convoys continued to run steadily to Tobruk, with only slight losses in spite of considerable air and U-boat activity. The change of Commanders-in-Chief had made it necessary to renew the agreement with Admiral Godfroy concerning the French squadron, all the more so because French opinion might easily have been inflamed by the coming British occupation of part of Madagascar.[1]

On the night of 14th/15th May the Italians made an attempt to repeat their spectacular attack of the previous December at Alexandria. The submarine *Ambra* succeeded in launching three human torpedoes, but these were dazzled by searchlights and worried by depth charges and patrol boats and failed to find the harbour entrance. An unexpected westerly set had not made their task easier. Four of the six Italians were captured immediately; the two others were at liberty in Alexandria for about a month before they were caught. The target for two of the human torpedoes had been the floating dock, in which the damaged *Queen Elizabeth* was being made seaworthy for passage to the United States. The *Valiant*, which had preceded her in dock, had left for Durban on 3rd April. The third human torpedo was to have attacked the submarine depot ship *Medway*.

Three British, three German, but no Italian submarines were lost at sea during April and May. On 1st May Hudson aircraft of No. 233 Squadron attacked *U.573* two hundred miles east of Gibraltar and damaged her so badly that she took refuge in Cartagena and was interned. The next day *U.74* was sunk some fifty miles to the east of that port by the combined efforts of a Catalina of No. 202 Squadron and the destroyers *Wishart* and *Wrestler*. On 28th May a Sunderland of the same squadron seriously damaged a submarine midway between the Balearic Islands and the North African coast, and sixty miles north-east of Tobruk the destroyers *Eridge*, *Hero* and *Hurworth* sank *U.568* after a tenacious hunt of over fifteen hours. This submarine had first been sighted by a Blenheim of No. 203 Squadron.

The first of the three British submarines to be lost was the gallant *Upholder*. The *Upholder*, *Urge*, and *Thrasher* had been ordered to establish a patrol line to the north-east of Tripoli on 15th April in order to intercept an important convoy bound for that port.[2] On the 14th, when on the way to take up their positions, both the *Urge* and the *Thrasher* heard distant explosions of depth charges from early morning until dusk. The *Thrasher* subsequently failed to establish communication with the *Upholder*, and a few days later the Italians announced

---

[1] For relations between Admiral Cunningham and Admiral Godfroy see Volume I of this history p. 138 ff and pp. 215-16.

[2] This was the convoy referred to on page 190.

that a torpedo-boat had sunk a British submarine in the Central Mediterranean on the 14th April. During her service with the 10th Flotilla the *Upholder* was credited with sinking two submarines, two destroyers, and 94,900 tons of merchant shipping, and her commanding officer, Lieut.-Commander M. D. Wanklyn, had been awarded the Victoria Cross and the D.S.O. She was on her twenty-fifth patrol in the Mediterranean and would afterwards have returned to the United Kingdom to pay off.

Two weeks later the *Urge* was lost without trace. She had left Malta for Alexandria on 27th April and nothing was heard of her again and no claim was made by the enemy. It may well be that she struck a mine shortly after sailing. It has already been mentioned that the few local patrol craft and minesweepers remaining at Malta were quite unable either to interfere seriously with the minelaying by German motor-boats which was being done almost nightly, or to keep the channels properly swept. There is no doubt that it was by striking a mine on the 8th May that the *Olympus*, bound for Gibraltar, was sunk only three miles from the Grand Harbour. She was carrying passengers from other submarines recently sunk or damaged in Malta harbour, and had 99 officers and men on board. Dawn was breaking as all those who had not been killed or trapped by the explosion began a forlorn swim. The land was just visible in the morning haze, but there was an easterly set, and air raids over Malta lessened the chances of the swimmers being sighted. No officers and only nine ratings reached the shore.

The Chiefs of Staff had been correct in believing that German aircraft were moving away from Sicily at the end of April, and that this was why the air attacks on Malta were waning. One bomber and one fighter group were moved to Russia, and 40 dive-bombers and 45 fighters were sent to reinforce *Fliegerführer Afrika*. These withdrawals and the losses which followed the arrival of the Spitfire reinforcements on 9th May greatly reduced the German effort from Sicily. However, the object had been achieved, at least for the time being, for Axis supplies were reaching North Africa with no interference from Malta and practically none from Egypt. *Luftflotte 2* had certainly done much to help General Rommel with his preparations.

It seems that as late as March Rommel had favoured the idea of capturing Malta early because he would not be in a position to attack Tobruk himself until the summer. Kesselring also was in favour of this, as he expected many German aircraft to be withdrawn from the Mediterranean before long. The Italians, however, did not think they could be ready before July. In April Rommel changed his mind, because he judged that the British in the Desert would be much stronger after May and decided that he could not defer his own attack until after the assault on Malta. Kesselring agreed with this view because of the good results of his air attacks, and on 13th April he reported that convoys or ships sailing independently could now pass close east or west of the island with little danger of being attacked. The British surface ships and submarines had been withdrawn, and the destruction of docks and storehouses had resulted in the elimination of Malta as a naval base, though not entirely as an air base. However, no British attacks had been made for some weeks on Tripoli, Sicily, or southern Italy by aircraft from Malta. From now on the plans for the attack on Tobruk took precedence over those for the assault on Malta, and although there was talk from time to time about a *coup-de-main* it came to nothing because preparations and training were not sufficiently far advanced. Kesselring was confident that the supplies for Rommel's offensive could be assured, and a point in favour of capturing Tobruk first was that the British air forces in Cyrenaica would be pushed farther east before the assault on Malta was to begin.

Although operation '*Herkules*', as it was called, was now postponed, planning and training went ahead. By mid-April the Germans had begun to take a more practical interest, and a joint German-Italian staff was set up. New plans jostled one another, but certain firm agreements were gradually reached. Valletta was to be the main objective; the attack was to be made against the southern part of the island; and the main point of disembarkation was to be in Marsa Scirocco. The south and east coasts were chosen in preference to the north because although they were rocky and steep they were believed to be less well defended, and Valletta could be reached without storming the Victoria Lines. Paratroops were to land first to secure the beach-heads for the main assault from the sea, which would be made by night. As the Italian paratroops were not trained to land in the dark the jump would be made in the afternoon. Because stone walls abounded over all but the craggiest parts of the island it would be necessary to seize landing strips before any troops could be flown in by aircraft or gliders. (*See Photo* 5.)

Crete had been captured without the help of sea-borne troops, but the defences of Malta were much stronger. The Italian Navy was to lift a first wave of 8,300 men with tanks and artillery in self-propelled lighters and other powered craft, to be followed by transports and supply ships. The Fleet would be ready to oppose any attempts by the British to intervene by sea, either from east or west. The German Navy was to provide a flotilla of submarines, and a most essential item was a special allowance to Italy of 40,000 tons of oil fuel and 12,000 tons of aviation spirit.

The proposed order of battle included an Airborne Corps of one Italian and one German parachute division, and one Italian airborne division; one Corps of two Italian divisions and one of three. There were in addition six Italian battalions, two tank battalions, some armoured cars, self-propelled artillery, motor-cyclists and ancillary units and a few German tanks; which indicates that there was no intention that the assault should fail through lack of troops.

Both Germans and Italians were well aware that German help in the air would be essential, and Field-Marshal Kesselring promised that the bulk of *Fliegerkorps X* and additional units from *Fliegerführer Afrika* would join *Fliegerkorps II* in Sicily. Eight to fourteen days after the fighting at Tobruk was over he would resume systematic attacks on Malta. The parachute and airborne divisions would be carried by German Ju. 52s and Italian Savoia 82s. Altogether there would be between 370 and 470 transport aircraft, of which 155 would be Italian.

On 1st May a meeting took place at Berchtesgaden at which both Führer and Duce were present. The senior partner made it clear that the attack in the Desert should take place at the end of May or early in June, and the assault on Malta in the middle of July—a programme which probably suited the Italian preparations quite well. Thus everything depended upon General Rommel's ability to forestall the British in the Desert and to capture Tobruk. He did both.

CHAPTER IX

THE LULL IN THE DESERT

(February – May 1942)

See Map 2

THE two previous chapters will have left no doubts as to the seriousness of the loss of the airfields in Western Cyrenaica from the point of view of the replenishment of Malta. It was only from Malta that the sea-traffic to North Africa could be attacked to good purpose, so the longer Malta was without adequately supplied striking forces the stronger would General Rommel become. It was only to be expected that General Auchinleck would be pressed to recapture the Western Cyrenaican airfields as soon as possible. Cause and effect were thus chasing each other in a circle.

The retreat of the 8th Army in January and February had stopped about thirty miles west of Tobruk. The line taken up ran inland from Gazala, where the coastal road passed through a narrow gap which was easily blocked. While the position had no important tactical features it did cover the tracks running east towards Acroma, as well as the Trigh Capuzzo and Trigh el Abd farther to the south. At the beginning of February the line was only very weakly held, but General Auchinleck ordered it to be made as strong as possible to preserve Tobruk as the base for a new offensive. In the light of subsequent events it is of interest to note that General Ritchie was told that if he was compelled to withdraw again he was not to allow his forces to be invested in Tobruk. He was to make every effort to prevent Tobruk being lost to the enemy, 'but it is not my intention,' wrote General Auchinleck, 'to continue to hold it once the enemy is in a position to invest it effectively. Should this appear inevitable, the place will be evacuated and the maximum amount of destruction carried out in it, so as to make it useless to the enemy as a supply base. In this eventuality the enemy's advance will be stopped on the general line Sollum-Fort Maddalena-Jarabub'—in other words, on the line of the Egyptian frontier. This order was the outcome of a decision taken by the Commanders-in-Chief on 4th February. They knew well the advantages the enemy would draw from gaining possession of Tobruk, but General Auchinleck was unwilling to lock up a garrison of at least one division, having regard to his strength and his other possible commitments. (The Persia-Iraq-Syria front was always in his thoughts.)

Admiral Cunningham, remembering how much it had cost in ships to maintain the garrison in 1941, strongly agreed. Air Marshal Drummond, representing the Air Officer Commanding-in-Chief, believed that we might well be unable to hold Tobruk, particularly as it would be impossible to provide it with fighter cover.

In addition to completing his defensive dispositions as soon as possible, General Ritchie was to organize a striking force with which to resume the offensive. He was also to study the possibility of regaining the airfields in the area Derna-Mechili-Martuba, or alternatively of preventing their use by the enemy—both these tasks without prejudice to the main one of defeating the enemy and reoccupying Cyrenaica. He might expect to have available three armoured divisions, two armoured brigade groups, one army tank brigade, and three infantry divisions. Most of these would be equipped and trained by the middle of April.

The Commanders-in-Chief communicated their intentions to the Chiefs of Staff on 7th February, but made no estimate of when the offensive would begin. The date, they said, would depend on the speed with which both sides would build up their armoured forces. They stated as a principle that to have a reasonable chance of beating the enemy on ground of his choosing we required a numerical superiority over the German tanks of 3 to 2 'owing to our inferiority in tank performance'. This principle, which was put forward by General Auchinleck, took account of many factors other than mere numbers. Leadership and training have often been referred to, and will be referred to again; there was also the time taken in overhauling and modifying newly arrived tanks, and the long time taken by a casualty to rejoin after being sent off to a base workshop—of which there were too few. In this connexion it should be mentioned that a Ministerial enquiry in England showed that reports from the Middle East had not exaggerated the defects of the Crusader tank in desert conditions. As for the Ordnance Workshops being too few, circumstances had been obstinately adverse. Of several that were ready to embark in October 1941 only two were on the sea by March 1942; the remainder had been shut out of two convoys mainly by drafts needed to replace battle casualties, and from a third because that convoy had suddenly been wanted for the Far East.

The Commanders-in-Chief's telegram of 7th February started a debate between London and Cairo which went on until May. The question was when could General Auchinleck start an offensive in the Western Desert. The War Cabinet and Chiefs of Staff had weighty reasons for wishing it to open very soon. General Auchinleck, supported by the other Commanders-in-Chief and by the Minister of State, was unwilling to start until he had the number of tanks that he believed essential for a reasonable hope of success: the object, as before, being to occupy Cyrenaica and press on into Tripolitania. Thus a great deal turned on the relative strength in tanks.

It is not necessary to follow in detail the rather tedious arguments about the British tanks which were put forward during the following three months. The whole episode recalls the dispute about aircraft strengths before 'Crusader' and shows what misunderstandings can arise and how misleading figures—especially telegraphed figures—can be. Broadly, London was primarily interested in the numbers of tanks despatched from the United Kingdom to the Middle East, while Cairo was concerned with tanks in fighting trim—a very different thing. Other disputes occurred about whether 'I' tanks were to be included in the calculations or not, and whether only tanks with units should count towards the three to two superiority or those in reserve as well.

The calculations of the enemy's future tank strength led to further argument. It was agreed that the Axis could spare no fresh armoured formations for Africa, except perhaps the Italian Littorio Division. It was also agreed that they would try to keep up the strength of the formations already in Africa, and had the tanks to do so. There was a difference of opinion as to what the 'establishments' of German and Italian armoured regiments were, and it will perhaps cause no surprise that Cairo's estimate was higher in each case than London's. Finally, London thought that the Middle East, although so well aware of the problems connected with tank replacements, tended to minimize unduly the enemy's difficulties.

The Middle East had other anxieties. On 17th February came the order to send the 70th Division to the Far East, and a warning that the 9th Australian Division would probably be removed from the Middle East as well.[1] On the same day the C.I.G.S., General Sir Alan Brooke, warned General Auchinleck that one division might have to return to India from Iraq, and that not more than one division would be sent to the Middle East from England during the next six months. 'I realize,' he wrote, 'that your plans for regaining Cyrenaica may have to be abandoned in favour of the defence of the Egyptian frontier and that you will be on little more than an internal security basis on your northern front . . . It is a question of reinforcing where we are immediately threatened . . .'

On 26th February the Prime Minister telegraphed to General Auchinleck:

> 'I have not troubled you much in these difficult days, but I must now ask what are your intentions. According to our figures you have substantial superiority in the air, in armour, and in other forces over the enemy. There seems to be danger that he may gain reinforcements as fast as or even faster than you.

[1] See page 126.

The supply of Malta is causing us increasing anxiety, and anyone can see the magnitude of our disasters in the Far East.

Pray let me hear from you. All good wishes.'

General Auchinleck replied the next day with a long examination of all the factors which ended with a very unpalatable conclusion. This was that to launch a major offensive before the 1st June would be to risk defeat in detail and possibly endanger the safety of Egypt.

The very same day the Chiefs of Staff signalled to the Commanders-in-Chief that Malta was of such importance that the most drastic steps were justifiable to sustain it.[1]

'We are unable to supply Malta from the west. Your chances of doing so from the east depend on an advance in Cyrenaica. The situation in Malta will be dangerous by early May, if no convoys have got through. . . . We appreciate that the timing of another offensive will depend on building up adequate tank superiority, and that its launching may necessitate taking considerable risks in other parts of Mideast Command. Nevertheless we feel that we must aim to be so placed in Cyrenaica by April dark period that we can pass substantial convoy to Malta.'

It is appropriate to recall how black at this moment seemed the immediate circumstances of the war, even if the entry of the United States made victory certain in the long run. In three weeks most of the British winter gains in Cyrenaica had been blown away. On 15th February had occurred the disaster of the fall of Singapore, quickly followed by the Allied collapse in the Netherlands East Indies. Then had come the Japanese invasion of Burma, and the prospect of losing that country was all too clear. Nearer home the escape through the Straits of Dover of the *Scharnhorst*, *Gneisenau* and *Prinz Eugen* had aroused bewilderment and indignation. The political situation was somewhat uneasy in spite of the overwhelming Vote of Confidence which the Prime Minister had obtained at the end of January, and public opinion was depressed and querulous.

The Defence Committee was deeply dissatisfied with General Auchinleck's conclusion, all the more so because the enemy in the Middle East seemed able to rebound after his reverses and we could not. Accordingly on 3rd March the Chiefs of Staff again pressed upon the Commanders-in-Chief the vital need of sustaining Malta by a convoy before May. In their opinion General Auchinleck's review was heavily biased in favour of the enemy and took no account of air power, in which we had temporarily the advantage in the desert.

[1] This was the signal referred to on page 161.

They considered that an attempt to drive the enemy out of Cyrenaica in the next few weeks was imperative for the safety of Malta and gave the only hope of fighting a battle while the enemy was still comparatively weak. Looking ahead, they pointed to the danger to the Levant-Caspian front if the enemy were allowed to build up in Africa a force which could pin down the Middle East's strength, already lessened by the needs of the Far East, to the defence of Egypt's western flank. Moreover we could not stand idle while the Russians were straining every nerve to give the enemy no rest. 'If our view of the situation is correct,' they wrote, 'you must either grasp the opportunity which is held out in the immediate future or else we must face the loss of Malta and a precarious defensive.'

To this the Commanders-in-Chief replied on 5th March agreeing that from the naval and air points of view there was nothing to gain and much to lose by waiting. But the battle would be primarily a land one, and the Army was not ready for it. A premature offensive might result in the piecemeal destruction of the new armoured forces now being built up, and would endanger the security of Egypt. The issue was therefore whether in the effort to save Malta they were to jeopardize our whole position in the Middle East.

This view angered the Prime Minister and troubled the Chiefs of Staff, and on 8th March Mr. Churchill asked General Auchinleck to come home for consultation. The General bluntly refused, saying that he felt unable to hand over his problems to anyone else even for ten days. He had given all the information there was about the tanks, and his coming home would not make it any more possible to stage an earlier offensive. Mr. Churchill saw in this refusal a manoeuvre to escape pressure and had it in mind to remove General Auchinleck. However he did not do so, and instead asked Sir Stafford Cripps, the Lord Privy Seal, to break a journey he was making to India in order to give General Auchinleck the War Cabinet's views. Sir Stafford would be joined by the Vice-C.I.G.S., Lieut.-General A. E. Nye, who knew the opinions of the Chiefs of Staff.

On 21st March Sir Stafford Cripps reported the outcome of his discussions. He was convinced that we were not strong enough in armour or in the air to make it possible for an offensive to be begun with reasonable hope of success before mid-May. Sir Stafford included a good deal of detail in his report, which was separately elaborated by General Nye, who had brought with him from the Prime Minister a formidable list of questions enquiring into everything from the build up of the armoured forces to the average ages of their commanders. General Nye, a very able and experienced Staff Officer, summarized the mass of facts which had led General Auchinleck to his conclusions. He also called attention to a factor which had frequently tended to slip out of sight—the need for proper training.

These reports were exceedingly unpleasing to the Prime Minister, who believed that his emissaries had failed to deal properly with the Middle East's arguments. Nevertheless the Defence Committee reluctantly accepted mid-May as the date for the offensive, only to be told by the Commanders-in-Chief on 2nd April that they could not bind themselves to begin even then, in spite of the very obvious and urgent need to do so as soon as possible.

On 9th April the Chiefs of Staff informed the Commanders-in-Chief of the Japanese threat to Ceylon, and the consequent danger to the Middle East's communications with the United Kingdom and to the oil supplies from Abadan. Ceylon must be given an air striking force, and at once. The Commanders-in-Chief were asked to send 30 Hurricane IIs, 20 Blenheim IVs and a squadron of Beaufort torpedo-bombers. The deeper implications of this telegram disturbed the Commanders-in-Chief even more than the loss of the aircraft, and they asked for some more information. On 23rd April the Chiefs of Staff replied with a stark review which led to the conclusion that if the Japanese pressed boldly and quickly westwards there would be a grave danger to India, and that the eventual security of the Middle East and of its essential supply lines would be threatened. This seemed to General Auchinleck to demand a complete reconsideration of Middle Eastern strategy. He told his colleagues that, in a general situation as desperate as the Chiefs of Staff had painted it, it would be taking a tremendous risk to launch an offensive in Libya; all their efforts should rather be applied to strengthening their defences and sparing everything they could for India in order to check the Japanese before it was too late.

Accordingly on 3rd May a proposal amplifying this conclusion was made to London, where, however, a very different view was held. In fact the wish to see the Middle East take the offensive had grown if anything stronger as things grew worse, in particular the situation at Malta. It may be recalled that on 23rd April the Chiefs of Staff had had to announce to Malta that she would get no convoy during May either from east or west.[1] The Prime Minister now explained that the Chiefs of Staff's review in question had been prepared on the British principle of facing the worst; when expounded to the House of Commons in Secret Session it had had a most exhilarating and heartening effect. He went on to show how the situation had now improved, and outlined the steps being taken to strengthen India, Ceylon, and the Eastern Fleet. He was grateful for the offer to denude the Middle East still further for the sake of the Indian danger, but the greatest help that the Middle East could give to the whole war at this juncture would be to engage and defeat the enemy in the Western Desert.

The reply to this appeal was discouraging in the extreme, for the

[1] See page 183.

Commanders-in-Chief signalled on 6th May that the latest comparison of tank strengths made it unjustifiable to attack before mid-June. 'To start earlier would incur risk of only partial success and tank losses, and might in the worst case lead to a serious reverse, the consequences of which in present circumstances are likely, in our opinion, to be extremely dangerous.' With this the Chiefs of Staff and the War Cabinet could not agree, and on 8th May the Prime Minister telegraphed their considered views, which were that the loss of Malta would be a disaster of the first magnitude to the British Empire and would probably be fatal in the long run to the defence of the Nile valley. 'We are agreed that in spite of the risks you mention you would be right to attack the enemy and fight a major battle, if possible during May, and the sooner the better. We are prepared to take full responsibility for these general directions leaving you the necessary latitude for their execution.' He went on to point out that the enemy might himself be intending to attack early in June.

But the Middle East Defence Committee felt unable as yet to accept these directions. They replied on 9th May putting forward the view that the fall of Malta would not necessarily be fatal to the security of Egypt for a very long time, if at all, provided our supply lines through the Indian Ocean remained uninterrupted. In its present almost completely neutralized state Malta was having very little influence on the enemy's maintenance in North Africa. It was, however, containing large air forces and if the enemy continued to use these for attacking the island it was doubtful whether the recapture of Cyrenaica would restore Malta's offensive power. Moreover, they believed that it would take at least two months to get a firm grip on Cyrenaica. And then came their deepest misgiving:

> 'We feel that to launch an offensive with inadequate armoured forces may very well result in the almost complete destruction of those troops, in view of our experience in the last Cyrenaican campaign. We cannot hope to hold the defensive positions we have prepared covering Egypt, however strong we may be in infantry, against a serious enemy offensive unless we can dispose of a reasonably strong armoured force in reserve, which we should not then have. This also was proved last December, and will always be so in terrain such as the Western Desert, where the southern flank of any defensive position west of the El Alamein-Qattara depression must be open to attack and encirclement. . . . We still feel that the risk to Egypt incurred by the piecemeal destruction of our armoured forces which may result from a premature offensive may be more serious and more immediate than that involved in the possible loss of Malta, serious though this would be.'

They agreed that there were signs that the enemy might be going to attack our strong positions at Gazala; this might result in his armoured forces becoming so weakened that our own would have a chance of destroying them.

For a moment the Chiefs of Staff were inclined to agree to postpone the offensive until mid-June, but they came to the conclusion that in the Middle East the danger to Egypt was being over-estimated. The War Cabinet agreed, and on 10th May the Prime Minister brought matters to a head with a telegram in the name of the War Cabinet, the Defence Committee, and the Chiefs of Staff:

> 'We are determined that Malta shall not be allowed to fall without a battle being fought by your whole army for its retention. The starving out of this fortress would involve the surrender of over 30,000 men—Army and Air Force—together with several hundred guns. Its possession would give the enemy a clear and sure bridge to Africa with all the consequences flowing from that. Its loss would sever the air route upon which both you and India must depend for a substantial part of your aircraft reinforcements. Besides this, it would compromise any offensive against Italy and future plans such as 'Acrobat' and 'Gymnast'.[1] Compared with the certainty of these disasters, we consider the risks you have set out to the safety of Egypt are definitely less, and we accept them.'

He repeated that General Auchinleck would be right to fight a major battle, if possible during May, and added that the very latest date for engaging the enemy which they could approve would be one which provided a distraction in time to help the passage of the June dark-period convoy to Malta.

This telegram in fact gave General Auchinleck the choice between complying and resigning. On 19th May he reported to the Prime Minister that he would carry out his instructions, but asked for confirmation that the primary object was to destroy the enemy's forces in Cyrenaica and ultimately to drive him from Libya, and not solely to stage a distraction to help the Malta convoy. There were now strong signs that the enemy was about to attack; if he did not, General Ritchie would be told to launch his offensive to fit in with the object of providing the greatest possible help to the Malta convoy. General Auchinleck added that owing to the narrowness of our superiority, both on land and in the air, the success of a major offensive was not in any way certain and in any event was not likely to be rapid or spectacular.

The Prime Minister replied that General Auchinleck's interpretation of his instructions was quite correct. The time had come for a trial

[1] See page 119 ff.

of strength in Cyrenaica. He realized, of course, that success could not be guaranteed: there were no safe battles. His confidence in the Army would be even greater than it was if General Auchinleck would go forward and take direct command. General Auchinleck replied that he had considered this point most carefully, but had decided that he must not become immersed in tactical problems in Libya. He might be faced with having to decide whether to continue to reinforce the 8th Army or to build up the northern front which he was now weakening in order to give General Ritchie all the help possible. Only at the hub could he keep a right sense of proportion, and his place was there.

The outcome of all this was that the enemy attacked first. It will be seen that he offered the British a chance of winning a really great victory, but they did not succeed in taking it. In conclusion it is of interest to note that when, in the following August, General Auchinleck was replaced by General Alexander, a separate Command was created for Persia and Iraq, because Mr. Churchill doubted whether the disasters in the Western Desert would have occurred if General Auchinleck 'had not been distracted by the divergent considerations of a too widely extended front'.

During the lull in the Desert from February to May the Royal Air Force had a great deal to do in the way of reorganization and preparation for the next active phase on land, while continuing all the time to harass the enemy as much as possible. In the course of the 'Crusader' campaign the Desert Air Force had been much weakened, the fighters in particular having suffered wastage much greater than the flow of replacements, in spite of the remarkable achievements of the salvage and repair units. The Hurricane Is had been outclassed, the supply of Tomahawks had dried up, few Hurricane IIs were arriving, and there had been only a trickle of Kittyhawks. As for bombers, the supply of Marylands was at an end, the Blenheims' engines were suffering terribly from the dust, the new Bostons were also having engine troubles, and the few Baltimores were having to be modified. Apart from these local worries there had been calls from time to time to help the Far East—and there might be more. Looking further ahead there was always the possibility of having to send substantial air forces to the Northern Front.

In July 1941 the Air Ministry had set a target for the Middle East Air Force of 62½ squadrons, to be reached in March 1942.[1] By the end of January there were 57 complete squadrons (including 5 in Malta) exclusive of various air transport, communication, photographic and survey reconnaissance, and Fleet Air Arm units. Another thirteen squadrons were forming or about to form. Thus, in spite of withdrawals

[1] See Volume II, page 289.

and diversions to the Far East, the intended figure was well within reach. In the meantime, however, the Air Ministry had reviewed Air Marshal Tedder's requirements, and in December 1941 a new target was set at 85½ squadrons by August 1942. In early March further additions were made to the figure aimed at, but by increasing the number of aircraft in every light bomber and tactical reconnaissance squadron it was possible to reduce the figure to 80. Of these, 3 were to be heavy bomber squadrons, and 35 short-range fighter squadrons—15 of which were to have Spitfires.

The introduction of heavy bombers into the Middle East programme deserves a word of explanation. The arrival of the first Liberator in December 1941 and its experimental use for bombing Tripoli has already been referred to.[1] In April 1942 the serious situation at Malta led the Commanders-in-Chief to ask for heavy bombers to deal with the Sicilian airfields. In May, by a stroke of good fortune, a detachment of Liberators arrived on its way to the Far East, under orders to attack the Ploesti oilfields before moving on.[2] The Commanders-in-Chief seized their opportunity, and at their urgent request these Liberators were retained and others bound for India were diverted to the Middle East, on the understanding that they were not to be used for local operations nor in a manner unsuited to their type. In addition two squadrons of Halifaxes were to be sent from the United Kingdom. The transfer of all these heavy bombers to the Middle East was in fact an exercise in strategic mobility, the intention being to switch them from one theatre to another as required.

The needs of the Middle East were not in dispute as far as aircraft were concerned, but the question of providing aircrews was hotly argued. The unsatisfactory state of operational training in the Middle East in 1941 was referred to in Volume II; in the spring of 1942 it had become worse. Reinforcements from the United Kingdom were as necessary as ever, but the Home Commands were now equally hard pressed. Bomber O.T.Us especially were strained to the limit; Bomber Command had been obliged to adopt a 'one pilot' policy for its heavy bombers, and the Middle East was eventually obliged to conform. Air Marshal Tedder's repeated requests for aircrew reinforcements came under heavy fire from the Air Ministry, but during these months it was mainly from the United Kingdom that the aircrews were sent.

While these plans were going forward for forming new squadrons and for building up aircrews and aircraft, steps were being taken to eradicate certain weaknesses in the Desert Air Force before it should again be called upon to support a major land offensive. One of the most important of these steps was the creation of a fighter group headquarters. Hitherto the mobile fighter force had consisted of two wings,

[1] See page 93.

[2] See page 245.

both directly under Air Headquarters. The new group was formed mainly by absorbing Nos. 258 and 262 Wing Headquarters, and became No. 211 Group, which had previously been disbanded when its area of responsibility in Cyrenaica had been overrun by the enemy. The first Commanding Officer was Group Captain K. B. B. Cross, who had been the senior Fighter Wing Commander during 'Crusader'. The new group was designed to control, for operational purposes only, three mobile fighter wings of four to six squadrons each. A central group operations centre was formed—in duplicate in order to be able to 'leap-frog'. It absorbed the operations centres of Nos. 258 and 262 Wing Headquarters, which were themselves replaced by two new Wing Headquarters (Nos. 239 and 243), and the already existing No. 233 was brought forward to complete the group. For administration and maintenance the three wings were to be responsible to Air Headquarters; for all air operations and for the control of early warning arrangements and airfield defence they would be commanded by the new group.

Great efforts were made to raise the standard of air firing among the fighter pilots, and shadow firing took the place of the current method of firing at a towed drogue or sleeve.[1] Navigation and ground-attack were strenuously practised. New tactics were developed for dealing with the Me. 109F. The radar coverage was now so much better—it could, for example, deal with low-flying aircraft—and the wireless observer screen so much more complete, that the employment of wing formations on offensive patrols could be dropped in favour of using flights of four to six aircraft. It was hoped that by this means the Me. 109Fs would find less to pick at.

For the day-bombers the main item of training was bombing practice, particularly with the new Boston aircraft. The usual height was between eight and ten thousand feet, with occasional high-level practices at fifteen thousand; experiments were also made in bombing from shallow dives. The day-bombers were now based at Bir el Baheira, only a few miles from the main fighter base at Gambut, and this was greatly to the advantage of both bomber and fighter pilots since one of the most important tactical changes at this time was in the system of giving fighter escorts to the day-bombers. The enemy's growing fighter defence and the greater speed of the Boston compared with the Maryland were two of the reasons for the change. One fighter wing now specialized in this duty; radio communication between fighters and bombers was developed; and procedures were agreed and adopted for the bombers as regards formation flying, climbing and cruising speeds, and avoiding flying 'down sun'.

In view of the shortage of day-bombers it was decided to aim at equipping every single-engined fighter to carry one or more bombs.

[1] Shadow firing means firing at the aircraft's own shadow on the ground.

This did not affect its performance as a fighter once its bombs had been released, and as a fighter-bomber it was capable of being bombed-up and put into the air much more quickly than a bomber. It also used much less fuel, which was an important point when supply became difficult, particularly in a rapid advance. By the end of May one Hurricane and three Kittyhawk squadrons had been so equipped, and others, both Hurricane and Kittyhawk, were gradually fitted up during the summer. During the time of the lull the weapon used was the 250-lb. bomb, though Kittyhawks which were delivered later came equipped to carry one bomb of 500-lb.[1]

In the realm of army/air co-operation there were not many developments. The transfer of the Air Support Control from the level of Corps headquarters to that of Army/Air headquarters enabled requests for air support received through the tentacles to be presented quickly and simultaneously to the Army and Air Force Commanders, or their nominees. A system of land markings was introduced to help pilots to fix their position in featureless surroundings; by day bold letters of the alphabet were used, and by night large Vs of lighted petrol in cans. In an attempt to solve the vexed problem of the bomb-line arrangements were made to pass hourly forecasts of the position of the most advanced British troops to Air Support Control, the forecasts being made two hours ahead. The difficult question of recognition from the air continued to be a subject for argument between the two Services, and the suggestion that the R.A.F. roundel should be painted on all vehicles had not been adopted before the next phase of active land operations began.

The retreat from Western Cyrenaica made it necessary to construct a number of new operational landing-grounds. The experience of the squadrons of the Desert Air Force had made them distinctly anxious about the protection that the army could give to their landing-grounds during a battle. There had been no permanent allotment of troops to this duty; such troops as were near were apt to become involved in some other task and the landing-grounds were frequently unprotected. Much the same applied to the anti-aircraft defence, for the army tended to regard the guns as available for other tasks. It is of interest to note that the air defence of the back areas had been the subject of a special enquiry by an inter-Service mission from England under Air Vice-Marshal D. C. S. Evill in December 1941. Shortage of equipment, vehicles, aircraft, and trained men prevented many of its recommendations being put into effect by the spring of 1942, but the principle of unified air defence—including anti-aircraft defence—had been

---

[1] The original fighter-bomber squadron, No. 80, was initially equipped to carry eight 40-lb. bombs. The 250-lb. bombs which replaced them were fitted with extension rods to give detonation above ground. Materials did not allow of supplying more than one squadron with bombs fitted with this device.

accepted. In the forward area the same principle was adopted, but not yet.

The measures which have been outlined for raising the operational efficiency of the Desert Air Force were accompanied by a drive for better administration. Ground organization in particular received attention, especially as regards the speeding up of rearming and refuelling—two very important aspects of intensive air operations. Under the vigilant eye of Air Vice-Marshal Coningham the Desert Air Force was thus preparing itself for the next intensive phase. But a lull on land does not necessarily mean a lull in the air, as will be seen from the summary of operations which follows.

When, early in February, the 8th Army's retreat was halted at Gazala, Air Marshal Tedder and Air Vice-Marshal Coningham found themselves faced with much the same problems as had arisen after the failure of 'Battleaxe'. Then, as now, the Army had needed a long spell of reorganization and preparation, while to the Air Force fell the duties of striking at the enemy's supply lines, attacking his air forces in Cyrenaica, and harassing his troops. Reconnaissance of all kinds—strategical, tactical and photographic—was in great demand, and there were in addition numerous defensive commitments in both the forward and the rear areas, as well as the protection of coastal shipping, especially on the sea route to Tobruk.

There was one important difference from the autumn of 1941; the heavy air attacks on Malta were causing her offensive contribution to wane until it was to become almost non-existent. In the fifteen weeks of the lull in the Desert the Wellingtons from Malta could only fly about sixty sorties against Tripoli, though they also attacked Palermo and sank the *Cuma* of 6,652 tons, the *Securitas* of 5,366 tons, and sank or damaged several other vessels.[1] The only aircraft from Egypt which could now reach Tripoli were the Liberators, but it was not until May that any number of these arrived. Consequently the attack on enemy ports amounted really to the attack of Benghazi, an off-loading place of great importance to the enemy because its use cut out the long road haul from Tripoli.

On Benghazi, then, the weight of the Wellingtons was mainly concentrated. The first attack was made early in February, and in three months the total day and night bomber sorties against the port and its surroundings, including the laying of mines off the harbour entrance, amounted to 741, or an average of 8 sorties every 24 hours. Some of the attacks were heavy; for example on 8th May twenty-eight aircraft bombed the port and ships in the offing. In May, when the enemy showed signs of preparing an offensive on land, the night

[1] See page 173.

attacks were supplemented by the Bostons and long-range Kittyhawks by day. It appears that ships usually entered harbour at dawn and unloaded during daylight; photographs gave an impression of much damage, but, judging from the enemy's statements of cargo unloaded, the interruption was not so serious as was hoped. The capacity of the port steadily rose, though without these attacks it would presumably have risen even faster.

Against the enemy's airfields only a much weakened force of day-bombers was at first available, for reasons already given. But the effort soon grew, and the developments in tactics and equipment brought good results. As a rule the Wellingtons went for the important airfields at Martuba, and the day-bombers attacked Derna, Berka, Benina, Barce and Tmimi. Kittyhawk fighter-bombers also took part. An example of good fighter co-operation was on 14th March, when during an attack on Martuba West the escorting fighters successfully beat off determined attacks by German and Italian fighters without damage to a single Boston. Unescorted raids, however, occasioned some losses, as for instance when two out of three Bostons did not return from attacking Barce on 21st March. A notable success was scored on 15th March when four Italian fighters were destroyed and six others damaged; a German communications aircraft was also destroyed. At about this time the Germans gave an order to their fighter units to counter such attacks very aggressively and to strike at R.A.F. airfields 'to regain air supremacy'.

Another commitment for the day-bombers during the lull was the attack of troops, transport and supply lines in the forward area, though the force available did not allow of more than about a hundred sorties. A certain amount of experience, however, was gained by the Beaufighters and by the Hurricane and Kittyhawk fighters and fighter-bombers in the attack of ground targets. Not the least successful were the night-flying Hurricanes of No. 73 Squadron, which had just been put through a special course. Flying on free-lance patrols, either singly or in pairs, they attacked camps and vehicles, reconnoitred airfields, and intercepted returning night-flying aircraft.

During the first half of the lull No. 208 Squadron continued to provide tactical reconnaissance of the enemy's troop positions and of movement around Derna, Martuba, Tmimi, Mechili and Tengeder. At the end of 'Crusader' the tactical reconnaissance squadrons were still equipped with Hurricane Is, and it had been decided to replace one flight in each squadron with Tomahawks. (The greater speed of this aircraft was to prove a big factor in keeping up the morale of the pilots engaged on this exacting work.) In mid-March No. 40 Squadron S.A.A.F., which had already received a few Tomahawks, took over from No. 208, which was then withdrawn to rest and refit. Various tactical methods were tried to counter the growing opposition by the enemy's fighters and to ensure the important work of reconnaissance being successfully accomplished. One way was for the Hurricane I to be accompanied by a Tomahawk as 'weaver'; another was to send it as a part of a fighter formation; a third method depended upon the greatly improved radar coverage, which made it possible for the tactical reconnaissance aircraft to work independently, the pilot being informed by the fighter controller of the approach or absence of any hostile aircraft in the area of his reconnaissance.[1]

The fighter force was based first at Gambut and El Adem, with Gazala as a forward refuelling field. The last two received much attention from German fighter-bombers, and Me. 109s equipped in this way met with considerable success. (The Italians also claimed to have attacked British airfields at Gambut by moonlight with C.R. 42s carrying glider bombs.) The prevalence of dust at El Adem limited the use of this airfield and the fighters became concentrated at Gambut and Gasr el Arid. The improved warning system allowed time for interception over the forward area even from these bases, while communications were greatly simplified and the anti-aircraft defence much strengthened.

During most of the lull the fighters were mainly committed to defensive tasks such as escorting the day-bombers and aircraft on tactical reconnaissance, defending Tobruk, and protecting the shipping route from Alexandria as well as road and rail communications and airfields. During April and May there was a renewal of the enemy's 'jumping' tactics by Me. 109s flying out of the sun; on 20th April, for instance, six to eight of them pounced on four Hurricanes near Tobruk, shot down two and damaged the other two so badly that they had to land. On another occasion, however, the British scored a similar success when six Macchi 200s were shot down over Tobruk.

The passage of the convoy from Alexandria to Malta in March was the occasion for a special effort to keep the enemy's air forces occupied. This led to many encounters; for example, the fighters, supporting raids by the army, destroyed three Me. 109s and damaged two others for the loss of five Kittyhawks and one Hurricane.[2] The Wellingtons joined in the same operation by attacking the naval base at Piraeus, the submarine base at Salamis, three airfields near Athens, two on Rhodes, and four on Crete.

Even after the attacks from Malta upon the sea route to North Africa had dwindled almost to nothing, the Germans made great use of their numerous transport aircraft to carry men and stores from Crete to Cyrenaica. On 12th May eight long-range Kittyhawks and

[1] One mobile radar unit, with a range of sixty miles, was sited on the sea-shore at Gazala point, as far forward as it could possibly be.

[2] Between 18th and 23rd March two other Me. 109s were destroyed by bombing, one Ju. 87 and one Me. 110 by A.A. fire, and two more Me. 109s were damaged by A.A. fire.

four Beaufighters intercepted twenty south-bound Ju. 52s escorted by three Me. 110s fifty miles off Derna; they shot down eight and damaged another, and destroyed a Me. 110, all for the loss of one Beaufighter. Thereafter the Germans used Me. 109s fitted with extra fuel tanks to escort their transport aircraft.

The principal targets for the enemy at this time were Tobruk, the British desert railway, the airfields—especially Fuka and Gambut—and troops in the forward area. During March the Germans had been concentrating their air forces in Sicily for neutralizing Malta, and for this purpose they withdrew units from Greece and Crete, and left *Fliegerführer Afrika* to make do with what he had.[1] During April there were a few attacks on Alexandria and towards the end of the month on the Suez Canal also—the first since February. The night-fighters of No. 89 Squadron took heavy toll of the enemy and it is probable that they shot down most, if not all, of the 4 Heinkels and 7 Ju. 88s lost during those few weeks. In May there were signs that General Rommel was preparing for something. German fighter activity increased, though the dive-bombers and fighter-bombers were unusually quiet, as if gathering their strength. Actually their numbers, as we have seen, were being increased, because Malta had been neutralized and some of the air forces in Sicily were being sent back to Greece and Crete, and others to North Africa. In the third week of May there was an increase in reconnaissance flights and dive-bombing. The British lines of communication, especially the railheads, were frequently attacked, and attempts by R.A.F. reconnaissance aircraft to find out what was going on met with increasing opposition. By now Nos. 40 S.A.A.F. and 208 Squadrons were both at work, the former with the 13th Corps and the latter with the 30th, operating from El Adem and Bir el Gubi respectively.

When it began to look as if an offensive might be expected during the moonlight period at the end of May, daily reconnaissance of the whole of the enemy's area was intensified and fighters were drawn upon to swell the reconnaissance resources. From 21st May the attack of 'strategic' targets (such as Benghazi) was lifted, and the Wellingtons of No. 205 Group, together with the light bombers, fighter-bombers and night-flying Hurricanes of the Desert Air Force set about the task of disorganizing and weakening the Axis air forces in order to offset, from the start, the superiority of the German fighters and the greater numerical strength of the enemy in the air. First on the list came the single-engined fighter bases at Martuba and Tmimi, and the twin-engined fighter and dive-bomber base at Derna. By 26th May over 160 tons of bombs were dropped on these airfields—mostly on Martuba. Photographs taken by day and night indicated that there

[1] General Fröhlich relinquished his appointment as *Fliegerführer Afrika* in March and was succeeded the following month by Generalleutnant Otto Hoffmann von Waldau.

had been considerable destruction, but German reports disclose less positive results. A feature of the night attacks at this time was the successful use of Fleet Air Arm Albacores, with their wide field of view and their ample flare-carrying capacity, as 'pathfinders' for the Wellingtons.

So passed the lull. For the Air Force it had been a difficult period, the urgent demands of operations on the one hand conflicting with the need of rest, refitting and training on the other. New problems had cropped up, as they always do; the four 20-mm. cannons of the Hurricane IICs were being affected by dust, the Allison engine in the Kittyhawk was giving trouble, and this aircraft, a difficult one to handle, was taking the Hurricane pilots longer than expected to master. In spite of all this, during the fifteen weeks from 7th February to 25th May the Middle East air force (including Malta's bombers, but excluding anti-shipping operations) flew nearly 14,000 sorties, which is an average of 130 sorties a day. In the Desert during this time 89 German and over 60 Italian aircraft were destroyed by all causes. The British losses, amounting to nearly 300, were relatively high, and were the price paid for an aggressive air policy and a fighter force composed for the most part of obsolescent aircraft.

The experience of the winter fighting had led General Auchinleck to decide upon two important changes in the organization of the army. It was not only the enemy who had noticed that the British armour, artillery and infantry had often been unsuccessful in concerting their action on the battlefield. General Auchinleck accordingly made up his mind 'to associate the three arms more closely at all times and in all places'. He thought that the British type of armoured division would be better balanced if it had less armour and more infantry—like a German Panzer division. In future, therefore, an armoured division would consist basically of one armoured brigade group and one motor brigade group. The former would contain three tank regiments, one motor battalion, and a regiment of field and anti-tank guns, and the latter three motor battalions and a similar artillery regiment. In addition, both types of brigade group would include light anti-aircraft artillery, engineers, and administrative units. The Army tank brigades, each of three regiments of 'I' tanks, would not form part of a division, but would continue to be allotted as the situation demanded.

The second decision concerned the infantry brigade. Here General Auchinleck thought that a permanent grouping of the various arms would make for better co-operation between them. In future, therefore, an infantry division would consist of three infantry brigade groups, each containing three battalions, a regiment of field and anti-tank guns and a proportion of light anti-aircraft artillery, engineers, and administrative units.

These changes made it necessary to alter the composition of certain units. A regiment of horse or field artillery, for compactness, was now to contain three batteries each of eight 25-pdrs and one battery of sixteen anti-tank guns. (The anti-tank batteries would be provided by the existing anti-tank regiments which would then disappear.) A motor battalion was to consist of three motor companies, and one anti-tank company of sixteen guns. An infantry battalion was to consist of a headquarter company, three rifle companies, and a support company of a mortar platoon, a carrier platoon, and an anti-tank platoon of eight guns.[1] The intention was to give the artillery the new 6-pdr anti-tank gun, and the infantry and motor battalions the 2-pdr.[2]

The tanks on both sides had undergone some changes since the fighting of the previous winter. The Crusader Mark II had slightly thicker frontal armour than the Mark I, but was no more reliable mechanically. The Germans had received so many reinforcements since the New Year that it must be assumed that almost all their tanks now carried thickened frontal armour, which was face-hardened—an important consideration in view of the fact that on the British side only the Stuart's 37-mm. gun was provided with capped ammunition. This among other factors in the struggle between guns and armour is discussed in Appendix 8.

Apart from these changes there were two important newcomers. The Germans had begun to receive a new model of Pzkw III, called 'III Special', armed with a long 5-cm. gun similar to the highly successful Pak 38 anti-tank gun. The extra length of barrel gave greater muzzle-velocity and penetration than the short 5-cm. with which the bulk of the Pzkw IIIs were still armed. Only nineteen of the new model took part in the early fighting at Gazala.

The British, for their part, had begun to receive their first American medium tanks—the M3 or General Grant—whose main armament was a 75-mm. gun firing either a high-explosive shell or a 14-lb. uncapped armour-piercing shot.[3] Its arrival was welcomed by the Middle East as 'a resounding event . . . for it provided the means of killing German tanks and anti-tank gun crews at ranges hitherto undreamed

---

[1] The carrier platoon was mounted on the small tracked Bren carriers.

[2] The development of the larger gun was referred to in the previous volume. The need had been foreseen as early as 1938, but in the stress of general rearmament two years elapsed before the new 6-pdr was ready for trials. The loss of the British Army's equipment in France in 1940 and the urgent need for anti-tank guns in England resulted in as many 2-pdrs being made as possible and it was some time before factories were ready to make the 6-pdr. In April 1941, long before the 6-pdr had come into use, the design of a 17-pdr was begun. See also M. M. Postan: *History of the Second World War, British War Production* (1952), page 194.

[3] Strictly speaking, some of these were the 'General Lee', an earlier but almost identical model.

LEGEND

British troops are shown in red,
German in blue and Italian in green

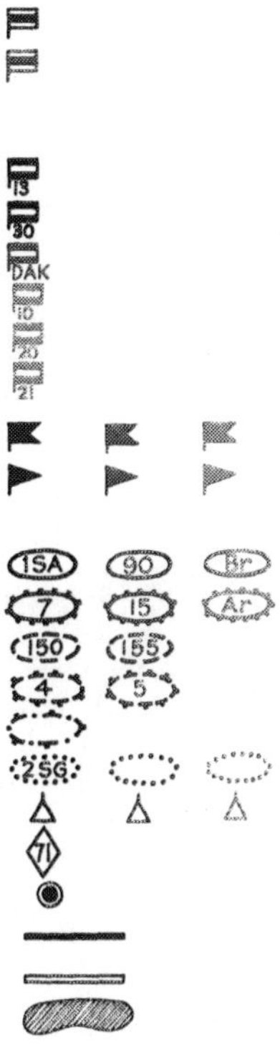

Headquarters of Armies

8th (Ritchie)
Panzerarmee Afrika (Rommel)

Headquarters of Corps

13th (Gott)
30th (Norrie)
D.A.K. (Nehring)
10th (Gioda)
20th (Baldassare)
21st (Navarrini)

Headquarters of Divisions
Heaaquarters of Brigades (or equivalent)

Divisions
Armoured Divisions
Brigades (or equivalent)
Armoured Brigades and Panzer Regiments
Armoured (British) Regiments
Other units and detachments
Recce. Patrols
Field Maintenance Centres
Airfields and landing grounds
Minefield: main alignment only
Dummy minefield " "
Full extent of mine marsh

Arabic terms

Dahar = plateau, lit. 'back'
Hagiag = barrier, escarpment
Maabus = steep cliff

Map 25

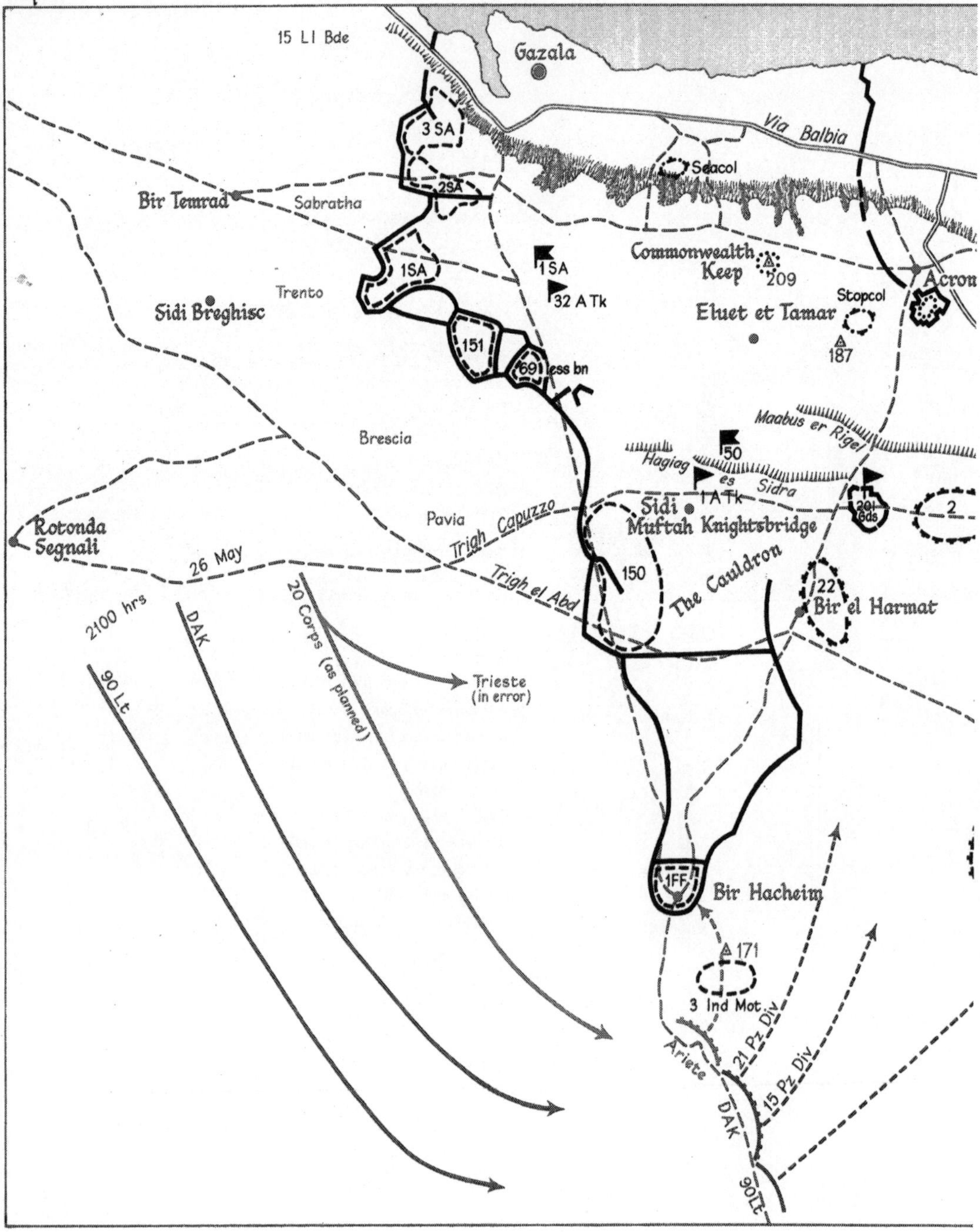

15 LI Bde
Gazala
Via Balbia
3 SA
2SA
Seacol
Bir Temrad
Sabratha
1SA
1 SA
32 A Tk
Commonwealth Keep
209
Acroma
Stopcol
Eluet et Tamar
187
Trento
Sidi Breghisc
151
69 less bn
Brescia
Maabus er Rigel
50
Hagiag es Sidra
1 A Tk
201 Gds
2
Sidi Muftah
Knightsbridge
Pavia
Trigh Capuzzo
Rotonda Segnali
26 May
Trigh el Abd
150
The Cauldron
22
Bir el Harmat
2100 hrs
DAK
20 Corps (as planned)
Trieste (in error)
90 Lt
1FF
Bir Hacheim
171
3 Ind Mot
21 Pz Div
15 Pz Div
Ariete
DAK
90Lt

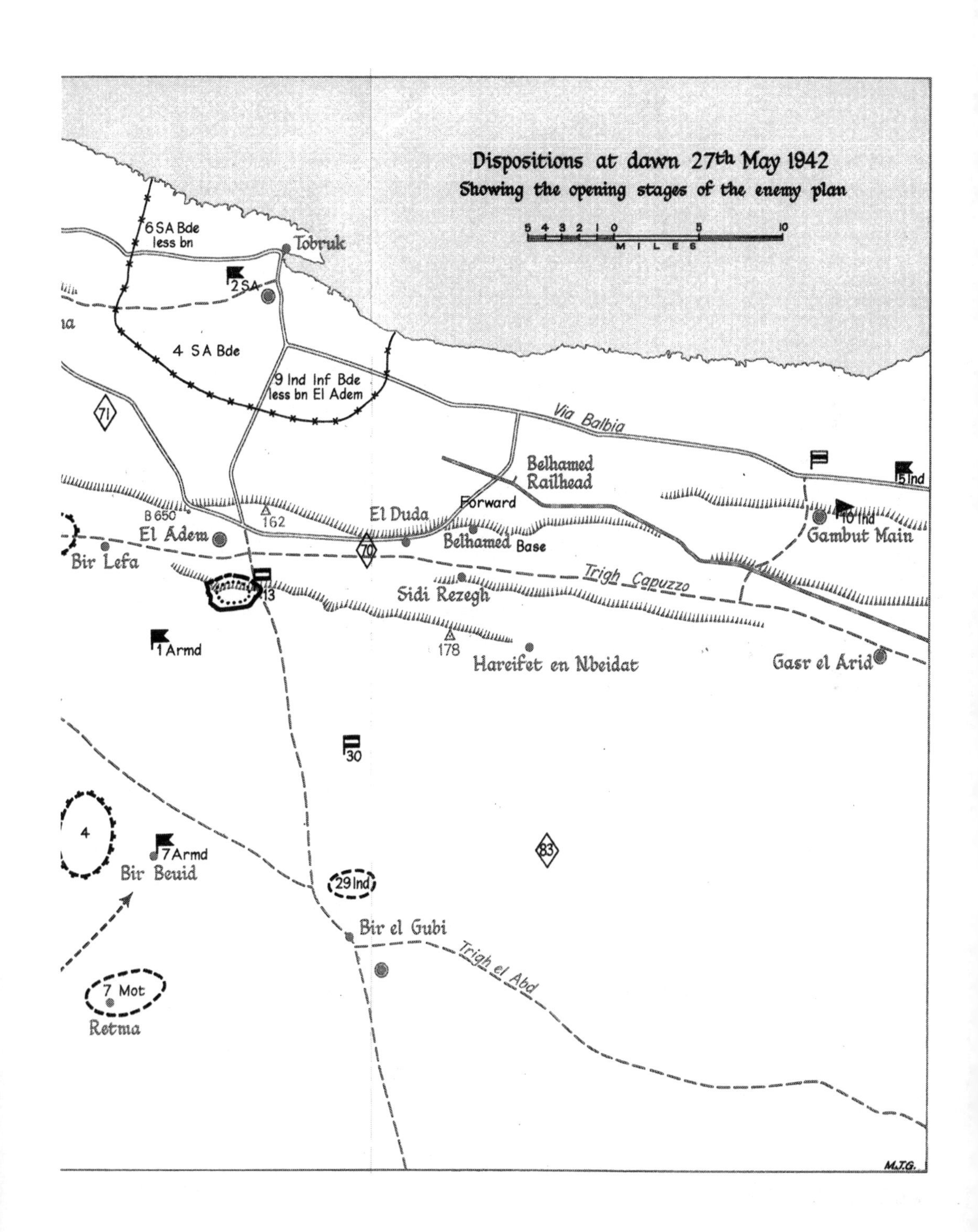

Dispositions at dawn 27th May 1942
Showing the opening stages of the enemy plan
5 4 3 2 1 0 5 10
MILES
6 SA Bde less bn
Tobruk
2 SA
4 SA Bde
9 Ind Inf Bde less bn El Adem
71
Via Balbia
Belhamed Railhead
5 Ind
Forward
10 Ind
Gambut Main
B 650
162
El Duda
El Adem
Bir Lefa
70
Belhamed Base
Trigh Capuzzo
13
Sidi Rezegh
1 Armd
178
Hareifet en Nbeidat
Gasr el Arid
30
4
7 Armd
Bir Beuid
83
29 Ind
Bir el Gubi
Trigh el Abd
7 Mot
Retma
M.J.G.

of. And this could be done from behind the heavy armour of a reasonably fast and very reliable tank'. In the turret was a high-velocity 37-mm. gun, similar to that of the Stuart. The Grant would have been better still if its 75-mm. gun had been mounted in the turret instead of in a sponson at one side, and if the latest armour-piercing ammunition had been available for it.[1]

The introduction of the Grant led to changes in the equipment of the British armoured regiments. There were obvious advantages in giving a regiment only one type of tank, but the whole programme depended upon what arrived from overseas and there were strong psychological reasons for giving every regiment some of the new and powerful Grants. The plan decided upon was for some regiments to have two squadrons of Grants and one squadron of Stuarts; others would have two squadrons of Crusaders and one squadron of Grants. Some armoured brigades would consist of regiments which had only American tanks, and others of Crusader-Grant regiments. This plan seemed to give the best compromise between speed of re-equipping and tactical and administrative advantages.

In the event the battle began before all the foregoing changes had been completed. Neither of the armoured divisions had changed over to the one armoured and the one motor brigade organization. Some progress had been made with the 'brigade groups' in the divisions of the 8th Army, but only 112 of the new 6-pdr anti-tank guns had arrived, so that many anti-tank batteries were still armed with the 2-pdr and many of the infantry and motor battalions had not got their anti-tank guns. Many artillery regiments had not yet changed over to the new organization. The three armoured brigades were up to strength in tanks, though some regiments had barely received all their Grants when the battle began.

It has been seen earlier in this chapter how reluctant General Auchinleck was to attack until he had the strength to beat the enemy decisively. Much work, however, had been put into the administrative preparations for an eventual offensive. Three forward bases were to be established: one at Tobruk containing 10,000 tons of stores, one at Belhamed of 26,000 tons, and a small one at Jarabub of 1,000 tons. The extension of the desert railway from Misheifa had begun as soon as the enemy's frontier garrisons had surrendered, and by the middle of February the working railhead was at Capuzzo. In spite of much interference from the air the line was pushed on to Belhamed, where a temporary railhead was opened late in May. All this time stores had been arriving by road, rail and sea, and by 25th May the forward bases were roughly four-fifths complete except for petrol, which fell short at Belhamed by about one-third. This shortage was mainly

[1] Both these failings were remedied in September with the coming of the 'General Sherman' tank.

caused by attacks on ships on the Tobruk run, nearly 400,000 gallons having been lost when the *Cerion* and *Crista* were severely damaged by enemy aircraft in March. In April and May two more petrol carriers, the *Kirkland* and *Eocene*, were sunk by U-boats. Altogether from February to May five destroyers, six supply ships, and one hospital ship were lost in coastal operations from U-boat and air attack, and other ships were damaged. It had been far from easy to find the warship and fighter escorts for the Tobruk convoys: larger and less frequent convoys could not have been run without exposing too many ships for long periods in Tobruk harbour. The Army did its best to help by using the land route to the fullest possible extent, and generally speaking the administrative preparations may be said to have placed the maintenance of the 8th Army on such a firm foundation that there should be no cause to fear a breakdown. It will be seen, however, that the valuable base at Belhamed—which held for example 1½ million gallons of motor fuel—became something of an embarrassment to General Ritchie. In the battle which came about instead of the intended offensive, this base was too close to the fighting.

By 10th May, the day on which General Auchinleck was told that he would be right to fight a major battle during May and the sooner the better, there were already indications that Rommel was preparing to attack on a big scale. The 8th Army, on the other hand, was by no means ready, except administratively, to attack, and the prospect of fighting on its prepared position was welcome. On 16th May General Ritchie issued an instruction in which he gave his intention as 'to destroy the enemy's armoured forces in the battle of the Gazala-Tobruk-Bir Hacheim position as the initial step in securing Cyrenaica'. The British dispositions in this area are shown on Map 25 and it will be noticed that the distances separating the positions held by the front-line brigade groups were considerable; for instance, from the Free French locality at Bir Hacheim to that of the 150th Infantry Brigade Group was about thirteen miles, and from there to the 69th Infantry Brigade Group was about six miles. Thus these localities were too far apart to be mutually supporting, but they were well dug and wired and held about a week's supplies and ample ammunition. The whole front from Gazala to Bir Hacheim was covered by fairly thickly sown minefields which at the southern end formed the sides of an inverted triangle with its apex at Bir Hacheim. These minefields were really a compromise solution to the problem of how far to extend the desert flank in the absence of any natural obstacle for it to rest on. If, for a given number of troops, the whole front were kept short it would be locally strong, but the enemy would be put to no great trouble in driving round it. If it were long it would be weaker, but if the enemy tried to drive round it he would have farther to go, and all his problems of supply would be increased. In the event the enemy did drive round: the minefields had an important bearing on the fighting, but like any other obstacle that is not under the close fire of the defence they could, in time, be breached.

Behind the main line were other widely separated positions intended to block the more defined tracks and centres of communication or to form pivots of manœuvre for the mobile forces. They are shown on the map at Commonwealth Keep, Acroma, Knightsbridge, and El Adem, but it must be noted that between the last two the escarpment is passable to vehicles in about five places only. The position shown at Retma was nearly ready a few days before the attack, but those at Pt 171 and Bir el Gubi were not begun until 25th May. The main forces under General Ritchie's command were:

13th Corps (Lieut.-General W. H. E. Gott)
 1st and 32nd Army Tank Brigades
 50th Division (Major-General W. H. C. Ramsden)
  69th, 150th and 151st Infantry Brigade Groups
 1st South African Division (Major-General D. H. Pienaar)
  1st, 2nd and 3rd South African Infantry Brigade Groups[1]
 2nd South African Division (Major-General H. B. Klopper)
  4th and 6th South African Infantry Brigade Groups
  9th Indian Infantry Brigade Group[2]

30th Corps (Lieut.-General C. W. M. Norrie)
 1st Armoured Division (Major-General H. Lumsden)
  2nd and 22nd Armoured Brigade Groups
  201st Guards (Motor) Brigade[3]
 7th Armoured Division (Major-General F. W. Messervy)[4]
  4th Armoured Brigade Group
  7th Motor Brigade Group
  3rd Indian Motor Brigade Group
  29th Indian Infantry Brigade Group[5]
  1st Free French Brigade Group

Directly under Army Command were:

 5th Indian Division (Major-General H. R. Briggs)
  10th Indian Infantry Brigade Group
  2nd Free French Brigade Group[6]
 'Dencol', a small column of all arms, comprising
  South African, Free French, Middle East Commando, and Libyan Arab Force troops.

---

[1] The last named came from 2nd S.A. Division, replacing 5th S.A. Brigade, which was at Matruh, not having fully re-formed after its destruction in November 1941.
[2] From 5th Indian Division (Army reserve), replacing 3rd S.A. Brigade.
[3] Redesignation of 200th (Guards) Brigade.
[4] In place of Major-General J. C. Campbell, V.C., killed in a car accident.
[5] From 5th Indian Division.
[6] Replacing 9th and 29th Indian Infantry Brigades.

Under orders to join the 8th Army were:

from Iraq:
  10th Indian Division (Major-General T. W. Rees)
    20th, 21st, and 25th Indian Infantry Brigades
from Egypt:
  11th Indian Infantry Brigade (of 4th Indian Division)
  1st Armoured Brigade.

On 20th May General Auchinleck had given General Ritchie in writing his views on the coming battle. He thought that the enemy might try to envelop the southern flank and make for Tobruk; alternatively he might break through the centre on a narrow front, widen the gap, and then thrust at Tobruk. General Auchinleck regarded the second course as the more likely and dangerous, and expected it to be accompanied by a feint to draw the British armour southward. He suggested that both armoured divisions should be disposed astride the Trigh Capuzzo west of El Adem, where they would be well placed to meet either threat. He saw the 8th Army as consisting of two parts: one, whose task was to hold the fort—in this case the quadrilateral Gazala-Tobruk-Bir el Gubi-Bir Hacheim; and the other whose task was to hit and destroy the enemy wherever he might thrust out. General Auchinleck had made it clear that he did not wish the armour to become engaged piecemeal. 'I consider it to be of the highest importance,' he wrote, 'that you should not break up the organization of either of the armoured divisions. They have been trained to fight as divisions, I hope, and fight as divisions they should. Norrie must handle them as a Corps Commander, and thus be able to take advantage of the flexibility which the fact of having two formations gives him.'

The senior commanders in the 8th Army, however, were by no means sure that the enemy's attack would be made against the centre. General Norrie thought that it would fall on the 13th Corps and be coupled with a thrust from the south, while General Ritchie expected an approach round the desert flank. There could be no certainty, and preparations would have to be made to meet a main attack against each Corps front or round the south of Bir Hacheim. The last possibility led to the 7th Armoured Division being placed farther to the south than General Auchinleck had suggested. Both armoured divisions were given various alternative roles for delaying the enemy and later counter-attacking in order to destroy him. If he advanced round the south of Bir Hacheim the 7th Armoured Division was to observe and harass him, and the 1st was to be prepared to join in either on the east or west of the 7th.

The basis of 13th Corps' plan was a resolute defence and local counter-attacks in each formation's area. For this purpose two regiments of the 32nd Army Tank Brigade were divided between the 1st South African and 50th Divisions. Two columns of all arms—'Stopcol' and 'Seacol'—were placed by the 2nd South African Division to guard the coastal plain from seaborne or airborne landings, and to hold the passage of the escarpment near Acroma. Naval patrols to guard against seaborne attack were also instituted. The 1st South African and 50th Divisions were each to earmark one brigade group and all the 'I' tanks for a future counter-offensive.

The whole British front was actively screened by armoured car patrols and small mobile columns. To these must be given the credit for preventing the enemy from reconnoitring the defensive positions and minefields.

At the meeting of Axis leaders held at Berchtesgaden on 1st May it was decided that General Rommel should attack at the end of May with the object of capturing Tobruk.[1] He was not to move farther east than the Egyptian frontier and was then to remain on the defensive while the main Axis effort turned to the capture of Malta, for which purpose some air forces would have to be withdrawn from North Africa. When his supply lines had been made safe by the elimination of Malta, Rommel was to invade Egypt.

Rommel's plan relied on boldness and speed. He had not a very high opinion of the state of training of the British, and doubted the ability of their commanders to handle armoured forces. In general his information about the British forces in the Middle East was accurate, but he underestimated the strength of the 8th Army in the forward area to the extent of one armoured brigade, one army tank brigade, and three infantry brigades. His knowledge of the tactical dispositions was incomplete, for he knew nothing of the defended locality at Sidi Muftah, and had only the vaguest idea of the mine marshes running down to Bir Hacheim.

He decided to start by creating the impression that a heavy attack was coming between the sea and the Trigh Capuzzo, and placed General Crüwell in command of the whole of this portion of the front.[2] In the afternoon of 26th May the troops in this sector were to close up to the British positions and dig in, covered by heavy dive-bombing and artillery fire. Noise and movement were to continue throughout the night. Meanwhile, in the moonlight, a mobile force led by Rommel himself was to sweep through Bir Hacheim with the Italian 20th

---

[1] See page 195.

[2] General Crüwell's Group consisted of 10th Italian Corps (Pavia and Brescia Divisions); 21st Italian Corps (Trento and Sabratha Divisions; H.Q. 15th German Lorried Infantry Brigade, with two light infantry regiments); and the bulk of the Army artillery.

Corps (Ariete Armoured and Trieste Motorized Divisions) on the inside of the wheel, and the 90th Light Division and the *D.A.K.*, now commanded by General Nehring, on the outside. Next morning the Panzer Divisions would turn north towards Acroma and get in rear of the British 13th Corps. The 90th Light Division was to move farther east and create havoc about El Adem and Belhamed. The 1st South African and 50th Divisions would then be attacked from both east and west, and their communications with Tobruk cut by a force (the Hecker Group) landed from the sea. The capture of Tobruk would follow. Four days were considered enough for the whole operation. To ensure supplies during these four days special arrangements were made for the *D.A.K.* to be closely followed by columns carrying the balance of four days' rations and water, ammunition for three days' fighting, and fuel for about 300 miles.

Some last-minute information about the presence of British mobile forces to the north-east of Bir Hacheim caused the plan to be modified. The Ariete Division was now to capture Bir Hacheim while the *D.A.K.* and the 90th Light Division made a wide sweep round to the south of it. The final plan is illustrated on Map 25.

The strength of the mobile force in tanks was approximately 332 German and 228 Italian. This does not include the Littorio Armoured Division which was only in process of arriving in the back area. Of the German tanks 50 were Pzkw IIs, 223 were IIIs, 19 were III Specials, with the long 5-cm. gun, and 40 were IVs.[1] Nearly all the Italian tanks were M 13/40 or M 14/41 mediums.

On the British side the reorganization of the armoured forces described on pages 213-4 had resulted in the following distribution of tanks in the 8th Army. The 1st and 7th Armoured Divisions and reserves—167 Grants, 149 Stuarts and 257 Crusaders; 1st and 32nd Army Tank Brigades (five regiments)—166 Valentines and 110 Matildas. The 1st Armoured Brigade, under orders to join, had 75 Grants and 70 Stuarts.

During May there had been substantial transfers of Axis aircraft to North Africa, and by the 26th it was estimated that the German and Italian numbers had risen to 270 and 460, of which about 400 in all might be serviceable. It is known now that the actual figures were 312 and 392, making a total of 704 of which 497 were serviceable. The Desert Air Force had some 320 aircraft, of which about 190 were serviceable.[2] Behind it, but not under Air Vice-Marshal Coningham's control, was the rest of the Royal Air Force in the Middle East, with some 739 serviceable aircraft. Similarly, on the Axis side, there were

[1] In reserve, but not all immediately available, were 10 Pzkw IIs, 38 IIIs, 19 III Specials, one IV, and 9 IV Specials. The IV Special was a new tank with a long and powerful 7·5-cm. gun, but very few reached Libya before August 1942.

[2] The Order of Battle of the Desert Air Force on the eve of the battle of Gazala is given in Appendix 5.

some 215 serviceable German aircraft in Greece, Crete and Sicily and over 775 Italian scattered throughout the Mediterranean, making a total, excluding Libya and Metropolitan Italy, of about 1,000 serviceable Axis aircraft. The British were therefore outnumbered in the whole theatre and also in the Desert. Moreover, in fighter aircraft performance, the Germans held the trump card in the Me. 109F.

CHAPTER X

THE BATTLE OF GAZALA

(26th May – 15th June)

See Map 25

THE Battle of Gazala is the name given to the series of actions which began on 26th May and ended four weeks later with the fall of Tobruk. The present chapter covers three phases. First, the failure of General Rommel's attempt to crack open the British positions from the rear—26th to 29th May. Second, his pause in the so-called 'Cauldron' to recover and re-establish his communications; here he was unsuccessfully attacked on 5th June with great loss to the British. Third, his counter-stroke which led to the defeat of the British armour between 11th and 13th June, after which General Ritchie decided to withdraw from the Gazala position.

In the afternoon of 26th May the Crüwell Group, covered by heavy artillery fire and bombing, began to make ground towards the British positions between Gazala and Sidi Muftah. Before dark a large concentration of vehicles was seen near Rotonda Segnali, and others were detected from the air moving north-east. These indications of coming activity in the northern sector were soon matched by reports from the 4th South African Armoured Car Regiment and patrols of the 2nd K.R.R.C. (7th Motor Brigade) who were observing and shadowing large columns of enemy vehicles heading south-east in the moonlight—that is, towards Bir Hacheim. If General Rommel expected operation '*Venezia*' to come as a surprise he was to be disappointed, but fortunately for him the British made but poor use of their information.

At 6.30 a.m. on the 27th Brigadier Filose, commander of the newly arrived 3rd Indian Motor Brigade, reported to General Messervy that he faced 'a whole bloody German armoured division'. It was in fact the Ariete Division and a few tanks of 21st Panzer Division, and a short fierce fight followed in which the 3rd Indian Motor Brigade, after doing some damage, was overrun. It lost about 440 officers and men and much of its scanty equipment, and the survivors were sent right back east of the frontier to re-form. At about 8.30 a.m. the 90th Light Division fell upon the Retma position, which was partly broken into, but Brigadier Renton extricated his troops and withdrew to

Bir el Gubi.[1] So much for the last-minute positions on the southern flank.

By 7.30 a.m. Brigadier G. W. Richards, commanding the 4th Armoured Brigade, knew that the enemy was present in unknown strength about twenty-five miles to the south-west, that the 7th Motor Brigade's mobile columns were withdrawing on Retma, and that the 3rd Indian Motor Brigade was being attacked. He was ordered by the 7th Armoured Division to take up a battle position south-east of the 3rd Indian Motor Brigade. As his brigade was moving to the assembly area, the 15th Panzer Division crashed into it, destroyed the 8th Hussars as a fighting unit, and roughly handled the 3rd Royal Tank Regiment. The Brigade in its turn inflicted considerable loss on the enemy but had to withdraw to near El Adem, followed some of the way by the 90th Light Division. Army Headquarters later ordered it towards Belhamed, and at length it leaguered about fifteen miles east of El Adem.

Another blow, which completed the disruption of the 7th Armoured Division, was soon to follow. Shortly after 10 a.m. its Advanced Headquarters was near Bir Beuid. Having clearly not grasped how quickly the enemy was moving it was surprised by German armoured cars and dispersed, and General Messervy, his G.S.O.1, and two other staff officers were captured. This unhappy news did not reach 30th Corps in intelligible form until the evening of the 27th, and was not believed at Army Headquarters until next day. Though General Messervy soon escaped, his Division was without effective command until the afternoon of 29th May.

General Norrie, commanding the 30th Corps, had meanwhile ordered the 1st Armoured Division to be ready to move south and give battle. These orders were passed to the 22nd Armoured Brigade, then about twelve miles north of the scene of 4th Armoured Brigade's encounter with the 15th Panzer Division. The 2nd Armoured Brigade, farther north still, between Knightsbridge and El Adem, also prepared to move south. Before 22nd Armoured Brigade was far on its way the two Panzer Divisions fell upon it and destroyed thirty tanks and a number of guns. General Lumsden then ordered the Brigade to fall back on Knightsbridge as a spring-board for a second stroke south-eastwards, while the 2nd Armoured Brigade attacked the German right flank from the east. This plan succeeded, and both brigades dealt the enemy some sharp blows as he followed up. In addition, the 1st Army Tank Brigade from north-west of Knightsbridge struck at the German left flank.

The rapid movements of both sides and the uncertainty about the 7th Armoured Division made it difficult for the Air Force to give full

[1] The Retma position was held by 2nd Rifle Brigade, 9th King's Royal Rifle Corps, C Battery R.H.A., and the Rhodesian Anti-Tank Battery of 4th Regiment R.H.A.

LEGEND

British troops are shown in red,
German in blue and Italian in green

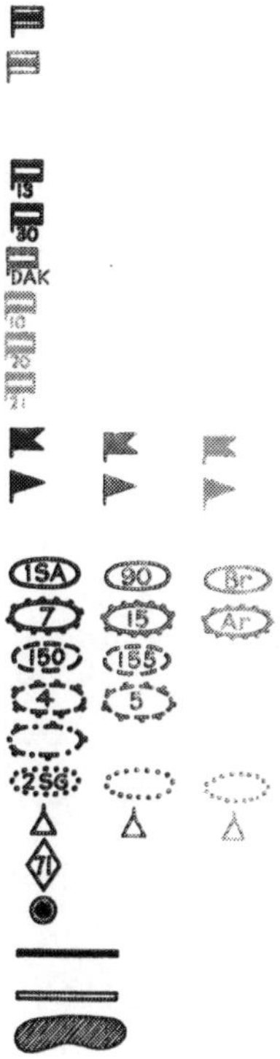

Headquarters of Armies

8th (Ritchie)
Panzerarmee Afrika (Rommel)

Headquarters of Corps

13th (Gott)
30th (Norrie)
D.A.K. (Nehring)
10th (Gioda)
20th (Baldassare)
21st (Navarrini)

Headquarters of Divisions
Heaaquarters of Brigades (or equivalent)

Divisions
Armoured Divisions
Brigades (or equivalent)
Armoured Brigades and Panzer Regiments
Armoured (British) Regiments
Other units and detachments
Recce. Patrols
Field Maintenance Centres
Airfields and landing grounds
Minefield: main alignment only
Dummy minefield " "
Full extent of mine marsh

Arabic terms

Dahar = plateau, lit. 'back'
Hagiag = barrier, escarpment
Maabus = steep cliff

Map 26

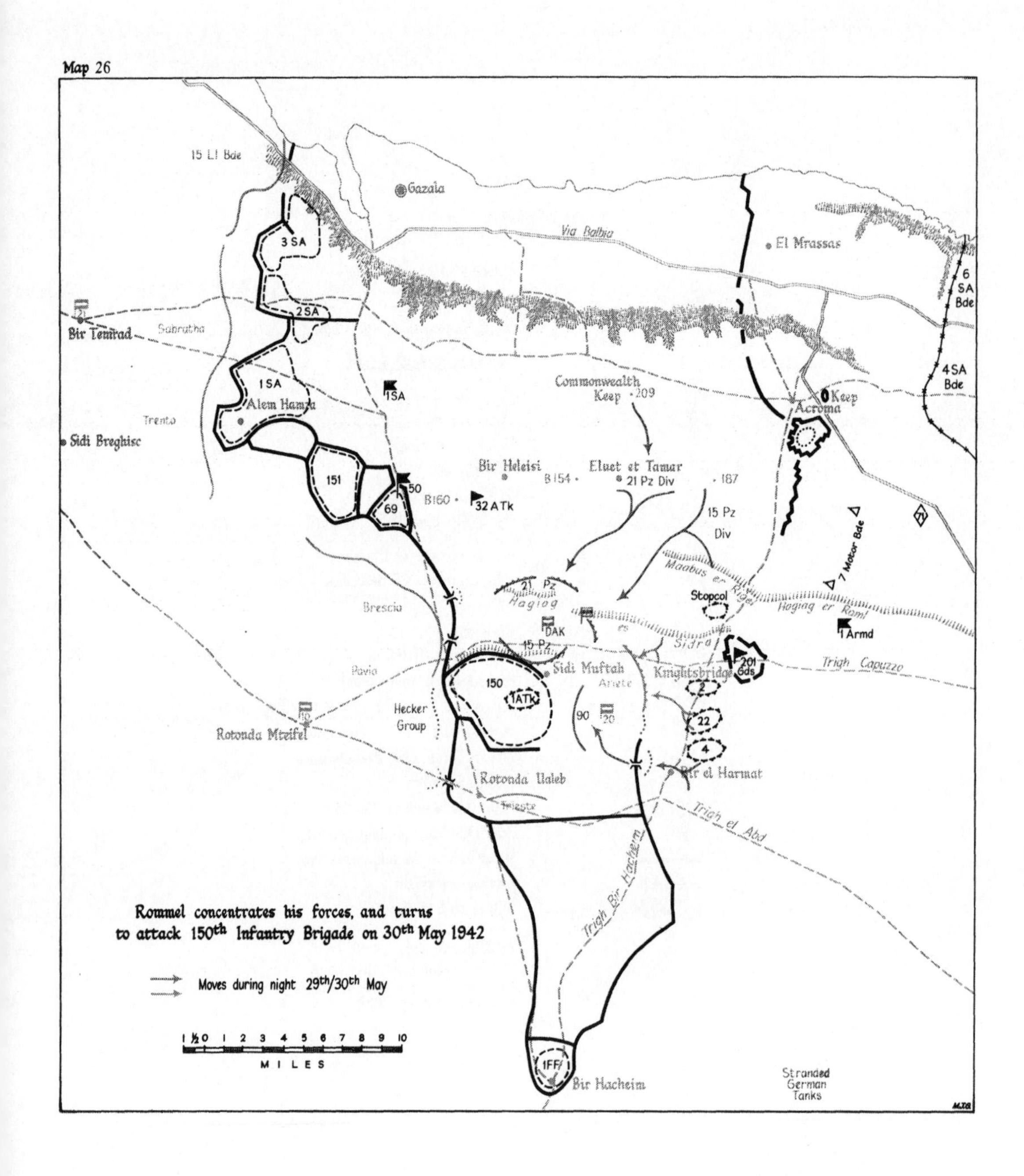
15 L I Bde
Gazala
Via Balbia
El Mrassas
6 SA Bde
3 SA
2 SA
Bir Temrad
Sabratha
1 SA
Alem Hamza
Trento
Sidi Breghisc
1 SA
Commonwealth Keep
209
4 SA Bde
Keep
Acroma
151
50
69
Bir Heleisi
B154
Eluet et Tamar
21 Pz Div
187
B160
32 A Tk
15 Pz Div
7 Motor Bde
Maabus er Rigel
21 Pz
Hagiag
Brescia
Stopcol
Hagiag er Rami
1 Armd
DAK
Sidra
15 Pz
201 Gds
Trigh Capuzzo
Pavia
Sidi Muftah
Ariete
Knightsbridge
150
1 ATk
2
22
Hecker Group
90
20
Rotonda Mteifel
4
Bir el Harmat
Rotonda Ualeb
Trieste
Trigh el Abd
Trigh Bir Hacheim
Rommel concentrates his forces, and turns to attack 150th Infantry Brigade on 30th May 1942
Moves during night 29th/30th May
MILES
1FF
Bir Hacheim
Stranded German Tanks

Map 27

Enemy dispositions are taken from captured records

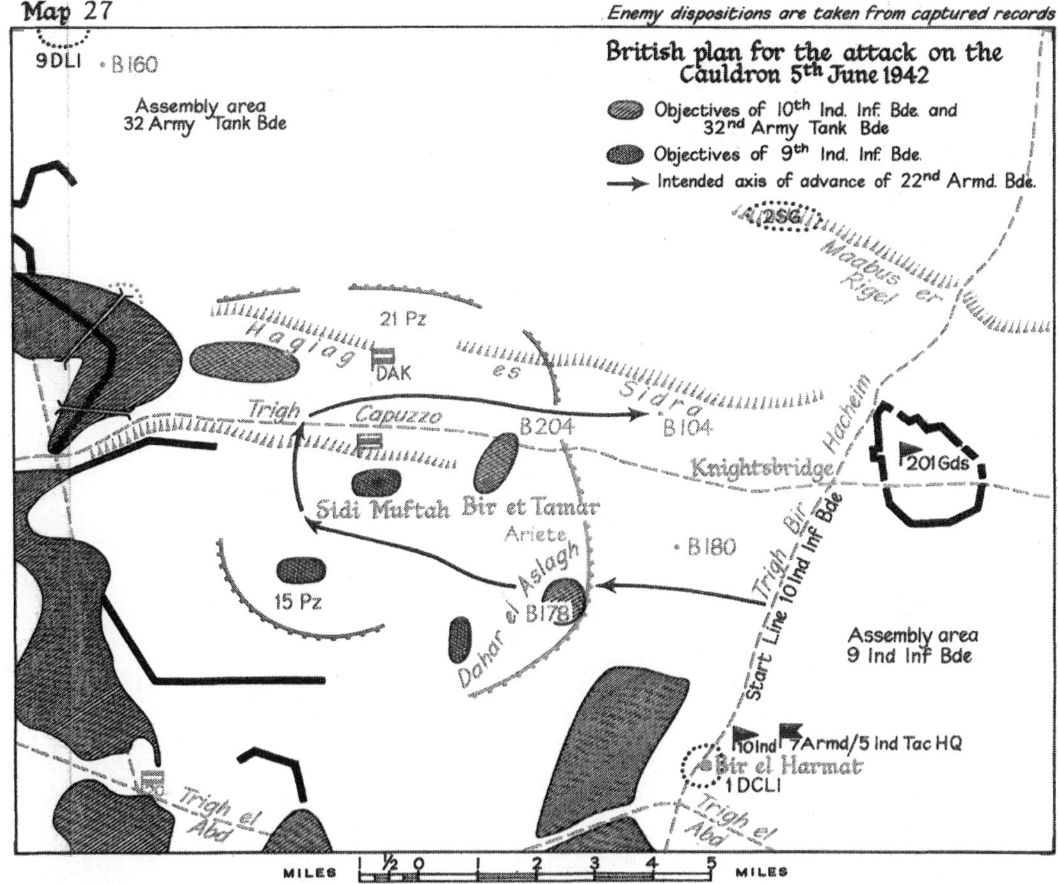

Map 28

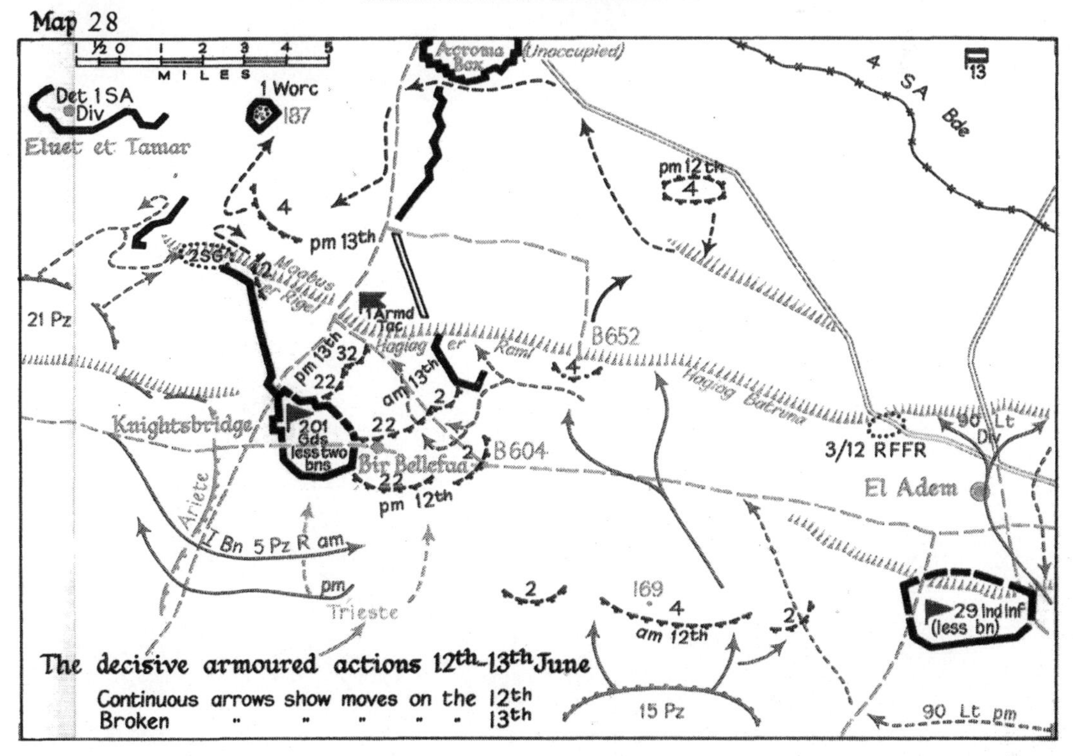

support to the Army, as it had intended to do. Only on the southern flank, in the direction of Bir Hacheim, Bir el Gubi and El Adem, were the day-bombers and fighter-bombers (the Kittyhawk was making its first appearance in this role) able to find suitable targets, many of which were provided by the 90th Light Division. Meanwhile the enemy's fighter patrols were active, reaching out as far as the British forward landing-grounds. Their fighters were also employed on tactical reconnaissance, while others escorted formations of dive-bombers. Six of the British fighter squadrons were withdrawn from Gambut for the night as a precaution, and at dusk the South African Bostons visited Tmimi airfields as 'intruders' and attacked aircraft in the dispersal areas, as they had done at Martuba the night before.

The day ended with the British higher command more satisfied with the day's fighting than was General Rommel. His Panzer Divisions had penetrated as far north as Bir Lefa and Maabus er Rigel, but had lost one-third of their tanks, and 15th Panzer was already short of fuel and ammunition; 90th Light was out of touch somewhere south of El Adem; the Ariete had failed to capture Bir Hacheim and had lost many tanks before sheering off to Bir el Harmat; and Trieste was apparently bogged down in the minefields well to the west. Thus his striking force lay scattered in the midst of enemy forces whose armoured formations, though battered, were by no means destroyed, and the supply columns which had followed the *D.A.K.* were in trouble south of Bir el Harmat, completely separated from the fighting troops.

Nevertheless General Rommel decided to advance again next day, though this move had to be confined to the 21st Panzer Division, for the 15th was out of fuel. It resulted in the capture of Commonwealth Keep after a stubborn defence, but that was all. General Lumsden had intended the 2nd and 22nd Armoured Brigades to attack the expected northward move in flank, and the 22nd remained watching the immobile 15th Panzer Division. The Ariete Division, moving northwards from Bir el Harmat, was attacked by the 2nd Armoured Brigade from the east and by the 1st Army Tank Brigade from the north-west, an engagement which ended slightly in favour of the British. Farther to the east the 4th Armoured Brigade reappeared on the scene at El Adem, attacked the 90th Light Division, and chased it south and west.

Air Vice-Marshal Coningham had agreed to use his fighters as much as possible in low-flying attacks on enemy columns. Most of the targets found were near El Adem and Bir Hacheim, though both the fighters and day-bombers made attacks in poor visibility on what was probably the 15th Panzer Division. The enemy's air forces provided cover over the area generally but made few attacks, probably because they were ignorant of the whereabouts of their own scattered troops.

At the end of 28th May General Ritchie was still satisfied with the progress of the battle. He considered rightly that Rommel's plan, which had been revealed by captured orders, had been badly upset. He estimated that the *D.A.K.* and Ariete together had about 250 fit tanks. He felt that his own forces were well placed to deal with what might come, and there was a good chance of destroying the enemy completely. He could concentrate against the enemy armour some 240 cruisers and 90 'I' tanks, and expected 40 more cruisers and 30 'I' tanks to arrive on the 29th.[1] General Auchinleck, too, was optimistic, but urged quicker action to destroy the enemy lest he should recover from the setback. There had in fact been a development of which the full significance had not yet been grasped—the Pavia and Trieste Divisions had begun to gap the minefields near the Trigh Capuzzo and Trigh el Abd in places not continually covered by fire.

See Map 26

General Rommel, for his part, was anxious. He had had about 200 tank casualties, his striking force was still scattered over a large area and his own Headquarters had been dispersed. The problem of supply was becoming more and more serious, because the route round Bir Hacheim, which the run of the battle had brought into temporary use, was proving vulnerable, and the Trigh Capuzzo and Trigh el Abd were still blocked by minefields, and also by the 150th Infantry Brigade, although this does not seem to have been realized as yet. Rommel decided that at all costs he must concentrate his forces on the 29th; that was as far ahead as he could see. Colonel Westphal, his senior operations officer, had taken upon himself to ask General Crüwell to come to the rescue by breaking through the 13th Corps' position towards Eluet et Tamar. Accordingly at dawn on 29th May the Sabratha Division attacked the South Africans north of Alem Hamza, but gained nothing and lost 400 prisoners.

Meanwhile, early in the morning, the supply vehicles from Bir el Harmat, led by Rommel himself, had succeeded in making their way up to the *D.A.K.* The Axis forces began to close in to the west and south-west of Knightsbridge and were attacked at 8 a.m. by the 2nd Armoured Brigade, which soon found itself in a fierce battle with German armour—21st Panzer Division to the north and 15th to the west—and with the Ariete Division to the south. Two regiments of the 22nd Armoured Brigade came to its help, and a violent artillery and tank action continued all day in a rising sandstorm which prevented the 4th Armoured Brigade reaching the battlefield, as it had been ordered to do. By evening both sides were severely battered and completely exhausted, but the Axis formations had partly succeeded

[1] The 1st Army Tank Brigade appears to have been left out of these calculations.

in concentrating; even the 90th Light Division had joined up. The commander of the 15th Panzer Division, General von Vaerst, had been wounded.

Again the British fighters and fighter-bombers had focused their attention on enemy transport. It might be thought that the concentration of enemy troops west and south-west of Knightsbridge would have produced some good targets for the day-bombers, but in fact these were not called upon to act until the evening. An accurate attack was made by nine Bostons of No. 12 Squadron S.A.A.F. against Commonwealth Keep, but an attempt to retake this place did not succeed.[1] At last light other Bostons bombed Derna harbour where a destroyer was seen alongside the mole.

On the enemy's side the fighters had been active. They attacked Gambut, and patrols flew over the battlefield escorting dive-bombers on no very obvious plan. Perhaps the key to this scrappy day in the air is supplied by an entry in General von Waldau's diary: '. . . Owing to a complete lack of information of our ground situation and plan of action, we were forced to resort to guess-work based on the results of aerial reconnaissance and the behaviour of the enemy's air force. We are sometimes obliged to make decisions without having the least idea whether they are appropriate to the over-all military situation.' The recorded losses during these three days were: British, 16 aircraft; German, 10; Italian, 7.

By the evening of 28th May it was clear to Brigadier C. W. Haydon, commanding the 150th Infantry Brigade, which stretched from the Trigh Capuzzo to the Trigh el Abd, that he was now threatened with attack from the east.[2] He therefore drew in his southern battalion, which had been holding up the advance of the Trieste Division, and prepared his brigade for all-round defence. On the morning of 29th May he was reinforced by the Tactical Headquarters of the 1st Army Tank Brigade, with the 44th Royal Tank Regiment and one squadron of the 42nd—thirty tanks in all.

The same day an interesting capture was made in the person of General Crüwell, who was shot down while flying over the battlefield in his Storch. With his capture there passed from the desert stage one of its outstanding figures. Crüwell had commanded the *D.A.K.* all through 'Crusader' in good times and bad, and, although he was frequently interfered with and to a large extent overshadowed by Rommel, he had shown himself to be a brave and energetic leader

---

[1] 39*th Panzerjäger Regiment* withdrew from Commonwealth Keep that evening, in accordance with Rommel's change of policy described on page 228.

[2] 150th Infantry Brigade consisted of 4th Battalion, East Yorkshire Regiment; 4th and 5th Battalions, The Green Howards; D Company, 2nd Battalion Cheshire Regiment (machine guns); 72nd Field Regiment R.A.; 25th/26thMedium Battery (7th Medium Regiment) R.A.; 259th (Norfolk Yeomanry) Anti-Tank Battery R.A.; 81st/25th Light A.A. Battery R.A.; 232nd Field Company R.E.

and a good judge of a tactical situation. Field-Marshal Kesselring, who was visiting the front, agreed to take over temporary command of the Crüwell group.

General Rommel had no illusions about his critical situation, and in particular about the shortage of ammunition and fuel in his Panzer divisions. He swiftly decided to abandon his plan of pressing on to the north and cancelled the landing from the sea; instead, he would hold off the British on the east with a thick anti-tank screen, and smash a wide gap in the minefields to the west. This would open up both a supply route and a way of escape, if need be. He was far from beaten, and the perils of the situation seem to have been matched by his confidence and determination.

On the British side there was a feeling of general satisfaction. The enemy's striking force seemed to be pinned against the minefields and would probably consume its remaining supplies during the next day. General Ritchie thought that there was a chance of shelling the armour to pieces, while his own tanks and motor brigades sought out and destroyed the supply columns. Indeed there seemed to be a prospect of making a counter-offensive, and General Auchinleck joined in with ideas of a possible advance to Bir Temrad, Sidi Breghisc and Rotonda Segnali, and of light mobile forces pushing on to Mechili and Benghazi. Quite rightly the British commanders were thinking big. But the basis of their hopes, which were that the enemy armour was cornered and wasting away, was soon to be shattered.

Early on the 30th May strong detachments of the *D.A.K.*, including 5th Panzer Regiment, were sent to open up a supply route to the west of Sidi Muftah. The operation was called off after eleven tanks had been lost, and it was then realized for the first time that the ground between the Trigh Capuzzo and the Trigh el Abd was well fortified and held by strong forces, including 'I' tanks. On the 31st May the Trieste and 90th Light Divisions joined in, but made little progress in the face of a defence which the German diaries record as skilful and stubborn. Next day, 1st June, after heavy dive-bombing, the assault was resumed, the attacking force having again been strengthened, this time by more artillery and by various units of the 21st Panzer Division. Early in the afternoon, after bitter fighting, the opposition was overcome by a series of concentric attacks. It is sad that General Rommel had felt able to withdraw so many troops from the northern and eastern sides of the area beginning to be known as 'the Cauldron', with which to overwhelm the single brigade, so stoutly defending more than five miles of front and facing attack from every direction at once.

By the time that the situation of the 150th Infantry Brigade was realized at Corps and Army Headquarters to be desperate it was too late to do anything effective to help. On 30th May the 2nd and 22nd Armoured Brigades of the 30th Corps had attacked the anti-tank screen which now faced them, but these attacks failed. Meanwhile half the 4th Armoured Brigade was sent southward on a wild-goose chase after some damaged enemy tanks. The same evening a column from the 201st Guards (Motor) Brigade set off westward along the Trigh Capuzzo from Knightsbridge with the object of occupying harassing positions. It ran into a watchful enemy and was driven back having lost five 25-pdr and seven 6-pdr guns and 157 men missing. For the moment the 30th Corps had shot its bolt.

During this time the British higher command undoubtedly seems to have kept in mind the enemy's probable embarrassments and even made a plan for the 13th Corps to attack towards Tmimi. This was postponed, however, because the enemy's armour in the Cauldron showed no signs of withdrawing, and General Ritchie considered that it must first be eliminated. He decided that on the night 1st/2nd June the 13th Corps was to establish a brigade group on the ridge Hagiag es Sidra, while the 30th Corps established another one west of Bir el Harmat. These and the locality of 150th Infantry Brigade (whose fate was not known) would be the jumping-off places for attacks to destroy the enemy in the Cauldron. General Auchinleck agreed with these preliminaries, but gave a warning that 'the enemy may yet try to resume the offensive, and, as we have learned, he has surprising powers of recovery'.

The British operations on the night 1st/2nd June were a fiasco. A single battalion of the 151st Infantry Brigade was launched at the Sidra ridge and failed to reach it, while the 10th Indian Infantry Brigade, hastily summoned from near Tobruk to establish the southern strongpoint, received its orders too late to be acted on. General Ritchie, who now knew that he had lost the 150th Infantry Brigade, thereupon began to make fresh plans which he hoped to put into effect 'in 48 to 72 hours'. From the Commander-in-Chief came another warning—this time that the loss of the Sidi Muftah position might mean that the initiative was passing to the enemy.

Indeed, although General Rommel had given up his original plan, at any rate for the time being, and although he had placed his armour on the defensive, he had no intention of doing nothing. Directly after capturing the Sidi Muftah locality, which made the position of his troops in the Cauldron much less precarious, he decided to capture Bir Hacheim, and on 2nd June sent the 90th Light and Trieste Divisions south for this purpose. By now he had lost two important members of his own staff, General Gause and Colonel Westphal having been wounded.

The main effort of the British fighters and fighter-bombers had been directed during 30th May to the attack of enemy transport driving through gaps in the minefields, and, as was to be expected, this brought on many encounters with German fighters, and twelve British aircraft were lost during the day. The tactical reconnaissance squadrons—No. 40 S.A.A.F. and No. 208—strove hard to keep their Corps Commanders informed of the latest moves on the ground, and during the afternoon the Bostons were sent to attack the large quantity of transport seen to eastward of the gaps. This they did, under heavy fighter escort, with apparently good results. Within an hour of their return the Bostons were off again, this time to attack concentrations farther east towards Knightsbridge. That night, because it was thought that the enemy was short of water, the Bostons attacked a known water-point at Tmimi.

The 31st May, in spite of many dust-storms, was an active day for the fighters and fighter-bombers, which attacked vehicles over a wide area. The German fighters were up in force, and sixteen British aircraft were lost against a loss of three German fighters and two dive-bombers. These heavy losses prompted Air Vice-Marshal Coningham to draw Air Marshal Tedder's attention to the serious matter of replacements, for squadrons were now reduced to seven or eight serviceable aircraft each.

It has been mentioned that early on 1st June the enemy's dive-bombers heavily attacked the 150th Infantry Brigade's position as a preliminary to its capture. British air operations, however, were seriously hampered by dust-storms, and indeed the Desert Air Force, whose strength was much reduced, needed a rest after the intense activity of the past few days. The attacks on Rommel's supply columns had added greatly to his anxieties, but they had been strongly opposed by fighters and anti-aircraft and small arms fire, and in the five days from the 27th May, during which the British fighters had flown over 1500 sorties, 50 out of 250 serviceable aircraft had been lost. There was now a dearth of Kittyhawks in reserve and it was therefore necessary to conserve the declining fighter force and to stop attacking from very low altitudes. An encouraging sign, however, was the arrival of the first Spitfires—six belonging to No. 145 Squadron. It was decided to use them on patrols high up, sometimes as cover to the Hurricanes, so that they could 'jump' enemy fighters without becoming embroiled in combat.[1]

The 2nd June was again a day of sandstorms, but next day the *Luftwaffe* began to attack Bir Hacheim in earnest. What with the numerous dive-bombers and the growing concentration of German and Italian troops in the area there was plenty for the R.A.F. to attack, and the scores of burning vehicles in full view of the Free French

[1] These were the first Spitfires to appear as fighters, but not the first to arrive in the desert. A special photographic unit of four Spitfires had arrived a few weeks previously.

garrison did much to keep up the morale of General Koenig's stout-hearted troops. At the end of 4th June he signalled to Air Vice-Marshal Coningham: 'Bravo! Merci pour la R.A.F.' which drew the immediate reply: 'Merci pour le sport'. In two days, apart from the damage done on the ground, ten Stukas, one Ju. 88, two Me. 109s, and three Italian aircraft had been shot down for the loss of thirteen British.[1] The shift of main interest to the Cauldron area on the following day gave the French a brief respite from attack.

The clearing away of all opposition from where the Trigh Capuzzo and Trigh el Abd crossed the minefields had made the enemy's supply position much easier. It did not mean, however, that his supply columns were now entirely secure, for apart from air attacks they suffered much during the first ten days of June from frequent raids by columns from the 1st South African Division, the 50th Division, and the 7th Motor Brigade. On 3rd June the 1st South African Brigade made a very well-handled raid on the Trento Division, in which Sergeant Q. Smythe, 1st Royal Natal Carbineers, won the Victoria Cross.

Partly, perhaps, to draw attention from Bir Hacheim and partly to upset the preparations for the British attack which General Rommel knew must come, he sent the 21st Panzer Division to make a strong demonstration towards Eluet et Tamar on 2nd June, in the course of which twelve tanks of the 5th R.T.R. (4th Armoured Brigade) were destroyed. No major tank actions then occurred for a few days because the armoured formations on both sides were busy reorganizing. On 2nd June the *D.A.K.* recorded that it had 130 serviceable tanks out of the 320 with which it began the battle, but that the number was now rising.

General Auchinleck still had the idea of making a bold thrust from 13th Corps' front towards Bir el Temrad, but General Ritchie stuck to his view (which was shared by his Corps Commanders) that he might not be able to hold the enemy's armour while such an advance was being made. For the same reason, and because of supply difficulties, he had given up the idea of making a wide turning movement round the southern flank. He decided that the first essential was to crush the enemy's forces in the Cauldron. To this end the 30th Corps would advance westward from the south of Knightsbridge, using infantry to drive a wedge through the enemy's anti-tank screen in the dark. The armour would then pass 'through this corridor into the

---

[1] These German figures are from enemy records. As always, therefore, they may include aircraft shot down by anti-aircraft fire or by small-arms fire from the ground. British Army diaries contain frequent reference to similar successes, and sometimes add that the pilot was taken prisoner.

rear of the enemy and close the gaps behind him'. The 13th Corps would co-operate by seizing the Sidra ridge and would later exploit the success gained in the Cauldron by advancing on Tmimi. Such was Ritchie's expressed intention early on 3rd June; the operation was to begin during the night 4th/5th.

The final plan for the attack on the Cauldron is illustrated in outline on Map 27. It was to be in two phases. In the first phase the 10th Indian Infantry Brigade (of Major-General H. R. Briggs's 5th Indian Division) was to capture the first objective in the early hours of 5th June after a really heavy artillery bombardment. The 32nd Army Tank Brigade (of 13th Corps), with 7th Green Howards under command, was then to capture the Sidra ridge. In the second phase the leading role would pass to General Messervy's 7th Armoured Division with the 9th Indian Infantry Brigade (of 5th Indian Division) under command, its object being to destroy the enemy in the Cauldron. The 1st Armoured Division, whose reorganized 22nd Armoured Brigade was now in the 7th Armoured Division (replacing the rather battered 4th Armoured Brigade), was to prevent the enemy breaking out to the north or north-east and was to be ready to exploit success westwards.

The system of command adopted for this very important operation deserves notice. In the first place, no single commander below the Army Commander was responsible for co-ordinating the attacks on the two fronts. This may have been because General Gott's 13th Corps was to have exploited west towards Tmimi, and not south through Sidra. On the 30th Corps' front there was no single commander either, for General Norrie had delegated the command to Generals Briggs and Messervy in turn and they worked out their parts of the plan as best they could. It is interesting to note that the 22nd Armoured Brigade was to help the 9th Indian Infantry Brigade in the second phase, but was to give its first thought to destroying the enemy's tanks. The infantry's action was to depend on any armoured engagement that might occur, but it was laid down that 'In case of armoured action infantry are self-protecting. They will not hamper the movement of 22nd Armoured Brigade.' The planned movement of 22nd Armoured Brigade was a right-handed sweep through the Cauldron, or, as one regiment put it, 'To mop up the enemy en route and be at B 104 for breakfast'. At the last moment the 1st Battalion, Duke of Cornwall's Light Infantry, which had arrived in Tobruk from Iraq on 3rd June, was rushed out to act as left flank-guard at Bir el Harmat. The Tactical Headquarters of the 7th Armoured and 5th Indian Divisions were together near Bir el Harmat.

The attack began in moonlight at 2.50 a.m. and made good progress. All the battalions of the 10th Indian Infantry Brigade (Brigadier C. H. Boucher) supported by tanks of the 4th R.T.R. reached their objectives with trifling loss. By daylight the 2nd H.L.I. were in the area B 204—Bir et Tamar, 4/10th Baluch Regiment at B 178, and 2/4th Gurkha Rifles at B 180. Soon afterwards the 50th Reconnaissance Battalion and the 107th Regiment R.H.A. (of 22nd Armoured Brigade Group) also arrived near B 180, and the 4th, 28th and 157th Field Regiments R.A. moved into positions near the Baluch Regiment and the Gurkhas. The 2nd Battalion West Yorkshire Regiment (of 9th Indian Infantry Brigade), who had been supported by a squadron of 4th R.T.R., reached their objective on the Dahar el Aslagh.

Unfortunately, the main reason for this prosperous beginning had been that the enemy's defensive positions lay farther to the west than had been thought and had escaped the weight of the British bombardment. Evil consequences were to follow quickly. The 22nd Armoured Brigade had begun its advance with 156 Grant, Stuart, and Crusader tanks, and the leading regiment had reached about two miles west of the Dahar el Aslagh when it ran into the concentrated fire of most of the German artillery. The whole brigade checked and wheeled north to between Bir et Tamar and B 178. The 2nd H.L.I. had meanwhile lost part of its objective to a local counter-attack; it did its best to consolidate under intense fire, but was unable to do so before a heavy attack led by tanks (probably of 8th Panzer Regiment) came in at noon. Part of this attack fell on the 22nd Armoured Brigade, which was soon embroiled. Because divisional orders had absolved—for so they were understood—the armour from responsibility for the infantry, the 22nd Armoured Brigade gave no help to the H.L.I., who were at length driven back to the Gurkhas' positions and were later ordered back to the Trigh Bir Hacheim to re-form. Farther south the 2nd West Yorkshires had been dangerously isolated and were withdrawn. Meanwhile the 32nd Army Tank Brigade's dawn attack on the Sidra ridge had been met by intense anti-tank fire and had run into an unsuspected minefield. The attack was called off but not before about 50 of the 70 'I' tanks in action had been lost.

The unpleasant turn taken by the battle was soon realized at the Tactical Headquarters of the 7th Armoured and 5th Indian Divisions, but each was occupied with its own problems and there was nobody in sole command to concert their actions. Each division determined to hold on, but was unable to do anything effective to regain the initiative. The 2nd Armoured Brigade Group (of one armoured regiment, one motor battalion, and one regiment R.H.A.) had been sent as a reinforcement from Eluet et Tamar to a point seven miles south of Knightsbridge. Here it was placed under command of 7th Armoured Division, but received from it a number of orders which cancelled each other out.

Early in the afternoon General Rommel judged that the situation was well in hand and his northern flank safe. He decided to strike east with the Ariete and 21st Panzer Divisions, and from the south towards Knightsbridge with part of the 15th Panzer Division, using a gap made in the minefield south-west of Bir el Harmat the previous day. This group first overran the D.C.L.I. and then, joined by other units from Bir Hacheim and by Rommel himself, dispersed in confusion the Tactical Headquarters of both British divisions, the Headquarters of the 9th Indian Infantry Brigade and two of its battalions (the third, 3/9th Jats, had been sent to reinforce the 2/4th Gurkhas), the Headquarters of the 10th Indian Infantry Brigade and the survivors of the 2nd H.L.I. Communication and control broke down completely. The Tactical Headquarters of the 7th Armoured Division took refuge in Knightsbridge and that of 5th Indian Division in El Adem, where the disorganized units of the 9th Indian Infantry Brigade, and most of the H.L.I., also assembled. The armoured regiments of the 22nd Armoured Brigade, under renewed attacks by the 15th Panzer Division, withdrew to leaguer east of the Trigh Bir Hacheim in no state to restore the situation; in the course of a dispiriting day they had lost some sixty tanks. The extent of all these reverses was not grasped for some time by the higher formations. It is true that towards midnight General Ritchie realized that a strong thrust had driven back the 5th Indian Division, but he hoped to play for time and reorganize his armour.

It had been a disappointing day for the Royal Air Force also. Once more it seems to have been impossible for the Army to lay down a satisfactory bomb-line, though there was at least one example of a successful attack early in the morning; this was made by the Bostons against positions south of Dahar el Aslagh. Either because of the need to conserve the day-bombers and fighter-bombers or because it was felt that they might get a chance of intervening with telling effect at a later stage of the battle, numerous requests for air support seem to have been turned down during the day. The enemy's air activity had been on a small scale.

There now remained in the Cauldron near B 180 the 4/10th Baluch Regiment, 2/4th Gurkha Rifles, 3/9th Jat Regiment, 50th Reconnaissance Battalion, the 4th, 28th and 157th Field Regiments R.A. and the 107th Regiment R.H.A. On these the storm broke on 6th June. First the Baluchis were overrun, and then, during the afternoon, the Gurkhas. By evening the same fate had overtaken the 50th Reconnaissance Battalion and all the artillery. This day was both a splendid and a tragic episode in the history of the Royal Artillery, for the gunners fought their guns to the last and died where they stood. From the infantry battalions a few sub-units and individuals escaped eastwards. No help reached the doomed units in the Cauldron, for although the 2nd and 4th Armoured Brigades had been placed under General

Messervy, who was now in sole command, he was unable in the prevailing confusion to bring them into action.

It was also unfortunate that the Desert Air Force could not help. Though low cloud seriously interfered with their operations, it was the absence of a clearly defined bomb-line which ruled out any employment whatever of the day-bombers in the battle area. Air Vice-Marshal Coningham had therefore to be content with using them, together with the fighter-bombers, to attack enemy columns beyond the fringe of the fighting. A good omen for the future, however, was the arrival of the first Hurricane IID tank-destroying aircraft, as yet untried, armed with two 40-mm. cannons. No 6 Squadron started operations with nine of them.

So ended the attempt to destroy the Axis forces waiting in the Cauldron for the attack they knew was bound to come. General Rommel had judged to a nicety the strength necessary to hold it, and had hoped to see the British exhaust themselves—as indeed they did. With his quick eye for the run of a battle he soon saw that their plan had gone astray, and showed his quality by being ready to take advantage of it. Of the courage and self-sacrifice of the British troops there is no doubt, as the enemy noted with admiration. Signs that two old lessons were being relearned—which was encouraging for the future—were the concentration of a strong force of artillery, and the use of infantry to effect a 'break in' by night in order to clear a passage for the armour. But there seems to have been a too optimistic view of the probable course of the battle after the hard core of the enemy's resistance had been reached. The British system of command was too complicated to deal with the unexpected, and was no match for the strong personal control of the enemy Commander. This caused an unfair burden to be laid on the divisional commanders and resulted in many fine troops being thrown away.

All this time the Trieste and 90th Light Divisions, together with other troops, had been trying unsuccessfully to capture Bir Hacheim with the help of the *Luftwaffe*—somewhat grudgingly given, to judge from General von Waldau's repeated complaints about the misuse of the air forces. But General Rommel was anxious to have done with Bir Hacheim before reverting to his original intention of attacking the main Gazala positions from the rear. After the successful outcome of the fighting in the Cauldron, he gave orders for Bir Hacheim to be captured on 8th June, and when that plan failed he sent the hard-worked 15th Panzer Division south to join the investing force. He still hoped to resume the northward move of his Army on the 9th.

Outside the ring at Bir Hacheim columns of the 7th Motor Brigade and 29th Indian Infantry Brigade and of the Free French themselves had been harassing the enemy's communications. As early as 6th June General Ritchie was in two minds whether to continue to hold Bir Hacheim: the enemy had now got a more direct route of supply, and if the 7th Motor Brigade were used, as Ritchie wished, to operate more intensively against this supply route west of the Cauldron, he doubted whether Bir Hacheim could still be supplied. However General Auchinleck advised against giving the place up, and Ritchie decided that General Koenig should hold on.

On 8th June the *Luftwaffe's* attacks on Bir Hacheim began to be much heavier, and early that morning they used no fewer than 45 Ju. 87s, three Ju. 88s, and ten Me. 110s, escorted by 54 single-engine fighters. The Free French were also heavily shelled and were engaged in repelling infantry attacks most of the morning. In the afternoon General Koenig reported that his troops were much exhausted, that they had had heavy casualties and were starting to consume their reserve supplies. He asked for a full-scale operation to relieve him, and for more air support. The first of these requests could not be met at short notice, but the Royal Air Force, who had been uncertain whether to give priority that day to Bir Hacheim or to the Cauldron area, now went all out to help the Free French. The British fighters flew 478 sorties—the highest total so far on any one day in the desert. In all, on the 8th, the British lost eight aircraft, the Germans one, and the Italians three. That night Hurricanes and Bostons dropped supplies for the garrison.

On 9th June the heavy shelling and the onslaught from the air continued unabated. On land the enemy made two furious attacks, broke into the defences and was thrown out. Unfortunately the British air effort was limited because many aircraft were temporarily unserviceable. The fighter-bombers managed to fly twenty-five sorties, and the fighters had several encounters, in which one German fighter and one bomber were shot down for the loss of two fighters, and another German fighter fell to British A.A. guns. Under cover of these operations two Hurricanes dropped medical supplies for the garrison. Meanwhile the 30th Corps had arranged for columns of the 7th Motor Brigade, the 29th Indian Infantry Brigade and the 4th Armoured Brigade to distract the enemy, but their attacks were not strong enough to do so, although part of 90th Light Division had to turn and defend itself against one of the columns. On the evening of 8th June a warning order had been issued to prepare to evacuate the garrison, and on 10th June General Ritchie decided that they should withdraw the same night. During the morning of 10th June a particularly heavy raid by twenty Ju. 88s and forty Ju. 87s, with some fifty Me. 109s and 110s in attendance, was made on Bir Hacheim, where in the whole day a total of 130 tons of bombs was dropped. As a further protection to his bombers the enemy kept fighter patrols over Bir Hacheim and also a screen over the El Adem area to intercept the British fighters coming from Gambut. Sweeps by Hurricanes and Spitfires nevertheless made some interceptions and two German aircraft were shot down for the loss of two British fighters.

During the day a strong group, under General Rommel's personal command, mainly from the *D.A.K.* (but without any tanks) had broken into the defences in the north and established itself. Late that night Rommel reported to *OKH* that he was confident of capturing Bir Hacheim next day. It is interesting to note that Field-Marshal Kesselring had been pressing Rommel hard to bring down stronger forces, including tanks, to hasten the capture, but Rommel wished to keep his tanks for more open fighting and thought that they would merely be thrown away on the minefields.

The moment for the withdrawal of the garrison was therefore well chosen. The 7th Motor Brigade ran a large convoy of lorries and ambulances to a point about five miles west of Bir Hacheim, and the Free French broke out to this rendezvous, not—as was to be expected—without some clashes. About 2,700 troops (including 200 wounded) of the original garrison of 3,600 were brought away. The defence of Bir Hacheim had served several purposes. At the outset it had made longer and more difficult the enemy's temporary supply route; it had caused him many casualties; and it gave the British a chance to recover from their defeat in the Cauldron. General Koenig's Brigade made a great impression upon the enemy by their courageous and enterprising resistance, and their success gave a well-won fillip to the pride of the Free French who, for the first time in the Middle East, had fought the Germans and Italians in a complete formation of their own.[1]

Between 2nd and 10th June the Desert Air Force had done its best to help the garrison. It had flown close on 1,500 sorties and lost 19 fighters in the process. During the same time the Germans had flown about 1,400 sorties against Bir Hacheim and lost at least 15 aircraft; the Italians lost at least 5. Both sides felt the strain of such a prolonged effort, and the maintenance crews deserve a word of recognition for their work which enabled many aircraft to make four, and even six, sorties in a day.

The 7th Motor Brigade, too, had made great efforts to support the Free French in their besieged position. Under Brigadier J. M. L. Renton, it was responsible for running in convoys of supplies, ammunition, and water, which it did on four nights between 31st May and 7th June. When it is remembered that the defended locality was

[1] The main units comprising the 1st Free French Brigade Group were: 2e *et* 3e *bataillons de légion étrangère; 2e bataillon de marche de l'Oubanghi; 1er bataillon d'infanterie de marine (coloniale); 1er bataillon du Pacifique; 1er régiment d'artillerie; 1er bataillon de fusiliers marins* (A.A.). An anti-tank company, engineers, signal, medical and administrative troops, all Free French, completed the Group. Their arms included 26 field guns, 62 anti-tank guns of various sizes and 44 mortars.

merely a piece of open desert almost entirely surrounded by minefields and to a varying extent by the enemy also, it will be appreciated that each of these supply runs was a tricky operation, and there was no certainty that they could continue for very long.

After the Cauldron battle General Auchinleck had feared that the enemy, unless fully engaged, might recover from his losses—although these had undoubtedly been heavy—and that a stalemate might occur. He considered nevertheless that the British armour should not now attack, but hoped that Rommel might be induced to do so and exhaust himself. The 8th Army would then strike westward against his rear from the 13th Corps' front at Alem Hamza. General Ritchie was also thinking on these lines, and on 6th June had actually ordered the 13th Corps to make a thrust westward. General Gott, after discussion with General Pienaar, decided upon a raid by not more than one brigade group between Bir Temrad and the coast, and on 7th June General Pienaar sent out a number of small detachments to find soft spots. No results were achieved and the South Africans suffered 280 casualties.

By 11th June the British defensive system had still not been cracked open. From the sea to south of Alem Hamza the original defences of the 1st South African and 50th Divisions were intact, while between this point and Acroma to the east were five new strong-points, each held by a garrison of roughly a battalion, a field battery, and a few anti-tank guns.[1] The 201st Guards (Motor) Brigade Group still held Knightsbridge, and now had the 2nd Scots Guards on the Maabus er Rigel to guard the crossing to Acroma. From Acroma a minefield had been completed to the sea. El Adem was held by the 29th Indian Infantry Brigade, which had one battalion on the escarpment where this is climbed by the Tobruk by-pass road. Tobruk itself was held by the 2nd South African Division, and there were other defended localities at Sidi Rezegh and Belhamed. Thus there was a framework of defences which might help to check or disrupt the enemy's further advance and serve to some extent as pivots of manœuvre for the British armour. The state of this arm must now be examined.

On 10th June General Ritchie estimated that he had about 250 cruiser and 80 'I' tanks fit to fight, though an analysis of unit records suggests that the true figures were: in the three armoured brigades 77 Grants, 52 Crusaders and 56 Stuarts, and in the 32nd Army Tank Brigade 63 'I' tanks. Attempts to bring the armour up to strength had been most complicated and not very successful, the basic cause being the differences between the three sorts of cruiser tank. To get the required tank with a suitable crew to the unit that wanted it was not

[1] The five were B 160, Bir Heleisi, B 154, Eluet et Tamar, and Pt 187.

easy. It led to sub-units being combined, or sometimes lent to other units. Even single tanks and crews had to be sent here and there. Regimental organization was disrupted, and the 1st Armoured Brigade, much to its disgust, had been used as a pool of immediate requirements. In fact expediency ruled, and any fairly well-filled till was raided for the benefit of empty ones. Units disliked this policy intensely. They complained also of many defects in their replacement tanks—of missing wireless equipment and of guns arriving rusted or in grease. All the armoured brigades had changed divisions at least twice, which was unsettling and led to administrative difficulties. But all in all the British armour was numerically still a factor of great importance. A cause for more anxiety was the shortage of artillery, for since 26th May the equivalent of seven field regiments had been lost.

General Rommel lost little time after the fall of Bir Hacheim in setting his forces in motion again. The *D.A.K.* had now 25 Pzkw IIs, 83 IIIs and 8 IVs, and, in addition, 27 III Specials which mounted a long 5-cm. gun, and 6 IV Specials which mounted a long 7·5-cm. gun. In all, 124 tanks apart from the Pzkw IIs, roughly equally divided between the two Panzer Divisions. There were also about 60 Italian cruisers. The enemy's losses had therefore been considerable, though the increase in the numbers of new and powerful types is significant. A serious matter was that one-third of the German infantry had become casualties. Nevertheless on 11th June General Rommel ordered 15th Panzer, 90th Light and Trieste Divisions to advance north-east towards El Adem while 21st Panzer Division demonstrated northwards from the Sidra ridge. These movements had not gone very far by nightfall, but they led General Norrie to see that the enemy had spread his forces on a very wide front, and he thought there was now an opportunity 'to go in and smash him'.

During the morning the British fighters began by protecting the withdrawal of the Free French. No enemy aircraft appeared on this flank until about 9 a.m., by which time the Brigade had got safely away. The *Luftwaffe* celebrated its release from Bir Hacheim by spreading its operations all over the place, but not until the afternoon had any targets been given to the Desert Air Force, and then the South African day-bombers with some of their escorting Kittyhawks carrying bombs attacked transport in the Knightsbridge area. One of the targets turned out to have been the *Panzerarmee's* battle headquarters, which reported some casualties.

See Map 28

Early on 12th June General Norrie, wishing to profit by the enemy's dispersal, had in mind a move south by the 2nd and 4th Armoured

Brigades, who would then turn east and attack the 15th Panzer Division.[1] General Messervy, however, feared that this would divide the British armour and decided that he must confer with Norrie. After leaving his Headquarters to do so he was headed off by the enemy near El Adem, and for some hours was out of touch with everyone. Meanwhile the two armoured brigades, east and west of Pt 169, where they were awaiting the order to move, resisted a not very vigorous attack by the 15th Panzer Division. This division had in fact been told to stay on the defensive because General Rommel had reason to expect (from an intercepted message) that the 4th Armoured Brigade was about to advance, and wished to let it blunt itself in so doing. Nothing much having happened by noon, Rommel ordered both Panzer Divisions to attack the 2nd and 4th Armoured Brigades—the 15th frontally and the 21st from the rear. These orders were to have disastrous consequences for the British.

At about this time, the whereabouts of General Messervy being still unknown, General Norrie decided to put all three armoured brigades under the 1st Armoured Division. General Lumsden quickly brought down the remains of the 22nd Armoured Brigade to the Knightsbridge area, where they were just in time to delay the advance from the west of a battle-group of 21st Panzer Division consisting of a battalion of 5th Panzer Regiment and some guns. The scanty and conflicting records make it impossible to disentangle the details of the ensuing fighting. However, by about 4 p.m. the 15th Panzer Division was outflanking the 2nd Armoured Brigade on the east and pushing the 4th Armoured Brigade northwards. General Lumsden now decided to shorten his eastern front by holding a line between B 652 on the Batruna escarpment and B 604 east of Knightsbridge—4th Armoured Brigade on the north, 2nd Armoured Brigade on the south. Owing to misunderstandings and enemy pressure the depleted regiments of the 4th Armoured Brigade were forced over the escarpment and down the other side. The 2nd Armoured Brigade reached and maintained its

---

[1] *British Armour on 12th June*

(i) 2nd Armoured Brigade: Queen's Bays; one squadron 8th Hussars; one squadron 4th Hussars; 4th County of London Yeomanry (including one squadron 8th Hussars) on loan from 22nd Armoured Brigade until 6 p.m.

(ii) 4th Armoured Brigade: 1st Royal Tank Regiment; 3/5th (composite regiment) Royal Tank Regiment; 6th Royal Tank Regiment.

(iii) 22nd Armoured Brigade: 3rd County of London Yeomanry (two squadrons).

(iv) Tank strengths:

	Grant	*Stuart*	*Crusader*
2nd Armoured Brigade	17	3	25
4th Armoured Brigade	39	56	—
22nd Armoured Brigade	27	5	34
	83	64	59

(v) In addition to the above

a. 32nd Army Tank Brigade—63 'I' tanks.

b. Detachment 2nd Royal Gloucestershire Hussars (with 7th Motor Brigade)—16 Stuarts.

appointed position and at nightfall the remnants of the 22nd came into position between it and Knightsbridge at Bir Bellefaa.

During the late afternoon of 11th June the enemy's moves north-east from Bir Hacheim had been seen from the air, and early on the 12th the presence of 90th Light Division near El Adem was confirmed. Owing to the lack of definite information from the Army as to a bomb-line in the Knightsbridge area it was decided to concentrate on 90th Light Division. Throughout the day, bombers, fighters, and fighter-bombers of the Desert Air Force shuttled to and fro, stopping only just long enough to rearm and refuel. Altogether nineteen separate attacks were made, and considerable damage seemed to have been done. The diary of 90th Light Division, however, refers to low-flying and bombing attacks throughout the whole day—in all about twenty attacks made by six to ten aircraft at a time—which, they said, had had no effect upon the morale of the division and had done only slight damage to their vehicles. The division was greatly disappointed, however, that not a single German aircraft showed itself, in spite of requests to the *Luftwaffe*.

The enemy's aircraft had nevertheless been very active all day, especially about Knightsbridge and Acroma. (During the evening the 15th Panzer Division was dive-bombed by its own Stukas.) At about 8 p.m. a large formation, reported as over 100 aircraft, appeared over El Adem, and six fighter squadrons engaged it in the biggest air combat of the battle. It was believed that eleven of the enemy had been destroyed for the loss of five British fighters. The German records disclose the loss of only two, and the Italian none. Altogether during the day eleven British aircraft were lost—the highest figure since 1st June. It was another record day for the fighters, which flew no less than 583 sorties.

The 12th June was a costly day for the British armour also.[1] In the heavy fighting during the afternoon it appears that full advantage of the prevailing haze and dust was taken by the German anti-tank gunners to push boldly forward, and they did great execution. General Lumsden realized that his losses had been heavy and considered that he could do no more than consolidate round Knightsbridge. General Norrie, while not yet aware of the losses, was thinking of further offensive action, but communication between the two commanders failed and Lumsden was left to make his own decision, which was to hold Knightsbridge for one more day.

Back at Army Headquarters General Ritchie was beginning to feel that the weakness of the British armour might allow the enemy to advance north and cut off the 1st South African and 50th Divisions. (This is exactly what Rommel intended to do.) In his opinion the

[1] By noon on 13th June the losses in the three Armoured Brigades had been reckoned as 105 tanks and in the Army Tank Brigade as 33.

choice lay between fighting the present battle out and withdrawing his whole force to the Egyptian frontier. The first course held the risk that the armour might be defeated and the infantry divisions cut off; the second course entailed a difficult withdrawal and the danger of becoming involved in a running fight, besides raising an awkward problem of what to do about Tobruk. General Ritchie decided to stand and fight, and General Auchinleck, who was visiting him, agreed. When the Prime Minister heard the news he telegraphed: 'Your decision to fight it out to the end is most cordially endorsed. We shall sustain you whatever the result. Retreat would be fatal. This is a business not only of armour but of will-power. God bless you all.'

As it seemed to General Ritchie on the evening of 12th June that the 13th Corps would now be in the centre of the battle, he placed the 1st Armoured Division under its command. Not being in touch with General Gott, General Lumsden did not get any orders until the next day. General Ritchie wished the armour to be kept concentrated and make full use of the support afforded by the infantry positions, and Gott's orders were for Lumsden to secure the area Acroma–Knightsbridge–Maabus er Rigel–Eluet et Tamar and engage the enemy actively whenever possible. Meanwhile the 30th Corps had ordered the 7th Motor Brigade to strike at the enemy's rear between El Adem and Knightsbridge. The 10th Indian Division, by General Ritchie's order, was to engage the enemy in the El Adem area.

The enemy's plan for 13th June was for the 15th Panzer Division to move west along the Hagiag er Raml and the 21st Panzer Division east along the Maabus er Rigel and thus cut off Knightsbridge. The 90th Light Division was recalled from the position it had reached near El Adem. During the morning, although the pressure was severe, the 2nd and 22nd Armoured Brigades and a few tanks of the 32nd Army Tank Brigade just managed to hold their own east of Knightsbridge. Then in the afternoon the 21st Panzer Division began its attack upon the position at the western end of Maabus er Rigel held by the 2nd Scots Guards supported by one battery of 11th Regiment R.H.A. and the 6th South African Field Battery. By 3 p.m. the danger here seemed so great that the 2nd and 4th Armoured Brigades (the latter from its overnight position north of the Hagiag Batruna) were ordered to help. There was little air activity on either side because of the dust-storms; indeed Gambut airfield was out of action for most of the day. A few small operations were carried out and there was one fight between a formation of Kittyhawks and some heavily escorted Ju. 88s in which four Kittyhawks were lost.

It was in the tail-end of one of these dust-storms that the final armoured clash of the day took place—a most confused action which lasted until dark and ended with the western part of the Scots Guards' position in enemy hands. For great gallantry on this day and on earlier occasions Lieut.-Colonel H. R. B. Foote, 7th Royal Tank Regiment, was awarded the Victoria Cross.

The 2nd Armoured Brigade was holding, with difficulty, the northern edge of the Rigel feature, and the 4th Armoured Brigade was withdrawing towards Acroma. It had meanwhile become clear that Knightsbridge was almost surrounded and General Gott ordered it to be abandoned the same night.

The British armour was now reduced to about 50 cruiser and 20 'I' tanks and was no longer in a position to recover its damaged tanks from the battlefield. Ever since the opening of the battle the British had striven hard to get damaged tanks into action again quickly, and a few figures will suffice to show not only what a large number of casualties had occurred, but what good work the tireless recovery and repair teams had been doing. Up to the 13th June no less than 417 damaged tanks had been recovered; of these 210 had already been repaired, 122 had been sent off to the base workshops, and the rest were under repair locally. (All this over and above the hundreds of 'roadside' repairs.) In addition, up to the previous day—there is no record for 13th June—138 damaged 'I' tanks of 13th Corps had been recovered, making a total of at least 555 tanks damaged and an unknown but undoubtedly large number destroyed or damaged beyond repair. In a sadly high proportion of these the crew, if not killed outright, must have been trapped when their tank caught fire, as so often happened after one had been penetrated—especially if it was a Crusader. There is ample evidence that the experienced crews were by this time only too well aware of the shortcomings of their own tanks. The Stuart, after many months of service, was now regarded as no more than a fast and reliable reconnaissance vehicle or a mobile artillery observation post. The Grant had justified the confidence placed in it: its 75-mm. gun had given good results in spite of its limited traverse and the fact that the best armour-piercing ammunition was not yet available, while its armour gave excellent protection —much better than the Crusader's. As for the British 2-pdr gun, the Middle East reported that the fighting had conclusively shown it to be outmatched and that its uncapped shot, which was all it had, broke up against the face-hardened plates of the German tanks. Armour-piercing capped and ballistic capped ammunition was required with 'the utmost urgency' to improve the performance of this gun and of the new 6-pdr anti-tank gun.

All through the battle the British supply arrangements had worked well in spite of many difficulties and the occasional capture of vehicles by a roving enemy. Only one field maintenance centre was actually overrun, but the course of the battle made it necessary to maintain most of the troops from the base at Belhamed, which placed a severe strain on the transport units. Yet there were no real shortages. Demands for 25-pdr ammunition were particularly heavy (estimated at one time as 20,000 rounds a day for the two armoured divisions alone) and issues were restricted to save transport, without however any apparent ill effect; indeed the restriction curbed wasteful expenditure and the practice of building up private reserves.

Work had been going steadily on to extend the railway towards Tobruk and to complete the lay-out of the railhead at Belhamed, and it was ironical that on the very day set for the opening of this railhead, 12th June, all work had to be stopped because of the tactical situation. Worse still, on 14th June it was decided that all stores must be removed from the Belhamed Forward Base. This task was begun immediately on a pre-arranged plan, and by 16th June almost everything had been cleared except nearly a million rations and a million and a half gallons of petrol. That morning General Ritchie decided that the petrol must be leaked away. By nightfall the men of the Base, half poisoned by fumes and with their boots rotted from their feet, had accomplished this depressing and dangerous task. And so the Belhamed base, which had cost so much to create, ceased to exist.

There remained of course Tobruk, with its great accumulation of stores and supplies, including 3 million rations, 2½ million gallons of petrol and 270,000 rounds of ammunition for guns of various calibres, a visible sign that the British had been determined that their offensive, when it came, should not fail for want of administrative backing. The question was whether this enormous stock would now be an invaluable asset or a hostage to fortune.

The work of the Wellington medium bombers was less closely connected with day-to-day events of the land fighting than that of the day-bombers, and it is convenient to consider their action over a longer period. No. 205 Group, under Air Commodore L. L. Maclean, had been working at high pressure since 26th May and by 13th June had flown 403 sorties—an average of 22 aircraft every night. Its two main tasks had been the mining of Benghazi harbour, which was done on four occasions, and the persistent attack of rearward airfields, especially Tmimi, Martuba, Berka and Derna. It will be realized that from Malta, only now beginning to recover from her terrible ordeal, no help could be given against targets in North Africa. Indeed, on the five nights from 8th June the Wellingtons of No. 205 Group were employed in attacking Italian ports and airfields in preparation for the passage of two important convoys to Malta, one from Gibraltar and one from Alexandria, the fortunes of which are related in Chapter XIII.

9. British 'I' tank Matilda.

10. Valentines near Knightsbridge, June 1942. These tanks served both as cruisers and 'I' tanks.

11. American Stuart light tanks being tried out in the desert, August 1941.

12. The American Grant, mounting a 75-mm gun in a sponson and a 37-mm high velocity gun in the turret.

13. British built cruiser Crusader; like Matilda and Valentine, it mounted a 2-pdr gun in a revolving turret.

14. A British tank transporter, with a Matilda up, on its way to the workshops.

15. German Pzkw III Special, with long 5-cm gun and spaced armour on the gun mantlet and front superstructure; captured after the Battle of Alam el Halfa.

16. Pzkw III Model H with short 5-cm gun and extra plate on the front superstructure; the first of such tanks to be captured being dismantled for examination, May 1941.

17. Captured Pzkw IV, with short 7·5-cm gun, being taken back for examination after the 'Crusader' battle.

18. Pzkw IV Special, with its powerful long 7·5-cm gun. One of the few to be taken intact.

19. German half-tracked armoured infantry carrier.

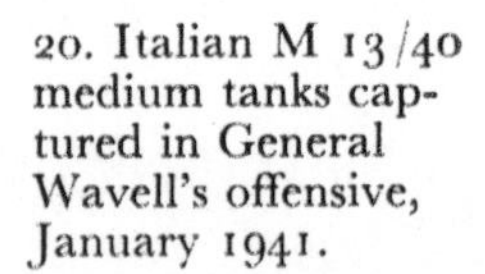

20. Italian M 13/40 medium tanks captured in General Wavell's offensive, January 1941.

21. British 2-pdr anti-tank gun firing portée.

22. A six-gun battery of 25-pdrs in action.

23. British 6-pdr anti-tank gun. (The muzzle is carrying a counter-weight.)

24. A 40-mm Bofors, British light A.A. gun, in position overlooking Bardia harbour, January 1942.

25. The chief tank killer of the time; the German 5-cm *Pak* 38 anti-tank gun, dug in and camouflaged.

26. The German 8·8-cm *Flak* 36, which proved to be a very effective anti-tank gun.

27. British 4·5-inch gun in action near El Alamein.

28. British 3·7-inch heavy A.A. gun dug in; a Service being held round one of the guns in Tobruk, August 1941.

29. A Bishop, the first British self-propelled gun to reach the Middle East, July 1942.

30. Humber armoured car bringing in Italian prisoners, June 1942.

31. Italian 75/18 self-propelled gun. (Spare tracks and sandbags being used to give extra protection.)

32. British Bren or Universal type carriers.

An air operation of a type new to the Middle East took place during this period. It was mentioned in the last chapter that a force of American Liberators, known as the Halverson Detachment, had arrived in Egypt to attack the Ploesti oilfields in Rumania. On the night of 11th/12th June thirteen of these aircraft took off from Fayid on the Suez Canal to make their attack. The plan was for them to depart individually at short intervals and to rendezvous shortly after dawn on the 12th in order to concentrate their bombing. Afterwards they were all to proceed to Habbaniya, in Iraq. In the event they did not join up, and most of the aircraft released their bombs either above the clouds at the estimated time of arrival or else immediately after breaking cloud. In the circumstances it is improbable that any damage was done. On the return flight four aircraft landed in Turkey, two in Syria and seven in Iraq. The American authorities had agreed that the Halverson Detachment should also take part in operations to cover the passage of the Malta convoys already referred to; seven Liberators did so, and their activities are included in the story of the 'Vigorous' convoy.[1]

It will be recalled that early in February the three Commanders-in-Chief had decided not to accept a second siege of Tobruk. General Auchinleck had accordingly laid down that the 8th Army was to make every effort to prevent Tobruk being lost, but was not to continue to hold it once the enemy was in a position to invest it effectively.[2] These words must have rung in General Ritchie's ears as he faced the hard facts of the situation on the evening of 13th June. So easy to say, so hard to do. The previous day he had made the decision to 'stand and fight', and that fight had now been lost. He no longer possessed an armoured force strong enough to protect the long southern flank from Alem Hamza to El Adem, nor could such a force be built up quickly. It was consequently only a matter of time before the enemy would cut the communications of the two divisions in the Gazala line. Therefore these divisions must be withdrawn, but where to? Not to Tobruk, where they could not prevent themselves being invested. The only position they were likely to be able to secure, behind which the armour could be built up and from which the enemy's desert flank could be harried, was the Egyptian frontier. By 7 a.m. on 14th June he had given orders to the 13th Corps to withdraw the 1st South African and 50th Divisions to the frontier, where they would be in Army reserve. At 9.30 he gave a guarded report to the Commander-in-Chief on the telephone and an hour later set forth his views in a long signal which reached Cairo at 1.15 p.m.

---

[1] See page 311.

[2] See page 197.

The question was: what to do about Tobruk? It seemed to General Ritchie that as long as Tobruk remained in British hands the enemy was unlikely to try to advance into Egypt, and the better would be the chances of rebuilding the 8th Army for a fresh offensive. Therefore there would be advantages in holding it for a time, even if it was completely invested. He would hope initially to hold the western half of the perimeter and the localities of El Adem and Belhamed. A mobile force would operate from the south, and help to keep the coastal road open as a supply route. There was a risk that this back door might be closed, but Tobruk had a month's supplies and if the situation could be restored within that time the place might be denied to the enemy and all the installations saved from destruction. The alternatives were therefore:

(a) to accept the risk of a temporary investment,
(b) to give up Tobruk and withdraw the whole Army to the frontier.

General Ritchie added that he could not guarantee the safety of the Gambut airfields after the 14th June, though he hoped the tactical situation would allow of their continued use as advanced landing-grounds. He then asked General Auchinleck the direct question: 'Do you agree to me accepting the risk of investment in Tobruk?'

This message crossed one that General Auchinleck had sent off at 11.30 a.m., at which time he was not fully aware of the state of the 8th Army nor of General Ritchie's precise intentions. He seems to have assumed that Ritchie, in choosing to 'stand and fight', had discarded altogether the idea of withdrawing the Army to the frontier and that, although it had become tactically necessary to disengage the 1st South African and 50th Divisions, they would re-enter the battle in the neighbourhood of, but outside, Tobruk. General Auchinleck's message ran:

'1. If in your opinion situation has so deteriorated that you can no longer leave 1 S.A. and 50 Divisions in main Gazala position without certain risk of their being cut off and isolated, then I agree to their withdrawal undesirable as this is in view of tactical advantage this bastion gives us.

2. While I realize that our armoured forces have been defeated and are now weaker in quantity as well as quality than those of enemy, I must stress my opinion that enemy, who so far has won all his successes with two German armoured and one German motor divisions, helped to some extent by one Italian motor division, cannot really be in a position to carry out large scale offensive operations for indefinite period at pace he has been doing. He must, I feel, have lost heavily, and we know his ammunition is short. Moreover, we are definitely superior to him in the air [sic].

3. This being so, Tobruk must be held and the enemy must not be allowed to invest it. This means that Eighth Army must hold the line Acroma-El Adem and southwards and resist all enemy attempts to pass it. Having reduced your front by evacuating Gazala and reorganized your forces, this should be feasible and I order you to do it.
4. If you feel you cannot accept the responsibility of holding this position you must say so.'

From this it is clear that General Auchinleck believed that the enemy's capabilities were not so great as to make it necessary to abandon Tobruk, and he was not prepared to allow the place to be invested.

General Ritchie did not see this message until he returned at 4 p.m. on 14th June from visiting his Corps Commanders. At 5.30 he telephoned to Cairo and spoke to the Deputy Director of Operations, who had just returned from a visit to the 8th Army, bringing with him the latest information. General Ritchie said that he accepted the task and would do his best, but that he could not guarantee to hold the line from Acroma to El Adem and southwards. If he failed, and was compelled to withdraw to the Egyptian frontier, he wished to accept the investment of Tobruk and again asked for the Commander-in-Chief's approval.

But General Auchinleck saw no reason to change his mind. If the enemy could be kept fighting there was a good chance of exhausting him. At 7.50 he issued another order, which was received at 8th Army just before midnight. In it he referred to the fatigue and losses of the Germans, and to the relative freshness of the troops from the Gazala position and in Tobruk. In order to destroy the enemy General Ritchie was first to deny the line Acroma-El Adem-Bir el Gubi. The message then described the type of offensive/defensive which was to be carried out. It ended with a summing-up:

'. . . 7(a) The general line Acroma-El Adem-El Gubi is to be denied to the enemy.
(b) Our forces will not be invested in Tobruk, and your army is to remain a mobile field army.
(c) The enemy's forces are to be attacked and destroyed as soon as we have collected adequate forces for an offensive.'

General Ritchie had already issued two important instructions, one before and one after receiving the message sent by the Commander-in-Chief at 11.30 a.m. The first gave as his intention 'To withdraw to the frontier and occupy the frontier defences', and laid down that the enemy was to be denied for as long as possible the western perimeter of Tobruk and El Adem. The 10th Indian Division was to protect the Gambut airfields until the Air Officer Commanding no longer required them, and was then to occupy Sollum and the Omars. A destination near the frontier was also given to the 5th Indian Division. The second instruction, timed 8.30 p.m., was addressed to General Norrie, and reflects the Commander-in-Chief's decision about Tobruk.

> 'Greatest danger present time is enemy investing Tobruk. Main contribution which 30 Corps can make is in conjunction with 13 Corps to prevent enemy closing eastern exits Tobruk. Your role therefore is to deny to enemy escarpment Pt 162 4141 to Belhamed [*approximately the line of the by-pass road, east of El Adem*]. To do this, necessary you will prevent enemy operating in area El Adem-Belhamed-Gubi and keep him as far west of this area as possible. I consider that enemy armour must be nearing exhaustion and may give us a few days' respite during which I will do my utmost to strengthen you. You are not restricted in the use of such armour as may be allotted to you. Having regard to your resources a mobile policy will probably best achieve your object and an organization will be set up to enable all available columns with their gun power to be concentrated on a threatened area. Great sacrifices may have to be incurred to achieve this end on which 13th Corps are so dependent.'

General Ritchie was clearly uneasy about the task he had undertaken, and at 11.10 p.m. he sent a further message to General Auchinleck explaining what he was doing to strengthen the 7th Armoured Division by giving it all the available motorized units and armour for employment on the southern flank. As soon as possible the artillery of the 1st South African and 50th Divisions would be reorganized with the same object. The danger was that the enemy would not allow time to do this, and might get astride the eastern exits from Tobruk, in which case a decision would be required whether to accept investment or order the garrison to fight its way out—which it could probably do, but with much disorganization and loss. Ships in Tobruk (diverted, because of damage or lack of speed, from the convoy intended for Malta) would bring the local stocks up to two months' supply.[1] Ritchie strongly recommended that if he failed to prevent the place being surrounded he should accept investment rather than order the garrison to fight its way out in difficult circumstances. He ended: 'If this is a correct interpretation of your ideas I accept responsibility'.

Meanwhile in London the decision to withdraw the two divisions from Gazala had aroused interest, and on 14th June the Prime Minister asked where they were to go. He presumed that there was no question of giving up Tobruk; as long as Tobruk was held no serious advance into Egypt was possible. To this General Auchinleck replied on 15th June giving the gist of his order to General Ritchie timed 7.50 p.m.

---

[1] In fact, only the *City of Calcutta* reached Tobruk; the *Aagtekirk* was sunk in the offing by German air attack. See page 309.

the previous evening. He said that the two divisions from the Gazala line would be available to help in denying to the enemy the general line Acroma-El Adem-Bir el Gubi. He repeated, in slightly shorter form, his summing up, and went on to say that he intended to build up a reserve in the area Sollum-Fort Maddalena with the object of launching a counter-offensive as soon as possible. The New Zealand Division from Syria and the 8th Armoured Brigade from the Delta had been ordered forward to the Western Desert.[1] But the Prime Minister had one more question: did General Auchinleck mean that, if the need arose, enough troops would be left in Tobruk to hold the place for certain? It happened that early on the morning of 16th June Auchinleck had given Ritchie an answer to his persistent question in a new form. Briefly, the garrison was not to be invested, but it might be isolated for short periods. In reply to the Prime Minister General Auchinleck said that his interpretation was correct. General Ritchie was putting into Tobruk what he considered to be an adequate force to hold it even if it should be temporarily isolated. El Adem would be held as a pivot of manœuvre, and all available mobile forces were to be used to prevent the enemy establishing himself east of El Adem or Tobruk.

After this summary of the exchanges that led to the decision to accept the temporary isolation of Tobruk, it is time to resume the story of events in the battle area where it was left on the evening of 13th June.

During the night 13th/14th June the 201st Guards (Motor) Brigade was withdrawn from Knightsbridge. That left intact the defended posts at B 154 and Eluet et Tamar—both manned by troops of the 1st South African Division; Pt 187 by 1st Battalion The Worcestershire Regiment and the 62nd Field Battery R.A. of 29th Indian Infantry Brigade Group; and Acroma and Commonwealth Keep each with a small garrison from the 2nd South African Division. The armour was more or less concentrated south and west of Acroma.

General Rommel intended to reap the benefits of his success of the previous day by cutting the coastal road, and did his utmost to goad on his tired troops. He failed, owing to the extreme fatigue of the *D.A.K.*, the well co-ordinated artillery fire and the determined defence of the garrisons of Eluet et Tamar and Pt 187, and the timely intervention of the 22nd and part of the 2nd Armoured Brigade. After further attacks Pt 187 had to be given up, but a resolute and successful

[1] The 8th Armoured Brigade belonged to the 10th Armoured Division, formerly the 1st Cavalry Division. The conversion of this division to armour had proceeded unavoidably by fits and starts, and it was not yet ready to take the field as a whole, mainly for want of transport.

rearguard action by the British armour and artillery, assisted by an attack by the day-bombers, held off the 15th Panzer Division until dark. Meanwhile the 21st Panzer Division heavily attacked Eluet et Tamar, penetrated part of the defences, and was driven out by artillery fire and a counter-attack by the Cape Town Highlanders.

Early that morning, 14th June, the 1st South African and 50th Divisions received their orders to withdraw from the Gazala line and make for destinations on the Egyptian frontier. A plan already existed for such a move, but now that the enemy was almost in Acroma and El Adem it had to be modified: 1st South African Division was to move by the coast road through Tobruk and the 50th Division was to break out south-west through the Italian 10th Corps and make its way south of Bir Hacheim and across country to the frontier. The 50th Division was to hold its positions until 6 p.m. that evening and the South Africans theirs until first light on 15th June.

General Pienaar protested against being made to withdraw by daylight in the face of a certainly aroused enemy, and it was agreed that he too should hold his positions until 6 p.m. on the 14th and that his rear parties should pass into Tobruk by 7 a.m. on the 15th. The 13th Corps had already ordered that Bir Heleisi (50th Division), B 154 and Eluet et Tamar (1st South African Division), Commonwealth Keep and Pt 187 (2nd South African Division) would be held until 9 p.m. on 14th June, after which the garrisons would be withdrawn by their parent formations. Furthermore 2nd South African Division, supported by 1st Armoured Division, would hold the line of the minefields from El Mrassas to Acroma until further orders, and their columns would operate as far west as the Tobruk by-pass road.

In both divisions all reserves of food, water, fuel, and certain stores were silently destroyed or made useless during the day, and in the 1st South African Division unessential units and vehicles were sent away early. The 1st South African Infantry Brigade, helped by a dust-storm, withdrew during the afternoon, and the 2nd and 3rd Brigades after dark. There then remained the rearguards, made up of detachments from the three brigades, each of a composite company of infantry with a few field, anti-tank and anti-aircraft guns, the whole commanded by Brigadier C. L. de W. du Toit. The withdrawal of the Division went well except for some casualties and damage from air attacks. The Germans near Acroma failed to move early enough to intercept the main bodies. This they could have done, because by first light on the 15th there were no troops facing them on the escarpment west of Acroma. Pt 187 had been given up; the remaining posts had been withdrawn by their parent formations during the night; and 13th Corps, deciding to get the 1st Armoured Division away to reorganize, had ordered it to withdraw at 10 p.m. on the 14th. However, between 8 and 9 a.m. on 15th June a battalion of German infantry and some tanks drove a small protective detachment of the 2nd South African Division from its position at El Mrassas and blocked the main road. On the wrong side of this block were the rearguards of 2nd and 3rd South African Brigades and some units of the 50th Division who had been obliged to take this route also. Brigadier du Toit and his headquarters had already passed by, so that effective command was lacking. At length Lieut.-Colonel J. E. S. Percy, 9th Durham Light Infantry, collected a miscellaneous force and in the afternoon broke through the German screen. The bulk of the South African rearguards did not seize the opportunity to follow, and towards dark they were captured or dispersed by the enemy. During its retreat the 1st South African Division lost 27 killed and 366 wounded or missing, and 13 guns.

General Ramsden, commanding the 50th Division, decided to break out just after dark in two main groups, one under Brigadier L. L. Hassell (69th Infantry Brigade) and the other under Brigadier J. S. Nichols (151st Infantry Brigade). In each group one battalion with supporting arms was detailed to smash a gap in the Italian positions and hold it open while the rest, in their self-contained columns, passed through. The afternoon dust-storm helped by concealing the preparations, and the break-out was made with great vigour. The 5th Battalion East Yorkshire Regiment and the 8th Battalion Durham Light Infantry made the gaps, and the columns, with a few exceptions, ran through the enemy's fire (and even over his positions) before gaining the open desert. The 9th Battalion Durham Light Infantry (of 151st Infantry Brigade) and its attached troops suffered various delays until the chances of getting through the thoroughly roused enemy seemed very slender. Lieut.-Colonel Percy decided instead to make for the coast road. He was joined by various stray detachments and reached Tobruk after the encounter at El Mrassas already described. The bulk of the division began to assemble east of the Egyptian frontier on 16th June.

It happened that on 14th June one of the important convoys for Malta—'Vigorous', already referred to—was passing between Crete and Cyrenaica. This attracted much of the air effort on both sides, Ju. 87s and 88s being sent to attack it and fighters of the Desert Air Force to protect it when it came within their range. To keep down the weight of attack on the convoy a few Bostons and a small force of Wellingtons had bombed airfields at Derna and elsewhere on the night of the 13th. On the following day, however, dust-storms interfered with flying, and the day-bombers were grounded until the evening, when they were urgently required to give air support in the Acroma area. Fighter activity was also seriously restricted. A few Italian aircraft and a small force of Me. 110s attacked troops withdrawing from Gazala along the congested coast road, but, like the

British, the enemy was preoccupied with the convoy, and his dive-bombers were almost wholly employed against it. Thus, for one reason or another, air activity over the Desert on 14th June was much less than usual.

On 15th June General Rommel wrote 'The battle has been won, and the enemy is breaking up.' This was unpleasantly near the truth, for although the 8th Army still occupied Tobruk, and had detachments at El Adem and Belhamed, it had been out-manœuvred and driven from its chosen battlefields and most of it was re-forming eighty miles away. Its force of cruiser tanks had been reduced to one weak brigade of composite regiments, the organization of most of its infantry divisions had been disjointed, and no significant reserves were within reach. The enemy, too, had suffered heavily, but although he had failed to round up the divisions in the Gazala line he had at last prised them loose, had defeated the British armour, and had made great captures of men and material. He was now almost within reach of his objective, which was Tobruk; moreover he was quite clear as to his object, which was to capture it quickly. The British, on the other hand, were by no means clear what they meant to do, and were soon to pay the penalty.

CHAPTER XI

THE BATTLE OF GAZALA (contd.): THE LOSS OF TOBRUK

ON 15th June General Rommel informed *Comando Supremo* that the enemy was probably withdrawing the bulk of his forces beyond the Egyptian frontier. Cavallero at once signalled to Bastico that the tactical success must be exploited and that a stalemate must be avoided, for the Axis forces could not undertake a long siege of Tobruk. Air forces would have to be withdrawn from North Africa at the end of June to assist in the capture of Malta, which was as necessary as ever; indeed Rommel's urgent request for 8,000 men could not be met because Hitler had placed a ban on the movements of German troops by sea until the situation round Malta had been cleared up. General Rommel, for his part, required no prodding. Baulked in his attempt to cut off all the troops retiring from Gazala he lost no time in setting his forces in motion eastwards. The 21st Panzer Division was directed on El Duda, and the 90th Light was ordered (for the third time in a week) to advance on El Adem.

Before describing the outcome of these orders it will be convenient to consider briefly how the 8th Army was trying to cope with the situation. General Ritchie had not yet had the Commander-in-Chief's approval for allowing Tobruk to be isolated (this was not given until 16th June) and could say no more than that Tobruk was to be a bastion upon which mobile operations could be based and that the 13th Corps was to deny it to the enemy. The 30th Corps would be responsible for the operations outside the perimeter, for which purpose General Norrie would have under his command the 7th Armoured Division, the 29th Indian Infantry Brigade at El Adem, and the 20th Indian Infantry Brigade at Belhamed. At the same time he was to complete the occupation of the positions on the frontier and organize a striking force with which to resume the offensive. The immediate problem was to strengthen the 7th Armoured Division, on which would largely depend any chance there might be of preventing the enemy from lapping round the southern flank of the 13th Corps. The only mobile formations available were the battered but resilient 4th Armoured Brigade and the 3rd Indian Motor Brigade. The flow of repaired tanks from the forward workshops was expected to be 15 to 25 a day, and about 9 a day were coming forward from Egypt; at this rate it would be several days before the 2nd and 22nd Armoured Brigades could be re-equipped. In these straits General Ritchie's reflections led him to turn to the idea of 'Jock' columns.

Since the very beginning of the war in the Western Desert these columns had been such a feature of the British mode of warfare that they deserve a word to put them into perspective. There is no doubt that they were a stimulating form of enterprise which at times caused the enemy anxiety and loss. Brigadier 'Jock' Campbell himself knew well their limitations, and in April 1942 General Auchinleck saw fit to lay down a policy for their use. Columns, he wrote, could harass or could carry out a pursuit against weak rearguards, but they could not drive home an attack against other than very weak resistance nor deny ground except for a very short time. He considered that their use tended to disperse resources (especially artillery) and to make the troops so accustomed to tip-and-run tactics that they might begin to regard all-out attack or protracted defence as exceptions rather than the rule. He therefore directed that columns should be sparingly used, and gave as examples of suitable tasks: raids on definite objectives; harassing, covering, and delaying operations ahead of a defensive position on a definite plan; support of armoured cars on reconnaissance; and, in certain circumstances, pursuit.

General Ritchie now felt that the column could help him in his predicament. He considered the enemy's tanks to be superior to his own, and that therefore the offensive weapon must be the field gun. On 16th June he issued instructions for infantry divisions to split into two, with an advanced mobile element of regimental groups (or columns) of all arms and a rear or static element occupying a sector of the frontier defences. A regimental column was to consist of the headquarters of a battalion or field regiment, a field battery, an anti-tank battery, an anti-aircraft troop, and a battalion of infantry (less one company) to provide local protection for the guns. But field guns were none too plentiful at this moment, and the arrival of the 1st South African and 50th Divisions in the frontier area was eagerly awaited. Not until 17th June was it known with any certainty what was their state of completeness. Meanwhile the Commander-in-Chief's attention was firmly fixed on El Adem, and he constantly urged the Army Commander to reinforce it, which was just what General Ritchie could not do.

Two battalions of the 29th Indian Infantry Brigade (Brigadier D. W. Reid) held the locality of El Adem, with the third battalion—the 3rd Royal Battalion 12th Frontier Force Regiment—holding a detached position to the north-west at B 650. On 15th June the 90th Light Division made three attacks on El Adem and was beaten off. During the afternoon an attack by the 21st Panzer Division on B 650 was also beaten off and the 7th Motor Brigade was credited with very effective co-operation. At 7.30 p.m. General Norrie spoke confidently to the Army Commander. He felt that El Adem would hold fast, but he did not then know that the 21st Panzer Division had just driven home an attack which overran and captured B 650 and its garrison. Next morning Norrie spoke very differently. He felt that his mobile troops were too few to guarantee support to the garrisons of El Adem and Belhamed for the next few days, and that without this support they could not be expected to hold out for long. He did not feel that the casualties which a last-ditch resistance would inflict on the enemy would compensate for the loss of these brigades. The Army Commander was not immediately available to give a ruling, but one was promised. A little after mid-day Norrie spoke to Messervy, saying that in his view there would have to be a complete withdrawal to the frontier. Meanwhile the 21st Panzer Division had passed on to El Duda, and the 90th Light had made another attack on El Adem while the two German reconnaissance units and the Ariete Division held off the attempts by 7th Motor Brigade to help. The 29th Indian Infantry Brigade continued to resist stoutly and the 90th Light Division, being in a bad way, was told to discontinue its attacks. At 5.30 p.m. General Ritchie (who had by now received the Commander-in-Chief's authority to allow Tobruk to be temporarily isolated) told General Norrie that the local situation must govern the decision whether or not to give up El Adem, and because he could not tell what the situation was he delegated the decision to General Norrie. A little later Norrie decided to evacuate El Adem the same night. General Messervy had already made arrangements, and the Brigade successfully slipped away during the small hours of 17th June. In the circumstances this withdrawal was unavoidable, yet the effect, as 90th Light Division noted in its diary, was that it removed the southern corner-stone from the advanced defence line of the fortress of Tobruk.

The concentration of enemy movement towards and around El Adem had given the Desert Air Force plenty of targets at a short distance from the Gambut airfields. On the 15th June the Bostons and the fighter-bombers were out in strength, as were the new tank-destroying Hurricanes. This meant heavy escort duties for the fighters, which had also to protect convoy 'Vigorous' as it returned to Alexandria. This convoy, as on the previous evening, was attracting a large part of the enemy's air effort, and the German bombers based in North Africa flew 193 sorties against it in the two days—another example of the interplay of sea, land, and air. Without this diversion the air attacks on the retreating 8th Army on the evening of 14th June and during the 15th could have been much heavier than they were. But in that case the British fighters could have opposed them in strength, and although the 8th Army no doubt gained some respite by the passage of the convoy at this particular moment, it is impossible to say how much.

The approach of the enemy so close to Gambut meant that Air Vice-Marshal Coningham was taking a risk in continuing to use these airfields. But if he withdrew the fighters thirty miles to Sidi Azeiz it would seriously limit the support they could give in the El Adem area. Behind a screen of patrols of No. 2 Armoured Car Company R.A.F. there were four infantry battalions and three and a half anti-aircraft batteries (ready to engage tanks if necessary) allotted to the close defence of the Gambut airfields for as long as he needed them, and Coningham decided to keep Gambut open for the time being and to remain there himself.

The next day, 16th June, was a particularly busy one for the Desert Air Force. In the El Adem-Sidi Rezegh area the Bostons made seven attacks and the fighter-bombers twenty. The 21st Panzer Division reported that it had been attacked for the first time by fighter-bombers firing a 2-cm. cannon which caused considerable losses in men and material.[1] In the afternoon enemy fighters became increasingly active. They intercepted some of the Boston formations and followed them back to their landing-grounds at Baheira. However, only once did the Me. 109s break through the escorting Kittyhawks, and no damage was done. It was undoubtedly a successful day for air support; co-operation between the 8th Army and the Desert Air Force worked well and the 21st Panzer Division had cause to report 'Continual attacks at quarter hour intervals by bombers and low flying aircraft', and to request urgent fighter protection.

On 17th June news of the withdrawal from El Adem seems to have travelled slowly, and did not reach the Desert Air Force until 3 p.m.—twelve hours after the event. The result was that for much of the day the Gambut airfields were in danger of attack from any columns of the enemy who might have by-passed the two remaining defended localities at Sidi Rezegh and Belhamed. As the British aircraft shuttled to and fro, the rearming and refuelling parties could hear the burst of their own bombs falling among the enemy's foremost troops. The attacks were concentrated on the area between Sidi Rezegh and Belhamed because requests for air support were coming from the 20th Indian Infantry Brigade but none from the 29th.

The 20th Indian Infantry Brigade was a new formation which had not trained as a brigade. It had arrived in the Desert from Iraq in the first week of June and by the 10th was holding a main position at Belhamed, with a detached battalion at Sidi Rezegh.[2] Late on 16th

[1] The Hurricane IID was not in fact a fighter-bomber, and its cannons were of 40-mm. calibre.

[2] 20th Indian Infantry Brigade (Brigadier L. E. Macgregor): 97th (Kent Yeomanry) Field Regiment R.A.; 1st Battalion, The South Wales Borderers; 1/6th Rajputana Rifles, 3/18th Royal Garhwal Rifles.

June the 21st Panzer Division bit into Sidi Rezegh, reported stubborn resistance, and did not press on. General Norrie, however, was weighing (as he had done at El Adem) the possible loss of the Brigade against the damage it might do to the enemy. At 10.30 a.m. on 17th June he decided that the Brigade was to hold on as long as possible but would withdraw if in imminent danger of being overrun.

We must now turn to the 4th Armoured Brigade. This Brigade had been hastily reconstituted and by 16th June consisted of the composite regiments 1st/6th and 3rd/5th R.T.R.; 9th Lancers, two squadrons strong; and a composite squadron from the 3rd and 4th County of London Yeomanry. It had under command the 1st R.H.A. and the 1st K.R.R.C. The brigade had about 90 tanks, but was undoubtedly a scratch affair as regards organization and equipment. On 16th June it had a brush with the enemy near Sidi Rezegh and leaguered about ten miles south-east of that place. On the morning of 17th June the tanks were busy with maintenance, and two columns, each consisting of a horse artillery battery and an infantry company, set out—one to Sidi Rezegh and one to Pt 178—to help the 20th Indian Infantry Brigade. Early in the afternoon General Messervy ordered the whole Brigade to an area south of the Trigh Capuzzo between Belhamed and El Adem, with a view to striking at the enemy's flank. Brigadier Richards doubted whether the area was suitable tactically, but before the brigade moved enemy columns appeared travelling rapidly eastward across it. These were in fact the 15th and 21st Panzer Divisions which Rommel had ordered to drive south-east and after a time to turn north to Gambut and cut the coast road. The British regiment closest to the enemy, the 9th Lancers near Hareifet en Nbeidat, faced north and engaged, and the 3rd/5th R.T.R. soon came into action south-west of them. A slogging-match followed in which the British were handicapped since their artillery fire-power had been dispersed, most of the guns being with the harassing columns. After a couple of hours' fighting it appeared that the enemy was pressing hardest against the 3rd/5th R.T.R. The 1st/6th R.T.R. was ordered across to help, but because of misunderstandings a part only of the regiment got into action. The enemy kept up his attacks with the sun behind, and at about 7 p.m. Brigadier Richards began to withdraw south-eastwards. The enemy followed up until nearly nightfall and in particular severely pressed the 9th Lancers. After dark Richards decided to withdraw to a Field Maintenance Centre south of the Trigh el Abd where he would replenish and be in a position to strike at any enemy advancing eastward next day. But the Germans, who had broken off the action on Rommel's orders, turned north, and a little after midnight the 21st Panzer Division reported that it had cut the coast road near Gambut. The 4th Armoured Brigade, with 58 fit tanks, spent

18th and 19th June in reorganization and maintenance, and was then ordered back to the Egyptian frontier.

By the time on 17th June that the 4th Armoured Brigade's battle was ending General Norrie had concluded that Belhamed was nearly cut off. He therefore ordered the 20th Indian Infantry Brigade to withdraw to Sollum during the night 17th/18th. This withdrawal was only partially successful, for in the small hours the 1st South Wales Borderers and 3/18th Royal Garhwal Rifles ran into the German road blocks; in their uncombined attempts to run the gauntlet at dawn they were scattered and captured almost to a man. Brigade Headquarters, 1/6th Rajputana Rifles, and 97th Field Regiment, which had taken other routes, escaped.

On 17th June, as soon as Air Vice-Marshal Coningham learned for certain that the El Adem locality was in enemy hands, he ordered the Gambut airfields to be evacuated. As the enemy air forces were too busy protecting their own troops to bother about the British airfields, the fighters flew safely away to Sidi Azeiz and the airfield defence troops withdrew. Most of the day-bombers moved back from Baheira to near Mersa Matruh; the rest withdrew the following day. The tactical reconnaissance aircraft of No. 40 Squadron S.A.A.F. were already within the Tobruk perimeter. That the Desert Air Force had been able to stay in action well forward until the last possible moment is proof of its good organization. From 15th to 17th June it had been operating with skeleton maintenance crews, and ready to move at one hour's notice. Yet the fighters had averaged 450 sorties, which means at least three flown by every available aircraft each day. The light bombers averaged 50 a day and dropped over 100 tons of bombs. Five German and three Italian aircraft had been shot down, while the British, not unexpectedly, lost sixteen.

Early on 18th June General Rommel reported to *OKH* that Tobruk was now invested and that an area extending to a distance of forty miles east and south-east of it had been cleared of the enemy. The *D.A.K.* lay to the east of the perimeter, the Ariete Division to the south-east, the 10th Corps to the south, and the 21st Corps and a few German infantry to the west. Thus the rear of the intended operation against Tobruk was now safe from interference, and the British had lost the use of the Gambut airfields. Axis units had reported the discovery of large stocks of all kinds, principally in the Belhamed area and to the east of Gambut.

As late as 10 p.m. on 17th June General Auchinleck, as yet unaware of the evacuation of Belhamed and the defeat of the 4th Armoured Brigade, issued an order to General Ritchie to hold Tobruk and keep the enemy west of the general line Tobruk-El Adem-Bir el Gubi, to hold the frontier, and to counter-attack when a suitable opportunity could be made. Ritchie had seen the Commanders of the 1st South African and 50th Divisions on 17th June, and estimated that nine 8-gun columns would be ready between 18th and 21st June. But by early morning on 18th June he realized that he was trying to do too much at once and signalled to the Commander-in-Chief that he was feeling the difficulty of acting aggressively against the enemy's southern flank near Tobruk and at the same time implementing the plans for defending the frontier.

General Auchinleck flew up at once to discuss the matter. The outcome was that Tobruk was to come directly under Army Headquarters while the 13th Corps would be responsible for defending the frontier and for operating westward of it—in other words, for helping Tobruk from outside. The 30th Corps was to pass into general reserve in the Matruh area, where it would form and train a striking force with which, in due course, to resume the offensive. The 13th Corps, given time, would have available for its mobile operations the 7th Armoured Division (4th Armoured Brigade, 7th Motor Brigade and 3rd Indian Motor Brigade), in all sixty-six tanks and six 'columns', and one brigade each from the 1st South African and 50th Divisions, each contributing three 'columns'. The rest of these two Divisions and the 10th Indian Division would occupy defensive positions on the frontier. Plans were made for two eventualities: one in which the enemy's main thrust was directed towards the frontier, and the other in which it was made against Tobruk. The second was thought to be the more likely, but in the event the speed with which the assault on Tobruk was mounted precluded any effective help being given by the 8th Army from outside.

At this time the support which the Desert Air Force could give was rapidly dwindling. Not only had it lost the use of the Gambut airfields, but the Army could give no security at Sidi Azeiz against fast-moving enemy forces, and the *D.A.K.* was known to be already well to the east of Tobruk. It was therefore necessary for Air Vice-Marshal Coningham to take the next step in his plans for withdrawal, namely to move the fighters back to airfields near Sidi Barrani. This meant that the whole fighter force, with the exception of No. 250 Squadron, whose Kittyhawks were equipped with long-range tanks, would now be out of range of Tobruk, but there was no alternative. The last aircraft took off from Sidi Azeiz on 19th June, and German reconnaissance troops were there next morning. The enemy's air forces were unusually quiet on the 18th and 19th June, being no doubt fully occupied in preparing to make a very special effort on the 20th.

Before turning to the attack on Tobruk it will be of interest to consider the gist of a very full appreciation sent by the Commanders-in-Chief to the Chiefs of Staff on 20th June, based on the situation as seen on the 19th. The Commanders-in-Chief had been informed nine days earlier that, provided Australia were not threatened with serious invasion within the next few days, they could assume that the 8th Armoured Division would reach Suez from the United Kingdom at the end of June and the 44th Division by mid-July. Further considerable reinforcements were known to be on the way.[1] In their appreciation the Commanders-in-Chief reiterated that their intention was to attack and destroy the enemy's forces at the earliest possible moment, and stated the tasks that had been given to General Ritchie. They went thoroughly into their probable strength in aircraft, guns, and tanks, making the comment that experience had now shown that 'as regards German tanks we require superiority of three to one in 2-pdr tanks and parity in Grants'. In spite of the recent set-backs morale was high. Tobruk was already being attacked, and could be given but little air support. However, the garrison approximated to the force thought necessary to meet the expected scale of attack, and there were about 90 days' supplies and ammunition. The water situation was reasonably satisfactory. 'We hope therefore that Tobruk should be able to hold out until operations for relief are successfully completed after resumption of our offensive.' They thought that, unless the enemy changed his whole policy for the reinforcement of North Africa, he must assume that the British strength in the Western Desert would increase out of proportion to his own. Moreover the present supply position of the Axis would not allow of further intensive and lengthy operations. 'There is no natural position east of Halfaya which enemy could hold successfully against superior forces. Therefore, should both Tobruk and frontier positions fall, enemy would be unlikely to attempt advance deep into Egypt unless our forces be decisively routed in the field or he has received considerable reinforcements.' This opinion is of particular interest in view of the enemy's reactions to his own success related in the next chapter.

See Map 29

The fortified perimeter which bounded the defensive area of Tobruk followed practically the same trace in June 1942 as it had when the 6th Australian Division captured the place from the Italians in January 1941, and throughout the long siege from April to December of that year. The original Italian defences consisted of a double ring of concrete works stretching in a rough semicircle eight or nine miles

[1] Several workshop units, together with over 7,600 R.A.F. and 1,000 Naval drafts, had just arrived at Suez. The convoy bringing the 8th Armoured Division contained also over 3,000 R.A.F. drafts. A further convoy, containing 7,500 Army, 1,000 R.A.F. and 900 Naval drafts, was due on 22nd June, and another of 8,000 Army, 1,300 R.A.F. and 800 Naval drafts on 18th July. The convoy bringing the 44th Division contained also eleven anti-aircraft regiments and various other units, and 3,000 Army and 2,800 R.A.F. drafts.

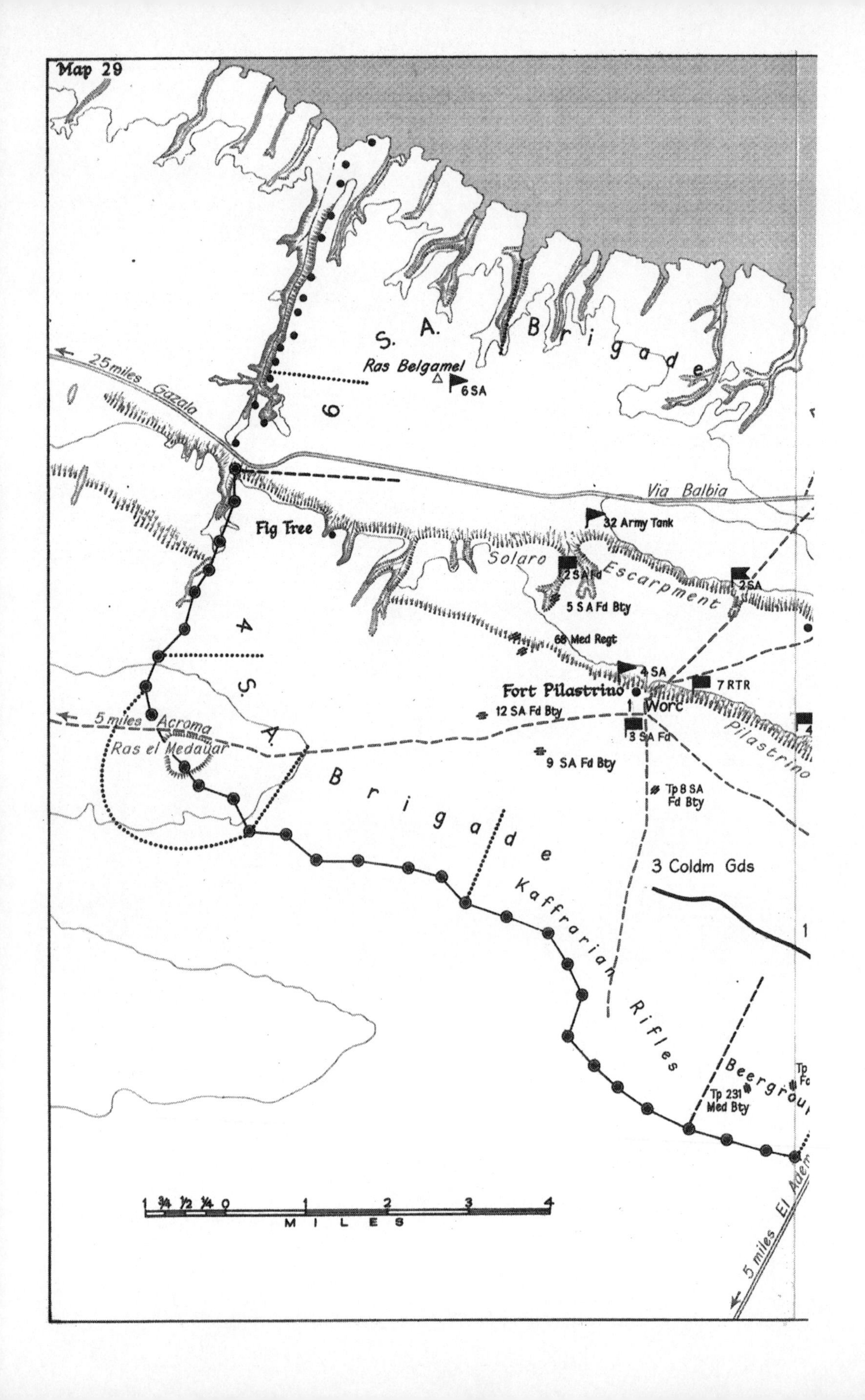
Map 29
S. A. Brigade
6
Ras Belgamel
6 SA
25 miles Gazala
Via Balbia
Fig Tree
32 Army Tank
Solaro Escarpment
2 SA Fd
2 SA
5 S A Fd Bty
68 Med Regt
4
S.
A.
4 SA
Fort Pilastrino
7 RTR
1 Worc
12 SA Fd Bty
5 miles Acroma
Ras el Medauar
3 SA Fd
Pilastrino
9 SA Fd Bty
Brigade
Tp 8 SA Fd Bty
3 Coldm Gds
Kaffrarian Rifles
Beergroun
Tp 231 Med Bty
5 miles El Adem
1 3/4 1/2 1/4 0 1 2 3 4
MILES

TOBRUK, 20th JUNE 1942
Showing main dispositions in the area of the attack

Div HQ   Bde HQ   Regt HQ

Approximate line of inner (Blue Line) minefield. Perimeter minefield is not shown.

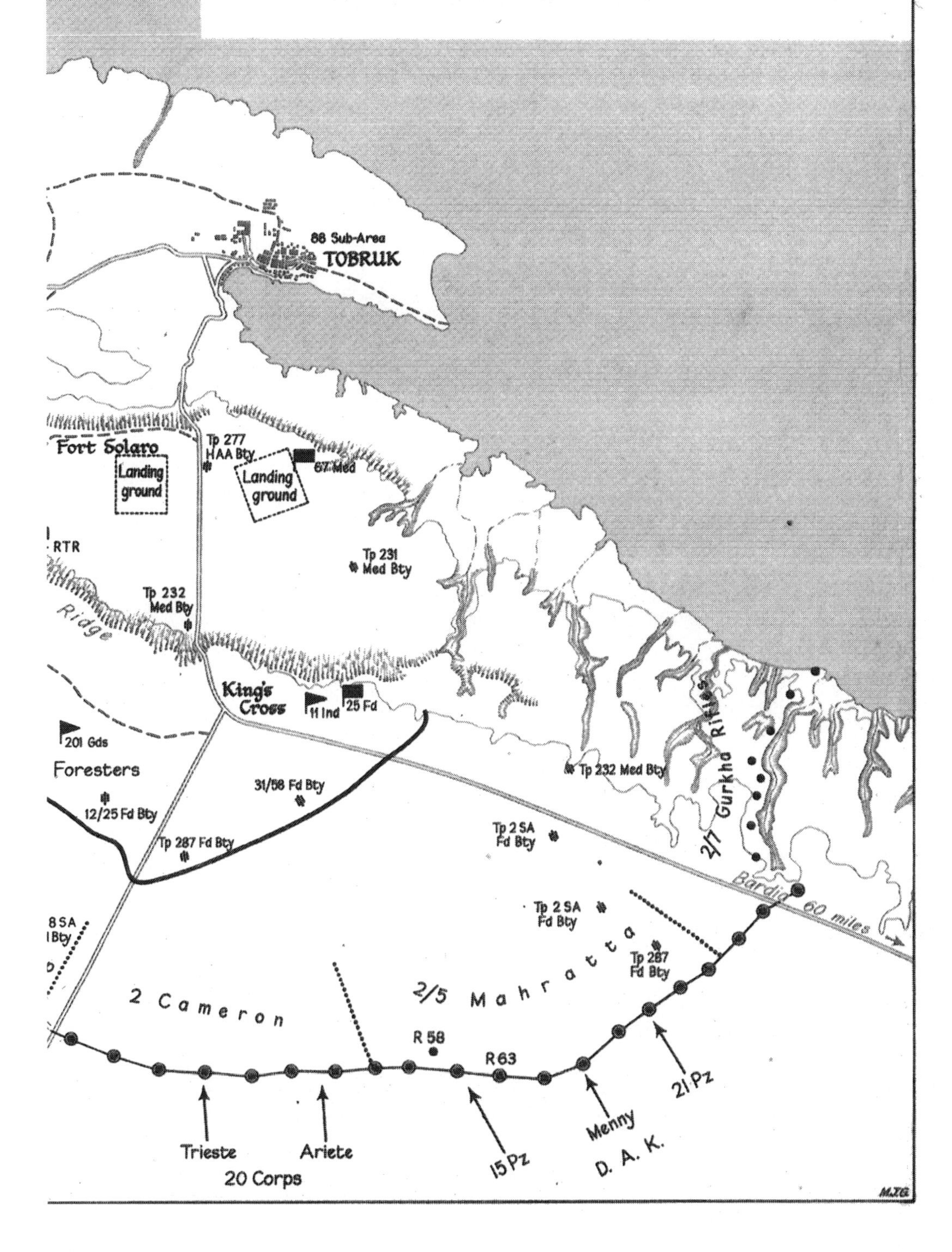

from the town, giving a length of some thirty miles of front. They had been protected by barbed wire obstacles and an anti-tank ditch, but when first captured from the Italians the works had been criticized on the ground that they were refuges rather than fire positions. Within the outer ring, and about two miles from it, the Australians had constructed a second system of defence in 1941, known as the Blue Line. Both the outer perimeter and the Blue Line had been thickly mined, and between them numerous tactical minefields had been laid. The ground was generally open and sloped down from the perimeter to the town and harbour in a number of steps, of which the most prominent are the Pilastrino ridge (so-called, but in reality an escarpment, not a ridge) and the Solaro escarpment.

The 2nd South African Division inherited these defences when it arrived in Tobruk at the end of March 1942, and there is considerable conflict of evidence as to their condition both then and in June. In February 1942 the Commanders-in-Chief had decided, and it was commonly known, that Tobruk was not again to stand a siege, and with the Gazala position ranking as more important it is probable that nobody was interested in keeping the defences of Tobruk in first-rate condition. The anti-tank ditch, for instance, had not been kept in repair and in places had caved in or silted up, and large amounts of barbed wire had been lifted for use elsewhere. Moreover, the garrison had made a sortie towards El Duda during 'Crusader', for which gaps were prepared in the obstacles. Elsewhere, too, large numbers of mines seemed to have been lifted, though whether they were mostly old Italian mines or newer British mines is uncertain. Indeed by June 1942 little accurate information about the minefields or the buried telephone lines seems to have been available. Something of the state of affairs was realized by the 2nd South African Division which had been spasmodically cleaning out the existing works, making alternative gun positions, and inspecting minefields by sample checks.

The 2nd South African Division, of only two brigades, which now formed the main contingent of the garrison, had neither the experience nor the training of the 1st. It was not entirely untried, however, having captured Bardia and Sollum in January. On 14th May Brigadier H. B. Klopper had taken over command from Major-General I. P. de Villiers, who had left for an appointment in South Africa. The new commander had held important staff and training positions but had little operational experience other than at Bardia, when he had been G.S.O.1. of the Division. The divisional staff had several newcomers in May 1942 and as a team was inexperienced.

Besides the 2nd South African Division there were three formations in Tobruk—the 32nd Army Tank Brigade (Brigadier A. C. Willison), the 201st Guards Brigade (Brigadier G. F. Johnson), and the 11th Indian Infantry Brigade (Brigadier A. Anderson). The 32nd Army

Tank Brigade now consisted of the 4th R.T.R. of three squadrons with 35 fit Valentines between them, and the 7th R.T.R. (with some reinforcements from the 8th and 42nd R.T.R.) of two squadrons with 26 fit Valentines and Matildas. The battalions of the 201st Guards Brigade were the 3rd Coldstream Guards, and the 1st Sherwood Foresters and 1st Worcestershire Regiment who had just been assigned to the Brigade. The Brigade commander was a newcomer to the Middle East who had only taken over on 17th June. The Coldstream Guards were up to strength, were fairly complete in equipment, and had ten 6-pdr anti-tank guns. The Sherwood Foresters were nearly up to strength and had most of their equipment, together with four 6-pdrs, which were new to them. The Worcestershires were still recovering from the sharp action at Pt 187 on 14th June; they were about 500 strong and had little besides their personal weapons. The 11th Indian Infantry Brigade consisted of a weak anti-tank company; the experienced 2nd Cameron Highlanders; the 2/5th Mahratta Light Infantry, which contained a high proportion of young reinforcements; and the 2/7th Gurkha Rifles, who had seen little fighting as yet. Under Brigadier Anderson's command there was also a composite battalion from the 1st South African Division named "Beergroup' after its commanding officer, Lieut.-Colonel J. M. de Beer.

The field artillery in Tobruk consisted of the 2nd and 3rd South African Field Regiments and the 25th Field Regiment R.A.[1] There were two medium Regiments R.A., the 67th and 68th, each with eight 4·5-inch guns and eight 155-mm. howitzers. Besides the infantry's anti-tank guns already mentioned there were the 6th South African Anti-Tank Battery and 'A' Battery 95th Anti-Tank Regiment R.A., both very weak. In all the garrison possessed fifteen 6-pdrs, thirty-two 2-pdrs, and eight anti-tank Bofors—not a very large provision. Anti-aircraft guns were also few: eighteen 3·7-inch guns of the 4th A.A. Brigade R.A. and the light guns of the 2nd South African L.A.A. Regiment. Eighteen 3·7-inch guns had been removed on 8th Army's orders on 16th June, and sent back to the frontier positions.[2]

Many units whose primary role was not fighting had been withdrawn from Tobruk, but there remained a number of administrative establishments, under control of Headquarters 88th Sub-Area (Brigadier L. F. Thompson). Apart from vehicles with units there were ten transport companies—British, South African, and Indian. All unwanted ships, mainly storeships and lighters, were sailed for Alexandria on 16th and 17th June. There remained a Naval Establishment under the Senior Naval Officer, Inshore Squadron, Captain P. N. Walter, R.N., with a Naval Officer in charge, Captain F. M. Smith,

[1] The 25th Field Regiment R.A. had, in addition to its own 12/25th and 31/58th Field Batteries, the 287th Field Battery R.A. and the 2nd South African Field Battery.

[2] See p. 28n.

R.N.R. No. 40 Squadron S.A.A.F. having been withdrawn, there were now no aircraft in Tobruk. An Air Support Tentacle, however, was left with General Klopper's Headquarters. As regards supplies, Tobruk was well provided, there being some 3 million rations, 7,000 tons of water, and 1½ million gallons of petrol. Stocks of field artillery ammunition stood at over 130,000 rounds, medium at about 18,000, two-pounder at 115,000, and six-pounder at 23,000.

On 15th June General Klopper took command of all troops within the perimeter, and at a conference held that day he told his subordinates that Tobruk would be held as part of the 8th Army's plan (which he outlined to them) and must be prepared to resist for three months. No tactical questions were discussed, probably because Klopper had not received his detailed orders from the 13th Corps. Brigadier Willison, however, who had been through the siege in 1941, when he had been the commander of the reserve, made privately to General Klopper some suggestions for changing the organization and dispositions based on his previous experience. This was taken in good part, but produced no change. A further proposal by Brigadier Johnson, whose brigade, together with the 32nd Army Tank Brigade, would be in reserve, that he and Brigadier Willison should set up a combined battle headquarters was apparently agreed to in principle, but seems to have been deferred as being premature until the direction of the enemy's attack was apparent.

On 16th June General Gott's headquarters were still in Tobruk, and at a meeting with the Army Commander he suggested that he should remain to take command. General Ritchie did not agree, and that afternoon Gott departed, leaving three of his staff to assist General Klopper in administrative matters. His final instructions to Klopper were to make three more sets of plans: for co-operating at once with the harassing forces outside Tobruk in keeping open its lines of communication, for re-establishing the Belhamed locality in conjunction with the 30th Corps, and for the withdrawal of the Tobruk garrison eastwards, covered on the south by the 30th Corps. This was a considerable addition to the already heavy burden on Klopper and his staff.

General Klopper held his next conference on 18th June but, beyond declaring that Tobruk was now besieged and would be held, he announced no new plans or dispositions. Brigadier Willison again offered some suggestions, his main point being that the chance of a landing by sea was very slight compared with an attack against the perimeter, and that the number of troops locked up in guarding the coast was excessive. Again he received a courteous hearing, but General Klopper seems to have been satisfied and quietly confident. He had written in this spirit to General Theron in Cairo on 16th June, and on the 18th signalled to General Ritchie that the position was very satisfactory, and that his harassing of the enemy was being effective.

The dispositions of the garrison at dawn on 20th June were as shown on Map 29, with the 6th South African Infantry Brigade in the north and north-west, and the 4th South African Infantry Brigade in the centre holding as far east as a point about one mile west of the El Adem road. From there to the sea was held by the 11th Indian Infantry Brigade, whose units from west to east were 'Beergroup', the 2nd Cameron Highlanders, the 2/5th Mahratta Light Infantry, and the 2/7th Gurkha Rifles. In garrison reserve the 201st Guards Brigade was disposed above, and the regiments of the 32nd Army Tank Brigade below, the Pilastrino ridge.

The 2nd and 3rd South African Field Artillery Regiments were supporting the two South African Infantry Brigades, and the 25th Field Regiment R.A. was supporting the 11th Indian Infantry Brigade. The 68th and 67th Medium Regiments R.A. were allotted to the western and eastern halves of the whole front. It was General Klopper's intention that the artillery should fight as a whole under his C.R.A., Colonel H. McA. Richards, but no orders to carry out this intention can be traced. Plans for counter-attacks—doubly important when the perimeter is long for the number of defending troops—remained nebulous as far as Divisional Headquarters were concerned, although Brigadier Johnson had on 16th June made some tentative arrangements with the commanding officers of the 25th Field Regiment R.A. and the 2nd South African Field Regiment. General Klopper's own Headquarters was divided into two separate portions and was centrally situated in the so-called Pilastrino caves, where the road from Pilastrino to the harbour crosses the Solaro escarpment.

The enemy had made several attempts to capture Tobruk's last outpost at Acroma, whose small garrison from the 2nd Transvaal Scottish and Die Middellandse Regiment resisted stoutly until withdrawn on 18th June. South African armoured cars and small mobile columns kept an eye on the enemy and reported him to be thickening up on the south-east, south, and west. From which of these directions would the attack come? It was General Auchinleck, distant in Cairo, who most clearly read the signs. At 6.30 a.m. on 20th June he signalled to General Ritchie: 'Enemy's movements yesterday show intention launch early attack Tobruk from east . . .' And an hour later, 'Am perturbed by apparently deliberate nature your preparations though I realize difficulties. Crisis may arise in matter of hours not days and you must therefore put in everything you can raise . . .' Before the first of these messages was sent the attack on Tobruk had already begun.

A word of explanation is called for about the sources from which the rest of this chapter is drawn. In the fighting at Tobruk on 20th and 21st June the British garrison was defeated and only a few escaped capture. Almost all the relevant contemporary documents are missing. The story has therefore had to be built up from the personal accounts of individuals after their return from captivity, and of those who avoided capture. Between their various versions there are many points of difference. The German records have been useful, but it is difficult to reconcile their timings with those given by British eye-witnesses from memory. The net result is that the sequence of events is probably fairly correct, though the actual timings are open to doubt. In some of the detailed fighting it is impossible to be sure what occurred.[1]

General Rommel had lost no time in deciding upon his front of attack, which was the same as he had chosen for the intended assault in the previous November—namely, the south-east. The positions of his German troops in the area El Adem-Belhamed-Gambut were well suited to this, and the plan was for the *D.A.K.* to attack the sector which happened to be held by the 2/5th Mahratta Light Infantry, with the 21st Panzer Division on the right, the 'Menny' group of the infantry of the 90th Light Division in the centre, and the 15th Panzer Division on the left. The 20th Italian Corps was to attack still farther to the left, which brought it opposite the front held by the Cameron Highlanders. Behind the *D.A.K.* would follow one division of the 10th Corps to occupy the captured posts, and its second division would be around El Adem. Farther south would be the newly arrived Littorio Division, while in the direction of Bardia and Sidi Azeiz the 90th Light Division, less the Menny group, together with the 3rd and 33rd Reconnaissance Units, would hold the attention of the British on the frontier.[2]

As regards timing, General Rommel decided that it would be better to take advantage of the disorganization that had followed the British defeat than to spend much time in making elaborate preparations. He had obtained the willing consent of Field-Marshal Kesselring to use the *Luftwaffe* at its greatest possible strength to deliver a highly concentrated attack on the front to be assaulted. Kesselring was, as

---

[1] The authors have been greatly helped by the South African official historians, whose lucid analysis of the fall of Tobruk appears in J. A. I. Agar-Hamilton and L. C. F. Turner: *Crisis in the Desert, May to July* 1942 (Oxford University Press, London and Cape Town, 1952) a volume in the series of Union War Histories.

[2] After the disaster to the 10th Italian Army in the winter of 1940/41, the Littorio Division was supposed to reorganize and refit, but was in fact drawn upon to make up the Ariete and Trieste to their new 'Africa' type establishments. In January 1942 it parted with some guns to the Ariete and later some guns and tanks to the Trieste. In addition, its transport was taken to form a central pool. Thus the Littorio Division which moved up to the Tobruk area was short of many of its units and had no engineers or supply services. It was only because Rommel insisted that its presence was essential that the Italians reluctantly sent it forward in this incomplete state.

we know, anxious to have done with Tobruk and turn again to Malta, and the clearly defined target no doubt made the idea an attractive one from his point of view, particularly as the distance from the nearest British airfields made it unlikely that there would be any appreciable opposition in the air.

General Rommel issued his orders for the attack on 18th June. Reconnaissances were to be made on the 19th; otherwise no movements towards the assembly positions were to begin before the late afternoon. This drew something of a protest from the *D.A.K.*, but a personal visit by Rommel quickly made it clear that the original order held good. An entry in the *D.A.K's* diary that evening gives a hint as to their doubts. It reads: 'The fact that the divisions will move during darkness into an assembly area with which they are unfamiliar will probably not work out badly.' Nor did it; the reconnaissances had no doubt been very thorough, and the handicap to the artillery in moving into their positions so late was to a large extent offset by the use of aircraft to open the bombardment of the perimeter defences.

In the event every bomber unit in North Africa was drawn upon, and some aircraft were even transferred there from Greece and Crete. The total force of serviceable aircraft actually used against Tobruk on 20th June consisted of some 80 to 85 bombers, 21 dive-bombers (Stukas) and 40 to 50 fighter-bombers, the majority German—a grand total of some 150 bombers of various types. In addition there were about 50 German and over 100 Italian fighters available as escorts. The nearness of the landing-grounds at Gazala and El Adem made possible the 'shuttling to and fro' remarked by eye-witnesses, and in this way the German aircraft flew no less than 580 bomber sorties in the day (30 of which were from Crete), and the Italians 177. The German share of the total bomber load was well over 300 tons and that of the Italians probably about 65 tons. Two Stukas were lost in a collision, one Me. 110 crash-landed, but the Italians suffered no losses.

A brief summary of the day's progress from the point of view of the attackers will serve as a background to the somewhat confused story of the defence. By 4 a.m. the troops were in position, well back from the perimeter. At about 5.20 the bombers began to pound the sector between the Tobruk-Bardia and Tobruk-El Adem roads. The Menny group then worked forward and shortly before 7 a.m. was ready to assault. The engineers made crossings over the anti-tank ditch and by 7.45 the tanks were ordered to advance. By now several of the foremost posts had been captured and the infantry were reported as making good progress. The first tanks of the 15th Panzer Division crossed the ditch at 8.30 and those of the 21st Panzer Division not long afterwards, having been delayed in traversing the minefield. The Ariete also crossed the ditch, but met strong opposition and failed to get through the wire. Part of 20th Corps was therefore ordered to follow 15th Panzer Division, which had driven back some British tanks 'in a stubborn fight' and was steadily advancing towards the road junction (King's Cross). By 1 p.m. the 21st Panzer Division had caught up and half an hour later Rommel announced that the dominating heights four to five miles from the harbour (i.e. King's Cross) had been captured. Shortly after 2 p.m. the harbour came under artillery fire. The 21st Panzer Division's advance was then directed on Tobruk, while the 15th was to protect its left flank by operating towards Fort Solaro. (It actually moved west above the Pilastrino ridge.) At 5 p.m. the 21st Panzer Division asked that fire on the town and harbour should cease, and at 5.15 reported that it was advancing from the airfield towards Tobruk. At 7 p.m. it reported that the town had been captured. At 8 p.m. General Rommel ordered the occupied areas to be mopped up, embarkations to be prevented, and the attack to be continued at first light next day.

The extremely heavy air and artillery bombardment, which was heaviest in the neighbourhood of Post R 63, effectively neutralized the defenders, and by about 7.45 a.m. a breach had been made between Posts R 58 and R 63 and the 2/5th Mahrattas had committed their reserve to an unavailing local counter-attack. At about 7 a.m. Brigadier Anderson had ordered the carrier platoon of 2/7th Gurkhas over to the threatened point, and had reported to General Klopper that his front had been penetrated but counter-measures had been taken and things were in hand. Klopper's reply gave Anderson to understand that a battalion of tanks and some infantry were being sent up to counter-attack.

Soon afterwards, Headquarters 11th Indian Infantry Brigade realized that events were taking an ugly turn and reported accordingly to the Division. At 9.30 Brigadier Anderson telephoned in person, for there was as yet no signs of the counter-attacking force which he was expecting to meet and steer into action to seal off the German penetration. By 10 a.m. resistance by the Mahrattas had ceased.

General Klopper's intention had been that the counter-attack force should be under command of 32nd Army Tank Brigade, who would make whatever arrangements were necessary with the Guards Brigade and 11th Indian Infantry Brigade. The orders issued do not seem to have been understood in this sense; at any rate Brigadier Johnson and Brigadier Willison never met, although the former, listening to the noise of battle, had already suggested opening a joint battle headquarters near King's Cross. Willison called Lieut.-Colonel W. R. Reeves of the 4th R.T.R. to his own headquarters and ordered him to counter-attack in the south-east sector. Reeves returned to his battalion and got his tanks on the move, but valuable time had been lost in the journey to and from Brigade Headquarters. Meanwhile, two companies of the Coldstream Guards and a platoon of anti-tank guns had been ordered to move to a point near King's Cross and to stand by for counter-attack. At about 9.30 the officer commanding this detachment met Colonel Reeves, whose tanks were just going into action and who had certainly not grasped that any infantry were to co-operate with him. The detachment commander reasonably decided that as there was no plan his small force could do nothing but await events.

Colonel Reeves took his battalion forward to hull-down positions covering known gaps in the Blue Line minefields. The German tanks appeared to be moving north and fanning out east and west, but their movements were slow and the fire of the tanks and of the 25th Field Regiment seemed to be holding them in check. Meanwhile Brigadier Willison had ordered the 7th R.T.R. to concentrate west of King's Cross, and Lieut.-Colonel Foote, moving ahead of his battalion, met Lieut.-Colonel Reeves. They agreed that the situation was serious but not desperate, and that there was a prospect of stopping the enemy on the Blue Line. Colonel Foote decided to bring his battalion up on the right (i.e. south) of the 4th, but first sought out Brigadier Anderson, to whom he imparted his opinion and decision. Anderson agreed, but asked that one squadron—the battalion had only two—should be sent south to support the Cameron Highlanders.

At Divisional Headquarters all seemed well enough. General Klopper had been expecting the assault to open with a feint and seems to have thought at first that a feint was in fact being made. (This is surprising in view of the concentration of aircraft and the tremendous din.) When it was clear that this was the real thing, it seemed at divisional headquarters that a counter-attack had been ordered in good time and the absence of news of its progress was taken to mean that nothing untoward was happening. Then came a reassuring report from Brigadier Anderson based on his conversation with Colonel Foote. Two troops of the 5th South African Field Battery and the 9th South African Field Battery were successively ordered to the King's Cross area, but nothing else was done. The Air Support Tentacle had reported to Advanced Air Headquarters what was known of the situation, and as a result nine Bostons escorted by long-range Kittyhawks were sent to attack vehicles concentrated near the gap in the perimeter.

Just before noon the German thrust began again in three prongs, all converging on King's Cross: one along the Bardia road, one from the south-east, and one from the south. The events and timings of the mêlée which followed are uncertain, but the result is quite clear. By about 2 p.m. all the artillery on and in front of the Blue Line had been destroyed with the exception of a few detachments. The 4th

R.T.R. had ceased to exist as a unit, and its surviving tanks, perhaps six, joined the 7th Battalion. The squadron sent to support the Cameron Highlanders had been recalled and was destroyed en route. Headquarters 11th Indian Infantry Brigade had been scattered and was moving to a rendezvous south of Tobruk town.

Although King's Cross had passed into enemy hands only vague information reached Divisional Headquarters until Brigadier Anderson arrived between 3 and 4 p.m. with some account of the situation. General Klopper, however, had already heard enough to make him uneasy, and at about 2 p.m. he ordered the Guards Brigade to form a new line facing east and to deny the Pilastrino ridge to the enemy. He ordered Brigadier Hayton, commanding 4th South African Brigade, to take over the Cameron Highlanders and 'Beergroup' and reorganize the defence in that area. He also instructed the 4th and 6th South African Brigades to prepare a company each to attack the German leaguers the same night.

The two parts into which the German advance now divided—the thrust of 21st Panzer Division towards Tobruk and the attack of 15th Panzer Division along the Pilastrino ridge—will here, for the sake of clarity, be treated separately.

At about 2.30 p.m. the 21st Panzer Division began to descend the escarpment from King's Cross by the road running north to Tobruk. It met and scattered the remains of the 7th R.T.R., and there was now nothing between it and Tobruk except the 9th South African Field Battery and a troop of the 5th, a troop of the 231st Medium Battery R.A. and four guns of the 277th Heavy Anti-Aircraft Battery R.A. The field guns delayed the advance until about 4 p.m. when they were forced westwards. Rommel wrote of the 'extraordinary tenacity' of a British strong-point near 'the descent into the town'; it was about here that some of 5th Panzer Regiment's tanks came under the close fire of the heavy anti-aircraft guns, which claimed to have disabled several of them.[1] At about 6 p.m. the leading German troops began to enter the town.

The German advance had naturally caused a crisis in No. 88 Sub-Area. The commander, Brigadier Thompson, after several personal reconnaissances, obtained General Klopper's agreement to put the demolition scheme in hand. At about 6 p.m., on his own initiative, he ordered demolitions to begin. Although time was now very short a large amount of damage was done to the petrol and water installations, and to the harbour facilities. Brigadier Thompson himself was taken prisoner, fighting on a roof. All craft had meanwhile been ordered to sail for Alexandria and left harbour under fire, partly covered by a smoke-screen laid by a M.T.B. The last craft, containing the naval demolition parties, was sunk in the harbour; Captain Smith was

[1] The German records of tank losses for the day are missing.

mortally wounded and Captain Walter wounded and captured. In all, two minesweepers and thirteen craft of various sorts escaped, and one minesweeper and a total of twenty-four launches, tugs, schooners, and landing craft were lost in harbour or on passage to Alexandria.

A crisis had also occurred at Divisional Headquarters. Reports during the afternoon were scanty, and at 4 p.m., while shells were falling around and a miscellaneous collection of men and vehicles were passing through, apparently from Pilastrino, tanks were seen to the east. General Klopper judged that his headquarters would be overrun in a matter of minutes, and ordered his staff to destroy their documents and disperse. A rendezvous was appointed at Sollum. The signal office, telephone exchange, and most of the wireless sets were destroyed; only a few sets in trucks survived. The German tanks, however, moved away, but Divisional Headquarters was now in a state of self-inflicted paralysis. At about 6.30 Klopper decided to move to the headquarters of the 6th South African Brigade at Ras Belgamel in the north-western sector, but his earlier decision to disperse his own headquarters had deprived him of the means of exercising command.

We must now return to the Pilastrino ridge, above (i.e. to the south of) which the 201st Guards Brigade was now disposed from a point about one mile south-west of King's Cross to Fort Pilastrino four miles away. From east to west were the Sherwood Foresters, Brigade Headquarters, the Coldstream Guards, and, in the Pilastrino area, the Worcestershires. These dispositions required some little time to take up; for instance two companies of the Coldstream Guards, as has been related, had been sent earlier in the day to near King's Cross. There was practically no natural cover at all and the rocky ground made digging almost impossible.

The attack by 15th Panzer Division along the ridge began at about 5 p.m. Two companies of the Sherwood Foresters were soon overrun, the Coldstream Guards were engaged, and at about 6.45 Brigade Headquarters was captured. It seems that a message reached the Sherwood Foresters from Brigade Headquarters that the brigade was surrendering, and their remnants ceased to resist. Major H. M. Sainthill, commanding the 3rd Coldstream Guards, extricated his No. 4 Company, some fifty survivors of the other companies, and six antitank guns, and withdrew to Fort Pilastrino. The Germans (whose role was to protect the flank of the advance on Tobruk town) did not follow up.

In the meantime Brigadier Hayton had told Lieut.-Colonel Geddes Page of the Kaffrarian Rifles, which lay west of 'Beergroup', to contact 'Beergroup' and the Cameron Highlanders. Some tanks were roaming about in this area and a shell destroyed the Kaffrarian

Rifles' wireless link. From the subsequent silence Brigadier Hayton concluded that the battalion had been overrun. At Fort Pilastrino he had no news of the general situation, and at about 4 p.m., on a report of tanks in the distance, he decided to move his headquarters four miles to Fig Tree. The move was confused, and for the next three hours the 4th South African Brigade was without command. Just about the time when this headquarters moved, Lieut.-Colonel I. B. Whyte, commanding the 3rd South African Field Regiment, unable to gain touch with the Brigadier or the C.R.A. or the divisional headquarters, decided that something must be done. He and Lieut.-Colonel O. W. Sherwell, of the 2nd South African Field Regiment, resolved to concentrate their guns (about fifty in number) at Fort Pilastrino and there withstand an enemy advance from the east. He then conferred with Lieut.-Colonel J. O. Knight of the Worcestershire Regiment and Major Sainthill of the Coldstream Guards and all agreed to fight it out where they were. But these stout-hearted officers were fated to have no chance to carry out their resolve.

The situation at nightfall was broadly as follows. In the extreme east the 2/7th Gurkha Rifles were resisting attempts to mop them up. In the south the Cameron Highlanders, 'Beergroup', and the Kaffrarian Rifles, which had been by-passed by the main German thrust, had prepared for all-round defence. The Coldstream Guards, the Worcestershire Regiment and Colonels Whyte and Sherwell with their guns were preparing to give battle at Pilastrino. The 6th South African Brigade had not been engaged and the 4th had dealt with demonstrations only. Brigadier Willison, with General Klopper's permission, was planning to break out with the survivors of his brigade, on wheels. In the administrative areas round the town and harbour there was confusion and chaos. Into the western sector of the perimeter there was a steady percolation of miscellaneous stragglers, the backwash of the day's fighting. General Klopper and some of his staff were at Headquarters 6th South African Brigade, but had lost control. The enemy had gone into leaguers for the night. At last light a small force of Bostons made an attack on targets in the south-eastern sector, and single Bostons came over during the night: this was all that the Royal Air Force could do.

Until the dispersal of Divisional Headquarters the signal communication with 8th Army had been fairly good, though there were considerable delays. By 4.30 p.m. the advance of enemy tanks to a mile west of King's Cross had been reported, and at about 6 p.m. came the news that the garrison had no tanks left and that the eastern sector had been badly mauled. A naval signal then brought word that tanks were approaching Tobruk harbour. It was at about this time that

General Klopper reached the 6th South African Brigade's head-quarters. He had decided that the position of his troops was hopeless and issued a warning order that all units should prepare for a mass break-out at 10 p.m. At 8.8 p.m. he sent a message to 8th Army: 'My HQ surrounded. Infantry on perimeter still fighting hard. Am holding out but I do not know for how long.' This message, received shortly after midnight, confirmed the impressions which had been steadily growing that the situation in Tobruk was desperate. Earlier in the day General Ritchie had ordered the 30th Corps to push the 7th Armoured Division northwards to Sidi Rezegh, but it is evident from the enemy's reports that the ring was in no danger of being broken. Indeed, writing shortly after the event, General Ritchie recorded that 'I deplore more than ever that I found it impossible in the circumstances to give General Klopper any material assistance by operations from outside. The fact is that I was being held off by considerable enemy forces which could so delay my advance as to make this impossible in the time the enemy took to reduce Tobruk.'

About 9 p.m. there began an exchange of messages by radio-telephone between the B.G.S. 8th Army and General Klopper, of which short notes exist. Brigadier Whiteley asked if the situation was in hand and for how long Klopper could hold out. The answer ran '. . . Situation not in hand. Counter-attack with Inf Bn to-night. All my tanks gone. Half my guns gone. Do you think it advisable I battle through? If you are counter-attacking let me know.' This was referred to General Ritchie, and the B.G.S. replied: 'Come out tomorrow night preferably if not tonight. Centre line Medauar-Knightsbridge-Maddalena. I will keep open gap Harmat-El Adem. Inform me time selected and route. Tomorrow night preferred. Destruction petrol vital.' With this General Klopper had to be content and a sad series of discussions took place with Brigadier Hayton, Brigadier Cooper, Colonel Richards, and others. Brigadier Anderson awaited orders near-by but took no part in the debate. Brigadier Hayton said that it was impossible to break out without transport and no one knew what had happened to the transport.[1] He advocated a stand in the western sector. Brigadier Cooper on the other hand was prepared to attempt a break-out. Other officers, among them the C.R.A., argued that the position was hopeless mainly because the artillery now had only the ammunition in its limbers which would not last long. They suggested that all mobile troops, at least, should escape.

At length at about 2 a.m. on 21st June General Klopper sent this message to 8th Army: 'Am sending mobile troops out tonight. Not possible to hold tomorrow. Mobile troops nearly nought. Enemy captured vehicles. Will resist to last man and last round.' This decision

[1] The 2nd South African Division had no troop-carrying transport, and for moves had to improvise by pooling unit vehicles, or be provided with Corps or Army transport.

was approved by most of his subordinates but viewed with misgiving by some. A certain amount of digging and other defensive preparations had been going on, and were continued. Some time between 5 and 6 a.m. however General Klopper changed his mind and concluded that the advantages that he could gain for the 8th Army by prolonging resistance would be negligible, and would not justify the casualties that must be expected. Some time about 6 a.m. General Ritchie at last made touch with Klopper, and this record of their exchange of messages remains:

> '*Army Comd.* Noted about mobile elements. In respect remainder every day and hour of resistance materially assist our cause. I cannot tell tactical situation and must therefore leave you to act on your own judgement regarding capitulation.
>
> Report if you can extent to which destruction P.O.L. effected.[1]
>
> *G.O.C.* Situation shambles. Terrible casualties would result. Am doing the worst. Petrol destroyed.
>
> *Army Comd.* Whole of Eighth Army has watched with admiration your gallant fight. You are an example to us all and I know South Africa will be proud of you. God bless you and may fortune favour your efforts wherever you may be . . .'

For both commanders these minutes in which each had to admit failure—the one to hold on, the other to help—must have been bitter indeed.

Soon after this General Klopper sent out *parlementaires* and it was not long before the German officers charged with receiving the surrender arrived at his headquarters. The orders to surrender took some time to communicate to units and were received with general amazement and often with disbelief. Once however they were understood there was a general destruction of weapons and equipment. Last to surrender were the Gurkha Rifles on the evening of 21st June, and the Cameron Highlanders—after a threat of extermination if they persisted in disregarding a general capitulation—on the morning of 22nd June. Numerous small parties and individuals did their best to escape, but the only considerable successful attempt was led by Major Sainthill of the Coldstream Guards. He collected 199 officers and men of his battalion, all his remaining anti-tank guns, and 188 men of other units. This column burst out of the perimeter in the south-west corner and near Knightsbridge was picked up and escorted to safety by South African armoured cars working with the 7th Armoured Division. There were some notable lesser attempts: Lieut. L. Bailie and Sergeant G. R. Norton of the Kaffrarian Rifles with a small party reached the El Alamein position 38 days after the fall of Tobruk.

[1] P.O.L. is the Army's abbreviation for petrol, oil and lubricants.

Sergeants J. H. Brown and C. A. Turner of the Coldstream Guards who, in carriers, had fallen behind Major Sainthill's column, struggled on and brought their men and machines safely in.

The number of prisoners taken at Tobruk is not known for certain, but was probably made up of:

British troops	19,000
South African Europeans	8,960
South African Natives	1,760
Indian troops	2,500
Total	32,220

or perhaps 33,000 in all.

The booty captured at Tobruk and Belhamed, and in various dumps in the desert, gave the Germans practically everything they needed except water. The *Panzerarmee's* figures show that of a total of over 2,000 tons of fuel about 1,400 tons were found at Tobruk and only 20 tons at Belhamed. Large quantities of ammunition, both British and German, were found, together with some 2,000 serviceable vehicles and about 5,000 tons of provisions.

The German casualties for 20th June are not known, but were certainly light. Their total casualties since the beginning of the fighting on 26th May were reported to *OKH* on 24th June as having been approximately:

Officers	300
N.C.Os	570
Other ranks	2,490

which represented about 15% of their strength. The officer casualties had been particularly high, reaching as much as 70% in the Panzer units and in the lorried infantry.

The fall of Tobruk came as a staggering blow to the British cause. For South Africa it was particularly tragic, since about one third of all her forces in the field went into captivity. The suddenness of the collapse, almost before it was generally realized that the place was again being besieged, made the shock all the greater. Tobruk had previously withstood a siege for seven months: how came it, then, that a garrison of much the same size could only resist for one day? First Singapore and now Tobruk. What hope was there, on this showing, of saving Egypt? Worse still, what was the matter with British arms?

Small wonder that the Prime Minister, who heard the news in Washington, felt that it was one of the heaviest blows of the war. This climax to a series of misfortunes and defeats was among the reasons which caused a motion expressing no confidence in the central direction of the war to be tabled in the House of Commons on 25th June.[1]

The reasons for the disaster are plain enough. In the first place it had been commonly known since February that there was no intention of accepting a second siege. This knowledge led to Tobruk not being properly prepared to withstand a siege or even a determined assault. It seems clear that in making their plans after the withdrawal from the Gazala positions neither General Auchinleck nor General Ritchie realized the full extent of the 8th Army's defeat. Had they done so, they would scarcely have attempted to carry out three simultaneous policies—to continue the battle in the Tobruk area, to organize the defence of the frontier, and to prepare for a counter-offensive. In the narrower field of tactics there can be no doubt that the commander and staff of the 2nd South African Division had not the experience to enable them in the difficult circumstances to make the best use of the forces available. Whether the best would have been good enough against Rommel and his *Panzerarmee*, exhilarated by success and by the nearness of the prize, is another matter—especially as he was supported by strong and concentrated air forces which had the stage practically to themselves because almost all the fighters of the Desert Air Force were out of range. The resulting onslaught was devastating; apart from the shelling nearly 400 tons of bombs were dropped in a short time on a very small sector of the defences.

For General Rommel the triumph must have been all the sweeter for having been so boldly and so easily won. It seemed to open the way for the quick conquest of Egypt. The world rang with his fame, and he was immediately promoted Field-Marshal. It was a great moment, and no Fate whispered that he would never experience a greater.

[1] It was defeated on 2nd July by 475 votes to 25.

CHAPTER XII

THE RETREAT TO EL ALAMEIN

IT had been the agreed intention of the Axis to follow the capture of Tobruk with an assault on Malta, and on 20th June Mussolini wrote to Hitler asking for his help over some of the problems connected with '*Herkules*', especially the provision of oil fuel for the Italian Navy. He reiterated the arguments in favour of the operation and pointed out that so many aircraft had now reached Malta that the island's offensive power had been largely restored and Axis shipping to Libya was again in difficulties. The next day came news of the capture of Tobruk, but Mussolini saw no reason to alter his directive of 5th May, which had authorized the Axis forces to advance as far as the Egyptian frontier and occupy Jarabub.

The new German Field-Marshal, however, was not to be robbed thus easily of the fruits of his victory. On 22nd June he sent his views to von Rintelen in Rome, asking him to put them to Mussolini and *OKW*. 'The first objective of the *Panzerarmee*—to defeat the enemy's army in the field and capture Tobruk—has been attained.' The condition and morale of his own troops, the quantities of transport and supplies he had captured, and the weakness of the British would enable him to chase them deep into Egypt. The main thing was to give them no time to form a new front behind which to gather reinforcements. The way to Alexandria and Suez would then be open. 'Request you ask the Duce to lift the present restriction on freedom of movement and to put all the troops now under my command at my disposal, so that I can continue the battle.' He made similar representations to Hitler.

Hitler, in spite of the advice of his naval staff, had been growing lukewarm about '*Herkules*', which he thought might end in Malta becoming a drain on Axis resources. He therefore welcomed Rommel's views and on 23rd June wrote to Mussolini strongly supporting them and urging the Duce to order the advance in Africa to continue until the enemy's forces were totally destroyed. A beaten army should always be pursued to the limit of the victor's resources. If the British and Americans were allowed to build up their strength in Egypt the situation would change greatly to the disadvantage of the Axis. Destiny was offering the Axis powers an opportunity which would not occur again.

The prospect of reaching the Suez Canal was irresistibly attractive to Mussolini. In spite of the doubts of his advisers he declared himself in agreement with Hitler: this was the moment to conquer Egypt. The main difficulty would be to keep the forces supplied, and Malta would therefore have to be neutralized. To do this the air forces in Sicily would have to be reinforced from Libya, Italy and Germany. On 25th June he sent Cavallero to Africa to set the new policy in train, by which time Rommel had already taken up the pursuit.

Cavallero found Kesselring in two minds—convinced at heart that the proper strategic course was to do '*Herkules*', and yet seeing the obvious advantages of giving no respite to the retreating enemy. The Axis air forces would not be strong enough to neutralize Malta and at the same time support extensive operations in Egypt against an enemy who was withdrawing towards his bases. Kesselring compromised by agreeing to an advance into Egypt providing that it should not be carried beyond El Alamein.

On 26th June Cavallero, Bastico and the rest went forward to see Rommel, whose headquarters by this time were near Sidi Barrani. Rommel explained that he was about to attack Mersa Matruh and push on to El Daba. From there he would move on either Alexandria or Cairo, which, if all went well, he would reach by the 30th. After this meeting Cavallero issued a directive in the name of *Comando Supremo* which declared that the successes must be fully exploited but took note of some of the difficulties. Malta had resumed its offensive role, and shipments to Tripoli would have to cease for the time being. Even those to Cyrenaican ports were threatened. The intention was to neutralize Malta again but in the meantime a crisis over supplies was inevitable. Every effort would be made to send some convoys to Benghazi and Tobruk, to increase air transport, and to use submarines, but for some time the Axis forces in Africa would have to live off their hump. This being so, the El Alamein positions would be seized as a jumping-off place, but further operations would be decided upon in the light of the general Mediterranean situation. It was essential to bring forward the German and Italian air forces as quickly as possible.

This directive was expanded by another from Mussolini on 27th June, which stated that when the present opposition was overcome the aim of the Axis forces should be to advance to the Suez Canal at Ismailia, in order to close the Canal and prevent the arrival of British reinforcements. Essential preliminaries were to occupy Cairo, mask Alexandria, and secure the rear of the armies against landings from the sea.

Thus it came about that the sudden fall of Tobruk may have saved Malta from assault. It had another and a very positive result: President Roosevelt agreed to send immediately three hundred Sherman tanks and a hundred 105-mm. self-propelled guns to the Middle East, in addition to a large number of aircraft.[1]

On 21st June the Commanders-in-Chief and the Minister of State had considered their future policy in the belief that Tobruk was on the point of falling. General Ritchie had reported that, of the two courses open to him, he considered that to delay the enemy on the frontier while he withdrew the main body of his army to Matruh was preferable to making a stand on the frontier. The Commanders-in-Chief agreed with this view and telegraphed a long appreciation to London. In outline this ran as follows.

The enemy was now the stronger in all types of troops required for fighting in open country and had plenty of transport. British troops in the Western Desert were now the equivalent of three and two-thirds infantry divisions weak in artillery; three armoured regiments of which two were partly trained and one was composite; two motor brigades and some armoured car regiments. The New Zealand Division was beginning to arrive at Matruh. Thus the force was not suitably composed for a campaign of manoeuvre. The situation in the air was fairly favourable. The plan for the frontier defences had been for infantry to hold defended localities while a strong armoured reserve stood ready to strike the enemy if he tried to penetrate or outflank the position. As this armoured reserve did not exist the infantry localities might be defeated in detail, and the frontier position could not therefore be held for long against a serious attack. East of the Egyptian frontier there were no natural or artificial obstacles on which to frame a satisfactory defensive position until Matruh was reached. At Matruh there were cramped defences for an infantry division, and south of it, at Sidi Hamza, a position which had been planned but not made. Between Matruh and Sidi Hamza there were minefields not covered by defended localities. Here too the plans for defence had assumed that an armoured reserve would exist, but, if it did not, infantry could cover the minefields. Work on the defences was being carried on. As Matruh was 120 miles from the Egyptian frontier and water was scarce in between, the administrative difficulties would impose a delay on the enemy, which would give our air force the opportunity to attack and cause still more delay. On the whole, to check the enemy on the Egyptian frontier while withdrawing the main body of the 8th Army to Matruh seemed to give the best chance of gaining time to re-organize and build up a striking force with which to resume the offensive.

[1] The Sherman was a great improvement on the Grant, because its 75-mm. gun was mounted in the turret instead of in a sponson at the side.

There would, however, be some serious consequences of a withdrawal to Matruh. Air attacks on targets in the Delta and as far as Suez and the Red Sea might increase, and daylight attacks by bombers escorted by fighters upon Alexandria would become possible. The move of our air force eastward would reduce its power to operate over the Central Mediterranean, to protect naval forces and shipping, and to strike at the enemy's North African ports. From this it followed that it would be impossible to run a convoy to Malta from the east, and might become impossible for our single-engined fighters to move between Malta and Egypt. The enemy would be able to supply North Africa more easily, and his naval forces, with greater freedom of action, could penetrate farther into the Eastern Mediterranean. Finally, there might be internal troubles in Egypt and a change in the Turkish attitude, while the nearness of the enemy to our main base would make it difficult for us to release forces for the northern front or elsewhere in the Middle East if the need arose.

The Defence Committee in London approved these measures in general but commented that sufficient emphasis had not been placed on the difficulties which would confront the enemy in staging an attack on the frontier positions. They felt that if there was to be merely a rearguard action on the frontier the Matruh position might be quickly overrun. If however the troops on the frontier made a resolute and determined defence the enemy's advance might be stopped altogether, or at the worst enough time could be gained to build up an armoured force to operate from Matruh. The Middle East Defence Committee replied with some asperity on 23rd June that there did not exist the minimum armoured force necessary to prevent the infantry formations on the frontier from being defeated in detail, and that, if this happened, there would not be enough troops left to hold Matruh. Mobile troops, strong in artillery and with full air support, would use the frontier positions to delay and damage the enemy while preparations were made to fight an offensive/defensive battle in the Matruh area. This course would deprive the enemy of the chance to use his armoured formations at high momentum in a decisive battle on the frontier, and would set him instead the formidable problem of invading Egypt in strength across a further 120 miles of waterless country. At Matruh a decisive battle could be fought with many advantages to the 8th Army.

In resisting the temptation to stand on the frontier the British commanders were undoubtedly wise. Whether they should have disengaged completely and withdrawn to the place where the passable desert is at its narrowest—that is, at El Alamein, where the Qattara depression approaches to within thirty-five miles of the sea—is another question. Rommel's problem in the previous December, though superficially similar, had in fact been different, for there was

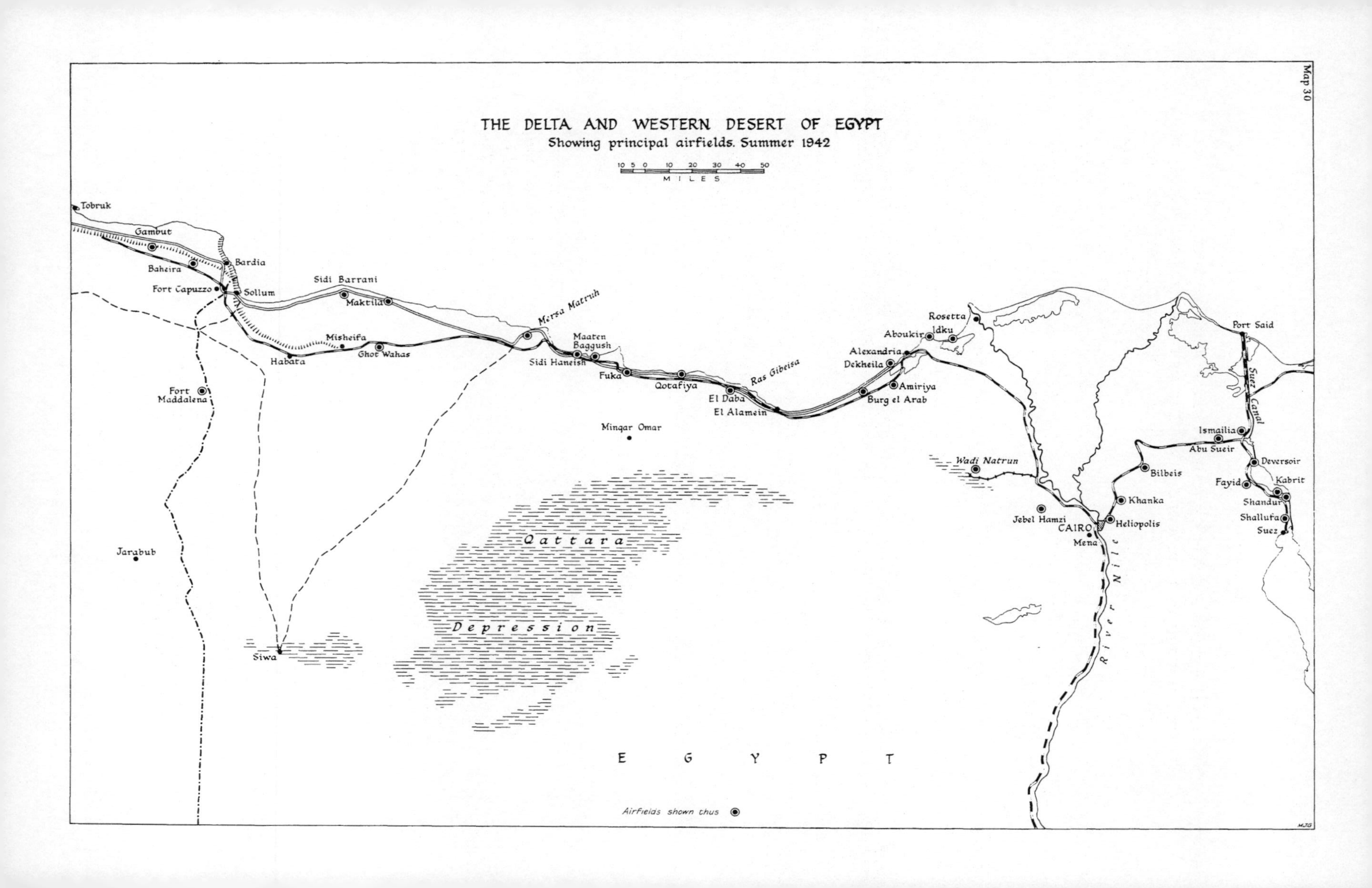
Map 30
THE DELTA AND WESTERN DESERT OF EGYPT
Showing principal airfields. Summer 1942
10 5 0 10 20 30 40 50
MILES
Tobruk
Gambut
Baheira
Bardia
Fort Capuzzo
Sollum
Sidi Barrani
Maktila
Misheifa
Ghot Wahas
Habata
Fort Maddalena
Jarabub
Siwa
Mersa Matruh
Maaten Baggush
Sidi Haneish
Fuka
Qotafiya
Ras Gibeisa
El Daba
El Alamein
Mingar Omar
Qattara
Depression
Burg el Arab
Amiriya
Dekheila
Alexandria
Aboukir
Idku
Rosetta
Wadi Natrun
Jebel Hamzi
CAIRO
Mena
Heliopolis
Khanka
Bilbeis
Abu Sueir
Ismailia
Port Said
Suez Canal
Deversoir
Fayid
Kabrit
Shandur
Shallufa
Suez
River Nile
E G Y P T
Airfields shown thus

at El Agheila a strong natural position to fall back upon, which was still a long way from Tripoli. The British Commanders-in-Chief, on the other hand, could not contemplate allowing the enemy to advance to the very doorstep of the Delta without making any attempt to stop him. The weakness of the plan was that at Matruh, no less than on the frontier, a strong armoured reserve was needed for an active defence. Unless the enemy was appreciably delayed on the frontier this strong armoured reserve would not exist.

The plan which emerged was for a strong force under Lieut.-General Gott to delay the enemy in order to gain time. This would enable the Royal Air Force to continue its attacks from landing-grounds as far west as possible, and would cover the destruction of stores—in particular, petrol and ammunition—that could not be got away. The 8th Army was to prepare to fight a decisive action in the Matruh area, and to the forces at the Army Commander's disposal were now added the Headquarters 10th Corps (Lieut.-General W. G. Holmes), the 10th Armoured Division and the New Zealand Division.[1]

The divisions under General Gott's command were the 7th Armoured, the 50th, and the 10th Indian, together with five armoured car regiments. Of the two armoured brigades in the 7th Armoured Division the 4th had two regiments and the 22nd only one. As regards the 1st South African Division General Ritchie had come to the conclusion that it was not at the moment in high fighting trim, and decided to send it to reorganize at El Alamein. It set off eastwards between 21st and 23rd June.

There was some discussion between Generals Ritchie and Gott about how long the enemy was to be held up on the frontier. As it turned out, he began to cross it on 23rd June and the delaying action proposed by General Auchinleck degenerated into an orthodox withdrawal. The demolition schemes, which were an important feature of the plan, were on the whole successful. It was perhaps just as well that the withdrawals begun by the 8th Army on 14th June had set off a train of prescribed actions which included the demolition of installations at Bardia and Fort Capuzzo and the deliberate leaking-away of 500,000 gallons of petrol.[2] The clearing of stores from Misheifa railhead began on 21st June and was almost complete on the 23rd. On that day the

---

[1] H.Q. 10th Corps was ordered from Syria to Egypt on 14th June. There was much shilly-shallying over its role, but it was ordered to the Western Desert on 20th June and arrived in the Matruh area during 21st and 22nd June. The 10th Armoured Division amounted to the 8th Armoured Brigade. On 23rd June this Brigade's tanks were taken from it to re-equip the 1st Armoured Division and the men returned to the Delta. The New Zealand Division arrived at Matruh from Syria between 19th and 24th June.

[2] According to the *Panzerarmee's* diary 500 tons of fuel and 930 tons of provisions were captured at Capuzzo.

water point at Habata was destroyed and on the 24th the ammunition dump at Misheifa was blown up. These actions must have handicapped the enemy, whose records indicate, however, that he met very little opposition on the ground from 23rd June onwards. But from 23rd June it is plain that the air attacks were really beginning to hurt.

See Map 30

If there was one lesson above all others that the Desert Air Force had learned during the recent fighting it was the need to have landing-grounds ready in depth; only in this way could anything like continuous air support be given to a retreating army. Accordingly Air Vice-Marshal Coningham took steps to prepare some of the chain of landing-grounds in Egypt for use at short notice, such as Matruh, Maaten Baggush, Sidi Haneish, Fuka, El Daba, Amiriya and Wadi Natrun. Only the essential maintenance parties were kept forward at the advanced landing-grounds.

It was now clearly necessary for the Air to take as much of the load off the Army as it could, and everything possible was done to increase the strength of the Desert Air Force. The training units in the Delta, already short of aircraft, had to part with their Hurricane IIs which went to re-equip No. 1 Squadron S.A.A.F., and to complete No. 127 Squadron R.A.F. Twenty Spitfires were asked for from Malta. Two Beaufighter Squadrons, Nos. 252 and 272, and the Alsace and Hellenic Hurricane Squadrons were withdrawn from No. 201 Naval Co-operation Group and given to the Desert Air Force with No. 234 Wing Headquarters to control them all. (After this the fighter defence of the Delta area rested solely on the few night-fighting Beaufighters and one or two Spitfires awaiting modification.) Of the bombers, No. 223 (Baltimore) Squadron at last received its full quota of aircraft and No. 14 (Blenheim) Squadron was added to the light bomber force for use at night.

Apart from these internal adjustments it was essential to have more aircraft. The strength of squadrons was falling, although the output from the Base Repair Depot had greatly improved—the expected total for June was 250—and by strenuous efforts the proportion of serviceable aircraft in squadrons had been not only kept up but actually raised. The Chiefs of Staff came to the rescue by ordering 21 Hurricane IICs, intended for India, to be diverted to the Middle East, to arrive at the end of June. They authorized some Blenheims, also destined for India, to be retained, and planned to send another 20 Hurricane IICs by 20th July, 32 Halifaxes by 5th July, and 22 Liberators during July and August. 42 Spitfires en route for Australia were, with the consent of the Australian Government, to be unloaded at Freetown for Takoradi early in July. The Halverson Detachment of

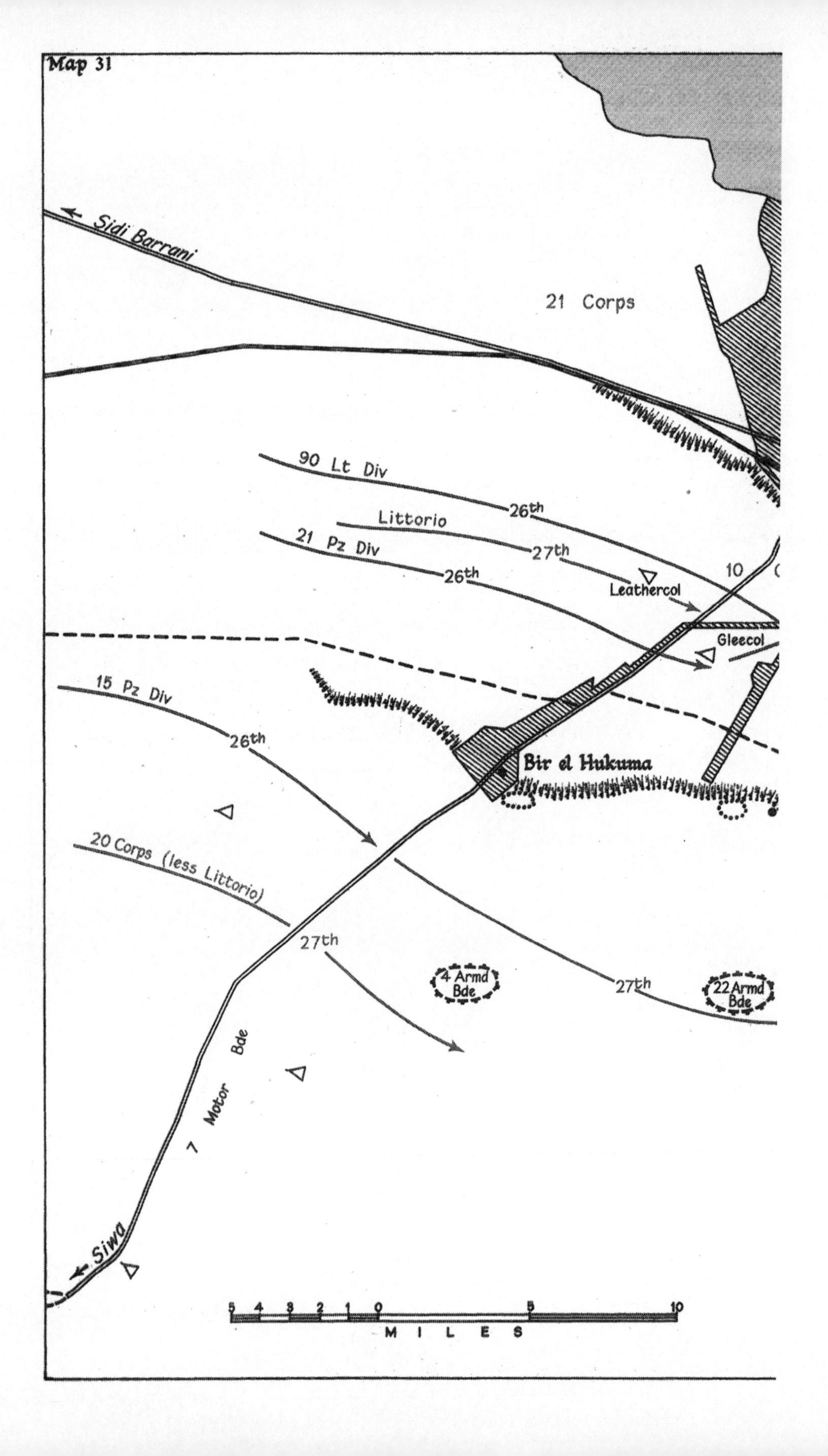
Map 31
Sidi Barrani
21 Corps
90 Lt Div
26th
Littorio
27th
21 Pz Div
26th
Leathercol
10
Gleecol
15 Pz Div
26th
Bir el Hukuma
20 Corps (less Littorio)
27th
4 Armd Bde
27th
22 Armd Bde
7 Motor Bde
Siwa
5 4 3 2 1 0 5 10
MILES

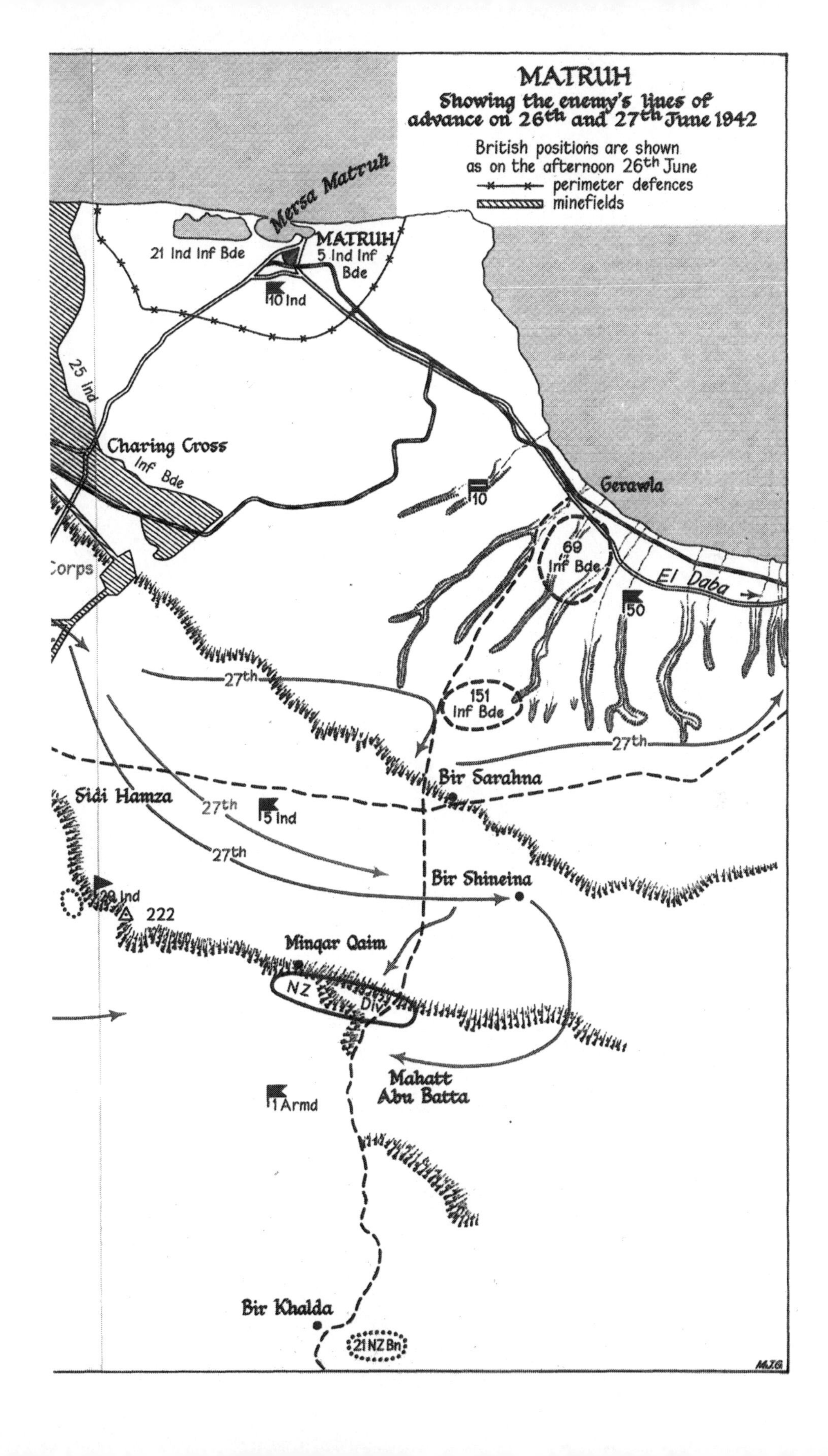
MATRUH
Showing the enemy's lines of advance on 26th and 27th June 1942
British positions are shown as on the afternoon 26th June
perimeter defences
minefields
Mersa Matruh
MATRUH
21 Ind Inf Bde
5 Ind Inf Bde
10 Ind
25 Ind
Charing Cross
Inf Bde
10
Gerawla
69 Inf Bde
El Daba
50
Corps
27th
151 Inf Bde
27th
Bir Sarahna
Sidi Hamza
27th
5 Ind
27th
Bir Shineina
29 Ind
222
Minqar Qaim
NZ Div
Mahatt Abu Batta
1 Armd
Bir Khalda
21 NZ Bn
M.J.G.

American Liberators became permanently established in Egypt and the restrictions that had been placed on its use were removed. In addition, the following American reinforcements were to be transferred to the Middle East: one Light Bombardment Squadron of 27 Hudsons, one Fighter Group of 80 Kittyhawks, one Medium Bombardment Group of 57 Mitchells, and one Heavy Bombardment Group of 35 Liberators—all to leave the U.S.A. late in June or early in July.[1]

The preponderance of fighters is illustrated by the composition of the Desert Air Force on 22nd June, when its squadrons consisted of: Fighters and Fighter-Bombers, twenty-two (11 Hurricane, 6 Kittyhawk, 1 Spitfire, 2 Tomahawk, 2 Beaufighter); Tactical Reconnaissance, two (Hurricane and Tomahawk); Light Bombers, four (two Boston, one Blenheim, and one Baltimore). At about the same time the comparative strengths of the three air forces in North Africa, in terms of aircraft serviceable or fit to fly almost immediately, were as follows. The Germans had 183 and the Italians 238, a total of 421. The Desert Air Force had 463 and behind them were a further 420 in the Middle East, against a figure for the Germans in the rest of the Mediterranean of 174, and for the Italians (excluding Metropolitan Italy) of nearly 500. Thus the present balance was slightly in favour of the Royal Air Force, but the enemy's total resources were the greater.

The decision to withdraw the 8th Army from the frontier was the signal for the light bombers of the Desert Air Force to turn on their maximum effort. Reconnaissance and fighter aircraft had kept watch on the enemy's movements, and the first attacks were made about Gabr Saleh. On 23rd June the light bombers flew 45 sorties and the fighter-bombers 30. That evening the fighters withdrew to Matruh and some of the bombers moved to El Daba to make room for them.

Next day, the 24th, after a long wait for fuel, the enemy advanced with the *D.A.K.* and the Italian 20th Corps south of the railway and 90th Light Division north, while the 21st Corps and later the 10th Corps followed the coast road. There were thus plenty of targets for the R.A.F. to attack, and the Baltimores and Bostons increased their sorties to 72, with another 30 by the fighter-bombers. The Beaufighters joined in by attacking transport well in rear of the advance. The *D.A.K.* mentions having had some casualties, but not how many, and observed 'No sign of the *Luftwaffe*'.

The German fighters were in fact only just moving in to Gambut and Baheira. The enemy, including Rommel himself, were learning what the Desert Air Force already knew—that much preparation and ample transport were required if aircraft were to be able to reach out

[1] The Hudsons (A 29) would leave Florida by air on 26th June; the Kittyhawks (Mk. II—P 40F with Packard Merlin engine) would leave the U.S.A. by aircraft carrier for Takoradi; the Mitchells (B 25) and the Liberators (B 24) would fly by single squadrons.

ahead of, or even to keep up with, a rapid advance by their own troops. When the Axis plan was suddenly changed from the attack on Malta to the invasion of Egypt their air forces were caught unprepared. The *Luftwaffe* was feeling the strain after its exertions of the past few weeks, especially at Bir Hacheim and Tobruk. A few reconnaissance aircraft came over the dense British columns, packed in places nose to tail along the coast road, but no attempt was made to turn the retreat into a rout.

See Map 31

The choice of Matruh as the place to fall back upon was not dictated by the existence of any easily defended natural position, but rather by the fact that, when Matruh had been of some value as a port which the Italians would have been glad to possess, the British had spent much time and trouble in preparing its defences. Some months later it became the base for the 'Crusader' offensive. Since then the rather cramped ring of field works near the coast had naturally not been kept in full repair. Farther inland the ground rises in two stages, marked by the line of the northern and southern escarpments. The Matruh-Siwa track and the coastal road cross the first of these escarpments at Charing Cross, and from here to the sea stretched a minefield. Above the southern escarpment a position had been planned near Sidi Hamza, but in the hard rock little had been dug. However a minefield of sorts ran from here towards Charing Cross and another short minefield had been laid along the Siwa track. East of Sidi Hamza a track descended the southern escarpment at Minqar Qaim.[1]

The plans to give battle in the Matruh area were worked out under pressure between 22nd and 24th June. The intention was simple enough: to occupy Matruh with the 10th Corps and the Sidi Hamza area with the 13th Corps; meanwhile Headquarters 30th Corps in rear would collect a reserve and organize an armoured striking force. The speed of the enemy's approach, the general confusion of the retreat, and the simultaneous arrival of reinforcements made the task of sorting out matters in the focal area of Matruh a very hectic one; the burden fell mostly upon 10th Corps, which was itself in the process of relieving the 30th. One of its minor troubles was caused by General Freyberg's protest against the static use of the New Zealand Division in the Matruh 'box', and he was allowed to change from 10th Corps to the 13th.

By 24th June the plan was reasonably firm. The 10th Corps was to have the 10th Indian Division at Matruh and the 50th Division some miles to the south-east about Gerawla.[2] In the inland sector the 13th

[1] Minqar: a promontory or cliff.

[2] On 21st June Brigadier J. S. Nichols succeeded Major-General T. W. Rees in command of the 10th Indian Division.

Corps would have the 5th Indian Division about Sidi Hamza, the New Zealand Division at Minqar Qaim, and the 1st Armoured Division in the open desert to the south-west. The 7th Armoured Division, both of whose armoured brigades had been transferred to the 1st, was acting as a covering force; it consisted of the 7th Motor Brigade, the 3rd Indian Motor Brigade, and the 69th Infantry Brigade of the 50th Division. The broad intention was that the enemy was to be held in front of Matruh and Sidi Hamza; if he penetrated between these places or swept round to the south he was to be struck in flank by the 13th Corps.

On 25th June General Auchinleck decided that the position of the 8th Army was so critical and the danger to Egypt so great that he ought to take command in person. He flew to Maaten Baggush and at 7 p.m. took over from General Ritchie. The Chief of the General Staff, Lieut.-General T. W. Corbett, remained at Cairo acting as the Commander-in-Chief's Deputy for all matters except those of the highest strategic or political importance. This action of General Auchinleck's serves as a reminder of the peculiar circumstances in which General Ritchie had been appointed to command the 8th Army. Very soon after the beginning of 'Crusader' General Auchinleck had decided that a change of commanders was necessary, and because the battle was in full swing he had to appoint someone thoroughly conversant with his own ideas and with the whole plan. There was no time to lose. At his headquarters he had such an officer, who, in addition, possessed the requisite energy and determination. The fact that General Ritchie had had no experience of exercising higher command had to be accepted. After the new Army Commander took over, he was visited for days at a stretch by General Auchinleck, who was at pains not to interfere with the execution of any plans, but saw to it that General Ritchie was kept fully aware of his own views. For a while this worked well enough: being new to the job and with less experience than many of his subordinates General Ritchie was no doubt glad of the opportunities to talk things over with the Commander-in-Chief.

But after 'Crusader' had petered out, the weakness of the system began to show and became more evident still after the enemy anticipated the British by attacking the Gazala position. General Ritchie had become accustomed to consult the Commander-in-Chief, not because he had not the strength of character to make decisions for himself, but possibly because he continued to think more as a staff officer than as a commander. General Auchinleck was in the tantalising position of feeling that he knew what ought to be done and at the same time of not wishing to cramp General Ritchie's style by telling him how to do it. Instead, he gave him suggestions, and there was an ever increasing exchange of views between Army Headquarters and Cairo.

The outcome of the Desert fighting was a matter of such supreme concern to General Auchinleck that he must often have been tempted, and was in fact pressed from London, to go and command the 8th Army himself. What held him back was the fact that his post was at the centre of affairs in the whole Middle East, and he felt he must not become absorbed in one part of it. The studious correctness of his relations with General Ritchie was in keeping with the British respect, amounting almost to reverence, for the chain of command. General Rommel, it will have been noticed, had no use for such niceties. His method of command was domineering and personal. He took charge whenever and wherever he thought the added impetus of his presence was most needed. This method has many obvious dangers, and indeed might be disastrous, but applied at critical moments by an expert tactician it had certainly produced results.

On assuming command of the 8th Army General Auchinleck at once changed the policy. He felt so weak in tanks and artillery that it was doubtful if he could hold on at Matruh and Sidi Hamza. He credited the enemy with a superiority in tanks that would enable them to pierce the British centre or envelop the southern flank; if either of these things happened, defeat in detail would probably result.[1] He was convinced of the need to preserve the 8th Army's freedom of action, and he therefore could not risk being pinned down at Matruh. At 4.15 a.m. on 26th June he issued fresh orders, the gist of which had been given to Corps Commanders just before midnight.

These orders laid down that he no longer intended to fight a decisive action at Matruh and Sidi Hamza. Instead, the enemy was to be fought over the large area between the meridian of Matruh and the El Alamein gap. General Auchinleck's aim in his own words was 'to keep all troops fluid and mobile, and strike at [the] enemy from all sides. Armour not to be committed unless very favourable opportunity presents itself. At all costs and even if ground has to be given up [I] intend to keep 8th Army in being and to give no hostage to fortune in shape of immobile troops holding localities which can easily be isolated.' To this end every infantry division was to reorganize itself into 'brigade battle-groups'—an idea which deserves a word of explanation.

In the last chapter it was described how General Ritchie, convinced of the need to exploit all the available gun-power, set about the creation of mobile columns from his existing divisions. The remainder, or static element, of each division was to occupy the frontier defences while the columns carried out their roving role towards Tobruk. The enemy did not allow time for anything much to be achieved in this way, but General Ritchie stuck to his idea—which must have had the

[1] In the early morning of 26th June the probable figures were: in 1st Armoured Division and 7th Motor Brigade about 155 tanks apart from 19 'I' tanks; Germans 60, and Italians 44. Less than 50 of the British tanks were Grants. Very few of the German 'Specials' were present.

blessing of the Commander-in-Chief—and on 22nd June ordered all infantry divisions to reorganize into 'brigade battle-groups', in which the principal arm would be the artillery, with detachments of other arms and only enough infantry to provide close escorts. In the circumstances little could be done towards carrying out this order, but when General Auchinleck changed the policy into one of 'fluid defence' he endorsed the idea of reorganizing divisions into forward and rearward elements and appointed destinations for the latter in the El Alamein positions.[1] In the 10th Corps the forward elements of the 50th and 10th Indian Divisions were each to consist of the divisional headquarters with one brigade group and all the divisional artillery. In the 13th Corps the New Zealand and 5th Indian Divisions were to be similarly 'streamlined'. It is noteworthy that General Freyberg invoked his charter, by which any change in organization would have had to be referred to his Government, and kept two of his brigades forward. Indeed, the reason for not having all three was that even by borrowing transport from the 10th Indian Division it was only possible to make two of the New Zealand Brigades mobile; the third, which had not yet arrived, was therefore held back east of El Alamein.

Whether the fluid tactics were appropriate to the occasion or not, they were certainly new and entirely unpractised. The British tactical doctrine for a withdrawal had for many years insisted that anything in the nature of a running fight must be avoided. Thus the 8th Army was facing a bewildering number of changes. Its Commander had been replaced; it was retreating before a thrusting enemy; it had barely prepared itself for one kind of battle when it was ordered to fight another; and in the midst of all this it was told to change its organization and its tactics. But before anything could be done in the way of reorganization, the enemy put an end to one uncertainty by starting to attack.

Meanwhile the Desert Air Force had continued to do its utmost to delay the enemy, whose leading troops had reached a point on the coast road about twenty-eight miles west of Matruh on the night of 24th June. Next morning 'thousands of enemy vehicles' were seen moving east from Misheifa, against which the Bostons made ten attacks and the Baltimores three, flying a total of 98 sorties during the day. Nor was this all, for the day-bombers were backed up by every possible fighter-bomber and 'ground-strafing' fighter, which flew between them 115 sorties. These attacks led to many entries in the *Panzerarmee's* diary: hourly attacks on 90th Light Division, causing over 70 casualties; repeated low-level and bomber attacks on the

---

[1] Little existed, as yet, in the way of defended localities between El Alamein station and the Qattara depression, and certainly nothing that could be called a 'line'.

Italian 20th Corps; the halting of the Littorio Division; the difficulty of getting fuel forward; and so on.

The bombers of No. 205 Group now forsook their attacks on Benghazi and the enemy's rearward airfields for more urgent tactical targets. The 'pathfinder' technique, by which the Albacores of the Fleet Air Arm illuminated targets at night for the bombers, has already been referred to. It was now made use of to enable bombing to be carried on round the clock. Starting two hours after the aircraft from the last daylight sorties had landed, Wellingtons, pathfinder Albacores, Bostons and Blenheims renewed the attacks on known concentrations. Between 9.30 p.m. and 4 a.m. eighty-six sorties were flown, and over one hundred tons of bombs dropped. The Italian 20th Corps reported uninterrupted bombing from 10.30 p.m. onwards. For the enemy this was more than a restless night—it was the beginning of an ordeal.

On 26th June the Desert Air Force excelled itself by flying 615 sorties, which was two and a half times the number of available aircraft. No. 233 Wing and its fighter squadrons, all of which had been withdrawn to Maaten Baggush to rest, were now ready to resume their operations. The day-bombers shuttled to and fro flying 118 sorties, while the fighter-bombers surpassed all previous efforts by flying 178. Early in the morning they dispersed a petrol convoy, which caused delay to both Panzer Divisions. The remaining fighters flew 310 sorties, and to do this some aircraft were flown on as many as seven sorties and some of the pilots flew five. Difficulties arose over the nearness of the bomb-line to the British troops, and another feature of the day was a brief reappearance of the *Luftwaffe* over the battlefield in strength. Six of the Boston raids were intercepted by fighters, and the Baltimores were also attacked. At 5 p.m. a force of twenty-six Ju. 88s and twenty-three Ju. 87s was intercepted about ten miles south of Minqar Qaim, but not before the New Zealanders had had sixty-two casualties. The enemy's losses in aircraft for the day were four, while the British lost twelve, including a Beaufighter and three Spitfires. The German claim was twenty-nine.

By the afternoon of 26th June the 10th Indian Division (5th, 21st and 25th Brigades) was in the Matruh defences, and the 50th Division (69th and 151st Brigades) was south of Gerawla, all under the 10th Corps. In the 13th Corps, the New Zealand Division (less the 6th Brigade) was on the southern escarpment about Minqar Qaim, and the 5th Indian Division (of one Brigade only, the 29th, and two field regiments) was divided into several detachments. One of these was near Sidi Hamza, one at Pt 222, and another at Bir el Hukuma. In addition this Brigade provided two columns ('Gleecol' and 'Leathercol') to operate between the two escarpments and cover the thinnest part of the minefields. The 1st Armoured Division was some miles away to the south-west, having been joined by both armoured brigades (4th and 22nd) and both motor brigades (7th, and 3rd Indian which was under orders to return to Amiriya to refit).[1] The enemy had made light contact on the previous day and Field-Marshal Rommel, who thought that the New Zealand Division was still at Matruh, decided to send the 90th Light Division between the escarpments to cut the coast road well to the east, while the *D.A.K.* drove off the 1st Armoured Division. For this purpose the 21st Panzer Division would move north of the Sidi Hamza-Minqar Qaim escarpment and the 15th Panzer south of it. The 20th Corps was to support the *D.A.K.* and the 10th and 21st Corps were to contain Matruh on the west.

The advance began late in the evening of 26th June, after the *D.A.K.* had been delayed by shortage of fuel and incessant air attacks in which their Headquarters and both Panzer Divisions and both Italian Corps reported considerable losses. The 90th Light Division, however, managed to pass through the thin minefield 'nose to tail' and scattered 'Leathercol', while the 21st Panzer did likewise to 'Gleecol'. That was all the fighting for the day, but the way was open for the further advance of 90th Light. Communications in the 29th Indian Infantry Brigade had broken down, but the impression gained was of a big break-through, and an attempt was made to withdraw most of the Brigade some miles to the east. The detachments at Sidi Hamza and Bir el Hukuma were ordered to stay where they were, but in fact the Brigade had become scattered and was only able to re-form as two small columns and a weak reserve. Conflicting reports of these happenings reached the higher headquarters and no one knew quite what had occurred. It seemed however that a hundred tanks had broken through and were being engaged by the columns of 29th Indian Infantry Brigade.

At daybreak on the 27th the enemy resumed the advance. The 90th Light Division found itself in an exposed position and was heavily shelled by the 50th Division, but came across an isolated battalion of the 151st Infantry Brigade—the 9th Durham Light Infantry—and almost destroyed it in a fierce action during which Private A. Wakenshaw won a posthumous Victoria Cross for his gallantry in continuing to serve an anti-tank gun when mortally wounded. Artillery fire prevented the enemy from following up this success, and the 90th Light Division, which was now very weary, withdrew some distance and lay low until the afternoon. Farther west on 10th Corps' front the 5th

---

[1] The 4th Armoured Brigade, commanded since 24th June by Brigadier A. F. Fisher, comprised 1st, 6th and 8th Royal Tank Regiment and one squadron 9th Lancers. In the 22nd Armoured Brigade were 3rd and 4th County of London Yeomanry. The 2nd Armoured Brigade was 'off the board' re-equipping various regiments; the first to be ready, the Bays, was to join 22nd Armoured Brigade on 28th June.

Indian Infantry Brigade had tried to advance southwards to strike the enemy near the minefield gap, but encountered opposition, probably from the Pavia Division of the 10th Corps, and failed to get up the northern escarpment.

During the morning the *D.A.K.*, unaware of the presence of the New Zealand Division, had not achieved very much. The 15th Panzer Division advanced east above the escarpment and the 21st Panzer Division below it. As a precaution the Littorio Division moved behind and to the north of the 21st. Almost at once the 15th Panzer was attacked by the 4th Armoured Brigade and the 7th Motor Brigade and was held up. The 21st Panzer meanwhile moved to below Minqar Qaim to block the passage down the escarpment which may have been thought to be a probable line of withdrawal for the quantity of vehicles reported to be facing 15th Panzer. At about 10 a.m. the 21st Panzer Division reported a large amount of transport below the escarpment as well, which was in fact the transport of the 5th New Zealand Infantry Brigade. These vehicles had to escape rapidly east, and climbed the escarpment to a point near Mahatt abu Batta. Soon after this an artillery duel began, while the main enemy columns moved on towards Bir Shineina. At noon, the 15th Panzer Division being still held up, and attempts to bring 20th Corps into action proving unavailing, the *D.A.K.* ordered 21st Panzer to attack the concentration at Minqar Qaim.[1] Field-Marshal Rommel drove the 90th Light Division on again, permitting it to move farther inland to avoid shell fire, but insisting that it was to cut the coast road by the evening. At 2 p.m. the 21st Panzer Division began to encircle Minqar Qaim, and the Littorio moved up to near Bir Shineina. The Ariete and Trieste Divisions were placed under command of the *D.A.K.*

See also Map 30

At 8th Army Headquarters General Auchinleck, waiting for the battle to develop, had been considering what to do if he were forced to withdraw. At 11.20 a.m. he sent personal messages to Generals Holmes and Gott telling them that if it became necessary both Corps would disengage, withdraw in concert to a line running from the escarpment just west of Fuka to Minqar Omar (thirty miles to the south) and there resume the battle. The signal for this would be the code word 'Pike'.

At 12.30 p.m. General Gott reported to Army Headquarters by telephone the impressions gained during a visit to the New Zealand Division at Minqar Qaim. The Division was being heavily shelled, and he had given General Freyberg permission to 'side step' if necessary. He had refused a request for some 'I' tanks because he wished to

[1] 21st Panzer Division is now known to have had only 5 Pzkw IIs and 16 Pzkw IIIs.

keep his armour concentrated. The B.G.S. 8th Army replied that he would arrange for the 10th Corps to attack southwards to relieve the pressure. At about 3 p.m. General Holmes received orders accordingly, and told the 50th Division to seize the line of the northern escarpment on either side of Bir Sarahna, starting at 7.30 p.m. During the night the 5th Indian Infantry Brigade was also to get on to the escarpment farther west.

By about 3.40 p.m. the 21st Panzer Division was attacking the New Zealanders from the north, north-east, and east. These attacks were easily held, but the enemy's eastern group, working round to the south, compelled the transport of the 4th New Zealand Brigade to withdraw westwards and sent that of the 5th New Zealand Brigade scurrying headlong to the south 'into the blue'. Moreover the attack from the south was threatening, and at about 4 p.m. General Freyberg asked the 1st Armoured Division for support. The 4th Armoured Brigade was just withdrawing to about ten miles west of Minqar Qaim, and the 3rd County of London Yeomanry were sent to the New Zealanders. They found a confused situation with New Zealand vehicles between them and the enemy, and were fired at by the New Zealand artillery. It happened that the Bays were just arriving from the east with a job lot of tanks to join 1st Armoured Division, and the double threat caused the enemy to stop attacking and prepare to defend himself.

General Gott's intention on 27th June had been to delay the enemy for as long as possible on the positions which his troops held at the start of the day, but in accordance with General Auchinleck's plans for a mobile defence he had issued instructions for withdrawal if this should be necessary. (These instructions were issued before the receipt of General Auchinleck's 'Pike' plan.) The first stage was to be to a line some eight miles from Fuka and covering it from the west and south. Divisions were to move there on roughly parallel routes, the 5th Indian on the north, the New Zealand Division in the centre, and the 1st Armoured to the south; each division would find its own rearguard. This stage was to begin on the receipt of a code word for each division, not necessarily at the same time. The second bound would be to the El Alamein line. The wording of Gott's instructions shows that he had clearly in mind Auchinleck's wish that the armour was not to be committed except in very favourable circumstances.

It seems clear, though the reasons are not recorded, that during the afternoon of 27th June General Gott came to the conclusion that the enemy's move against Minqar Qaim threatened to split his Corps in two. He had been told by General Auchinleck that no formation was to become isolated and pinned to its ground, and he apparently decided that he must soon withdraw. He had already reported to 8th Army that the 1st Armoured Division was to bring its armour into reserve at the end of its present engagement (with 15th Panzer Division), and at about 5 p.m. a garbled message from 13th Corps reached General Lumsden which appeared to convey the news that the New Zealand Division had left Minqar Qaim and that he (Lumsden) had discretion to withdraw east of the Bir Khalda track. This he did not do. A somewhat similar message—untimed—was sent to the New Zealand Division. Both are inexplicable, and there is no clue as to who sent them, other than that the use of the word 'I' in each suggests that it may well have been General Gott.

At 5 p.m. General Freyberg was wounded by a shell splinter and handed over command of his Division to Brigadier L. M. Inglis of the 4th New Zealand Infantry Brigade. Inglis knew that General Gott had said that the New Zealand Division's ground was not vital and decided that the Division must withdraw that night, for as far as he could see it was almost surrounded and his artillery ammunition was down to about 35 rounds a gun. But he was by no means clear where to go. Soon after 5 p.m. a veiled enquiry over the radio telephone elicited from 13th Corps a reply that was understood to mean Bab el Qattara, twenty miles south-west of El Alamein, which indicated the *second* stage of the Corps' plan for withdrawal. Brigadier Inglis accordingly appointed a rendezvous in the neighbourhood of the El Alamein line.

At 7.20 p.m. the 13th Corps issued the code words to begin the *first* stage of withdrawal and gave destinations for the 5th Indian and 1st Armoured Divisions near Fuka. There is little doubt that General Gott was trying to conform to the Army Commander's 'Pike' plan and it is noteworthy that although the New Zealand Division's code word was included in this message, there is no mention of any destination for it—a possible explanation being that this had already been given and that the New Zealand Division was not expected to rendezvous in the Fuka area at all.

As soon as he had issued his code words General Gott reported his action to 8th Army, who thereupon issued 'Pike' to the 10th Corps, hoping thereby to cancel the attack that General Holmes had been ordered to carry out and start the 10th Corps withdrawing. Before describing the fortunes of the 10th Corps it will be convenient to round off the events of the night in 13th Corps' sector.

At about 9.15 p.m. General Lumsden visited the New Zealand Division, and Brigadier Inglis suggested that the 1st Armoured Division should co-operate in a combined withdrawal in the moonlight, but General Lumsden did not agree, partly, presumably, because he had orders from 13th Corps as to his route and partly because his refill of petrol lay at Bir Khalda. But he agreed to take under his wing the 21st New Zealand Battalion which was protecting the petrol dump and the transport of the 5th New Zealand Infantry Brigade.[1] Brigadier

[1] In the event the New Zealand units withdrew independently.

Inglis then carried out his own bold plan, which was for the 4th New Zealand Brigade, in whose state of training he had great confidence, to clear a gap for the rest of the Division to pass through. This was brilliantly successful, and caused heavy casualties in the 1st Battalion 104th Regiment. The 4th Brigade attacked eastward with bomb and bayonet and broke through after a wild mêlée during which the exploits of Captain C. H. Upham led, after further acts of gallantry in July, to the award of a Bar to the Victoria Cross he had won in Crete. Brigadier Inglis at the last moment decided that his headquarters, his reserve group and the 5th Brigade would not directly follow the 4th, which would have meant driving through the thoroughly stirred-up enemy, but would move south for a couple of miles and then turn east. A complication was that the 5th Brigade's transport had been scattered during the afternoon and could not be reached, so that the men had to cling like bees to the available vehicles and even to guns. Before the column eventually broke clear it crashed into a German tank leaguer, creating pandemonium: it was a dazed 21st Panzer Division which reported to *D.A.K.* that it had repulsed all attacks. Having dealt this hard blow the New Zealand Division reunited at its rendezvous by the next night, 28th June, having had over 800 casualties in the three days.

The 1st Armoured Division, which had received no petrol or supplies during the day, first moved to Bir Khalda to replenish, and started eastward just after midnight. It reached its area fifteen miles south-east of Fuka during the forenoon of 28th June.

We must now turn to the 10th Corps.

At 5.30 p.m. on 27th June General Holmes received information (which seems to have been premature) that the enemy had cut the coast road east of Gerawla. He decided, nevertheless, not to cancel the attack he had been ordered to make, but, as bad luck would have it, his headquarters were out of touch with 8th Army from 7.30 p.m. until 4.30 a.m. next day and only then did the 10th Corps learn that the 13th Corps was withdrawing and that General Auchinleck had decided to put the 'Pike' plan into effect. Meanwhile the 10th Corps' attack took place but achieved nothing. In the 50th Division the 151st Infantry Brigade hit the air, and the 69th met stiff opposition and failed to get on to the escarpment. The 5th Indian Infantry Brigade fared no better. The code word 'Pike' came too late to be acted upon that night.

At dawn on the 27th the fighters and the Bostons moved back to El Daba and the Baltimores to Amiriya. They were quickly fit for action again but information about the fighting on that day had been so meagre that it was impossible to lay down a clearly defined bomb-line. The Desert Air Force therefore turned its attention to the area west of the battle, where for most of the day it found plenty of good targets. The precaution was taken of maintaining fighter sweeps over the Matruh area, but the enemy's air activity was only slight. During the night the Wellingtons, led as before by pathfinder Albacores, and reinforced by Bostons and R.A.F. Liberators, continued the attacks on enemy concentrations.

On the morning of 28th June General Auchinleck had very little information about the situation of the two Corps, but at 11.45 a.m. he sent them a message saying that the enemy was reported to have a detachment at Maaten Baggush and clearly intended to attack Matruh from the south. The 10th Corps was not to be cut off but was to withdraw towards Fuka keeping above the northern escarpment. This crossed a message from General Holmes reporting that the enemy had cut the coastal road seventeen miles east of Matruh, and saying that he had three choices: to force the road block by a direct attack, to break out southwards and then turn east, or to concentrate both his divisions and fight it out. General Auchinleck replied 'No question of fighting it out. No time to stage deliberate attack along road for which there is probably no objective. You will slip out to-night with whole force on broad front, turn east on high ground and rally El Daba. 13 Corps will cover you.'

The 13th Corps, however, was in no position to do so. General Gott was first told at 3.30 p.m. that he was to help, but not until 9.30 p.m. did he receive 8th Army's signal that the break-out was to begin at 9! In the general confusion and uncertainty no effective help could be arranged by the 13th Corps; it was obviously unable to comply with 8th Army's order to send back some of the New Zealand Division. During the evening the 21st Panzer Division crashed into the remains of the 29th Indian Infantry Brigade at Fuka. Brigadier Reid had been given discretion to withdraw if he were in imminent danger of being cut off, and he had collected transport to do so, but the attack was too swift for him and only small parties of survivors escaped. Late that evening the *D.A.K.* noted that the lengthening of the lines of communication was throwing a strain on the supply services, but the rapid advance on the 28th had quite made up for the initial delays.

The advance of the enemy columns east of Matruh had also made it necessary to withdraw the Bostons to Amiriya. The fighters, however, were kept forward about El Daba, for it had become known that the enemy's bombers and dive-bombers were moving up, and the protection of the 8th Army became the main occupation of the Desert Air Force. As it happened, there was surprisingly little air action against the withdrawing troops, the 203 sorties flown by the *Luftwaffe* that day being nearly all devoted to reconnaissance and defensive fighter tasks. At the special request of 10th Corps British fighter-bombers were sent out to deal with some guns that were firing on the road near Sidi Haneish. These formed part of a group of 90th Light Division, which later reported that they had been attacked by low-flying aircraft and the guns forced to change position. These attacks were made by the Kittyhawks of Nos. 3 R.A.A.F., 112, and 250 Squadrons and the Hurricanes of No. 274. That evening the airfields at El Daba seemed to be in some danger, but the 29th Indian Infantry Brigade's stand was made about twelve miles from the most westerly airfields still in use and gave time for a fighter wing to be flown off. The rest of the fighters remained to cover the 10th Corps next day. During the night 105 sorties were flown by Wellingtons, Liberators, Albacores, Blenheims, and Bostons, mainly against vehicles in the neighbourhood of Charing Cross.

General Holmes had made a simple plan for his break-out. The 50th and 10th Indian Divisions were to hold their positions during daylight on 28th June and at 9 p.m. were to burst out southwards for thirty miles and then turn east for a rendezvous near Fuka. The enemy had himself been attacking the 25th Indian Infantry Brigade intermittently, and part of the 151st Infantry Brigade became engaged towards dusk. The 21st Indian Infantry Brigade, which had been brought over from Matruh towards Gerawla, had two sharp actions with groups of the 90th Light Division. Then came the time to break out. Both divisions had planned to do this by brigade groups moving in variously organized columns. As might be expected it led to a spirited rough-and-tumble. Nearly every column ran across an enemy leaguer at one point or another and the confusion on both sides was indescribable. To break clear was made still more difficult by the presence of the enemy at Fuka, and the 10th Indian Division suffered particularly heavy losses in men and vehicles. General Holmes's Corps Headquarters barged its way through, like the rest, and was sent back to take over the 'Delta Force', which was being hastily formed, while the two divisions set about re-forming in rear of the El Alamein positions. The scattering of the 10th Corps upset General Auchinleck's plan for occupying these positions, and on 29th June he directed that the 30th Corps (1st South African, 50th, and 10th Indian Divisions) should take the right sector, and the 13th Corps (New Zealand and 5th Indian Divisions) the left. The two armoured divisions, 1st and 7th, the latter being an armoured division in name only, were to be in army reserve.

After remaining at El Daba to cover the remnants of the 10th Corps getting away from Matruh on 29th June, the fighter squadrons were withdrawn. During the night 29th/30th heavy attacks were made by Wellingtons, Bostons and Blenheims against the landing-ground at Sidi Barrani and other targets presented by road transport. On the 30th, when the enemy was already in contact with the El Alamein positions, every available aircraft was brought to bear in order to gain a little breathing space for the 8th Army. One of the troubles was the lack of information from the Army. Bomb-lines given by formations were often contradictory, and there were no requests for air support. Air Vice-Marshal Coningham's Advanced Headquarters were well forward, and in choosing his targets he used air reconnaissance reports and information brought back by the attacking aircraft. The enemy's columns were seen to be closely packed, and against them the Baltimores made three attacks and the Bostons six. A total of sixty-three sorties was flown in addition to the Kittyhawks' twenty-seven. The attack fell heaviest on the 90th Light Division, which was 'rather shaken' by it. The weather then took a hand; dust hid many targets, and sandstorms spread to the landing-grounds, causing the day-bombers to scatter over a wide area in search of places to land. There was hardly any enemy air activity, probably because the German fighters were in the process of moving forward to Fuka. That night the road, railway, and landing-grounds at Fuka received the concentrated attack of thirty-seven Wellingtons.

The mining of the harbour and destruction of the port facilities were successfully accomplished at Sollum on 23rd June and at Matruh on the 28th. In addition, at Matruh the water installations were destroyed and the water contaminated. The 'A' lighters continued to supply the Army with essential stores until the last possible moment.[1] Bombardment from the sea was considered, but the Naval Liaison Officer with the 8th Army reported on 30th June that it would be of little use as the troops were much dispersed and most of the fighting was taking place too far inland.

Ever since the fall of Tobruk Field-Marshal Rommel had been striving to hustle the British and prevent them from forming a front behind which to absorb the land and air reinforcements they were likely to receive. General Auchinleck's object had been to keep the 8th Army in being. Although it had suffered severe losses in men and material and was much disorganized, it was bewildered rather than demoralized; its framework still existed and it was certainly capable of further efforts, as events were soon to show. But this did not alter the fact that it was now back in a 'last ditch' position. Rommel was certain to waste no time, no matter how exhausted his troops might be and no matter what they lacked—including the full support of their air force, which was still struggling to make its way forward. The task before the 8th Army and the Desert Air Force was clear; they must at all costs parry the blow that was surely coming.

True to form, Rommel acted with the greatest vigour, and on 1st

[1] An 'A' lighter was an early form of tank landing craft.

July launched an attack just south of El Alamein. The fighting thus begun lasted on and off the whole month. When it died down both sides were exhausted, but the British were still in possession of the vital ground. This fighting is described in Chapter XIV.

CHAPTER XIII

MALTA AND THE WAR AT SEA (June – September 1942)

IN spite of the tremendous importance of replenishing Malta, the hard decision had been taken in April that the island would have to hold out without a convoy until mid-June.[1] It was eventually decided to run two convoys, one from each end, so as to encourage the enemy to spread his naval and air forces in opposing them.

Ever since the severe losses suffered by the Royal Navy at the end of 1941 the Commanders-in-Chief had been pressing for shore-based aircraft to make up for the absence of battleships and carriers in the Mediterranean Fleet—bombers and torpedo-bombers to replace the battleships, and long-range fighters to give the cover that had previously been provided from carriers. The Chiefs of Staff had agreed, but so far these aims had not been achieved and the Italian Fleet had now gained confidence. British aircraft of all types were too few and the crews had not the necessary experience in attacking warships, nor were their weapons all that could be desired—for instance, they needed an armour-piercing bomb heavier than 500-lb. and a more effective torpedo. Worst of all, instead of the Army advancing, as had been hoped, and capturing the airfields in the bulge of Cyrenaica, the enemy had struck first, and the passage of the June convoys coincided with the height of a land battle which was going badly for the British. Thus it happened that, instead of a starving Malta being saved by a victory in the Desert, it required all that the island base could do to help to save Egypt. The interplay of cause and effect in the battle for supplies has been remarked upon before; it reached its climax in the summer and autumn of 1942.

Plans for the two convoys (operation 'Harpoon' from the west and 'Vigorous' from the east) differed only in matters of detail from previous ones. Reconnaissance and striking force aircraft were more numerous than before. At Malta there were six Baltimores, four Wellingtons fitted with A.S.V. and three P.R.U. Spitfires for reconnaissance;[2] and six torpedo Wellingtons and one squadron of Beauforts as striking force with one squadron of Albacores for anti-submarine patrols. In

[1] See page 183.

[2] A.S.V. was a radar device for detecting the presence of surface vessels. P.R.U. means 'Photographic Reconnaissance Unit'.

Egypt there were one squadron of Marylands, one of A.S.V. Wellingtons and one of Hudsons for reconnaissance; and one squadron of Beauforts and, it was hoped, one of Liberators as striking force. In addition there were two squadrons of Albacores, one of A.S.V. Swordfish, one of Sunderlands and various Blenheims and Wellesleys available to maintain continuous anti-submarine patrols.[1] The sailing of the convoys was to be preceded by the bombing of enemy ports and airfields in Italy, Sicily, Sardinia, North Africa and Crete, and over Cyrenaica these attacks were to be continued during their passage. To simplify problems of giving fighter cover from Malta and of berthing and unloading after arrival, 'Harpoon' was to arrive at Malta one day before 'Vigorous', but if conflicting demands for either striking forces or cover arose, 'Vigorous' was to have the prior claim. Over Malta itself the superiority which had been won after the second *Wasp* trip on 9th May had got to be maintained, and on 3rd June and again on the 9th more Spitfires—fifty-nine in all—were flown in from H.M.S. *Eagle*. This brought the total number available on the island to ninety-five.[2] There was a night-flying Beaufighter flight, and a squadron of the coastal type was added for long-range cover and escort duties.[3] So far as anti-aircraft ammunition was concerned, daily expenditure had been getting less since 10th May when the fast minelayer *Welshman* had arrived with fresh stocks; to make sure, however, that there should be plenty, the *Welshman* with a further load of ammunition was to accompany the 'Harpoon' convoy as far as the Narrows and then go on alone at 28 knots to reach Malta at first light on the day the convoy was due. The only recent replenishment of aviation spirit had come to Malta early in May in the submarine *Olympus* but there was enough to cover immediate requirements.

---

[1] The squadrons which took part were:

	Malta	*Egypt*
Albacore	No. 830 (F.A.A.)	Nos. 821 & 826 (F.A.A.)
Baltimore	No. 69	
Beaufort	No. 217	No. 39
Blenheim		Nos. 203 and 13 (Hellenic)
Hudson		No. 459 (R.A.A.F.)
Maryland		No. 203
Spitfire	No. 2 P.R.U.	
Sunderland		No. 230
Swordfish (A.S.V.)		No. 815 (F.A.A.)
Wellesley		No. 47
Wellington (torpedo)	No. 38	
Wellington (A.S.V.)	No. 221 (Detachment)	No. 221

[2] These were divided between Nos. 126, 185, 249, and detachments from Nos. 601 and 603 squadrons.

[3] Night-flying Beaufighters—No. 1435 Flight. Coastal Beaufighters—No. 235 Squadron on detachment from the U.K.).

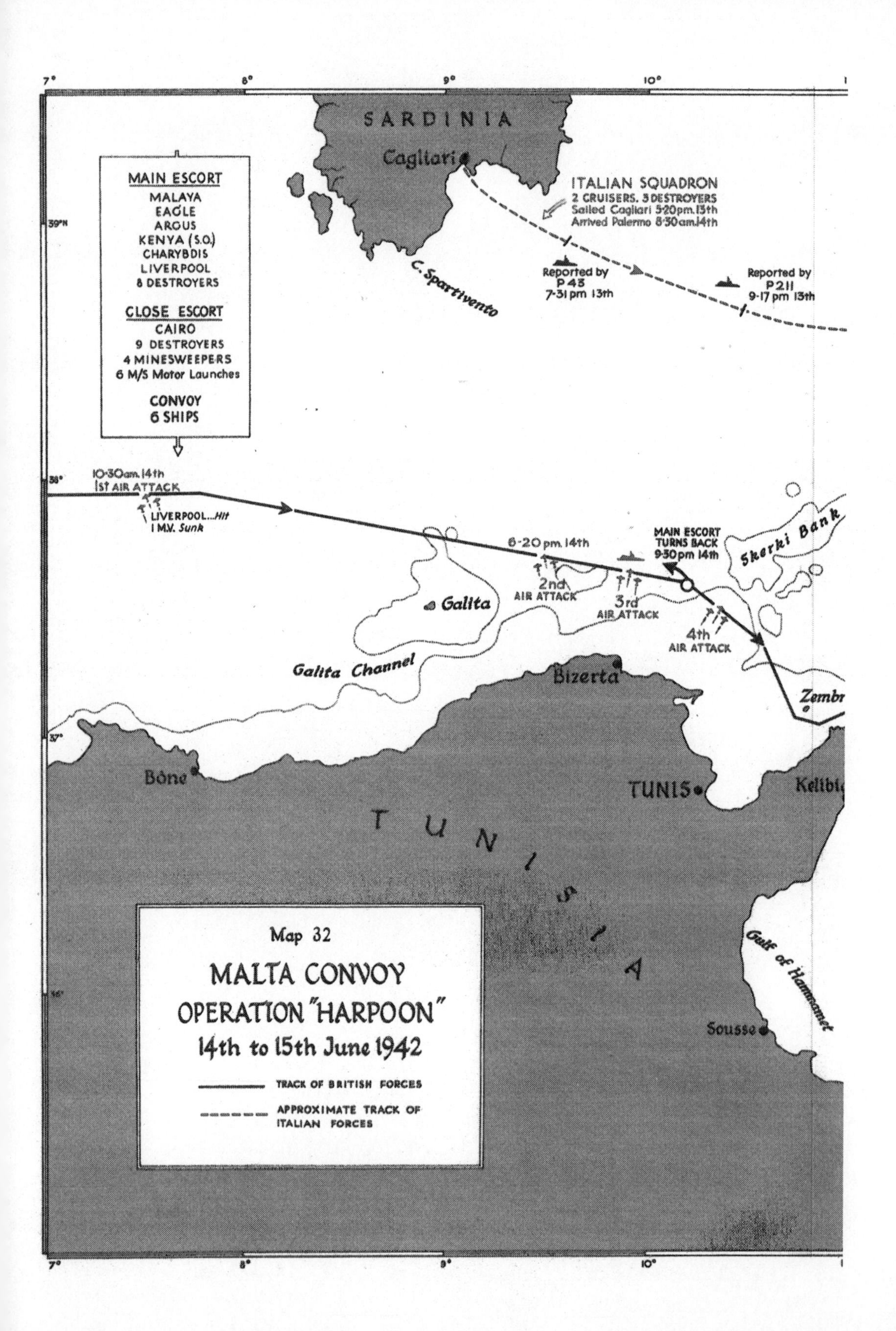
SARDINIA
Cagliari
ITALIAN SQUADRON
2 CRUISERS. 3 DESTROYERS
Sailed Cagliari 5·20pm.13th
Arrived Palermo 8·30am.14th
C. Spartivento
Reported by
P43
7·31pm 13th
Reported by
P211
9·17pm 13th
MAIN ESCORT
MALAYA
EAGLE
ARGUS
KENYA (S.O.)
CHARYBDIS
LIVERPOOL
8 DESTROYERS
CLOSE ESCORT
CAIRO
9 DESTROYERS
4 MINESWEEPERS
6 M/S Motor Launches
CONVOY
6 SHIPS
10·30am.14th
1st AIR ATTACK
LIVERPOOL...Hit
1 M.V. Sunk
6·20 pm.14th
2nd
AIR ATTACK
3rd
AIR ATTACK
4th
AIR ATTACK
MAIN ESCORT
TURNS BACK
9·30pm 14th
Skerki Bank
Galita
Galita Channel
Bizerta
Zembr
Bône
TUNIS
Kelibi
TUNISIA
Gulf of Hammamet
Sousse
7°
8°
9°
10°
39°N
38°
37°
36°
Map 32
MALTA CONVOY
OPERATION "HARPOON"
14th to 15th June 1942
TRACK OF BRITISH FORCES
APPROXIMATE TRACK OF
ITALIAN FORCES

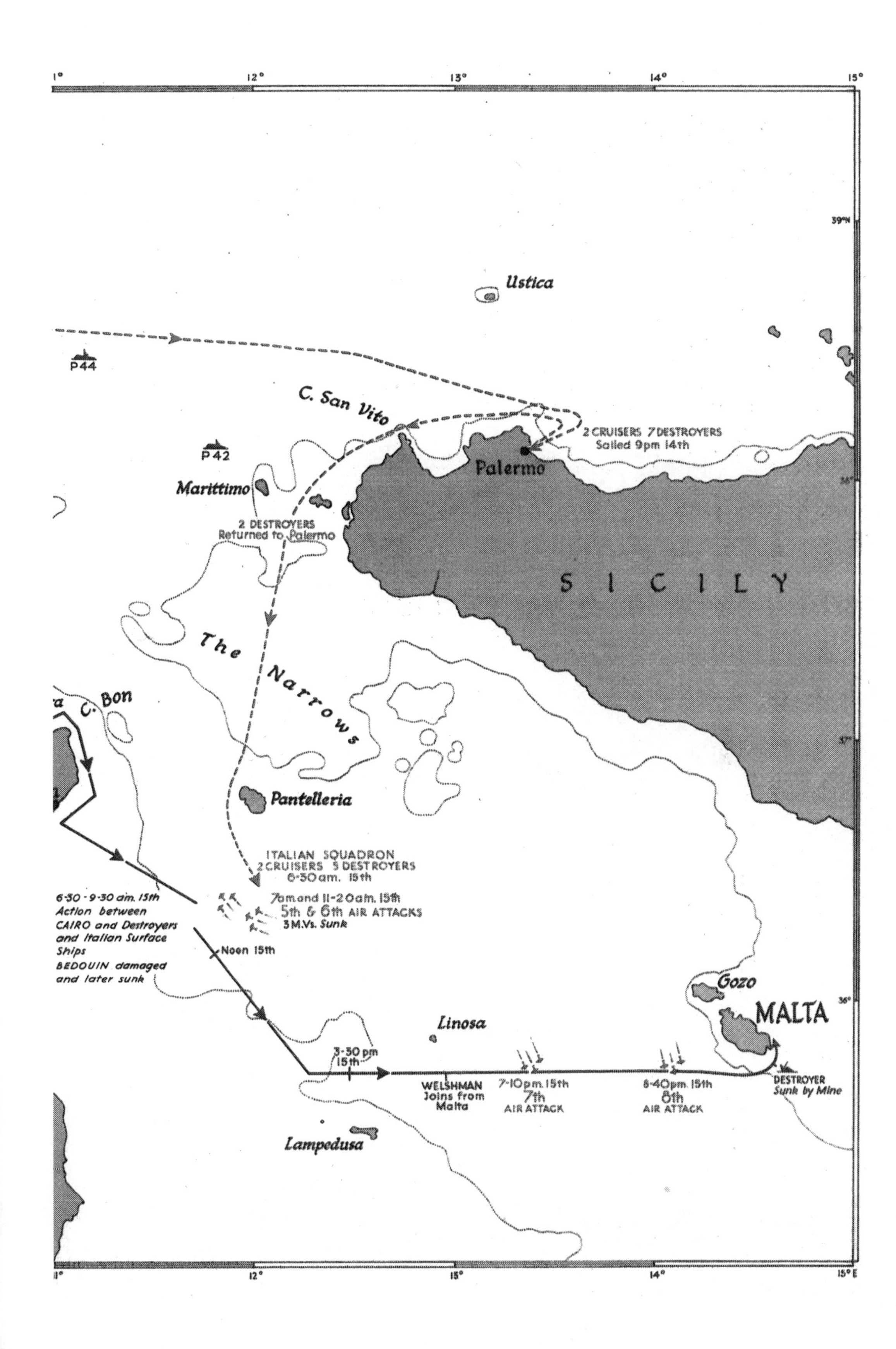

Ustica
P44
C. San Vito
2 CRUISERS 7 DESTROYERS
Sailed 9pm 14th
P42
Palermo
Marittimo
2 DESTROYERS
Returned to Palermo
SICILY
The Narrows
C. Bon
Pantelleria
ITALIAN SQUADRON
2 CRUISERS 5 DESTROYERS
6-30 am. 15th
6-30 - 9-30 am. 15th
Action between
CAIRO and Destroyers
and Italian Surface
Ships
BEDOUIN damaged
and later sunk
7am and 11-20 am. 15th
5th & 6th AIR ATTACKS
3 M.Vs. Sunk
Noon 15th
Gozo
MALTA
Linosa
3-30 pm
15th
WELSHMAN
Joins from
Malta
7-10 pm. 15th
7th
AIR ATTACK
8-40 pm. 15th
8th
AIR ATTACK
DESTROYER
Sunk by Mine
Lampedusa

OPERATION "HARPOON"

The action on 15th June 1942

Cruisers .... ▷ ▷ Destroyers .... > >
Convoy .... Cairo ....
Fleets .... Hunts ....
Italian Cruisers .... Italian Destroyers ....
Air attack ....

Position of convoy at 0630: 36° 23′ N; 11° 45′ E

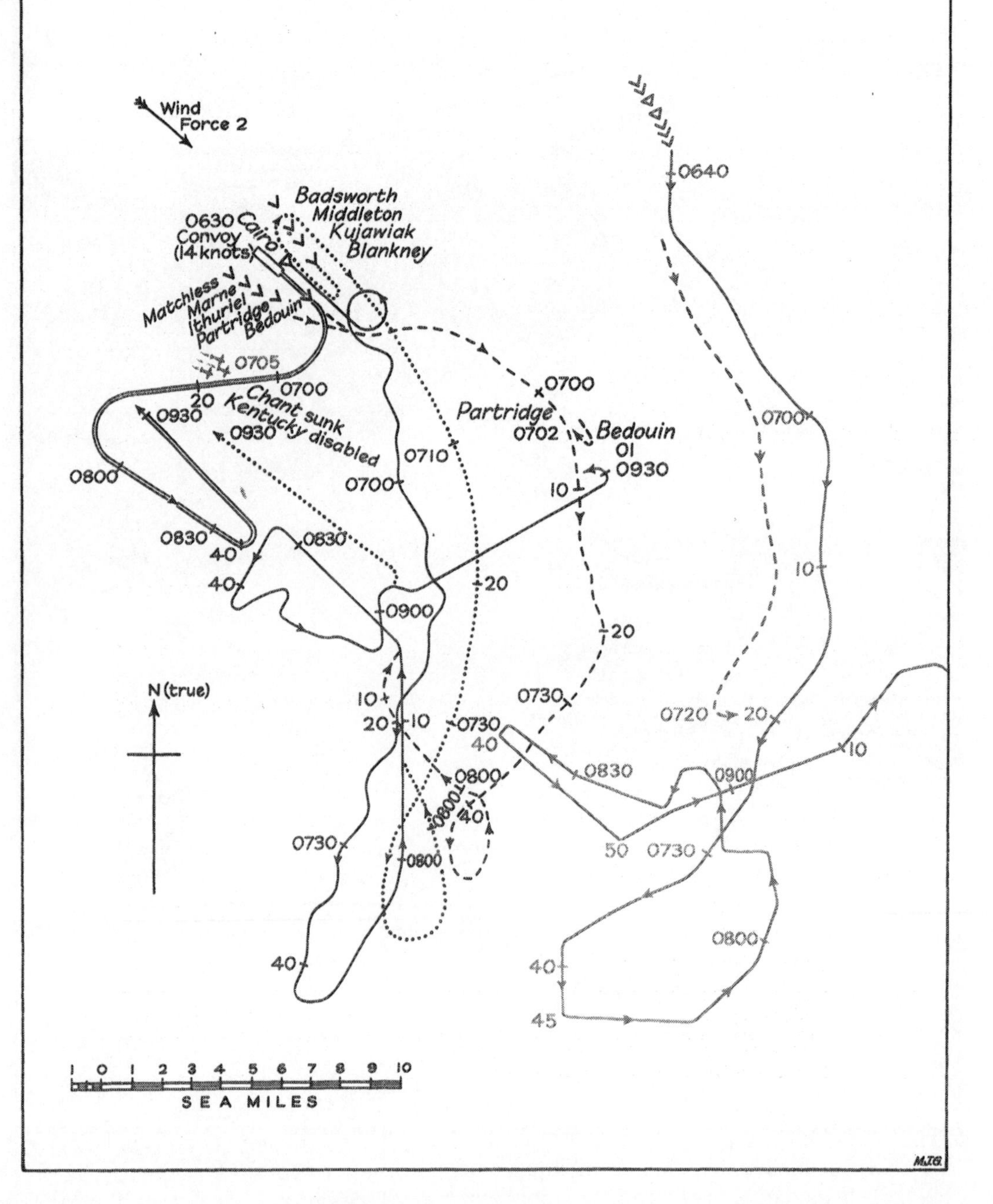

See Map 32

The six ships of the 'Harpoon' convoy were to be covered as far as the Skerki Channel by the main covering force—the battleship *Malaya*, the *Eagle* and *Argus*, carrying only twenty-two fighters between them, the cruisers *Kenya*, *Liverpool* and *Charybdis* and eight destroyers.[1] From there only the anti-aircraft cruiser *Cairo* (Captain C. C. Hardy) and five Fleet and four Hunt class destroyers, known, as had become the custom, as Force X, were to continue to Malta. Until it came within range of those Spitfires equipped with long-range tanks, Force X would depend for fighter cover on the very few available Beaufighters. Four fleet minesweepers and six minesweeping motor launches were also to accompany the convoy to sweep it into harbour and subsequently reinforce the seriously depleted minesweeping flotilla at Malta. The tanker *Brown Ranger*, with her own escort, not accompanying the convoy but cruising independently along its route, was to refuel the smaller warships, particularly those of Force X, so that they might turn back on reaching Malta without drawing on the island's precious stock of oil. Finally, four submarines were stationed on a line between Cagliari in Sardinia and the western end of Sicily to report and attack the enemy if sighted. Vice-Admiral A. T. B. Curteis was to command the operation, flying his flag in H.M.S. *Kenya*. His forces were weak in comparison with those of the previous July and September, but, even so, they had been assembled with difficulty, for since the closing months of 1941 the Royal Navy had lost many ships and had shouldered heavy new responsibilities. However, there were grounds for hoping that the escort would be strong enough. The main units of the Italian Fleet, which were at Taranto, were more likely to dispute the passage of the convoy from the east, and the enemy's air effort would be divided between the two convoys and the battle in the desert.

Five of the merchantmen, the British *Troilus*, *Burdwan* and *Orari*, the American *Chant* and the Dutch *Tanimbar*, left the Clyde on the 5th June and entered the Mediterranean during the night of the 11th/12th. The sixth ship, the American tanker *Kentucky*, joined from Gibraltar, and by the morning of the 12th convoy and escort were at full strength and steaming east at 12 to 13 knots. Shadowing by German and Italian aircraft began early on the 13th and the convoy was reported by at least one submarine. During that day the *Cairo* and eleven destroyers were refuelled from the *Brown Ranger*, and three destroyers from the *Liverpool*. By dawn on the 14th the convoy was approaching the area in which attacks by the enemy's twenty bombers and fifty torpedo-bombers based in Sardinia would begin. The morning was

[1] Stowage for aircraft in these two old carriers compared unfavourably with that in more modern carriers such as the *Ark Royal*. Embarked for this operation were: in *Eagle* 16 Hurricanes of Nos. 801 and 813 Squadrons and 4 Fulmars of No. 807 Squadron; in *Argus* 2 Fulmars of No. 807 Squadron and 18 Swordfish of No. 824 Squadron.

21

bright and clear. Such wind as there was came from astern and in order to operate their aircraft the *Eagle* and *Argus* would have to expose themselves outside the shelter of the main screen.

Attacks began at 10.30 with shallow dive-bombing by two groups of Italian fighter-bombers. These did no harm, but half an hour later twenty-eight Savoia torpedo-bombers, escorted by twenty Macchi fighters, and ten Cant high-level bombers came in simultaneously. They torpedoed the *Liverpool* and the Dutch ship *Tanimbar*, and the merchantman sank within a few minutes. The *Liverpool*, hit in the engine room and reduced in speed to 3 or 4 knots, was ordered back to Gibraltar. Towed by one destroyer and screened by a second she seems to have drawn attention away from the convoy, and was fortunate indeed not to be hit from the air again. Meanwhile the main body went east undisturbed, until at 6.20 p.m., when still 150 miles from Sicily, it was attacked from that island by ten German Ju. 88s. They were difficult to see, but the Fleet Air Arm fighters worried them, and although both carriers had narrow escapes no ship was damaged. Next came a heavy combined attack at 8 p.m. The torpedo-bombers were again Italian, but the bombers were German Ju. 88s and there were some Ju. 87 dive-bombers too. In the middle of all this a periscope was sighted, first ahead of the convoy and then close to the *Malaya*, and the explosion of depth charges was added to that of bombs and anti-aircraft shell. The *Argus* escaped several torpedoes from the Savoias only by her handiness under helm, but, although the timing of the attacks was better than it had been during the forenoon, the enemy had no further success. The Fleet Air Arm fighters were doing valiantly, but during the combined attacks they had been busy with the much more numerous enemy fighters and had little time left for the bombers. During daylight on the 14th seven British fighters were lost from the *Eagle* and *Argus*. The enemy's recorded losses for the day amounted to seventeen aircraft.

At 9 p.m. four Beaufighters from Malta arrived to take over from the hard worked naval airmen and at 9.30, as the Skerki Channel was reached, Admiral Curteis hauled round to the west with the main covering force while the convoy (now of five ships) and Force X, the *Cairo*, nine destroyers, four minesweepers and six minesweeping motor launches stood on under Captain Hardy. Around 10 o'clock one more shallow dive-bombing attack came out of the dusk ahead, but had no success. This ended the fighting on the 14th.

In the previous September the route chosen for the convoy had passed close to Sicily to avoid minefields; this time it was thought better to hug the African shore. Captain Hardy accordingly altered course to pass inside Zembra island. Attacks by enemy aircraft and submarines were to be expected again next day; but now, during darkness and in narrow waters, motor torpedo boats were more to be feared. As it happened, the sea was too rough for these craft and the night passed quietly.

The threat from heavy surface ships did not seem great; the enemy had never yet sent any south of the Narrows to dispute the passage of a convoy, and perhaps it was too readily assumed that he never would. In point of fact the Italian VII Division, the 6-inch cruisers *Eugenio di Savoia* (Flag of Admiral A. da Zara) and *Montecuccoli* and three destroyers had left Cagliari on the evening of the 13th with orders to intercept fast enemy ships which might be sent on to Malta in advance of the main British force. None was reported and the VII Division was told to enter Palermo and await orders. British submarines had seen the Italian ships between Sardinia and Sicily, and Wellingtons from Malta were sent to attack them. Unfortunately the Wellington carrying the main supply of flares crashed on taking off and the others had to return without attacking. Having spent daylight of the 14th in Palermo the Italian ships (now two cruisers and seven destroyers) were spotted as they put to sea at dusk, but their subsequent course could not be determined. At Malta, Admiral Leatham judged they would pass through the Straits of Messina and join the Italian main Fleet which had left Taranto at 2.30 that afternoon. A Fleet Air Arm patrol was therefore stationed above the Straits and a striking force of Albacores held in readiness. That was all that Malta could do, for its Wellingtons and Beauforts were about to be launched against the Italian battleships which were clearly steering to intercept the convoy coming from Alexandria.

On hearing that the Italians had left Palermo Admiral Curteis had a difficult decision to make. Should he send either or both of his remaining cruisers to reinforce Captain Hardy or keep them to defend his carriers against tomorrow's air attacks from Sardinia? It was a gamble either way. He was short of fighters and the *Eagle*, *Argus* and *Malaya* had pitifully weak anti-aircraft armaments. Admiral Curteis judged that the Italian ships were unlikely to enter an area in which they might expect to come under heavy air attack from Malta, but he considered that even if they took this risk the existing escort was strong enough to prevent them from doing harm. He therefore decided against sending either ship, and his decision was subsequently upheld by the Admiralty. Thus, Captain Hardy, with five Fleet destroyers, four Hunts, and one rearmed old cruiser with guns no bigger than the Hunts', was to find himself, while hampered by five merchantmen, facing two modern 6-inch cruisers and five Fleet destroyers.[1]

The VII Division had, in fact, been ordered to attack the British force to the south of Pantelleria at first light on the 15th, and it was at daybreak that Captain Hardy, then thirty miles south of the island, received his first news of the enemy from one of five Beaufighters on

[1] Two Italian destroyers had been sent back to Palermo with engine defects.

their way to patrol above his ships. A few minutes later, just before 6.30, the Italian ships could be seen hull down against the brightening sky to the east. At once the *Bedouin* led out the other four Fleet destroyers to engage and hold them off, while the *Cairo* and the rest of the escort made smoke to cover the convoy which was ordered to alter course towards the Tunisian coast. If time could be gained an air striking force from Malta might turn the scale.

See Map 33

At 6.40 on 15th June the Italian cruisers opened accurate fire at over eleven miles, and five minutes later some of the Fleets replied, although they could as yet scarcely reach the enemy. The *Cairo* and the Hunts, as soon as they had screened the convoy with smoke, followed to join in the battle which for an hour took a southerly course with the faster Italians altering gradually round to the south-west, presumably to try to get a glimpse of the convoy. It was to their advantage to keep at a range at which the smaller but more numerous British guns could not all reach them, and, although the range from the Fleets was down for a time to five miles or less, the *Cairo* and the Hunts, who were farther to the west, cutting corners so as to keep between the enemy and the convoy, were never able to engage the Italian cruisers.

Soon after 7 o'clock the two leading Fleets, the *Bedouin* and *Partridge*, were hit and stopped and the fight passed them by. The Italian destroyers *Vivaldi* and *Malocello*, who had been having difficulty in keeping up, had been detached to harass the convoy; under fire from the British destroyers the *Vivaldi* had also been brought to a standstill. At 7.20 Admiral da Zara sent his remaining three destroyers to help the *Vivaldi* and continued the action with his two cruisers alone. These ships appear to have split their armament much of the time, each using two turrets to engage the Fleets and two to engage the *Cairo*. Twenty minutes later Captain Hardy, ordering his destroyers to concentrate on the *Cairo*, turned back towards the convoy followed by the Italian cruisers. At about this time the convoy had resumed its south-easterly course but as Captain Hardy approached, with the enemy following warily, he ordered the convoy to reverse its course once more, and at 8.30 the *Cairo* and destroyers again laid a smoke screen to hide the convoy's movements. Admiral da Zara at first tried to work round to the west, but he was now in the position of having to follow rather than to lead the enemy. He probably feared torpedo attack if he pressed too hard and at 8.40 he hauled right round to the east and stood away. Ordering the Hunts to stay with the convoy, Captain Hardy followed with the *Cairo* and the three remaining Fleets, but by 9.30 the enemy cruisers were out of sight and he turned back to the convoy. During the engagement the *Cairo* had received two 6-inch hits and the Italian cruisers had also been hit, but only the damage to the *Bedouin*, *Partridge* and *Vivaldi* was of any consequence.

Although the Italian ships had been held off, they had delayed the convoy for three hours from reaching the comparative safety of the short-range fighter cover from Malta, and by drawing away the main anti-aircraft defence they had exposed the convoy to air attack and thus to still further delay. Captain Hardy had felt it necessary to use the *Cairo* and all his destroyers to meet the immediate threat from a superior surface force, but scarcely had he left the convoy when eight Ju. 87s arrived. The Beaufighters which had originally reported the enemy had returned to Malta and no other fighters made contact until 9.30. The convoy had thus no defence except its own guns and those of the minesweepers, and the dive-bombers had little difficulty in sinking the *Chant* and disabling the *Kentucky*. In the circumstances it was fortunate that this was all. One of the sweepers, the *Hebe*, took the *Kentucky* in tow and the convoy proceeded with its speed thus reduced to about 6 knots.

An hour after the enemy cruisers had disappeared the convoy was once again steering south-east with the escort at full strength except for the *Bedouin* and *Partridge*. Long-range Spitfires were overhead, though nearly at the limit of their range, and after successfully driving off some German bombers at 10.40 they had to go back before the relief flight arrived. At 11.20, when the next attack came in, the convoy was again without cover and another merchantman, the *Burdwan*, was disabled. Malta was still 150 miles away, further air attacks were likely, and the Italian ships might come back at any moment. Captain Hardy decided to push on with the remaining two merchant ships—the *Troilus* and *Orari*—at their best speed, and sacrifice the *Kentucky* and *Burdwan*. It was a bitter decision to have to make. He left the *Hebe* to sink the *Kentucky* and the Hunt destroyer, *Badsworth*, to sink the *Burdwan*. There was one more, happily unsuccessful, dive-bombing attack before the Malta umbrella was reached.

It is not quite clear why Admiral da Zara broke off action when he did: perhaps he wished his destroyers to rejoin before continuing the engagement. Indeed in detaching his destroyers at all he seems to have shown more concern for the damaged *Vivaldi* than for concentrating on the destruction of the British, who had, he believed, a second cruiser present, possibly a heavy one. He mentions in his report on the battle that a mined area, of which he thought the British would be aware, lay between the convoy and Malta. He judged that the British would aim to pass north of this minefield, between it and Pantelleria. By standing to the east himself he would be in a position to renew the action at will and perhaps draw the enemy over the mines. Be that as it may, shortly after 9 o'clock he recalled his destroyers, except the

Premuda which was towing the *Vivaldi* into Pantelleria, and by 11.15 the *Oriani* and *Ascari* had rejoined. These destroyers had been attacked at 10.35 by four Fleet Air Arm Albacores, and at about the same time the cruisers had been attacked by two Beauforts escorted by sixteen Spitfires. Although a large number of Me. 109s were covering the Italian ships they did not succeed in interfering with the attacks; these, however, did no harm. This was all that Malta could manage to send at the time, the Wellingtons and the remainder of the Beauforts having just landed after attacking the Italian main Fleet.

Admiral da Zara now steered south over much the same water as during the morning's engagement. Here, soon after 1 p.m., he found the *Hebe* trying to overtake the convoy after her unsuccessful attempts to sink the *Kentucky*, and she was presently hit. Receiving a report from the *Hebe* at 1.41, Captain Hardy left the convoy, which was now some twenty-five miles south of the Italian ships, and with the *Cairo* and his three large destroyers stood towards the enemy. Hardly had the Italian ships come in sight when, at 1.55, they turned away to engage a target to the westward. This could only be the *Bedouin* and *Partridge*, but Captain Hardy now felt bound to turn back to his convoy, already more than ten miles off, though it meant leaving the damaged destroyers to their fate.

The *Partridge* had been ready to steam again by 7.45 and by 10 o'clock, in spite of interruptions by two Italian destroyers, she had the more seriously damaged *Bedouin* in tow. Progress was so slow that the Captain of the *Bedouin* decided to make for the Tunisian coast. When at 1.20 the Italian cruisers had been sighted again, the *Partridge* had slipped her tow, laid smoke around the *Bedouin* and then stood away in the hope of drawing the enemy's fire. This gallant intention was frustrated when at 2.25 an Italian aircraft torpedoed and sank the *Bedouin*; the *coup de grâce* to the *Kentucky* and perhaps to the *Burdwan* also came from the air about this time. The Italian cruisers, themselves under air attack from what must have been German or Italian aircraft, did not pursue the *Partridge* for long. She was next attacked by German bombers; her rudder was jammed hard over by near misses and took more than an hour to clear. She arrived at Gibraltar on the 17th—the same day as the *Liverpool*—miraculously enough without further incident. Survivors from the *Bedouin* were picked up by an Italian hospital ship after dark on the 15th.

At 3.30 Captain Hardy rejoined the convoy and two hours later, when south of Linosa, he was reinforced by the *Welshman* (six dual-purpose 4-inch guns) who had reached Malta that morning and had been sent out as soon as her stores were unloaded. By this time, unknown to Captain Hardy, the Italian ships were well on their way home. They had used a great deal of ammunition; the British convoy was entering the zone allocated to Italian submarines; and the danger of air attack from Malta was increasing. The Italian Admiralty decided that further action against the convoy should be left to submarines and aircraft, and recalled Admiral da Zara. German bombers made two further attacks before dark without doing damage. There still remained the danger from mines. It had been intended that the minesweepers should sweep ahead of the convoy as it approached the harbour. It was not now possible for the *Cairo* and destroyers to return westward without more fuel and ammunition and they too had to make for harbour. After the day's happenings it was perhaps not surprising that misunderstandings should arise as to the precise channel to be swept and the order in which ships should arrive. The *Badsworth* and the Polish *Kujawiak* (both Hunt class) and the *Orari*, *Matchless* and *Hebe* all struck mines. The *Kujawiak* sank, but the others were only slightly damaged and were able to reach the Grand Harbour.

Next evening, the 16th, the *Cairo* and the four undamaged destroyers—two Fleets and two Hunts—sailed for Gibraltar. They were repeatedly bombed the following day while passing along the North African coast but received no serious damage. That evening they joined Admiral Curteis who was waiting for them with the *Kenya* and *Charybdis*. The *Malaya* and the two carriers had gone on to Gibraltar.

The 15,000 tons of stores which reached Malta in the two merchantmen were quickly unloaded. Four merchantmen had been lost—two sunk by air attack and two disabled by air attack and subsequently sunk. Of the escort, the *Bedouin* had been disabled by gunfire and sunk by a torpedo-bomber, and the *Kujawiak* had been sunk by a mine. A cruiser had been damaged by a torpedo-bomber, one destroyer by gunfire, and two others and a sweeper by mines. The Italians had one destroyer damaged by gunfire. The Royal Air Force had lost five aircraft, the Fleet Air Arm seven, and the enemy at least twenty-two. It was a disappointing affair in which one British 6-inch cruiser might have turned the scale. For one 6-inch cruiser and the five Fleet destroyers should have been able to drive off Admiral de Zara's ships while the *Cairo* and the Hunts remained with the convoy and might perhaps have saved it from some, if not all, of its losses from air attack.

In the Eastern Mediterranean the complementary operation 'Vigorous' had been taking place, conducted from the headquarters of No. 201 Naval Co-operation Group R.A.F. by Admiral Harwood and Air Marshal Tedder. Once again Rear-Admiral Vian was in command afloat. Three months earlier, in March, in a gale of wind from the right quarter, his light cruisers and destroyers had held off a much heavier enemy force for two and a half hours.[1] In the long days of midsummer the conditions could hardly be so favourable, but if a superior force was met his intentions were again:

> 'To use smoke to cover the convoy and, when practicable, for the protection of our ships'

and

> 'To drive off the enemy by torpedoes, or by the threat of torpedoes, and to inflict early casualties by gunfire on two selected enemy ships.'

His plan was an elaboration of the March plan, but this time much would depend on whether the Italian Fleet could be damaged or discouraged by air striking forces and submarines, while the convoy and its escort were still at a safe distance. A suggestion that Admiral Somerville should bring the *Warspite* and two or three carriers from the Eastern Fleet through the Canal to strengthen the escort had been rejected as exposing these valuable ships to too great a risk from the air.

Nevertheless both convoy and escort were larger than in March. Admiral Vian again flew his flag in the *Cleopatra*, which with the *Dido* and *Euryalus*, and the *Hermione* from the Eastern Fleet, made four light cruisers armed with the dual-purpose 5·25 inch low- and high-angle gun. Three 6-inch cruisers, the *Newcastle* (Flag of Rear-Admiral W. G. Tennant), *Birmingham*, and the smaller *Arethusa*, had come from the Eastern Fleet, making seven cruisers in all and one anti-aircraft cruiser, the *Coventry*. Of the twenty-six destroyers, ten were from the Eastern Fleet. To the main escort were added four corvettes, two minesweepers to sweep ahead of the convoy entering Malta, four M.T.Bs and two unarmed rescue ships. The former battleship *Centurion*, unarmed except against air attack, was to masquerade as a fully armed capital ship.

See Map 34

In earlier operations submarines had been stationed in the approaches to Taranto and Messina, from where they made some valuable reports but had little opportunity to attack. This time the nine available boats from the 1st and 10th Flotillas were to act as a moving screen parallel to the convoy's route on the critical day while it was passing through the Central Mediterranean; on the preceding and following days they were to patrol in the areas through which the Italian Fleet was most likely to pass.

Some forty aircraft were available as a striking force, Wellingtons and Beauforts at Malta, and Beauforts at a landing-ground in Egypt near the Libyan border, all armed with torpedoes; in addition there were the United States Liberator bombers at their temporary base at

---

[1] See page 164ff.

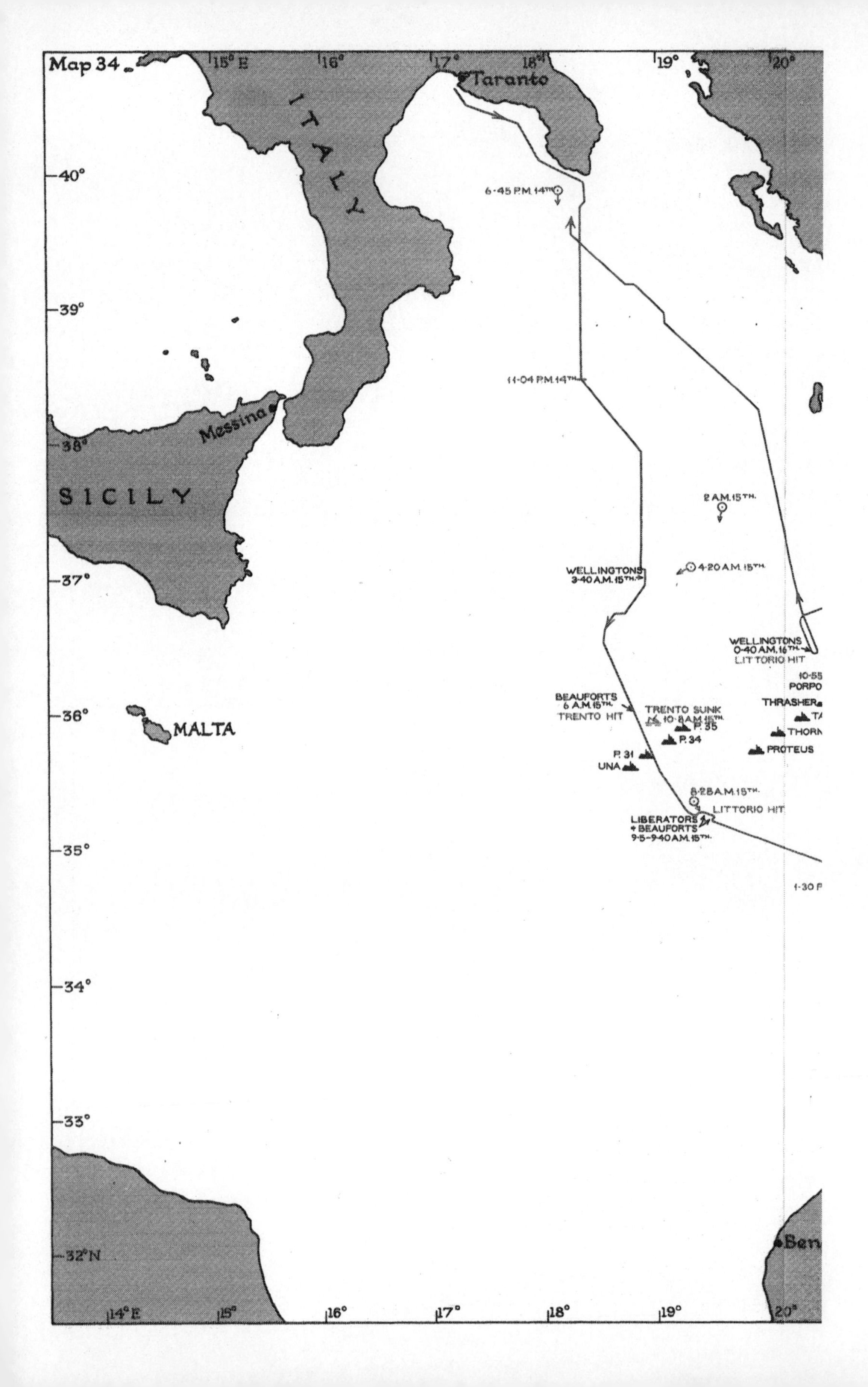

Map 34
ITALY
Taranto
SICILY
Messina
MALTA
6·45 P.M. 14TH
11·04 P.M. 14TH
2 A.M. 15TH.
4·20 A.M. 15TH.
WELLINGTONS
3·40 A.M. 15TH.
WELLINGTONS
0·40 A.M. 16TH.
LITTORIO HIT
BEAUFORTS
6 A.M. 15TH.
TRENTO HIT
TRENTO SUNK
10·8 A.M. 15TH.
THRASHER
PROTEUS
P. 35
P. 34
P. 31
UNA
8·28 A.M. 15TH.
LITTORIO HIT
LIBERATORS
+ BEAUFORTS
9·5–9·40 A.M. 15TH.

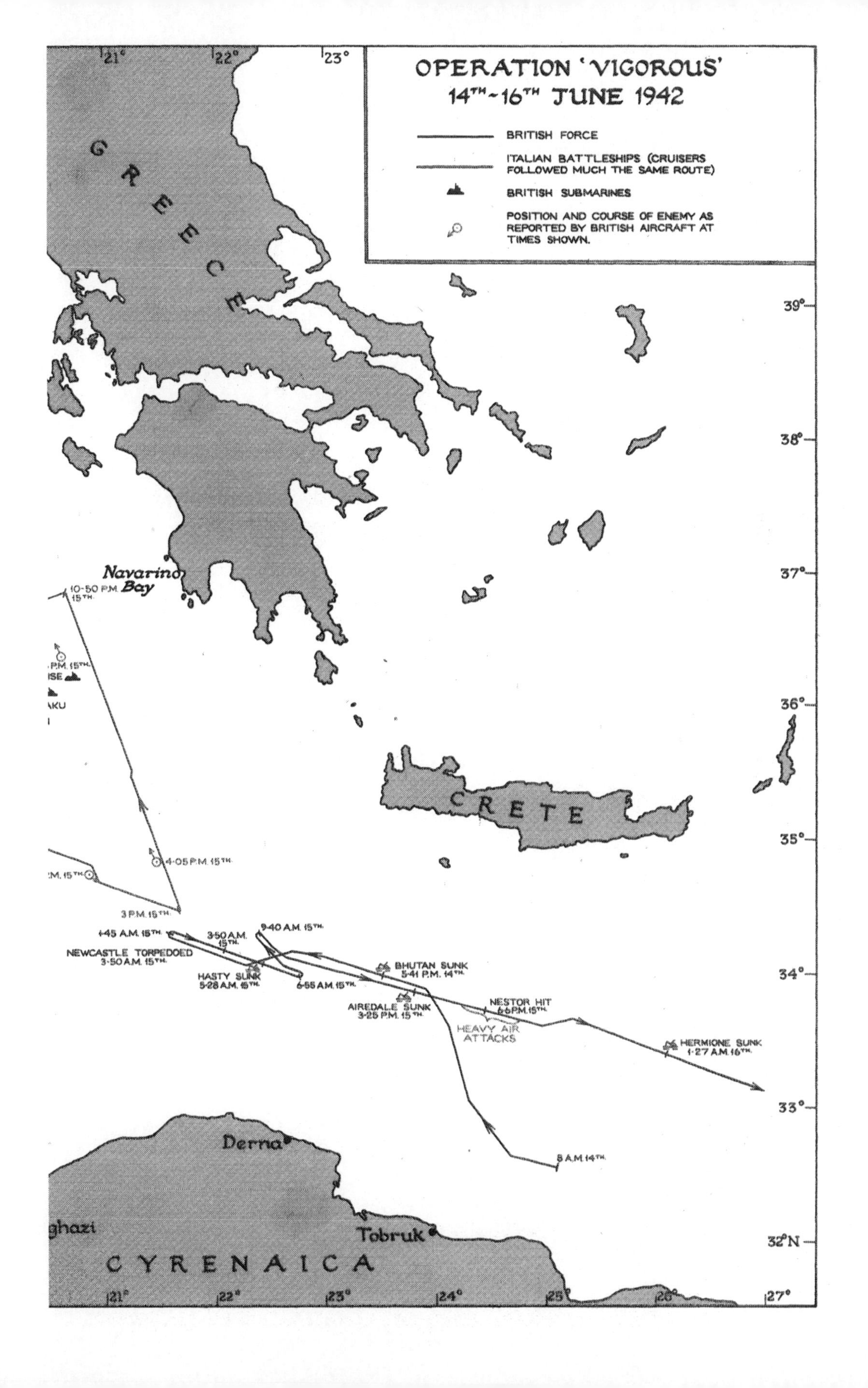

OPERATION 'VIGOROUS'
14TH–16TH JUNE 1942
BRITISH FORCE
ITALIAN BATTLESHIPS (CRUISERS FOLLOWED MUCH THE SAME ROUTE)
BRITISH SUBMARINES
POSITION AND COURSE OF ENEMY AS REPORTED BY BRITISH AIRCRAFT AT TIMES SHOWN.
GREECE
Navarino Bay
10-50 P.M. 15TH.
4-05 P.M. 15TH.
3 P.M. 15TH.
1-45 A.M. 15TH.
3-50 A.M. 15TH.
9-40 A.M. 15TH.
NEWCASTLE TORPEDOED 3-50 A.M. 15TH.
HASTY SUNK 5-28 A.M. 15TH.
6-55 A.M. 15TH.
BHUTAN SUNK 5-41 P.M. 14TH.
AIREDALE SUNK 3-25 P.M. 15TH.
NESTOR HIT 6-6 P.M. 15TH.
HEAVY AIR ATTACKS
HERMIONE SUNK 1-27 A.M. 16TH.
8 A.M. 14TH.
CRETE
Derna
Tobruk
CYRENAICA
21°
22°
23°
24°
25°
26°
27°
39°
38°
37°
36°
35°
34°
33°
32°N

Fayid. These were the Halverson Detachment, which had attacked the Rumanian oilfields on 12th June and which the U.S. Chiefs of Staff had allowed to be used against the Italian Fleet if it should leave harbour while the convoys were at sea. These striking forces were not, in the opinion of the Commanders-in-Chief, numerous enough to ensure that the Italian Fleet would be turned from its purpose, but no more aircraft could be provided. Fighter cover for the convoy would be given at first by short-range fighters and then by Beaufighters and long-range Kittyhawks, to the limit of their endurance.[1] Success would depend more than ever on frequent and accurate reporting of the Italian Fleet, without which it could be neither attacked nor evaded.

To disguise for as long as possible from the enemy that a convoy was being got ready, the eleven ships were loaded at various ports between Beirut and Alexandria. A part of the convoy was to sail from Port Said some thirty-six hours ahead of the main body; these ships were to go almost as far west as Tobruk before turning back to meet the rest. It was hoped by this means to draw the Italian Fleet to sea prematurely, expose it to attack, and make it run short of fuel.

The decoy convoy, escorted by the *Coventry* and eight destroyers, sailed on the 11th June as arranged. On the evening of the 12th, when about to turn east to rendezvous with the main body, one of the merchant ships (the *City of Calcutta*) was damaged in an attack by Ju. 87s and 88s and had to be sent in to Tobruk. The main body was met off Alexandria on the afternoon of the 13th. The Norwegian *Elizabeth Bakke* had been unable to keep up and so the convoy was already reduced to nine. During the night enemy aircraft dropped flares continually, but the bombing that followed did no harm. By the morning of the 14th the escort was complete except for the motor torpedo boats, sent back because the weather was too rough. During that forenoon, two of the corvettes had to part company by reason of defects, and the Dutch *Aagtekirk* proved too slow and was also detached. She and her escort were later attacked by forty German Ju. 87s and 88s twelve miles off Tobruk and the *Aagtekirk* was sunk.

Although the convoy was well inside 'Bomb Alley' between Crete and Cyrenaica, there were few signs of enemy aircraft between daybreak and 4.30 p.m., thanks largely to the British fighters. Some of these had been detached at short notice from the land battle to intercept enemy striking forces on their way out from Cyrenaican airfields to attack the convoy.[2] The convoy was now passing out of range of the British short-range fighters and between 4.30 and 9.15 there were seven attacks in which some 60 or 70 Ju. 87s and 88s in all took part. Some of the enemy were intercepted by long-range Kittyhawks and

---

[1] Coastal Beaufighters of Nos. 252 and 272 Squadrons and night-flying Beaufighters of No. 227 Squadron; Kittyhawks, each fitted with a long-range tank, of No. 250 Squadron.

[2] See page 251.

Beaufighters, but around 6 p.m. the *Bhutan* was sunk; another merchantman, the *Potaro*, was hit and damaged but was able to stay with the convoy. The two rescue ships picked up the *Bhutan's* survivors and were sent in to Tobruk.

Shortly before sunset a submarine nearly torpedoed the destroyer *Pakenham*, and a few minutes later the fighter patrol reported six M.T.Bs to the north-westward. Presently the *Euryalus* could discern them hull down on the starboard bow. Four British fighters directed to attack were held off by the M.T.Bs' own escort of German fighters. As darkness fell the dropping of flares began again, evidently to help submarines and M.T.Bs as well as the bombers which were still making sporadic attacks.

Various sightings on the 13th had confirmed the departure of a large British convoy from eastern Mediterranean ports, and by that evening the Italian Admiralty were confident that its destination was Malta. The convoy from Gibraltar had already been reported, and it was deduced that the British intention was to split the Axis opposition between the two, but the Italians decided to use the principal ships of their Fleet against the convoy from the east. At 2.30 p.m. on the 14th, the battleships *Littorio* (Flag of Admiral Iachino) and *Vittorio Veneto*, the 8-inch cruisers *Gorizia* and *Trento*, the 6-inch cruisers *Garibaldi* and *Duca D'Aosta* and twelve destroyers left Taranto with orders to intercept the British convoy. If the convoy maintained the course and speed reported, this could happen at about 9 a.m. next morning.

First news of the Italian ships came from a Baltimore from Malta searching for the cruisers from Palermo which subsequently attacked Captain Hardy. It sighted the main force at 6.45 p.m. clearing the Gulf of Taranto, and made an accurate report except that it identified the battleships as *Cavour* class. This signal reached Admiral Harwood at 10.27 p.m. The results of a photographic reconnaissance of Taranto at 8 p.m., which showed that it was not the *Cavours* but the faster and more powerful *Littorios* which had left harbour, did not reach him until after 8 o'clock next morning.

By 11 p.m. it was evident to Admiral Vian that the enemy might be met with early next morning. In the fine weather and light breeze which prevailed, he could not hope to hold off such a force all day, and he therefore asked Admiral Harwood if he wished him to retire. Admiral Harwood's intention was for the convoy to make as much ground to the west as possible while leaving sea-room for the submarines and aircraft to attack the Italian Fleet, and he replied that the convoy should continue west till 2 a.m. on the 15th and then turn back along the same track. This intricate manœuvre had only just been completed when Admiral Tennant's flagship, the *Newcastle*, was torpedoed by a M.T.B., but after the damaged compartments had been shored she was still capable of 24 knots. An hour and a half later the destroyer *Hasty* was also torpedoed by a M.T.B. and had to be sunk.

No further news of the Italian ships reached Admiral Harwood until 2.24 next morning, when the air reported only one battleship, two cruisers and two destroyers. It placed the enemy some 220 miles north-west of the convoy at 2 a.m., which except for the longitude was not far wrong. By 5.25 the Commander-in-Chief had decided that the risks of a return to 'Bomb Alley' outweighed those of an advance towards the Italian Fleet. He therefore ordered the convoy to turn to the west again and at 6.55 Admiral Vian complied. Admiral Harwood was, of course, hoping that the Italian Fleet would presently suffer losses from air and submarine attack, if indeed it had not already done so. For at midnight four Wellingtons of No. 38 Squadron, the night torpedo-bombers, had been despatched from Malta, followed three hours later by nine Beauforts of No. 217 Squadron. The Wellingtons found the Italian battleships at 3.40 but the enemy's smoke screen was so effective that only one Wellington was able to attack and both its torpedoes missed. At dawn, which was around 6 o'clock, the Beauforts took up the attack and drove it home with great determination. On return to Malta they claimed hits on both Italian battleships, but in fact it was the 8-inch cruiser *Trento* which they had torpedoed and stopped.

P.31, *P.34* and *P.35* of the 10th Submarine Flotilla had all sighted the Italian Fleet between 5.45 and 7 a.m. Only *P.35* was near enough to attack, but just as she was about to fire she was baulked of almost certain success when her battleship target altered course to avoid the Beauforts' torpedoes. *P.35* had a second chance, but it was at long range and her torpedoes missed. However, her luck was not entirely out, for all three submarines closed the damaged *Trento* as soon as the main body of the Fleet had passed, and shortly after 10 a.m. *P.35* hit her with two torpedoes causing the fore magazine to explode before she sank.

At 9 a.m. eight Liberators—seven U.S.A.A.F. and one R.A.F.—after a flight of more than five hours scored one bomb hit on the *Littorio*, the Italian flagship, but it did not seriously inconvenience her. The Americans, however, believed that both battleships had been heavily hit. Meanwhile twelve Beauforts of No. 39 Squadron had been sent out from Sidi Barrani to synchronise their attacks with those of the Liberators and then proceed to Malta as they would have insufficient fuel to return. Unfortunately they were intercepted by Me. 109s on the way; two were shot down and five were forced to abandon the operation. The remaining five attacked the Italian ships as the Liberators were leaving the scene—their timing had been nearly perfect. They too reported hitting a battleship but in fact they scored no hits, and the Italian Fleet less the *Trento* and two destroyers stood on.

Learning from an air report timed 8.28 a.m. that the enemy fleet, still apparently intact, was within 150 miles of the convoy and steering towards it, Admiral Harwood decided to turn the convoy east once more until he knew the results of the air and submarine attacks. At 9.40 this was done. Then came the claim of the Malta Beauforts to have hit both Italian battleships at 6 a.m. and at 11.51 Admiral Harwood ordered the convoy to resume its course for Malta. He informed Admiral Vian of the supposed damage to the Italians and added that a further air attack was intended in the afternoon. He repeated an earlier signal 'Avoid contact until aircraft have attacked, which should be by 10.30. If air attack fails, every effort must be made to get convoy through to Malta by adopting offensive attitude. Should this fail, and convoy be cornered, it is to be sacrificed, and you are to extricate your forces, proceeding to the eastward or the westward.' But no further reports about the enemy came through and the Commander-in-Chief began to suspect that the *Trento* might be the only Italian ship damaged. He did not know what damage our own ships had suffered nor how they stood for fuel and ammunition, and at 12.45 he signalled Admiral Vian giving him discretion either to comply with his order to turn west again, or to continue eastward in the hope of carrying out a night destroyer attack should the enemy stand on.

By 1.45 p.m., when Admiral Vian received the signal ordering him to turn again for Malta, he already knew from a recent air report that the Italian Fleet was standing on with both battleships intact, whereas his own two biggest ships were damaged, the *Birmingham* only two hours earlier by a near miss and the *Newcastle* by M.T.B. attack the previous night. He decided to continue eastward and await his Commander-in-Chief's reaction to this latest information. At 2.20 p.m. he received Admiral Harwood's signal freeing his hands and he held on to the east. An hour later in a further air attack the destroyer *Airedale* was disabled and had to be sunk.

Meanwhile, at 3 p.m., the Italian Fleet, rather more than 100 miles astern, had hauled round to the north-west. The Italian Admiralty had ordered that, if no opportunity of an engagement before 4 p.m. existed, Admiral Iachino was to take his ships to Navarino in readiness to challenge a fresh attempt by the British next day to break through to Malta.

To Admiral Harwood, on receiving air reports of this change of course, it seemed probable that the Italians were returning to Taranto and at 4.25 p.m. he signalled to Admiral Vian that now was the golden opportunity to get the convoy to Malta. He inquired whether the Hunts, *Coventry*, minesweepers and corvettes had enough fuel and ammunition for the one-way trip. If so he wished the convoy to turn at once, and the cruisers and Fleet destroyers to part company after dark and return to Alexandria. When Admiral Vian received this signal he was busily engaged with some of the heaviest air attacks of the passage. A general reversal of course was out of the question, and it was 6.30 before he could collect the information on which he reported that the Hunts had less than 30% of ammunition left and were using that up fast. He considered that they had not enough for the passage to Malta. In the meantime Admiral Harwood had modified the plan, intending to send to Malta only the four fastest from the seven remaining merchant ships and adding the *Arethusa* and two Fleet destroyers to the escort, but when he received Admiral Vian's reply he ordered him to return to Alexandria with his whole force. That night the escort suffered its heaviest casualty when the cruiser *Hermione* was hit by two torpedoes from the *U.205* and sank in twenty minutes with the loss of 88 officers and men. Next morning the Australian destroyer *Nestor*, which had been damaged in air attacks, had to be scuttled. In the evening of the 16th Admiral Vian arrived at Alexandria and sent on part of the convoy to Port Said.

Meanwhile the Italian Fleet on its north-westerly course had narrowly escaped attack by submarines of the 1st Flotilla on the evening of the 15th, and shortly after midnight had been attacked by five Wellingtons of No. 38 Squadron from Malta. One of them scored a hit with a torpedo on the *Littorio*, which put her out of action for more than two months. On learning of this damage the Italian Admiralty recalled their Fleet to Taranto, where it arrived a few hours before Admiral Vian reached Alexandria.

There is little to be said in summing up this disappointing operation. The convoy had first been turned back not because of any damage that the enemy's aircraft, submarines or M.T.Bs had been able to inflict, but because, as had been feared, the small British and American air striking force had been unable to do serious damage to the Italian Fleet.[1] While this Fleet remained intact the British surface escort had little hope of fighting the convoy through. When, at length, the Italian Fleet seemed no longer to bar the way to Malta, anti-aircraft ammunition was running short and seven Beaufighters had been lost; the means of defending the convoy against further air attacks outside the reach of short-range fighters were therefore insufficient. The conduct of the whole operation had been hampered by meagre information, and some important signals had taken a long time to get through. It is doubtful, however, whether even a continuous flow of speedy and accurate reports would have radically affected the action taken, for without the use of the airfields in Western Cyrenaica the British were too heavily handicapped.

[1] See pages 308-9.

Out of seventeen merchantmen in the two convoys only two had arrived at Malta; six had been sunk and nine turned back. The 15,000 tons of cargo unloaded from these two ships would enable the island, given a good harvest, to last out so far as food was concerned until the end of September, but in Lord Gort's opinion the stocks of aviation spirit were being used up too quickly. The instructions he had received were to prolong the island's resistance as much as possible. For this adequate fighter defence was essential and, until future supplies of aviation spirit were assured, existing stocks must be preserved for the fighters at the expense of the striking force. The Commanders-in-Chief, while seeing Lord Gort's point, felt that everything depended on the land battle and that Malta must continue to strike against enemy shipping even at some risk to the island's stock of fuel. The Chiefs of Staff agreed with Lord Gort to the extent of ordering strikes to be restricted to those giving extremely good chances at close ranges. Except for Beauforts, the passage of aircraft to Egypt via Malta was to be suspended. To maintain stocks for fighters, a more regular supply by submarine was to be encouraged.

In fact, during July, the submarines *Parthian* and *Clyde* arrived from Gibraltar with aviation spirit, ammunition and special stores, and fifty-nine more Spitfires were flown in from the *Eagle* in two ferrying trips on the 15th and 21st. Making her third trip with special stores, H.M.S. *Welshman* came in under cover of the first ferry trip, arriving at Malta on 16th July. Italian cruisers which might have disputed her passage had been heavily bombed in Cagliari and had just been transferred to Naples. Towards the end of the month Admiral Harwood felt able to send the 10th Submarine Flotilla back to Malta. Not only had the bombing lessened but the minesweepers which had arrived with the 'Harpoon' convoy had been able to make the approaches safer. As will be seen, these submarines soon began to make their presence felt again.

Fearing just such a recovery of Malta's power to strike, with aircraft as well as with submarines, the enemy had increased the severity of his bombing attacks during the first half of July, concentrating chiefly on the island's airfields, where 17 aircraft were destroyed on the ground and many more damaged.[1] In the fortnight the defending fighters flew nearly 1,000 sorties; 36 Spitfires (out of 135) were lost in combat, but the enemy lost 65 aircraft from all causes and had been forced first to increase the ratio of escort fighters to bombers and later to fall back on tip-and-run attacks by fighter-bombers. This was a notable success for the island's air defences.

On the 15th, just as the enemy air attacks had again died down, Air Vice-Marshal Lloyd handed over as A.O.C. Malta to Air Vice-

---

[1] During the whole month over 700 tons of bombs were dropped, mostly in the first fortnight.

Marshal K. R. Park. Lloyd had arrived in Malta in June 1941, just as the heavy attacks of the year were waning. He had been in command throughout the much heavier attacks of 1942, when his example of personal courage and tenacity of purpose had been a source of inspiration to the hard-pressed squadrons of the Royal Air Force. His services were not to be lost to the Middle East, however, for he was to join Air Marshal Tedder's staff.

Towards the end of July the British fighters at Malta changed their tactics, and began to fly out to intercept the enemy over the sea as a regular routine. This may seem an obvious thing to do, but before strong German air reinforcements arrived in Sicily in December 1941 the fighters had gone even farther than this by attacking the enemy on his own airfields. Gradually, however, the British had been forced out of the sky over Sicily, and the time came when, greatly outnumbered, it was all they could do to survive over Malta. Now, as July 1942 drew to a close, there were again enough fighters to go out to meet the enemy, and these tactics Park was to employ with great success.

Before carrying the story of Malta further it is necessary to see how the maritime war in the Mediterranean had been affected by what was happening in North Africa. As has already been described, the British withdrawal from the Gazala position was taking place at the same time as operations 'Harpoon' and 'Vigorous'; five days after these had ended Tobruk fell, and by 28th June the enemy was at Matruh in possession of airfields within 160 miles of Alexandria. Faced with the possibility of fighter-escorted bomber attacks and with the danger that Alexandria itself might be captured, Admiral Harwood dispersed the Fleet to Haifa, Port Said and Beirut, and moved merchant shipping and warships not required for active operations, such as the repair ship *Resource*, south of the Canal. A wonderful job was done in completing the temporary repairs to the *Queen Elizabeth* so that she could be undocked and sent to the comparative safety of Port Sudan, where she stayed a few weeks before leaving for permanent repairs in America. At Alexandria arrangements were made to block the harbour and destroy stores and the facilities of the port. Admiral Harwood and his operations staff moved to Ismailia on 2nd July. On the 30th June the submarine depot ship *Medway*, on her way to Haifa where it was intended to base the Submarine Flotillas, was torpedoed and sunk by *U.372*. Happily only thirty lives were lost, but the *Medway* herself was a serious loss and with her went nearly ninety spare torpedoes. Forty-seven of these were later recovered.

Circumstances had relieved the Royal Navy of the duty of supplying Tobruk but it could still lend its support to the Army along the coast with its gunfire, and between the 12th and 20th July a number of bombardments, referred to again in Chapter XIV, were carried out by cruisers and destroyers against the area around Mersa Matruh with varying success. Towards the end of the month, as the front stabilized, the danger to Alexandria receded, and on 8th August Admiral Harwood returned there with his staff. The harbour, however, was still within easy range of fighter-escorted bombers, and the Fleet continued to be based on Levant and Canal ports.

A delicate situation arose over Admiral Godfroy's squadron when it became necessary to evacuate Alexandria. The British were naturally anxious lest these French ships should fall into German hands. Admiral Godfroy was confident that he could always avoid this, if necessary by scuttling, and he refused to sail for any of the ports suggested either by the British Government or by President Roosevelt, who did his best to mediate. Fortunately the march of events resolved the difficulty.

See Map 35

The failure of the June convoys had led, of course, to immediate planning for a further attempt to supply Malta; indeed, before Admiral Vian's ships were back in Alexandria the Prime Minister had minuted to the First Lord and Admiral Pound that Lord Gort must be able to tell the Maltese that the Navy would never abandon Malta.

Neither in 'Vigorous' nor in 'Harpoon' had the sea and air forces been strong enough. Next time they would have to be given priority over all other demands, for on the success or failure of 'Pedestal' (as it was to be called) would hang the fate of Malta and hence in all probability of the Nile valley. The enemy's advance into Egypt had made air support in the Eastern Mediterranean more difficult than ever, so that the next convoy would be run from the west only. The escort would have to be powerful enough to brush off the main Italian Fleet, if this should venture into the western basin, and it was realized that the portion of the escort continuing on to Malta should be much stronger than it was in 'Harpoon'. Fighters, at first from carriers and later from Malta, should be numerous enough to match the opposing fighters and still leave others to deal with bombers and torpedo-bombers. The air striking force at Malta should be able to attack enemy airfields in addition to ships. It was known that the enemy was increasing his air forces in Sicily and Sardinia in anticipation of a further British attempt. Both sides, indeed, had realized that the issue was of great consequence, and were bracing themselves for a trial of strength.

The carriers *Victorious* (Flag of Rear-Admiral A. L. St. G. Lyster), *Indomitable* and *Eagle* and the battleships *Nelson* and *Rodney* formed the

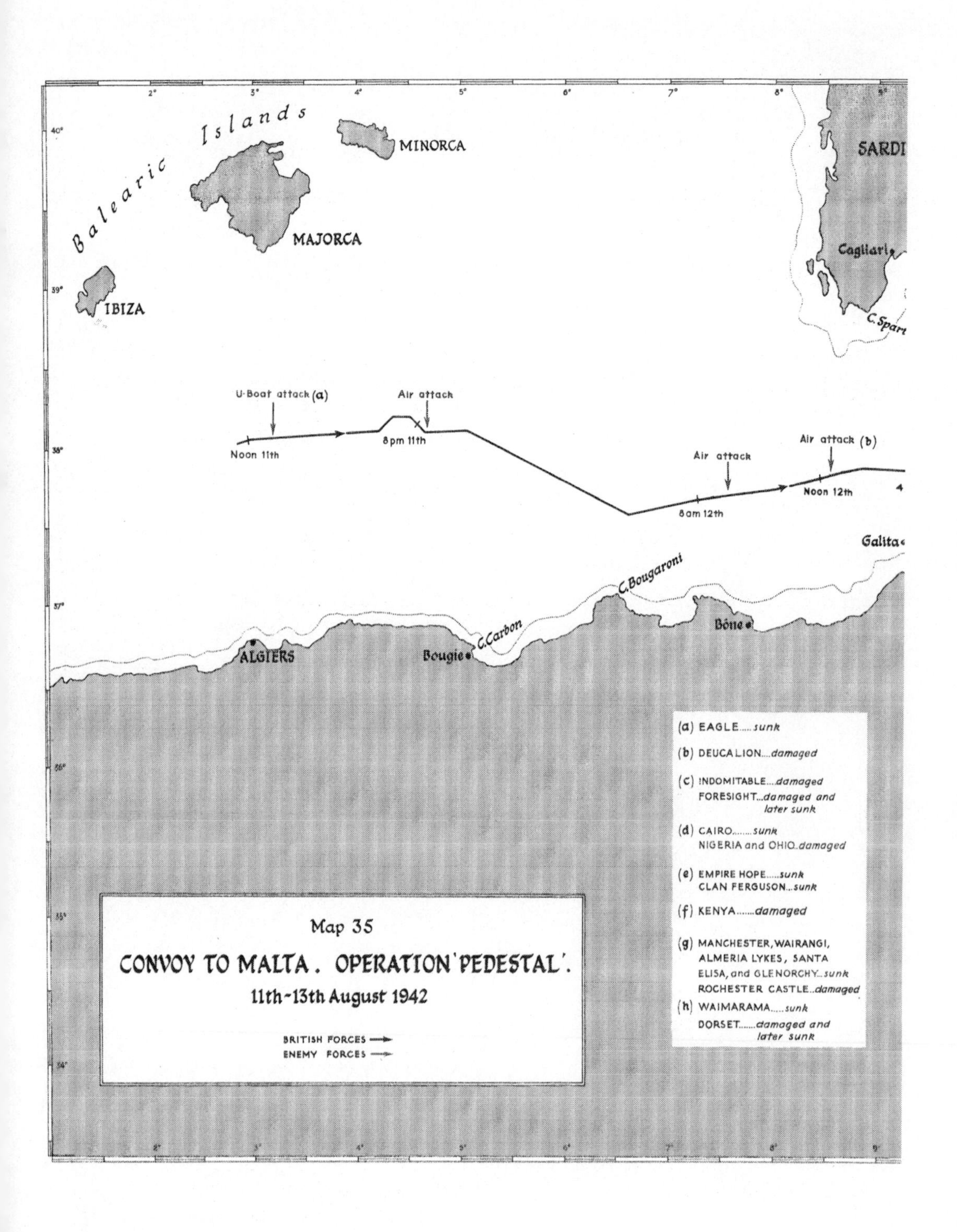
Balearic Islands
MINORCA
MAJORCA
IBIZA
SARDI
Cagliari
C. Spart
U-Boat attack (a)
Air attack
Noon 11th
8pm 11th
Air attack
Air attack (b)
8am 12th
Noon 12th
Galita
C. Bougaroni
C. Carbon
Bône
ALGIERS
Bougie
(a) EAGLE.....sunk
(b) DEUCALION....damaged
(c) INDOMITABLE....damaged
FORESIGHT...damaged and later sunk
(d) CAIRO.......sunk
NIGERIA and OHIO..damaged
(e) EMPIRE HOPE.....sunk
CLAN FERGUSON...sunk
(f) KENYA.......damaged
(g) MANCHESTER, WAIRANGI, ALMERIA LYKES, SANTA ELISA, and GLENORCHY...sunk
ROCHESTER CASTLE..damaged
(h) WAIMARAMA.....sunk
DORSET.......damaged and later sunk
Map 35
CONVOY TO MALTA. OPERATION 'PEDESTAL'.
11th–13th August 1942
BRITISH FORCES
ENEMY FORCES

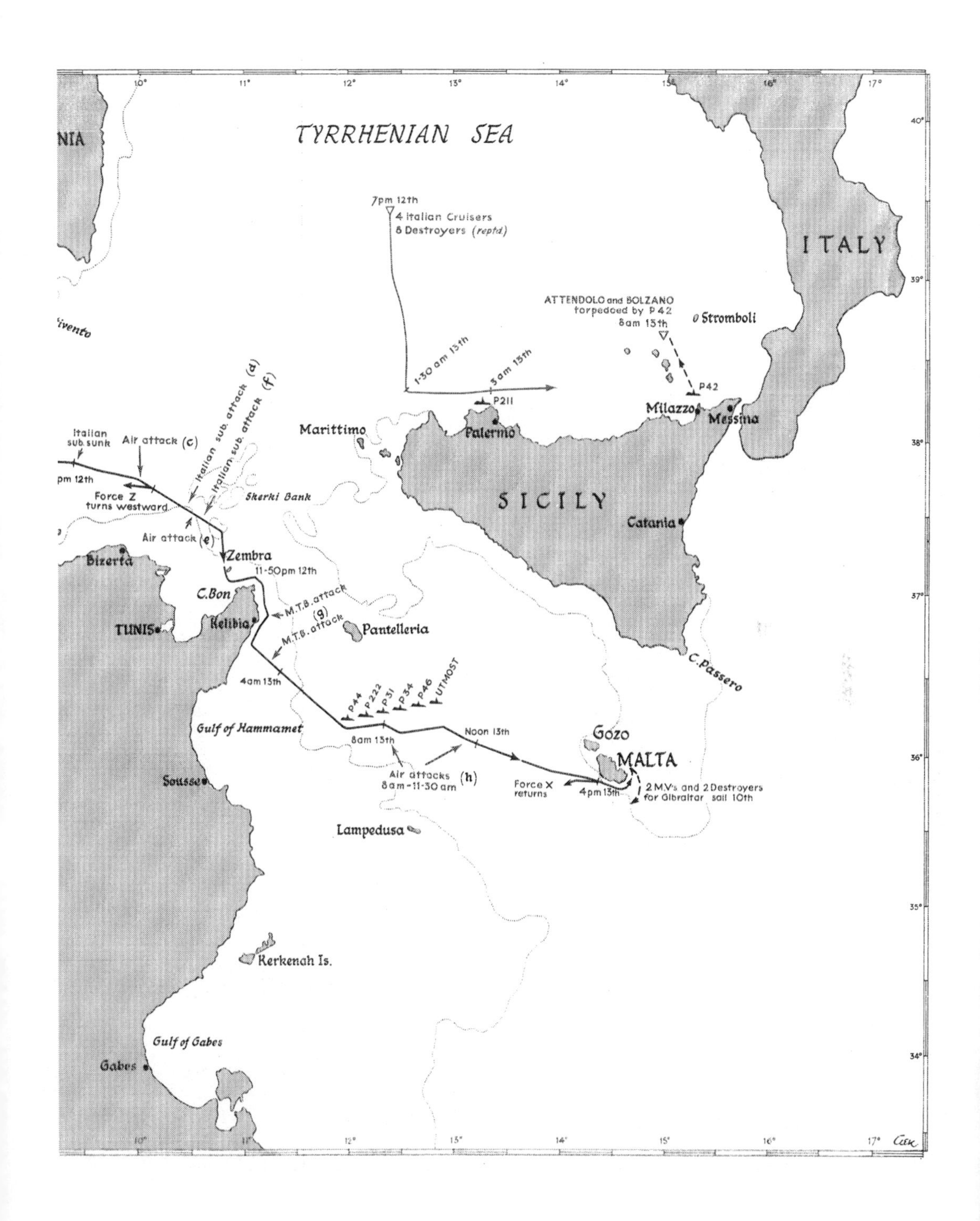

TYRRHENIAN SEA
NIA
ITALY
7pm 12th
4 Italian Cruisers
8 Destroyers (reptd)
ATTENDOLO and BOLZANO
torpedoed by P42
8am 13th
Stromboli
1-30 am 13th
5 am 13th
P211
P42
Milazzo
Messina
Palermo
Marittimo
SICILY
Catania
Italian sub. attack (d)
Italian sub. attack (f)
Italian sub. sunk
Air attack (c)
pm 12th
Force Z turns westward
Skerki Bank
Air attack (e)
Zembra
11-50pm 12th
Bizerta
C.Bon
M.T.B. attack
(g)
M.T.B. attack
TUNIS
Kelibia
Pantelleria
C.Passero
4am 13th
P44
P222
P31
P34
P46
UTMOST
Gulf of Hammamet
8am 13th
Noon 13th
Gozo
MALTA
Air attacks (h)
8am-11-30 am
Force X returns
4pm 13th
2 M.V's and 2 Destroyers for Gibraltar sail 10th
Sousse
Lampedusa
Kerkenah Is.
Gulf of Gabes
Gabes

main strength of the escort.[1] The suspension of North Russian convoys after the disaster to convoy P.Q.17 in July made it easier to spare ships from the Home Fleet, and the American victory at the battle of Midway Island had made it less urgent to reinforce the Eastern Fleet. The sailing of the *Nelson* and *Rodney* to join the Eastern Fleet was postponed and the *Indomitable* was brought back all the way round the Cape. Between them the carriers had embarked 72 fighters—Hurricanes, Fulmars and Martlets—and 28 Albacores. Three modern light cruisers with dual-purpose guns (*Sirius*, *Phoebe* and *Charybdis*) were to have the special duty of defending the carriers from air attack. Together with 12 destroyers this powerful fleet would form Force Z, which was to turn back at the Skerki Channel. Force X, which was to continue on to Malta, comprised the 6-inch cruisers *Nigeria* (Flag of Rear-Admiral H. M. Burrough), *Kenya* and *Manchester*, the anti-aircraft cruiser *Cairo* and a further 12 destroyers. Vice-Admiral E. N. Syfret, his flag in the *Nelson*, was to command the whole operation. It will be noticed that both in ships and in aircraft this escort was much stronger than in 'Harpoon'; it was in fact the most powerful force ever to accompany a Malta convoy.

At the end of July there were 80 serviceable fighters at Malta, but as the weekly wastage averaged 17 it was planned to give them a last minute fillip, and H.M.S. *Furious* was to fly off another batch of Spitfires under cover of the main operation. Two fleet oilers and a tug escorted by four corvettes were provided for refuelling ships on passage, and a further eight destroyers would be available for incidental duties, such as escorting the *Furious* back to Gibraltar. Another ocean tug was to be attached to Force X—an innovation following the experience of operation 'Harpoon'. Two submarines were to patrol, one off Palermo and the other off Milazzo, while six others to the south of Pantelleria were to provide a screen to the convoy. It was expressly intended that they should be seen on the surface and reported by enemy aircraft in order to deter enemy surface ships from attacking the convoy.

The air forces at Malta were strongly reinforced from the United Kingdom and Egypt, and the maximum numbers of aircraft serviceable at any one time during the operation were 100 Spitfires, 36 Beaufighters, 30 Beauforts, 3 Wellingtons, 2 Liberators, 2 Baltimores, 3 F.A.A. Albacores and Swordfish. This does not include reconnaissance aircraft, of which there were 5 Baltimores, 6 P.R.U. Spitfires and 5 Wellington VIIIs.

---

[1] *Victorious:* Nos. 809 and 884 Squadrons—16 Fulmars;
No. 885 Squadron—6 Hurricanes;
Nos. 817 and 832 Squadrons—14 Albacores.
Indomitable: No. 806 Squadron—10 Martlets;
Nos. 800 and 880 Squadrons—24 Hurricanes;
Nos. 827 and 831 Squadrons—14 Albacores.
Eagle: Nos. 801 and 813 Squadrons—16 Hurricanes.
(*See Photo* 37.)

While the main convoy was coming east, the two merchantmen which had arrived at Malta in operation 'Harpoon' were to return to Gibraltar escorted by two destroyers. In the Eastern Mediterranean the Fleet would stage a diversion with a dummy convoy and station submarines in suitable positions in case the Italians put to sea.

The convoy of 14 large ships—11 British and 3 American, including the 15-knot tanker *Ohio* (on loan to the Ministry of War Transport) carrying 12,000 tons of oil—passed through the Straits of Gibraltar early on 10th August. Admiral Syfret with the bulk of the escorting men-of-war had accompanied it from the Clyde. Enemy aircraft started shadowing soon after daylight on the 11th, and thereafter the convoy was under continuous observation in spite of the British fighters. The *Furious* began flying off her Spitfires for Malta shortly after noon, but this was interrupted when at 1.15 the *Eagle* was torpedoed. The German submarine *U.73* had dived undetected through the port screen and convoy columns to attack the carrier which was on the starboard quarter of the convoy. Four torpedoes hit her on the port side and she sank in eight minutes, happily without heavy loss of life; many of her survivors were picked up by the tug attached to Force X. The *Eagle*, it will be recalled, had played a prominent part in the Mediterranean Fleet's opening moves against the Italians, in the course of which she had been severely shaken by numerous near misses. After repairs she had joined Force H early in 1942 to replace the much more modern *Ark Royal* (which was also torpedoed by a German submarine), and since then 182 Spitfires had successfully reached Malta off her flying deck. Together with the *Wasp* the *Eagle* had sustained Malta during the island's greatest need and when she was sunk she was with the last Malta convoy to be seriously opposed. The *Furious* resumed her task of flying off Spitfires to Malta—37 arrived safely—and then went back to Gibraltar; on the way one of her destroyer escort, H.M.S. *Wolverine*, rammed and sank the Italian submarine *Dagabur*.

Sardinia was still nearly 200 miles away when, at 8.45, just as the sun was setting, the first air attack on the convoy began. The 36 German bombers and torpedo-bombers were difficult for the F.A.A. fighters to see in the failing light, but the guns did good work and no ships were damaged. That night Liberators and Beaufighters attacked airfields in Sardinia, destroying and damaging several aircraft and setting a hangar on fire. Next morning, the 12th, German attacks began at 9.15. This time F.A.A. fighters intercepted them twenty-five miles clear of the convoy, and those of the enemy that succeeded in getting through did no harm. The main effort from Sardinia came at midday—an elaborate combined attack by some 70 aircraft strongly escorted by fighters. First came 10 Italian torpedo-bombers carrying, as it turned out, a new type of circling torpedo known as a *motobomba*.

They were followed by a few German fighter-bombers. The main force of Italian torpedo-bombers was intended to come in about five minutes after these earlier attacks had upset the formation of the ships and drawn their fire, but they were late and dropped their torpedoes at long range having been seriously upset by the F.A.A. fighters on the way. The ships of the convoy had been given plenty of practice since leaving the Clyde and were manœuvring together like a squadron of warships; they turned to avoid these various attacks, none of which was successful. The Italian torpedo-bombers were followed at about 1.15 by some 20 German dive-bombers and, although this attack too was broken up by fighters, one merchantman, the *Deucalion*, was damaged, and as she could not keep up she was ordered to follow an inshore route along the Tunisian coast. Here, in the evening, after she and her escort had repelled one attack, she was hit by torpedo-bombers and blew up. The last of this series of attacks which had begun at midday was made on the *Victorious*; at 1.45 an Italian aircraft dropped a heavy armour-piercing bomb which broke up on the flight deck without exploding.

The convoy passed some twenty miles north of Galita Island and spent the rest of the afternoon successfully avoiding submarines. Admiral Syfret was well content with the vigilance of the anti-submarine screen, which, although it had failed to detect the submarine which sank the *Eagle*, had foiled many another attack; moreover during the afternoon the Italian submarine *Cobalto* was sunk by the destroyer *Ithuriel*.

At 6.30 that evening the attacks from Sicily began about 120 miles from the island. Again the bombers and torpedo-bombers were escorted by fighters, but, as before, the Savoias dropped their torpedoes at long range and once again the convoy was turned away to avoid them. This time however the destroyer *Foresight* was hit and later had to be sunk. The bombers made the *Indomitable* their main target, some of the Ju. 87s coming down to 1,000 feet. The carrier received three hits, her flight deck was put out of action, and her fighters had to return to the *Victorious*. (*See photo* 38).

At 7 p.m., when this big attack from Sicily was over and the convoy was approaching the Skerki Channel, Admiral Syfret turned his ships of Force Z away and left Admiral Burrough with Force X to take the convoy on. An hour later, while the convoy was changing its formation from four columns to two for easier manœuvring in narrow waters, the *Nigeria*, the *Cairo* and the tanker *Ohio*, one of the most important ships in the convoy, all received underwater damage—now known to have been caused by torpedoes fired by the Italian submarine *Axum*. The *Nigeria* turned back for Gibraltar with an escort, and Admiral Burrough shifted his flag to the destroyer *Ashanti*: the *Cairo* had to be sunk; the *Ohio* struggled on. The convoy had been turned away to the south to avoid the danger, and in the process became bunched up. Many of the destroyers were busy with damaged ships. In this state, while trying to form two columns in the gathering dusk, the convoy was attacked by 20 German bombers and torpedo-bombers. The convoy had lost its two fighter-direction ships, *Nigeria* and *Cairo*. The long-range fighters from Malta were being fired on by their own ships, and the enemy's task was easy. The *Empire Hope* was hit by a bomb and had to be sunk. The *Clan Ferguson* was torpedoed and blew up. The *Brisbane Star*, also hit by a torpedo, was able to hold on and eventually reached Malta. Soon after this attack the *Kenya* was torpedoed by the Italian submarine *Alagi* but fortunately she was able to remain with the convoy.

But worse was to come. To avoid the minefields in the Sicilian Narrows the route lay south of Zembra Island and then hugged the coast as far south as Kelibia. The ships were now badly strung out. Three destroyers were minesweeping ahead followed by the *Kenya*, *Manchester* and two merchant ships. This, the main body, was fast being overhauled by Admiral Burrough in the *Ashanti*. Another three destroyers were rounding up the remaining nine merchantmen. The destroyer *Bramham* was rejoining after the *Deucalion* had been sunk, and the cruiser *Charybdis* and the destroyers *Eskimo* and *Somali* had been sent by Admiral Syfret to replace the warships lost, but would not overtake for some hours. The main body passed Cape Bon at midnight. Forty minutes later M.T.B. attacks began and lasted until the convoy was well past Kelibia and on course for Malta. The *Manchester* was the first ship to be torpedoed. The other ships hit were all stragglers, the *Wairangi*, *Rochester Castle*, *Almeria Lykes*, *Santa Elisa* and *Glenorchy*. They were attacked between 3.15 and 4.30 about fifteen miles south-east of Kelibia while taking a short cut to overhaul the main body. Only the *Rochester Castle* survived and she, 'merrily doing 13 knots', caught up with the main body at 5.30, two hours after being torpedoed. By then the *Charybdis*, *Eskimo* and *Somali* had joined Admiral Burrough, making the main force up to two cruisers and seven destroyers with the *Rochester Castle*, *Waimarama* and *Melbourne Star*. The *Ohio* escorted by one destroyer was slowly catching up. Further astern was the *Port Chalmers* with two destroyers. The *Dorset* was following alone and lastly the torpedoed *Brisbane Star* was still hugging the Tunisian coast intending to make for Malta at nightfall. At 7.30 a.m. Admiral Burrough sent back the *Eskimo* and *Somali* to help the *Manchester*. It was just a year since the Captain of the *Manchester* had succeeded in bringing his ship to Gibraltar after being torpedoed during convoy operation 'Substance'; this time, however, he decided that the *Manchester* was too badly crippled and scuttled her. The two destroyers were able to rescue those of her company who had not reached shore, and took them to Gibraltar.

Daylight relieved the merchantmen and their escort from further attack by motor torpedo boats, but opened the way again for air attacks. To Admiral Burrough, at that time, there seemed to be a grave risk of attack by surface warships also. Air reconnaissance on the previous evening had found one 8-inch and three 6-inch cruisers and eight destroyers some eighty miles north of the western end of Sicily steering south. This looked dangerous, for they could easily have reached the convoy by dawn next day; in fact at 1.30 a.m. they had turned east along the north coast of Sicily, and further reports had shown them holding on to the east. They had been attacked, but not heavily, by aircraft from Malta, where the main striking force was being held back in case the battleships at Taranto put to sea.

At 8 a.m. air attacks on the main body started again, and although Beaufighters and long-range Spitfires from Malta were patrolling over the convoy the *Waimarama* was hit and blew up. The destroyer *Ledbury*, skilfully handled, saved some of her crew out of a blazing sea. In further attacks an enemy bomber crashed on board the *Ohio*, and the *Ohio's* engines were disabled by four or five near misses; the *Dorset* was hit and stopped, and the *Rochester Castle* was set on fire but was able to continue with the convoy. Two destroyers were left with the cripples. There was one more attack about 11.30 which did no harm. Malta was now within eighty miles, and further attacks on the main body were held off by short-range Spitfires. At 4 p.m. Admiral Burrough handed over his remaining three merchant ships to the minesweeping force from Malta and turned westward on his return passage to Gibraltar with two cruisers and five destroyers. Two hours later the *Port Chalmers*, *Melbourne Star* and *Rochester Castle*, the last very low in the water, entered the Grand Harbour.

There were still the *Dorset*, *Ohio* and *Brisbane Star*. The two first were lying helpless, the two destroyers with them having found them unmanageable in tow. Air attacks were frequent and at 7 p.m. both ships were hit again and the *Dorset* sunk. With the help of the minesweepers the *Ohio* was at last taken in tow, but the tow parted again after a further attack and fresh wires were passed, while the *Ohio* became even more unwieldy. But at length persistence won, and on the morning of the 15th the vital tanker entered harbour with destroyers lashed alongside to steer her and push her ahead. (*See Photo* 39.) The *Brisbane Star* had already arrived. After some difficulty with unhelpful French Boarding Officers she had left the Tunisian coast as planned at nightfall on the 13th and reached Malta next afternoon in spite of air attacks on the way.

In addition to the serious casualties to ships there had been a heavy loss of aircraft, the Fleet Air Arm having lost thirteen in addition to the sixteen that went down with the *Eagle*. The Royal Air Force had lost five and the enemy thirty-five, including those shot down over Malta.

The two empty merchant ships from Malta had an undisturbed run to Gibraltar, but the return passage of Admiral Burrough's ships was very different. They had to run the gauntlet again of motor torpedo boats, submarines and aircraft. Several ships were nearly hit, but they rejoined Admiral Syfret without suffering damage and the combined force reached Gibraltar on the 15th. In the Eastern Mediterranean the diversion passed without incident; 'the only point of interest,' reported Admiral Harwood, 'was that considerable disappointment was expressed by the merchant ships taking part when they found they were not going through to Malta.'

In paying tribute to the men who had fought the convoy through, on the sea and in the air, Admiral Syfret felt that all would desire to give first place to the courage and determination of the masters, officers and men of the merchant ships. 'The memory of their conduct will remain an inspiration to all who were privileged to sail with them.' This was echoed by Admiral Leatham in reporting on the five merchant ships which arrived at Malta. He made special mention of the *Ohio*, the destroyers *Penn*, *Bramham* and *Ledbury*, who, with the minesweeper *Rye*, had brought her at long last into harbour, and the *Brisbane Star* who had played a lone hand after being damaged and had come triumphantly through. There was particular satisfaction when Captain D. W. Mason, Master of the *Ohio*, received the George Cross for his outstanding services.

To oppose the passage of the 'Pedestal' convoy the enemy had assembled more than 600 aircraft in Sardinia and Sicily. Of these some 200 were German, many being reinforcements sent for the occasion from Crete and North Africa. Six Italian and three German submarines had been stationed between the Balearics and the Algerian coast, eleven Italian submarines in the approaches to the Skerki Channel, and one near Malta lying in wait for stragglers. A new minefield was laid off Cape Bon the day before the convoy was expected, and south of Cape Bon twenty-three M.T.Bs were on patrol, four of which were German. In spite of the British attempt to assemble a formidable force, the enemy fighters usually appeared in considerably greater strength than those which the carriers or Malta could put up, and it is a measure of the quality of the British fighters and of the gunfire and asdic training of the ships that the convoy reached the approaches to the Skerki Channel with only one merchantman damaged. After that it was a disappointment that only five of the fourteen merchantmen arrived at Malta. It was the skilful attack by the Italian submarine *Axum* and her luck in picking two fighter-direction ships as targets which started things going wrong. This success opened the way for further successes in the air attack at dusk. Thereafter the convoy became strung out and presented many easy targets to M.T.Bs during darkness and to aircraft the following day. The results are therefore not surprising. Indeed, the Italians seem to have missed an opportunity of doing even more damage. The ships which had been reported in the Tyrrhenian sea the previous evening had in fact comprised three 8-inch and three 6-inch cruisers and eleven destroyers—a formidable enough force even if the British escort had not been reduced to the damaged *Kenya*, the *Charybdis*, and ten destroyers. The Italian orders were to attack the British convoy early on the 13th to the south of Pantelleria. Powerful air forces, however, had been reported assembled on Malta's airfields and it was considered essential that the Italian warships should be well protected by fighters. But the bombers and torpedo-bombers from Sicily also needed fighter protection, and there were not enough fighters for both duties. Eventually Mussolini was called upon to arbitrate between the rival claims of the Italian Naval Staff and Field-Marshal Kesselring, and he decided that the fighters should protect the bombers. The orders for the warships were then altered. Some of the Italian warships were ordered to return to harbour; others were directed through the Messina Straits to reinforce three 6-inch cruisers at Navarino Bay which had been ordered to attack the British force reported at sea with a convoy in the Eastern Mediterranean.[1] In the course of their passage along the north coast of Sicily, these reinforcements were attacked by the British submarine *P.42*, which torpedoed the 8-inch cruiser *Bolzano* and the 6-inch cruiser *Attendolo*. Both cruisers eventually reached harbour but neither came into service again. In conclusion, it should be mentioned that the Italian battleships, for which the main air striking force at Malta had been held back, could not put to sea because they had no fuel. After the Italian operations against the two Malta convoys in June, Mussolini had warned Hitler that stocks of fuel were exhausted and that further British attempts to supply Malta could be opposed only by submarines and aircraft.

The 'Pedestal' convoy was the last of the Malta convoys to be seriously opposed and it is appropriate here to summarize what these convoys had achieved.[2] In the six and a half months from Italy's entry into the war to the end of 1940, twenty-one ships carrying 160,000 tons of cargo were discharged at Malta without loss, and stocks were

---

[1] The Royal Air Force at Malta tried to discourage the Italian warships from standing on towards the convoy by transmitting in plain language messages concerning air attacks, real and imaginary, about to be made upon them. In the event this stratagem had no effect, as *Supermarina* had cancelled the orders for attacking the convoy before any of these British signals were intercepted.

[2] See also the summary on page 155.

built up to a reserve of seven months. The arrival of the *Luftwaffe* then prevented the intended figure of eight months' reserve being reached. During the twenty months from January 1941 to August 1942 forty-six merchant ships discharged 320,000 tons. The following table shows in more detail what arrived at Malta in this period and at what cost in ships. Not that the price paid was confined to sunk and damaged ships and aircraft destroyed; the Malta convoys tied up, for weeks on end, fast and valuable merchant ships and diverted appreciable naval and

The Supply of Malta

January 1941 *to August* 1942

Date of arrival	Convoy or Ship	Supply ships			Cargo unloaded in thousands of tons
		Started	Arrived	Sunk at Sea (T Torpedo bombing; B Bombs)	
1941					
10 Jan.	During Op. 'Excess'*	3	3	—	78 (10 Jan. and 23 Mar.)
23 Mar.	M.W.6	4	4	—	
21 Apr.	Breconshire	1	1	—	7
(Apr.)	Parracombe	1	—	1 (Mine)	0
10 May	During Op. 'Tiger'	7	7	—	40†
21 July	Op. 'Substance'	6	6	—	40†
19 Sept.	Empire Guillemot	1	1	—	6†
24 Sept.	Op. 'Halberd'	9	8	1 (T)	50
(Nov.)	Empire Pelican Empire Defender	2	—	2 (T)	0
18 Dec.	Breconshire	1	1	—	7
1942					
7 Jan.	Glengyle	1	1	—	7
18 Jan.	M.F.3	4	3	1 (B)	21
27 Jan.	Breconshire	1	1	—	7
(Feb.)	M.F.5	3	—	2 (B)	0
23 Mar.	M.G.1*	4	3	1 (B)	7·5
10 May	Welshman	1	1	—	0·3†
15 June	Op. 'Harpoon'	6	2	4 (B & T)	15
15 June	Welshman	1	1	—	0·3†
(June)	Op. 'Vigorous'	11	—	2 (B)	0
16 July	Welshman	1	1	—	0·3
14 Aug.	Op. 'Pedestal'	14	5	9 (B, T & M.T.B.)	47
TOTAL		82	49	23	

During this period there were also 31 supply trips by submarine.

*One ship from Convoy 'Excess' seriously damaged and three ships from Convoy M.G.1 sunk by bombing after arrival.

†Approximate tonnage

33. Photograph found in an enemy dug-out of German A.A. gunners in action; the gun is a 2-cm *Flak*.

34. A crashed Stuka (Ju. 87 dive-bomber), taken the moment after impact.

35. Boston bombers of the Royal Air Force take off from a desert airfield, leaving plumes of dust in their wake.

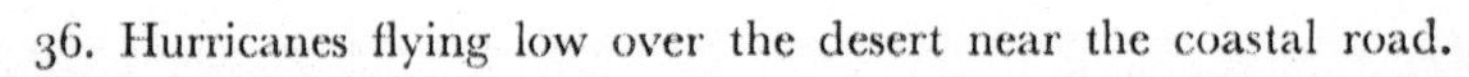

36. Hurricanes flying low over the desert near the coastal road.

37. Operation 'Pedestal', August 1942, showing some of the escorting warships, including the three carriers H.M.S. *Victorious*, *Indomitable*, and *Eagle* (nearest the camera).

38. Operation 'Pedestal': H.M.S. *Indomitable* hit by German dive-bombers, 12th August 1942.

39. Operation 'Pedestal': the damaged tanker *Ohio* being nursed into harbour by two destroyers.

40. Malta: tugs bustling round the crippled tanker *Ohio* in the Grand Harbour.

air forces to their defence. Moreover, many other operations had to be staged, in the desert as well as at sea, to help to sustain Malta and enable it to make its vital contribution to the campaign in the Middle East. Among these operations, the most important had been the air ferrying from Gibraltar which had made heavy demands on the aircraft carriers. Between August 1940 and the last of this type of operation at the end of August 1942, 670 Hurricanes and Spitfires were flown in to Malta from the decks of carriers in the Western Mediterranean in nineteen separate operations.

After 'Pedestal' Malta had still several months of extreme hardship and anxiety to endure before the long ordeal was over. Of the 47,000 tons unloaded from the convoy, 15,000 were black and white oils and 32,000 general supplies. On these the island could hold out until early December, but on rations so meagre that the health of the people was bound to suffer. In August the fortnightly individual sugar ration stood at 14 oz, fats at 7 oz, and corned beef at 14 oz. Early in September the daily ration of bread for men between 16 and 60 years was raised to 14 oz, while the normal remained at 10½ oz. At this time the daily calorific value of the diet, including the meal from the Victory Kitchens, was 1,690 for adult male workers and 1,500 for women and children. A properly balanced diet of 1,500 calories will support life for some months but only at the cost of rapid loss of weight and physical powers. The pre-war figure for Maltese not engaged in manual labour was assessed at 2,500; manual workers had eaten substantially more. (In the United Kingdom the calorific value of the available daily ration did not fall below 2,800 throughout the war.) In August it was at length decided to begin the slaughter of Malta's livestock on a large scale. This would make it unnecessary to import fodder and would free grazing and fodder-growing land for producing food for human consumption; the fresh meat thus provided was bought by the Government for the Victory Kitchens.

Stocks of aviation spirit were still too low to permit the build-up of much larger air striking forces at Malta. Supply by submarine or by the *Welshman*, which was being fitted to carry this dangerous cargo, was intended to ensure that at all events the fighters would have enough. The wastage of fighters had to be made good and on 17th August a further 29 Spitfires were flown in from H.M.S. *Furious*.

The retreat on land and the move of the Fleet from Alexandria greatly increased the distances which the Royal Navy and the Royal Air Force had to cover in attacking Axis shipping. Benghazi could be reached with worth-while bombloads only by Liberators, and even Tobruk, which was now being used by the enemy for his smaller supply ships, was farther from British bases than Benghazi had been before the retreat. Moreover, in June and again in August nearly all the submarines had been diverted from their anti-shipping patrols to take part in convoy operations; others had been employed in supplying Malta. After the loss of the *Medway* it was decided to base the 1st Submarine Flotilla on Beirut, where there had previously been a French submarine base. At the end of July the Commanders-in-Chief asked for more submarines for the Central and Eastern Mediterranean, and during August and September these arrived, many of them from the 8th Flotilla at Gibraltar. A request for more destroyers from which to build up again a surface striking force at Malta could not be met, owing to the general shortage. Although the enemy was routeing many of his ships via Greece and Crete direct to Derna and Tobruk, the Fleet Air Arm Albacores could not reach even the Crete-Tobruk traffic. Not to be denied, the Fleet Air Arm and Royal Air Force together devised a plan to refuel Albacores behind the enemy's lines far to the west of the main battle area. On 9th/10th July six Bombays from No. 216 Squadron carried 1,500 gallons of petrol and 60 gallons of oil to a landing-ground near Fort Maddalena from where, after refuelling, ten Albacores of No. 826 Squadron took off to attack a convoy to the south-west of Crete. That no enemy ships were sunk was certainly not due to any lack of enterprise. It was in July also that a Beaufort's crew, which had been made prisoner after a forced landing, overpowered the Italian crew of the seaplane in which they were being flown to Italy and brought it safely to Malta where it was later used in the British service.

From June to September Malta's aircraft and those of No. 201 Group operating from Egypt flew close on 1,000 sorties in searching for enemy shipping; and more than 3,300 were flown on anti-shipping strikes. Taken all in all, August was the most profitable month of the four, and a few typical exploits may be mentioned to enliven the bare figures given in the following tables. On the 17th the *Rosolino Pilo*, of 8,326 tons, when thirty-five miles off Lampedusa, blew up and sank as a result of the combined action of six Beauforts of No. 86 Squadron and submarine *P.44*. On the 27th Beauforts of No. 39 Squadron and Beaufighters of No. 227 Squadron (some carrying bombs) attacked the *Istria* of 5,400 tons, which also blew up and sank. These same squadrons sank the *Sanandrea*, a tanker of 5,077 tons, on the 30th. One of the most successful submarine patrols of this period was that of H.M.S. *Porpoise*. She sank the *Ogaden*, of 4,553 tons, on the 12th August, and, four days later, damaged the *Lerici*, of 6,070 tons, so severely that she had to be sunk by her escort; on the 22nd the Italian torpedo boat *Cantore* blew up on one of the mines laid by *Porpoise* in the Gulf of Sollum at the commencement of her patrol. Earlier in the month, on the 7th, *Porpoise* had sunk the German merchant vessel *Wachtfels*, of 8,467 tons, ten miles north-west of Milos Island in the Aegean.

Number and tonnage of Italian and German merchant ships of over 500 tons sunk at sea or in port in the Mediterranean
June – September 1942

(Compiled from Italian post-war and German war records)

Month	By surface ships	By submarine	By aircraft	By mine	By combined Naval and Air action	Total
June	—	2— 2,565	3— 16,701	1— 750	—	6— 20,016
July	2— 3,877	1— 792	4— 10,919	—	—	7— 15,588
Aug.	—	7— 40,036	3— 12,020	1— 4,894	1— 8,326	12— 65,276
Sept.	—	5— 13,249	5— 20,948	—	2— 2,737	12— 36,934
TOTAL	2— 3,877	15— 56,642	15— 60,588	2— 5,644	3— 11,063	37— 137,814

Over the same period 17 vessels of less than 500 tons, totalling some 2,500 tons, were also sunk.

The tonnage of general military cargoes and fuel unloaded in North Africa over the same period, and the percentage lost on the way, are shown in the table following:

Cargoes disembarked in North Africa and Percentage lost on passage

(From figures given by the Italian Official Naval Historian)[1]

Month 1942	Type	Cargo disembarked in North Africa (tons)	Percentage lost on the way
June	General Military Cargo	26,759	23
	Fuel	5,568	17
July	General Military Cargo	67,590	6 (both)
	Fuel	23,901	
August	General Military Cargo	29,155	25
	Fuel	22,500	41
Sept.	General Military Cargo	46,165	20 (both)
	Fuel	31,061	

[1] M. A. Bragadin: *Che ha fatto la Marina?*

As usual Allied submarines found many things to do on patrol besides attacking shipping. Coastal railways in Sicily and southern Italy were a favourite target. Gunfire could be used against the trains themselves, and guns or raiding parties could destroy bridges. Mine-laying submarines were busy along the North African coast and in the channels between Greek islands. To lessen the weight of enemy air attack from Crete during operation 'Vigorous', British and French parties had been landed from two Greek submarines to raid airfields and succeeded in destroying several aircraft and some bombs and petrol. A similar attempt was made from the submarine *Una* to raid Catania airfield on the night of the 11th/12th August, before the arrival of the 'Pedestal' convoy, but it was unsuccessful. Two British submarines were lost during the four months covered by this chapter. On 11th August H.M.S. *Thorn* was sunk to the south-west of Crete by two Italian torpedo boats. During September H.M.S. *Talisman* was lost on passage from Gibraltar to Malta—probably early on the 17th when the Italians claimed that a torpedo boat had sunk a submarine off the Tunisian coast.

Surface warships of the Mediterranean Fleet made frequent anti-shipping sweeps along the coast during August and September but without success. Bombardments in the El Daba area were carried out on 29th August and 14th September. (A raid on Tobruk on 13th September is described in Volume IV.) In the second half of August transport and protection for a further movement of about 12,000 troops in and out of Cyprus had to be provided; the transport *Princess Marguerite* was sunk by a German U-boat, but the casualties were fortunately light.

The ships of the 15th Cruiser Squadron had taken the opportunity during these two months for a quick docking at Massawa where a floating dock was now working. On 12th September their commander, Sir Philip Vian, had been succeeded by Rear-Admiral A. J. Power, and next day Rear-Admiral I. G. Glennie was succeeded in command of the Mediterranean destroyer flotillas by Commodore P. Todd. Towards the end of the month Commodore J. G. L. Dundas replaced Rear-Admiral J. H. Edelsten as Chief of Staff.

During the period covered by this chapter the enemy lost ten submarines. On 2nd June *U.652* was sunk by aircraft north of Sollum. The *Veniero* was sunk on 7th June and the *Zaffiro* on the 9th, both to the south of Majorca and both by aircraft from Gibraltar—the first by a Sunderland and the second by a Catalina. On 9th July another Italian, the *Perla*, surrendered after depth charge attacks to the corvette *Hyacinth* which towed her proudly into Beirut. The *Perla* was one of the four Italian submarines in the Red Sea in the spring of 1941 which had made a successful passage from Massawa to Bordeaux. She was now taken into British service and later lent to the Greek

Navy. Two days after the capture of the *Perla*, South African anti-submarine whalers helped by a Walrus aircraft destroyed the *Ondina*, and on 4th August another combined effort, this time between destroyers and aircraft off Haifa, sank the *U.372* which just five weeks earlier had sunk H.M.S. *Medway*. In the same area, on 10th August, the trawler *Islay* sank the *Sciré*, the Italian submarine which had long been used for the transport of human torpedoes and was notable for the successful attacks on the *Queen Elizabeth* and *Valiant*. Next came the destruction of the *Cobalto* and *Dagabur* during operation 'Pedestal', and finally the *Albastro* was sunk by a Sunderland flying boat on 14th September off Algiers.

Down in the Gulf of Aden, enemy submarines, presumably Japanese, had made their appearance again in September, but had sunk only two ships. At the opposite extreme, just outside the limits of Admiral Harwood's command, the Italian 'Sea Devils' had been making trouble again at Gibraltar. On 14th July explosions occurred in three British merchant ships in the commercial anchorage, and on 15th September, in spite of a further tightening of precautions against this form of attack, the British *Ravenspoint* was damaged and settled on the bottom in thirty feet of water. These attacks were suspected, correctly, to be the work of divers wearing a form of shallow-water diving dress who fixed small explosive charges, known as limpets, to the hulls of their targets. It is now known that the Italians used an interned merchant ship, the *Folgore*, at Cadiz as the secret base for their work against Gibraltar. Before making these two attacks, they had rented a villa on the seashore near La Linea in Spanish territory at the head of Gibraltar Bay, and had adapted to their purpose another interned Italian merchant ship, the *Olterra*, which was moored off Algeciras.

Although this chapter has run concurrently with the critical period of the fighting in the Desert, it has been devoted almost exclusively to the story of three Malta convoys. It is therefore appropriate to recall that the supply of Malta was only an episode—although a most important one—in the long struggle to keep the rival forces in North Africa supplied.

The problems facing the two sides in this struggle were totally different. On the Axis side, the sea passage across the Mediterranean was at most 600 miles. This gave the Axis Powers the chance to send over any urgent requirements at short notice, and on occasion they did so with great effect. The whole length of the route, however, was in danger of attack by British submarines, aircraft, and surface warships, and, as has been seen, the Italian and German losses were considerable. When Italy entered the war her merchant fleet was at once reduced by more than one-third through the loss by internment of those of her ships then outside the Mediterranean.[1] By September 1942 she had lost about half the remainder, and with them much of the flexibility which the short sea passage to Africa conferred upon her.[2]

The problem confronting the British was on a much larger scale, partly because their forces in the Middle East had to be self-dependent, and therefore much bigger, and partly because the distances were so vast. Almost every man and thing had to be brought across the oceans, from Australasia, India, or South Africa, but mostly from the United Kingdom or North America round the Cape—a distance of some 14,000 miles. Yet if this route was long, and subject to tedious delays, it proved at least to be sure. Indeed, in the 'W.S.' series of military convoys (U.K. to Suez), which carried nearly all the men, only one ship was lost on passage.[3] Among the numerous cargo ships plying to the Middle East, the losses, though not negligible, amounted to no more than three per cent of the cargoes embarked. According to the Italian Official Naval Historian the comparable figure for Axis losses in supplying North Africa between June 1940 and May 1943 was over sixteen per cent.[4]

---

[1] In June 1940 Italy possessed 792 ships of over 500 tons totalling 3,350,000 gross tons. The comparable British figure was over 20,000,000.

[2] Bragadin: *Che ha fatto la Marina?* page 608.

[3] The s.s. *Soudan* of convoy W.S. 18 was sunk on 15th May 1942 by a mine laid by the German raider *Thor* 150 miles south-west of the Cape of Good Hope. See also p. 353n.

[4] Bragadin: *op. cit.*, page 598.

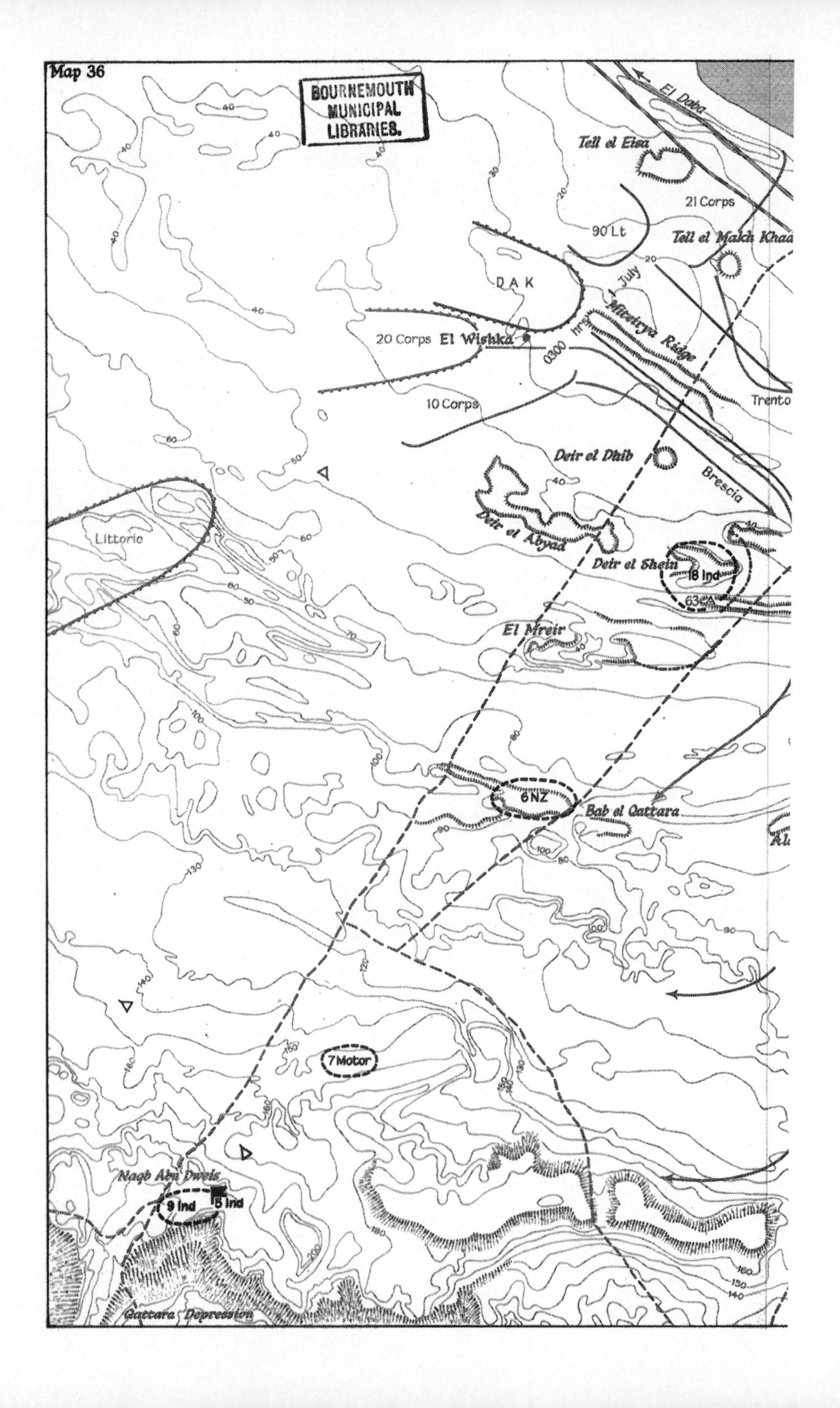

BOURNEMOUTH MUNICIPAL LIBRARIES.

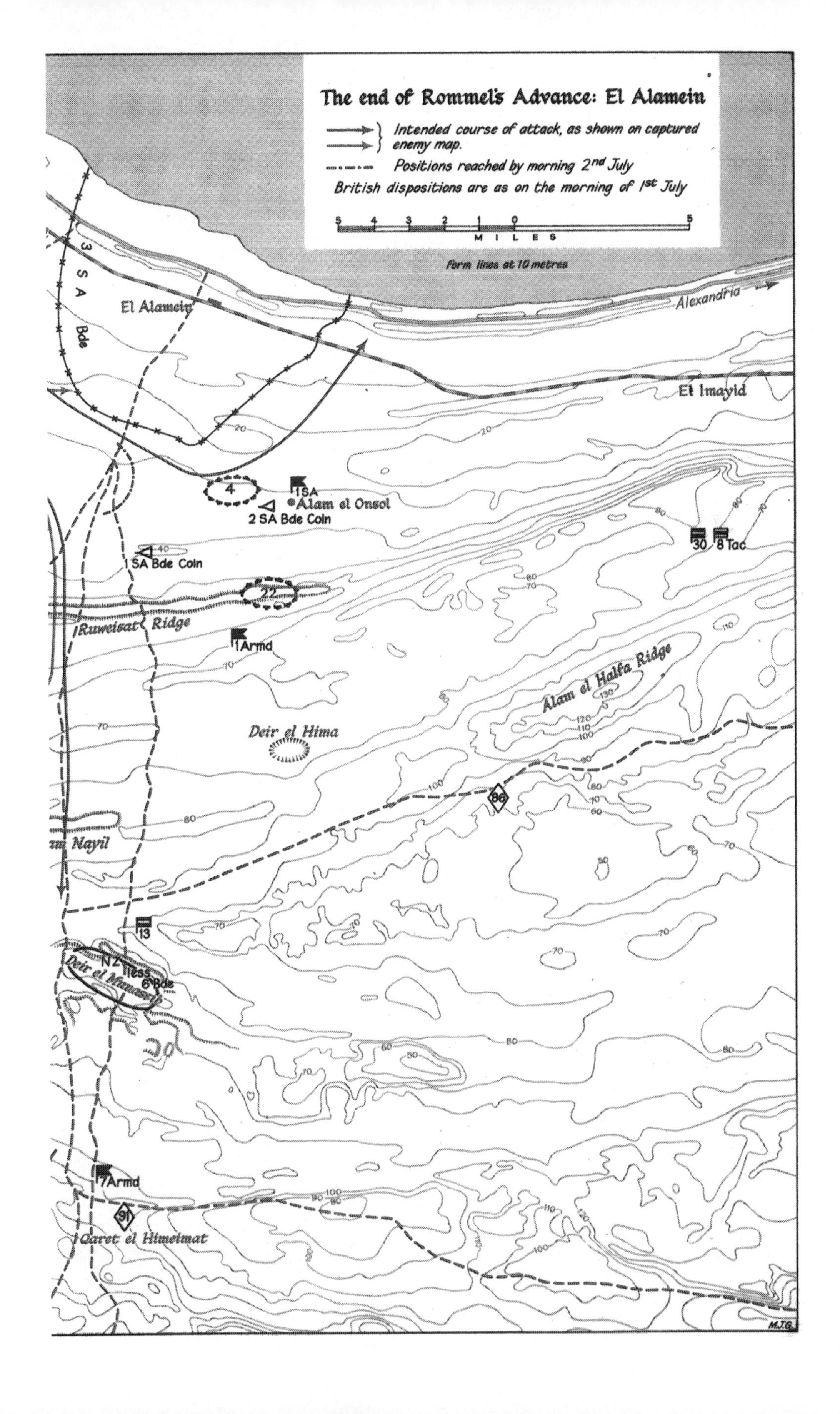
The end of Rommel's Advance: El Alamein
Intended course of attack, as shown on captured enemy map.
Positions reached by morning 2nd July
British dispositions are as on the morning of 1st July
MILES
Form lines at 10 metres
Alexandria
El Alamein
3 SA Bde
El Imayid
4
1 SA
Alam el Onsol
2 SA Bde Coln
1 SA Bde Coln
30
8 Tac
22
Ruweisat Ridge
1 Armd
Alam el Halfa Ridge
Deir el Hima
86
Alam Nayil
13
NZ
6 Bde
Deir el Munassib
7 Armd
91
Qaret el Himeimat
M.J.G.

CHAPTER XIV

THE FIGHTING IN THE EL ALAMEIN LINE

See Map 36

THE last days of June saw General Auchinleck striving to plug the gap between El Alamein and the lip of the Qattara Depression, partly with troops who had been there for some days, and partly with those who had escaped from Matruh. Meanwhile reinforcements from Palestine and Iraq were on the way. Field-Marshal Rommel, for his part, had but one thought—to hustle the British and prevent them settling down. If the momentum of his pursuit could be made to carry him past El Alamein, he felt confident of reaching the Delta without much further opposition. For this reason he drove his men unmercifully. (A plaintive entry in the diary of the 90th Light Division shows that they were not even allowed time to bathe in the sea.) Many were the complaints of exhaustion and shortages, but all were brushed aside in furtherance of the policy of allowing the British no respite.

It had been understood in the *Panzerarmee* that after the capture of Tobruk there would be a pause of at least six weeks. When, as it turned out, there was no pause at all, the supply and transport services were taken unawares and had more than they could do to keep up with the spearheads which were being persistently driven forward by the energetic Army Commander. No use could be made of the railway, for not a single repairable locomotive had been left behind by the British.[1] Captured stocks of all kinds were considerable and undoubtedly of great value, but did not provide the complete answer, for they took time to distribute and absorb.[2] The air forces, in particular, were seriously short of transport. Water and ammunition were causes of constant anxiety. In spite of all this the Field-Marshal, by his devil-take-the-hindmost methods, drove his advanced troops into contact

[1] The railway started to run in a very small way in August. About 300 wagons had been left behind at El Daba, but they were constantly bombed by the R.A.F. and by the time the Axis had shipped over a few Diesel locomotives there was hardly any serviceable rolling-stock. Work was begun on extending the line from Belhamed to Tobruk harbour, but was never finished.

[2] According to the *Panzerarmee's* administrative diary it was the captured stocks of provisions that took the army to El Alamein. About half the casualties among German vehicles had been replaced by captured ones.

with the so-called 'Alamein line' on the 30th June, on the same day that many of the retreating British reached it. Indeed there were several brushes in the desert inland of El Daba between small parties, many of them not very sure of the identity of the others, but all determined to make the Alamein line as quickly as possible.

The thirty-eight miles of desert between the Qattara Depression and the coast near the wayside railway station of El Alamein has no prominent features except the rocky hills which border the salt marshes and sand-dunes of the depression itself. From these hills, some 700 feet above sea level, the ground falls gradually to the coast, so that it is everywhere almost flat. Patches of loose sand alternate with areas which allow of free movement. There are occasional mounds ('tells') of which two—Tell el Eisa and Tell el Makh Khad—should be noted; several shallow saucers of various sizes, called 'deirs'; and numerous low ridges, among which the Miteirya, Ruweisat, and Alam el Halfa ridges play a prominent part in the story. The ridges generally are of hard rock, barely covered with loose sand, which made the construction of field defences extremely laborious and the rapid consolidation of a captured position well-nigh impossible.[1]

Some work had already been done. Since before the war the 'Alamein line' had been recognized as the possible site of a position for defending the Delta of Egypt—a glance at a map is enough to show why—and various troops and civil labour gangs had been employed there from time to time. But when preparations began for 'Crusader' and for the defence of the Syria-Iraq front, work at El Alamein naturally fell very low on the list of things to be done.

The plan had been to create three defended localities, about fifteen miles apart, at El Alamein, Bab el Qattara (also known as Qaret el Abd), and Naqb Abu Dweis. The defences of the first had been dug and were partly wired and mined; at the second they had been dug, but there was no minefield; at the third very little had been done. A water pipeline had however been laid right across the front from El Alamein to Naqb Abu Dweis, though owing to changes in the dispositions it turned out to be of little use. General Norrie wished to create other localities in the gaps, one of them to be sited at Deir El Shein, just north of the western end of the Ruweisat Ridge. No work had yet been done on any of these. Such was the slender framework of the position to which the British were withdrawing: the term 'Alamein line' at this time meant only a line on the map.

It was General Auchinleck's intention that part of the Army should

[1] The Arabic names on the map are a guide to the topography, e.g.:

Naqb or *Bab*, a pass or cutting.
Qaret, a low hill.
Alam, a cairn or rock.
Sanyet, a deep well.
Deir, a depression.

hold positions to canalize and disorganize the enemy's advance, while the remainder, keeping mobile, should strike at his flanks and rear. Infantry divisions were to organize their mobile components into 'artillery battle-groups' whose actions were to be co-ordinated by Divisional Commanders in person. Corps Commanders were to ensure that the maximum forces were concentrated at the decisive point, even if this should be outside their own sector. Everyone and everything which did not fulfil an immediate tactical purpose was to be sent to the rear—an instruction which, however sound tactically, favoured the spread of discouraging rumours.

It may be thought that General Auchinleck should have declared that it was now 'Backs to the Wall' and that the Army, reinforced by every possible man and gun from Egypt, and fully supported by the Middle East air force, would die where it stood. Certainly such an order would have cleared away much bewilderment and doubt, for some of the measures adopted at this time seemed to the men in the ranks inconsistent with a firm determination to fight. To this extent a clear and resolute call would have been all to the good. Yet there was no denying that the enemy was on the crest of the wave. He had soundly defeated the British at Gazala, Tobruk, and Matruh. British losses in men and equipment had been very high. Now, almost within sight of a most coveted prize, Rommel would certainly press on with all his might. His troops were tired, no doubt, but so was the 8th Army, which, unlike the enemy, had not been stimulated by a run of success. The Alamein positions were not complete and the British formations were mostly weak and disorganized. On the whole General Auchinleck felt that, although he had a good chance to stop Rommel, and firmly intended to try, it would be wrong to ignore the possibility that once more his own rather loosely-knit army might be outmanoeuvred or outfought. Above all, he decided, it must be kept in being. Therefore it might have to retreat again.

One of the most awkward problems that can confront a Commander-in-Chief, still hoping for the best, is how to prepare for the worst without causing such alarm and despondency that the worst is almost bound to occur. Nowhere would this problem have been more delicate than in Egypt—a sovereign State not at war with the Axis. Neither the Egyptian authorities nor the people could be expected to be enthusiastic about measures for flooding their precious cultivation, or for demolishing their public utilities. But the British did their work discreetly, the Egyptian authorities gave their co-operation, and the country remained remarkably calm. To this happy result the Minister of State, Mr. Casey, the Ambassador, Sir Miles Lampson, and their staffs contributed not a little. It was certainly a fortunate outcome, for a breakdown of internal security in Egypt would have gone far towards ensuring a British defeat. As it was, defensive positions were constructed west of Alexandria and a large amount of land to the south was flooded. A fortified area was organized between the Wadi Natrun and the edge of the Delta. Defences were built near Mena and the Pyramids, to cover the close approaches to Cairo. Rearward communications were improved and boat bridges were thrown across the Nile. The Royal Navy organized a Nile Flotilla of armed small craft. All G.H.Q. schools were closed and every available fighting man found his place in some improvised unit or formation. All administrative establishments and stocks were cleared from the Western Delta.

General Auchinleck intended, if he failed to stop the enemy at El Alamein, to fight step by step through Egypt, and in the last resort to hold the Suez Canal with part of his force while the remainder withdrew along the Nile. Plans for these operations were made, taking advantage of the work already done to develop Aqaba and link it by road to the new branch of the Hedjaz railway from Ma'an.[1] G.H.Q. made ready to move to Gaza and leave an operational section in Cairo. A 'scorched earth' policy was examined but it was decided that, broadly speaking, nothing essential to the existence of the Egyptian people should be destroyed.[2] The list of demolitions to be prepared was nevertheless a long one, and included wireless stations, telegraph and telephone systems, transportation and electricity systems, oil and petrol installations and stocks, and stocks of cotton, silk and coal. No flooding in the Delta was to be done until the need became compelling. All these plans were no doubt wise and necessary, but as they could not be kept secret they furnished rich material for the gossip which, especially in back areas, thrives on emergencies.

The fighting in the El Alamein positions during July was almost continuous and often very heavy, and much of it is difficult to follow. A broad outline will serve as a background against which to view the details later. The outstanding feature is that the enemy's triumphant rush was not merely checked but was stopped.

The month began with a typical Rommel operation—a replica of his successful stroke at Matruh. He intended to penetrate just south of the El Alamein locality with the object of cutting the coast road and to make a sweep with his armour towards the south. The thrust was successfully opposed by the 30th Corps in the north, and the 13th Corps tried to attack the enemy's southern flank. This phase melted into another in which the 30th Corps still barred the way while the 13th Corps tried to outflank the enemy by manœuvring north and

---

[1] See Volume II, Chapter XI.

[2] e.g.: irrigation works, water systems in towns, flour mills, kerosene, stocks of cereals, cotton seed, vegetable oils, sugar, tea.

north-west. This attempt failed. On 10th July the 30th Corps attacked near the coast at Tell el Eisa, throwing the enemy on the defensive. General Auchinleck next tried twice, both times unsuccessfully and with heavy loss, to break through the enemy's centre—on the Ruweisat Ridge between 14th and 16th July, and again on this ridge and at El Mreir on the 21st and 22nd. In these attacks the 13th Corps took the main part. After a short pause the 30th Corps again attacked near Tell el Eisa and the Miteirya Ridge. This too was a failure, and General Auchinleck then decided that he must make a long pause to rest, reorganize, and re-train his sadly battered army.

Meanwhile a great deal of work had been done on defences designed to give depth to the position, and on plans—in case withdrawal should be necessary—for keeping the 8th Army in being and for continuing the fight for the Delta.

It has been seen how, towards the end of June, the Desert Air Force had done its utmost to take the pressure off the retreating 8th Army by attacking the enemy's troops, transport, and supplies. Nevertheless, the pursuit had been carried out remarkably quickly, but only by a comparatively small force which had become tired and weakened by shortages of all kinds. The idea of giving the Axis forces no respite from air attack throughout the twenty-four hours had now begun to be translated into action.

By July the Desert Air Force had been pressed back into the lap of the Egypt-based portion of the Royal Air Force, and there were not enough airfields to go round. The light bombers and the main force of fighters were therefore allotted the airfields in the Amiriya area, with main bases in the Canal zone and at Cairo, and the medium and heavy bombers were forced to move back to Palestine.

In July, with the front stabilizing, a new peak of intensity of air effort was reached. From the 1st to the 27th the Royal Air Force in Egypt and the Levant flew close on 15,400 sorties, apart from those against ships, which gives the impressive average of 570 sorties every twenty-four hours. Of this achievement General Auchinleck wrote in his Despatch: '. . . Our air forces could not have done more than they did to help and sustain the Eighth Army in its struggle. Their effort was continuous by day and night, and the effect on the enemy was tremendous. I am certain that, had it not been for their devoted and exceptional efforts, we should not have been able to stop the enemy on the El Alamein position, and I wish to record my gratitude and that of the whole of the Eighth Army to Air Chief Marshal Tedder, Air Marshal Coningham, and the air forces under their command.'[1]

[1] Air Marshal Tedder was promoted to Air Chief Marshal on 1st July, 1942.

The pattern of air operations throughout the month did not vary greatly. It covered broadly three types: operations directed against the enemy's supply lines, those against his air forces—in the air and on the airfields—and those in more direct support of the Army. The emphasis was on the last of these when the Army was attacking or being attacked; during the comparative lulls part of the air effort was lifted on to other objectives—notably Benghazi, Tobruk and Matruh, and occasionally Heraklion and Suda Bay in Crete.

Throughout the month British aircraft roamed up and down the front and deep into enemy territory on offensive and defensive tasks and on reconnaissances of all kinds—strategical, tactical, survey and photographic. It was inevitable that the losses should be heavy; in fact the Royal Air Force lost 113 aircraft from all causes against about 80 German and 18 Italian.

One result of the long retreat had been that the machinery for army/air co-operation had slipped out of gear. Indeed, it was to be some time before it was again in full working order. On many occasions good targets were reported by the tactical reconnaissance aircraft without the information being passed on to the bombers. The bomb-lines were often drawn so far to the west as almost to rule out any close support at all; moreover the wishes of Divisions and Corps in this respect seem to have differed from those of the Army. In an attempt to improve matters the Army undertook to be able to predict the position of its foremost troops two hours ahead, leaving the R.A.F. to decide how close to these positions they could attack. This was not entirely successful, and there were many complaints of British aircraft being fired at by their own troops, and also of British troops being bombed by their own aircraft. German and Italian diaries disclose similar occurrences on their side, and it is interesting to read that on 3rd July the *Fliegerführer Afrika*, General von Waldau, was complaining that the lack of co-operation between the *Panzerarmee* and the *Luftwaffe* made it difficult to judge the course of events, for information from his Air units did not agree with that supplied by the Army.

It is noteworthy that on the British side the first essential for good co-operation was lacking, for General Auchinleck was directing his operations from an Advanced Headquarters near El Imayid fifteen miles east of El Alamein, while Air Vice-Marshal Coningham's Headquarters were forty miles away, close to the Main Headquarters of the 8th Army at Amiriya. Towards the end of the month matters improved a little, and with good information coming from units on the ground the Air Force could operate much closer to the British positions, to the great satisfaction of the troops who were often able to pass back the results immediately. At about this time the enemy began to disperse his vehicles by day much more widely than before, which made them less profitable as targets. By night, however, the combination of target illuminating by the Albacores and attacks by the Wellingtons often caught concentrations of vehicles in leaguer and interfered seriously with the work of maintenance. More than that, the harassing effect of 'round the clock' bombing was noted with growing frequency in the enemy's diaries, and Rommel himself referred to it as the main feature of the violent and bloody battles of July.

For the British, perhaps the most serious feature of the month was the wastage in fighters. Although the proportion of aircraft fit to fly had been high, the strength of many squadrons had fallen below one half—Kittyhawks being especially scarce. This fact gives added interest to the opinion of General von Waldau, who wrote on 25th July: '. . . Although the enemy has lost a great many of his fighter aircraft during the last two months, there has been so far no apparent sign of a decrease in flying ability or combat performance. Combat effectiveness has been maintained, and indeed increased, by the assignment of new and excellently trained Spitfire squadrons from England. The employment of the Spitfire has given the enemy the confidence he needs to hold his own against our Me. 109s.'

The pursuit to El Alamein had made advanced landing-grounds available to the enemy at El Daba, only 90 miles from the naval base at Alexandria, 185 miles from Cairo, less than 250 miles from the main Army and R.A.F. depots, installations, and airfields in the Delta and Canal zone, and little more from Suez itself. These distances were much less than from Crete, and it was to be expected that there would be daylight attacks by bombers with fighter escort on Alexandria, and minelaying and bombing by night on the Canal and the busy terminal port of Suez. This threat was serious, for anti-aircraft guns were few for so many targets, and the fighters had necessarily to be mainly concentrated in the forward area. Yet except for fairly large raids nightly from the 3rd to the 7th July, when he lost four He. 111s, and again between the 25th and 30th, when he lost two more He. 111s and two Ju. 88s, the enemy showed no inclination to use his bombers to attack the sensitive spots in the British back area. The emphasis was almost all on giving support to the Army.

The attacks just mentioned achieved nothing at Alexandria. There was some damage to a pumping station and a fuel tank at Port Said, and mines were dropped in the Canal, which closed it to shipping for about a week. Mines were laid and bombs were dropped among ships off Suez, but the only casualty was one water boat. On 28th July the Boom Defence Vessel *Punnet* was badly damaged and H.E.M.S. *Fawzia*, employed on coastguard duty in the Red Sea, was sunk. But the great volume of shipping, bringing the reinforcements with which the British were enabled to fight back, continued to arrive and unload with very little interference, just as they had done the previous year during the lull before 'Crusader'. Now, as then, the Germans and

Italians seem not to have realized how important it was for them to dislocate the busy port of Suez, focal point for the arrival of British reinforcements of all kinds.

The nearness of the enemy's airfields had, as described in the previous chapter, led to the evacuation of Alexandria by the Mediterranean Fleet at the end of June, and preparations were made for demolishing the port and blocking the harbour. The cruisers and destroyers were divided into two bombarding forces, one based at Haifa, the other at Port Said, and four times between 12th and 20th July some of these ships were called upon to bombard the Matruh area by night with the aid of flares dropped by Albacores of the Fleet Air Arm. These bombardments sank two merchant vessels and added to the damage to the port and other shipping already caused by R.A.F. bombs. Thereafter, the enemy restricted his coastal shipping to still smaller ships, landing craft, and sailing vessels. Supplies passing through Mersa Matruh fell considerably in consequence.

July was a disappointing month for the enemy, who started with high hopes of a quick success at the gateway to Egypt. Within a week these hopes had almost vanished, and before the month was out there were doubts whether the Axis forces would even be able to hold on. Mussolini, accompanied by Cavallero and von Rintelen, had flown over to Cyrenaica on 29th June, in readiness to be in at the kill. He spent some time discussing the relative merits of Cairo and Alexandria as objectives; what was more to the point, he ordered the Italian air forces to be reinforced, which led to arguments with the Germans over the supply of oil fuel for the Italian Navy. He did not visit the front, and Rommel did not visit him. On 20th July, by which time it was evident that there would be no early triumph, he returned to Italy.

Marshal Cavallero, who was pointedly promoted to that rank a few days after Rommel had been made a Field-Marshal, applied himself energetically to the task of building up the Italian forces, by now woefully weak and disorganized. He arranged for seven infantry battalions and four artillery regiments, as well as tanks, armoured cars and self-propelled guns, to be sent over from Italy; most of the men were to be flown, and the tanks were to come in barges. The Folgore Parachute Division was being sent to Africa at once, and would be followed by the Pistoia and Friuli Divisions. Meanwhile the Germans had begun to fly reinforcements from Crete to Tobruk—over 2,000 had arrived by 5th July—and a start had been made in bringing over the 164th Light Africa Division, to be followed towards the end of the month by the Ramcke Parachute Brigade.

On 21st July Rommel made a long and depressing report to *OKH*

—a report of the failure of his plans. His German troops had been fighting for eight weeks without a break and had lost heavily. He had been obliged to spread them all along the front to stiffen the Italians, who were a constant anxiety to him. Having done this he did not fear a wide break-through, but the position would be critical until the 164th Division had arrived, a mobile reserve had been formed, and the front covered by obstacles. The Germans were down to 30 per cent. of their effective strength and the losses in experienced men were particularly serious, as the replacements were found to be only partly trained.

Reviewing the British situation, he rated high the New Zealand and 9th Australian Divisions which had had time to train in Syria and Palestine. He praised the British field artillery for its versatility and for its plentiful supplies of ammunition, and noted that the medium and heavy artillery was being strengthened. The British supply situation was very favourable because of the convenient harbours and network of railways. The Royal Air Force, now concentrated in Egypt, was attacking everything—sea traffic, the *Luftwaffe*, and the ground organizations, as well as the forward troops. His own supply situation was precarious, owing to air attacks on Tobruk and Matruh. Food was adequate (thanks to captures) and there was enough fuel for the present type of operations but not for a large offensive. Captured transport was plentiful, but suffered from lack of spare parts, and the daily loss from air attack was thirty vehicles. In short, he wrote, the Alamein position could be kept supplied, but stocks for an advance could not be built up. He pressed for more shipping space to be allotted to German reinforcements, and for 'Special' tanks, armoured cars, 5-cm. and 8·8-cm. anti-tank guns, and recovery vehicles. It was important to reinforce the air forces in Africa, not only to protect the troops and their supplies, but to enable attacks to be made on railway traffic and on shipping at Suez and in the Canal.

In fact, as Cavallero and Kesselring no doubt noticed, Rommel was reciting a list of the evil consequences which they themselves had feared would follow if the *Panzerarmee* failed to break through at El Alamein. To Kesselring in particular the situation was most unsatisfactory, for on the one hand Rommel was pressing for more air action in Egypt and on the other hand he himself had already been obliged to divide his air strength by concentrating a large force of German aircraft in Sicily (including more than half the Ju. 88s available in the Mediterranean area) in order to resume the attacks on Malta. And at this moment von Waldau was reporting that his fighters were steadily decreasing and that his fuel situation was critical.

We now turn to consider the July operations in more detail.

On 30th June Rommel had two obvious choices—to attack as soon as possible or spare a little time in learning about the ground and the British dispositions. He chose the former course, and paid heavily for being in such a hurry. The British dispositions were as shown on Map 36, but the enemy did not know of the presence of the South Africans and expected to find the 18th Indian Infantry Brigade at Deir el Abyad. Rommel's plan was for the 90th Light Division and the *D.A.K.* to penetrate between the El Alamein defences (held, he supposed, by the remains of the 50th Division) and Deir el Abyad, starting at 3 a.m. on 1st July. The 90th Light would then make for the coast and cut off El Alamein from the east—just as they had done at Matruh. Meanwhile the *D.A.K.* would swing south to Alam Nayil (which meant a night march of twenty-two miles) to take the British 13th Corps in the rear. One Italian division was to attack El Alamein from the west, another was to follow 90th Light, and the Italian 20th Corps was to follow the *D.A.K.* and deal with Bab el Qattara. The Littorio Armoured Division and the German reconnaissance units were to protect the southern flank.

The 90th Light Division, still badly in need of rest, reached its assembly area in good time. The *D.A.K.* ran into some very bad going, and at 1.30 a.m. on 1st July reported that it could not be ready to attack at the time ordered. One of its trials was an early sandstorm, and only by a continuous firework display of light signals were its units able to keep in touch. The 21st Panzer Division became mixed up with the 15th and at 6 a.m. was in dire confusion; it only needed a heavy air attack to make its misery complete. At 6.15 this, too, took place.

The 90th Light soon lost direction, strayed too far north, collided with the El Alamein defences, and became pinned down. It did not resume its advance until early in the afternoon. Nor had the *D.A.K.* fared much better, for in its belated attempt to circle round Deir el Abyad—it was now broad daylight—it discovered that Deir el Shein was in British hands, and General Nehring decided to attack it.

The 18th Indian Infantry Brigade, under a temporary commander, was newly arrived from Iraq.[1] Two of its three battalions had never been in action. Helped by the South African Engineers the Brigade had laboured for three days to construct defences in the rocky ground and now had section posts, a thin wire obstacle, and a partial minefield. It was short of small arms ammunition. It had received a small reinforcement of nine Matilda tanks manned by scratch crews, and was

[1] 18th Indian Infantry Brigade (Lieut.-Colonel C. E. Gray, 2/3rd Gurkha Rifles, in temporary command) was for the moment under command of 1st S.A. Division. Its battalions were 2/5th Essex Regiment, 4/11th Sikh Regiment, 2/3rd Gurkha Rifles. It had no artillery but on 30th June and during the night 30th June/1st July it received twenty-three 25-pdr guns drawn from 97th, 121st, and 124th Field Regiments R.A.; also the anti-tank company of the Buffs, which had been in possession of its sixteen 6-pdr guns for only a fortnight.

struggling to organize itself on the latest column idea. The supporting artillery was drawn from three different regiments and was short of signal equipment. Fortunately, whatever else was lacking, the small garrison at Deir el Shein had courage and determination in good measure.

For some time before 9 a.m. on 1st July registration by enemy artillery foretold an attack. Then came a demand to surrender, which was refused. Heavy shelling was followed by infantry attacks and by about 1 p.m. the enemy, aided by the dust, managed to gap the minefield in the north-east corner. Through this gap passed about a dozen enemy tanks, but the defence was hotly maintained and not until 4 p.m. did the arrival of eight more enemy tanks turn the scale. Many guns were knocked out and by 5 p.m. the Matildas were also out of action and the greater part of the position had been overrun. The brunt of the fighting had been borne by the 2/5th Essex Regiment and the 4/11th Sikhs, for the attack had not fallen on the 2/3rd Gurkhas. Various parties continued to resist and it was not until after 7 p.m. that all was over. The Brigade's gallant defence had not only dislocated the enemy's plan but had gained several precious hours during which the 1st Armoured Division, which had been almost out of petrol and whose 4th Armoured Brigade was stuck in an unsuspected tract of soft sand, was able to replenish and regroup.

The first intimation that Deir el Shein was in trouble reached the 30th Corps through the 1st South African Division at 1.30 p.m. The 1st Armoured Division was ordered to intervene, but at 2.30 received word from its armoured cars that all seemed quiet at Deir el Shein. At 4.30, on a more urgent order from the Corps, the 22nd Armoured Brigade (the 4th was still in trouble in the sand) was sent out and clashed with enemy armour—in fact part of the 15th Panzer Division—to the south of Deir el Shein and drove it west.

Meanwhile the 90th Light Division had had a bad afternoon. Under cover of the dust it had extricated itself from the El Alamein defences and resumed its advance eastward at about 1.30 p.m. It soon came under fire from the guns of all three South African Brigade Groups. Something like a panic occurred, and when this was checked the Division went to ground. Rommel tried to get it moving, but was himself pinned down for a while, and failed. He seems to have persuaded himself that he had achieved at least the beginnings of a break-through, although the Italians had had no success, 90th Light was digging in, and the *D.A.K.* had got no farther than Deir el Shein, having only thirty-seven tanks left out of fifty-five. It reported having been bombed many times during the day and complained of the inactivity of the *Luftwaffe*. Incessant air attacks by night had scattered the supply columns, and the logistic situation was still bad. In particular fuel and ammunition were running short. In spite of all this Rommel decided to go on with the same plan, influenced, perhaps, by urgent news from Kesselring that the British Fleet had left Alexandria. He only changed his mind when, early next morning, 2nd July, the 90th Light again failed to make any headway in the face of artillery and machine-gun fire. Rommel then called off the *D.A.K.* from its intended sweep round the British rear, in order to throw its weight into the attempt to break through to the coast road; this move was to start in the afternoon.

Meanwhile General Auchinleck, realizing that the defended localities of Bab el Qattara and Naqb Abu Dweis were in danger of being isolated and captured, decided to abandon them and make his defence more compact. The New Zealand Division was to withdraw its 6th Brigade from Bab el Qattara, leaving there only a column, and prepare for a mobile role. The 5th Indian Division was to prepare for a similar role at Qaret el Himeimat. On the morning of 2nd July it seemed that Rommel would concentrate his efforts on bursting through near El Alamein, and General Auchinleck decided that an opportunity would occur for a counter-attack. While the 30th Corps held the expected thrust the 13th Corps would attack towards Deir el Abyad from two directions—the 1st Armoured Division westwards, moving south of the Ruweisat Ridge, and the rest of the Corps northwards. Exploitation would be towards the coast. This plan, which aimed at wresting the initiative from the enemy, would have had some chance of succeeding if the 13th Corps had been a Corps in anything but name. In reality it was very weak and becoming weaker by separating (or, as some would say, disintegrating) into its 'mobile artillery battle-groups', the latest development of the 'Jock' columns which, in the Commander-in-Chief's own words of the previous April, could not 'press home an attack against anything but very weak resistance'.[1]

The renewed German thrust and the British counter-attack began almost simultaneously on the afternoon of 2nd July. The weight of the first was taken successfully by the 1st South African Brigade and by a column of the 10th Indian Division, called 'Robcol'.[2] When General Pienaar asked that his Brigade should be given armoured support or else be withdrawn to Alam el Onsol, it was replaced by another column of the 50th Division—'Ackcol'.

The 90th Light Division had fared no better than before and complained bitterly of being attacked every twenty or thirty minutes by 15, 18 or even 21 bombers with strong fighter protection. Wide dispersion saved them from having a great many casualties, but the attacks had a bad effect on morale. South of the Ruweisat Ridge the 4th Armoured Brigade clashed with the 15th Panzer Division, and the 22nd

[1] See pp. 254 and 286-7.

[2] 'Robcol' consisted of part of 11th (H.A.C.) Regiment R.H.A., 11th Field Regiment R.A., two companies 1/4th Essex Regiment, three platoons 1st Royal Northumberland Fusiliers, and a detachment of The Guides Cavalry.

with the 21st Panzer Division in engagements which lasted until dark, when the enemy withdrew to south of Deir el Shein. The Armoured Brigades, which had been well supported by their divisional artillery, by the New Zealand columns, and by a column from the 7th Motor Brigade, remained in possession of the field. The enemy, however, regarded the result as indecisive, and Rommel resolved to try again next day, starting with a probe forward to find the weak spots in the British line. In general, the *D.A.K.* was to renew its eastward thrust, the 20th Corps to advance on its southern flank, and the 10th Corps to hold El Mreir. The combined strength in tanks of the two Panzer Divisions was only 26. The British air activity during the night was said to be very exhausting, though in fact the main weight of attack fell on ammunition and petrol dumps near the coast; one explosion at Ras Gibeisa was so violent that it destroyed the Wellington which had caused it.

General Auchinleck, too, had made no change in his object, but placed the 1st Armoured Division under the 30th Corps and ordered the 13th Corps to advance north-west of Deir el Shein in order to threaten the enemy's rear. The two Corps were to start as soon as they could on 3rd July. This time the British armour awaited attack, and a sharp action took place south of the Ruweisat Ridge lasting an hour and a half, at the end of which the German troops are known to have been near their limit.[1] In spite of constant urgings they made almost no progress. Thus the main thrust was firmly held. Farther south, in 13th Corps, the New Zealanders began the day well. Soon after 7 a.m. their columns opened fire on what turned out to be the artillery and some infantry of the Ariete Division, advancing on the southern flank of the *D.A.K.* The Italians replied, but got the worst of the exchanges, and the 19th Battalion of the 4th New Zealand Brigade assaulted and overran them, capturing some 350 prisoners and 44 guns, besides other weapons and much transport. The 5th New Zealand Brigade, sent to cut off the expected retreat of the Ariete, attacked El Mreir, found to be held by the Brescia Division, and by dawn on 4th July had secured a position near the western end of the depression.

The twenty-four hours ending at dusk on 3rd July had seen the Royal Air Force make its greatest effort to date in flying 900 sorties (or nearly four times as many as the enemy) of which the Desert Air Force flew 770. Bombs had been dropped on troops and vehicles at the rate of ten tons every hour.[2]

---

[1] On 3rd July the 4th Armoured Brigade had 18 Grants, 33 Stuarts and 12 Valentines; 22nd Armoured Brigade had 20 Grants, 28 Stuarts and 8 cruisers.

[2] The squadrons operating were: *Night of 2nd/3rd July*—Nos. 37, 38, 40, 70, 104, 108, 148 and 162 R.A.F.; Nos. 821 and 826 F.A.A.; Halverson Detachment (Liberators), U.S.A.A.F. *Day of 3rd July*—Nos. 33, 55, 73, 80, 112, 145, 208, 213, 223, 250, 252, 260, 272 and 274 R.A.F.; Nos. 1, 2, 4, 5, 12 and 24 S.A.A.F.; Nos. 3 and 450 R.A.A.F.; No. 335 Hellenic; The Alsace, Free French.

The day's fighting had convinced Rommel that he would have to call off his major attacks for the time being. He reported to *OKH* that his divisions were down to 1,200 or 1,500 men each, and that it was scarcely possible to supply the army at night since the road and tracks were almost completely blocked by the enemy's air action. The fighting strength of the Italians was very low. For these reasons he expected to have to remain on the defensive for at least a fortnight.

The 4th of July was a day of disjointed engagements which had no significant results, and the records are contradictory. General Auchinleck seems to have sensed the enemy's condition and felt that they might be on the point of retreating; he even gave orders to prepare for a pursuit. It is true that the enemy had become alarmed at the situation on the Ruweisat Ridge owing to the action of the British armour, and by 3 p.m. it did look as if some withdrawal was afoot. Both Corps were ordered to be ready to pursue, but the armoured brigades, probing forward, met an anti-tank screen which held them up. (According to the enemy this screen was a scratch affair, thrown together in great haste.) The 13th Corps did no more than order the New Zealanders to carry out a limited advance at El Mreir. This had already been planned by Brigadier Kippenberger and took the form of a raid by the 23rd New Zealand Battalion. General Auchinleck persisted with his idea of loosing the 13th Corps towards the enemy's rear, and 5th July was spent in moving to jumping-off places. He then decided that he had not the superiority to justify the dispersal of his forces in making such a wide movement, and a new plan was made by which each Corps was to operate towards Deir el Shein. The outcome was a number of actions by columns without very much result. One column from the 7th Motor Brigade, however, having evaded observation, reached Fuka on the evening of 7th July and shelled one of the landing-grounds for half an hour. It withdrew in the dark and rejoined its brigade after some brushes with the enemy. The same night a detachment of Special Air Service troops under Major D. Stirling, guided by a patrol of the Long Range Desert Group, raided two other landing-grounds nearby. The Italians recorded that altogether seven C.R. 42 fighters were lost on the ground.

Meanwhile Rommel was regrouping his forces, his object being to relieve his armour and draw it into reserve. The Italian 10th and 21st Corps were to take over from the *D.A.K.*, the 90th Light Division, and the 20th Corps. The move of 21st Panzer Division, made on 4th July in accordance with this plan, was apparently the cause of the British idea that the enemy was beginning to retreat. The regrouping was supported by the *Luftwaffe*, which made several Stuka attacks, chiefly on the New Zealanders. (The reappearance of the Stukas 'after a long absence' was said to have raised the morale of the German troops.)

Rommel now began to take particular interest in the southern sector, where he hoped to cut off the New Zealand Division, which he had noticed as being rather far forward. But General Auchinleck, as has been seen, had given up the idea of making a wide sweep from the south; instead he now planned to attack in the north, near the coast, where success would present a threat to the enemy's main line of supply. The 13th Corps was accordingly drawn back, and next day the 21st Panzer Division made a full-dress attack on Bab el Qattara, which had been given up. Rommel began to think that an opportunity had occurred for a thrust towards Qaret el Himeimat, and his reconnaissance troops did in fact reach this area on 10th July. At that moment, however, the new battle in the north demanded his whole attention, and nothing significant came of these moves in the south.

The lull in the enemy's attempts to break through the British front had enabled the Royal Air Force to lift some of the weight of its attacks back to more distant targets. The 5th July saw a resumption of attacks on the enemy's airfields, and that night No. 205 Group began to turn its attention once more to the ports; the Wellingtons went to Tobruk and next night the Liberators attacked Benghazi. Meanwhile in the Desert Air Vice-Marshal Coningham had decided to curtail offensive sweeps for a few days and direct most of his fighters to fighter-bombing, and the *D.A.K.* diary for 7th July records that the fighter-bomber attacks on that day had been especially unpleasant. Another form of activity was an attempt by the Beaufighters to interfere with the German air transport traffic from Crete; on the 8th and 9th three large formations were in fact intercepted near Tobruk and some slight loss inflicted.

On 8th July General Auchinleck ordered General Ramsden (who had just succeeded Norrie in command of the 30th Corps) to capture, as a first step, the low ridges Tell el Eisa and Tell el Makh Khad. The defences were rightly thought to be manned by Italians and, as seen on air photographs, were not highly developed. From these objectives mobile battle groups would move south towards Deir el Shein and raiding parties would make for the landing-grounds about El Daba. The 13th Corps was to prevent the enemy reinforcing the coastal sector from the south and was to be ready for any opportunity to attack; for this purpose the 2nd Armoured Brigade was to come under its command on 9th July, moving by day in order to attract the enemy's attention in the wrong direction.

The 9th Australian Division (Lieut.-General Sir Leslie Morshead) had been moving up from Alexandria and came under command of the 30th Corps on 3rd July. Since its relief from Tobruk the Division had been working on the construction of defences in Syria and was not in suitable training for very mobile operations. The final plan for the

30th Corps' attack required the Division to capture Tell el Eisa, while the 1st South African Division (less one brigade) captured Tell el Makh Khad. Each division was to prepare to exploit on its own front. The 44th R.T.R. (which included one squadron of the 8th R.T.R.) with 32 Valentine tanks came under command of the Australians, and 8 Matildas were allotted to the South Africans. The raiding parties for El Daba were provided by the 1st Armoured Division.

The attack began at 3.30 a.m. on 10th July with a bombardment of unusual intensity—one German diary likened the sound to the drum-fire of the First World War. The Sabratha Division on either side of the coast road made little resistance. Many of the British tanks became bogged in salt marshes near the road, but eight went on with the 26th Australian Infantry Brigade, who by 7.30 a.m. had cleared the Italians from all their positions east of the railway. By about the same time the South Africans had taken their first objective. By 10 a.m. the Australians were consolidating the ground they had gained and were preparing to attack the western end of the ridge; the South Africans had taken Tell el Makh Khad and were occupying covering positions.

The headquarters of the *Panzerarmee* were only a few miles away on the coast, and in Rommel's absence the officer in charge, Lieut.-Colonel von Mellenthin, hurriedly collected part of the 382nd Regiment (of the 164th Division, then in process of arriving by air) and with some machine-gunners and anti-aircraft guns improvised a new front just in time to stop the Australians crossing the line of the railway. Meanwhile Rommel, who had spent the night at Bab el Qattara, had been speeding north, collecting a battle-group of the 15th Panzer Division on the way. That evening a counter-attack broke into the position of the 26th Australian Brigade and was thrown out again.[1] In all about 1,500 prisoners were taken, mostly Italians. The fighters of the Desert Air Force had had a particularly strenuous time, patrolling over the battle and sweeping ahead, and together with the fighter-bombers flew more sorties in the day than ever before. Seven enemy air formations, some of which included C.R. 42 fighter-bombers, were intercepted.

At 6.30 a.m. on 11th July the 2/24th Australian Battalion, supported by the 44th R.T.R., attacked the western end of Tell el Eisa ridge. Soon after midday the whole feature was in their hands. A small column of tanks, infantry in carriers, and field and anti-tank guns had been sent off to raid Deir el Abyad, and on the way it caused about a battalion of Italian infantry to surrender. It was later held up at the Miteirya Ridge, from which, after being bombed and constantly

[1] Of the four Pzkw IIIs captured in this fighting, one had the new spaced armour referred to in Appendix 8. They had been knocked out by 2-pdrs, sited well forward and firing in enfilade, penetrating the comparatively vulnerable sides of these tanks.

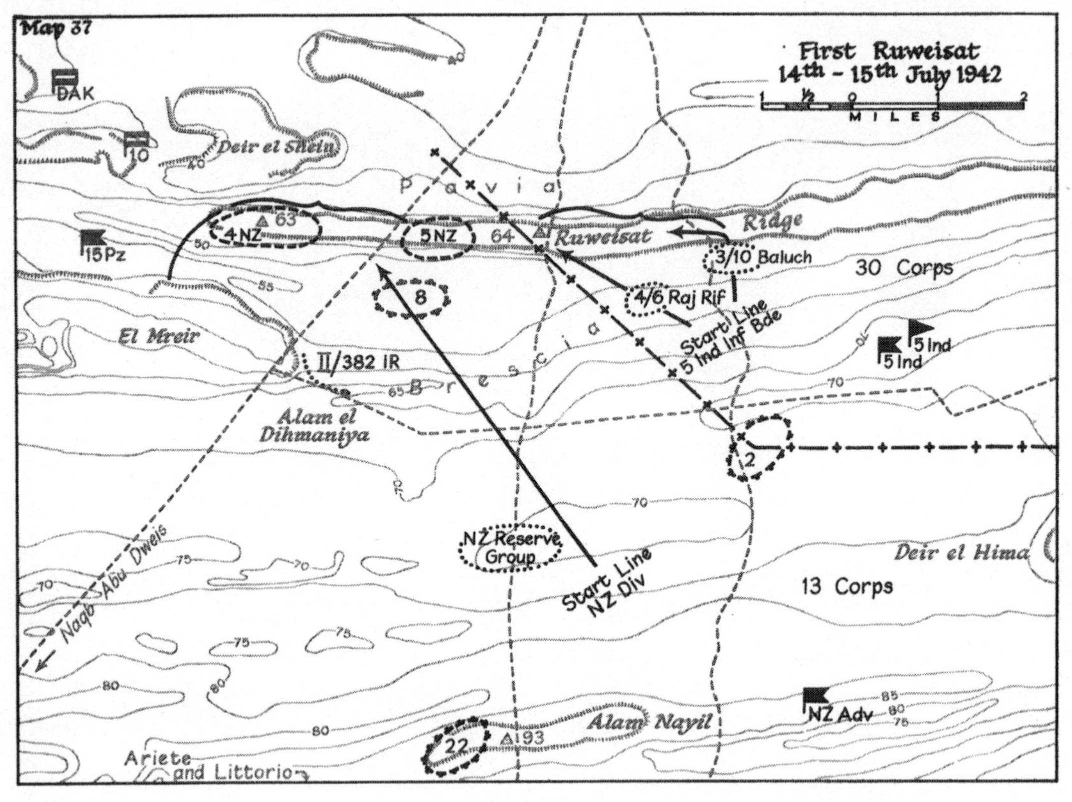
Map 37
First Ruweisat
14th - 15th July 1942
MILES
DAK
10
Deir el Shein
Pavia
Ridge
4 NZ
63
5 NZ
64
Ruweisat
15 Pz
3/10 Baluch
30 Corps
8
4/6 Raj Rif
Start Line
5 Ind Inf Bde
El Mreir
II/382 IR
Brescia
5 Ind
5 Ind
Alam el
Dihmaniya
2
NZ Reserve
Group
Deir el Hima
Naqb Abu Dweis
Start Line
NZ Div
13 Corps
NZ Adv
Alam Nayil
22
193
Ariete
and Littorio

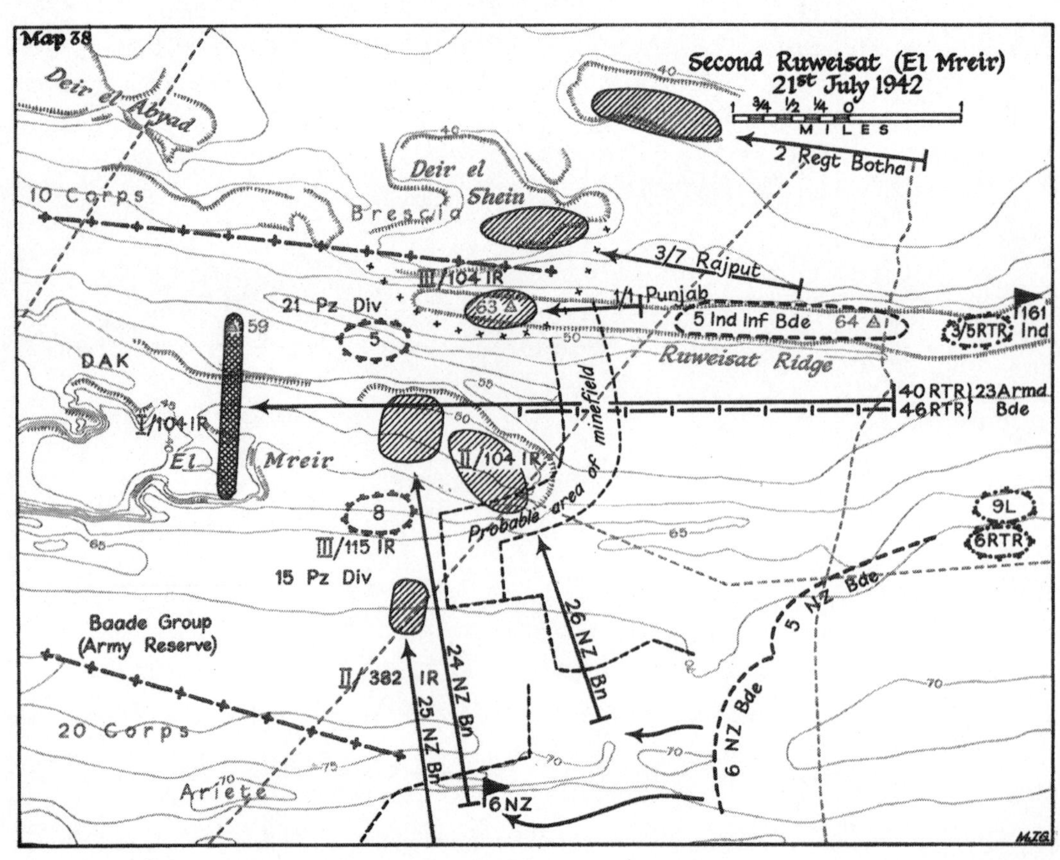
Map 38
Second Ruweisat (El Mreir)
21st July 1942
MILES
Deir el Abyad
Deir el
Shein
2 Regt Botha
10 Corps
Brescia
3/7 Rajput
III/104 IR
1/1 Punjab
21 Pz Div
63
5 Ind Inf Bde
64
161
Ind
3/5 RTR
59
5
Ruweisat Ridge
DAK
40 RTR
46 RTR
23 Armd
Bde
I/104 IR
El
Mreir
II/104 IR
Probable area of minefield
8
9L
6 RTR
III/115 IR
15 Pz Div
5 NZ Bde
Baade Group
(Army Reserve)
26 NZ Bn
II/382 IR
24 NZ Bn
25 NZ Bn
20 Corps
6 NZ Bde
Ariete
6 NZ
MJG

First Ruweisat
Showing plan and positions reached by dawn 15th July

Axes of advance
Objectives
Inter Corps boundary

Second Ruweisat
(El Mreir) 21st July 1942

Showing 13th Corps plan and British and enemy dispositions on evening of attack

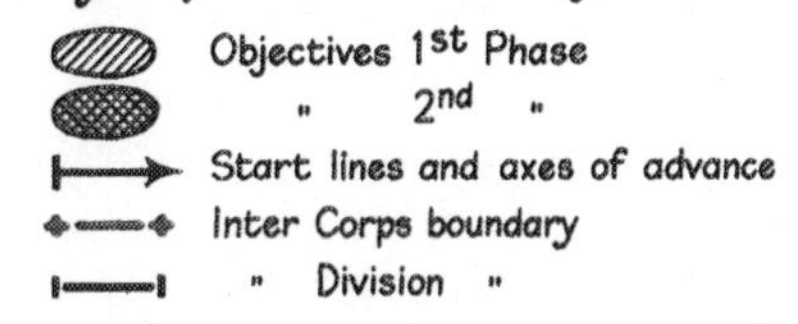

Enemy dispositions are taken from captured records; the position of the minefields can only be regarded as approximate.

shelled, it was forced to withdraw in the evening to the El Alamein perimeter.

During the day the enemy had sent over a number of large formations of Ju. 87s and 88s with strong fighter escorts, and several were met and turned back by the British fighters. Another attempt by the long-range fighters of Nos. 252 and 272 Squadrons to intercept the air transport traffic from Crete was successful; one Beaufighter and one Ju. 52 were lost and two aircraft on each side were damaged. That night a Halifax bomber from No. 10 Squadron joined the Wellingtons attacking Tobruk; this was the first operation by this type of heavy bomber in the Middle East.

On 12th and 13th July the enemy attacked the Tell el Eisa salient, and also tried to cut if off by attacking the Alamein 'box', but had no success. On 14th July another counter-attack, made after considerable bombing, failed, and next day the main interest shifted to the Ruweisat Ridge, where General Auchinleck had launched a new attack.

See Map 37

Having drawn several German units to the rescue of the Italians in the coastal sector, General Auchinleck sought to keep the enemy worried by striking another blow as quickly as possible—this time against the Pavia and Brescia Divisions in the centre. This decision led to a costly and partly successful action on and about the Ruweisat Ridge between 14th and 17th July.

The Commander-in-Chief's object was 'to break through the enemy's centre and destroy his forces east of the track El Alamein—Abu Dweis and north of the Ruweisat Ridge'. The 13th Corps was to secure the western end of the ridge at Pt 63 by a night attack and then exploit north-west; the 30th Corps was to protect the right flank by securing the eastern part of the ridge and was also to attack southwards from the Tell el Eisa salient to secure the low ridge at Miteirya.[1] The artillery fire plans of both Corps were to be co-ordinated by the Brigadier, Royal Artillery, 8th Army, but the attack was at first to be silent. Little was known of the enemy's dispositions except that they had various scattered posts to the south of the ridge, mostly held by Italians.

The formations chosen for the attack were: in 30th Corps, the 5th Indian Infantry Brigade (of the 5th Indian Division); in 13th Corps, the New Zealand Division, with its 5th Brigade on the right and the 4th on the left. On 14th July it was decided that the operation would take place that night. General Gott was to lay down the hour of arrival

---

[1] On some editions of the maps in use in July 1942 Pt 63 is shown as Pt 64. It is here called Pt 63 to distinguish it from a Pt 64, also on the Ruweisat Ridge, close to which was drawn the boundary between the two Corps.

of both Corps on the objective, and made it 4.30 a.m. on 15th July.

In his own orders General Gott defined the intention of 13th Corps as 'to secure Point 63'. The 1st Armoured Division was to protect the left flank of the New Zealanders from first light on the 15th July and be ready to exploit to the north-west with armoured forces if a favourable opportunity should occur after that time. The Division was to place its 'Wall Group' in support of 30th Corps.[1]

The 1st Armoured Division's order stated that the Division would co-operate in the attack of the two Corps, and went on: '2 Armd Bde will be prepared to move on centre line of the inter-Corps boundary [i.e. through Point 64] with the tasks of (a) exploiting success of the NZ Div to the NW, (b) countering any counter-attack by the enemy armour against NZ Div which may develop from the NE, North or NW.' The 22nd Armoured Brigade was to be prepared to move from Deir el Hima to a prescribed area north of Alam el Dihmaniya with the task of protecting 'the southern and western flank of the NZ Division attack from first light 15th July, particularly against attack by enemy armd forces'. In fact, the Brigade was moved on the evening of the 14th to Alam Nayil to deal with some enemy tanks reported approaching from the south-west.

The New Zealand Division, with some six miles to cover from its start-line to its objective, began its advance at 11 p.m. The night was moonless but visibility was good, and Albacores were busy illuminating and dive-bombing groups of transport behind the enemy's lines. Both brigades moved on narrow fronts because of the shortage of riflemen. Shortly after midnight minefields were met, and soon the enemy's flares began to go up and his machine guns opened fire. The assaulting troops, guided by the lines of tracer, tackled (with the bayonet) any post that was near, and the advance swept on. But cohesion and control suffered, and many posts were unnoticed or left to be mopped up—it was hoped—by the reserve troops.

By a little before dawn the 5th New Zealand Brigade had reached its objective on the right, but its left battalion had become completely dispersed, having, among other adventures, attacked and killed the crews of three stationary tanks. Its third battalion, the 22nd, had advanced steadily in rear without finding much mopping up to do. Most of the anti-tank guns had been unable to keep in their correct positions and were some way back. Failures in wireless sets and difficulties over cable-laying made communication with Divisional Headquarters intermittent, and within the brigade it had broken down

---

[1] 'Wall Group' was a temporary collection of columns under the command of Brigadier R. B. Waller. Its composition fluctuated, but its main units were 3rd Regiment R.H.A.; two batteries 104th Regiment R.H.A.; one battery 11th (H.A.C.) Regiment R.H.A.; 11th Field Regiment R.A. (less one battery); Composite Guards Battalion (3rd Coldstream Guards, 2nd Scots Guards); 1/4th Essex Regiment; 9th Rifle Brigade; detachments 1st Royal Northumberland Fusiliers and 1st The Buffs.

altogether. The left brigade—the 4th—had become partly scattered for much the same reasons, but on the left had reached its objective and had a number of anti-tank guns well forward. Digging was impossible in the rock and much equipment was still missing. A good haul of prisoners had been made, but behind the forward troops were many centres of resistance still unsubdued. The Divisional Reserve Group, including the three field regiments, was still south-west of Alam el Dihmaniya, out of supporting range.

At this time—just before dawn—the 5th Indian Infantry Brigade's right battalion (3/10th Baluch Regiment) was held up east of Pt 64. The left battalion (4/6th Rajputana Rifles) had got out of control at the very start, and when it advanced it was caught in flank by heavy fire and fell back in disorder. The 1/4th Essex Regiment had not been committed.

Of the armour, the 22nd Armoured Brigade was close to Alam Nayil and the 2nd Armoured Brigade was still near Deir el Hima.[1]

On the enemy's side there was much confusion and no little anxiety as refugees from the Brescia and Pavia spread alarming stories. North of Alam el Dihmaniya, however, a detachment of some eight or ten tanks of 8th Panzer Regiment happened to have been passed unnoticed in the dark. When it was light the Commander saw the 22nd New Zealand Battalion to his north and at once attacked it. In the short sharp duel which followed the four New Zealand anti-tank guns on their portées were soon knocked out, and the tanks then closed in on the infantry, who were in the open with practically no cover. The choice was between extermination and surrender, and about 350 were taken prisoner. The tank commander hurried his prisoners off westward and withdrew.

Brigadier Kippenberger, who had seen something of this episode, had gone to report personally to General Inglis and was sent on by him to contact the British armour. He saw Brigadier Briggs and General Lumsden, and by 7 a.m. the 2nd Armoured Brigade had moved off in a north-westerly direction. Two of its regiments became involved with minefields and with a locality known as 'Strong Point 2'. The third, finding that the 5th Indian Infantry Brigade was renewing its attack, joined in to help it, and by 10 a.m. the Baluch Regiment had reached the ridge. An hour later the reorganized Rajputana Rifles, with artillery support and helped by the tanks, attacked Pt 64. By the early afternoon they had taken it.

---

[1] On 15th July 2nd Armoured Brigade consisted of 6th Royal Tank Regiment (including one squadron 10th Hussars); 3rd/5th (composite) Royal Tank Regiment; 9th Lancers (including one squadron 2nd Royal Gloucestershire Hussars). Total tanks: 46 Grants, 11 Stuarts and 59 Crusaders.

The 22nd Armoured Brigade consisted of 3rd County of London Yeomanry and was joined during the afternoon by the Royal Scots Greys, whose first action it was as an armoured regiment. Total tanks: 31 Grants, 21 Stuarts and 23 Crusaders.

Meanwhile the New Zealanders were collecting their scattered detachments and trying to consolidate. One platoon, commanded by Sergeant K. Elliott, had had an astonishing morning. When the tanks overran his Battalion—the 22nd—Sergeant Elliott and his men escaped northwards only to find themselves in an Italian defended locality. Sergeant Elliott, though wounded, decided to attack. He and his party, which now included some men of the 21st and 23rd Battalions, reduced five posts and took over 200 prisoners before returning to where they had started. For his gallantry and initiative Sergeant Elliott, who had been wounded three times, was awarded the Victoria Cross.

But the main trouble still existed, for near Alam el Dihmaniya and in various other positions south of the Ruweisat Ridge there were still centres of resistance which frustrated persistent attempts to run vehicles forward in support of the foremost troops. There were no infantry to deal with these pockets except the 26th New Zealand Battalion of the Divisional Reserve Group which, like the two armoured regiments, was more or less pinned down. Gradually, however, the opposition was worn down by shell fire, and one by one the positions were taken.[1] By 4 p.m. some vehicles were beginning to reach the ridge.

During the night the enemy had thought that a large raid was in progress. When Rommel realized that the Pavia and Brescia had collapsed he began to rush German troops to the spot: from the north, the 3rd Reconnaissance Unit and part of 21st Panzer Division, and from the south the 33rd Reconnaissance Unit and the Baade Group of 15th Panzer Division, which had been attached to 90th Light Division for the intended operations at Qaret el Himeimat. These were all placed under General Nehring, who at 3 p.m. ordered a counter-attack. At 5 p.m. it was launched.

The 4th New Zealand Brigade had already had many casualties from shelling and mortaring. It was short of ammunition because of the delay to its vehicles, and it had no artillery support. By 5 p.m. the visibility was bad, owing to dust and smoke. Out of the haze and under cover of heavy shell fire the German attack came in, headed by armoured cars of the Reconnaissance Units. The anti-tank defence soon collapsed, and, as in the early morning, the infantry were then practically helpless. About 380 were made prisoner, among them Captain C. H. Upham, who, for his gallantry during this night and day, and at Minqar Qaim in June, attained the great distinction of being awarded a Bar to his Victoria Cross. At about 6 p.m. the enemy

[1] 'Strong Point 2' surrendered to a detachment of the 6th N.Z. Field Regiment and yielded 180 prisoners and several anti-tank guns, including two of 8·8 cm. In 'Strong Point 3' about a hundred prisoners and six anti-tank guns were taken. The anti-tank gunners in each case were Germans.

turned against the area of Brigade Headquarters, where there was but one-2 pdr, and captured nearly everyone, including Brigadier Burrows, who later managed to escape. At about 6.15 p.m. part of the 2nd Armoured Brigade came into action, and stopped the enemy's eastward advance. At dusk the enemy broke off the action, and, when at 10 p.m. news of the reverse reached General Gott, he ordered General Inglis to hold a shortened front from Pt 64 to the south-west of Alam el Dihmaniya.

Elsewhere than on the Ruweisat Ridge nothing much had happened during 15th July. The 90th Light Division and the Ariete, probing north, were easily held off by the 22nd Armoured Brigade and by columns of the 7th Armoured Division.[1] Formations of Ju. 87s and 88s had made several attempts to intervene in the fighting, but most of them had been driven off. The British fighter-bombers had one of their busiest days; in good weather conditions and with abundant targets they shuttled to and fro flying nearly 150 sorties.

That night the enemy was still anxious. They had expected the British night attack to be followed by an armoured thrust, and were uneasy lest this might still happen. The best counter seemed to be to regain the lost ground, and early on 16th July an unsuccessful attack was made against the 5th Indian Infantry Brigade's position near Pt 64. There were clear signs—including intercepted signals—that another attempt would be made, and there was time to make a good artillery plan and reinforce the 2nd Armoured Brigade by a regiment from the 22nd. At 7.30 p.m. the new attack came in and was repulsed.

On 16th July the Australians had regained some ground in a small operation at Tell el Eisa, but the enemy shelled and mortared the area so persistently that it was given up as not worth the cost. The day was remarkable for a record number of sorties—641—flown by the fighters and fighter-bombers. At dawn on the 17th July the 24th Australian Brigade, supported by a squadron of the 44th R.T.R. and strong fighter cover, carried out a limited attack towards Miteirya. The Australians had some initial success and captured about 800 men of the Trieste Division. They were then heavily shelled and bombed and were counter-attacked by a hastily collected German force, in which the hard-worked Reconnaissance Units were again prominent, and the 24th Australian Brigade suffered over 300 casualties. The situation then stabilized with the Australians consolidating a little north of Tell el Makh Khad.

The three days' fighting had cost the New Zealand Division 1,405 officers and men killed, wounded or missing. These sad losses were aggravated by a bitter feeling that the Division had been let down by

---

[1] The 7th Armoured Division consisted in the main of 7th Motor Brigade and three armoured car regiments. The only tanks were eight Stuarts of 1st Royal Tank Regiment in 7th Motor Brigade.

the armour. The New Zealanders' attack, made in difficult circumstances, had been largely successful, for which they deserve full credit. Most of the things that had gone wrong were of the kind that do go wrong in a complicated night operation for which there has not been time to prepare thoroughly—particularly as regards finding out about the enemy's dispositions. But the Commander-in-Chief had felt that the situation demanded another blow at the weakening enemy, and no more time could be spared.

There is no doubt that General Inglis had understood at Corps conferences that from first light on 15th July British tanks would protect his division either by exploiting beyond it, or, if there were no exploitation, by supporting it closely. Although in the written order issued by General Lumsden the armoured brigades were required to 'be prepared' to move on definite tasks, they expected an executive order before moving. This fact probably reflects the dislike of the armoured forces—the result of much painful experience during 'Crusader'—to be tied to the protection of the infantry at the expense of their wider role. Whatever they did they could not guarantee that no enemy tanks would ever approach the infantry, who, after all, should have the support of the field and anti-tank guns. So General Lumsden reserved to himself the decision to commit his armoured brigades, realizing that much would depend upon timely information of how the battle was going. As has been seen, the battle went fairly well in front but for most of the day the situation in the wake of the advance was far from clear, and the supporting weapons found their way barred by pockets of resistance which had not been dealt with. Many suggestions could be made as to what should have been done, but they would all be open to criticism as owing much to wisdom after the event. But it is fair to say that co-operation between an armoured division (as distinct from 'I' tank units) and one or more infantry divisions had not been really studied and had certainly not been practised.

The Desert Air Force had done its utmost to help the Army during this fighting, and the system of notifying targets to the air had been working better. Fighters, reconnaissance aircraft, bombers and fighter-bombers had all played their part, and during the three days no less than 1,900 sorties were flown solely in support of the land battle, which was equivalent to at least two trips a day by every available aircraft. This says as much for those who kept the aircraft in the air as for those who flew in them. The 17th July was marked by a new enterprise—the first daylight raid by the heavy bombers on Tobruk. A force of eight R.A.F. and U.S.A.A.F. Liberators approached the port from the sea and attacked it successfully without suffering any loss.

See Map 38

By 18th July General Auchinleck had come to the conclusion that the enemy was in a very bad way—the Italians even on the point of collapse—and that the best way of inflicting a major defeat would be to strike again strongly in the centre. (This in spite of the fact that the German armour, after rushing frantically to and fro, was now known to be about Deir el Abyad and El Mreir.) This estimate of the enemy's condition was substantially correct. A *Panzerarmee* report of 21st July (referred to on page 338) shows that both the Germans and Italians had lost much of their field artillery and about half their anti-tank guns; their men were reduced to a third of their strength and it was stated that since 10th July the Italians had lost the equivalent of four divisions. On 21st July the Germans had 42 fit tanks and the Italians about 50.[1]

With regard to the British troops, the 1st South African and 9th Australian Divisions were still fairly well up to strength. The New Zealand and 5th Indian Divisions had each two brigades. The 7th Armoured Division was being reconstituted as a highly mobile force to comprise the 4th Light Armoured Brigade (of armoured cars and Stuart tanks), the 7th Motor Brigade and the 69th Infantry Brigade. The 1st Armoured Division had 61 Grant and 81 Crusader tanks, besides 31 Stuarts, and there were others in immediate reserve or transit. All the foregoing formations were battle-worthy in a greater or less degree, and, in addition, two fresh formations were now available —the 161st Indian Motor Brigade and the 23rd Armoured Brigade Group. The former had come from Iraq and had been working for some time on defences in the Delta; the latter belonged to the 8th Armoured Division (whose coming was referred to on page 260) and had reached Suez on 6th July. It consisted of three regiments each of about 50 tanks, of which 6 were close-support Matildas and the rest Valentines.[2]

On 19th July the attack was fixed for the evening of the 21st and during the next two days elaborate instructions were issued, principally for the pursuit and for co-operation with the air. The main role was given to the 13th Corps, which was to break through at Deir el Shein

[1] The two Panzer Regiments had together: Pzkw IIs, 6; IIIs, 27; III Specials, 6; IVs, 1; and IV Specials, 2. Total, 42. About another 100 awaited repair.

[2] The voyage of the 8th Armoured Division illustrates once again that there can be many a slip in war. The Commander of the 24th Armoured Brigade was sent ahead by air to prepare for the arrival of his brigade, which was known to be wanted urgently. Unfortunately H.M.T. *Scythia*, carrying the headquarters and two of the regiments of his brigade, was delayed at Cape Town for repairs. Another ship (U.S.S. *Orizaba*, carrying part of the Support Group) was sent on to Bombay by mistake, and the third (the *Elysia*), sailing independently, was sunk by two Japanese raiders. The 23rd Armoured Brigade had to take the place of the 24th. All the tanks had to be passed through the Base Ordnance Workshops, where considerable work on them was found to be necessary. In the circumstances it was no mean achievement to equip the brigade in time, but not until 17th July did it receive its last tanks, and even then there were many defects and deficiences.

and Deir el Abyad and exploit westwards. It was to make a subsidiary attack in the south and prepare to pursue to El Daba and Fuka. The 30th Corps was to contain the enemy on its front by vigorous local action, and it too was to be ready to pursue towards El Daba. Wellingtons and flare-carrying Albacores were to attack targets in the central sector during the night 21st/22nd, and would be followed at first light by as many light bombers and fighter-bombers as possible.

General Gott's plan was for the 5th Indian Division to capture Deir el Shein and Pt 63 (of unhappy memories) and for the New Zealand Division to capture the eastern end of the El Mreir depression. The inter-divisional boundary gave the whole Ruweisat Ridge to the 5th Indian Division. In the second phase the 1st Armoured Division was to go through and capture an area about Pt 59, whereupon the 5th Indian and New Zealand Divisions would go forward about two miles and consolidate the ground won. The 7th Armoured Division's task up to then would be to harass. The part of the plan which dealt with subsequent action need not be considered.

The formations chosen for the first phase were the 161st Indian Motor Brigade and the 6th New Zealand Brigade.[1] The 22nd Armoured Brigade was to protect the southern flank, and the 2nd was to be prepared to frustrate any enemy counter-attack against the infantry after the first objective had been captured. The second phase was an advance to Pt 59, to be made by the 23rd Armoured Brigade (less one regiment lent to the 30th Corps to operate with the Australians). The artillery support would be provided by about nine field regiments. The two infantry divisions were each to clear half of a wide lane through the minefields; in 5th Indian Division's area, close to the Ruweisat Ridge, this was to be done by the 9th Indian Infantry Brigade, which had the further task of occupying the second objective.

Some features of the British plan may here be emphasized. It had the merit of placing the main operations under one Corps Commander. It aimed at striking at the point where the remains of the German Panzer Divisions were concentrated—probably in the belief that if they were defeated the rest of the front would crumble. It assumed that the minefields could be detected and lanes cleared in time for the 23rd Armoured Brigade's drive into battle. It gave key tasks to two inexperienced formations, and once again it allowed insufficient time for the study of a multitude of details. It saw the wood well ahead, but lost sight of many nearby trees.

On 18th July both General Lumsden and Brigadier Briggs had been wounded in an air attack. Major-General A. H. Gatehouse, then commanding the 10th Armoured Division in the Delta, was sent up to take command of the 1st Armoured Division. He arrived on the evening of

---

[1] The 161st Indian Motor Brigade (Brigadier F. E. C. Hughes) consisted of 1/1st Punjab Regiment; 1/2nd Punjab Regiment; 3/7th Rajput Regiment.

the 20th, by which time the plan for the coming battle and the role of his division had been decided upon.

Unlike the 'First Ruweisat' the night attack was made with strong artillery support, but in spite of much trouble to ensure the early intervention of the 2nd Armoured Brigade, should it be needed, the experience of the 6th New Zealand Brigade was sadly reminiscent of the week before. The New Zealanders reached their objective after some sharp fighting during which several companies went astray and many vehicles failed to arrive. The 25th Battalion was ordered to move up between the other two. There was great anxiety at General Inglis's headquarters when, at about 3.30 a.m., a report came from Brigadier Clifton that enemy tanks were at large even at that early hour. It appears that the 8th Panzer Regiment was preparing to make an immediate counter-attack in the dark when General Nehring intervened and ordered both Panzer Regiments to attack at 5.15 a.m. instead. When this took place a great volume of fire caught the New Zealanders in their exposed position in the El Mreir depression. Their anti-tank guns were nearly all knocked out, as were the two tanks and the armoured car of the Armoured Division's liaison officers. Communication with the guns broke down. In this counter-attack the Brigade was overrun. Brigadier Clifton, who was taken prisoner, disguised himself as a Private and escaped after spending the day in tending the wounded. It seems that the two regiments of the 2nd Armoured Brigade (the third was on the Ruweisat Ridge) both tried to go forward when they heard of the tank attack on the New Zealanders, but one was held up by anti-tank fire and the other by mines. The 6th New Zealand Brigade's total losses in this action were nearly 700 officers and men.

The 161st Indian Motor Brigade's attack also experienced varying fortunes. Its northern flank was protected by the seizing of a small depression by the 2nd Battalion Regiment Botha, from the South African Division. On the right the 3/7th Rajput Regiment broke into Deir el Shein but was turned out after a confused hand to hand struggle. On the left the 1/1st Punjab Regiment was held up by fire short of Pt 63, but at 8 a.m. the reserve battalion, the 1/2nd Punjab, successfully renewed the attack and captured 190 prisoners. Surprisingly enough the enemy was taken off his guard, somewhat shaken perhaps by the appearance of the 23rd Armoured Brigade thundering past, as will presently be related.

The events of the night had had their effects upon the mine-clearing operations of both divisions, and by daylight the lanes did not extend very far. The 23rd Armoured Brigade's advance was to begin at 8 a.m., and at 6.25 General Gatehouse suggested that it should be cancelled because he was very doubtful if the mines had been sufficiently cleared. General Gott considered that it was so important to take advantage of the enemy's uneasiness (revealed in wireless intercepts) that the operation must go ahead, but that its centre line should be shifted about a mile to the south. This change should take the Brigade through what he understood (wrongly) to be a mine-free area and farther from the enemy's position on Ruweisat Ridge which the Indian Division had so far failed to take. A breakdown in wireless communication, however, prevented the new orders reaching Brigadier Misa.

Just about 8 a.m. the 23rd Armoured Brigade, with the 40th R.T.R. on the right and the 46th on the left, started along the centre line originally ordered.[1] After advancing about a mile and a half the 40th R.T.R. came under heavy shell and anti-tank gun fire and then struck a minefield; seventeen tanks had by now been lost. In spite of this set-back fifteen tanks had reached their objective by shortly after 10 a.m. and were hotly engaged from both flanks. Soon only eight remained, three of which were too badly damaged to fight. Meanwhile the 46th R.T.R. had struck another part of the same minefield and met much the same opposition. After losing about thirteen tanks its squadrons fanned out; some tanks joined the other regiment on the objective and some tried to work round south of the El Mreir depression and were never seen again. By 11 a.m. the remains of the two regiments were strongly attacked by the 21st Panzer Division and were ordered to withdraw. This gallant and disastrous action, on its first day of battle, cost the Brigade 203 casualties, with about 40 tanks destroyed and 47 badly damaged. The Germans followed up the withdrawal past Pt 63, but soon after midday Rommel called them off. While all this had been happening attempts were being made to bring the 2nd Armoured Brigade into action in support of the 23rd and of the New Zealanders who were thought to be still holding out in the El Mreir depression.[2] This entailed the clearing of more mines farther south. By 4 p.m. a narrow lane had been cleared and at 5 p.m. the 9th Lancers followed by the 6th R.T.R. began to move through the gap. They soon came under shell and anti-tank fire from both flanks; five tanks were set ablaze, others were being hit, and after forty minutes the acting Divisional Commander called off the attempt as hopeless.[3] Under cover of smoke laid by the 1st R.H.A. and fire by the 6th R.T.R. the tanks reversed singly through the narrow lane, now partly

---

[1] The 23rd Armoured Brigade Group (Brigadier L. Misa) consisted of 40th and 46th Royal Tank Regiments, and 50th Royal Tank Regiment (detached to 9th Australian Division); 5th Regiment R.H.A.; 73rd Anti-Tank Regiment R.A.; 37th Light Anti-Aircraft Battery R.A.; 7th Rifle Brigade.

[2] Evidence of the straits to which the British armour had by this time been reduced is the fact that 2nd Armoured Brigade on this day, although nominally composed of 9th Lancers, 6th Royal Tank Regiment and 3rd/5th Royal Tank Regiment, contained detachments of nine armoured regiments.

[3] Brigadier A. F. Fisher had taken over command when General Gatehouse was wounded at about 9 a.m.

blocked by casualties. Seven more were badly damaged, bringing the total losses in this brigade to twenty-one.

Elsewhere on the 13th Corps' front little had happened. The 22nd Armoured Brigade had protected the left flank without incident, and the 7th Armoured Division had been engaged on a minor operation on the extreme south. It remains to tell of the fighting in the 30th Corps' sector.

At 6 a.m. on 22nd July the 9th Australian Division attacked—the 26th Brigade at Tell el Eisa and the 24th at Tell el Makh Khad. An immediate counter-attack followed and tough fighting went on the whole morning. The Australians gained the upper hand and by early afternoon they held the whole low ridge at Tell el Eisa and had advanced about a mile south of Tell el Makh Khad. On this day Private A. S. Gurney, A.I.F., won a posthumous Victoria Cross for destroying, single-handed, several enemy machine-gun posts. In the afternoon General Ramsden ordered the second phase, an attack on Miteirya, to begin at 7 p.m.

This attack was made by the 24th Australian Brigade and the 50th R.T.R., who, although equipped with Valentine tanks, had trained as part of an armoured division but not in close support of infantry. In the event armour and infantry advanced independently, having failed to marry. For an hour the tanks milled about on the objective, and at dark withdrew as had been planned, having had twenty-three of their number knocked out.

Meanwhile at 5 p.m. General Gott had ordered the 5th Indian Division to capture Pt 63 and Deir el Shein during the night. The 3/14th Punjab Regiment (of 9th Indian Infantry Brigade) made the attack at about 2 a.m. Loss of direction led to confusion, but a second attempt in daylight nearly succeeded in reaching Pt 63. The Battalion came under intense fire from three sides, the Commanding Officer was killed, two Company Commanders were missing, a third and the Adjutant were wounded, control was lost, and the result was failure.

General Auchinleck's final attempt to make the enemy crack began in the northern sector on 26th July. The 30th Corps was reinforced for the purpose by the 1st Armoured Division (less 22nd Armoured Brigade), the 4th Light Armoured Brigade and the 69th Infantry Brigade. The object was to break through between Miteirya and Deir el Dhib, and to extend the penetration to the north-west. The 13th Corps was to contain as many of the enemy as possible, and made elaborate arrangements to simulate another attack on its own front.

Briefly, the plan required the South Africans to make and mark by midnight 26th/27th July a wide gap in the enemy's minefields south-east of Miteirya. By 1 a.m. the 24th Australian Infantry Brigade was to capture the eastern end of the Miteirya ridge with one battalion and then exploit north-west. The 69th Infantry Brigade was to pass through the 'South African gap' to Deir el Dhib and was also to make, mark, and protect gaps in any further minefields. Through these gaps would then pass the 2nd Armoured Brigade to El Wishka, followed by the 4th Light Armoured Brigade which would raid the enemy's communications.

The timing soon fell behind, but by 3 a.m. the Australians had taken their objective. By 1.30 a.m. news had been received that the gaps were partly cleared, and the 69th Brigade began to advance. In crossing the minefield there was a good deal of confusion, but two battalions passed through and by about 8 a.m. had reached their objectives. Two specially formed anti-tank groups did not fare so well; many of the units missed their way and only one small detachment was within a mile of the foremost infantry by first light.

Now followed a period of doubt and muddle. The reports from the front were confused and conflicting, particularly in regard to the minefield gaps. There was confusion between the South African gaps, the gaps behind the Australian battalion, and the gaps which the 69th Brigade was expected to make. All this caused the advance of the 2nd Armoured Brigade to be delayed. The enemy, perhaps grasping that the leading troops were isolated, counter-attacked, and though the 6th R.T.R. tried to come to the rescue it had trouble with mines and heavy anti-tank fire, and the two battalions—the 6th Durham Light Infantry and the 5th East Yorks—were both overrun. Meanwhile the 2/28th Australian Battalion had been under heavy fire which prevented the proper clearing of the passage for the supporting weapons and for the Valentines of 50th R.T.R. Before the tanks could find such gaps as existed they were heavily fired on; thirteen were destroyed or damaged and the unsupported 2/28th Australian Battalion was overrun. In this sad failure there had been about 400 casualties in the 24th Australian Brigade and 600 in the 69th Brigade.

During the night 26th/27th raids were made on landing-grounds near Sidi Haneish by Special Air Service troops, guided, as usual, by the Long Range Desert Group. About thirty aircraft were thought to have been destroyed or damaged. The Germans recorded that three of theirs were destroyed and two damaged by tank fire [sic]; the Italian figures are not known. On the 27th the Desert Air Force had its busiest day since the 17th, though the exertions of the past few weeks were having their effect upon the numbers of aircraft serviceable, especially fighters. In spite of this the day-bombers and fighter-bombers earned a special word of praise from the 8th Army for their co-operation on this day.

The July actions at Ruweisat, El Mreir, and Miteirya showed clearly the value of infantry trained to attack by night. But they also showed that, besides the all too familiar anti-tank gun, the anti-tank mine was now making it very difficult for the armour to carry on with what current tactics held to be the next phase, namely, to provide tank support for the foremost troops at dawn, or to pass through them in order to exploit success. It was a regrettable fact that the failure of all these operations caused a lack of confidence in the British armour to spread in the 8th Army. Some critics were so outspoken and unfair that they had to be openly rebuked. Nevertheless, the problem of co-operation between infantry and armour in the attack was as yet unsolved. It will be seen later how the 8th Army tried to tackle it in the great offensive in October.

It has already been seen that Field-Marshal Rommel had decided quite early in July that he must go over to the defensive. By the end of the month the 8th Army had also exhausted itself, and on 31st July General Auchinleck issued instructions to his Corps Commanders to strengthen their defences, rehearse the plans for meeting attack, and rest, reorganize, and train the troops. He thought it unlikely that the enemy could muster the strength to make a serious attack during August. Plans were to be made for a new British offensive, but the programme of reinforcements would not allow this to start before mid-September. Thus July ended with a stalemate on the ground. More than twenty years earlier the front lines between Switzerland and the North Sea had stagnated for months behind barbed wire: now, in Egypt, the front between the Qattara Depression and the Mediterranean was being sown with belts of mines, which, unless a means of crossing them could be found, looked like depriving the armoured forces of their mobility—for there was no way round, no open desert in which to manœuvre.

The fighting during July had been costly and, except in the air, was in many respects disappointing, but it brought the Axis advance to a standstill and put a stop to the run of British disasters. It would be wrong to underrate its importance, and a special word of recognition is due to those who fought through this period in the most trying conditions, parched by heat and sandstorms and pestered by loathsome swarms of flies. That horrible affliction, the desert sore, was common. These and other forms of the ten plagues had to be endured day after day in cramped or exposed positions or in roasting-hot tanks. Small wonder that tempers were short or that strain and malaise set hasty tongues wagging. But it is to the lasting credit of the troops that, although they suffered heavily, they nevertheless responded to every demand made upon them. This could not have happened with a dispirited army. The 8th Army was certainly perplexed and puzzled by the continual changes of plan and the switching of formations and units here and there. There was a feeling, too, that as our enterprises seemed to start well and end badly there must be something wrong with the machine somewhere. But underlying all this was the plain fact that the fabulous Rommel had been stopped and it was well known that fresh troops and equipment were arriving in the country.[1] Moreover the soldier could see and hear for himself the almost ceaseless hammering by the Royal Air Force, and the effect was most stimulating, for seeing is believing and it was good to know that the enemy was receiving worse than he was giving.

At the same time it would be unfair and ungenerous not to recognize the remarkable achievement of the German troops. They had been fighting just as long, and in many cases longer. They had all the same discomforts of the terrain and the climate with the added handicap of an uncertain supply line under constant attack by an aggressive air force. They had almost no rest and very little prospect of relief. Small groups of units or sub-units were constantly being flung together for some desperate enterprise—usually to plug some gap—and it is astonishing how often they brought it off. The German soldier always seemed capable of making one more supreme effort.

But everyone has his limit, and General Auchinleck persisted with his costly and hurried attacks because he felt that the Italians had reached theirs and the Germans must be nearing theirs too. Was he right in doing so? Perhaps the best commentary is that of Rommel himself, who wrote to his wife on 17th July: 'Things are going downright badly for me at the moment, at any rate in the military sense. The enemy is using his superiority, especially in infantry, to destroy the Italian formations one by one, and the German formations are much too weak to stand alone . . .' And again the next day: 'Yesterday was a particularly hard and critical day. We pulled through again but it can't go on like this for long, otherwise the front will crack.'

---

[1] The adjective applied to Rommel is no exaggeration. Auchinleck had written a letter to his Commanders pointing out that Rommel was not a superman and that to refer to him as such was bad for morale and was to stop.

CHAPTER XV

THE MOMENTOUS DECISIONS OF JULY AND AUGUST 1942

WHILE the 8th Army and the Desert Air Force were engaging the enemy at El Alamein, the Prime Minister, President Roosevelt and their advisers had been hammering out decisions which were to shape the course of the war. The work had not been easy and Mr. Churchill has written of it: 'During this month of July, when I was politically at my weakest and without a gleam of military success, I had to procure from the United States the decision which, for good or ill, dominated the next two years of the war. This was the abandonment of all plans for crossing the Channel in 1942 and the occupation of French North Africa in the autumn or winter by a large Anglo-American expedition.'[1] After many exchanges of opinion and a visit to London by the President's representatives, Mr. Hopkins, General Marshall and Admiral King, the final decisions were taken on 25th July. There was to be no cross-Channel expedition in 1942. Administrative preparations for the invasion of France (probably in 1943) were to continue, and 'full steam ahead' was ordered on the planning of an Allied landing in French North Africa to take place not later than 30th October 1942. This operation was named 'Torch' and will be described in Volume IV of this history.

It was obvious that these decisions would greatly affect, and would be affected by, the course of events in the Middle East, and during July Mr. Churchill gave his attention increasingly to that theatre. There were other reasons for this interest. Early in the month the outcome of the fighting in the Western Desert had been in doubt, to say the least, and public opinion in the United Kingdom (and indeed in America) was disturbed. Press reports from Cairo had seemed to be too optimistic and gave rise to doubts whether the High Command in the Middle East grasped the full seriousness of the situation. There was a feeling that with better generalship Rommel could have been defeated, and there were doubts whether the senior British commanders were up-to-date in their methods, especially of mechanized warfare. Nor was it felt that army/air co-operation had been as good

[1] Winston S. Churchill: *The Second World War* Volume IV (1951) p. 390. See also the forthcoming volume by J. M. A. Gwyer: *History of the Second World War, Grand Strategy*, Volume III.

as it might be, and after three years of war we had apparently not matched the enemy in such vital weapons as tanks and anti-tank guns.

Apart from these important domestic matters, the question of Russian relations drew the Prime Minister's thoughts eastward. He was anxious to meet Premier Stalin, and would have to perform the difficult tasks of explaining to him that there would be no second front in Europe in 1942 and of convincing him of the soundness of Anglo-American policy. It was very necessary to find out what were the Russian plans for the defence of the Caucasus front, which was vital to the Middle East and seemed to be in grave danger from the German advance in Southern Russia. Directly after the decisions of 25th July had been reached Mr. Churchill telegraphed to General Auchinleck an outline of the new policy, pointing out how 'Torch' would fit in with 'Acrobat'—the advance from Cyrenaica into Tripolitania. He added that the C.I.G.S., General Sir Alan Brooke, was flying out to Cairo to explain the future plans.

Mr. Churchill was also thinking of visiting the Middle East himself. On 31st July came Premier Stalin's invitation to Moscow. Early on 3rd August the Prime Minister left England in an American Liberator and reached Cairo with only one stop—at Gibraltar. General Brooke arrived the same day from Malta, where he had been visiting. General Wavell came from India and Field-Marshal Smuts from South Africa to join in the consultations.

All through the early summer of 1942 the Commanders-in-Chief in the Middle East had felt the need of authoritative strategical guidance. To them the conflicting requirements of the Desert and northern fronts were very real. Indeed the northern front had been an anxiety amidst all the vicissitudes of the year up to date. Threats to it might occur from a hostile advance on Syria and Iraq through Turkey, or on Persia from the Caucasus; there was also the danger of internal disorder in those unstable countries (Syria, Iraq and Persia), which might have serious consequences for our bases and supplies of oil. The difficulty was to estimate when these dangers might become acute, and to find the forces to meet them while continuing to sustain the Desert front. Such guidance as had come from London had so far been of little help. For instance in May the view at the War Office was that the threat to the northern front was unlikely to occur before the autumn of 1942, but the Russians would not disclose their dispositions or plans in that quarter. It was in fact lack of information about the Russians rather than about the Germans which made the situation so hard to judge. Early in June the C.I.G.S. told General Auchinleck that he considered the danger to the northern front was in no way lessened. The very same day Mr. Churchill told the Minister of State that the best opinion in England did not expect the Germans to advance smoothly or rapidly into the Caucasus; that the Russians, though anxious, were in very good heart; and that the forces on either side seemed well matched. None of this did much to help the men on the spot to shoulder their hard, practical responsibility or to absolve them from it.

On 9th July, soon after Rommel's attack at El Alamein had been repulsed, the Middle East Defence Committee asked for guidance from London. They pointed out that since Japan had entered the war large diversions of land and air forces from the Middle East to the Far East had caused great risks to be run on the northern front. In fact the Russians had been relied on to guard this approach to Egypt and the Persian Gulf, and now the new German offensive in Russia seemed to be gaining at least an initial success. Almost the whole of the battle-worthy forces in the Middle East were concentrated in the Desert and it would be impracticable to transfer them to the northern front at this moment. Nor was there much hope of doing so in the future, for if the battle in the Desert went badly there would be no forces to spare, and if it went well it would be necessary to exploit any success to the utmost with the object of regaining Cyrenaica. But the challenge of a German advance into Northern Persia might arise by mid-October, and the less likely one of a move through Anatolia into Syria and Iraq by mid-September. To meet these threats there were in Persia, Syria, and Iraq part of two infantry divisions, some weak Allied contingents and almost no air forces. The matter was therefore urgent. The deficiency in Iraq and Persia was one armoured division and either four or six infantry divisions, depending on whether the situation in the Desert would improve enough to allow of the 44th and 51st Divisions, now on their way to Egypt, being sent to the northern front. If the campaign in Russia went badly for the Russians, and if more troops for the Middle East could not be provided in time, a choice between two serious decisions would have to be made: whether to transfer forces from Egypt to the northern front, thus securing the Persian oilfields but losing Egypt, or to continue to put the defence of Egypt first, thus risking the loss of the Persian oilfields. 'We have not got the forces to do both', the telegram concluded, 'and if we try to do both we may fail to achieve either. We request your guidance and instructions on this issue.'

The Chiefs of Staff were unable to reply to this enquiry until the discussions with the Americans on the policy for the conduct of the war had been concluded, for the issues raised by the Middle East were far-reaching. On 12th July, however, the Prime Minister sent his views to General Auchinleck. Only too well was it realized, he said, that the Japanese threat to India and the defeats in the Western Desert had stripped bare the Middle East's northern front. It was impossible to send six or even four divisions from England or America to reach the northern front by the end of October. The only solution was to defeat or destroy Rommel, thus enabling the forces in the Middle East to be regrouped. Meanwhile an extra division (the 56th) would be sent in August and yet another was being got ready; if the Russian southern front showed signs of breaking it might be possible to withdraw a British division from India. If General Auchinleck could not defeat Rommel, all would depend on the Russian front holding. There was no reason to assume that it would not. Even if it broke it was unlikely that any substantial enemy forces could operate in Persia as early as October, and the General Staff felt that the onset of winter in the Caucasus might postpone the threat until the spring of 1943. Mr. Churchill was confident that General Auchinleck would defeat Rommel; if this happened, and if the Russians prevented the Germans breaking into Persia or Syria in 1942, it would be time to consider a British advance into Tripolitania.

General Auchinleck replied that he took this to mean that the Prime Minister accepted the risk to the northern front, and hence to Iraq and the oil. Whether it was a justifiable risk he himself could not say. He would continue to apply all his available resources to destroying the Germans in the Desert as soon as possible. He had constantly in mind an advance into Tripolitania, remote as the prospect might seem.

When July ended with a stalemate in the Desert, and with no prospect of resuming the offensive until mid-September, the Commanders-in-Chief were still in a dilemma. They naturally wished to secure both the western and northern fronts, for which they estimated they needed two fresh armoured and five infantry divisions, some 18,000 extra vehicles, and a large number of aircraft. It seemed most unlikely that reinforcements on this scale could be provided and more unlikely still that there would be the ships to carry them. In this perplexity the Commanders-in-Chief attended a meeting held by Mr. Churchill soon after his arrival in Cairo, at which there were also present Field-Marshal Smuts, General Wavell, the C.I.G.S., and the Minister of State, Mr. Casey.

At this meeting General Brooke presented and amplified the reply of the Chiefs of Staff to the queries raised by the Middle East Defence Committee on 9th July. The Chiefs of Staff considered that if everything went wholly in the enemy's favour a force of between three and five divisions supported by two or three hundred aircraft might advance from Tabriz and Astara during October, and that its progress might be rapid until the snow fell in December. An advance through Turkey or a seaborne/airborne expedition against Cyprus or the Levant was unlikely. Nor were the Germans likely to send large reinforcements to Africa while their offensive in Russia continued. The

Chiefs of Staff believed that there was a reasonable chance of defeating Rommel in the near future, but unless he were cleared out of Tripolitania there was little hope of transferring large land forces from the Desert to the northern front; the air requirements in the Desert would remain large whatever happened. They had then considered the balance-sheet of the forces in the Middle East and, assuming that all the reinforcements allotted or likely to be allotted were sent to the northern front, concluded that the shortage there in November would be one and a half armoured and two infantry divisions; in January 1943 it would be one armoured brigade and two infantry divisions.[1] Nevertheless the Chiefs of Staff felt that the available troops might just be able to hold German infiltration into North Persia this autumn and winter. In the air prospects seemed better, for it was probable that by 31st December the Middle East would have most of the 95 squadrons that it needed for all its commitments.

If, however, the Germans completely defeated the Russians and were determined to drive the British from the Middle East, a grave situation might arise during the spring of 1943. Against the effort that the enemy might then be expected to make from both directions, the Middle East would need a maximum of nine armoured and twenty-four infantry divisions, and it seemed certain that what could be provided would fall short of these figures by one and a half armoured and seven infantry divisions.

The Chiefs of Staff had then gone on to suggest a policy. In framing it they had been greatly influenced by a recent report by the Oil Control Board that if Abadan and Bahrein were lost nearly 13½ million tons of oil a year would have to be found from American and other sources. To carry this oil about the world 270 tankers would have to be added to the existing Allied tanker fleet, and this could not be done. The loss of Abadan and Bahrein would therefore be 'calamitous', and might lead to a 20 per cent cut in our various activities. The Chiefs of Staff had concluded:

> '(a) The capture of Cyrenaica and Tripolitania is [the] best contribution to Middle East security, since it is doubtful if total requirements can otherwise be met, even at [the] expense of trans-Atlantic movement of American forces; you should therefore strain every effort towards defeating Rommel and exploiting your success to the limits of Italian Africa.
>
> (b) A spreading of Middle East base installations by judicious thinning out from Egypt may well be advisable, and this is

[1] On 4th August the following reinforcements were in sight. Allotted—51st and 56th Divisions from U.K., 5th Division from India: possible—2nd Division from India, and one armoured division from U.S.A.

> for you to judge; much will depend on whether you are able to defeat Rommel. Should the worst arise, i.e., if we were unable to send you adequate forces and the Russian southern front broke, you must hold on to the Abadan area in the last resort—even at the risk of losing the Egyptian Delta. At present, however, we do not consider that circumstances in any way justify a large-scale withdrawal of forces and installations from Egypt, involving abandonment of that country.
>
> We realise that whole Middle East position mainly depends on success against Rommel or [the] continued resistance of Russia. Neither can be prejudged. . . .'

The Prime Minister then spoke, explaining the recent discussions with the Americans and outlining the future course of Allied grand strategy. As for the Middle East, he thought that the Caspian Sea, the Caucasus and a neutral Turkey together formed a good shield for our northern flank, provided that the Russians held the Caucasus chain, with British air support if necessary. He was not yet prepared to divert anything from Egypt until a decision had been reached in the Western Desert. The battle there was of vital importance to the whole war, and it would be wrong to withdraw forces which could take part in it in order to prepare what could only be a weak defence in the north.

With this policy of first things first the meeting agreed, and the arguments for it were strengthened when, later in the month, the Prime Minister and General Brooke received from Premier Stalin and Marshal Voroshilov positive assurances that the Caucasus would be held. Before the meeting ended, however, General Auchinleck pointed to a practical difficulty, namely that the limiting factor was likely to be transport. The numbers of vehicles available and in sight were not enough to enable him to conduct a big offensive in the Desert and at the same time prepare a mobile defence in northern Persia, and he might find the threat from the Caucasus developing just as he was in the middle of his advance. No one at the meeting had anything to say about this possibility, and some other discussion followed. General Wavell described the risks he was running in India, and confirmed his interest in seeing the Germans prevented from approaching the Persian Gulf; this was why he had offered the 5th and 2nd Divisions. He asked what the chances were of a successful battle in the Western Desert, and General Auchinleck replied that for the time being the 8th Army was exhausted and that if he was to destroy the enemy—as he intended—he must wait until his reinforcements were ready, which would not be until mid-September. He would not commit himself to any date, but would of course seize any favourable opportunity for action. The Prime Minister then said that final decisions on policy would be taken on his return from Moscow and that meanwhile nothing was to be done which would in any way detract from our effort in the Western Desert.

Mr. Churchill could now devote himself to the main purpose of his visit to the Middle East—an examination of how the war was being conducted there. He had been from the first very favourably impressed by General Auchinleck. In the autumn of 1941, when the General had withstood—wrongly, in the Prime Minister's opinion—all pressure to launch an early offensive, Mr. Churchill had been struck by his 'unquestioned abilities, his powers of exposition, his high, dignified, and commanding personality'.[1] He had strongly approved of General Auchinleck's conduct at the crisis of 'Crusader' and had assured him of his confidence on several occasions during the recent campaign. On the other hand he had been displeased by the leisurely plans for the summer of 1942 and by General Auchinleck's rejection of the suggestion that he should take personal command of the 8th Army in May.[2] Mr. Churchill had also had doubts about the conduct of the most recent fighting, and was displeased by General Auchinleck's estimate that he would be unable to resume the offensive before the middle of September.

Mr. Churchill and the C.I.G.S. now carried out a brisk programme of interviews and inspections in Cairo and the Western Desert. They met many senior army and air officers, including in particular General Gott, and visited the Australian and South African Divisions. On 6th August Mr. Churchill discussed his impressions with General Smuts, Mr. Casey and General Brooke. He concluded, and his advisers agreed, that a drastic and immediate change should be made to impart a new and vigorous impulse to the Army and restore confidence in the High Command. A new start and vehement action were needed to animate the vast but baffled and somewhat unhinged organization. General Auchinleck should be appointed to command the land forces in Persia and Iraq, which would be separated from the Middle East. The choice of the new commanders was soon made. Mr. Churchill at first wished General Brooke to become Commander-in-Chief, Middle East, but gave up the idea because General Brooke, who was sorely tempted to accept, felt it his duty to remain as C.I.G.S. The Chiefs of Staff's machine was working smoothly and he thought that a change of C.I.G.S. and Chairman of the Chiefs of Staff's Committee at such a critical time might be extremely unsettling. The choice then fell on General the Hon. Sir Harold Alexander, commander-designate of the British land forces in 'Torch', and Lieut.-

[1] Winston S. Churchill: *The Second World War*, Volume III (1950) p. 361.

[2] *Op. cit*: Volume IV (1951) pp. 260 ff, 328-9.

General B. L. Montgomery was selected to replace him. Lieut.-General Gott was to command the 8th Army.[1]

The War Cabinet, to whom these suggestions were submitted for approval, did not welcome the idea of dividing the Middle East into two Commands, for reasons which will be referred to presently. In any case they thought that the appointment suggested for General Auchinleck would convey the impression that a Command was being created in order to let him down lightly. He would be unlikely to retain confidence in himself or to inspire it in others if he were transferred to a reduced, though important, position.

Mr. Churchill then took up the cudgels for General Auchinleck in whom, as the head of an army with a single and direct purpose, he said he had complete confidence. General Auchinleck had shown high-minded qualities of character and resolution; he had restored the battle of Sidi Rezegh and only recently had stemmed the retreat at El Alamein. If he had taken command of the 8th Army when he, Mr. Churchill, urged him to, we might have won the Gazala battle. The need of making an abrupt change in the Command against Rommel was the sole reason for the present proposals, and General Alexander ought not to be embarrassed with remote cares at a moment when all our fortunes turned upon the speedy and decisive defeat of Rommel. Mr. Churchill could not advise that General Auchinleck should be cast aside as unfit to render any further services. General Wavell had not lost his reputation when he was removed from the Middle East; nor would General Auchinleck. The nation would admire the array of distinguished commanders—Alexander, Wavell and Auchinleck—facing their responsibilities on the vast front which extended from Cairo to Calcutta.

Before the War Cabinet's agreement had been received chance dictated a further change. On 7th August the Bombay aircraft in which General Gott had taken passage to Cairo on leave (unknown to Air Headquarters, Western Desert) was forced down by two German fighters and then destroyed on the ground. Among the killed was General Gott. His death was deeply felt throughout the Army, where he was greatly liked and respected for his frank, courteous and unruffled manner, his easy natural leadership and his personal courage. He had had more experience of the Desert than any other commander, having served there almost without a break from the beginning, through good times and bad. Indeed, he is known to have felt that he had been there almost too long, and himself believed that fresh blood was required. Although he was ready to do whatever was required of

[1] General Brooke, according to his diary for 4th August, thought that Montgomery would be a better choice than Gott for the 8th Army, and noted that General Auchinleck thought so too. He (Brooke) put this forward to the Prime Minister, who, however, decided in favour of Gott, and Brooke did not feel strongly enough about the choice to oppose it further.

him he would have welcomed a change. It may therefore be doubted whether he would have been the man to breathe new life into the 8th Army, but it was sad to think of an eventual victory in the desert without him there to share in it.

To succeed him the C.I.G.S. recommended Lieut.-General Montgomery, and this was approved in spite of the great embarrassment caused by having to present the Americans with a second change of commanders of the British component of 'Torch'. On 8th August Mr. Churchill informed General Auchinleck of the decisions, and offered him the new Persia and Iraq Command. General Auchinleck felt unable to accept the post, which he believed to be strategically unsound and unworkable, but was given a few days to think it over. General Alexander arrived in Cairo the same day and formally assumed command in the Middle East on 15th August. Lieut.-General Montgomery took over the 8th Army, and Lieut.-General B. G. Horrocks the 13th Corps. General Alexander chose as his Chief of General Staff Major-General R. L. McCreery, who had been head of the Armoured Fighting Vehicles branch at G.H.Q. and had served on General Alexander's staff before.

On 10th August Mr. Churchill gave General Alexander a directive, written in his own hand on a sheet of Embassy notepaper, and initialled also by General Brooke:

> '1. Your prime and main duty will be to take or destroy at the earliest opportunity the German-Italian Army commanded by Field-Marshal Rommel together with all its supplies and establishments in Egypt and Libya.
>
> 2. You will discharge or cause to be discharged such other duties as pertain to your Command without prejudice to the task described in paragraph 1 which must be considered paramount in His Majesty's interests.'

General Alexander's first concern was with the morale of the 8th Army. He found the troops resolute, but puzzled by retreats which they had not understood. 'A more serious cause of discouragement was the knowledge that our defeat had been due in part to inferiority of equipment: there is nothing so sure to cause lack of confidence.' Mr. Churchill had expressed the opinion a week earlier that wherever the fault for the present serious situation might lie, it was certainly not with the troops and only to a minor extent with their equipment. But the references in this volume to the performance of British and German tanks and anti-tank guns, particularly in Appendix 8, show that in several respects the British equipments in 1941 and the first half of 1942 were not the equal of the German.

General Alexander made it known that there was to be no more withdrawal, and that the basic formation would be the division, which was not to be split up into detachments except temporarily for a definite task. General Montgomery, thinking on similar lines, set to work at once to inspire confidence and enthusiasm in his Army. His address to the officers of Army Headquarters made a tremendous impact, of which word soon spread. The defence of Egypt lay at El Alamein, he said, and if the 8th Army could not stay there alive it would stay there dead. There would be no more backward looks. The hard times were over; ample reinforcements were at hand, and if Rommel chose to attack so much the better. Meanwhile they would begin to plan the campaign that would 'hit Rommel and his army for six right out of Africa'. This campaign would not begin until everything was completely ready. He asked for confidence and faith that everything he said would come to pass. All this and more was put over with a Cromwellian fervour, and the effect was electric. By a strenuous programme of tours and visits, with the objects of seeing and being seen and heard, of getting to know and becoming known, the new Commander strove to impress his personality upon his whole Army. He certainly succeeded.

One of General Montgomery's first acts was to concentrate his whole Headquarters at Burg el Arab, where it would be in close touch at all levels with Air Vice-Marshal Coningham's Headquarters. This was a visible sign of the determination to tighten and strengthen the links which had bound the 8th Army and the Desert Air Force, but had worked loose during the disasters of June. Now the two Services were to work in double harness, and, as will be seen, in their first big test—at Alam el Halfa—their mutual confidence was to be renewed in an unmistakable manner.

On 21st August Mr. Churchill, who on his return from Moscow had spent two days with the 8th Army, sent his impressions to the War Cabinet in a long telegram.

> 'A complete change of atmosphere has taken place . . . the highest alacrity and activity prevails . . . the roads are busy with the forward movement of troops, tanks and guns . . . our army will eagerly meet the enemy should he attack and I am satisfied that we have lively, confident, resolute men in command working together as an admirable team under leaders of the highest military quality.'[1]

All this was true, for, although there had been no lack of activity and energy before, it was now that a renewed, strong sense of purpose made itself widely felt. Officers and men who had borne the burden and heat of the disasters of June and the hard slogging of July felt

1 The telegram is printed almost in full in *The Second World War*, Volume IV (1951) pp. 465-467.

braced and invigorated. Particularly encouraging were the signs of growing strength for all to see, and in this respect the new commanders were fortunate, for they came upon the scene just as the balance was swinging decidedly in the British favour.

The flow of equipment and stores of all kinds had been well maintained throughout the year in spite of diversions to the Far East, as the following figures show.

From the United Kingdom

1942	Guns	Tanks	Vehicles	Ammunition and various stores (tons)
January	118	60	1,949	64,788
February	120	143	2,196	77,026
March	196	74	2,007	66,433
April	462	264	3,172	66,217
May	182	113	1,406	45,740
June	682	179	3,810	75,790
July	374	114	4,573	74,461
August	446	254	3,289	72,192
September	209	34	1,512	27,072

From North America

1942	No. of ships	Tanks	Vehicles
January	13	102	1,479
February	18	192	2,430
March	33	251	4,848
April	28	73	5,433
May	25	25	5,646
June	28	3	7,694
July	23	33	4,618
August	22	132	3,371
September	28	407	3,016

In view of the large numbers of tanks it is of interest to note that on 15th March 1942 there were 1,383 tanks of all kinds in the Middle East, of which 746 were in workshops.

Of the supplies dealt with by the Royal Army Service Corps during the summer of 1942, 10 per cent. came from the United Kingdom, 30 per cent. from Canada and the United States, and 60 per cent. from India and elsewhere.

The numbers of men arriving in W.S. convoys from the United Kingdom between January and August, both inclusive, were as follows:

Land Forces, in formations, miscellaneous units, reinforcements and drafts.	149,800	including the 8th Armoured, 44th and 51st Divisions.
Royal Air Force	32,400	
Royal Navy	9,800	excluding those carried in H.M. ships.

In addition, about 32,400 had come from India, mostly as reinforcements.

If these figures seem to be very high, a reason is that an underdeveloped region which becomes an important theatre of war becomes also a bottomless pit. Setting up the bases and armed forces in the Middle East was like gradually transplanting a complete modern society with all its complicated needs. Almost every activity known in ordinary life was being carried out there by someone in uniform. There was therefore a constant demand for men to fill the establishments of many sorts of units, some newly created, and others of longer standing which had been reduced by various causes. Since November 1941 the Army alone had suffered nearly 102,000 casualties in battle.[1] Sickness too was a steady drain, although by no means a heavy one thanks to the progressive skill of the medical services in applying their science to a host of problems under the conditions of war.[2]

Some reorganization and a great deal of training were needed in the 8th Army, but the tactical situation demanded first that much work should be done to strengthen the defensive positions. Not until after the battle of Alam el Halfa (described in the next chapter) was it possible for General Montgomery to introduce a programme of rigorous training to prepare the army for the offensive which was to drive the enemy from Egypt and Libya.

The Royal Air Force had its problems too, though it was spared an upheaval among its High Commanders. As with the Army, its real

[1] British 49,000; Australian 2,700; New Zealand 9,500; South African 20,400; Indian 17,300; Colonial 540; Free French 1,360; Polish 480; Czech 100.

[2] Some illustrative figures from the 8th Army for the first six months of 1942 are:

	Approximate average strength	*Sick admitted to medical units*
January	88,000	4,488
February	101,000	5,730
March	122,000	5,119
April	124,000	5,300
May	126,000	4,135
June	100,000	4,954

period of rest, reorganization and training was to come after the battle of Alam el Halfa; until then there was very little opportunity for any of these. Indeed August brought with it some new problems: for example, how to balance the requirement of providing fighter cover for the 8th Army with that of defending the base areas in Egypt, now so close to the enemy's growing air forces. It was known that German and Italian parachute troops had arrived in the forward area during July, and gliders had been seen at Tobruk. The possibility of airborne landings on airfields and vulnerable points could not be disregarded. Steps were therefore taken to stiffen the anti-aircraft and ground defences, and all the Hurricane squadrons in the Desert Air Force were given training in night fighting, to supplement No. 73 Squadron which had already specialized in night operations.

The retreat to the El Alamein line had thrown the Air Force back on itself, and created a need for many more airfields. This was met partly by enlarging existing sites but principally by developing new ones—fifteen around Amiriya and along the Alexandria-Cairo road, for example. The work was done by the Royal Engineers, under the direction of the Chief Engineer, Aerodromes, on a policy laid down by the Air Officer Commanding-in-Chief. In spite of some difficult terrain, unreliable native labour, and scarcity of suitable machinery, these new landing-grounds were provided at remarkable speed. Looking ahead, the Army had to organize and equip airfield construction units whose task it would be to provide the Desert Air Force with landing-grounds during a long and rapid advance.

The increasing participation of the United States in the Middle Eastern war was a development of the highest importance. In September 1941 President Roosevelt had directed the Secretary of War to furnish lend-lease aid to the Middle East. In November 1941 two missions were set up—one in Cairo, the United States Military North African Mission, under Major-General Russell L. Maxwell, and one in Baghdad, the United States Military Iranian Mission, under Brigadier General Raymond A. Wheeler. The main work of these missions was to direct constructional and industrial projects to be carried out by American firms, whose methods were on the admirable and sweeping American scale.

When, in December 1941, the United States entered the war, the British hoped that the American Missions might merge into a single organization to deal with all aspects of the war in the Middle East. After much discussion, however, the two Missions remained, with the tasks of keeping in touch with the appropriate military commanders, routeing lend-lease material, and training men in the use and maintenance of American equipment. More precisely, General Maxwell concerned himself with the establishment in Eritrea of a large plant for erecting bomber aircraft, with taking over and developing the port of Massawa, and with other projects. General Wheeler was at first mainly interested in the development of ports, roads and railways in Iraq, but in April 1942 his mission was instructed to concentrate on expanding the route for supplying Russia through Persia.[1]

As early as February 1942 the Americans decided to militarize their undertakings in North Africa and Persia, but this plan became whittled down by the competing demands of preparing for operations in Europe in 1943. In June 1942 a new command was set up—the 'United States Army Forces in Middle East'. General Maxwell was appointed Commanding General and became a member of the Middle East War Council.[2] The new command took over the North African Mission, and later the Iranian Mission also, which in August became the U.S. Persian Gulf Service Command.

On 28th June 1942 the 'U.S. Army Middle East Air Force' came into existence with Major-General Lewis H. Brereton as its first Commanding General. It has been related how, directly after the fall of Tobruk in June, President Roosevelt came to the rescue with offers of equipment, notably tanks and self-propelled guns.[3] At the same time the Americans decided that instead of supplying aircraft to build up squadrons of the R.A.F. in the Middle East they would establish complete formations and units of their own. This change of policy made Air Chief Marshal Tedder anxious lest it should cause the flow of American types of aircraft to the R.A.F. to cease, or at any rate to fall behind the programme, while the American squadrons were becoming established and acclimatized. By the middle of July eleven R.A.F. fighter squadrons were at half strength, and two of these together with five others were still equipped with Hurricane Is or Tomahawks; a further nine squadrons had no operational aircraft at all.[4] Tedder was told to expect 100 Kittyhawks in July and comparable numbers during the next few months, Baltimores at the rate of 60 a month, and various other aircraft. At the end of July the intake of Hurricanes and Kittyhawks had not made up for the losses, while the newly arrived Kittyhawk IIs with Merlin engines were being issued

---

[1] Brigadier General Don G. Shingler relieved Brigadier General Wheeler in April 1942.

[2] This Council had been formed in 1941, its permanent members being the Minister of State, the Commanders-in-Chief, H.M. Ambassadors in Egypt and Iraq, the Governors of Cyprus and Aden, the High Commissioner to Palestine, a representative of the Government of India, and the Prime Minister of South Africa. See volume II of this History, page 240.

[3] See pages 278-9.

[4] During the intensive six weeks from 24th May to 7th July when 202 British fighter aircraft of all types were lost on operations, some of the Kittyhawk squadrons' losses had been 100 per cent. of their original numbers. Such a rate of wastage had not been allowed for in planning for aircraft replacement. The Americans, for example, were working on a basis of 20 per cent. wastage per month.

to the U.S.A.A.F. squadrons, which had yet to train up to desert standards. The problem of integrating an inexperienced air force with a seasoned one had arisen at a rather precarious time. The process began slowly with the introduction of American fighter section leaders into squadrons of the Desert Air Force, with whom they went out on operational flights to be 'blooded', later to be followed by entire squadrons. Thus, until the American squadrons were ready, the position looked better on paper than it was in practice.

On 11th August Tedder was told that it had been decided to limit the R.A.F. strength in the Middle East to 65 squadrons and that the U.S.A.A.F. would provide 24, making a total combined strength of 89 squadrons. In theory this meant that there was no longer any need to equip several of the unarmed R.A.F. squadrons, but there still remained the problem of replacing obsolescent aircraft with newer types.[1] For example, of 513 Kittyhawks expected during the period April to August only 251 had arrived, and at the end of August there were no more than 58 fit to fight.

It has been mentioned that when Mr. Churchill announced his idea of setting up a new Army Command in Persia and Iraq the War Cabinet did not at first agree. After the rebellion in Iraq in June 1941 control of the land forces in that country and in Persia had been transferred to the Commander-in-Chief, India, for the reasons given on pages 128-9. The Chiefs of Staff had intended, however, to give it back to the Middle East if the Germans looked like moving through Southern Caucasia. In January 1942 the Middle East did in fact assume control, but for a different reason, namely that General Wavell in India was fully occupied in facing the new threat from the Japanese. Now, in August 1942, the Prime Minister was so much impressed by the need for the Commander-in-Chief, Middle East, to devote all his energies to defeating Rommel that he wanted to free him from responsibility for Persia and Iraq. With India looking east and Cairo looking west the solution seemed to be to create a third command to deal with the intermediate, or northern, front.

General Auchinleck opposed the idea, for he had always thought that the land and air forces in Persia and Iraq should be under the same command as those in the Middle East. The War Cabinet felt that the arguments in favour of a unified command were even stronger than they had been in January, owing to the threat to the Caucasus. The Chiefs of Staff studied the problem anew, and on 14th August reported that the plan would introduce many complications but no insurmountable difficulties. London would inevitably be drawn in to settle many questions, such as, for example, those of competing claims

[1] Most of these unarmed fighter squadrons were in fact equipped by March, 1943.

for shipping space. The Minister of State would have to retain Persia and Iraq in his field of action. Contacts with Turkey should remain in the hands of the Commander-in-Chief, Middle East, who would have to take account of the interests of the new Command. The Middle East Joint Planning Staff could serve both Commands. As regards the air, the Chiefs of Staff saw no reason to alter their view that there must be a single Air Officer Commanding-in-Chief over the whole area, who would allot air forces to an 'Air Officer Commanding Persia and Iraq' and delegate control of them to him. The entire R.A.F. organization in the Middle East had been based on the strategic mobility and flexibility of air forces, and control of every aspect of operations, maintenance and supply was therefore centred in Air Headquarters, Middle East. The Air Officer Commanding-in-Chief alone was in a position to ensure that the available resources were most suitably and economically used, and to work the machinery which had been devised for the purpose.

The War Cabinet had telegraphed to say that they still had misgivings about the Prime Minister's plan, but that as he was on the spot with General Smuts and the C.I.G.S., who both agreed with it, they were prepared to agree also. Mr. Churchill presided over a meeting in Cairo on 18th August to thrash the matter out, and after hearing various views he ruled on 21st August that the Persia and Iraq Command ('PAIC') was to be set up at once.[1] General Auchinleck having finally refused the appointment, General Sir Maitland Wilson, from the 9th Army in Syria, was to take command immediately.[2] The decision was based upon circumstances rather than logic. It clearly indicated a wish to relieve General Alexander of some of the distractions from which General Auchinleck had suffered, although with Syria remaining in the Middle East Command there might still be a 'northern front'. The real easing of the burden on the Commander-in-Chief, Middle East, was the appointment of a commander of known energy and ability for the 8th Army. In August 1943 General Auchinleck became Commander-in-Chief, India, for the second time, succeeding General Wavell who was appointed Viceroy of India.

Such, then, were the circumstances of General Auchinleck's removal from the post of Commander-in-Chief, Middle East, after he had held it for just over a year. Like General Wavell he had known success and failure, and like him he left to make way for a fresh eye and an unstrained hand. He had had several clashes of opinion with the Prime Minister, yet no one was more generous in praise of his qualities than Mr. Churchill himself. In spite of the disasters that had befallen his Army he had retained to a remarkable degree its admiration and high

[1] A short account of the early life of 'PAIC' is given in Appendix 6.

[2] General Wilson was succeeded in command of the 9th Army by Lieut.-General W. G. Holmes.

regard. When he left, the prevailing sentiment was: 'There goes a fine man; all the same, it will not hurt us to have a change.' Perhaps it was felt that he was not a lucky general—it was Napoleon who placed luck among the necessary attributes of a general—and who would not rather serve under a lucky one?

His relations with General Ritchie have already been commented on;[1] it may well be that he asked too much of that loyal, energetic, but inexperienced commander. His own personal interventions in the battle met with wide approval, but his attempts while the fight was on to improvise organizations and tactical methods lessened the confidence of many of his commanders in his judgement. It showed that he had the enterprise and courage to try out new ideas, but there were some who thought him too easy of approach and ready to listen to advice from too many people.

In all the stir of the Prime Minister's visit it was perhaps natural that thoughts should dwell more upon the future than upon the past, more upon the blow that was in store for the Axis forces than upon the mauling they had already received. In retrospect the vital importance of the July fighting stands out clearly, and to General Auchinleck belongs the credit for turning retreat into counter-attack. His forecast of mid-September as the earliest date by which the Army could be ready for an 'all out' offensive may not have been popular in London, but it was realistic and reasonable. In the event, this offensive began on 23rd October, and its success should not be allowed to overshadow the earlier achievements of those who made it possible.

The month of August saw the British gathering strength, with their supply position assured and their High Command reorganized on promising lines. On the Axis side things were very different. There the flow of reinforcements and supplies was unsatisfactory and was causing friction between the Germans and the Italians, while some rather ineffective changes in the system of command were being made.

In July Field-Marshal Rommel had frequent cause to complain about the administrative situation. Early in August he informed *OKW* that the supplies reaching the front only met the daily needs; nothing was left over to go towards reserves. He repeated his constant complaint that the Italians took for themselves too great a share of the valuable cargo-space. Above all, he wanted more German troops.

In fact there appear to have been in Italy enough men, vehicles, stores, and supplies to meet many of the German and Italian requirements. The trouble was to get all these things to the front in the right order and proportions. Apart from the dangers of British attack by sea and air there were many obstacles to overcome. For example, there

[1] See pages 285-6.

were not enough Italian escort vessels (mainly for want of fuel) or coastal cargo ships; the capacity of Tobruk, Bardia and Matruh to handle cargo was too small; load-carrying vehicles were too few and many were threatened with breakdown because of the shortage of spare parts. Moreover, the coastal road was in bad repair and the desert railway was scarcely working.

In Rommel's opinion the Italians were mismanaging the lines of communication. Only in Rome could this be put right. There the German representative who dealt with *Comando Supremo* in matters concerning the movement of men, stores, and supplies to Africa was the Military Attaché, General von Rintelen, who, Rommel thought, had not enough status or drive to look after German interests properly. He would have liked to see this responsibility given to Kesselring.

Cavallero realized that something must be done to improve matters but felt that the Germans were interfering too much in Italian affairs. Early in August he obtained the Duce's agreement to a reorganization of the command in North Africa. From 16th August the German-Italian Army under Rommel was to become directly responsible to *Comando Supremo* for operations. Bastico, now promoted to Marshal, was thus cut out of the chain of command, which suggests that Cavallero thought that *Comando Supremo* would be more successful in dealing with Rommel than Bastico had been. As a link between *Comando Supremo* and the *Panzerarmee* a Delegation from the former ('*Delease*') was to be set up in Africa under General Barbasetti di Prun. The *Panzerarmee* was to deal with this Delegation over non-operational matters, and was to attach to it German army and air force representatives. In outline the duties of the Delegation were as follows: to arrange for the supply of the Italian forces fighting in Egypt; to co-ordinate Italian and German administrative traffic of every kind; to control the lines of communication area as defined by *Comando Supremo* from time to time; to command and administer Italian troops in transit to and from the front. It had also certain responsibilities for the defence of the lines of communication and for the discipline of Italian troops.

In fact the new organization took a long time to get into its stride, and in consequence did not produce results in time to be of much use.

LEGEND

30 21	Corps HQ
NZ 164 Trento	Div HQ
9 Ind	Brigades
8	Armoured Brigades
	Units or detachments
	British minefield, main alignment
	" " dummy minefield
	Forward line of enemy minefield

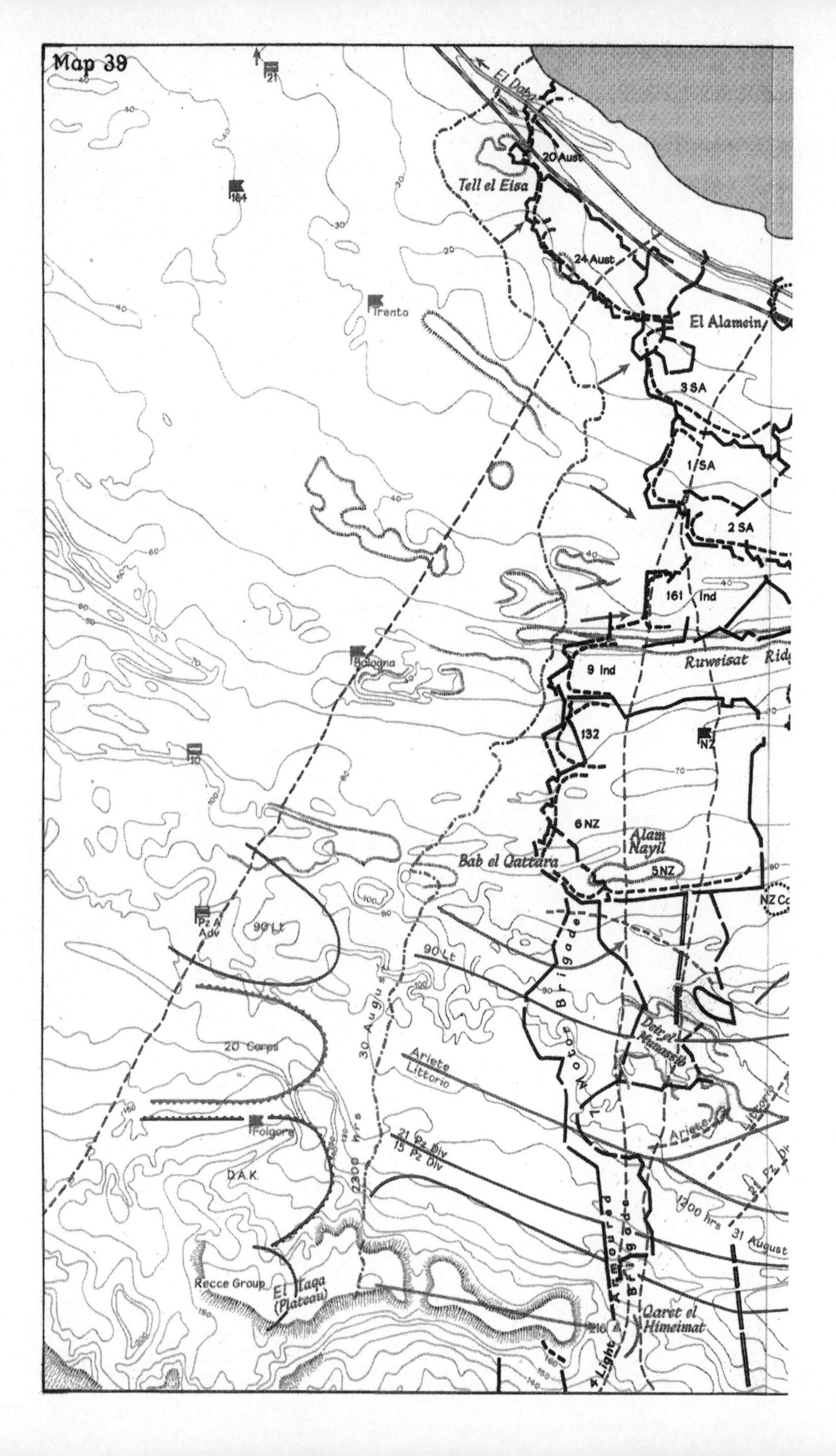

Map 39
El Daba
20 Aust
Tell el Eisa
24 Aust
El Alamein
Trento
3 SA
1 SA
2 SA
161 Ind
Ruweisat Ridg
9 Ind
Bologna
132
NZ
6 NZ
Alam Nayil
5NZ
Bab el Qattara
NZ Co
Pz A Adv
90 Lt
90 Lt
Motor Brigade
Deir el Munassib
20 Corps
30 August
Ariete
Littorio
Ariete
Littorio
21 Pz Div
15 Pz Div
21 Pz Div
Folgore
D.A.K.
2300 hrs
1200 hrs 31 August
Recce Group
El Taqa (Plateau)
Qaret el Himeimat
4 Light Armoured Brigade

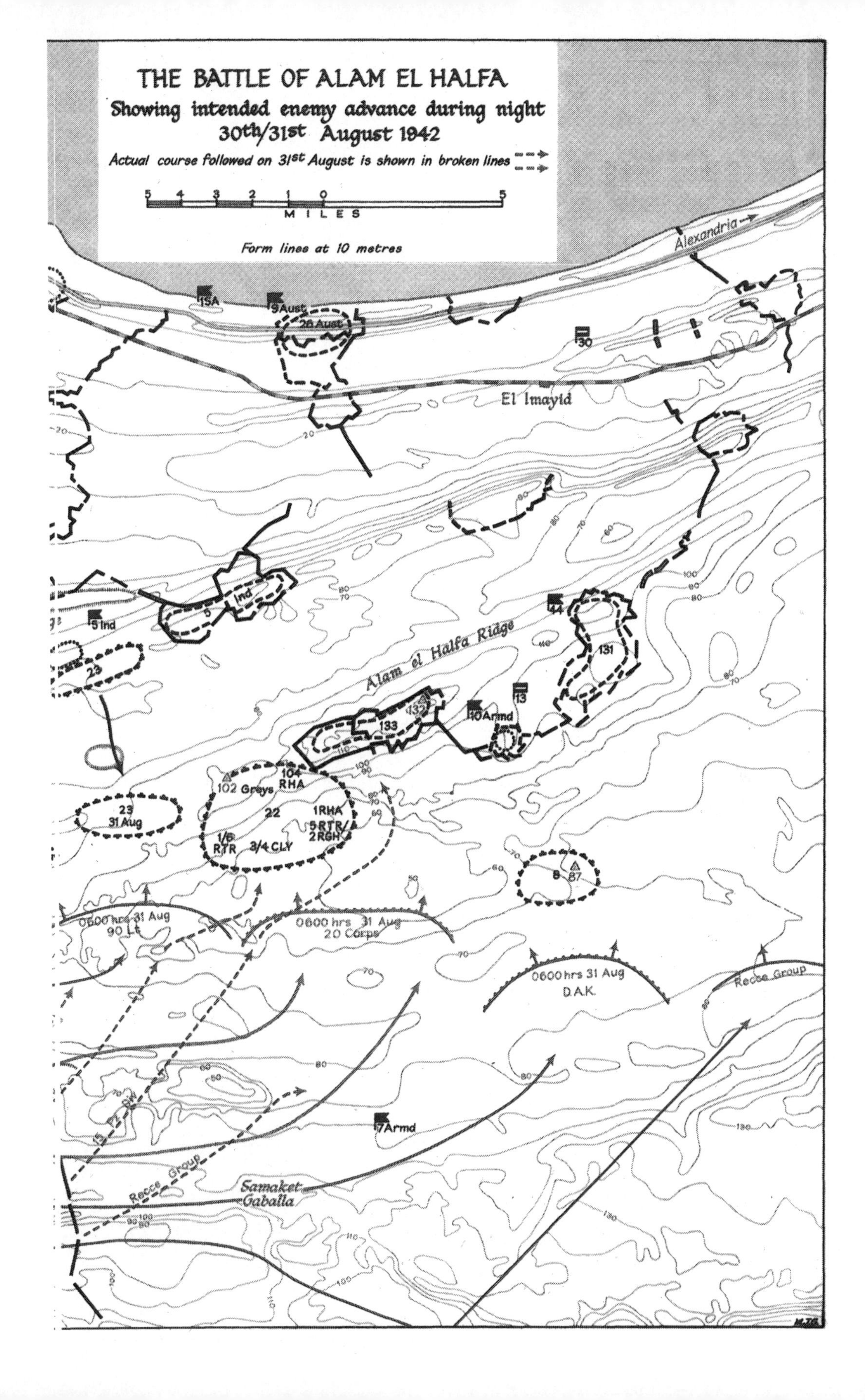
THE BATTLE OF ALAM EL HALFA
Showing intended enemy advance during night 30th/31st August 1942
Actual course followed on 31st August is shown in broken lines
5 4 3 2 1 0 5
MILES
Form lines at 10 metres
Alexandria
1SA
9 Aust
26 Aust
30
El Imayid
Ind
5
5 Ind
23
Alam el Halfa Ridge
44
131
13
10 Armd
133
132
104 RHA
102 Greys
23 31 Aug
22
1 RHA
5 RTR
2 RGH
1/6 RTR
3/4 CLY
8
87
0600 hrs 31 Aug 90 Lt
0600 hrs 31 Aug 20 Corps
0600 hrs 31 Aug D.A.K.
Recce Group
7 Armd
Recce Group
Samaket Gaballa

CHAPTER XVI

AUGUST 1942 AND THE BATTLE OF ALAM EL HALFA

See Map 39

IT often happened in the desert war that the comparatively quiet periods which separated the major engagements on land gave the air forces little chance of easing off, although they, like the armies, needed to refit and reorganize and generally renew their strength. The month of August 1942 was no exception.

In the first place it was clearly necessary for the British to continue to attack the enemy's supply line, and the parts played by Malta's sea and air forces and by the aircraft of No. 201 Group in doing this were described in Chapter XIII. The serious loss of ships led the enemy to make more use of the air route from Crete, and no less than 500 transport aircraft were being used in the Mediterranean area to carry men and supplies for the German forces in Egypt and Libya.[1] It was difficult for the Beaufighters to intercept this traffic, but they had some success at the Cyrenaican end, while the Wellingtons and Liberators attacked the bases in Crete, where they doubtless caused some disorganization and damage.

At this time the main Axis port in North Africa was Tobruk. From here cargoes were moved forward mainly by road, and to some slight extent by railway, and by coasting vessels or barges to Bardia, Sollum or Matruh. Tripoli had almost dropped out of use and only the biggest Axis ships were using Benghazi, which the Liberators alone could reach. Tobruk therefore became the principal target for the night-bombers, and during the month it was attacked night after night almost without a break. Together with raids on the subsidiary ports no less than 1,646 sorties were flown; in other words, fifty bombers on the average were out every night attacking Tobruk and the minor ports and the shipping in or lying off them.

It is a truism that good information is the basis of all successful planning, and the three Services depended upon air reconnaissance to provide them with much of it. Over the sea this important work was done by aircraft based on Malta and by the specialized squadrons of

[1] The German airlift of men to North Africa in 1942 was on a large scale. From April to June 22,912 men were ferried across for the Army and 6,645 for the *Luftwaffe*. In July and August these figures rose to Army 24,606 and *Luftwaffe* 11,620.

No. 201 Group. Over the land it was done by No. 240 (later renumbered No. 285) Reconnaissance Wing. Strategic reconnaissance was the task of Spitfires of No. 2 Photographic Reconnaissance Unit and Baltimores of No. 1437 Flight. Between them they covered the ports and landing-grounds along the North African coast as far west as Derna, and penetrated inland as far as Siwa and Jarabub. In so doing they were able to report when movement on the coast road offered suitable targets for the Beaufighters. No. 208 Squadron undertook most of the tactical reconnaissance, both visual and photographic, its tasks being to watch the forward area for movement, observe for the artillery, and locate targets for the air support squadrons. The Tomahawk Is and Hurricanes I and IIA with which No. 208 Squadron was still equipped suffered heavily at the hands of enemy fighters, but a proposal to rearm it with Spitfires was not approved by the Air Ministry, on the ground that the Spitfires were too valuable for low-altitude work. This decision was disappointing to those who had learned the value of good battlefield reconnaissance.

Soon after the middle of the month distinct signs of a trend of movement towards the southern sector of the El Alamein line began to be apparent, and the enemy's fighters seemed anxious to discourage any inquisitiveness on the part of the British. New tactics were therefore tried, in which the tactical reconnaissance aircraft were sent out with an escort of two or even three fighter squadrons each, in search of information which should give a clue to the enemy's intentions. In this way the essential information was obtained. It has been said that in war each side gets the information it deserves: certainly the 8th Army and Desert Air Force had good reason to be grateful to No. 208 Squadron for the information it strove so hard to obtain. It was exacting work, and during the month the Squadron flew 242 sorties and lost eight pilots and eight aircraft. Fifteen other aircraft were damaged.

The essential fact is that the enemy's preliminary moves had been detected, and towards the end of the month this led to plenty of targets being found for the fighter-bombers and light bombers. Whereas these had flown in all 481 sorties against battlefield targets up to the 20th August, in the next ten days they flew 492. On the 21st August 'round the clock' bombing began again, with the Wellingtons also attacking battlefield targets. The *Panzerarmee* later reported that the continual heavy air attacks by day and night before the commencement of the operation against Alam el Halfa caused many casualties to men and much damage to equipment and affected the morale of both German and Italian troops.

It was of course realized that the enemy's air forces must not be allowed to grow stronger unmolested, and attacks on their landing-grounds, especially those from which the German fighters and dive-bombers were known to operate, were carried out throughout the month. A notable success was gained on the night 8th/9th August and the following day, when Qotafiya was attacked repeatedly and ten aircraft are known to have been destroyed or damaged. The total effort expended in this type of attack was equivalent to six aircraft attacking one landing-ground or another every day of the month.

During August the *Fliegerführer Afrika*, General von Waldau, left to take command of *Fliegerkorps X* based on Greece and Crete. He was succeeded by Major-General Hans Seidemann, previously Chief of Staff of *Luftflotte* 2, who held the appointment until the end of the North African campaign. The month was largely spent by the enemy's air forces in North Africa in building up their strength. They were greatly handicapped by shortage of fuel, especially during the first half of the month. Thereafter the German fighters were very active, which necessitated the strong British air escorts already referred to. Elsewhere in the Mediterranean the enemy air forces were mainly occupied in making a few weak and unsuccessful attacks on Alexandria and Port Said, and in opposing the passage of the 'Pedestal' convoy (described in Chapter XIII). Excluding the fighter-bombers, the British fighters in North Africa flew an average of over 160 sorties on offensive and protective tasks every day.

Thus although the clash on land did not occur until the end of the month, the Royal Air Force had already done a great deal towards weakening the enemy by attacking his air forces, his troops and transport, his supply routes, ports and ships. On all these tasks, other than anti-shipping operations and those from Malta, the Middle East flew an average of 260 sorties every day. At least 61 aircraft (33 German and 28 Italian) were destroyed in North Africa for the loss of 52 British—a remarkable result considering that it was the British who were for most of the time carrying the war to the enemy. For the whole of the Mediterranean and Middle East the figures for August were: German 92, Italian 46, and British 122.

The month of August had been a depressing time for Rommel, conscious of his failure in July, irritated by the stalemate, and never able to forget that shiploads of men and equipment were daily drawing nearer to Suez. His own prospects of reinforcement were slight, and he calculated that he must either attack the British before they could benefit from the convoys expected early in September or give up the initiative altogether.

His study of the tactical situation convinced him that General Montgomery would give battle on the present ground, for a mere delaying position would not have had so much work done on it. The defences in the northern and central parts of the front, as far south as Alam Nayil, seemed to be well developed and strongly held, but between this point and the Qattara depression they were very different. With his fondness for manœuvre Rommel saw a chance of applying his familiar design of a break-through in the south followed by a sweep up towards the coast, cutting the main road and taking the defenders of the northern sector in rear. To carry out this plan he would want to make an approach march by moonlight, which meant that the operation must begin at the end of August. The operation would be the first phase of a renewed attempt to capture the Suez Canal.

This brought to a head the troublesome matter of supplies. Consumption had been greatly in excess of the amounts arriving by sea, and stocks of all kinds—particularly fuel and ammunition—were running dangerously low.[1] Rommel reported on the 22nd that, if the *Panzerarmee* was to attack at the end of August, shipments of about 6,000 tons of fuel and 2,500 tons of ammunition must reach Libya by specified dates between 25th and 30th August. *Comando Supremo* promised to do everything possible, and sent seven ships, carrying 10,000 tons of fuel, half for the *Panzerarmee* and half aviation spirit for the *Luftwaffe*. (In the event four of the seven ships were sunk.) These were to be followed by others a few days later.[2] By 29th August only about 1,500 tons had arrived at Tobruk for the army, but for the reason already given Rommel could not merely postpone his attack until everything was ready. He decided to take a chance on gaining a quick success, and notified *OKH* that the shortage of fuel and ammunition would restrict the coming offensive to the vicinity of El Alamein and that it would start the next evening.

A further trouble over petrol lay in getting it distributed. Tobruk is 350 miles by road from El Alamein and the process of moving supplies from ship to consumer took a long time. At the forward end Rommel could not afford to run very low unless he was sure that fresh supplies were being fed into the 'pipeline', which consisted mainly of road transport and itself consumed a large quantity of the precious petrol. Apart from this it suffered appreciable losses from air attack. It seems that the fuel available on 30th August was, if a promise by Kesselring to help the *Panzerarmee* from the *Luftwaffe's* stock is taken into account, enough for about 150 miles per vehicle with the troops, and about 250 miles per vehicle elsewhere.

Another cause of anxiety to Rommel was the state of his own health.

---

[1] See table on page 327.

[2] The following ships reached Tobruk with fuel for the Army: on 23rd August, *Alberto Fassio* (with 1,140 tons); on 25th *Kreta* (225); on 28th *Giorgio* (120); on 30th *Gualdi* (837). The *Giorgio* seems to have caused some confusion because she carried 2,474 tons, nearly all for the *Luftwaffe*, of which the Army expected to get more than it did. Other ships arriving at Benghazi and Tobruk between the 23rd and 30th August carried in all about 1,200 tons of ammunition. In the same period the following were sunk: on 27th August *Istria* (with 407 tons of fuel) and *Dielpi* (464), and on 30th *Sanandrea* (2,411) nearly all for the Army. The *Abruzzi* was damaged by air attack on 1st September; the *Picci Fassio* was sunk on the 2nd, and the *Bianchi* and *Padenna* on the 4th, on which day the *Sportivo* reached Tobruk.

He had long been suffering from a stomach complaint which was now aggravated by the mental and physical strain of the past weeks and by the climate. On 22nd August he informed *OKH* that he was ill, and asked for a substitute in time for the coming offensive. He suggested Guderian, but was informed on the 24th that no suitable Panzer General was available. If necessary the Führer would agree to Kesselring assuming supreme command in Africa, with Nehring as Army Commander and von Vaerst as Commander of the *D.A.K.* Rommel replied that he now felt well enough to command the operation under medical supervision, but would then have to take a long cure in Germany. In these circumstances it is not surprising that the old fire and enthusiasm were lacking, and that the Rommel of Alam el Halfa was not the Rommel of Gazala and Tobruk.

Map No. 39 shows the outline of the plan of attack, which was simple and bold. The striking force, having concentrated stealthily between Bab el Qattara and the plateau at El Taqa, would move forward at 11 p.m. on 30th August. The advance was at first to be eastward, but a subsequent wheel to the left would bring the whole force into line facing north. Reconnaissance Units 3 and 33 would then be on the eastern or outer flank; next, the *D.A.K.*; then the 20th Italian Corps; then the 90th Light Division; and lastly a strong mixed group under 10th Corps whose purpose was to hold open the 'hinge'.[1] From these positions the striking force would advance north at 6 a.m. and encircle the enemy. This meant that the *D.A.K.* had seven hours in which to go thirty miles and be ready to advance again to the attack. Seeing that this distance had to be covered at night over almost entirely unreconnoitred ground, known to be mined, but to an unknown extent, and against a degree of opposition that could only be guessed at, it is evident that the timing was, to say the least, wildly optimistic. In the event the plan failed to achieve either the surprise or the speed upon which its success depended. As for surprise, General Montgomery and his Intelligence Staff had read the signs correctly and were expecting just such a move, for which the 8th Army and the Desert Air Force were consequently ready. As for speed, the enemy had rightly appreciated that minefields can be crossed but had failed to allow anything like enough time for doing so.

On the remainder of the front the troops of 10th and 21st Corps, the Ramcke Parachute Brigade and the 164th Division were to hold their positions, and make raids during the night of 30th/31st August to mislead the British and capture prisoners for purpose of identification. From daylight 31st August the *Luftwaffe* was to support the striking

[1] On 30th August the *D.A.K.* had (omitting Pzkw IIs) 93 IIIs, 73 III Specials, 10 IVs and 27 IV Specials: total 203. Thus about half its tanks were the powerful 'Specials'. Since 25th May at least 90 III Specials and 20 IV Specials had reached the country, mostly during the last few weeks. The Italians had 243 medium tanks, many of which were almost worn out.

force and maintain fighter patrols over it; Italian fighters were to protect the 20th Corps. There was to be no preliminary air action against the British positions.

General Montgomery confidently expected that the enemy's blow would be directed against the 13th Corps' sector. To the north lay the 30th Corps consisting of three Divisions—the 9th Australian, 1st South African and 5th Indian—all in considerable depth. The 23rd Armoured Brigade of three regiments of Valentine tanks was in Corps Reserve near the eastern end of the Ruweisat ridge.

The 13th Corps (Lieut.-General B. G. Horrocks) consisted of:

New Zealand Division
  5th and 6th N.Z. Infantry Brigades and the 132nd Infantry Brigade;[1]
44th Division
  131st and 133rd Infantry Brigades;
7th Armoured Division
  4th Light Armoured Brigade and 7th Motor Brigade Groups;
10th Armoured Division
  8th and 22nd Armoured Brigade Groups.

The turned-back left flank of the New Zealand Division formed a stiff shoulder which could remain in place without the support of the relatively weak 7th Armoured Division to the south. In rear of the New Zealand Division's position was the Alam el Halfa ridge, originally chosen by General Auchinleck to be a defended locality, and now strongly fortified and held by the 44th Division. General Horrocks's plan was for the New Zealand and 44th Divisions to hold their ground to the last, while in the south the 7th Armoured Division, on its wide front, was to delay and harass the enemy as much as possible. It was so likely that the enemy would try to seize the Alam el Halfa ridge that the 22nd Armoured Brigade was placed in dug-in positions at the western end, where the fire of its tanks and the 6-pdr anti-tank guns of its motor battalion could be united with that of the supporting artillery in a strong defensive fire plan. The 8th Armoured Brigade was placed to the east, on the flank of the enemy's expected line of advance. Various stratagems were adopted to mislead the enemy.[2]

---

[1] The 4th New Zealand Brigade was away refitting.

[2] For example, the planting in No Man's Land of a bogus map purporting to show the state of the going behind the British lines. This map certainly found its way to H.Q. *Panzerarmee* as intended, but there is no direct evidence that it had anything to do with the change of plan described on page 386. The fact remains that the enemy experienced great difficulty with the going, and used up a lot of fuel in consequence.

It is interesting to note that General Montgomery was even now planning his own offensive, which eventually took place in October. For this purpose he intended to form a corps strong in armour—the 10th Corps—on the lines of the *D.A.K.* He therefore told General Horrocks that in repelling the enemy at Alam el Halfa he was on no account to allow the British armour to become mauled. The Army Commander's basic idea at this time was to build up and train the 8th Army before launching it in an 'all out' attempt to destroy the enemy.

The role of the Desert Air Force in the coming battle was to make continuous attacks on the enemy in the forward area by day and night, consistent with preventing the *Luftwaffe* from intervening. As things turned out the air played a very important part, so that the comparative strength of air forces on both sides at the end of August is of particular interest. Since the convoy operations in mid-August, described in Chapter XIII, the defence of Sicily and the attacks on Malta had devolved almost entirely upon the Italian Air Force, while German air strength was being moved to the help of Rommel. Some fighters had come from Russia and the long-range bomber force in Crete had been built up to 229 aircraft, about half of which were serviceable. In North Africa, where their activity had been kept low, the Axis air forces had grown to about 720 aircraft in all, of which about 450 were serviceable. In the Western Desert the British could muster 565, of which roughly 400 were serviceable, apart from a small number of Fleet Air Arm aircraft. Behind them No. 205 Group had 140 medium and 25 heavy bombers, of which rather more than half were available at a time. There were also the small force of Liberators, the few Fortresses and some of the newly arrived Mitchells and Kittyhawk IIs of the United States Army Air Force.[1] The numerical balance was thus fairly even; indeed in fighters it was almost exactly so, though most of the British fighters were still Hurricane Is and IIs.

The Order of Battle of the Desert Air Force during the battle of Alam el Halfa, including other air formations available in support, is given in Appendix 5.

It has already been described how the southward moves of the enemy's striking force had been detected from the air. At last light on 30th August the final concentrations were seen and were quickly attacked by Wellingtons and flare-dropping Albacores. In 30th Corps' sector the raids and diversionary attacks took place just before and after midnight; the strongest was made against the 9th Indian

[1] The Mitchell was classified as a medium bomber, although its role was the same as that of the Desert Air Force's light bomber. From now on, therefore, the term 'day-bombers' will be used to denote both medium and light bombers operating in daylight.

Infantry Brigade on the Ruweisat ridge, where some ground was lost and regained by a counter-attack at dawn. Each of the three South African Infantry Brigades also carried out raids during the night, in one of which 56 Italian prisoners were taken.

By about 2 a.m. on the 31st the enemy's striking force had reached the first minefield, not without some intermingling of units and other confusion. Strongly opposed by the 7th Motor and 4th Light Armoured Brigades, it was soon in difficulty with the mines, and under renewed attack from the air made desperately slow progress.[1] General Nehring was wounded in an air attack and his Chief of Staff, Colonel Bayerlein, took temporary command of the *D.A.K.* At about 9 a.m. Rommel arrived; in view of the depressing start he was inclined to call a halt. After discussion with Bayerlein, however, he decided not to give up without trying to capture Alam el Halfa, and the attack intended for 6 a.m. was ordered to begin at noon. The wheel was to be slightly reduced, bringing the *D.A.K.* into the position originally intended for the 20th Corps, that is, opposite the western half of the Alam el Halfa ridge, instead of the eastern. Nothing could have suited the British better.

The *D.A.K.* had great difficulty in forming up on account of a dust-storm, which however saved them from air attack since flying was hampered for much of the day. They got off to a late and ragged start —15th Panzer Division at about 1 p.m. and 21st Panzer an hour later. Two miles south of the 22nd Armoured Brigade's position two squadrons of Crusader tanks had been stationed to decoy the enemy on to the Brigade's dug-in Grants and the 6-pdr anti-tanks guns of its motor battalion—1st The Rifle Brigade.[2] The 15th Panzer Division did not take the bait, but headed east, followed forty-five minutes later by 21st Panzer. The 22nd Armoured Brigade therefore showed some of its tanks, whereupon 21st Panzer wheeled round and headed for the 3rd/4th County of London Yeomanry in the centre. A fierce duel began in which the Royal Scots Greys, the 1st and 104th Regiments R.H.A., and part of the 44th Divisional Artillery joined to give the enemy tanks a hot reception. The 15th Panzer Division to the north-east circled round to threaten 5th R.T.R./2nd R.G.H. on the left of the Brigade's line, but darkness was falling, the consumption of fuel over bad 'going' had been heavy, and General von Vaerst, now in command of the *D.A.K.*, called the attack off. General Bismarck of the 21st Panzer Division had been killed earlier in the day.

---

[1] At 6.55 a.m. 30th Corps received the message 'Is it a good day for a concert party to visit fwd area?' The answer recorded was 'NO'.

[2] On 31st August the 22nd Armoured Brigade (Brigadier G. P. B. Roberts) had four regiments: Royal Scots Greys; 1st/6th Royal Tank Regiment; 5th Royal Tank Regiment/2nd Royal Gloucestershire Hussars; 3rd/4th County of London Yeomanry. Each regiment had one light squadron of Stuarts or Crusaders and two heavy squadrons of Grants. Total: 40 Stuarts, 34 Crusaders, and 92 Grants.

Elsewhere nothing much had occurred. The 7th Armoured Division had fallen back before the Reconnaissance Group; the Littorio and Ariete Divisions had come up on the left of the *D.A.K.* with the Trieste behind them, and the 90th Light Division and the 10th Corps Group faced the New Zealand Division's southern flank.

On the British side General Montgomery was well satisfied with the day's events. As soon as both Panzer Divisions had been identified he had placed 23rd Armoured Brigade (less three squadrons) at General Horrocks's disposal and by 1 p.m. it had moved into the gap between the New Zealand Division and the 22nd Armoured Brigade, under command of the 10th Armoured Division (Major-General A. H. Gatehouse), thus strengthening the Alam el Halfa area by 100 Valentine tanks.

By nightfall the dust had subsided and the Royal Air Force came out in strength. The arena in which the enemy lay was lit up by flares, and tremendous havoc was caused by the night-bombers among the concentrations of transport. A night of continuous bombing left a pall of smoke from countless petrol fires and burning vehicles. Of this and the next few nights the *D.A.K.* recorded that not only was the damage very great but officers and men were badly shaken and their fighting capacity considerably reduced by the enforced dispersal, lack of sleep, and the strain of waiting for the next bomb.

Early on 1st September the 15th Panzer Division began to work round the east flank of 22nd Armoured Brigade. The 21st Panzer Division was inactive, probably from lack of petrol, having been unable to replenish during the night. The 8th Armoured Brigade had already been ordered to move across and make contact with the 22nd but when they tried to do so they found that the 15th Panzer Division had established a strong anti-tank screen which held them off.[1] However, this tactical success brought the enemy little advantage for at about noon Rommel announced that there was little hope of getting enough petrol forward and that he was going over to the defensive where he stood.

As soon as General Montgomery was satisfied that the enemy's main force was committed to the Alam el Halfa area, he ordered the 30th Corps to thin out and form reserves, and move the 2nd South African Brigade to a position north of Alam el Halfa. He called forward a brigade of the 50th Division from airfield protection, in which it was replaced by a brigade of the newly arrived 51st Division. The 5th Indian Infantry Brigade was placed under the New Zealand Division, and General Freyberg was warned to get ready to attack southwards from Alam Nayil towards Himeimat.

[1] On 1st September 8th Armoured Brigade (Brigadier G. W. Richards) consisted of: 3rd Royal Tank Regiment, the Nottinghamshire Yeomanry, and the Staffordshire Yeomanry, with, in all, 12 Crusader and 72 Grant tanks; 74th and 97th Field Regiments R.A. and 65th Anti-Tank Regiment R.A.

Early on the same day the 9th Australian Division had carried out a long-prepared operation to the west of Tell el Eisa. The 2/15th Australian Battalion, supported by a force of day-bombers, sprang a surprise on the enemy, but a fierce struggle ensued in which communications became disrupted and the bridgehead through which a raiding party was to issue could not be held. About 140 prisoners of the 164th (German) Division were taken and the Australians had 135 casualties. Seven Valentine tanks of the 40th R.T.R. were knocked out.

The 1st September marked the end of the main battle from the enemy's point of view, although he was to be given no respite from the air. The day-bombers, including the few American Mitchells, had dropped, in the course of 111 sorties that day, some 80 tons of bombs. The British fighters flew 372 sorties and prevented several attempts by Stukas to retaliate, forcing them to abandon their dive-bombing tactics and take to level-bombing, for which they were ill-adapted. That night the Wellingtons were again active over the rearward area of the *D.A.K.* and used some 4,000-lb. bombs with devastating effect. The heavy bombers visited Tobruk and ports in Crete, and attacked and damaged the *Picci Fassio* and *Abruzzi* at sea.

During the morning of 2nd September Rommel gave orders for a deliberate withdrawal, spread over several days, to positions just west of the British minefields. In a report to *OKW* he gave as his reasons the shortage of petrol, the bad start, the delay imposed by mines and the incessant air attacks by day and night. He had just had word of the sinking of the *Picci Fassio*; this meant that even if the *Bianchi* and *Sportivo* arrived safely it would be 7th September before petrol supplies could be assured.[1]

Although it was clear to General Montgomery that Rommel had shot his bolt, he resisted the temptation to start a general counter-attack. He judged the 8th Army to be unready, and going off at half-cock would only make it harder to prepare for the decisive blow he had in mind. He therefore ordered that the enemy was to be harassed vigorously, but that the only staged attack would be the one being prepared by General Freyberg with the object of closing the minefield gaps behind the enemy's striking force. This was now timed to take place on the night of 3rd/4th September.

As a preliminary step the 132nd Infantry Brigade was relieved by the 5th Indian Infantry Brigade, and became available for the attack. The front was to extend for about 4½ miles east from the 'hinge' at Alam Nayil, though the three minefields would canalize the attack into two separate lines of advance. The objectives of the first phase on the northern edge of the Deir el Munassib were about three miles distant; for the second phase—a further advance of three miles—the 151st Infantry Brigade would come under General Freyberg's command on

[1] The *Bianchi* was sunk on the 4th. See page 382n.

4th September. The 7th Armoured Division was to exert pressure westward from Samaket Gaballa all the time.

General Freyberg's plan was to attack at 10.30 p.m. on 3rd September with the 132nd Infantry Brigade on the right (west) and the 5th New Zealand Brigade on the left, each with one squadron of Valentine tanks, from 46th and 50th R.T.R. respectively. The operation was to begin silently, but six field and two medium artillery regiments were to be ready in support. The 6th New Zealand Brigade was to create a diversion by raids at about 11 p.m. and was to secure the 132nd Brigade's right flank.

The raids by the 6th New Zealand Brigade found the enemy on the alert and raised a hornet's nest. Unfortunately the 132nd Brigade had had much difficulty in reaching its start-line, which it crossed nearly an hour late.[1] The enemy was by then thoroughly roused and met the advancing infantry with machine-gun and mortar fire. There was much straggling and general confusion, which took some time to sort out. The Brigade Commander (Brigadier C. B. Robertson) was severely wounded and Brigadier Clifton, of the 6th New Zealand Brigade, who had gone forward to reconnoitre, drove into an enemy position and was captured.[2] On the left the 5th New Zealand Brigade's attack went in punctually and after brisk fighting reached its objective—indeed the 28th Maori Battalion penetrated beyond it, captured several enemy posts and did much damage to transport. Shortly after noon the enemy counter-attacked and was beaten off, and a second attempt was broken up by the fire of the New Zealand Divisional Artillery, backed up by the day-bombers.[3]

The enemy's vigorous reaction (which, after all, was only to be expected) made it unlikely that a renewal of the attack would succeed. Rather than leave the troops out in very exposed positions General Freyberg advised a complete withdrawal, with which Generals Horrocks and Montgomery agreed. It was carried out after dark, but not without further losses. The attempt to close the minefield gaps had therefore failed. It had caused the enemy no more than passing concern, a disappointing result in view of the high casualties, the New Zealanders having lost 275 officers and men and the 132nd Brigade—whose first battle it was—697 killed, wounded, and missing.

On 2nd September there had been even more British aircraft operating over the Desert than on the previous day, and on the 3rd Field-Marshal Kesselring issued a Special Order exhorting *Luftwaffe* pilots to protect their sorely oppressed comrades of the *Panzerarmee*.

[1] The 132nd Infantry Brigade consisted of 2nd The Buffs, 4th and 5th Royal West Kent Regiment, one squadron 46th Royal Tank Regiment, and 227th and 432nd Anti-Tank Batteries R.A.

[2] He escaped at Matruh and was recaptured after several days' trudging in the Desert.

[3] The New Zealand Divisional Artillery was reinforced by the 58th Field Regiment R.A., 64th Medium Regiment R.A., and one Battery 7th Medium Regiment R.A.

He ordered Seidemann to provide the army with dawn-to-dusk cover against low and high flying aircraft, and, taking a leaf from the R.A.F.'s book, he arranged for a continuous air attack to be made that night on the area occupied by the 5th Indian Division. This began shortly before 10 p.m. and lasted all night, but caused very few casualties.

The 3rd September had been another strenuous day for the Royal Air Force. Counting reconnaissance flights and the operations of the previous night the sorties for the twenty-four hours reached the record total of 957, and 230 tons of bombs were dropped. This marked the climax of a period of three days in which circumstances had been unusually favourable for the use of a strong air force in support of a defensive land battle. The British dispositions were well known and changed but little, so that there were no difficulties over identification; everything within a clearly defined arena was hostile, and free to be attacked. Moreover, the enemy's troops and vehicles advancing—and later retreating—over the stony surface had little opportunity to provide themselves with any cover and were consequently very exposed and vulnerable. Into this arena more than 750 bombloads had been dropped in the seventy-two hours. In all, a force of less than 500 available aircraft had flown 2,500 sorties in support of the 8th Army, which is equivalent to 35 aircraft in the air every hour, day and night. In addition, the United States Army Air Force had contributed nearly 180 sorties with its Liberators, Mitchells and Kittyhawk IIs.[1]

During the next few days the enemy withdrew to the westernmost of the three British minefields, followed up lightly by the 7th and 10th Armoured Divisions. The R.A.F. also harassed the enemy but less intensively than hitherto. This was partly because sandstorms interfered and partly because the wastage in British fighters now made it necessary to use most of them on fighter sweeps to counter the enemy's activity in the air, rather than as escorts to the day-bombers. By 7th September the battle had died down and General Montgomery began to reorganize his Army and to take in hand the important matter of training the new 10th Corps. His decision not to recapture the high ground at Himeimat is an interesting instance of looking ahead, his reason being that he had already decided to mislead the enemy into thinking that the British offensive would be made in the south, and he therefore thought it wise to leave him with a good vantage-point from which to observe the bogus preparations.

In the week's fighting the Germans had 1,859 killed, wounded, and

---

[1] Up to 4th September the *D.A.K.* estimated its own losses from air attacks to have been 110 killed and 305 wounded; 170 vehicles (including one tank) destroyed and 270 (including two tanks) damaged, besides a quantity of other equipment.

missing, and the Italians 1,051. German losses of equipment included 33 guns, 298 vehicles and 38 tanks destroyed, and large numbers were damaged; the Italians lost 22 guns, 97 vehicles and 11 tanks. The British had 1,750 casualties, and 67 tanks and 15 anti-tank guns put out of action. In the air the losses from all causes were 36 German aircraft, 5 Italian, and 68 British.

Thirty-one of the British tank casualties were Grants; five in the 22nd Armoured Brigade and thirteen in the 8th were destroyed, and the rest damaged. Of the other British tank losses twenty-one were suffered by those Valentines which were being used as 'I' tanks, a role for which they were no longer thought suitable. Indeed, the Middle East felt that they had no assault tank capable of tackling strongly defended positions: the Valentine was too light, the Matilda too slow, and both still mounted only a 2-pdr gun. The Matilda's long and valuable service was in fact coming to an end, for on 6th September the War Office was asked not to send out any more to the Middle East.

The extent of the British success at Alam el Halfa is to be measured less by its material results than by its effect on morale. To the Axis the battle seemed to put an end to their hopes of reaching the Delta. To the British it appeared as a clear-cut victory in which Rommel had been defeated at his own game. True, the minor operations at Tell el Eisa had achieved little, and the attempt to close the minefield gap was a failure. Of far greater importance, however, was the stimulus that had been given to morale: the confidence of the 8th Army in itself, in its Commander, and in the Royal Air Force, rose to quite new heights. What had been plain for all to see was the benefit of concentrating resources, which was made possible by a particularly accurate forecast of what Rommel was going to do. This meant that the enemy's striking force could be met on ground of the defenders' choice by a tremendous volume of fire: from the air with a rain of projectiles ranging from machine-gun bullets to 4,000-lb. bombs, and from the ground with the concentrated fire of field and medium artillery, anti-tank guns, and the guns of the dug-in tanks, notably the Grants.

The true view of this success on the desert battlefield is that it was the complement of the successes at sea against the enemy's shipping, for these lay at the root of all his shortages. The cumulative effect of the work of the Royal Navy and Royal Air Force had been to weaken the *Panzerarmee*, and the battle of Alam el Halfa supplied the finishing touch to this phase of the combined struggle.

CONCLUSION

In the ten months of campaigning covered by this volume, that is from November 1941 to September 1942, both sides had experienced success and failure. The worst disasters had befallen the British, and yet the end of the period found them in a better position in this theatre than their opponents, and able to prepare once more to give the Desert pendulum a push westwards. It has been seen that each side possessed the advantage in striking power when its forces were reasonably close to their bases; conversely, they were much weaker when reaching out at full stretch. It follows that somewhere between the extreme positions there should have been a place where both sides could maintain forces comparable in size. This was in fact the case from February to May 1942 at Gazala, where the Axis forces were served by the port of Benghazi and the road from Tripoli, and the British by Tobruk and the road and railway from Alexandria.

Here, after three months of preparation, a trial of strength took place between the comparable forces, in which the 8th Army was decisively defeated. Seizing his opportunity General Rommel took Tobruk almost in his stride and then made the fateful decision to pursue as far as he could, to Cairo, perhaps, or even to the Canal. The plan to halt on the Egyptian frontier at a convenient distance ahead of Tobruk was scrapped. The air forces which should then have taken part in an attack on Malta had suddenly to join in an improvised pursuit and support the army as best they could. The result was that Malta began to strike again, with disastrous consequences for Axis shipping. Not only was Rommel's land front now a long way ahead of the nearest port—Tobruk—but owing to the heavy losses at sea the supplies to be fed into the road system ran short in many important respects, notably ammunition and petrol.

Thus it happened that the British, after their long retreat and some very anxious moments, were nevertheless able to hold their vital bases. Their lean days were over. Their strength on land was growing every day. The first American Sherman tanks and self-propelled anti-tank guns were arriving, and the 6-pdr was rapidly replacing the 2-pdr anti-tank gun—changes which made for a great increase in confidence. The Royal Air Force in the Middle East was becoming a powerful influence in the war at sea and on land, the American squadrons were becoming acclimatized and battleworthy, and the Desert Air Force was looking forward with relish to the prospect of playing havoc with a retreating enemy.

By September 1942 the monthly figures for Allied world-wide

shipping losses had fallen well below the desperately high figure for June, though mastery of the U-boats was still not in sight. Attacks by the Royal Air Force on Germany were steadily becoming heavier (the first '1,000 bomber raid' on Cologne was made on 30th May) and United States heavy bombers were beginning to operate by day over occupied territory in Europe. In southern Russia there was heavy fighting near Stalingrad, and in the Caucasus the Germans were still advancing, though more slowly than before. In the Far East the British had been driven out of the whole of Burma and were awaiting the end of the monsoon to start what looked like being the long process of winning the country back again. In the Solomon Islands the great battle of attrition on Guadalcanal had begun, and in New Guinea the Japanese attempt to seize Port Moresby by an advance over the Owen Stanley range had been held. The battle of Midway Island, in which the Japanese had lost heavily, had removed the danger to shipping in the Indian Ocean from aircraft carriers; and the Allied landing in Madagascar had reduced the danger from submarines—German as well as Japanese—by depriving them of a potential fuelling base. These results were of great importance to the Middle East, which depended so largely upon shipping from India and Australia and up the east coast of Africa. To sum up: while the situation viewed as a whole gave no cause for complacency, there were hopeful signs that the enemy was being held and that some of the crises were past. German morale was still high, but that of the Italians was sinking fast.

Now, in the autumn of 1942, in this general setting the Allies were preparing to seize the strategic initiative in the Mediterranean area. They were to do this by assailing the enemy from both directions—from Egypt and from French North Africa. Both these operations depended basically upon the merchant ships, escort vessels, fleet cover, air patrols, air striking forces and securely held ports, fuelling stations, and naval and air bases which go to make up maritime power. This power had been relentlessly working for a long time to build up the 8th Army and Desert Air Force; it was now about to be applied in another and more spectacular way. For while the assault to be made on the confined front at El Alamein would be of necessity a bludgeon blow, the complementary operation in French North Africa would be a swoop from the sea in the grand manner. Together they were destined to change the course of the war.

CHRONOLOGY OF MAIN EVENTS FROM

Items within square brackets [ ] are

1941	General	Mediterranean Sea
Sept.		[Operation to reinforce Malta with aircraft] [German submarines reach the Mediterranean] [24-28 'Halberd' convoy to Malta]
Oct.	2 Allocation of Lend-Lease funds to the Middle East 24 Germans capture Kharkov	[Force K arrives at Malta]
Nov.	1 Ninth Army formed U.S. Military North African Mission set up in Cairo 22-28 Rostov lost and retaken by the Russians	9 Force K sinks the '*Duisburg*' convoy 13 Loss of H.M.S. *Ark Royal* after reinforcing Malta with aircraft 16-19 & 21-22 Mediterranean Fleet and Forces H and K operating in support of 'Crusader' 25 Loss of H.M.S. *Barham*
Dec.	7-8 Japanese attack Pearl Harbour and land in Malaya 11 Germany and Italy declare war on U.S.A. 22 First Washington Conference to decide Allied policy	13 Action off Cape Bon 14 Loss of H.M.S. *Galatea* 17 First Battle of Sirte 19 Disaster to Force K 19 Italian human torpedoes attack Alexandria harbour: H.M.S. *Queen Elizabeth* and *Valiant* damaged

SEPTEMBER 1941 TO SEPTEMBER 1942

not included in the present volume

Western Desert	Red Sea and East Africa	Persia and Iraq
Tobruk besieged 18 Eighth Army formed 19-27 Second stage of relief of Australians in Tobruk	[East Africa Command formed] [Gondar area: 25 Italians at Wolchefit surrender] [Blockade of French Somaliland continues]	[British and Russian forces enter Teheran] Start of development of supply route to Russia
Tobruk besieged 9 Western Desert Air Force formed 12-15 Third stage of relief of Australians in Tobruk	[Preparations to attack Gondar] [Blockade of French Somaliland continues] 21 Red Sea transferred to Mediterranean Station	
Tobruk besieged 18 'Crusader' begins	[Gondar: 27 General Nasi surrenders] [End of campaign in Italian East Africa] [Blockade of French Somaliland continues]	U.S. Military Iranian Mission set up in Baghdad
1 First attempt to relieve Tobruk fails: British pause to regroup 5 British advance resumed 10 Relief of Tobruk 16 Enemy withdraws from Gazala 25 British troops enter Benghazi	[Blockade of French Somaliland continues]	

CHRONOLOGY OF MAIN EVENTS FROM

Items within square brackets [ ] are

1942	General	Mediterranean Sea
Jan.	1 United Nations Declaration 29 Treaty of Alliance between U.K., Soviet Union and Persia	Three small convoys reach Malta from Alexandria
Feb.	2-7 Egyptian Cabinet crisis 15 Fall of Singapore 25 Mr. Lyttelton leaves, temporarily succeeded by Sir Walter Monckton	12-15 Convoy from Alexandria fails to reach Malta
March	20 Sir Stafford Cripps visits Middle East	Heavy air attacks on Malta 7, 21, 29 Three operations to reinforce Malta with aircraft 11 Loss of H.M.S. *Naiad* 22 Second Battle of Sirte 23 Convoy reaches Malta only to be sunk in harbour
April	3 Admiral Cunningham leaves, temporarily succeeded by Admiral Pridham-Wippell	10 Force H leaves Gibraltar for Madagascar Air attacks on Malta reach their peak Tenth Submarine Flotilla leaves Malta 15 H.M. the King awards Malta the George Cross 20 U.S.S. *Wasp* reinforces Malta with Spitfires

SEPTEMBER 1941 TO SEPTEMBER 1942

not included in the present volume

Western Desert	Red Sea and East Africa	Persia and Iraq
2 Bardia surrenders 17 Sollum and Halfaya surrender 21 Axis forces advance from Mersa Brega 28 British evacuate Benghazi and retire towards Gazala	[Blockade of French Somaliland continues]	12 Command of Troops in Iraq passes from India to the Middle East
2 Eighth Army stabilizes the line Gazala-Bir Hacheim	[Blockade of French Somaliland continues]	16 Tenth Army formed
Lull in the Desert continues	[Blockade of French Somaliland continues]	
Both sides preparing for major operations		

CHRONOLOGY OF MAIN EVENTS FROM

Items within square brackets [ ] are

1942	General	Mediterranean Sea
May	4 Mr. R. G. Casey becomes Minister of State, Middle East 5 British forces land on Madagascar 8 General Dobbie leaves Malta; succeeded by General Lord Gort 20 Admiral Sir Henry Harwood arrives as Naval C.-in-C. U.S.A.A.F. strategic bomber force arrives	Air attacks on Malta gradually decrease 9 U.S.S. *Wasp* and H.M.S. *Eagle* reinforce Malta with Spitfires 18 H.M.S. *Eagle* repeats the operation 14-15 Failure of human torpedo attack at Alexandria
June	Peak sinkings in Atlantic 4-6 Japanese naval defeat at Midway Island Formation of U.S. Army Command and U.S. Middle East Air Force 18-25 Second Washington Conference 27 General Eisenhower appointed C.-in-C. Allied Expeditionary Force	3, 9 Two operations to reinforce Malta with Spitfires 12-16 'Harpoon' convoy reaches Malta from the west; 'Vigorous' from the east turns back
July	Anglo-American agreement on operation 'Torch' 24 Germans occupy Rostov U.S.A.A.F. tactical air forces begin to arrive in the Middle East	1-14 Heavy air attacks on Malta renewed 15, 21 Two operations to reinforce Malta with Spitfires 10th Submarine Flotilla returns to Malta
August	4-10 Mr. Churchill in Cairo 12 He attends the First Moscow Conference 15 General Alexander succeeds General Auchinleck as C.-in-C. 16 Germans reach Maikop in the Caucasus 24 Allied Force H.Q. set up in London for 'Torch'	10-15 'Pedestal' convoy to Malta 11 Loss of H.M.S. *Eagle* 11,17 Two operations to reinforce Malta with Spitfires 12 Loss of H.M.S. *Manchester*
Sept.	Peak of struggle for Stalingrad	

SEPTEMBER 1941 TO SEPTEMBER 1942

not included in the present volume

Western Desert	Persia and Iraq
10 War Cabinet orders General Auchinleck to attack during May 26 Axis forces attack Gazala—Bir Hacheim positions	
5-6 The 'Cauldron' disaster 10 Bir Hacheim evacuated 11-12 Defeat of the British armour 14 Decision to withdraw from the Gazala positions 21 Loss of Tobruk 25 General Auchinleck takes direct command of 8th Army at Matruh	
1-5 Rommel's attempt to break through at El Alamein defeated 10-26 Repeated British attacks end indecisively Both sides exhausted	
13 General Montgomery takes command of 8th Army 30-31 Axis offensive begins: Battle of Alam el Halfa	U.S. Persian Gulf Service Command set up 21 Persia and Iraq Command (PAIC) set up. General Maitland Wilson appointed to command
2 Rommel begins to withdraw 7 Battle over British prepare to take the offensive	

APPENDIX 1

Principal Commanders and Staff Officers in the Mediterranean and Middle East

(The ranks given are in some cases 'acting' ranks.
Some brief temporary appointments are omitted.)

ROYAL NAVY

Commander-in-Chief, Mediterranean: Admiral Sir Andrew B. Cunningham; Admiral Sir H. D. Pridham-Wippell (from 1st April 1942); Admiral Sir Henry H. Harwood (from 20th May 1942)

Chief of Staff: Rear-Admiral J. H. Edelsten; Commodore J. G. L. Dundas (from September 1942)

Additional Chief of Staff, R.N., at Middle East H.Q. Cairo (also represented Commander-in-Chief, East Indies): Commodore H. G. Norman.

V.A. 1st Battle Squadron and Second-in-Command, Mediterranean Fleet: Vice-Admiral Sir H. D. Pridham-Wippell (to 1st April 1942)

R.A. Mediterranean Aircraft Carriers: Rear-Admiral D. W. Boyd (to 21st January 1942)

R.A. 7th Cruiser Squadron: Rear-Admiral H. B. Rawlings (to 15th January 1942)

R.A. 15th Cruiser Squadron: Rear-Admiral Sir Philip L. Vian; Rear-Admiral A. J. Power (from 12th September 1942)

R.A. Destroyers: Rear-Admiral I. G. Glennie; Commodore P. Todd (from 13th September 1942)

Senior Officer, Force K: Captain W. G. Agnew (to end of March 1942)

Vice-Admiral in Charge, Malta: Vice-Admiral Sir Wilbraham T. R. Ford; Vice-Admiral Sir Ralph Leatham (from 19th January 1942)

Flag Officer attached Middle East: Rear-Admiral H. T. Baillie-Grohman (appointment lapsed July 1942)

Flag Officer Commanding, Red Sea and Canal Area: Vice-Admiral R. H. C. Hallifax

R.A. Alexandria: Rear-Admiral G. A. Creswell

R.A. Training Establishments: Rear-Admiral R. J. R. Scott (from February 1942)

Flag Officer Force H: Vice-Admiral Sir James F. Somerville; Vice-Admiral E. N. Syfret (from 10th January 1942)

Commander-in-Chief, East Indies: Vice-Admiral G. S. Arbuthnot (to June 1942)

Senior Naval Officer Persian Gulf: Rear-Admiral (retd.) C. M. Graham (serving as Commodore 2nd Class); Commodore C. F. Hammill (from February 1942)

THE ARMY

Commander-in-Chief: General Sir Claude Auchinleck; General the Hon. Sir Harold Alexander (from 15th August 1942)

Deputy Commander-in-Chief: General Sir Thomas Blamey, who was also G.O.C. Australian Imperial Force. *This appointment lapsed on General Blamey's departure in January* 1942

Principal Staff Officers

General Staff branch: Lieutenant-General A. F. Smith;
Lieutenant-General T. W. Corbett (from 30th March 1942);
Lieutenant-General R. L. McCreery (from 23rd August 1942)

Quarter-Master-General's branch: Major-General B. O. Hutchinson;
Major-General A. R. Selby (from 10th May 1942);
Major-General G. Surtees (from 15th September 1942)

Adjutant-General's branch: Major-General N. W. Napier-Clavering;
Major-General R. M. Scobie (from 16th February 1942);
Major-General C. D. Moorhead (from 14th August 1942)

Lieutenant-General, Administration: Lieutenant-General T. S. Riddell-Webster;
Lieutenant-General Sir Wilfrid Lindsell (from 1st July 1942)

British Troops, Egypt

Lieutenant-General J. H. Marshall-Cornwall
Lieutenant-General W. G. Holmes (from 13th November 1941)
Lieutenant-General R. G. W. H. Stone (from 1st February 1942)

8th Army

Lieutenant-General Sir Alan Cunningham
Lieutenant-General N. M. Ritchie (from 26th November 1941 to 25th June 1942)
Lieutenant-General B. L. Montgomery (from 13th August 1942)

9th Army

General Sir Maitland Wilson
Lieutenant-General W. G. Holmes (from 21st August 1942)

10th Army

Lieutenant-General E. P. Quinan

Persia and Iraq Command

General Sir Maitland Wilson (from 21st August 1942)

Sudan

Lieutenant-General Sir Noel Beresford-Peirse
Lieutenant-General B. O. Hutchinson (from 5th May 1942)

Formations

1st Australian Corps: Lieutenant-General J. D. Lavarack
3rd Corps: Lieutenant-General D. F. Anderson

10th Corps: Lieutenant-General W. G. Holmes; Lieutenant-General H. Lumsden (from 10th August 1942)

13th Corps: Lieutenant-General A. R. Godwin-Austen; Lieutenant-General W. H. E. Gott (from 6th February 1942); Lieutenant-General B. G. Horrocks (from 14th August 1942)

30th Corps: Lieutenant-General V. V. Pope; Lieutenant-General C. W. M. Norrie (from 5th October 1941); Lieutenant-General W. H. C. Ramsden (from 8th July 1942); Lieutenant-General Sir Oliver Leese (from 10th September 1942)

4th Indian Corps: Lieutenant-General T. W. Corbett; Lieutenant-General W. J. Slim (from 30th March 1942)

21st Indian Corps: Lieutenant-General A. G. O. M. Mayne

1st Armoured Division: Major-General H. Lumsden; Major-General F. W. Messervy (temporary); Major-General A. H. Gatehouse (temporary); Major-General A. F. Fisher (temporary); Major-General R. Briggs (from 21st August 1942)

7th Armoured Division: Major-General W. H. E. Gott; Major-General F. W. Messervy (from 6th February 1942); Major-General J. M. L. Renton (from 19th June 1942); Major-General A. F. Harding (from 17th September 1942)

8th Armoured Division: Major-General C. W. Norman; Major-General C. H. Gairdner (from 23rd August 1942)

10th Armoured Division: Major-General J. G. W. Clark; Major-General A. H. Gatehouse (from 9th April 1942); Major-General E. C. N. Custance (temporary)

31st Indian Armoured Division: Major-General R. H. Wordsworth

5th Division: Major-General H. P. M. Berney-Ficklin

6th Division (later *70th*)*:* Major-General R. M. Scobie

44th Division: Major-General I. T. P. Hughes

50th Division: Major-General W. H. C. Ramsden; Major-General J. S. Nichols (from 12th July 1942)

51st Division: Major-General D. N. Wimberley

56th Division: Major-General E. G. Miles

70th Division: Major-General R. M. Scobie; Major-General G. W. Symes (from 18th February 1942)

6th Australian Division: Major-General E. F. Herring

7th Australian Division: Major-General A. S. Allen

9th Australian Division: Major-General Sir Leslie Morshead

New Zealand Division: Lieutenant-General B. C. Freyberg, V.C. who was also G.O.C. 2nd New Zealand Expeditionary Force; Major-General L. M. Inglis (from 27th June 1942 to 16th August 1942)

1st South African Division: Major-General G. L. Brink; Major-General D. H. Pienaar (from 10th March 1942)

2nd South African Division: Major-General I. P. de Villiers; Major-General H. B. Klopper (from 14th May 1942)

4th Indian Division: Major-General F. W. Messervy; Major-General F. I. S. Tuker (from 2nd January 1942)

5th Indian Division: Major-General A. G. O. M. Mayne; Major-General H. R. Briggs (from 12th May 1942)

6th Indian Division: Major-General J. N. Thomson

8th Indian Division: Major-General C. O. Harvey

10th Indian Division: Major-General W. J. Slim; Major-General T. W. Rees (from 30th March 1942); Major-General J. S. Nichols (from 22nd June 1942); Major-General A. B. Blaxland (from 22nd July 1942)

Malta

Governor and Commander-in-Chief: Lieutenant-General Sir William Dobbie

Governor (from 7th May 1942) and *Supreme Commander* (from 15th May): General the Viscount Gort, V.C.

General Officer Commanding: Major-General D. M. W. Beak, V.C.; Major-General R. M. Scobie (from 6th August 1942)

ROYAL AIR FORCE

Command Headquarters

Air Officer Commanding-in-Chief: Air Chief Marshal Sir Arthur W. Tedder

Deputy Air Officer Commanding-in-Chief: Air Marshal R. M. Drummond

Senior Air Staff Officer: Air Vice-Marshal H. E. P. Wigglesworth

Air Officer-in-Charge of Administration: Air Vice-Marshal G. C. Pirie

Chief Maintenance and Supply Officer: Air Vice-Marshal G. G. Dawson

Egypt

No. 201 *Group:* Air Vice-Marshal L. H. Slatter

No. 202 *Group (became Air Headquarters, Egypt on* 1*st December* 1941)*:* Air Commodore T. W. Elmhirst; Air Vice-Marshal K. R. Park (from 11th January 1942); Air Vice-Marshal W. A. McClaughry (from 8th July 1942)

No. 205 *Group:* Air Commodore L. L. Maclean; Air Commodore A. P. Ritchie (from 1st May 1942)

No. 206 *Group:* Air Commodore C. B. Cooke; Air Commodore C. F. Smylie (from 12th July 1942)

No. 216 *Group (formed on* 21*st May as a Ferry Group and re-formed on* 9*th September* 1942 *as an Air Transport and Ferry Group):* Group Captain B. H. C. Russell; Air Commodore W. W. Straight (from 10th September 1942)

Western Desert

Air Headquarters, Western Desert: Air Vice-Marshal A. Coningham

No. 211 *Group (formed on* 15th *January, disbanded on* 3*rd February and re-formed on* 12*th March* 1942)*:* Air Commodore H. B. Russell; Group Captain K. B. B. Cross (from 12 March 1942); Group Captain G. L. Carter (from 5th April 1942)

Palestine and Transjordan

(became Air Headquarters, Levant on 1st December 1941)

Air Headquarters: Air Commodore L. O. Brown

No. 213 *Group (formed on* 1*st December as Advanced A. H. Q. Levant and became No.* 213 *Group on* 15*th December* 1941)*:* Group Captain S. D. MacDonald; Group Captain R. A. R. Mangles (from 2nd October 1942)

Iraq

Air Headquarters: Air Vice-Marshal J. H. D'Albiac; Air Vice-Marshal H. V. Champion de Crespigny (from 9th March 1942)

No. 214 *Group (formed on* 1*st January* 1942)*:* Group Captain R. M. Foster

No. 215 *Group (formed on* 1*st May* 1942)*:* Air Commodore H. B. Russell

Aden

Air Vice-Marshal F. G. D. Hards

East Africa

(became No. 207 Group on 15th December 1941)

Air Commodore W. Sowrey
Air Commodore M. L. Taylor (from 11th June 1942)

Sudan

(No. 203 Group)

Air Commodore C. B. S. Spackman
Air Commodore R. G. Parry (from 11th February 1942)

Malta

Air Vice-Marshal H. P. Lloyd
Air Vice-Marshal K. R. Park (from 15th July 1942)

APPENDIX 2

Appointments held by the Principal Italian and German Commanders and Staff Officers mentioned in this volume

ITALIAN

Aimone-Cat, General Mario: commander of 5th Squadra in North Africa

Barbasetti di Prun, General Curio: head of the delegation from Comando Supremo (Delease) in August 1942

Bastico, Marshal Ettore: C-in-C Armed Forces in North Africa

Cavallero, Marshal Ugo: Chief of Staff of the Italian Armed Forces

Da Zara, A: Vice-Admiral commanding VII Division

Gambara, General Gastone: commander 20th Corps until December 1941, then Chief of Staff North Africa

Iachino, Admiral Angelo: C-in-C Afloat

Marchesi, General Vittorio: succeeded General Aimone-Cat on 6th November 1941

Navarrini, General Enea: commander 21st Corps

GERMAN

Bayerlein, Colonel Fritz: Chief of Staff D.A.K.

Bismarck, Major-General Georg von: commander of 21st Panzer Division from February 1942; killed August 1942

Crüwell, Lieut.-General Ludwig: commander of D.A.K. until captured in May 1942

Fröhlich, Major-General Stefan: Fliegerführer Afrika until April 1942

Gause, Lieut.-General Alfred: Chief of Staff, Panzergruppe Afrika

Geisler, General Hans-Ferdinand: commander of Fliegerkorps X until August 1942

Kesselring, Field-Marshal Albert: commander of Luftflotte 2, and from December 1941 C-in-C South

Loerzer, General Bruno: commander of Fliegerkorps II

Nehring, Lieut.-General Walther: commander of D.A.K. from June 1942 until wounded August 1942

Neumann-Silkow, Major-General Walther: commander of 15th Panzer Division; died of wounds December 1941

Raeder, Grand Admiral Erich: C-in-C German Navy

Ravenstein, Major-General Johann von: commander of 21st Panzer Division until captured November 1941

Rintelen, General Enno von: Military Attaché and German General at H.Q. Italian Armed Forces, Rome

Rommel, Field-Marshal Erwin: commander Panzergruppe Afrika, and later of German-Italian Panzerarmee Afrika

Seidemann, Major-General Hans: Fliegerführer Afrika from August 1942

Sümmermann, Major-General Max: commander of 90th Light Division; killed December 1941

Vaerst, Lieut.-General Gustav von: commander of 15th Panzer Division from December 1941

Waldau, Lieut.-General Otto Hoffmann von: Fliegerführer Afrika from April to August 1942; then commander of Fliegerkorps X

Westphal, Colonel Siegfried: chief operations officer, H.Q. Panzerarmee Afrika

APPENDIX 3

Main Strength of Mediterranean Fleet and Force H between November 1941 and October 1942

(Because of essential maintenance not all the ships in this list would be available continuously for immediate service, but no ship out of action at the times shown for more than a few days has been included)

THE MEDITERRANEAN FLEET

(*Does not include ships lent from Eastern Fleet*)

Early November 1941	*End of* 1941	*Mid March* 1942 immediately before 2nd Battle of Sirte	*Early September* 1942
Battleships: Queen Elizabeth Barham Valiant	None	None	None
Aircraft Carriers: None	None	None	None
Cruisers, 6-inch: Ajax Neptune Hobart (R.A.N.) Aurora Penelope	Ajax	Penelope	Orion Arethusa
5·25-*inch:* Naiad Galatea	Naiad Dido Euryalus	Cleopatra Dido Euryalus	Cleopatra Dido Euryalus
A.A. Cruisers: None	Carlisle	Carlisle	Coventry
Destroyers: 21	26	19	15
Submarines: (including those based on Gibraltar) 30	28	25	27

FORCE H

(*The name lapsed in April and was not revived until October* 1942)

Battleships:	Malaya	Malaya	Malaya	Malaya
Aircraft Carriers:	Ark Royal	Argus	Eagle Argus	None
Cruisers:	Hermione	Hermione	Hermione	Charybdis
Destroyers:	6	8	8	4

Italian Fleet and German Submarines in the Mediterranean

(*Ships seriously damaged and under repair are not included*)

	Early November 1941	*End of* 1941	*Mid March* 1942 immediately before 2nd Battle of Sirte	*Early September* 1942
Battleships:	Littorio Vittorio Veneto Doria Cesare Duilio	Littorio Doria Cesare Duilio	Littorio Duilio Cesare	Littorio Vittorio Veneto Roma Duilio Cesare Doria
Cruisers, 8-*inch:*	Trieste Trento Gorizia	Trento Gorizia	Trento Gorizia	Gorizia Trieste
6-*inch:*	Di Giussano Cadorna Bande Nere Da Barbiano Duca D'Aosta Montecuccoli Attendolo Duca degli Abruzzi Garibaldi	Cadorna Bande Nere Duca D'Aosta Montecuccoli Attendolo Garibaldi	Eugenio di Savoia Duca D'Aosta Montecuccoli Attendolo	Eugenio di Savoia Duca D'Aosta Montecuccoli Garibaldi Duca degli Abruzzi Cadorna
5·25-*inch:*	None	None	None	Regolo
Fleet Destroyers:	32	25	26	28
Submarines: *Italian**	44	50	33	35
German	14	21	20	16

*These figures are for submarines operating in the Mediterranean; in addition there were a number operating in the Atlantic.

APPENDIX 4

Outline Distribution of British Land Forces in the Middle East and Mediterranean theatre at the end of October 1941

Note: Certain discrepancies at times may be noticed between these outline distributions of forces and the more detailed distributions given in the text or in footnotes. The explanation is that in the field lower formations were often detached from their parent formations for tactical reasons.

8TH ARMY[1]

13th Corps:
- New Zealand Division
- 4th Indian Division
- 1st Army Tank Brigade

30th Corps:
- 7th Armoured Division
- 4th Armoured Brigade Group
- 1st South African Division
- 22nd Guards Brigade Group

2nd South African Division
2nd South African Infantry Brigade Group
29th Indian Infantry Brigade Group
161st Indian Infantry Brigade

Tobruk
70th Division; 32nd Army Tank Brigade

9TH ARMY[2]

10th Armoured Division
1st Australian Corps:
- 6th Australian Division
- 7th Australian Division
- 9th Australian Division

5th Independent Cavalry Brigade
3rd Indian Motor Brigade
One unbrigaded battalion

Transjordan Frontier Force
Free French Forces
Greek Independent Brigade Group

Egypt: 1st Armoured Brigade Group; 5th Indian Division; 38th Indian Infantry Brigade; five unbrigaded battalions
Sudan: Sudan Defence Force; two unbrigaded battalions
Cyprus: 50th Division; one armoured regiment; one unbrigaded battalion
Aden: One battalion
Malta (under control of C.-in-C. Middle East from 11th March to 15th May 1942): Four infantry brigades

---

[1] For a more detailed distribution of the 8th Army on the eve of 'Crusader' see p. 37.

[2] Many of the formations listed were short of weapons, transport, and other equipment in varying degree.

Outline Distribution of British Land Forces in the Middle East and Mediterranean theatre at the end of May 1942

8TH ARMY[1]

13th Corps:
- 50th Division
- 1st South African Division
- 2nd South African Division
- 9th Indian Infantry Brigade Group

30th Corps:
- 1st Armoured Division
- 7th Armoured Division
- 1st Armoured Brigade Group
- 3rd Indian Motor Brigade
- 29th Indian Infantry Brigade Group
- 1st Free French Brigade Group

5th Indian Division
10th Indian Division
5th South African Infantry Brigade
11th Indian Infantry Brigade Group
2nd Free French Brigade Group
Middle East Commando

9TH ARMY[2]

H.Q. 10th Corps
9th Australian Division
New Zealand Division

10TH ARMY[2]

6th Indian Division
8th Indian Division
252nd Indian Armoured Brigade Group

Egypt[2]*:* 10th Armoured Division; 9th Armoured Brigade Group; 161st Indian Motor Brigade; 25th Indian Infantry Brigade Group; five unbrigaded battalions; H.Q. 4th Indian Division

Palestine[2]*:* 5th Indian Infantry Brigade; Transjordan Frontier Force; 1st Greek Brigade Group; 1st Polish Division; Arab Legion

Sudan: 1st Sudan Defence Force Infantry Brigade; 2nd Sudan Defence Force Infantry Brigade; four unbrigaded battalions

Cyprus: 7th Indian Infantry Brigade; two armoured regiments; four unbrigaded battalions

Aden: One Indian Camel Regiment; one battalion

Malta: Four infantry brigades

---

[1] For a more detailed distribution see p. 217.

[2] Many of the formations listed were short of weapons, transport, and other equipment in varying degree.

APPENDIX 5

Royal Air Force Orders of Battle

See Maps 2 *and* 30

ABBREVIATIONS

A.C.—Army Co-operation; Amb.—Ambulance; A.S.R.—Air/Sea Rescue; A.T.—Air Transport; B.T.—Bomber Transport; Com.—Communications; Det.—Detachment; F.—Fighter; F.B.—Fighter-bomber; G.R.—General Reconnaissance; L.B.—Light Bomber; L.R.—Long-range; M.B.—Medium Bomber; N.C.—Naval Co-operation; N.F.—Night fighter; O.T.U.—Operational Training Unit; P.R.—Photographic Reconnaissance; S.E.—Single-engine; Strat.R.—Strategical Reconnaissance; Sur.R.—Survey Reconnaissance; Tac. R.—Tactical Reconnaissance; T.B.—Torpedo-bomber; T.D.—Tank-destroyer; T.E.—Twin-engine.

R.A.F. Middle East Command, 11th November, 1941

Formation or Squadron	*Location*	*Aircraft*	*Role*
H.Q., R.A.F., M.E. (Cairo)			
Units under direct control of H.Q., R.A.F., M.E.			
Nos. 2 P.R.U.	Heliopolis	L.R. Hurricane I/ Beaufighter IPR	P.R.*
267		Lodestar/Audax/ Proctor	A.T.
No. 201 (N.C.) Group (H.Q. at Alexandria)			
No. 2 (Yugoslav)	Aboukir	D.O. 22	G.R.
No. 13 (Hellenic); R.N. Flt.	Dekheila	Anson; Fulmar	G.R.; T.B.
No. 272 (Less det. with W.D.A.F.)	Idku	Beaufighter IC	L.R.-T.E.-F.
Sea Rescue Flt.		Wellington IC	A.S.R.
Adv. G.R. Base at Fuka. (Became Adv. H.Q. No. 201 Group on 7th December, 1941, and No. 235 Wing on 15th January, 1942)			
No. 39 (Less det. with W.D.A.F.)	Maryut (Alexandria)	Beaufort I/Maryland	T.B. and G.R.
No. 203 (Less det. with W.D.A.F.)	Burg El Arab	Blenheim IV	G.R.
No. 230	Kasfareet (Canal)	Sunderland	G.R.

Formation or Squadron	*Location*	*Aircraft*	*Role*
NO. 202 GROUP (H.Q. at CAIRO) (Became A.H.Q., EGYPT, on 1/12/41)			
No. 117 (Less det. with W.D.A.F.)	BILBEIS	Wellesley	B.T.
No. 216 (Less det. with W.D.A.F.)	KHANKA	Bombay	B.T.
No. 223	SHANDUR	Maryland	Temp. O.T.U.
No. 250 Wing (H.Q. at ISMAILIA)			
No. 73 (Less det. with No. 252 Wing)	PORT SAID	Hurricane I	S.E.-F.
No. 1 G.R.U.	ISMAILIA	Wellington I/IC	G.R.
No. 252 Wing (H.Q. at ALEXANDRIA)			
No. 73 (Det. from PORT SAID)	AMIRIYA	Hurricane I	S.E.-F.
No. 213 (Det. from CYPRUS)	MATARIYA (Heliopolis)	Hurricane I	S.E.-F.
NO. 203 GROUP (H.Q. AT KHARTOUM)			
No. 6	WADI HALFA	Gladiator/ Hurricane I/ Blenheim IV/ Lysander	Tac. R.
No. 6 (Det.)	KUFRA		
No. 47	ASMARA	Wellesley	L.B.
NO. 205 GROUP (H.Q. AT SHALLUFA)			
Nos. 37; 38	SHALLUFA	Wellington IC	M.B.*
Nos. 70; 148	KABRIT	Wellington IC; IC/II	M.B.*
No. 108	FAYID	Wellington IC	M.B.*
H.Q., R.A.F. IN PALESTINE AND TRANS-JORDAN (JERUSALEM) (Became A.H.Q., LEVANT, on 11/12/41)			
No. 263 Wing (H.Q. at BEIRUT)			
No. 335 (Hellenic)	AQIR (Palestine)	Hurricane I	S.E.-F.
Free French (F)	RAYAK (Lebanon)	Morane 406	S.E.-F.
Free French Flt.	DAMASCUS (Syria)	Blenheim IV	L.B.
Free French Com. Flt.	BEIRUT	Various	Air Com.
No. 259 Wing (H.Q. at NICOSIA)			
No. 213 (Less det. with No. 202 Group)	NICOSIA (Cyprus)	Hurricane I	S.E.-F.
No. 815 (F.A.A.)	LAKATAMIA (Cyprus)	Albacore/Swordfish	T.B.

Formation or Squadron	Location	Aircraft	Role
A.H.Q., ADEN (Became H.Q., British Forces, ADEN, on 14/4/42)			
No. 8 (Less det. with W.D.A.F.)	ADEN	Blenheim I/IV/ Vincent	L.B.
A.H.Q., IRAQ (HABBANIYA)			
No. 52	HABBANIYA	Audax	Tac. R.
No. 244	SHAIBAH	Vincent	L.B.
No. 261	MOSUL	Hurricane I	S.E.-F.
A.H.Q., EAST AFRICA (NAIROBI) (Became No. 207 Group on 15/12/41)			
No. 3 (S.A.A.F.)	AISCIA (Ethiopia)	Mohawk	S.E.-F.
No. 41 (S.A.A.F.)	GILGIL (Kenya)	Hartbeest	L.B.
No. 34 (S.A.A.F.) Flt.	PORT REITZ (Kenya)	Anson	G.R.
No. 35 (S.A.A.F.) Flt.	NAIROBI (Kenya)	Junkers 86	G.R.
H.Q., R.A.F., MEDITERRANEAN (VALLETTA) (Became known as A.H.Q., MALTA, in December, 1941)			
Nos. 18; 107	LUQA	Blenheim IV	L.B.
40 (Det. from U.K.); 104		Wellington IC	M.B.
69		Maryland	G.R.
Nos. 126; 249	TAKALI	Hurricane IIA/B	S.E.-F.
Nos. 185	HAL FAR	Hurricane I/IIA/B/C	S.E.-F.
828 (F.A.A.) 830 (F.A.A.)		Swordfish/Albacore	T.B.

Formation or Squadron	*Location*	*Aircraft*	*Role*
A.H.Q., W.D. (Adv. H.Q. at Bir Khamsa; Rear H.Q. at Maaten Baggush)			
Units under direct control of A.H.Q., W.D.			
Nos. 1 (R.A.A.F.) Amb. Unit	Fuka	D.H. 86	Air Amb.
60 (S.A.A.F.) Flt; 1437 Flt.		Maryland	Sur.R.; Strat. R
39 (Det. from No. 201 Group)		Beaufort I/Maryland	T.B. and G.R.
203 (Det. from No. 201 Group)		Blenheim IV	G.R.
(Nos. 39 and 203 employed in 'CRUSADER' on G.R. within range of Desert flank)			
Nos. 31 (Det. from Lahore (India)); 117 (Det. from No. 202 Group)	Maaten Baggush	D.C. 2	A.T.
(Nos. 31 and 117 formed one Sqdn.)			
216 (Det. from No. 202 Group)		Bombay	B.T.
Com. Flt.; 826 (F.A.A.)		Various; Swordfish/ Albacore	Air Com.; T.B.
(No. 826 employed in 'CRUSADER' on night reconnaissance and bombing in forward area)			
Nos. 33	Jarabub	L.R. Hurricane I	L.R.-S.E.-F.
113		Blenheim IV F	L.R.-T.E.-F.
No. 272 (Det. from No. 201 Group)	Gerawla	Beaufighter IC	L.R.-T.E.-F.

Formation or Squadron	*Location*	*Aircraft*	*Role*
No. 253 (A.C.) Wing (H.Q. at Ghot Wahas) (Absorbed by A.H.Q., W.D., later in November, 1941)			
Nos. 208; 451 (R.A.A.F.)	Sidi Barrani	Hurricane I	Tac. R.
No. 237 (Rhodesian)	Gerawla	Hurricane I	Tac. R.
No. 258 Wing (H.Q. at Bir Khamsa)†			
Nos. 1 (S.A.A.F.); 94	Maaten Baggush	Hurricane IIA/B; I	S.E.-F.
Nos. 2 (S.A.A.F.) 3 (R.A.A.F.)	Sidi Haneish	Tomahawk	S.E.-F.
238		Hurricane IIA/B	S.E.-F.
No. 274	Fuka	Hurricane IIA/B	S.E.-F.
No. 262 Wing (H.Q. at Sidi Haneish)†			
Nos. 4 (S.A.A.F.); 112; 250	Sidi Haneish	Tomahawk	S.E.-F.
229		Hurricane IIA/B	S.E.-F.
No. 80 (Began operations on 20/11/41)	Fuka	Hurricane I	F.B.
No. 260	Maaten Baggush	Hurricane I	S.E.-F.
No. 269 Wing (H.Q. at Sidi Haneish)†			
No. 30	Sidi Haneish	Hurricane I/IIA/B	S.E.-F.
R.N.(F) (F.A.A.)		Hurricane I	S.E.-F.
No. 3 (S.A.A.F.) Wing (H.Q. at Maaten Baggush)			
No. 11	Maaten Baggush	Blenheim IV	L.B.
No. 12 (S.A.A.F.)	El Daba	Maryland	L.B.
No. 21 (S.A.A.F.)	Qotafiya	Maryland	L.B.
No. 24 (S.A.A.F.) (Employed on reconnaissance until December, 1941)	Fuka	Boston III	L.B.
No. 270 Wing (H.Q. at Fuka)			
Nos. 8 (One Flt. det. from Aden); 45; 55 (No. 55 at disposal of W.D.A.F. for short time only)	Fuka	Blenheim IV	L.B.
Nos. 14; 84	Maaten Baggush	Blenheim IV	L.B.
Lorraine (Free French)	Abu Sueir	Blenheim IV	L.B.

*Available to reinforce W.D.A.F. in support of 'Crusader', but not under its control.

†Shortly before 'Crusader' the fighter wings were reorganised so that No. 262 Wing became entirely composed of Hurricane squadrons (Nos. 1 (S.A.A.F.), 94, 229, 238, 260 and 274) and No. 258 Wing of Tomahawk squadrons (Nos. 2 (S.A.A.F.), 3 (R.A.A.F.), 4 (S.A.A.F.), 112 and 250) together with the Hurricanes of the R.N.(F) Squadron. Nos. 30 and 80 squadrons came directly under A.H.Q., W.D., and H.Q. No. 269 Wing eventually came under the control of No. 201 Group as H.Q. No. 234 Wing. Both Nos. 262 and 258 Fighter Wings were then concentrated in the Bir Khamsa area on the eve of the offensive.

NOTES

1. The above Order of Battle does not include the many administrative and ground units of all kinds supporting the flying squadrons, such as maintenance and repair and salvage units; supply and transport columns; radar and wireless observer units; signal units; and R.A.F. armoured car companies. Because of the absence of large civilian industries the R.A.F. in the Middle East had to be almost entirely self-sufficient for repair and other technical requirements. Poor landline facilities coupled with the vast distances traversing the theatre also involved a very heavy signals commitment, and the R.A.F. had to provide its own substitute for the Observer Corps, too. Some idea of the additional effort involved can be gained from the following figures. Of the total R.A.F. strength in the Middle East in September, 1941, of nearly 57,000 officers and men, nearly 7,000 were absorbed in unloading and erecting aircraft at their arrival ports and flying them to Egypt, the great majority across Africa; 6,500 alone were absorbed in providing signal communications; and the observer and warning systems employed a further 3,700. Besides these, and excluding the flying squadrons themselves, there was a variety of other essential units employing large numbers of men.

2. Bomber aircraft were re-classified early in the period covered by this volume—see page 93.

Western Desert Air Force, 26th May, 1942

Formation or Squadron	*Location*	*Aircraft*	*Role*
A.H.Q., W.D. (ADV. H.Q. AT GAMBUT; REAR H.Q. AT MAATEN BAGGUSH)			
Units under direct control of A.H.Q., W.D.			
No. 1 (R.A.A.F.) Amb. Unit	GERAWLA	DH 86/86B	Air Amb.
No. 2 P.R.U. (Det. from H.Q., R.A.F., M.E.)	GAMBUT	Spitfire VB	P.R.
No. 15 (S.A.A.F.)	AMIRIYA	Blenheim IVF	L.R.-T.E.-F. and Tac. R.
No. 15 (S.A.A.F.) (Det.)	KUFRA	Blenheim IVF	L.R.-T.E.-F. and Tac. R.
No. 40 (S.A.A.F.); 208	EL ADEM	Hurricane I/ Tomahawk	Tac. R.
No. 60 (S.A.A.F.)	SIDI BARRANI	Maryland	Sur. R.
No. 1437 Flt.	MAKTILA	Maryland/Baltimore I	Strat. R.
Com. Flt.	MAATEN BAGGUSH	Various	Air Com.
No. 3 (S.A.A.F.) Wing (H.Q. at BAHEIRA)			
Nos. 12 (S.A.A.F.) 24 (S.A.A.F.)	BAHEIRA	Boston III	L.B.
223		Baltimore I	L.B.
NO. 211 GROUP (H.Q. AT EL ADEM)			
No. 233 Wing (H.Q. at GAMBUT)			
Nos. 4 (S.A.A.F.); 5 (S.A.A.F.)	GAMBUT	Tomahawk	S.E.-F.
2 (S.A.A.F.); 260		Kittyhawk I	S.E.-F.
No. 239 Wing (H.Q. at GAMBUT)			
Nos. 3 (R.A.A.F.); 112; 250 450 (R.A.A.F.)	GAMBUT	Kittyhawk I	S.E.-F.
No. 243 Wing (H.Q. at GAMBUT)			
Nos. 33; 274	GAMBUT	Hurricane IIA/B	S.E.-F.
80		Hurricane IIC	S.E.-F.
145		Spitfire VB	S.E.-F.
(No. 145 began operations on 1st June, 1942)			
No. 73	EL ADEM	Hurricane IIA/B/C	S.E.-N.F.

Formation or Squadron	Location	Aircraft	Role
AVAILABLE TO REINFORCE W.D.A.F., BUT NOT UNDER ITS CONTROL			
NO. 205 GROUP (H.Q. AT ISMAILIA)			
No. 231 Wing (H.Q. at QOTAFIYA)			
Nos. 37; 70; 108	EL DABA	Wellington IC	M.B.
(No. 108 also had Liberator II aircraft which were not available for tactical operations)			
No. 236 Wing (H.Q. at EL DABA)			
Nos. 104 (Less det. in MALTA); 148	EL DABA	Wellington II; IC	M.B.
No. 238 Wing (H.Q. at SHALLUFA)			
No. 38 (Less T.B. aircraft)	MAATEN BAGGUSH	Wellington IC	M.B.
No. 40	SHALLUFA	Wellington IC	M.B.
SQDNS. OF NO. 201 (N.C.) GROUP (H.Q. AT ALEXANDRIA)			
Nos. 252; 272	QASABA	Beaufighter IC	L.R.-T.E.-F.
Nos. 821 (F.A.A.); 826 (F.A.A.)	MAATEN BAGGUSH	Albacore	T.B.
(Nos. 821 and 826 employed on night reconnaissance and bombing in forward area when supporting operations in the Desert)			

NOTE

Prior to the Battle of Gazala it became the policy for all aircraft of the W.D.A.F. fighter force to be equipped for the alternative role of fighter-bomber. Owing to lack of materials only four squadrons (one of Hurricanes and three of Kittyhawks) had been converted to a dual role by 26th May, 1942.

Western Desert Air Force, 1st September, 1942

Formation or Squadron	Location	Aircraft	Role
A.H.Q., W.D. (Adv. H.Q. at Burg El Arab; Rear H.Q. at Wadi Natrun)			
Units under direct control of A.H.Q., W.D.			
No. 1 (R.A.A.F.) Amb. Unit	Wadi Natrun	D.H. 86/86B	Air Amb.
Com. Flt.		Various	Air Com.
No. 285 Wing (H.Q. at Burg El Arab)			
Nos. 2 P.R.U. (Det. from H.Q., R.A.F., M.E.)	Burg El Arab	Spitfire VB	P.R.
208		Hurricane IIA/ Tomahawk	Tac. R.
1437 Flt.		Maryland/Baltimore	Strat. R.
No. 60 (S.A.A.F.) (One Flt. only)	Wadi Natrun	Maryland	Sur. R.
No. 3 (S.A.A.F.) Wing (H.Q. at Amiriya)			
Nos. 12 (S.A.A.F.); 24 (S.A.A.F.)	Amiriya	Boston III	L.B.
55; 223		Baltimore II; III	L.B.
Attached			
81st (U.S.A.A.F.) (Operating with the R.A.F. L.Bs.)	Deversoir	Mitchell II	M.B.
No. 211 Group (H.Q. at Amiriya)			
Attached			
66th (U.S.A.A.F.)	Amiriya	Kittyhawk II	S.E.-F.
No. 7 (S.A.A.F.) Wing (H.Q. at Amiriya)			
Nos. 6; 7 (S.A.A.F.)	Amiriya	Hurricane IID; I/IIB	T.D.; F.B.
127; 274		Hurricane IIB	S.E.-F.
(Hurricane Is of No. 7 (S.A.A.F.) equipped to carry 24 x 9 lb. Jefferis bombs)			
No. 233 Wing (H.Q. at Amiriya)			
Nos. 2 (S.A.A.F.); 4 (S.A.A.F.)	Amiriya	Kittyhawk I; I/Tomahawk	S.E.-F.
5 (S.A.A.F.)		Tomahawk	S.E.-F.
260		Kittyhawk I/II	S.E.-F.
No. 239 Wing (H.Q. at Amiriya)			
Nos. 3 (R.A.A.F.); 112; 250; 450 (R.A.A.F.)	Amiriya	Kittyhawk I	S.E.-F.
No. 243 Wing (H.Q. at Amiriya)			
Nos. 33; 213	Amiriya	Hurricane IIC	S.E.-F.
145; 601		Spitfire VB	S.E.-F.
73		Hurricane IIC	S.E.-N.F.
No. 244 Wing (H.Q. at Amiriya)			
Nos. 1 (S.A.A.F.); 238	Amiriya	Hurricane IIB	S.E.-F.
80		Hurricane IIC	S.E.-F.
92		Spitfire VB/C	S.E.-F.

Formation or Squadron	*Location*	*Aircraft*	*Role*
AVAILABLE TO REINFORCE W.D.A.F., BUT NOT UNDER ITS CONTROL			
SQDNS. OF NO. 205 GROUP (H.Q. AT ISMAILIA)			
No. 231 Wing (H.Q. at ABU SUEIR)			
Nos. 37; 70	ABU SUEIR	Wellington IC	M.B.
No. 236 Wing (H.Q. at JEBEL HAMZI)			
Nos. 108; 148	JEBEL HAMZI	Wellington IC	M.B.
No. 238 Wing (H.Q. at KABRIT)			
Nos. 40; 104	KABRIT	Wellington IC; II	M.B.
SQDNS. OF NO. 201 (N.C.) GROUP (H.Q. AT ALEXANDRIA)			
Nos. 252; 272	IDKU	Beaufighter IC/VIF	L.R.-T.E.-F.
Nos. 821 (F.A.A.) Nos. 826 (F.A.A.)	DEKHEILA	Albacore	T.B.
(Nos. 821 and 826 employed on night reconnaissance and bombing in forward area when supporting operations in the Desert)			

NOTE

No. 73 Squadron had been employed almost exclusively in a night-fighter role since early 1942. Prior to the Battle of Alam el Halfa all the remaining Hurricane squadrons were trained for the alternative role of night-fighter to support No. 73 Squadron in the event of enemy airborne attack on airfields.

APPENDIX 6

The Persia and Iraq Command (P.A.I.C.)[1]

See Map 40

When British and Russian troops withdrew from Teheran in October 1941 it was arranged that the Russians should retain a zone in north Persia. The southern boundary of this zone ran from the west of Lake Urmia through Zenjan and Kazvin and thence eastwards. This arrangement was still in force when General Wilson took up the new Persia and Iraq Command. Two broad tasks were given to him. The first was to secure at all costs from land and air attack the oilfields and oil installations in Persia and Iraq. The second was to send to Russia from the Persian Gulf ports as many supplies and stores as possible without prejudicing the first task.

General Wilson opened his Headquarters in Baghdad on 15th September, leaving a liaison section to represent him at G.H.Q. Middle East. He took over the existing organization to control the base and lines of communication in Persia and Iraq, and placed its Commander at Basra, the focal point. General Wilson had in Persia and Iraq the 31st Indian Armoured Division (one in name only), the incomplete 6th and 8th Indian Divisions, and half a dozen unallotted Indian infantry battalions. There was also a Corps Headquarters—21st Indian Corps (Lieut.-General A. G. O. M. Mayne)—but the artillery, engineer, signal and administrative units necessary to form a balanced field army were short or absent. It was however the want of vehicles rather than of troops which handicapped General Wilson's planning.

At this time the Royal Air Force in Iraq, commanded by Air Vice-Marshal H. V. Champion de Crespigny, had only one squadron—a tactical reconnaissance unit—suitable for army/air support. This squadron was stationed near Mosul in Iraq, with one flight at Kermanshah in Persia. By the turn of the year, however, there were in Iraq two squadrons of light bombers and in Persia two of short-range fighters, one of tactical reconnaissance aircraft and a strategical reconnaissance flight. The units in Persia were under the control of Air Headquarters 'Deeforce', commanded by Air Commodore R. M. Foster. This was a nucleus headquarters formed to control any squadrons which might be required to assist the Russians in the Caucasus or, alternatively, to support operations in north Persia.

It was clearly desirable to keep the enemy out of the area between the river Araxes and Hamadan, particularly because here were the best sites in north Persia for airfields. Yet as things stood General Wilson saw little chance of holding it if the enemy attacked in strength. Nevertheless he intended to send forward to the Araxes whatever mobile forces he could

---

[1] See page 376

Map 40
PERSIA & IRAQ
1942
50 0 50 100
MILES
U. S. S. R.
L. Van
R. Araxes
Astara
TURKEY
L. Urmia
Tabriz
CASPIAN SEA
Mianeh
Zenjan
Kazvin
Mosul
TEHERAN
Kirkuk
Oil pipe
Hamadan
Qum
Khanikin
Kermanshah
PERSIA
BAGHDAD
L. Habbaniya
Mussayib
R. Tigris
Andimishk
Maidan i Naftun
IRAQ
R. Euphrates
Oil pipe
Oil pipe
Basra
Shaibah
Abadan
Bandar Shahpur
PERSIAN
GULF
M.J.G.

maintain, and delay the enemy as long as possible. The situation improved as time passed and the Russians continued to resist the Germans. Reinforcements for P.A.I.C. were arriving, but as the danger of attack receded it became unnecessary to send a force northwards. This was doubly fortunate. First, because the Russians were not at all helpful, and friction was avoided. Secondly, because General Wilson was able to limit his force in Persia to one division and one motor brigade at Qum and Andimishk (in the British zone) and to station the rest in training areas in Iraq, where the winter climate was much better than in north Persia. By November the German lack of decisive success before the start of the Russian winter, the British victory in the Western Desert, and the launching of 'Torch' further improved the prospect. There was now little fear of the war spreading to Persia before April 1943, and General Wilson's force had grown to a respectable size by reinforcements from England, India and the Middle East. There had been added 3rd Corps Headquarters, 5th and 56th Divisions, 5th Indian Division, 7th Armoured Brigade, and 10th Indian Motor Brigade. A considerable Polish force, too, was assembling in Iraq although it was not yet ready for operations. P.A.I.C. was not destined, however, to become an active Command. By February 1943 the war had swung away from it and a big reduction in its troops was beginning.

Although no important operations had taken place in Iraq or Persia since Rashid Ali's revolt in 1941, the troops in those countries accomplished a huge administrative task. This had been set by the decisions, made in 1941, to create in Iraq a base for ten divisions and thirty squadrons of aircraft; and to develop to the greatest possible extent a supply route to Russia through Persia. These decisions were to some extent conflicting, and were very difficult to carry out, because everything had to be done from scratch at a time when British resources, especially in technicians, were being used to the limit.

There were in Iraq and Persia no industries of importance except oil. Communications were therefore undeveloped, and the men and things which in industrialized countries can be turned to military uses—skilled workers, power-plant, workshops, machine-tools and so on—were wanting or scarce. The Persian Gulf ports were primitive, except for the oil port at Abadan, and Maqil—the modern port of Basra. The river transport was crude and unorganized. The railways in Iraq were efficient, but were of two different gauges and had much less capacity than was needed. The Trans-Persian railway had been opened in 1938, but an extension from Teheran to Tabriz was still under construction in 1942; it reached Mianeh by the end of the year. The Trans-Persian line was an astonishing feat of engineering and crossed country of every kind from desert to mountain. But these physical conditions made it a very difficult railway to operate: to give only two examples, water for the locomotives seldom existed in the right places, and rolling-stock needed specially strong couplings to stand the strain of very steep gradients. The railway could handle no more than about 200 tons a day. The roads of Iraq were mostly fair-weather tracks; in Persia the main north-south roads had been made for motors but had not been designed for heavy convoys and were in bad repair. Motor transport in both countries worked on the familiar hit-or-miss Eastern system and was limited in quantity. Distances were great: from Basra to Mosul is some 550 crow-flight miles and to the Caspian sea is nearly as far. Finally there was the climate, for in summer both countries are amongst the hottest in the world and in most of Persia the winter is extremely severe.

General responsibility for the work was shared by the Middle East and India, and local responsibility fell upon the forces in Iraq and Persia. A great deal of help was given by the United Kingdom Commercial Corporation and the Anglo-Iranian Oil Company.[1] There was no time to allow of a carefully phased programme of developments, and in a sense everything had to be done at once. Ships had to be unloaded in ports which were being improved, and supplies carried forward over roads and railways which were being reshaped to suit installations which were themselves being laid out. Work in Iraq at first had had priority, and had made considerable progress by the time that P.A.I.C. was formed. Base depots had been established in the Basra-Shaibah area and an advanced base at Mussayib was nearly ready. Railway and roads had been much improved and a fleet for inland water transport on the Tigris—to improve the river's navigability was an undertaking in itself—had been collected. In Persia not so much, but yet much, had been done; the army had concentrated its efforts on ports, railway and roads, and the U.K.C.C. on organizing road convoys and local transport and erecting vehicles received from overseas. When operations in north Persia became more likely than operations in north Iraq the administrative problem became more difficult because it was quite impossible to develop the Persian L. of C., and at the same time to send along it the supplies to stock operational depots in advance of need as well as a quota of 'aid to Russia'. General Wilson therefore took the risky decision that he would rely, for a start, upon the establishments in Iraq to sustain operations in north Persia. Work went ceaselessly on and General Wilson's luck held. The threat from the Caucasus receded, and in November 1942 he was able to take over from the U.K.C.C. the organization of road transport in Persia. Moreover American help was now at hand. Almost from the first it had been realized that British resources could never be sufficient to carry out the planned scale of development, and in August 1942 it was decided that the United States Army should take over the working of the ports and railway in Persia. The first elements of the U.S. Persian Gulf Service Command (Major-General Donald H. Connolly) arrived in October 1942 and the main units began to arrive in December. Welcome as was this relief, the British and Indian forces in Iraq and Persia could justly feel that they had already done much of the heavy work of preparation and had done it well.

---

[1] The U.K.C.C. was an organization set up by the British Government to acquire, broadly speaking, commodities from sources which were also open to the enemy. Its activities were diverse.

APPENDIX 7

A Note on Artillery Weapons

(For particulars of the performance of anti-tank guns see Appendix 8. See also photos 21 *to* 31.*)*

On the outbreak of war the field and medium artillery equipment of the British Army and the various Commonwealth contingents was in a very backward state, consisting as it did of weapons which, with some improvements, were legacies from the First World War. The decision to abolish the shrapnel shell had made it possible for the War Office to consider replacing the existing 18-pdr gun and 4·5-inch howitzer by a single weapon which, by using different charges, could combine the steep angle of descent of a howitzer with the relatively long range of a gun. This led to the design of the 25-pdr 'gun-how', which was to make such a name for itself in the desert. But in the stress and urgency of the general re-armament of the Services it was impossible to produce everything at once, and many stop-gap measures had to be adopted. One of these was to alter some of the existing 18-pdrs to serve as '18/25-pdrs', with many but not all of the merits of the new 25-pdrs. Some of these converted guns were in the Middle East in June 1940 when the war with Italy began, but there were also many unconverted 18-pdrs and old 4·5-inch howitzers which had a very short range; there were also some 3·7-inch howitzers—light weapons designed for carriage by pack-animals or porters. The reason was that from September 1939 to May 1940 the French front had had priority, and the Middle East had to make do with what was left over. The loss in June of all the British equipment in France made things even worse for the Middle East, because very little could be spared from the United Kingdom until the forces there were at least partly re-equipped. There was an added difficulty over ammunition, because production for the 18-pdrs and 4·5-inch howitzers had ceased on the introduction of the 25-pdr, so that the position was bound to be bad until the rearming of the Middle East with 25-pdrs could be completed. As it turned out, they did not even begin to arrive until November 1940, and as late as May 1942 there were still some 18-pdrs in use as anti-tank guns.

On the outbreak of war the medium artillery was in much the same state, for the existing 60-pdr gun and 6-inch howitzer were badly out-ranged by their continental counterparts. To remedy this serious defect the 60-pdr was re-lined and its bore reduced from 5 inches to 4·5, pending the production of a new 4·5-inch gun. An attempt was made to convert the 6-inch howitzer, but this was unsuccessful, and a new 5·5-inch 'gun-how' was evolved. These two new equipments, the 4·5-inch gun and the 5·5-inch gun-how, had a much longer range than the weapons they replaced, but here again their appearance in the Middle East was long delayed. To supplement the 6-inch howitzers a number of American 155-mm howitzers were sent out towards the end of 1941, though they too lacked range. By May 1942 the first of the 5·5-inch gun-hows were on the way, and the 4·5-inch guns were arriving in good numbers, though their use was limited for some time by unreliable ammunition.

The question of mobility had naturally become of great importance with the replacement of the horse by a mechanical vehicle for drawing the gun and its limber. In 1935 the vehicles known as 'Dragons', which had been developed for this purpose on tank and tractor chassis, were discarded in favour of four-wheel-drive vehicles. The mobility of the existing British medium pieces had been improved by fitting them with pneumatic, in place of steel, tyres.

Another system, which was used for the anti-tank guns, was to mount the whole gun on a carrying vehicle from which it was run off before coming into action. This was known as the 'portée'. A further development was for the gun to fire from the platform of its carrying vehicle. This method had been adopted in the Desert at the beginning of the war, when the 37-mm Bofors guns had practised firing from their 15-cwt trucks. When the 2-pdr anti-tank gun was introduced the War Office did not consider that it need be able to fire from the vehicle, and stipulated only that the gun should be capable of moving portée or towed. In spite of this view the Middle East made its own arrangements for strengthening a 30-cwt truck chassis to take the shock of discharge of a gun firing from the portée position. This method met with considerable success, and these guns sometimes fired off their own wheels and sometimes off the portées, but by 1942 the habit of firing from the portée was discouraged because the gun and its vehicle were so conspicuous that a great many had been knocked out.

The British had themselves very nearly solved this problem as far back as 1927, when, in connexion with the Experimental Armoured Force, they had carried out trials with an 18-pdr mounted on a tracked chassis, not as an anti-tank gun but as a close support weapon. The 18-pdr was not a suitable gun for this purpose and there may have been some confusion between the role of a tank which carried a gun and that of a gun which looked like a tank; at all events the idea of the self-propelled (S.P.) gun was dropped for the time being. There was an attempt to revive it in August 1940 for the anti-tank role, and a year later some 2-pdrs were mounted on a lightly-armoured carrier chassis for the purpose, but this was not a success and in any case the 2-pdr was already recognized as being too weak. At about the same time the experiment was tried of mounting a 25-pdr in an armoured box on the chassis of a Valentine tank, to serve as a support weapon for armoured formations. The first of these 'Bishops', as they were called, reached the Middle East during July 1942, but they had a poor range and were too slow. They were supplemented, and eventually replaced, by the 'Priest', which was an American 105-mm howitzer mounted on the chassis of a Grant tank. The Priest began to reach the Middle East during September 1942.

Anti-aircraft

In 1937 an urgent need arose for the Army to have a mobile anti-aircraft gun of comparable performance to the naval 2-pdr, and it was decided to adopt the 40-mm Bofors, which was already in production in Sweden. For heavier guns there were still some 3-inch veterans of the First World War. The new 3·7-inch was being given either a static or a mobile mounting, the former being for use in the Air Defence of Great Britain and at certain ports overseas. With these two guns—the 3·7 and the Bofors—the heavy and light anti-aircraft batteries in the Middle East were mainly equipped. (*See also p.* 28n).

In 1940 an attempt was made to find a dual-purpose anti-aircraft and anti-tank weapon for issue to arms other than the artillery, but no suitable weapon was readily available. Even if the Bofors could have been obtained in the necessary numbers, it was regarded as unsuitable for use by the infantry.

To reinforce the light anti-aircraft defence of such places as airfields, ports, railheads and field maintenance centres it was decided to issue 20-mm guns. Most of these were Oerlikons, but a large number of captured weapons, especially Italian, were also used.

German

By 1939 the Germans had standardized five artillery equipments, which were all still in use in 1942. These were the 10·5-cm gun, the 10·5-cm light field howitzer, the 15-cm gun, the 15-cm medium field howitzer, and the 21-cm howitzer. Two infantry guns—the 7·5-cm light and the 15-cm medium—had likewise been introduced by 1939 and were still in use in 1942. German guns were normally towed by half-tracked vehicles. This means a vehicle with a pair of wheels in front and a pair of tracks behind. The Germans set great store by them and had developed a whole series, of which the biggest could tow 18 tons. They were much used also for troop-carrying. By Spring 1942 the Germans in Libya had few of their own guns mounted on tracks, but the need had been foreseen by OKH in the previous August and experiments had been made with improvised mountings. In the following months many guns of Czech and Russian make were brought over, mounted on Pzkw I or half-tracked chassis and used principally as anti-tank guns.

The 8·8-cm Flak 36 deserves particular mention. Its conspicuous successes against tanks during 'Battleaxe' in June 1941 had been gained by siting it in defended localities and concealing it as well as possible—not an easy matter for such a big weapon. A new trailer (No. 201) was then introduced, towed by an 8-ton half-tracked vehicle, which enabled the gun to come into action against ground targets extremely quickly. Drawn in this way the gun was able to take part in mobile actions, and did so with great effect.

Italian

The Italians entered the war with a large number of artillery equipments, many of which were old and of foreign make, and many unsuitable for desert warfare. The low capacity of the armament industry made it very difficult to replace their heavy losses of 1940 and early 1941, but under German influence they made great efforts and produced several good weapons. They also made much progress with tractors of various kinds and with self-propelled guns mounted on tank chassis. Some of their new equipments came into use in Libya early in 1942; for example, a battery of the new 90/53 anti-aircraft gun (S.P. version) and two batteries of the 75/18 S.P. gun came over with the Littorio Division at the beginning of the year and went into action with the Ariete. Some of the less well equipped Italian divisions were helped by the loan of German weapons, notably the 8·8-cm dual-purpose gun.

The Italian weapons in the following table are typical examples of mobile equipments; there were too many varieties to give a complete list.

Some particulars of the principal Field Branch Artillery weapons used in the Middle East before September 1942

British

(1) Weapon	(2) Weight in action (tons)	(3) Calibre (inches)	(4) Weight of HE projectile (lb.)	(5) Maximum range (yards)	(6) Remarks
18-pdr gun	1·55	3·3	18	9,800	
3·7-in. how	0·75	3·7	20	6,800	
4·5-in. how	1·5	4·5	35	6,600	
18/25-pdr	1·6	3·45	25	11,800	
25-pdr gun/how	1·75	3·45	25	13,400	Also fired an AP shot.
60-pdr gun	5·5	5	60	15,100	
4·5-in. gun	5·7	4·5	55	20,500	
6-in. how	4·5	6	100	11,400	
5·5-in. gun/how	5·7	5·5	100	16,200	
U.S. 155-mm how	4	6·1	95	12,775	Increased in a later Model to 16,500 yds.

German

(1) Weapon	(2) Weight in action (tons)	(3) Calibre (inches)	(4) Weight of HE projectile (lb.)	(5) Maximum range (yards)	(6) Remarks
7·5-cm (I.G. 18) light infantry gun	0·39	2·95	12	3,800	Also fired hollow charge.
15-cm (s.I.G. 33) medium infantry gun	1·5	5·9	83·6	4,700	
10·5-cm (le. F.H. 18) light field howitzer	2	4·14	32·5	11,700	Also fired AP, tracer and hollow charge.
10·5-cm (K. 18) medium gun	5·5	4·14	33·3	20,860	
15-cm (s.F.H. 18) medium field howitzer	5·4	5·9	95·7	14,600	Also fired hollow charge.
15-cm (K. 18) gun	12·5	5·9	94·6	26,800	
21-cm (Mrs. 18) howitzer	16·4	8·2	250	18,250	

ITALIAN

(1) Weapon	(2) Weight in action (tons)	(3) Calibre (inches)	(4) Weight of HE projectile (lb.)	(5) Maximum range (yards)	(6) Remarks
47/32 gun (Mod. 35)	0·26	1·85	5·2	3,800	Normal close support and anti-tank weapon of Italian Army. See also page 444.
75/27 gun (Mod. 11 and 12)	1	2·95	14	9,000	Also fired hollow charge.
75/18 gun/how (Mod. 34 and 35)	SP approx 12	2·95	14	10,280	Replacing 75/27. SP version on M 13/40 chassis.
100/17 how (Mod. 14)	1·4	3·94	29	10,000	Of old Austrian design. Also fired hollow charge.
105/28 gun	?	4·13	35	14,800	
149/13 how	?	5·9	93·6	9,560	

NOTES

1. The second figure in the Italian title is the length of the weapon in calibres.
2. For explanation of hollow charge ammunition see page 438.

Anti-Aircraft Artillery

The British anti-aircraft guns shown below were all provided with S.A.P., A.P. and H.E. types of ammunition. The German and Italian anti-aircraft guns were also provided with suitable natures of ammunition for field and anti-tank roles.

British

Weapon	Weight in action (tons)	Calibre (inches)	Weight of projectile (lb.)	Muzzle velocity (feet per second)	Ceiling (feet)	Practical rate of fire (rds per minute)	Remarks
Bofors (40-mm)	2·0 to 2·5	1·58	2	2,800	23,600	120	
3-in.	8	3	16½	2,000	25,200	20 to 25	
3·7-in. (Marks I to III)	7·5 to 8	3·7	28	2,600	41,000	8 to 10*	*Later increased to 20 by use of automatic loading and fuze-setting gear.

German

Weapon	Weight in action (tons)	Calibre (inches)	Weight of projectile (lb.)	Muzzle velocity (feet per second)	Ceiling (feet)	Practical rate of fire (rds per minute)	Remarks
2-cm Flak 30	0·72	0·79	0·25	2,950	12,460	120	
8·8-cm Flak 36	5·5	3·46	20	2,690	34,770	15 to 20	See also p. 443

Italian

Weapon	Weight in action (tons)	Calibre (inches)	Weight of projectile (lb.)	Muzzle velocity (feet per second)	Ceiling (feet)	Practical rate of fire (rds per minute)	Remarks
20-mm M/35 Breda	0·32	0·79	0·297	2,750	8,000	120	
75/46 (Mod. 34)	3·3	2·95	14·3	2,350	27,200	20	Many other 75s existed of various nationalities.
90/53	5·1	3·54	22·2	2,756	39,300	15 to 20	Towed. Also a SP version on M 13/40 tank.

APPENDIX 8

A Note on Tanks, Armour and Anti-tank Guns

See photos 9 to 20

1. The second volume of this History contains an account (on page 174) of British and German tank production and some particulars (in Appendix 5) of the tanks and anti-tank guns in use in the Middle East up to the early autumn of 1941. The purpose of this Note is to summarize briefly the information there given and to bring it into line with the events of the present volume. The general position at the beginning of 'Crusader' is stated on page 26 ff.

2. *Explanation of terms and abbreviations used:*

A *shell* is a projectile with a cavity filled with high explosive (HE) or smoke, and is usually fitted with a fuze. An *Armour piercing* (AP) shot is a solid projectile. *Armour piercing capped* (APC) is a shot or shell with a steel cap to prevent shattering on impact. A *ballistic cap* (BC) is a long pointed cap which helps the shot to maintain its velocity, and thus improves penetration at longer ranges. *Homogeneous armour* is armour of approximately the same composition and hardness throughout its thickness. The *hardness* of armour is its capacity to resist deformation; it is usually measured by the Brinell scale. *Machinable quality armour* (MQ) is homogeneous armour soft enough to be machined by ordinary commercial methods; its Brinell figure is less than about 400. *Toughness* is the capacity of armour to absorb energy before fracturing. Toughness and hardness are largely opposing properties, the relation of which has to be balanced. *Face-hardened armour* has a hard face, but a tough back.

German terms:

Panzerkampfwagen (Pzkw) or tank
Panzerabwehrkanone (Pak) or anti-tank gun
Kampfwagenkanone (Kwk) or tank gun
Flugabwehrkanone (Flak) or anti-aircraft gun
Panzergranate (Pzgr) or armour-piercing shell or shot
Pzgr 40 was a special light armour-piercing shot with a core of tnugsten carbide.

3. Owing to financial stringency between the wars, and to a policy which for many years assumed that another major war was not to be expected, the British had allowed research and experiment on tanks to dwindle almost to nothing. When events compelled them to rearm they had no clear idea of the sort of war they might have to fight; there were demands for light and cruiser tanks, which seemed necessary for highly mobile warfare, and for 'I' tanks capable of acting against troops in fortified

positions. As war with Germany drew near, and the idea grew that it would be defensive in its opening stages, the emphasis on 'I' tanks increased. As a result of the campaign in France the British Army was practically disarmed; its losses included nearly 700 tanks and 850 anti-tank guns. The cry was now to rearm rapidly for home defence, for which purpose cruiser tanks, whose speed and mobility had been so well exploited by the Germans, were wanted in preference to 'I' tanks. But production cannot be switched about at a moment's notice, and the choice was not between a good tank and a better one, but between a fairly good tank and no tank at all. The result was that some of the armoured divisions had to be rearmed with 'I' tanks. Similarly, it was decided to persist in the manufacture of the 2-pdr tank and anti-tank gun, even though this meant delaying the production of the 6-pdr.[1] It took a long time to make up for these bad starts, and it was in the Middle East that the handicaps were most severely felt.

The Germans, on the other hand, had given the tank much careful study, and by 1939 they had four types in production, all thoroughly tested, and had even been able to try them out in the Spanish Civil War. In this way they had overcome the inevitable teething troubles. They had wisely allowed for larger weapons and heavier armour to be added if necessary, without interfering with the basic design, and they had standardized most of the parts and fittings so that they could spread manufacture over a large number of firms. When an alteration was wanted—as it was after the Germans had tested the British tanks and weapons captured in France—there was little delay in getting it done. They regarded the Matilda with respect; it was noted that she mounted a good gun, and that only the 8·8-cm Flak could penetrate her frontal armour.

4. Late in 1940 and during 1941 the Germans made three important changes in their equipment. They replaced the 3·7-cm tank gun by a short barrelled 5-cm, and began to replace the 3·7-cm anti-tank gun by a very efficient long barrelled 5-cm. They also increased the protection on their Pzkw III and IV medium tanks by adding plates of face-hardened steel at certain places. All Pzkw IIIs which came to North Africa mounted the larger gun but not all had the extra plates. It is not possible to tell what proportion of up-armoured tanks fought during 'Crusader', but subsequent examination of the battlefield suggested that there had been a considerable number.

The extra plates proved to have great power of resistance. The fact that they were face-hardened was not realized by the British until March 1942, when trials of the Grant's 75-mm gun were being carried out against a captured Pzkw III. The discovery led to further tests. The plates were found to break up the 2-pdr uncapped shot at all ranges, and gave protection against the 6-pdr and the Grant's 75-mm at anything over 500 yards. It was some consolation that after one or two hits the securing bolts (or more probably, studs) began to split or shear off.

The Germans, however, had not meant their extra plates to be anything but a stop-gap, and towards the end of 1941 they introduced

[1] See p. 214n.

Pzkw III J and Pzkw IV F1 in which extra plates were dispensed with and the basic frontal armour was increased from 30-mm to 50-mm. A further surprise was in store for the British when they found that this armour also was face-hardened. These were among the tanks which began to arrive at Benghazi and Tripoli at the turn of the year and which fought in some numbers at Gazala.

5. The next step was to increase the gun power of both Pzkw III and IV. In the case of the III this was done by replacing the short 5-cm gun by the long-barrelled 5-cm which had proved so good in the anti-tank role. This model was the 'III Special', and began to arrive in time for the fighting at Gazala in May 1942. Pzkw IV was similarly up-gunned by having its short 7·5-cm replaced by a long 7·5, which made it formidable indeed. This 'IV Special' appears in *D.A.K's* returns (this 'outstandingly good' tank) for the first time in June 1942, but only arrived in ones and twos. The gradual arrival of the Specials is shown by a few figures from the German records. Thus, the *D.A.K.* had:

On 11th June: 110 IIIs of which 27 were Specials, and 14 IVs of which 6 were Specials.
On 27th July: 63 IIIs of which 16 were Specials, and 13 IVs of which 9 were Specials.
On 12th August: 135 IIIs of which 56 were Specials, and 24 IVs of which 16 were Specials.
On 30th August (the eve of Alam el Halfa): 166 IIIs of which 73 were Specials, and 37 IVs of which 27 were Specials.

The III Specials were still further improved by being fitted with 'spaced armour', of which the first example was found on a tank abandoned at Tell el Eisa after the fighting of 10th July 1942. It consisted of an extra 20-mm plate separated from the basic 50-mm armour of the gun mantlet and the front superstructure by an air space of four inches or more, and secured to it by long bolts. Its purpose was to destroy the AP cap and so reduce the power of a projectile to penetrate the plate behind.

6. All these improvements were examined on captured tanks, and the various types of plates were analysed and tested. The results of the tests for hardness, although they show considerable variation, explained the remarkable resistance of the German frontal armour.[1] The British did not use hardened plate of such thickness themselves, nor had they the most suitable ammunition with which to attack it.

7. In addition to introducing new equipments the Germans made many improvisations, especially by turning existing guns (mostly captured) into self-propelled weapons, some for close support and others as anti-tank guns. First came the 4·7-cm gun of Czech manufacture mounted on a Pzkw I chassis, and then a few 7·5 mounted on 3-ton armoured half-track

[1] Tests carried out in the U.K. gave the following approximate Brinell values for the Pzkw III Model H—the quality varied no doubt with the manufacturer: front nose plate basic 500-600 and additional plates 600-800; driver's front plate basic 500-550, additional plates 600; turret front 400-500. The 50-mm frontal plates of the Model J had a Brinell value of approximately 550, but the hardening extended deeper. Similar tests showed that Italian tank armour was of homogeneous machinable quality throughout.

vehicles. Another notable newcomer, prominent at Gazala, was the 7·62-cm Russian gun, of which the self-propelled version was mounted either on a 5-ton half-track vehicle or a tank chassis. This gun had better penetration than the 5-cm Pak and was a valuable addition to the German anti-tank defences; 117 had arrived with the *Panzerarmee* by May 1942.

8. On the British side, by July 1942 the obsolescent Matilda had been almost completely replaced by the Valentine, which, more reliable than the Crusader and faster than the Matilda, had to act both as a cruiser and as an 'I' tank.

The mechanical weaknesses of the Crusader were the subject of a special enquiry under Mr. C. R. Attlee in the spring of 1942. The finding was that this tank had been pressed into production before the pilot model had been adequately tested. The situation had called for haste, and speedy production was essential; it had been obtained at the cost of mechanical reliability and fighting efficiency.

In July 1942 yet another complaint against the Crusader was made by the Middle East, who had been comparing Grant and Crusader casualties. While the latter's hull and turret were found to have been repeatedly holed by 5-cm projectiles, the former had stood up well to these; most penetrations had been made by 7·62 or 8·8-cm projectiles. Firing trials were then held against Crusader II, which was found to give much less protection than had been expected of a tank on a '50-mm armour basis'.[1] This was bad, for it was important that crews should have confidence in the armour of their tank.

9. By May 1942 the American Stuart tank, previously employed as a cruiser, had come to be treated as a light tank suitable for reconnaissance and observation work. (The Americans had never regarded it as anything but a light tank.) The Grant was welcomed as a great advance on the Crusader. It had defects, such as its lack of speed across country, the restricted arc of fire of its 75-mm gun mounted in a sponson at one side, its delicate sighting gear, and the tendency of the gun mantlet to jam. The armour, however, was excellent and the crews had great confidence in the tank. Its 75-mm gun was not primarily an anti-tank weapon, being a standard American field gun with a good HE performance. It thus corresponded more to the short 75 carried by the Pzkw IV. The Grant carried also a 37-mm high-velocity gun in the turret, similar to the Stuart's, so the position was that the 75 could engage targets with HE shell or with a moderately good AP shot at much longer ranges than could the 37 with its good, though small, APCBC shot.

10. This matter of different types of ammunition was of great importance. A few close-support 'I' tanks and Crusaders could fire HE or smoke from their 3-inch howitzers, but the Grant was the only tank to fire both HE and AP, which gave it the means of countering not only tanks but also anti-tank guns. The AP shot fired by the British 2-pdr and 6-pdr, and by the 75-mm on the Grant, would have been more use

[1] The expression 'armour basis' was commonly used to denote the thickness of armour that a shot travelling horizontally would have to penetrate. Plates sloping away from the vertical could, for lightness and economy, be made thinner. Examples of this can be seen in the table on p. 439.

against face-hardened armour had they been capped. But only the 37-mm shot was fitted with both piercing and ballistic caps, which gave it a slightly better performance than the 2-pdr against face-hardened armour. The 25-pdr was provided with a proportion of uncapped AP shot, as was the 40-mm Bofors, which was primarily an anti-aircraft weapon.

The German policy was to provide different natures of ammunition for nearly every gun, so that it could be used in more than one role. For example, the 8·8-cm was supplied with time-fuzed HE for anti-aircraft work, with percussion-fuzed HE for field targets, and with base-fuzed AP shell with piercing and ballistic caps for attacking armour. Similarly the small 2-cm, nominally a flak gun, was expected to take on aircraft, armoured cars, light tanks, machine-gun nests, lorries or troops on the move. The tank and anti-tank guns (3·7-cm, 5-cm and the Russian 7·62-cm) all had HE and capped armour piercing, and a small quantity of 'Pzgr 40'. This was a special high velocity shot, commonly called 'arrowhead', effective against armour at short range; as will be seen from the table on p. 443 its performance fell off badly at longer ranges. By the summer of 1942 the Germans had introduced 'hollow charge' ammunition for their low-velocity weapons. Unlike the usual AP projectile this depended not upon the force of impact but on controlled explosive action, and was intended to provide their infantry guns and field howitzers with some means of attacking armour plate. It also improved the AP performance of the short 7·5-cm Kwk.

The British had naturally been anxious to devise some method of increasing the power of the 2-pdr gun, while awaiting the arrival of the 6-pdr. A new High Velocity shot was introduced in small quantities in the summer of 1942, but being uncapped it suffered from shatter. More promising was the choke-bore 'Littlejohn conversion', but this had to be re-designed when the Germans were found to be using spaced armour and was not in time to be used. The Royal Army Ordnance Corps' Base Workshops and Ammunition Depots in the Middle East were not equipped to fit caps to 2-pdr shot, but they made a brave effort to meet the deficiency in capped 75-mm ammunition by adapting captured German APCBC shell for use in the Grant's 75-mm gun. Encouraged by a highly satisfactory trial they lost no time in converting some 15,000 rounds and rushed them up to the 8th Army about the end of May. Thereafter the story is less clear, but it seems that, for one reason or another, little use was made of this composite ammunition which had so ingeniously been made available.

The Middle East were very worried about the time taken to match the improvements made by the Germans, let alone get ahead of them. They urged that the 6-pdr should be provided with the best possible ammunition, but were told that, although this was in hand, neither piercing nor ballistic capped shot would be available for the 2-pdr and 6-pdr until 1943. The position with the Grant was more encouraging, because tests of the APCBC projectile (M61) in the Middle East showed that it could penetrate the Pzkw III's 62-mm plates at 1,000 yards. This ammunition was not available until after the battle of Alam el Halfa.

Thickness in Millimetres of some of the plates on British, German and Italian Tanks

The number of degrees shows the inclination of the plate to the vertical. Where no inclination is given the plate is vertical.

BRITISH

Type	Hull		Superstructure		Turret		Remarks
	Front nose plate	Sides	Front Glacis plate	Driver's front plate	Front	Sides	
Crusader II	33* at 29°	28	20 at 60°	40	49* at 7°	24 at 45°	*Figures for Mark I were 27 and 39.
Valentine II	60 at 21°	60	30 at 68°	60	65 rounded	60	
Matilda II	78 rounded	40*	47 at 67°	75	75 at 10°	75	*Plus a 25-mm skirting plate.
Stuart	44 at 25°	25	16 at 66°	38 at 12°	38 at 12°	32	
Grant	50 rounded	38	38 at 53°	50 at 30°	57 rounded	57 rounded	

GERMAN

Type	Front nose plate	Sides	Front Glacis plate	Driver's front plate	Turret Front	Turret Sides	Remarks
Pzkw III Model H	30 + 32 at 52°	30	25 at 84°	30 + 32 at 9°	30 at 15°	30 at 25°	See footnote[1]
Model J	50 at 52°	30	25 at 84°	50* at 9°	30* at 15°	30 at 25°	*Sometimes 20-mm spaced armour added.
Model L	50 at 52°	30	25 at 84°	50 + 20 at 9°	57 + 20 at 15°	30 at 25°	Spaced armour is standard.
Pzkw IV Model E	50 at 12°	20 + 20	20 at 73°	30 + 30 at 10°	30 at 11°	20 at 26°	
Model F (1 and 2)	50 at 12°	30	25 at 73°	50 at 10°	50 at 11°	30 at 26°	

[1]It is probable that extra plates were fitted to some tanks of earlier models also.

ITALIAN

Type	Front nose plate	Sides	Front Glacis plate	Driver's front plate	Turret Front	Turret Sides	Remarks
M 13/40	30 rounded	25	25 at 81°	30 at 11°	40 at 16°	25 at 22°	The armour on M 14/41 was practically the same.

Some particulars of British and Enemy tanks 1941/42

BRITISH

Type	Weight tons	Crew	Main armament	Type of ammunition	Secondary armament[1]	Thickest armour (see also previous table)	Engine B.H.P.	Cross-country speed m.p.h.[2]	Remarks
Cruiser A 13	14·75	4	one 2-pdr	AP shot	one ·303-inch m.g.	30-mm	340	12	62 of these were in 7 Armd Bde on 27th November 1941.
Crusader Mark II	19	4	one 2-pdr	,,	one 7·92-mm m.g.	49-mm	340	12	The close-support tank was armed with a 3-inch howitzer firing HE or smoke to a max. of barely 2,000 yards.
Matilda Mark II	26·5	4	one 2-pdr	,,	one 7·92-mm m.g.	78-mm	175	6	ditto
Valentine Mark II	16	3	one 2-pdr	,,	one 7·92-mm m.g.	65-mm	131	8	
Stuart Mark I	12·5	4	one 37-mm	APCBC shot	two ·30-inch m.gs.	44-mm	250	15	American tank also known as the 'Honey'.
Grant Mark I	28·5	6	one 75-mm (in sponson) one 37-mm (in turret)	75-mm AP shot and HE 37-mm APCBC shot	one, two or three ·30-inch m.gs.	57-mm	340	10	The Grant was preceded by the Lee which was almost identical.

GERMAN

Type	Weight tons	Crew	Main armament	Type of ammunition	Secondary armament[1]	Thickest armour (see also previous table)	Engine B.H.P.	Cross-country speed m.p.h.[2]	Remarks
Pzkw III Model H	20	5	one 5-cm (short)	APCBC, Pzgr 40 and HE	two 7·92-mm m.gs.	62-mm	300	11	
Model J	22	5	one 5-cm (long)	,,	,,	50-mm	,,	12	
Pzkw IV Model E	22	5	one 7·5-cm (short)	APCBC, HE and hollow charge	,,	60-mm	,,	10	
Model F2	23·25	5	one 7·5-cm (long)	APCBC, Pzgr 40, HE and smoke	,,	50-mm	,,	10	

ITALIAN

Type	Weight tons	Crew	Main armament	Type of ammunition	Secondary armament[1]	Thickest armour (see also previous table)	Engine B.H.P.	Cross-country speed m.p.h.[2]	Remarks
M 13/40	13·5	4	one 47-mm	AP and HE	three 8-mm m.gs.	40-mm	105	8	M 14/41 was an improved version with a 125 h.p. engine.
M 14/41	14·7								

[1] M.Gs. carried for A.A. purposes are omitted.
[2] Speed across country is greatly affected by the surface. These figures are a guide to comparative speeds in the Desert.

Tank and anti-tank guns

Expected penetration in millimetres of homogeneous armour plate

An angle of impact of 30° to the normal has been taken simply as a basis for comparison. In battle the angle of impact may be anything from 0° to 90°. As a rough guide it may be taken that at short ranges the penetration of a shot striking normally to the surface would be about one and a quarter times that of the figure given for 30°. At 60° it would be rather less than half.

Further work on captured German documents has led to some revision of the figures given in Appendix 5 of Volume II of this History. It is still necessary, however, to point out that while the figures give an idea of the relative expected performances of the various projectiles, they cannot be taken as a definite forecast of how any one particular shot or shell will behave.

BRITISH

Weapon	How moved or mounted	Weight of shot or shell (lb.)	Muzzle velocity (feet per second)	250 yds.	400 yds.	500 yds.	750 yds.	1,000 yds.	1,500 yds.	2,000 yds.
2-pdr	Towed or portée; and tank gun of Crusader, Matilda and Valentine	2 AP shot	2,600	58	—	52	46	40	—	—
6-pdr Mark II	Towed or portée	6·25 AP shot	2,675	—	—	79	72	65	52	—
25-pdr (not primarily an anti-tank gun)	Towed	20 AP shot	1,550	—	—	63	58	54	—	—
37-mm	Turret of Stuart and Grant	1·92 APCBC shot	2,900	58	—	53	48	47	—	—
75-mm M 2	Sponson of Grant	14 AP shot	1,930	—	—	61	—	53	46	38

GERMAN

Weapon	How moved or mounted	Weight of shot or shell (lb.)	Muzzle velocity (feet per second)	250 yds.	400 yds.	500 yds.	750 yds.	1,000 yds.	1,500 yds.	2,000 yds.
2·8-cm s.Pz.B.41 (tapered bore 1·1/0·787-in.)	Towed or lorry-borne	0·28 composite non-rigid shot	4,600	(50)	41	36	30	—	—	—
3·7-cm Pak 35/36 (L/45)	Towed or lorry-borne	1·5 APC shell	2,500	32	29	28	—	—	—	—
		0·78 Pzgr 40	3,378	40	32	28	—	—	—	—
5-cm Kwk (L/42)	In Pzkw III H and early J	4·5 APCBC shell	2,240	56	—	53	46	(40)	—	—
		1·94 Pzgr 40	3,440	83	—	60	42	—	—	—
5-cm Pak 38	Towed	4·5 APCBC shell	2,700	67	—	61	56	50	—	—
5-cm Kwk 39 (L/60)	In Pzkw III J Special and L	1·94 Pzgr 40	3,930	109	—	77	46	—	—	—
7·5-cm Kwk (L/24)	In Pzkw IV E and F 1	14·9 APCBC shell	1,350	—	—	46	42	41	—	—
		9·75 hollow charge	1,476		about 75-mm irrespective of range					
7·5-cm Kwk 40 (L/43)	In Pzkw IV Special F 2	15 APCBC shell	2,428	—	—	89	—	79	70	62
7·62-cm Pak (R)	Towed. SP version on 5-ton half-tracked lorry	14·81 APCBC shell	2,165	—	—	(79)	—	(70)	(61)	(53)
		9·25 Pzgr 40	2,789	—	—	(84)	—	(68)	—	—
8·8-cm Flak 36 (L/56)	Towed on trailer 201	21 APCBC shell	2,600	—	—	112	—	103	92	83

Figures in brackets are estimated.
All the above German weapons were also provided with a HE shell, slightly lighter in weight than the AP projectile.
The figures under the German guns give the length in calibres.

ITALIAN

Weapon	How moved or mounted	Weight of shot or shell (lb.)	Muzzle velocity (feet per second)	250 yds.	400 yds.	500 yds.	750 yds.	1,000 yds.	1,500 yds.	2,000 yds.
20-mm M/35 Breda	Towed	0·308 AP shot	2,750	29	27	24	—	—	—	—
47/32 (Model 37)	Towed. Also gun of M 13/40 and M 14/41 tanks	3·25 AP shell	2,060	—	48	—	38	32	—	—

APPENDIX 9

Some particulars of British and Enemy Aircraft in use in the Middle East and Mediterranean Theatre during the Period of this Volume

The figures in these tables are no more than a general guide to the characteristics and capabilities of each type of aircraft. The performance is affected by the climate, the skill of the pilot, the accuracy of navigation, and by the uncertainties of flying in the presence of the enemy. For these reasons a safety margin has to be imposed, so that the operational range—not to be confused with the radius of action—is always much less than the still air range. Broadly speaking, after allowing for the running of the engines on the ground and for the climb to the height quoted, the still air range is the distance that can be flown in still air until the tanks are empty.

NOTES: (i) The most economical cruising speed is the speed at which the greatest range is achieved.

(ii) The height given in column IV is the optimum height for the maximum speed.

Details of the following types of aircraft also in use during the period of this Volume but not included below will be found in Appendix 6 of Volume II.

British—Anson, Audax, Battle, Blenheim Mk. I, Gladiator, Hartbeest, Ju. 86, Lysander, Morane 406, Martlet Mk. III, Potez 63, Skua, Swordfish, Vincent, Walrus and Wellesley.

Italian—Ca. 311, Cant. Z. 501, C.R. 32 and S.81.

FIGHTER AIRCRAFT

BRITISH

Aircraft	Fuel and Still Air Range at Most Economical Cruising Speed		Most Economical Cruising Speed in Miles Per Hour	Maximum Speed in Miles Per Hour	Armament	Remarks
	Galls.	Miles				
Beaufighter Twin-engine monoplane Crew 2	550	1,515	226 at 15,000 ft.	324 at 11,750 ft.	6 × ·303 4 × 20 mm	
Blenheim Mk. IVF Twin-engine monoplane Crew 2	466	1,615	170 at 15,000 ft.	266 at 11,800 ft.	7 × ·303	
Fulmar Mk. II Single-engine monoplane Crew 2	155	820	170 at 10,000 ft.	253 at 10,000 ft.	8 × ·303	Fleet Air Arm.
Hurricane Mk. I Single-engine monoplane Crew 1	97	600	180 at 15,000 ft.	316 at 17,750 ft.	8 × ·303	
Hurricane Mk. IIA and B Single-engine monoplane Crew 1	97 183(a)	480 970	200 at 15,000 ft.	342 at 22,000 ft.	8 × ·303(A) or 12 × ·303(B)	(a) With two extra tanks. Could carry 2 × 250 lb bombs in lieu of tanks.
Hurricane Mk. IIC Single-engine monoplane Crew 1	97 183(a)	470 960	212 at 20,000 ft.	339 at 22,000 ft.	4 × 20 mm	(a) With two extra tanks. Could carry 2 × 250 lb bombs in lieu of tanks.
Hurricane Mk. IID Single-engine monoplane Crew 1	97	495	176 at 2,000 ft.	316 at 19,000 ft.	2 × 40 mm 2 × ·303	

FIGHTER AIRCRAFT

BRITISH (*continued*)

Aircraft	Fuel and Still Air Range at Most Economical Cruising Speed		Most Economical Cruising Speed in Miles Per Hour	Maximum Speed in Miles Per Hour	Armament	Remarks
	Galls.	Miles				
Kittyhawk Mk. I Single-engine monoplane Crew 1	123 166(a)	780 1,050	210 at 15,000 ft.	345 at 15,000 ft.	4 × ·50	American design and manufacture. (a) With extra tank. Could carry one 500 lb bomb in lieu of tank.
Kittyhawk Mk. II Single-engine monoplane Crew 1	131 174(a)	795 1,075	240 at 20,000 ft.	345 at 14,700 ft.	4 or 6 × ·50	American design and manufacture. (a) With extra tank. Could carry one 500 lb bomb in lieu of tank.
Spitfire Mk. VB Single-engine monoplane Crew 1	85	480	208 at 20,000 ft.	375 at 20,250 ft.	4 × ·303 2 × 20 mm	
Spitfire Mk. VC Single-engine monoplane Crew 1	84 114(a)	469 648	226 at 20,000 ft.	369 at 19,500 ft.	8 × ·303 or 2 × 20 mm+ 4 × ·303 or 4 × 20 mm	(a) With extra tank.
Tomahawk Single-engine monoplane Crew 1	132 175(a)	695 825	185 at 15,000 ft.	340 at 16,000 ft.	2 × ·50 4 × ·303	American design and manufacture. (a) With extra tank.

BOMBER AIRCRAFT

(including bomber transport and bomber reconnaissance)

BRITISH

Aircraft	Still Air Range with Associated Bombload		Most Economical Cruising Speed in Miles Per Hour	Maximum Speed in Miles Per Hour	Armament	Remarks
	Miles	Bombload				
Albacore Single-engine biplane Crew 2 or 3	521	1 Torpedo or 1,500 lb	105 at 6,000 ft.	163 at 4,800 ft.	2 × ·303	Fleet Air Arm. Figures relate to use as torpedo-bomber.
Baltimore Mk. III Twin-engine monoplane Crew 3	950 2,030	2,000 lb Nil	190 at 15,000 ft.	301 at 11,000 ft.	10 × ·300 4 × ·303	American design and manufacture. The Marks I and II were of only slightly lower performance.
Beaufort Mk. I Twin-engine monoplane Crew 4	1,390	1 Torpedo or 1,650 lb	160 at 5,000 ft.	236 at 5,000 ft.	4 × ·303	
Beaufort Mk. II Twin-engine monoplane Crew 4	1,285	1 Torpedo or 1,650 lb	160 at 5,000 ft.	260 at 14,500 ft.	4 × ·303	
Bisley (Blenheim Mk. V) Twin-engine monoplane Crew 3	1,230	1,000 lb	170 at 15,000 ft.	244 at 6,000 ft.	5 × ·303	

BOMBER AIRCRAFT

(including bomber transport and bomber reconnaissance)

BRITISH (*continued*)

Aircraft	Still Air Range with Associated Bombload		Most Economical Cruising Speed in Miles Per Hour	Maximum Speed in Miles Per Hour	Armament	Remarks
	Miles	Bombload				
Blenheim Mk. IV Twin-engine monoplane Crew 3	1,460	1,000 lb	180 at 15,000 ft.	266 at 11,800 ft.	5/6 × ·303	
Bombay Twin-engine monoplane Crew 4	1,500 330	(a) (b)	120 at 10,000 ft.	159 at 10,000 ft.	2 × ·303	Bomber transport aircraft. (a) With 10 troops. (b) With 24 troops. Could carry up to 2,000 lb of bombs.
Boston Mk. III Twin-engine monoplane Crew 4	1,020	2,000 lb	200 at 15,000 ft.	304 at 13,000 ft.	8 × ·303	American design and manufacture.
Catalina Flying Boat Twin-engine monoplane Crew 9	1,395 2,950	2,000 lb Nil	123 at 5,000 ft.	177 at 5,000 ft.	2 × ·303 2 × ·50	American design and manufacture.
Dakota Twin-engine monoplane Crew 3	1,520 1,910 3,220	(a) (b) (c)	160 at 10,000 ft.	220 at 10,000 ft.	None	Transport aircraft. (a) With 31 troops. (b) With 26 troops. (c) With 8 troops.

BOMBER AIRCRAFT

(including bomber transport and bomber reconnaissance)

BRITISH (*continued*)

Aircraft	Still Air Range with Associated Bombload		Most Economical Cruising Speed in Miles Per Hour	Maximum Speed in Miles Per Hour	Armament	Remarks
	Miles	Bombload				
Do. 22 Seaplane Single-engine monoplane Crew 3	1,430	Nil	186 at 13,120 ft.	217 at 13,120 ft.	4 × 7·9 mm	
Halifax Mk. II Four-engine monoplane Crew 6	1,900 500	3,000 lb 13,000 lb	195 at 15,000 ft.	260 at 18,500 ft.	8 × ·303	
Hudson Mk. III Twin-engine monoplane Crew 4	1,420 2,370	1,400 lb Nil	145 at 5,000 ft.	253 at 15,000 ft.	7 × ·303	American design and manufacture.
Hudson Mk. VI Twin-engine monoplane Crew 4	1,140 2,240	1,400 lb Nil	150 at 5,000 ft.	253 at 5,600 ft.	7 × ·303	American design and manufacture.
Liberator Mk. II Four-engine monoplane Crew 8	1,940 2,730	8,000 lb 4,500 lb	180 at 15,000 ft.	262 at 14,000 ft.	5 × ·50 4 × ·303	American design and manufacture.

BOMBER AIRCRAFT

(including bomber transport and bomber reconnaissance)

BRITISH (*continued*)

Aircraft	Still Air Range with Associated Bombload		Most Economical Cruising Speed in Miles Per Hour	Maximum Speed in Miles Per Hour	Armament	Remarks
	Miles	Bombload				
Maryland Twin-engine monoplane Crew 3	1,210 1,080	1,500 lb 2,000 lb	176 at 15,000 ft.	278 at 11,800 ft.	8 × ·303	American design and manufacture.
Sunderland Flying Boat Mk. I Four-engine monoplane Crew 10	1,850 2,425	1,900 lb Nil	142 at 5,000 ft.	188 at 6,500 ft.	7 × ·303	
Wellington Mk. I and IC Twin-engine monoplane Crew 6	2,550 1,200	1,000 lb 4,500 lb	165 at 10,000 ft.	235 at 15,500 ft.	6 × ·303	
Wellington Mk. II Twin-engine monoplane Crew 6	2,450 1,750 1,400	1,250 lb 3,500 lb 4,500 lb	175 at 15,000 ft.	247 at 17,000 ft.	6 × ·303	
Wellington Mk. VIII Twin-engine monoplane Crew 6	1,580 1,900 2,200	2,750 lb 1,500 lb Nil	137 at 1,000 ft.	205 at 15,500 ft.	6 × ·303	Equipped with A.S.V. Could carry two torpedoes.

FIGHTER AIRCRAFT
UNITED STATES

Aircraft	Fuel and Still Air Range at Most Economical Cruising Speed		Most Economical Cruising Speed in Miles Per Hour	Maximum Speed in Miles Per Hour	Armament	Remarks
	Galls.	Miles				
Kittyhawk Mk. II Single-engine monoplane Crew 1	131 174(a)	795 1,075	240 at 20,000 ft.	345 at 14,700 ft.	4 or 6 × ·50	(a) With extra tank. Could carry one 500 lb bomb in lieu of tank.

BOMBER AIRCRAFT
(including bomber transport and bomber reconnaissance)
UNITED STATES

Aircraft	Still Air Range with Associated Bombload		Most Economical Cruising Speed in Miles Per Hour	Maximum Speed in Miles Per Hour	Armament	Remarks
	Miles	Bombload				
Liberator Mk. II Four-engine monoplane Crew 8	1,940 2,730	8,000 lb 4,500 lb	180 at 15,000 ft.	262 at 14,000 ft.	5 × ·50 4 × ·303	
Mitchell Mk. II Twin-engine monoplane Crew 5	1,150	3,000 lb	210 at 15,000 ft.	295 at 15,000 ft.	4 × ·50 1 × ·30	

FIGHTER AIRCRAFT

GERMAN

Aircraft	Fuel and Still Air Range at Most Economical Cruising Speed		Most Economical Cruising Speed in Miles Per Hour	Maximum Speed in Miles Per Hour	Armament	Remarks
	Galls.	Miles				
Ar. 196 Single-engine monoplane Crew 2	132	600	120 at 6,000 ft.	195 at sea level	3 × 7·9mm 2 × 20 mm	Used mainly for reconnaissance. Could carry 220 lb of bombs.
Me. 109E Single-engine monoplane Crew 1	88	655	200 at 16,500 ft.	355 at 18,000 ft.	2 × 7·9 mm 2 × 20 mm	
Me. 109F Single-engine monoplane Crew 1	88	650	200 at 17,000 ft.	395 at 22,000 ft.	2 × 7·9 mm 3 × 20 mm	
Me. 110 Twin-engine monoplane Crew 2	280	930	200 at 18,000 ft.	360 at 20,000 ft.	6 × 7·9 mm 2 × 20 mm	

BOMBER AIRCRAFT

(including bomber transport and bomber reconnaissance)

GERMAN

Aircraft	Still Air Range with Associated Bombload		Most Economical Cruising Speed in Miles Per Hour	Maximum Speed in Miles Per Hour	Armament	Remarks
	Miles	Bombload				
BV. 138 Flying Boat Three-engine monoplane Crew 5 to 6	1,140	1,400 lb	120 at sea level	175 at sea level	2 × 15 or 20 mm 1 × 13 mm	
He. 111 Twin-engine monoplane Crew 5 to 6	1,510	2,200 lb	180 at 17,000 ft.	240 at 14,000 ft.	7 × 7·9 mm 2 × 20 mm	
Hs. 126 Single-engine monoplane Crew 2	530	620 lb	130 at 13,000 ft.	230 at 13,000 ft.	5 × 7·9 mm	Army co-operation aircraft.
Ju. 52 Three-engine monoplane Crew 3 to 4	530-790	Nil	132 at sea level	165 at sea level	5 × 7·9 mm	Transport aircraft. Freight 4,000-5,060 lb.
Ju. 87 Single-engine monoplane Crew 2	360	1,100 lb	160 at 15,000 ft.	245 at 15,000 ft.	3 × 7·9 mm	Dive-bomber (*Stuka*).
Ju. 87D Single-engine monoplane Crew 2	720	2,200 lb	180 at 15,000 ft.	255 at 13,500 ft.	4 × 7·9 mm	First operated in Middle East in Feb. 1942.
Ju. 88 Twin-engine monoplane Crew 4	1,310	2,200 lb	194 at 16,400 ft.	295 at 14,000 ft.	7 × 7·9 mm 1 × 20 mm	

FIGHTER AIRCRAFT

ITALIAN

Aircraft	Fuel and Still Air Range at Most Economical Cruising Speed		Most Economical Cruising Speed in Miles Per Hour	Maximum Speed in Miles Per Hour	Armament	Remarks
	Galls.	Miles				
C.R. 42 Single-engine biplane Crew 1	77	535	150 at 13,100 ft.	270 at 13,100 ft.	2 × 12·7 mm	Employed as a fighter-bomber in 1942.
G.50 Single-engine monoplane Crew 1	69	530	170 at 14,500 ft.	300 at 14,500 ft.	2 × 12·7 mm	
M.C. 200 Single-engine monoplane Crew 1	70	570	170 at 15,000 ft.	310 at 15,000 ft.	2 × 12·7 mm	
M.C. 202 Single-engine monoplane Crew 1	96	445	190 at 18,000 ft.	345 at 18,000 ft.	2 × 12·7 mm	
Re. 2000 Single-engine monoplane Crew 1	146	1,125	175 at 15,000 ft.	320 at 15,000 ft.	2 × 12·7 mm	
Re. 2001 Single-engine monoplane Crew 1	146	900	190 at 18,000 ft.	345 at 18,000 ft.	2 × 12·7 mm 2 × 7·7 mm	

BOMBER AIRCRAFT

(including bomber transport and bomber reconnaissance)

ITALIAN

Aircraft	Still Air Range with Associated Bombload		Most Economical Cruising Speed in Miles Per Hour	Maximum Speed in Miles Per Hour	Armament	Remarks
	Miles	Bombload				
B.R. 20 Twin-engine monoplane Crew 4	1,350	2,200 lb	175 at 13,000 ft.	255 at 13,500 ft.	1 × 12·7 mm 2 × 7·7 mm	
Cant. Z. 506 Seaplane Three-engine monoplane Crew 4 to 5	1,130	1,750 lb	140 at 13,000 ft.	230 at 13,000 ft.	1 × 12·7 mm 3 × 7·7 mm	
Cant. Z. 1007b Three-engine monoplane Crew 4 to 5	1,650	1,100 lb	160 at 15,000 ft.	280 at 15,000 ft.	2 × 12·7 mm 2 × 7·7 mm	
Ju. 87 Single-engine monoplane Crew 2	360	1,100 lb	160 at 15,000 ft.	245 at 15,000 ft.	3 × 7·9 mm	Dive-bomber (*Stuka*)
S. 79 Three-engine monoplane Crew 4 to 5	1,190	2,750 lb	155 at 13,000 ft.	255 at 13,000 ft.	3 × 12·7 mm 2 × 7·7 mm	Used, when modified, as a torpedo-bomber.
S. 82 Three-engine monoplane Crew 4 to 5	2,200	3,200 lb	172 at 10,000 ft.	205 at 7,000 ft.	3 × 7·7 mm 1 × 12·7 mm	
S. 84 Three-engine monoplane Crew 4 to 5	1,360 1,230	1,760 lb 4,400 lb	170 at 15,000 ft.	280 at 15,000 ft.	4 × 12·7 mm	

APPENDIX 10

Overleaf

APPENDIX 10

Details of Arrivals of Aircraft in Middle East by Various Routes November 1941 – September 1942

	1941		1942									Totals	
	Nov.	Dec.	Jan.	Feb.	March	April	May	June	July	Aug.	Sept.		
1. *From U.K.*													
A. *Takoradi route*													
Beaufighter						5	17	31	28	49	51	181	
Blenheim	16	60	52	7			23	42	136	101	51	488	
Boston				4	10	2		5				21	
Hurricane	26	93	186	87	71	111	13	122	78	83	163	1,033	
Lysander			3									3	
Maryland				1								1	
Moth		1								1		2	
Spitfire						15		6	4	3	50	78	
Tomahawk			4				3					7	Total: 1,814
B. *By Air via Malta*													
Baltimore								1				1	
Beaufighter	1	32	3	21	25	13	3		4		1	103	
Beaufort	4	1	2	6	12	5	10	4	12	22	11	89	
Bombay	1											1	
Fortress	1											1	
Halifax									24	2		26	
Hudson			3		10	13	42	4	42	24	16	154	
Liberator									2	15	1	18	
Lodestar									1			1	
Maryland	2	3		1			1				1	8	
Spitfire (P.R.U.)					4		1		2	3		10	
Sunderland					1							1	
Wellington	17	19	18	32	90	61	57		24	35	32	385	Total: 798
C. *By Sea and Air through the Mediterranean*													
Hurricane	34											34	
Spitfire					31	46	76	59	59	66		337	Total: 371*

D. *By Sea via the Cape*													
Anson					12	4	22		4	10	12	64	
Coudron Goelland											1	1	
Coudron Simoun			1			2					1	4	
Dewoitine							2			1		3	
Potez						2						2	
Spitfire							18	8	16			42	Total: 116
2. *From U.S.A.*													
A. *By Sea via the Cape*													
Baltimore	4	9	15	30	46	50	42	25	8		9	238	
Boston	23	32	7									62	
Fairchild										6		6	
Harvard	2	21	18	9								50	
Kittyhawk	62	135	116	42	108	11	16	16	23	79	97	705	Total: 1,061
B. *Takoradi route*													
Kittyhawk							40	35			50	125	Total: 125
C. *By Sea and Air via the Cape*													
Baltimore								11	16	29	14	70	Total: 70
D. *By Air*													
Dakota										12		12	
Fortress								9				9	
Hudson										59	24	83	
Liberator			4				25					29	
Lodestar										21		21	
Marauder										19	30	49	
Mitchell										57		57	Total: 260
												Grand Total: 4,615	

*Of these, 48 reached Egypt by the end of September. The rest stayed in Malta—the majority permanently.

APPENDIX 11

Operational Code Names

BRITISH

'Battleaxe'	Operation in the Western Desert, June 1941
'Crusader'	British offensive, November 1941. The Winter Battle
'Harpoon'	Convoy to Malta from the west, June 1942
'Vigorous'	Convoy to Malta from the east, June 1942
'Pedestal'	Convoy to Malta from the west, August 1942
'Acrobat'	Advance from Cyrenaica into Tripolitania
'Gymnast'	Plan for landings in French North Africa (later became 'Torch')

ENEMY

'*Herkules*'	Plan for the capture of Malta
'*Venezia*'	Attack on the Gazala position, May 1942

INDEX

Ships of all nationalities are in their alphabetical places *in italics*. Groups, Wings, Squadrons and other units of the R.A.F. are under Royal Air Force. Squadrons of the F.A.A. are under Fleet Air Arm. Squadrons of the R.A.A.F. and S.A.A.F. are under Royal Australian Air Force and South African Air Force. Corps, Divisions, Brigades and Battalions of the British forces are under those headings. Cavalry and armoured units are listed under Regiments. Other units and branches of the Army are under their titles: e.g. Royal Artillery. Formations of the German and Italian Armies are under German Army or Italian Army.

Aagtekirk, m.v.: 248n, 309
Abdiel, H.M.S.: 2, 25, 173
Abruzzi: 382n, 388
'Ackcol': 342
'Acrobat': importance of, 119, 142; and withdrawals from Middle East, 123, 125-6, 133; and retreat to Gazala, 153; mentioned, 204
Acroma: defence of, 217, 238, 242-3, 247; loss of, 264
Admiralty: and human torpedoes, 115; and reinforcements, 117, 124; and convoys to Malta, 182, 303; on 10th Submarine Flotilla, 185; and long-range bombers, 190
Adriatico: 106
Agedabia: airfield raided, 89; actions at, 91-2, 140-1; air attacks on, 150
Agnew, Captain W. G.: 103-4
Aimone-Cat, General Mario: 21
Aircraft: reclassification of bombers, 93; particulars of, 445-56; arrivals of in Middle East, 458-9
Airedale, H.M.S.: 312
Airfields: in an advance, 13; in Cyrenaica affecting Malta, 156, 161, 200, 280; in a retreat, 282
Air Ministry: 94, 205-6
Air Officer Commanding-in-Chief, Middle East: *see* Tedder, *and for joint action*, Commanders-in-Chief
Air Support: and lessons from Operation 'Battleaxe', 13-4; control of, 14, 208; in Operation 'Crusader', 14-5, 19, 35, 51, 76, 94, 98-9; problems of bomb-line, 35, 83, 208, 234-5, 293, 296, 336; indentification in, 35, 55, 208; first use of fighter-bombers for, 43; comparison of British with enemy, 71; in retreat to Gazala, 138-9, 146-7; further development of, 208; first use of tank-destroying Hurricanes in, 235; in Battle of Gazala, 245, 255-6, 258; in defence of Tobruk, 259; in withdrawal to Matruh, 280-2; and round the clock bombing, 288, 337; in withdrawal to El Alamein, 295-6; in fighting at El Alamein, 335-7; in Battle of Alam el Halfa, 385, 391
Ajax, H.M.S.: 43, 96, 105
Alagi: 320
Alam el Halfa: Battle of, 383-91
Albastro: 329
Alberto Fassio: 382n
Alexander, General the Hon. Sir Harold: *see also* Commanders-in-Chief; and 'Gymnast', 121; on training, 153; replaces Auchinleck, 205, 367-9; Prime Minister's directive to, 369; and morale of 8th Army, 369-70; and Persia and Iraq Command, 375-6; his burden eased, 376
Alexandria: air attacks on, 212, 337, 381
Almeria Lykes, s.s. (American): 320
Aly Maher Pasha: 130
Ambra: 192
Anderson, Brigadier A.: and operation 'Crusader', 75; at Tobruk, 261-2, 267-9, 272
Ankara: 87-8, 113
Antelat: capture of, 142-3
Anti-Submarine Group, 25th (South African): 90
Aphis, H.M.S.: 76, 96
Arethusa, H.M.S.: 308, 313
Argus, H.M.S.: mentioned, 117, 178; and fighter reinforcements for Malta, 163, 182; and 'Harpoon' convoy, 301-3
Ark Royal, H.M.S.: and fighter reinforcements for Malta, 108, 162; mentioned, 117, 301n, 318
Armies:
8th: formation of, 1-2; command of, 1, 61, 285-7, 367-9; and operation 'Crusader', 7, 10, 15, 17, 34-8, 42-4, 46, 54, 71; and Long Range Desert Group, 9; supplies and reinforcements for, 10-11, 73, 91, 135-6, 142, 205, 216, 243-4, 371-2; strength and state of, 29-31, 34, 143, 198, 216-20, 226, 252, 286, 296, 333, 359, 366, 369-72, 388, 412-3; mentioned, 56, 73, 77, 85, 98, 148, 291, 293-4, 336, 373, 393; air support for, 86, 256, 294, 358, 380, 390; co-operates with Desert Air Force, 98, 370; in retreat to Gazala, 151, 197, 209; Panzerarmee's views on, 154; and Malta convoy, 164; and a resumed offensive, 201; reorganisation of, 213, 286-7; in Battle of Gazala, 216-9, 238, 252, 392; and defence of Tobruk, 245-9, 252-3, 259, 271-3, 275; its withdrawal to Matruh, 279-81; its withdrawal to El Alamein, 287, 292-6; in fighting at El Alamein, 332-3, 335, 361; lacks confidence in armour, 359; morale of, 369-70; in Battle of Alam el Halfa, 383, 388, 391
9th: 1, 376, 412-3
10th: 129, 413

Armistice, French: 120
Armstrong, Brigadier B. F.: 43
Army in Middle East: *see also* 8th, 9th *and* 10th Armies; strength and state of, 3, 6; reorganization of, 3-4; training of, 5, 26; losses of, 9; and airfields, 13, 373; wireless difficulties of, 36-7; distribution of, 412-3
Artillery Weapons: note on, 427-33
Ascari: 306
Ashanti, H.M.S.: 319-20
Athens: air attacks on airfields at, 211
Attendolo: 323
Auchinleck, General Sir Claude: *see also* Commanders-in-Chief; organizes his forces, 1-4, 213, 286-7; and command in Western Desert, 1, 205, 286; and northern front, 1, 81, 126, 197, 205, 362-4; and operation 'Crusader', 2-6, 11-12, 23-4, 42, 52, 56, 70, 73, 96-7, 101, 121; and Tobruk, 22-5, 197, 245-9, 253, 255, 258-9, 264, 275; and General Cunningham, 60-1; and an advance into Tripolitania, 119, 135, 362, 364; and diversions and withdrawals, 123, 125-7, 199; and reinforcements, 127, 199, 366; and Persia and Iraq command, 128-9, 205, 367-8, 375-6; and retreat to Gazala, 135, 142-3, 145-7; and Godwin-Austen, 152; on weakness in armour, 153; and G.O.C. Malta, 161; and timing of a resumed offensive, 183-4, 198-202, 204-5, 215-6, 366-7; and Western Cyrenaican airfields, 197; and priority of commitments, 204-5, 363-4; replaced by Alexander, 205, 267-9, 376; and Battle of Gazala, 218, 226, 228-9, 231, 236, 238, 242, 275; on 'Jock' columns, 254, 342; and a withdrawal to Matruh, 281, 285; commands 8th Army, 285-6; and Ritchie, 285-6, 377; and withdrawal to El Alamein, 286-7, 290-1, 293-6; and fighting at El Alamein, 331-6, 342-5, 347, 352-3, 357, 359-60; and defence of Egypt, 334; praises R.A.F., 335; and operation 'Torch', 362; on shortage of transport, 366; Prime Minister's views on, 367-8, 376; fine qualities of, 367-8, 376-7; becomes C.-in-C., India, 376
Aujila: capture of, 50
Aurora, H.M.S.: and enemy convoys, 103-4, 106, 113-4; in convoy operations, 111; leaves Malta, 172
Australian Government: 23-4, 127, 282
Avon Vale, H.M.S.: 165, 172
Axis Armistice Commissions: 120
Axum: 319, 322

Bach, Major: 95-6
Badsworth, H.M.S.: 305, 307
Bagnold, Colonel R.A.: 8
Baheira: air attacks on, 17
Bande Nere: 169, 171, 174
'Barbarossa': 131
Barbasetti di Prun, General Curio: 378
Barbiano: 109
Barce: air attacks on, 17, 87, 210
Bardia: bombardment of, 43; air attacks on, 93n; captured, 95-6; as supply base, 378
Barham, H.M.S.: 109, 117
Barrowclough, Brigadier H. E.: 50, 68
Bastico, Marshal Ettore: and North Africa command, 20, 378; and Tobruk, 21, 79; and Rommel, 49n, 97-8, 152; and reinforcements, 69,76; and defence of Cyrenaica, 79-80, 84-5; and advance to Gazala, 145, 151-2; and an advance into Egypt, 278
Bathurst, H.M.A.S.: 124
Battalions:
- 2/13th Australian: 25,65
- 2/15th Australian: 25, 388
- 2/28th Australian: 358
- 3/10th Baluch: 349
- 4/10th Baluch: 233-4
- 2nd, The Black Watch: 43n, 45
- 1st, The Buffs: 82, 348n
- 2nd, The Buffs: 389n
- 2nd, The Cameron Highlanders: at Tobruk, 262, 264-5, 268-71; and surrender, 273
- The Cape Town Highlanders: 250
- 2nd, The Cheshire Regiment: 227n
- 3rd, Coldstream Guards: and operation 'Crusader', 85n, 86, 88; and retreat to Gazala, 138n; at Tobruk, 262, 268, 270-1; mentioned, 273; and fighting at El Alamein, 348n
- Die Middellandse: 264
- 1st, The Duke of Cornwall's Light Infantry: 232, 234
- 6th, The Durham Light Infantry: 358
- 8th, The Durham Light Infantry: 251
- 9th, The Durham Light Infantry: 251, 289
- 4th, The East Yorkshire Regiment: 227n
- 5th, The East Yorkshire Regiment: 251, 358
- 1st, The Essex Regiment: 61, 65, 69
- 1st/4th, The Essex Regiment: 342n, 348n, 349
- 2/5th, The Essex Regiment: 340n, 341
- 3rd, Frontier Force Regiment: 354
- 4th, The Green Howards: 227n
- 5th, The Green Howards, 227n
- 7th, The Green Howards: 232
- 2/3rd Gurkha Rifles: 340n, 341
- 2/4th Gurkha Rifles: 233-4
- 2/7th Gurkha Rifles: at Tobruk, 262, 264, 267, 271, 273
- 2nd, Highland Light Infantry: 233-4
- 3/9th, The Jat Regiment: 234
- The Kaffrarian Rifles: 270-1
- 2nd, The King's Own Royal Regiment: 43n
- 1st, The King's Royal Rifle Corps: 45, 257
- 2nd, The King's Royal Rifle Corps: 138n, 223
- 9th, The King's Royal Rifle Corps: 224n
- 2/5th, Mahratta Light Infantry: 262, 264-5, 267
- 28th Maori: 58, 389
- 19th New Zealand: 62, 69, 343
- 20th New Zealand: 68-9
- 21st New Zealand: 64, 292, 350
- 22nd New Zealand: 59n, 348-50
- 23rd New Zealand: 344, 350

Battalions—*cont.*
24th New Zealand: 67
25th New Zealand: 355
26th New Zealand: 67, 350
1/1st Punjab: 354n, 355
1/2nd Punjab: 354n, 355
3/14th Punjab: 357
4/16th Punjab: 48n
1/6th, Rajputana Rifles: 256n, 258
4/6th Rajputana Rifles: 349
3/7th Rajput Regiment: 354n, 355
50th, Reconnaissance Corps: 74, 233-4
2nd, Regiment Botha: 355
1st, The Rifle Brigade: 137, 138n
2nd, The Rifle Brigade: 45, 224n
7th, The Rifle Brigade: 356n
9th, The Rifle Brigade: and operation 'Crusader', 91n; and retreat to Gazala, 138n, 141n; and fighting at El Alamein, 348n
3/18th, Royal Garhwal Rifles: 256n, 258
1st, The Royal Natal Carbineers: 231
1st, The Royal Northumberland Fusiliers: 342n, 348n
4th, The Royal Northumberland Fusiliers: 61-2, 74n; *now see* 50th, Reconnaissance Corps
1st, The Royal Sussex Regiment: 48n
4th, The Royal West Kent Regiment: 389n
5th, The Royal West Kent Regiment: 389n
2nd, Scots Guards: and operation 'Crusader', 40n, 85n, 86; and retreat to Gazala, 138n, 141, 143; and Battle of Gazala, 238 242; and fighting at El Alamein 348n
1st The Sherwood Foresters: 262, 270
4/11th, Sikh Regiment: 48n, 340n, 341
1st, The South Wales Borderers: 256n, 258
2nd, The Transvaal Scottish: 264
3rd, The Transvaal Scottish: 47
1st The Welch Regiment: 149
2nd, The West Yorkshire Regiment: 233
1st, The Worcestershire Regiment: 249, 262, 270-1
2nd, The York and Lancaster Regiment: 43n
'Battleaxe': training in, 5; army/air co-operation in, 13; German tactics in, 28; mentioned, 53, 209; lessons of, 101
Bayerlein, Colonel Fritz: 386
Beak, Major-General D. M. W.: 161
Beamish, Air Commodore G. R.: 139
Beckett, Brigadier C. T.: 179
Bedouin, H.M.S.: 304-7
Beeley, Rifleman J.: 44
'Beergroup': 262, 264, 269-71
Belhamed: capture of, 61; lost, 68; destruction of base at, 244; attacked, 256-7; withdrawal from, 258
'Bencol': 85-6, 88-9
Benghazi: air attacks on, 16-7, 60, 70, 87, 102, 190, 209-10, 288, 325, 336, 345; defence of, 16; as supply base, 135-6, 379; mining of, 136, 244; fall of, 149-51
Benina: air attacks on, 17, 60, 87, 210; capture of, 88, 99
Beresford-Peirse, Lieut.-General Sir Noel: 1
Berka: air attacks on, 17, 60, 87, 210, 244
Bhutan, m.v.: 310
Bianchi: 382n, 388
Bir el Gubi: mentioned, 33; actions at, 39-40, 75-9
Bir el Khireigat: action at, 9
Bir Hacheim: air attacks on, 51, 225, 230, 236; capture of, 235-7
Birmingham, H.M.S.: 308, 312
Bismarck, Major-General Georg von: 386
Blamey, General Sir Thomas: 23
Bolzano: 323
Bonaventure, H.M.S.: 117
Borain, Brigadier C. E.: 95
Böttcher, General Karl: 53, 58, 64
Boucher, Brigadier C. H.: 232
Boyd, Rear-Admiral D. W.: 158
Bragadin, Captain M. A.: 70n, 106n, 189n, 327n, 330n
Bramham, H.M.S.: 320, 322
Brauchitsch, Field-Marshal von: 132
Breconshire, H.M.S.: carries supplies to Malta, 110-14, 155-6, 158-60, 164, 170, 324; sinks, 171; mentioned, 178
Brereton, Major-General Lewis H.: 374
Brigades and Brigade Groups:
Armoured:
1st Army Tank: equipped, 4; and operation 'Crusader', 30, 37, 61, 94-5; strength and state of, 69, 220; and Battle of Gazala, 217, 224-5, 226n, 227
32nd Army Tank; formed, 5; arrives at Tobruk, 25; and operation 'Crusader', 30, 38, 43, 61; in Battle of Gazala, 217, 219, 232-3, 242; strength of, 220, 238, 240n, 241n, 262; in defence of Tobruk, 261, 263-4, 267
1st: to join 8th Army, 218, 220; strength and state of, 220, 239; re-equipped, 281n
2nd: strength and state of, 73, 137-8, 240n, 241n, 349n; and retreat to Gazala, 137-8, 141, 144-5; in Battle of Gazala, 217, 224-6, 229, 233-4, 239-40, 242-3, 249; re-equipped, 254, 289n; in fighting at El Alamein, 345, 348-9, 351, 354-6, 358
4th: equipped, 4-5; and operation 'Crusader', 8, 28, 37, 38n, 39-49, 54, 56, 62, 63n, 67-8, 75, 81-4; relief of, 88, 136; in Battle of Gazala, 217, 224-6, 229, 231-2, 234, 236, 239-40, 242-3, 253, 257-9; and withdrawal to El Alamein, 289-91; in fighting at El Alamein, 341-3; strength of, 343n; *now see* 4th Light
4th Light: in fighting at El Alamein, 353, 357-8; in Battle of Alam el Halfa, 384, 386
7th: equipped, 4-5; strength of, 30, 48; in operation 'Crusader', 37, 38n, 39-42, 44, 46-9, 54, 56; withdrawn to Egypt, 62; for Far East, 125

Brigades and Brigade Groups—*cont.*
Armoured—*cont.*
8th: for Western Desert, 249; state of, 281n; in Battle of Alam el Halfa, 384, 387; losses of, 391
22nd: for Middle East, 4; strength and state of, 5, 12, 30, 48-50, 63n, 65n, 88, 91, 136-7, 240n, 281, 343n, 349n; in operation 'Crusader', 37, 38n, 39-42, 45-50, 54, 62, 63n, 73n, 88-9, 91-2, 136-7; mentioned, 67; losses of, 91, 234, 391; in Battle of Gazala, 217, 224-6, 229, 232-4, 240-2, 249; re-equipped, 254; and withdrawal to El Alamein, 289; in fighting at El Alamein, 341-3, 348-9, 351, 354, 357; in Battle of Alam el Halfa, 384, 386-7, 391
23rd: 353-6, 384, 387
24th: 353n
Infantry:
18th Australian: 23, 25
24th Australian: at Tobruk, 22; relief of, 25; in fighting at El Alamein, 351, 357-8
26th Australian: 346, 357
14th (British): 38, 43
16th (British): 25, 38, 43
23rd (British): 38, 44, 78
69th (British): and Battle of Gazala, 216-7, 251; and retreat to El Alamein, 285, 288, 293; in fighting at El Alamein, 357-8
131st (British): 384
132nd (British): 384, 388-9
133rd (British): 384
150th (British): 73-4, 216-7, 226-30
151st (British): and Battle of Gazala, 217, 229, 251; and retreat to El Alamein, 288-9, 293, 295; in Battle of Alam el Halfa, 388
1st Free French: raids by, 164; in Battle of Gazala, 217, 230-1, 235-7
2nd Free French: 217
22nd Guards: on the frontier, 9; and operation 'Crusader', 39, 56, 73, 77, 81, 85, 89, 91; and retreat to Gazala, 137; *now see* 200th Guards
200th Guards: and retreat to Gazala, 137-8, 141, 143, 145; state of, 138; redesignation of, 217n; *now see* 201st (Guards) Motor
5th Indian: and operation 'Crusader', 9, 37, 52, 82, 85; and Battle of Gazala, 217; at Matruh, 288; and withdrawal to El Alamein, 289-91, 293; in fighting at El Alamein, 347, 349, 351; in Battle of Alam el Halfa, 387-9
7th Indian: and operation 'Crusader', 9, 37, 39n, 41, 48, 50, 57n, 69, 82, 85; and retreat to Gazala, 141, 145, 149, 151

Brigades and Brigade Groups—*cont.*
Infantry—*cont.*
9th Indian: and Battle of Gazala, 217, 232-4; in fighting at El Alamein, 354, 357; in Battle of Alam el Halfa, 385-6
10th Indian: 217, 229, 232
11th Indian: and operation 'Crusader', 9, 37, 39n, 52, 73, 75-7; leaves Tobruk, 145; to join 8th Army, 218; and defence of Tobruk, 261-2, 264, 267, 269
18th Indian: 340-1
20th Indian: 218, 253, 256-8
21st Indian: 218, 288, 295
25th Indian: 218, 288, 295
29th Indian: and operation 'Crusader', 38; and Battle of Gazala, 217, 235-6, 238, 249, 253-6; and retreat to El Alamein, 288-9, 294-5
38th Indian: 73
4th New Zealand: and operation 'Crusader', 37, 50, 57, 61, 68, 81; and retreat to El Alamein, 291, 293; mentioned, 292; in fighting at El Alamein, 343, 347, 349-50; refitting, 384n
5th New Zealand: and operation 'Crusader', 37, 50, 59, 61, 69, 73-5; and retreat to El Alamein, 290-3; in fighting at El Alamein, 347-8; in Battle of Alam el Halfa, 384, 389
6th New Zealand: and operation 'Crusader', 37, 50, 61-2, 65, 67-8; and retreat to El Alamein, 288; in fighting at El Alamein, 342, 354-5; in Battle of Alam el Halfa, 384, 389
1st Polish Carpathian: at Tobruk, 23, 25, 38; and operation 'Crusader', 44, 81-2
1st South African: and operation 'Crusader', 37, 50, 52, 54, 57, 62-4, 66-7, 69, 73; in Battle of Gazala, 217, 231, 250; in fighting at El Alamein, 342
2nd South African: and operation 'Crusader', 94; and Battle of Gazala, 217, 250-1; in Battle of Alam el Halfa, 387
3rd South African: and operation 'Crusader', 38, 95-6; and Battle of Gazala, 217, 250-1
4th South African: and operation 'Crusader', 38, 96; and Battle of Gazala, 217, 264, 269, 271
5th South African: and operation 'Crusader', 37, 43, 46-7, 49; destruction of, 50, 54, 66; refitting, 94, 217n; in fighting at El Alamein, 343
6th South African: and operation 'Crusader', 38, 96; and Battle of Gazala, 217, 264, 269-72
Motor:
7th (British): and Battle of Gazala, 217, 223-4, 231, 235-7, 240n, 242, 259; and retreat to El Alamein, 285,

Brigades and Brigade Groups—*cont.*
Motor—*cont.*
286n, 289-90; in fighting at El Alamein, 343-4, 353; in Battle of Alam el Halfa, 384, 386
201st Guards: under Ritchie's command, 217; in Battle of Gazala, 229, 238, 249; at Tobruk, 261-2, 264, 267, 269-70
3rd Indian: and Battle of Gazala, 217, 223-4, 253; and retreat to El Alamein, 285, 289
9th Indian: 217
161st Indian: 353-5
Briggs, Brigadier (later Major-General) H. R.: and operation 'Crusader', 48; and retreat to Gazala, 149; and Battle of Gazala, 217, 232
Briggs, Brigadier R: and retreat to Gazala, 138, 141, 143-4; and fighting at El Alamein, 349; wounded, 354
Brindisi: air attacks on, 15-6
Brink, Major-General G. L.: 12, 37, 43
Brisbane Star, m.v.: 320-2
British Ambassador in Egypt: 130, 374n
British Ambassador in Iraq: 374n
British Ambassador in Washington: 120
British Government: *see* War Cabinet, *and* Defence Committee
Brooke, General Sir Alan, Chief of the Imperial General Staff: mentioned, 121n; and withdrawals, 126, 199; in Cairo with Churchill, 362, 364, 367, 376; visits Russia, 366; and Middle East Commands, 367, 368n, 369; and directive to Alexander, 369
Brown Ranger, tanker: 301
Burdwan, m.v.: 301, 305-6
Burma: threat to, 128: under Wavell's command, 128; Japanese invade, 200
Burrough, Rear-Admiral H. M.: 317, 319-22
Burrows, Brigadier J. T.: 351

Cairo, H.M.S.: escorts U.S.S. *Wasp*, 182; in 'Harpoon' convoy, 301-2, 304-7; in 'Pedestal' convoy, 317, 319-20
Campbell, Brigadier (later Major-General) J. C.: and action at Bir el Khireigat, 9; and operation 'Crusader', 44-5; killed, 217n; and 'Jock' columns, 254
Cantore: 326
Cape Bon: action off, 109-10
Cape Matapan: action off, 170
Capo Faro: 106
Carabiniere: 160
Caracciolo: 90
Carlisle, H.M.S.: in convoy operations, 101-11, 157, 159, 164-5, 172
Carlo del Greco: 87n
Casey, Rt. Hon. R. G.: appointed Minister of State, 129-30; and Dobbie, 186; and a withdrawal to Matruh, 279; and northern front, 362; mentioned, 364; and Middle East Command, 367; and Middle East War Council, 374n; and Persia and Iraq, 376
Castel Benito: air attacks on, 17
Castel Vetrano: air attacks on, 94
Casualties: at Tobruk, 25-6, 274; in operation 'Crusader', 45, 47, 50, 57, 62, 93, 96-7, 152; in retreat to Gazala, 152; at Malta, 185; in Battle of Gazala, 223, 236, 238-9, 251; in retreat to El Alamein, 293; at El Alamein, 343, 351, 355-6, 358; Army, Nov. 1941–July 1942, 372; at Alam el Halfa, 388-91
Catania: attempted raid on, 328
Cauldron, The: fighting in, 231-5
Cavallero, Marshal Ugo: and operation 'Crusader', 84-5; and advance to Gazala, 145-6; and Malta, 174-5, 278; and a pursuit into Egypt, 278, 338; and reinforcements, 338; and North Africa Command, 378
Centurion, H.M.S.: 308
Cerion, petrol carrier: 216
Chakdina, H.M.S.: 90
Champion de Crespigny, Air Vice-Marshal H. V.: 424
Chant, s.s. (American): 301, 305
Chantala, H.M.S.: 90
Chappel, Brigadier B. H.: 43
Charing Cross: air attacks on, 295
Charybdis, H.M.S.: escorts U.S.S. *Wasp*, 182' 187; in 'Harpoon' convoy, 301, 307; in 'Pedestal' convoy, 317, 320, 323
Chief of the Air Staff: *see* Portal
Chief of the Imperial General Staff: *see* Dill *and* Brooke
Chiefs of Staff: and Tobruk, 24, 259; and Auchinleck, 24; on future offensive plans, 119; and operation 'Gymnast', 121-2; and priority of commitments, 121-2, 363-6; on diversions and withdrawals, 123, 125, 202; and reinforcements, 125-6, 136, 282, 299, 365; and Persia and Iraq, 128-9, 375-6; and Malta, 161, 183, 186-7, 193, 200-2, 314; and Dobbie, 186; and timing of a resumed Desert offensive, 203-4; on northern front, 364-6; and Brooke, 367
Churchill, Rt. Hon. Winston S.: *see* Prime Minister
Ciano, Count: 111n
Cigno: 110
City of Calcutta, s.s.: 248n, 309
Clan Campbell, s.s.: 159-60, 164, 171
Clan Chattan, s.s.: 159-60
Clan Ferguson, s.s.: 320
Cleopatra, H.M.S.: 163-9, 308
Clifton, Brigadier G. H.: 65, 355, 389
Clyde, H.M.S.: 314
Cobalto: 319, 329
Cocker, H.M.S.A.S.: 90
Comando Supremo: *see* Italian High Command
Combined Chiefs of Staff's Committee in Washington: 177
Commander-in-Chief, India: *see* Wavell
Commander-in-Chief, Mediterranean: *see* Cunningham, *and, for joint action*, Commanders-in-Chief
Commander-in-Chief, Middle East: *see* Auchinleck, *and, for joint action*, Commanders-in-Chief

Commanders-in-Chief: and operation 'Crusader', 6, 12n, 126, 133; and operation 'Acrobat', 119, 125-6, 133; and capture of Sicily, 119-20; on operation 'Gymnast', 120-1; and diversions and withdrawals, 123-7, 133, 202; and northern front, 124, 126-7, 362, 364; and Middle East situation, 125, 260, 362; and reinforcements, 126-7, 206, 260, 299, 326, 364; on Minister of State, 129; and retreat to Gazala, 153; and Malta, 161, 182-3, 200-1, 314; mentioned, 177; and long-range bombers, 190; and Tobruk, 197, 245, 259-61, 279; and timing of a resumed offensive, 198, 201-3; on a withdrawal to Matruh, 279-81; and 'Vigorous' convoy, 309; need strategical guidance, 362, 364; and Middle East War Council, 374n

Commandos, No. 11 (Scottish): 21-2

Commonwealth Keep: capture of, 225; air attacks on, 227

Coningham, Air Vice-Marshal A: commands Western Desert Air Force, 12; and air support, 14, 94, 336; and operation 'Crusader', 14, 18, 51, 55, 74, 83, 94, 98; and an advance into Tripolitania, 138-9; and retreat to Gazala, 146-7; and the lull, 209; mentioned, 220, 296, 370; and Battle of Gazala, 225, 230-1, 235, 247, 256, 258-9; and use of landing-grounds, 282; and fighting at El Alamein, 335, 345

Convoys: *see also* 'Harpoon', 'Vigorous' *and* 'Pedestal':
- (enemy) to North Africa, 15-6, 19-20, 69-70, 79, 87, 94, 102-7, 109-14, 117, 139, 158-9, 162-3, 173, 189-91, 193-4, 197, 326, 329; losses, 16, 19-20, 106, 189, 326-7, 330;
- (British) and operation 'Crusader', 38, 90; to Malta, 110-14, 155-62, 164-73, 177, 180-5, 202, 204, 211, 244-5, 248, 251-2, 255, 299-325, 329; between Egypt, Cyprus and Levant, 90; to North Africa, 136, 192, 216, 329-30; to Middle East, 31, 121-3, 126, 128, 260n, 329-30, 372; losses, 216, 314, 322

Cooke, Captain G. C.: 109

Cooper, Brigadier F.: 96, 272

Corbett, Lieut.-General T. W.: 285

Corps:
- 10th: arrives in Middle East, 2; and withdrawal to El Alamein, 281, 284, 287-9, 291-5; to be strong in armour, 385; training of, 390
- 13th: Western Desert Force becomes, 1; and operation 'Crusader', 7-8, 10, 34, 37-9, 41, 46, 48-50, 52, 56, 81-2, 88; and relief of Tobruk, 64, 67, 73-4, 77; to drive enemy from Cyrenaica, 81; supplies for, 135; and retreat to Gazala, 137, 142, 146-8, 151; works with No. 40 Squadron S.A.A.F., 212; command of, 152, 217, 369; and Battle of Gazala, 218, 220, 226, 229, 231-2, 238, 242-3, 245; in defence of Tobruk, 248, 250, 253, 259, 263; and a withdrawal to Matruh, 284-5; and withdrawal to El

Corps—*cont.*
- 13th—*cont.*
  Alamein, 287-8, 292-5; in fighting at El Alamein, 334-5, 340, 342-5, 347-8, 353-4, 357; in Battle of Alam el Halfa, 384
- 30th: forms, 1; command of, 2, 345; and operation 'Crusader', 7, 9-10, 12, 34, 37-9, 41, 46, 48-50, 52, 54-5, 63, 73, 78, 101; mentioned, 65, 75; leaves for frontier area, 81; air support for, 94, 212; in Battle of Gazala, 217, 224, 229, 231-2, 236, 242; and defence of Tobruk, 248, 253, 263, 272; and withdrawal to Matruh, 259, 284; and withdrawal to El Alamein, 295; in fighting at El Alamein, 334-5, 341-8, 354, 357; in Battle of Alam el Halfa, 384-5, 386n, 387
- 1st Australian: 126
- 21st Indian: 424

Corvette Group, 10th: 90

Coventry, H.M.S.: 308-9, 312

Cox, Brigadier C. H. V.: 78

Crete: effect of loss of, 1; air attacks on, 164, 211, 388

Cripps, Rt. Hon. Sir Stafford: 201

Crista, petrol carrier: 216

Cross, Group Captain K. B. B.: 207

Cruiser Squadrons:
- 7th: 46, 158
- 15th: 110, 163, 328

'Crusader': timing of, 2-3, 12, 23, 25, 31; plan for, 5-10, 12-5, 19, 23, 31, 37-8, 103; supplies for, 10-12, 90-1; air operations related to, 15-9; and relief of Tobruk, 23-5, 78; effect of enemy armour in, 28; reviewed, 33, 70-1, 96-102; the operation, 38-96; losses in, 40, 43, 99; air support in, 99; mentioned, 105, 128, 140, 152-3, 159, 161, 205, 207, 210, 227, 261, 284-5, 332, 337, 352, 367; and operation 'Acrobat', 119, 142; and operation 'Gymnast', 120-1; and withdrawals and diversions, 123, 125-6, 133

Cruttwell, C. R. M. F.: 143

Crüwell, Lieut.-General Ludwig: and operation 'Crusader', 39-42, 44, 46-7, 49, 53, 55-8, 62, 64, 71, 74, 77, 85, 91, 101; and action at Agedabia, 141; and Battle of Gazala, 219, 223, 226; captured, 227; his abilities, 227-8

Cuma: 209

Cunningham, Lieut-General Sir Alan: commands 8th Army, 1, 37; and operation 'Crusader', 5-8, 14, 37, 39, 41-2, 46, 48-50, 52, 54-6, 60; and air support, 14; worried about tank losses, 52; General Auchinleck's opinion of, 60-1; relieved of 8th Army command, 61

Cunningham, Admiral Sir Andrew B.: *see also* Commanders-in-Chief; and Tobruk, 24-5, 90, 197; and operation 'Crusader', 24, 97; reinforcements for, 90, 124; and operations against enemy convoys, 109-16, 163; depleted forces of, 111, 117, 173; and First Battle of Sirte, 112; and human torpedo

Cunningham, Admiral—*cont.*
attacks, 115; and withdrawals from Mediterranean, 123-5; and convoy operations, 157, 159-60, 164, 166, 177; on air reconnaissance, 157; leaves Mediterranean Command, 177-8; his achievements, 177-8; on Malta, 178
Curteis, Vice-Admiral A.T.B.: 301-3, 307
Curtin, Rt. Hon. John: 24
Cyprus: defence of, 2
Cyrenaica: enemy withdrawal from 33, 84, 96; British reoccupation of, 161, 198; air attacks on airfields in, 164; effect of loss of airfields in, 173

Dagabur: 318, 329
D.A.K. (Deutsches Afrika Korps): mentioned, 28, 95, 227, 385; leaves Bardia, 39, 41; and operation 'Crusader', 44, 46-7, 50, 53, 56, 58-62, 66, 77, 84, 89, 92; air attacks on, 55, 57; strength and state of, 139n, 231, 239, 249, 383n; and advance to Gazala, 141, 144-9, 152; in Battle of Gazala, 220, 225-6, 228, 237, 249; and Tobruk, 258-9, 265-6; and advance to El Alamein, 283, 289-90, 293-4; in fighting at El Alamein, 340-5; in Battle of Alam el Halfa, 383, 386-8, 390n
Da Mosto: 106
Daniel, Commodore C. S.: 182, 187
Davy, Brigadier G. M. O.: 40, 44-5, 47
Da Zara, Admiral A.: 303-7
De Beer, Lieut.-Colonel J. M.: 262
Defence Committee: and recapture of Cyrenaica, 3; sends 22nd Armoured Brigade to Middle East, 4; and plan to capture Sicily, 119; and command in Iraq, 129; and Malta, 183, 204; and timing of a resumed offensive, 200, 202, 204; and a withdrawal to Matruh, 280
De Giorgis, Major-General Fedele: 95-6
Deir el Shein: defended locality at, 332; lost, 340-1
'Delease': 378
'Dencol': 217
Derna: air attacks on, 16-7, 41, 60, 102, 210, 212, 227, 244, 251; capture of, 85; as supply base, 135
Deucalion, m.v.: 319-20
De Villiers, Major-General I. P.: 38, 94-5, 261
Dido, H.M.S.: 117, 163-5, 308
Dielpi: 382n
Dill, Field-Marshal Sir John, Chief of the Imperial General Staff: 121n
Divisions:
Armoured:
1st: for Middle East, 4, 31; arrival of, 73, 88, 136; command of, 136-7, 354; strength and state of, 136, 147-8, 153, 220, 286n, 353; in retreat to Gazala, 141-9, 151; in Battle of Gazala, 217-8, 224, 232, 240, 242, 250; and a withdrawal to Matruh, 285; and withdrawal to El Alamein, 289, 291-3, 295; in defence of Alamein, 341-3, 346, 348, 354, 357

Divisions—*cont.*
Armoured—*cont.*
2nd: 1
7th: strength and state of, 4, 30, 99, 220, 353; and operation 'Crusader', 29, 37, 39, 40n, 46, 48, 50, 53-4, 62, 66-7, 73, 78, 81-2, 85, 88; relief of, 136; and Battle of Gazala, 217-8, 224, 232-3; at Tobruk, 248, 253, 259, 272-3; and withdrawal to Matruh, 281, 285; and withdrawal to El Alamein, 295; in fighting at El Alamein, 351, 354, 357; in Battle of Alam el Halfa, 384, 387, 389-90
8th: state of, 27n; arrival of, 260, 353, 372
10th: state of, 249n; at Matruh, 281; mentioned, 354; in Battle of Alam el Halfa, 384, 387, 390
31st Indian: 424
Cavalry:
1st: 249n
Infantry:
12th African: 1
6th Australian: 126, 260
7th Australian: 126
9th Australian: and defence of Tobruk, 22; question of its withdrawal, 126-7, 199; rated high by Rommel, 339; in fighting at El Alamein, 345-6, 356n, 357; strength of, 353; in Battle of Alam el Halfa, 384, 388
2nd (British): 365n, 366
5th (British): 365n, 366
6th (British): 2, 25; *now see* 70th (British)
18th (British): 123, 126
44th (British): arrival of, 260, 363, 372; in Battle of Alam el Halfa, 384, 386
50th (British): arrival of, 2; in Iraq, 123; and Malta convoy, 164; and Battle of Gazala, 217; 219-20, 231, 238, 241, 245-6, 248, 250-1, 254, 259; and retreat to El Alamein, 281, 284-5, 287-9, 291, 293, 295; in fighting at El Alamein, 340, 342; in Battle of Alam el Halfa, 387
51st (British): arrival of, 363, 365n, 372; in Battle of Alam el Halfa, 387
56th (British): 364, 365n
70th (British): and operation 'Crusader', 38, 42, 44, 46, 48-9, 52, 61-2, 68-9; for Far East, 126, 199
4th Indian: and operation 'Crusader', 7, 9, 37, 46, 56, 59, 69, 73, 75, 77-8, 81-2, 85; command of, 137; and retreat to Gazala, 141-2, 147-9; mentioned, 152, 218
5th Indian: in Cyprus, 2; and Battle of Gazala, 217, 232-4, 248; and retreat to El Alamein, 285, 287-8, 291-2, 295; in fighting at El Alamein, 342, 347, 353-4, 356-7; in Battle of Alam el Halfa, 384, 390
6th Indian: 424
8th Indian: 424

Divisions—*cont.*
Infantry—*cont.*
10th Indian: to join 8th Army, 218; and Battle of Gazala, 242, 247, 259; and retreat to El Alamein, 281, 284, 287-8, 295; in fighting at El Alamein, 342
17th Indian: 123, 126
1st South African: and operation 'Crusader', 12, 37, 41-2, 53, 94; and Malta convoy, 164; and Battle of Gazala, 217, 219-20, 231, 238, 241, 245-6, 248-51, 254, 259; mentioned, 261-2, 340n; strength and state of, 281, 353; and withdrawal to El Alamein, 295; in fighting at El Alamein, 341, 346; in Battle of Alam el Halfa, 384
2nd South African: and operation 'Crusader', 38, 52, 56, 69, 73, 77, 94-5; and Battle of Gazala, 217, 219, 238, 249-51, 261, 272n; strength and state of, 261, 272n; mentioned, 275
New Zealand: and operation 'Crusader', 7, 37, 39n, 41, 48, 50, 52, 54, 61-9, 73; to stay in Middle East, 127; for Western Desert, 249; at Matruh, 279, 281, 284, 287; at Minqar Qaim, 288-92; and withdrawal to El Alamein, 292-5; rated high by Rommel, 339; in fighting at El Alamein, 342, 347-8, 351, 354; strength of, 353; in Battle of Alam el Halfa, 384, 387, 389
Dobbie, Lieut.-General Sir William, Governor and C.-in-C., Malta: and supplies for Malta, 155-6, 160-2, 183; and air attacks on Malta, 181-2; leaves Malta, 186
Dominions: flow of munitions from, 3-4
Doria: 111-2
Dorset, m.v.: 320-1
Drew, Lieut.-Colonel H. D.: 68
Drummond, Air Marshal R. M.: 198
Duca D'Aosta: 310
Duca Degli Abruzzi: 105
Duilio: 111
Dundas, Commodore J. G. L.: 328
Du Toit, Brigadier C. L. de W.: 250-1

Eagle, H.M.S.: and fighter reinforcement of Malta, 163, 187-8, 300, 314; in dock, 182; in convoy operations, 301-3, 316, 318-9, 321
Edelsten, Rear-Admiral J. H.: 328
Egypt, King of: 130
Egypt: *see also* Egyptian Government; defence of, 1, 52, 124, 127, 201, 333-4, 363; internal security, 1, 333; political crisis in, 130
Egyptian Government and Ministers: 130
El Adem: advance on, 73, 77; and Battle of Gazala, 224-5; and investment of Tobruk, 245-50; action at, 254; evacuated 255-6
El Agheila: Rommel withdraws to, 92; air attacks on, 150
El Alamein: defences at, 2, 332; fighting at in July, 334-59
El Daba: bombardments of, 328; air attacks on, 331n; skirmishes near, 332; use of airfields, 337
El Duda: capture of, 61-2; Germans attack, 65-6, 75
El Mreir: actions at, 335, 343-4, 353-7
Elizabeth Bakke, m.v.: 309
Elliott, Sergeant K.: 350
Elysia, s.s.: 353n
Embry, Air Commodore B. E.: 13
Empire Defender, m.v.: 109, 324
Empire Guillemot, m.v.: 108, 324
Empire Hope, m.v.: 320
Empire Pelican, m.v.: 109, 324
Eocene, petrol carrier: 216
Eridge, H.M.S.: 192
Eskimo, H.M.S.: 320
Eugenio di Savoia: 303
Euryalus, H.M.S.: bombards Halfaya defences, 41; and enemy convoys, 110; at Alexandria, 117; bombards Rhodes, 163; in convoy operations, 164-7, 169, 308, 310
Evill, Air Vice-Marshal D.C.S.: 208
'Excess': 324

Fabio Filzi: 87n
Fadden, Rt. Hon. Arthur: 23-4
Falk, H.M.S.A.S.: 90
Falmouth, H.M.S.: 124
Far East: reinforcement of, 122-8, 173
Farndale, H.M.S.: 90
Fawzia, H.E.M.S.: 337
Field Maintenance Centres:
No. 50: 56n
No. 62: 56, 62, 65
Field Supply Depots: 10
Filose, Brigadier A. A. E.: 223
First Sea Lord: *see* Pound
Fisher, Brigadier A. F.: 289n, 356n
Flag Officer Commanding North Atlantic: 182
Flamingo, H.M.S.: 90
Fleet Air Arm: as 'pathfinders', 16, 213, 288; and operation 'Crusader', 17-8; attacks enemy shipping, 159, 326; and Malta convoys, 165, 302-3, 306, 318-9; strength in Malta, 185; reinforcements for, 188n; losses, 302, 307, 321; and bombardment of Matruh, 338
Squadrons:
No. 800: 317n
801: 301n, 317n
806: 317n
807: 301n
809: 317n
813: 301n, 317n
815: 300n
817: 317n
821: 300n, 343n
824: 301n
826: 159, 300n, 343n
827: 317n
828: 160, 171
830: 105, 300n
831: 317n

Fleet Air Arm—*cont.*
Squadrons—*cont.*
No. 832: 317n
880: 317n
884: 317n
885: 317n
Fliegerführer Afrika: *see* Fröhlich, Waldau *and* Seidemann
Flo, H.M.S.A.S.: 90
Folgore: 329
Foote, Lieut.-Colonel H. R. B.: 243, 268
Force B: sent to Malta, 105; and enemy convoys, 106; mentioned, 110; in convoy operations, 164, 166, 170-1
Force H: and operation 'Crusader', 19, 38; mentioned, 103, 318; and fighter reinforcements for Malta, 108, 163-4; strength of, 117, 133, 410; possible removal of battleship from, 123; reinforcements for, 156; in convoy operations, 156; command of, 162-3; and Diego Suarez operation, 182
Force K: and operation 'Crusader', 19, 38; reasons for formation of, 103; and enemy convoys, 70n, 103-9, 111-4, 158; mentioned, 110; in convoy operations, 112-4, 157, 159-60, 164; losses of, 114, 124; ceases to exist, 173
Force W: 182
Force X: 301-2, 317-9
Force Z: 317, 319
Ford, Vice-Admiral Sir Wilbraham, Vice-Admiral, Malta: 111, 157-8
Foresight, H.M.S.: 319
Fort Capuzzo: capture of, 48
Foster, Air Commodore R. M.: 424
Free French Movement: 44, 120
Freeman, Air Chief Marshal Sir Wilfred: 14
French Government: 120
Freyberg, Major-General B. C.: commands New Zealand Division, 37; and operation 'Crusader', 61, 64, 66-8; and use of New Zealand formations, 284, 287; and withdrawal to El Alamein, 290-1; wounded, 292; and Battle of Alam el Halfa, 387-9
Fröhlich, Major-General Stefan: 21, 98, 212
Fuka: air attacks on, 11, 17, 212, 296; loss of, 294-5; raid on, 344
Fulmine: 104
Furious, H.M.S.: 317-8, 325

Gabr Saleh: actions at, 40-4; air attacks on, 283
Galatea, H.M.S.: 110
Gallant, H.M.S.: 180
Gambara, General Gastone: 49n, 79-80, 85
Gambut: air attacks on, 9, 17, 211-12, 227; capture of, 50; loss of airfields at, 255-8
Gardner, Captain P. J.: 44
Garibaldi: 310
Gatehouse, Brigadier (later Major-General) A. H.: and operation 'Crusader', 37, 40, 68, 82; and fighting at El Alamein, 354-5, 356n; and Battle of Alam el Halfa, 387
Gause, Lieut.-General Alfred: 19, 229
Gazala: air attacks on, 17, 41; enemy stand at, 81-3; Battle of, 223-52, 392
Geisler, General Hans-Ferdinand: 21, 98
Geissler, Colonel Erich: 151
George VI, H.M. King: 179, 185-6
German Admiralty: 20
German Air Force: see *Luftwaffe*
German Army: *see also* D.A.K.; strength and dispositions of, 6-7, 26-31, 39, 48, 139-40, 199, 220; supplies for, 6, 15, 95; losses of, 9, 40, 50, 59, 69; wireless difficulties of, 37; and capture of Malta, 194-5
Armies:
Panzerarmee Afrika: strength and state of, 139n; views on 8th Army, 153-4; on booty captured, 274, 281n, 331n; and Tobruk, 275, 277, 331; on British air attacks, 287, 380; supplies for, 331, 382
Groups:
Armoured Group Africa: formed, 19-20; *now see* Panzerarmee Afrika
Divisions:
Africa (later 90th Light): command of, 19-20; state of, 29, 34, 139n, 331; and operation 'Crusader', 40, 64, 67, 80, 86; mentioned, 140n; and advance to Gazala, 148-9, 152; and Tobruk, 220, 265; in Battle of Gazala, 223-5, 227-9, 235-6, 239, 241-2, 253-5; and advance to El Alamein, 283, 289-90, 295; attacked by Desert Air Force, 287, 296; in fighting at El Alamein, 340-2, 344, 350-1; in Battle of Alam el Halfa, 383
164th Light: and fighting at El Alamein, 339, 346; in Battle of Alam el Halfa, 383, 388
15th Panzer: command of, 20; strength and state of, 29-30, 34, 63n, 74, 82n, 91, 139n, 145n; and operation 'Crusader', 39-42, 45, 47-9, 54-60, 63-7, 75, 77, 86, 91; and advance to Gazala, 140, 143-5, 147; in Battle of Gazala, 224-7, 234-5, 239-42, 250, 257; in attack on Tobruk, 265-7, 269-70; and advance to El Alamein, 289-90, 292; in fighting at El Alamein, 340-2, 346, 350, 354; in Battle of Alam el Halfa, 386-7
21st Panzer: in action at Bir el Khireigat, 9; strength and state of, 9, 29-30, 34, 63n, 82n, 91, 139n, 140n, 145n, 290n; command of, 20; and operation 'Crusader', 39-42, 45, 47-9, 54-6, 58-60, 64-7, 71, 74-5, 77, 86, 91; and advance to Gazala, 143-4, 149; in Battle of Gazala, 223, 225-6, 228, 231, 234, 239-40, 242, 250, 253-7; in attack on Tobruk, 265-7, 269; and advance to El Alamein, 289-91, 293-4; in fighting at El Alamein, 340, 343-5, 350, 354, 356; in Battle of Alam el Halfa, 386-7
Brigades:
15th Lorried Infantry: 219n
Ramcke Parachute: 338, 383

German Army—*cont.*
Regiments and Units:
155th Regiment: 34n, 46-7, 53n
382nd Regiment: 346
361st Afrika Regiment: 46-7, 50, 53n
104th Lorried Infantry Regiment: 47, 95, 293
115th Lorried Infantry Regiment: 58-9
5th Panzer Regiment: and operation 'Crusader', 40, 47, 49, 54-5, 57-9; Battle of Gazala, 228, 240, 269
8th Panzer Regiment: and operation 'Crusader', 54n, 66, 76, 82; reinforcement of, 87; in Battle of Gazala, 233; in fighting at El Alamein, 349, 355
39th Panzerjäger Regiment, 227n
900th Engineer Battalion: 53n
2nd Machine-Gun Battalion: 82, 141
3rd Reconnaissance Unit: and operation 'Crusader', 38, 58-9; and advance to Gazala, 148-9; to hold British on frontier, 265; in fighting at El Alamein, 350-1; in Battle of Alam el Halfa, 383
33rd Reconnaissance Unit: and operation 'Crusader', 38, 55, 57; and advance to Gazala, 148-9; to hold British on frontier, 265; in fighting at El Alamein, 350-1; in Battle of Alam el Halfa, 383
German High Command of the Armed Forces: *see* OKW
German High Command of the Army: *see* OKH
German Navy: 194
German soldiers: achievements of, 360
Germany: preoccupied with Russia, 2-3; declares war on United States, 121; British estimate of capabilities of, 126; and war in Russia, 132
Gioda, General: 80n
Giorgio: 382n
Giulio Cesare: 111
Giussano: 109
'Gleecol': 288-9
Glengyle, H.M.S.: and supplies for Malta, 156, 158, 160, 324
Glennie, Rear-Admiral I. G.: 328
Glenorchy, s.s.: 320
Glenroy, H.M.S.: 11, 90
Gnat, H.M.S.: 25
Gneisenau: 162, 200
Godfroy, Admiral: 192, 316
Godwin-Austen, Lieut.-General A. R.: commands 13th Corps, 1, 37; and operation 'Crusader', 8, 37, 46, 49, 52, 62, 67, 69, 73-4, 77-8, 81-3, 85, 88-9; mentioned 54-5; and retreat to Gazala, 135, 141, 143, 146-8, 151; relinquishes command, 152
Goebbels, Dr.: 108
Gorizia: 169, 310
Gort, General the Viscount, Governor and Supreme Commander, Malta: 186, 314, 316
Gott, Major-General (later Lieut.-General) W. H. E.: commands 7th Armoured Division, 37; and operation 'Crusader', 39-44, 46-7, 62-3, 68, 75, 78, 81-3, 85; mentioned, 54, 232, 367; commands 13th Corps, 217; and Battle of Gazala, 238, 242-3; and Tobruk, 263; and a withdrawal to Matruh, 281; and withdrawal to El Alamein, 290-2, 294; and fighting at El Alamein, 347-8, 351, 354-5, 357; to command 8th Army, 368; killed, 368; his abilities, 368
Gould, Petty Officer T. W.: 174
Governor of Aden: 374n
Governor of Cyprus: 374n
Gray, Lieut.-Colonel C. E.: 340n
Greece: effect of loss of, 1
Greek Navy: 328-9
Gualdi: 382n
Gurkha, H.M.S.: 157
Gurney, Private A. S.: 357
'Gymnast': 120-3, 204

'Halberd': 324
Halfaya: bombardment of, 41; air attacks on, 93, 96; captured, 95-6
Halverson Detachment: and attack on Ploesti oilfields, 206, 245; established in Egypt, 282; and 'Vigorous' convoy, 309; in Desert operations, 343n
Hardy, Captain C. C.: 301-6, 310
Hargest, Brigadier J.: 50
'Harpoon': 299-307, 314-8, 324
Harwood, Admiral Sir Henry: *see also* Commanders-in-Chief; becomes C.-in-C., Mediterranean, 178; and long-range bombers, 190; and convoy operations, 307, 310-13, 322; sends 10th Submarine Flotilla to Malta, 314; disperses Mediterranean Fleet, 315-6; mentioned, 329
Hassell, Brigadier L. L.: 251
Hasty, H.M.S.: 90, 165, 311
Havock, H.M.S.: in convoy operations, 165, 167, 169-70; destroyed, 180
Haydon, Brigadier C. W.: 227
Hayton, Brigadier A. A.: 96, 269-72
Hebe, minesweeper: 305-7
Heraklion: air attacks on, 336
'Herkules': 194, 277-8
Hermione, H.M.S.: in Force H, 117; and fighter reinforcement of Malta, 163; and 'Vigorous' convoy, 308, 313
Hero, H.M.S.: and relief of Tobruk, 25; in convoy operations, 165, 168; sinks *U*.568, 192
High Commissioner to Palestine: 374n
Hindustan, H.M.I.S.: 124
Hitler, Adolf: and German domination in Mediterranean, 21; and use of Bizerta, 69-70, 106; and Japan, 131; commands German Army, 132; mentioned, 145; and Malta, 175, 195, 277; meets Mussolini at Berchtesgaden, 195, 219; and an advance into Egypt, 277-8; and command in North Africa, 383
Hobart, H.M.A.S.: 43, 117, 124

Holmes, Lieut.-General W. G.: commands 10th Corps, 2, 281; and withdrawal to El Alamein, 290-1, 293-5
Home Fleet: 155
Hopkins, Harry L.: 361
Horrocks, Lieut.-General B. G.: commands 13th Corps, 369; and Battle of Alam el Halfa, 384-5, 387, 389
Hotspur, H.M.S.: 90
Hughes, Brigadier F. E. C.: 354n
Human torpedoes: attack Fleet at Alexandria, 115, 124, 192; attack ships at Gibraltar, 329
Hurworth, H.M.S.: 192
Hutchison, Captain C. A. G.: 170
Hyacinth, H.M.S.: 90, 328

Iachino, Admiral Angelo: and Malta convoys, 111, 113, 168-70, 172, 310, 312
Indomitable, H.M.S.: carries aircraft to Far East, 125, 127; mentioned, 158; and 'Pedestal' convoy, 316-7 ,319
Indus, H.M.I.S.: 124
Inglis, Brigadier L. M.: and operation 'Crusader', 50; and retreat to El Alamein, 292-3; and fighting at El Alamein, 349, 351-2; mentioned, 355
Inshore Squadron: 11, 24-5, 118
Iraq: and reinforcements for Far East, 122; defence of, 124, 126, 363; command in, 128-9, 375-6, 424-6; internal security of, 362
Iridio Mantovani: 106-7
Isaac Sweers: 109, 157, 173
Iseo: 106
Islay, trawler: 329
Istria: 326, 382n
Italian Admiralty: sails convoy to Africa, 105; and 'Harpoon' convoy, 307; and 'Vigorous' convoy, 310, 312-3
Italian Air Force: supplies for, 6, 15, 94; strength and state of, 6, 14-5, 21, 76, 87, 140, 178, 181; and operation 'Crusader', 18, 39, 41, 50-1, 60, 87; losses of, 18, 60, 89, 94, 99, 150, 179, 184, 188, 210-11, 213, 227, 231, 236-7, 241, 258, 336, 344; carries supplies to Africa, 79; attacks Force K, 104; and advance to Gazala, 142, 150; and Malta convoys, 165, 167, 169-71, 301-2, 306, 318-9; attacks Malta, 170-1, 178-9, 181, 184, 385; operations during the lull, 211; and Battle of Gazala, 225, 241, 258; and Tobruk, 266; and Battle of Alam el Halfa, 384; and defence of Sicily, 385
  Squadra:
    5th: 21
Italian Army: strength and dispositions of, 6, 29-30, 139-40, 199, 220, 383n; supplies for, 6, 15, 95; and operation 'Herkules', 194-5
  Corps:
    10th: under Rommel's command, 80n, 139n; in Crüwell Group, 219n; in Battle of Gazala, 250, 258, 265; and advance to El Alamein, 283, 290; in fighting at El Alamein, 343-4; in Battle of Alam el Halfa, 383, 387
Italian Army—*cont.*
  Corps—*cont.*
    Mobile (20th): command of, 19-20, 49n; and operation 'Crusader', 74, 77, 84, 89; mentioned, 80; and advance to Gazala, 139-41, 148-9, 151-2; in Battle of Gazala, 219-20, 265, 267; and advance to Matruh, 283, 288; and advance to El Alamein, 290; in fighting at El Alamein, 340, 343-4; in Battle of Alam el Halfa, 383-4, 386
    21st: command of, 19-20, 139n; and operation 'Crusader', 84; in Crüwell Group, 219n; and Tobruk, 258; and advance to El Alamein, 283; in fighting at El Alamein, 344; in Battle of Alam el Halfa, 383
  Divisions:
    Ariete: and operation 'Crusader', 8, 34, 39-40, 42, 49, 53, 55-8, 62-68, 75, 85-6; command of, 20; strength and state of, 29-30, 82n, 139n, 265n; losses of, 67; occupies Benghazi, 151; in Battle of Gazala, 220, 223, 225-6, 234, 255, 258; in attack on Tobruk, 266; and advance to El Alamein, 290; in fighting at El Alamein, 343, 351; in Battle of Alam el Halfa, 387
    Bologna: 20, 86, 139n
    Brescia: command of, 20, 139n; and operation 'Crusader', 78, 86, 88-9; in Crüwell Group, 219n; in fighting at El Alamein, 343, 347, 349-50
    Folgore Parachute: 338
    Friuli: 338
    Littorio: mentioned, 220; and Battle of Gazala, 265; and advance to El El Alamein, 288, 290; in fighting at El Alamein, 340; in Battle of Alam el Halfa, 387
    Pavia: command of, 20, 139n; and operation 'Crusader', 86; in Crüwell Group, 219n; in Battle of Gazala, 226; and advance to El Alamein 290; in fighting at El Alamein, 347, 349-50
    Pistoia: 338
    Sabratha: 139n, 219n, 346
    Savona: 19-20, 95
    Trento: command of, 20, 139n; and operation 'Crusader', 78, 86; in Crüwell Group, 219n; in Battle of Gazala, 231
    Trieste: command of, 20, 139n; and operation 'Crusader', 34, 53, 55, 68, 75-6, 85-6; mentioned, 80, 220; in Battle of Gazala, 225-9, 235, 239; reinforcement of, 265n; and advance to El Alamein, 290; in fighting at El Alamein, 351; in Battle of Alam el Halfa, 387
Italian East Africa: end of campaign in, 1
Italian High Command: and need to capture Tobruk, 19, 21-2; and supplies, 76, 145, 378, 382; and operation 'Crusader', 79-80, 84, 95; and advance to Gazala, 145; and

Italian High Command—*cont.*
Battle of Gazala, 253; on an advance into Egypt, 278; Panzerarmee directly responsible to, 378
Italian Naval Staff: 323
Italian Navy: mentioned, 15, 157; in convoy operations, 103, 109-14, 158-9, 163, 326; losses of, 106, 174; in action off Cape Bon, 109-10; and supplies to North Africa, 109, 163; in First Battle of Sirte, 112-3; and human torpedo attacks, 115, 124, 192; strength of, 117, 156, 173, 178, 411; and Force H, 123, 156; and Malta convoys, 156-7, 160, 164-70, 183, 303-13, 316, 323; gains confidence, 159, 299; in Second Battle of Sirte, 166-70, 172; and guns, 170; and capture of Malta, 194; oil fuel for, 277, 323, 338
Tenth Light Flotilla: 115
'Italuft': 21
Italy: declares war on United States, 121
Ithuriel, H.M.S.: 319

Jackal, H.M.S.: 190-1
Jackman, Captain J. J. B.: 61-2
Jaguar, H.M.S.: 114
Jalo: capture of, 8, 50; mentioned, 79
Japan: her entry into war, 80, 96, 121, 131-3, 363; attacks Thailand and Malaya, 128; and threat to Burma, 128; reaches agreement with Russia, 131; and Tripartite Pact, 131
Japanese Government: 131
Jarabub: deception at, 8; air action at, 17
Jervis, H.M.S.: 115, 165, 190-1
'Jock' columns: 254, 286, 342
Johnson, Brigadier G. F.: 261, 263-4, 267
Jumna, H.M.I.S.: 124

Kandahar, H.M.S.: 114
Kelvin, H.M.S.: 165
Kentucky, tanker: 301, 305-6
Kenya, H.M.S.: and 'Harpoon' convoy, 301, 307; and 'Pedestal' convoy, 317, 320, 323
Kesselring, Field-Marshal Albert: becomes C.-in-C., South, 21; and operation 'Crusader', 84; and system of command, 98; arrives in Rome, 108; and Rommel's offensive, 145-6; and Malta, 175, 193-5, 265-6, 278; takes temporary command of Crüwell group, 228; and Battle of Gazala, 237; and Tobruk, 265-6; and an advance into Egypt, 278; and 'Pedestal' convoy, 323; his commitments, 339; mentioned, 342, 378, 383; and supplies for Panzerarmee, 382; and Battle of Alam el Halfa, 389
Keyes, Lieut.-Colonel G. C. T.: 22
King, Fleet Admiral E. J.: 361
Kingston, H.M.S.: 165, 169-70, 180
Kipling, H.M.S.: 90, 165, 190-1
Kippenberger, Brigadier H. K.: 344, 349
Kirkland, petrol carrier: 216
Klopper, Major-General H. B.: commands 2nd South African Division, 217, 261; and defence of Tobruk, 263-4, 267-73
Knight, Lieut.-Colonel J. O.: 271
Knightsbridge: mentioned, 78, 224; fighting round, 238-43
Koenig, Brigadier General M-P.: 231, 236-7
Kopanski, Major-General S.: 38, 82
Kreta: 382n
Kufra: capture of, 8
Kujawiak: 307

Lance, H.M.S.: 103, 111
Lanciere: 170
Latona, H.M.S.: 25
Leatham, Vice-Admiral Sir Ralph, Vice-Admiral, Malta: 158, 303, 322
'Leathercol': 288-9
Ledbury, H.M.S.: 321-2
Legion, H.M.S.: 109-10, 164-5, 170-1
Lerici: 326
Libeccio: 104
Libyan Omar: capture of, 48
Lismore, H.M.A.S.: 124
Littorio: in convoy operations, 111; in Second Battle of Sirte, 166, 169; and 'Vigorous' convoy, 310-11, 313
Lively, H.M.S.: and enemy convoys, 103, 190-1; in convoy operations, 111, 165; in Second Battle of Sirte, 168-9
Liverpool, H.M.S.: 301-2, 306
Lloyd, Air Vice-Marshal H. P., Air Officer Commanding, Malta: 148, 181, 314-5
Loerzer, General Bruno: 21
Lomax, Brigadier C. E. N.: 43
Long Range Desert Group: strength and state of, 8; reconnaissances by, 8-9; and operation 'Crusader', 9, 89; and fighting at El Alamein, 344, 358
Luftwaffe: strength and state of, 6, 14-5, 76, 87, 140, 178, 212, 266, 283-4, 385; 8·8-cm. gun manned by, 28n; carries supplies to North Africa, 79, 94, 211; attacks Malta, 93, 118, 157-8, 161-2, 170-1, 178-9, 181-2, 184, 212; system of command in, 98; covers convoys to Africa, 158; and Malta convoys, 166, 169-71, 251-2, 255, 301-2, 305, 307, 309, 318-21, 323-4; and Russian campaign, 184; and capture of Malta, 195; losses of, 381
(in North Africa) supplies for, 6, 15, 381-2; attacks Bir el Khireigat, 9; losses of, 9, 16-8, 43, 51, 60, 99, 150, 210, 227, 236-7, 241, 258, 336, 381; and operation 'Crusader', 15, 18, 39, 41, 43, 50-1, 57, 60, 76, 87, 92; and advance to Gazala, 142, 150; operations during the lull, 210-12; and Battle of Gazala, 225, 230, 235-6, 239, 241, 256, 258; and attack on Tobruk, 265-6; and advance to Matruh, 288; and advance to El Alamein, 294; lack of co-operation between Panzerarmee and, 336; attacks targets in Egypt, 337; mentioned, 339; and fighting at El Alamein, 341, 344, 347, 351; operations in August, 381; and Battle of Alam el Halfa, 383-5, 389-90
(in Balkans) strength and state of, 14-5, 212; operations and losses of, 191, 211, 221, 266

Luftwaffe—*cont.*
(in Sicily) arrival of, 76, 80,174; strength of, 118, 174, 181, 212, 221, 322; operations of, 181-2; withdrawals from, 186, 193; reinforcement of, 278
Luftflotte 2: command of, 21; and Malta, 70, 193; mentioned, 98, 381
Fliegerkorps II: command of, 21; arrives in Sicily, 108; and Malta, 182, 195; strength of, 188
Fliegerkorps X: protects convoys to North Africa, 20; command of, 21, 98; mentioned, 71; and Malta, 195
Lumsden, Major-General H.: wounded, 137, 354; commands 1st Armoured Division, 217; and Battle of Gazala, 224-5, 240-2; and withdrawal to El Alamein, 292; and fighting at El Alamein, 349, 352
Luqa: air attacks on, 182
Lyster, Rear-Admiral A. L. St. G.: 316
Lyttelton, Rt. Hon. Oliver: and operation 'Crusader', 12n; and relief of Tobruk garrison, 24; and capture of Tripoli, 119; and defence of northern frontier, 124; and command in Iraq and Persia, 128; becomes Minister of Production, 129; his usefulness as Minister of State, 129; and timing of a resumed offensive, 198

Macgregor, Brigadier L. E.: 256n
Maclean, Air Commodore L. L.: 244
Malaya: Japanese attack on, 121, 128
Malaya, H.M.S.: in Force H; and fighter reinforcements for Malta, 163; and 'Harpoon' convoy, 301-3, 307
Maleme: air attacks on, 79
Malocello: 304
Malta: *for* Governor *see* Dobbie, *for* Supreme Commander *see* Gort, *for* Vice-Admiral *see* Ford *and* Leatham, *for* A.O.C. *see* Lloyd *and* Park; air forces at, 15, 159, 162, 205, 299-300, 317, 323; as striking base, 70, 94, 155, 161, 178, 185, 193-4, 197, 203, 209, 211, 244, 299, 314, 392; air attacks on, 93-4, 108, 118, 148, 157-8, 162-3, 166, 170, 173-5, 178-82, 184-5, 188, 193-4, 206, 209, 212, 244, 278, 314; reinforcements and supplies for, 108, 110-13, 117, 155-73, 177, 181-4, 187, 189, 193, 197, 200-1, 204, 244-5, 251-2, 299-314, 316-26, 329; an Axis assault on, 156, 174-5, 186, 193-5, 277-8; as a staging post, 161, 185; living conditions at, 162, 181, 186, 325; first Spitfires for, 162; defence and defences of, 170, 179, 181-2, 186, 194, 201, 203-4; awarded George Cross, 185; mine-laying around, 188; in grave peril, 189
Malta Defence Committee: 181, 186
Maltese Government: 186
Manchester, H.M.S.: 317, 320
Mantovani: 106
Manxman, H.M.S.: 155
Manzetti, General Ferruccio: 89n
Maori, H.M.S.: 109, 162
Maraua: air attacks on. 87
Marchesi, General Vittorio: 21
Marcks, Colonel Werner: 140, 151
Maritza: 105
Marriott, Brigadier J. C. O.: commands 22nd Guards Brigade, 37, 85, 137; and retreat to Gazala, 141
Marshall. General G. C.: 361
Martuba: air attacks on, 17, 41, 210, 212, 225, 244
Mason, Captain D. W.: 322
Matchless, H.M.S.: 307
Matruh (Mersa): consequences of a withdrawal to, 280; demolitions at, 296; bombardment of, 316, 338; air attacks on, 336, 339; as a supply base, 378
Matsuoka, Mr.: 131
Maxwell, Major-General Russell L.: 373-4
McCreery, Major-General R. L.: 369
Me. 109F: superiority of, 14, 76, 93, 100, 162, 221; and Spitfire, 337
Mediterranean Fleet: and operation 'Crusader', 19, 38, 51, 102; tasks of, 19, 117; and Inshore Squadron, 24; and Tobruk, 25-6, 90, 262, 315; its superiority in Mediterranean, 76; losses of, 108, 117, 133, 155-6, 173, 185, 299, 301, 315; in action off Cape Bon, 109-10; and enemy convoys to Africa, 109-14, 163, 173, 190-1, 325-6, 391; in convoy operations, 110-11, 113-4, 155-60, 164-72, 301-14, 316-22; in First Battle of Sirte, 112-3; and human torpedo attacks, 115, 124, 192; strength of, 117, 178, 409; effect of German submarines on, 118; and reinforcements for Malta, 155-6, 160, 172, 299-300, 323-5; bombards Rhodes, 163; in Second Battle of Sirte, 166-9, 172; and Cunningham, 177-8; lacks fighter cover, 178; supports 8th Army, 315, 338; dispersed, 315-6, 325, 338, 342; bombards Mersa Matruh, 316; stages diversionary operation, 318; reinforcements for, 326, 372; in anti-shipping sweeps, 328; and defence of Egypt, 334
Medway, H.M.S.: and human torpedoes, 192; sunk, 315, 326, 329
Melbourne Star, m.v.: 320-1
Mellenthin, Major (later Lieut.-Colonel) F. W. von: 139, 346
Menzies, Rt. Hon. Robert: 23
Merchant Navy: 25-6, 172, 178
Messervy, Major-General F. W.: and operation 'Crusader', 9, 37; mentioned, 57; commands 1st Armoured Division, 137; and retreat to Gazala, 138, 141, 143-4, 146, 148, 151; on training, 153; and Battle of Gazala, 223-4, 232, 234-5, 240, 255, 257; captured, 224
Mickl, Colonel Johann: 64, 66, 68
Micklethwait, Captain St. J. A.: 167-9
Middle East: estimated Axis air strength in, 14-5; withdrawals and diversions from, 122-8, 133, 363; threatened from the north, 126-8, 363; instability of countries in, 127; needs Minister of State, 129; situation in, 133; command in, 367-8; general review, 392-3

Middle East Defence Committee: and postponement of operation 'Crusader', 12; on northern front, 124; on timing of a resumed offensive, 203-4; on a withdrawal to Matruh, 280; asks for guidance, 363
Middle East Joint Planning Staff: 376
Middle East War Council: 374
Miers, Commander A. C. C.: 174
Minister of State in the Middle East: *see* Lyttelton, Monckton *and* Casey
Minqar Qaim: New Zealand Division at, 288-293
Misa, Brigadier L.: 356
Miteirya: mentioned, 332; actions at, 335, 357-9
Mobile Naval Base Defence Organisation: 123
Monckton, Sir Walter: 130, 181, 198
Monginevro: 87n
Montecuccoli: 303
Montezemolo, Colonel: 76, 79
Montgomery, Lieut.-General B. L.: commands 8th Army, 368-9, 376; and state of 8th Army, 370, 385, 390; mentioned, 381; and Battle of Alam el Halfa, 383-5, 387-9, 391
Morshead, Major-General L. J.: 22, 345
Musaid: capture of, 48
Mussolini, Benito: and German domination in Mediterranean, 21; and command in North Africa, 49n; and Tunisian ports, 69-70; mentioned, 80; and withdrawal to El Agheila, 92; and advance to Gazala, 145, 151; on supplies, 152; meets Hitler at Berchtesgaden, 195, 219; and fuel for Italian Navy, 277, 323, 338; on operation 'Herkules', 277; and an advance into Egypt, 277-8, 338; and 'Pedestal' convoy, 323
Myriel, water carrier: 90

Nahas Pasha: 130
Naiad, H.M.S.: bombards Halfaya defences, 41; and enemy convoys, 110, 112; at Alexandria, 117; sunk, 163
Naples: air attacks on, 15, 60
Napoli: 113
Navarrini, General Enea: 20
Nehring, Major-General Walther: commands D.A.K., 220; and fighting at El Alamein, 340, 350, 355; and Battle of Alam el Halfa, 383, 386
Nelson, H.M.S.: 316-7
Neptune, H.M.S.: and operation 'Crusader', 43; and enemy convoys, 105, 113-4; in convoy operation, 111
Nestor, H.M.A.S.: 313
Netherlands East Indies: Allied collapse in, 200
Neumann-Silkow, Major-General Walther: 63, 77
Newcastle, H.M.S.: 308, 310, 312
New Zealand Artillery:
6th Field Regiment: 350n
New Zealand Government: 14-5, 127, 287
New Zealand Railway Construction Companies: 10th and 13th: 10
Nicholl, Captain A. D.: 114, 180
Nichols, Lieut.-Colonel (later Major-General) J. S.: 69, 251, 284n
Nigeria, H.M.S.: 317, 319-20
Nizam, H.M.S.: 25
Norrie, Major-General C. W. M.: commands 30th Corps, 2, 37, 217; and operation 'Crusader', 7-8, 37, 42, 46, 48, 50, 54, 56, 64, 66-9, 74-5, 77-8, 81, 94-5; on British tanks, 27; mentioned, 41, 345; and retreat to Gazala, 146; and Battle of Gazala, 218, 224, 232, 239-41, 248, 253, 255, 257-8; and fighting at El Alamein, 332
North Africa Command (Axis): 20
Nye, Lieut.-General A. E., Vice-Chief of the Imperial General Staff: 201

Oasis Force: tasks of, 8; mentioned, 10; and operation 'Crusader', 38, 50-1, 89
O'Conor, Captain R. C.: 114
Ogaden: 326
Ohio, tanker: 318-22
OKH: and operation 'Crusader', 80, 84; and Battle of Gazala, 237, 274; and Tobruk, 258; Rommel reports to, 338-9, 344; and Battle of Alam el Halfa, 382-3
OKW: estimate British strength, 20; and operation 'Crusader', 79, 95; on entry of Japan, 132; and an advance into Egypt, 277; and supplies for Rommel, 377; and Battle of Alam el Halfa, 388
Olterra: 329
Olympus, H.M.S.: 193, 300
Ondina: 329
Orari, m.v.: 301, 305, 307
Oriani: 306
Orizaba, U.S.S.: 353n

P.31, H.M.S.: 311
P.34, H.M.S.: 311
P.35, H.M.S.: 311
P.36, H.M.S.: 160, 165-6
P.39, H.M.S.: 172
P.42, H.M.S.: 323
P.44, H.M.S.: 326
Padenna: 382n
Page, Lieut.-Colonel Geddes: 270
Pakenham, H.M.S.: 310
Pampas, m.v.: 164, 170-2, 178
Park, Air Vice-Marshal K. R., Air Officer Commanding, Malta: 315
Parracombe, s.s.: 324
Parramatta, H.M.A.S.: 90
Parthian, H.M.S.: 314
Partridge, H.M.S.: 304-6
Pass of Balmaha, s.s.: 25
Pearl Harbour: attack on, 121, 132
'Pedestal': 316-25, 328-9, 381
Penelope, H.M.S.: and enemy convoys, 103-5, 113-4; in convoy operations, 111, 157, 160, 164-5, 170, 172, 180-1
Penn, H.M.S.: 322
Peony, H.M.S.: 90
Pepys Column: 85, 88
Percy, Lieut.-Colonel J. E. S.: 251

Perla: 328-9
Persia: defence of, 124, 129, 363; Treaty of Alliance with, 129; internal security of, 362
Persia and Iraq Command: creation of, 205, 375-6; offered to Auchinleck, 369, 376; Wilson takes command of, 376; early life of, 424-6
Pétain, Marshal: 120
Petrella, water-carrier: 11
Phoebe, H.M.S.: 25, 317
Piazzoni, General: 80
Picci Fassio: 382n, 388
Pienaar, Brigadier (later Major-General) D. H.: and operation 'Crusader', 50, 64, 66; mentioned, 217; and Battle of Gazala, 238, 250; and fighting at El Alamein, 342
Piraeus: air attacks on, 211
Ploesti oilfields: air attacks on, 206, 245, 309
Poland, Captain A. L.: 167-9, 190-1
Polish Artillery: 1st Carpathian Field Regiment: 95
Pope, Lieut.-General V. V.: 1-2
Porpoise, H.M.S.: 326
Port Chalmers, m.v.: 320-1
Port Said: air attacks on, 337, 381
Portal, Air Chief Marshal Sir Charles, Chief of the Air Staff: 18, 123
Potaro, m.v.: 310
Pound, Admiral Sir Dudley, First Sea Lord and Chief of Naval Staff: and withdrawals from Mediterranean, 123; and supplies for Malta, 159, 316; mentioned, 177
Power, Rear-Admiral A. J.: 328
Premuda: 306
Prendergast, Lieut.-Colonel G. C.: 8
Pridham-Wippell, Vice-Admiral H. D.: 109, 178, 182
Prime Minister and Minister of Defence (Rt. Hon. Winston S. Churchill): and command in Western Desert, 1; on use of 50th (British) Division, 2; and operation 'Crusader', 3, 15; and Tobruk, 23-4, 248-9; and Auchinleck, 24, 201, 204-5, 367-9; and operation 'Gymnast', 120-2; visits Washington 121-2; and diversions and withdrawals, 123-5, 127-8; and northern front, 124, 362-4, 366; and reinforcements, 127, 364; tells Wavell to look East, 128; and defeat of British armour, 153; and Malta, 182, 187, 200, 203-4, 316; and timing of a resumed offensive, 199, 201-5; obtains Vote of Confidence, 200; and Persia and Iraq Command, 205, 375-6; and Battle of Gazala, 242; and fall of Tobruk, 275; and operation 'Torch', 361; visits Middle East and Russia, 362, 364, 366, 376; on priority of commitments, 363-4, 366-7; and Middle East commanders, 367, 368n; his directive to Alexander, 369; on state of 8th Army, 369-70
Prime Minister of Australia: *see* Menzies, Fadden *and* Curtin
Prime Minister of South Africa (Field-Marshal Smuts): forms South African administrative H.Q., 2; in Cairo with Churchill, 362, 364, 376; and Middle East Command, 367; and Middle East War Council, 374n; and Persia and Iraq Command, 376
Prince of Piedmont: 175
Prince of Wales, H.M.S.: 123
Princess Marguerite, transport: 328
Prinz Eugen: 162, 200
Prisoners: in operation 'Crusader', 46, 48, 50, 63, 67, 82-3, 96-7; in retreat to Gazala, 150; in Battle of Gazala, 226; at Tobruk, 274; at Alamein, 346, 349-51, 355; at Alam el Halfa, 386, 388
Procida: 105
Punnet, boom defence vessel: 337

Qotafiya: 381
Queen Elizabeth, H.M.S.: and human torpedo attacks, 115, 192, 329; mentioned, 117; repairs to, 315
Quinan, Lieut.-General E. P.: 129

Raeder, Admiral: 175
Ramsden, Major-General W. H. C.: commands 50th Division, 217; and Battle of Gazala, 251; commands 30th Corps, 345; and fighting at El Alamein, 345, 357
Ras Gibeisa: air attack on, 343
Ravenspoint, s.s.: 329
Ravenstein, Major-General Johann von: 55, 57-8, 64
Rawlings, Rear-Admiral H. B.: 105, 158
Red Sea: opened to American shipping, 3
Rees, Major-General T. W.: 218, 284n
Reeves, Captain J. W.: 182
Reeves, Lieut.-Colonel W. R.: 267-8
Regiments:
  Central India Horse: 39n
  3rd County of London Yeomanry (Sharpshooters): and operation 'Crusader', 40n, 88; and retreat to Gazala, 138n; and Battle of Gazala, 240n, 257; and retreat to El Alamein, 289n, 291; in fighting at El Alamein, 349n; 3rd/4th in Battle of Alam el Halfa, 386
  4th County of London Yeomanry (Sharpshooters): and operation 'Crusader', 40n, 88; and retreat to Gazala, 138n; and Battle of Gazala, 240n, 257; and retreat to El Alamein, 289n
  The Guides Cavalry: 342n
  4th Hussars: 240n
  7th Hussars: 40n
  8th Hussars: and operation 'Crusader', 48, 68; in Battle of Gazala, 224, 240n
  10th (Royal) Hussars: and retreat to Gazala, 138n, 144-5, 153; in fighting at El Alamein, 349n
  11th Hussars: 85n, 86, 138n
  The King's Dragoon Guards: and operation 'Crusader', 40, 43n, 62-3, 88
  9th Lancers: and retreat to Gazala, 138n, 144, 145n, 153; and Battle of Gazala, 257; and retreat to El Alamein, 289n; in fighting at El Alamein, 349n, 356

Regiments—*cont.*
12th Lancers: 73, 88
New Zealand Divisional Cavalry: 95
Nottinghamshire Yeomanry: 387n
The Queen's Bays: and retreat to Gazala, 138n, 143-5; in Battle of Gazala, 240n; and retreat to El Alamein, 289n, 291
The Royal Dragoons: 73
2nd Royal Gloucestershire Hussars: and operation 'Crusader', 40n, 85n, 88; in Battle of Gazala, 240n; in fighting at El Alamein, 349n; in Battle of Alam el Halfa, 386
The Royal Scots Greys: 349n, 386
Staffordshire Yeomanry: 387n
Royal Tank Regiment:
1st Battalion (also 1st/6th): and operation 'Crusader', 43n, 45; in Battle of Gazala, 240n, 257; and retreat to El Alamein, 289n; in Battle of Alam el Halfa, 386n
2nd Battalion: 30n, 40n, 45
3rd Battalion (also 3rd/5th): and operation 'Crusader', 40, 88-9; in Battle of Gazala, 224, 240n, 257; in fighting at El Alamein, 349n, 356n; in Battle of Alam el Halfa, 387n
4th Battalion: and relief of Tobruk, 25; and operation 'Crusader', 43n, 45, 66, 82n; in Battle of Gazala, 232-3, 262, 267-9
5th Battalion: and operation 'Crusader', 40n, 68; in Battle of Gazala, 231; in Battle of Alam el Halfa, 386
6th Battalion: and operation 'Crusader', 40n, 45; in Battle of Gazala, 240n; and retreat to El Alamein, 289n; in fighting at El Alamein, 349n, 356, 358
7th Battalion: and operation 'Crusader', 43n; in Battle of Gazala, 243, 262, 268-9
8th Battalion: and operation 'Crusader', 50, 61n, 75, 95; and retreat to El Alamein, 289n; in fighting at El Alamein, 346
40th Battalion: 356, 388
42nd Battalion: 48, 227
44th Battalion: and operation 'Crusader', 48, 61n, 62, 95; in Battle of Gazala, 227; in fighting at El Alamein, 346, 351
46th Battalion: 356, 389
50th Battalion: 356n, 357-8, 389
4th South African Armoured Car: 223
6th South African Armoured Car: 38
Reid, Brigadier D. W.: commands Oasis Force, 38; and operation 'Crusader', 50-1, 89; mentioned, 254; and retreat to El Alamein, 294
Renown, H.M.S.: 182, 187
Renton, Brigadier J. M. L.: 223, 237
Repulse, H.M.S.: 123
Resource, repair ship: 315
Rhodes: bombardment of, 163; air attacks on, 211
Ribbentrop, Herr von: 131
Richards, Brigadier G. W.: 224, 257, 387n
Richards, Colonel H. McA.: 264, 272
Rintelen, General Enno von: and supplies, 70, 378; mentioned, 277; and an advance into Egypt, 338
Ritchie, Lieut.-General N. M.: commands 8th Army, 61, 285; and operation 'Crusader', 62-3, 66-70, 73-5, 77-8, 81, 85, 88, 92, 95, 97; and Coningham, 98; and retreat to Gazala, 142-3, 145-9, 151; and Godwin-Austen, 152; and Tobruk, 197, 245-9; and timing of a renewed offensive, 198, 204; mentioned, 205; and Battle of Gazala, 216, 218, 223, 226, 228-9, 231-2, 234, 236, 238, 241-2, 244; and Tobruk, 197, 245-9, 253, 255, 258-9, 263-4, 272-3, 275; and timing of a resumed offensive, 198, 204; forces of, 217, 238; and 'Jock' columns, 254, 286; his tasks, 260; and a withdrawal to Matruh, 279, 281; relieved of command, 285; and Auchinleck, 285-6
'Robcol': 342
Roberts, Brigadier G. P. B.: 386n
Roberts, Lieutenant P. S. W.: 174
Robertson, Brigadier C. B.: 389
Rochester Castle, m.v.: 320-1
Rodney, H.M.S.: 316-7
Rommel, General (later Field-Marshal) Erwin: and operation 'Crusader', 7, 9, 21, 31, 38-42, 44, 47-50, 53-9, 61, 66, 69, 71, 74-8, 84-6, 89, 91-2, 95-6, 132; supplies and reinforcements for, 19-21, 69, 76, 126, 145, 159, 193-4, 197, 219, 226, 339, 377-8, 381-2; his command, 19-20, 80, 286; and Tobruk, 20-1, 31, 38, 41, 44, 64, 103, 193-5, 219, 258, 265-7, 269, 275, 277, 392; and Bastico, 21, 97-8; nearly captured, 34, 56; criticizes Italians, 79; regains initiative, 96, 133; his abilities, 97, 152; and Kesselring, 98; and advance to Gazala, 139-49, 151-3; and Malta, 193, 219; and a resumed offensive, 212, 216, 219; and Battle of Gazala, 219, 223, 225-31, 233-5, 237-41, 249, 252-3, 257; and Crüwell, 227; promoted Field-Marshal, 275; and an advance into Egypt, 277-8, 392 ; mentioned, 280, 283, 361, 364-6, 369-70; and advance to El Alamein, 289-90, 296 ; and fighting at El Alamein, 296-7, 331-4, 340-6, 356, 359-60, 363, 381; on failure of his plans, 338-9; and Battle of Alam el Halfa, 381-3, 386-8, 391; his health, 382-3
Roosevelt, President: mentioned, 120-1, 316; and reinforcements for Middle East, 127, 182, 187, 278-9, 374; and operation 'Torch', 361; and lend-lease, 373
Rosolino Pilo: 326
Rostov: Russians recapture, 132
Rowallan Castle, s.s.: 158-60
Royal Air Force in Middle East: *see also* Western Desert Air Force; strength and state of, 12, 14-5, 20, 31, 178, 205-6, 213, 220, 374-5, 385, 392, 414-9; reinforcement and rearmament of, 13, 76, 93, 205-6, 365, 372, 374-5; and aircraft maintenance, 13, 92; tasks of, 15, 209, 211, 373; and attacks on enemy shipping, 16, 70, 93, 102, 107-8,

Royal Air Force in Middle East—*cont.*
159, 189-90, 325-6, 391; its superiority in Mediterranean, 76; attacks enemy transport aircraft, 79; and withdrawals and diversions, 123, 205-6; and convoy operations, 156-7, 164-5, 190-1, 251, 309-11; problems of, 372-5
(in North Africa) strength of, 6, 14-5; and operation 'Crusader', 8, 15-8, 38, 41, 51, 60, 62-3, 68-9, 71, 76, 80, 93, 98-9; losses of, 9, 51, 99, 150, 211, 213, 227, 230-1, 236-7, 307, 311, 336, 347, 381; and Tobruk, 271; and retreat to Gazala 150; attacks Benghazi, 190; operations during the lull, 209-13; and Battle of Gazala, 224-5, 227, 229-30, 234, 236-7, 244; and a withdrawal to Matruh, 281; August operations, 379-81; and Battle of Alam el Halfa, 385, 387-91
(in Malta) strength and state of, 14-5, 159, 162, 179, 317; operations and losses of, 15, 17-8, 51, 70, 79, 93-4, 99, 148, 150, 157-60, 162, 170-1, 173, 179, 181-2, 184-5, 188, 209, 211, 213, 302-3, 306, 312-5, 321, 326, 379; supplies and reinforcements for, 156, 182-3, 187-8, 193
Groups:
No. 201 (Naval Co-operation): and operation 'Crusader', 19; and Malta convoys, 157, 307; strength and state of, 173, 282; and enemy shipping, 326, 379-80
204: 12
205: helps Desert Air Force, 12; operations of, 16, 70, 150, 212, 244, 288, 345; strength and state of, 385
211: 139, 207
Wings :
No. 233: 207, 288
234: 282
239: 207
240 (later 285): 380
243: 207
258: 79, 207
262: and operation 'Crusader', 79, 86; and retreat to Gazala, 142; replaced, 207
266: 123, 125
267: 122
270: 94, 96
Squadrons:
No. 6: 235
10: 347
11: 57, 93
13 (Hellenic): 300n
14: 57, 96, 282
18: 106
21: 150
30: 128
33: and operation 'Crusader', 50, 86, 93; and retreat to Gazala, 144; and fighting at El Alamein 343n
37: 343n

Royal Air Force in Middle East—*cont.*
Squadrons—*cont.*
No. 38: attacks Tripoli 15; and Malta convoys, 300n, attacks Italian Fleet, 311, 313; and fighting at El Alamein, 343n
39: and enemy shipping, 159, 163, 171, 311, 326; and Malta convoys, 300n
40: 343n
45: and operation 'Crusader', 51, 57, 93n, 96; leaves for Far East, 123
47: 300n
55: 343n
69: 103, 300n
70: 343n
73: 210, 343n, 373
80: 43, 208n, 343n
84: and operation 'Crusader', 57, 93n, 96; leaves for Far East, 123
86: 326
89: 212
104: 343n
107: 106
108: 343n
112: 51, 295, 343n
113: 50, 123
126: 300n
127: 282
145: 230, 343n
148: 343n
162: 343n
185: 179, 300n
202: 192
203: 192, 300n
208: and operation 'Crusader', 86; and retreat to Gazala, 140; withdrawn, 210; works with 30th Corps, 212; and Battle of Gazala, 230; and fighting at El Alamein, 343n; state of, 380; its operations in August, 380
211: 123
213: 343n
217: 300n, 311
221: 189, 300n
223: 282, 343n
227: 309n, 326
229: 179
230: 174, 300n
233: 192
235: 300n
237 (Rhodesian): 86
249: 300n
250: and retreat to Gazala, 149; and defence of Tobruk, 259; and retreat to El Alamein, 295; and 'Vigorous' convoy, 309n; and fighting at El Alamein, 343n
252: and Malta convoys, 157, 309n; for Desert Air Force, 282; and fighting at El Alamein, 343n; to intercept air transport traffic, 347
260: 343n

Royal Air Force in Middle East—*cont.*
Squadrons—*cont.*
No. 261: 128
272: and operation 'Crusader', 93; and retreat to Gazala, 147; and Malta convoys, 157, 309n; and enemy convoys, 191; for Desert Air Force, 282; and fighting at El Alamein, 343n; to intercept air transport traffic, 347
274: 295, 343n
335 (Hellenic): 282, 343n
601: 300n
603: 300n
Alsace: 282, 343n
Lorraine: 57, 96
Flights:
No. 1435: 188, 300n
1437 (Strategical Reconnaissance): 15, 380
Survey: 15
Other Units:
Aircraft Replacement Pool: 12
No. 1 Armoured Car Company: 142
No. 2 Armoured Car Company: 142, 256
No. 2 Photographic Reconnaissance Unit: 15, 300n, 380
Royal Artillery: *see also* Royal Horse Artillery
Brigades:
4th Anti-Aircraft: 262
7th Light Anti-Aircraft: 179
10th Heavy Anti-Aircraft: 179
Regiments:
4th Heavy Anti-Aircraft: 179n
7th Heavy Anti-Aircraft: 179n
10th Heavy Anti-Aircraft: 179n
32nd Light Anti-Aircraft: 179n
65th Light Anti-Aircraft: 179n
74th Light Anti-Aircraft: 179n
65th (Norfolk Yeomanry) Anti-Tank: 48n, 138n, 387n
73rd Anti-Tank: and operation 'Crusader', 75, 82n; and retreat to Gazala, 138n; in fighting at El Alamein, 356n
76th Anti-Tank: 137, 138n
1st Field: 48n, 57, 138n
4th Field: 233-4
8th Field: 138n
11th Field: 342n, 348n
12th Field: 187
25th Field: and operation 'Crusader', 48n, 57n; at Tobruk, 262, 264, 268
28th Field: 233-4
31st Field: 82n
51st Field: and operation 'Crusader', 45n, 75, 85n; and retreat to Gazala, 138n
58th Field: 389n
60th Field: 45, 45n, 64n
72nd Field: 227n
74th Field: 387n
97th Field (Kent Yeomanry): at Belhamed, 256n, 258; in fighting at El Alamein, 340n; in Battle of Alam el Halfa, 387n

Royal Artillery—*cont.*
Regiments—*cont.*
121st Field: 340n
124th Field: 340n
144th Field: 43n
157th Field: 233-4
7th Medium: and operation 'Crusader', 48n, 75; in Battle of Gazala, 227n; in Battle of Alam el Halfa, 389n
64th Medium: 389n
67th Medium: 95, 262, 264
68th Medium: 57n, 95, 262, 264
4th Searchlight (R.A./R.M.A.): 179n
Batteries:
6th Light Anti-Aircraft: 138n
37th Light Anti-Aircraft: 356n
43rd Light Anti-Aircraft: 138n
44th Light Anti-Aircraft: 138n
57th Light Anti-Aircraft: 57n
81st/25th Light Anti-Aircraft: 227n
122nd Light Anti-Aircraft: 91n
197th Light Anti-Aircraft: 138n
225th Light Anti-Aircraft: 179n
277th Heavy Anti-Aircraft: 269
'A' 95th Anti-Tank: 262
227th Anti-Tank: 389n
237th Anti-Tank: 145n
259th Anti-Tank (Norfolk Yeomanry): 227n
432nd Anti-Tank: 389n
12/25th Field: 262n
31/58th Field: 262n
62nd Field: 249
203rd Field: 64n
287th Field: 262n
25/26th Medium: 227n
27/28th Medium: 138n
211th Medium: 95
231st Medium: 269
Royal Australian Air Force:
Squadrons:
No. 3: in operation 'Crusader', 51, 93; withdrawal to El Alamein, 295; and fighting at El Alamein, 343n
450: 343n
451: 41, 96
459: 300n
Royal Engineers:
2nd Field Company: 43n
54th Field Company: 43n
232nd Field Company: 227n
1st Field Squadron: 138n
7th Field Squadron: 138n
Royal Horse Artillery:
Regiments:
1st: and operation 'Crusader', 43n, 65; and Battle of Gazala, 257; in fighting at El Alamein, 356; in Battle of Alam el Halfa, 386
2nd: and operation 'Crusader', 40n, 63n, 91n; and retreat to Gazala, 138n, 141n
3rd: 45, 45n, 348n
4th: and operation 'Crusader', 40n, 45, 63n, 64n; in Battle of Gazala, 224n
5th: 356n

Royal Horse Artillery—*cont.*
Regiments—*cont.*
11th (Honourable Artillery Company): and retreat to Gazala, 137, 138n, 145n; in Battle of Gazala, 242; in fighting at El Alamein, 342n, 348n
102nd (Northumberland Hussars) Anti-Tank: and operation 'Crusader', 40n, 63n, 91n; and retreat to Gazala, 138n, 141n
104th: and operation 'Crusader', 43n, 65-6; in fighting at El Alamein, 348n; in Battle of Alam el Halfa, 386
107th: 43n, 65-6, 233-4
Battery: 'C', 40n, 224n
Royal Malta Artillery: 179
Regiments:
3rd Light Anti-Aircraft: 179n
11th Heavy Anti-Aircraft: 179n
Battery: 14th Heavy (Relief) Anti-Aircraft, 179n
Royal Navy: *see* Mediterranean Fleet
Russell, Brigadier D.: 82
Russell, Brigadier H. E.: 2
Russia: German operations in, 20, 128, 132; probable resumption of German offensive in, 126
Ruweisat Ridge: mentioned, 332; actions at, 335, 347-51, 353-7
Rye, minesweeper: 322

Sagona, tanker: 115
Sainthill, Major H. M.: 270-1, 273-4
Salamis: air attacks on, 211
Salvia, H.M.S.: 90
Samos, s.s.: 25
Sanandrea: 326, 382n
Santa Elisa, s.s. (American): 320
Scharnhorst: 162, 200
Schmitt, Major-General Artur: 95-6
Scirè: 115, 117, 329
Scobie, Major-General R. M.: commands Tobruk garrison, 25, 38; and operation 'Crusader', 42, 46, 48, 61, 69
Scott-Cockburn, Brigadier J.: 39
Scythia, H.M.T.: 353n
'Seacol': 219
Sea Communications: between Italy and North Africa, 16, 173; control of in Mediterranean, 96, 124-5, 329-30; effect of North African fighting on, 315
Securitas: 209
Seidemann, Major-General Hans: 381, 390
Sherwell, Lieut.-Colonel O. W.: 271
Shingler, Brigadier General Don G.: 374n
Shuntien, m.v.: 90
Sicily: air attacks on, 17, 79, 148, 150, 206
Sidi Barrani: air attacks on, 295
Sidi Muftah: defended locality at, 223; 150th Brigade at, 227-9
Sidi Omar: capture of, 48
Sidi Rezegh: airfield captured, 40; action at, 44-8; British capture, 62; enemy capture, 67; air attacks on, 256
Sikh, H.M.S.: 109-10, 165, 168
Singapore: fall of, 200
Sirius, H.M.S.: 317
Sirocco: 170
Sirry, Hussein, Pasha: 130
Sirte: air attacks on, 60; First Battle of, 112; Second Battle of, 166-70, 177
Slatter, Air Vice-Marshal L. H.: 157
Smith, Captain F. M.: 262, 269
Smuts, Field-Marshal: *see* Prime Minister of South Africa
Smythe, Sergeant Q.: 231
Sollum: capture of, 95-6; demolitions at, 296
Somali, H.M.S.: 320
Somerville, Vice-Admiral Sir James: receives replacements, 117; and withdrawals, 123; relinquishes command of Force H, 163; and convoy operations, 184, 308
Soudan, s.s.: 330n
South African Air Force: in operation 'Crusader', 51
Squadrons:
No. 1: 282, 343n
2: 343n
4: 343n
5: 343n
12: attacks enemy raiding column, 9; and operation 'Crusader', 57, 87; state of, 87; and Battle of Gazala, 227; and fighting at El Alamein, 343n
21: 57, 87, 93
24: 9, 76, 343n
40: relieves No. 208 R.A.F., 210; works with 13th Corps, 212; and Battle of Gazala, 230; at Tobruk, 258; withdrawn from Tobruk, 263
South African Artillery:
Regiments:
2nd Light Anti-Aircraft: 262
2nd Anti-Tank: 57n, 138n
2nd Field: 262, 264, 271
3rd Field: 262, 264, 271
5th Field: 95n
7th Field: 95, 138n
Batteries:
6th Anti-Tank: 262
2nd Field: 262n
5th Field: 268-9
6th Field: 242
9th Field: 268-9
19th Field: 145n
21st Field: 144
Southwold, H.M.S.: 171
Special Air Service Brigade (later 1st S.A.S. Regiment): raids Gazala and Tmimi, 17; and operation 'Crusader', 89; and fighting at El Alamein, 344, 358
Sportivo: 382n, 388
Stalin, Premier: 362, 366
Stephan, Colonel: 40
Stirling, Major D.: 344
Stokes, Commander G. H.: 109-11, 117
'Stopcol': 219

Submarines:
(British) and enemy convoys, 107, 158, 174, 189, 326; carry supplies to Malta, 155, 173, 189, 325-6; losses of, 74, 189, 192-3; strength of, 178; in convoy operations, 326; tasks of, 328
(German) arrive in Mediterranean, 108; operations and losses of, 117-8, 174, 192, 216, 328-9; strength of, 118, 178, 411
(Italian) operations and losses of, 117, 174, 328-9; strength of, 178, 411
Submarine Flotillas:
1st: 308, 313, 326
8th: 326
10th: at Malta, 185, 314; and 'Vigorous' convoy, 308, 311
'Substance': 320, 324
Suda Bay: air attacks on, 336
Suez: air attacks on, 17
Suez Canal: air attacks on, 212; mining of, 337; enemy plan to capture, 382
Sümmermann, Major-General Max: 80
Support Groups:
1st: relieves 7th, 137; state of, 138; and retreat to Gazala, 140-1, 143-5
7th: on the frontier, 9; and operation 'Crusader', 39, 41-2, 44, 45n, 49, 54, 56, 62-5, 75, 81, 84-6, 88-9; relief of, 137-8
8th: 353n
Sutlej, H.M.I.S.: 124
Syfret, Rear-Admiral E. N.: 162-3, 317-20, 322
Syria: defence of, 124, 126, 363; internal security of, 362

Takali: air attacks on, 182
Takoradi air route: aircraft deliveries by, 13, 282, 283n
Talabot, m.v.: 164, 170-2, 178
Talisman, H.M.S.: 21, 328
Tamet: raid on, 89
Tanimbar, m.v.: 301-2
Tanks:
American:
Stuart light: arrive in Middle East, 4; description of, 28, 71, 100, 214, 243
M3 (Grant): arrival of, 214; description of, 214-5, 243; distribution of, 215; mentioned, 279n
Sherman: for Middle East, 278-9
British: supply of, 4-5, 31; description of, 27-8; distribution of, 30-1, 215; losses of, 91-2, 100, 233, 243, 391; repair of, 243; performance of, 369, 434-44
Matilda: arrive in Middle East, 4; description of, 27, 391
Crusader: defects of, 5, 27, 71, 198; changes in, 214
Valentine: description of, 27, 391; distribution of, 220
German: performance of, 369, 434-44
Pzkw II, III, IV: description of, 26-7, 214, 346n; supply and distribution of, 30, 214, 220; losses of, 92, 100, 239
Tanks—*cont.*
Italian: distribution of, 30, 220; losses of, 100; particulars of, 441
M13/40: description of, 27
M14/41: 220
Note on tanks, armour and anti-tank guns: 434-44
Tedder, Air Marshal (later Air Chief Marshal) Sir Arthur: *see also* Commanders-in-Chief; and operation 'Crusader', 3, 18, 24, 97-8; and maintenance, 13; and relief of Tobruk, 24-5; and retreat to Gazala, 147; and Malta, 181; and Dobbie, 186; mentioned, 198, 315; and rearmament and reinforcement, 206, 230, 374; commitments of, 209; and operation 'Vigorous', 307; and support for 8th Army, 335; promoted Air Chief Marshal, 335n; on airfield construction, 373; and Persia and Iraq, 376
Tell el Eisa: actions at, 335, 345-7, 357, 388
Tennant, Rear-Admiral W. G.: 308, 310
Thailand: Japanese attack on, 128
Thermopylae, m.v.: 157
Theron, Major-General F. H.: 2, 263
Thompson, Brigadier L. F.: 262, 269
Thorgrim, H.M.S.A.S.: 90
Thorn, H.M.S.: 328
Thrasher, H.M.S.: 174, 192
'Tiger': 136, 324
Tirpitz: 162
Tmimi: air attacks on, 17, 41, 43, 210, 212, 225, 230, 244
Tobruk: siege of, 10-11, 24, 28, 44, 53, 70, 78-9, 259; air attacks on, 17, 22, 25, 212, 336, 339, 345, 352, 379, 388; question of Axis attack on, 19-22, 29, 31, 38-9, 41, 103, 193-5, 219-20; importance of, 22; defence and defences of, 22, 33, 52, 67, 197-8, 245-51, 253-5, 258-64; relief of Australian troops in, 23-5; actions at, 44-9, 264-73; as a supply base, 90-1, 135, 215, 244, 325, 378, 382; fall of, 273-5, 277-9, 296, 392
Tobruk Garrison: 22-5, 29-30, 38
Todd, Commodore P.: 328
Torbay, H.M.S.: 21, 174
'Torch': 367, 369
Toscano, Vice-Admiral Antonino: 109
Treaties, etc.: Anglo-Soviet-Persian, 129; Anglo-Egyptian, 130; Tripartite Pact, 131; Soviet-Japanese Pact of Neutrality, 131
Trento: 104, 169, 310-12
Trieste: 104-5
Tripoli: air attacks on, 15-7, 79, 93, 102, 148, 150, 206, 209
Tripolitania: air attacks on, 17, 149; defence of, 84, 152; supplies to, 94; plans to advance into, 119-20, 199, 364; enemy air forces in, 140
Troilus, m.v.: 301, 305
Tuker, Major-General F. I. S.: commands 4th Indian Division, 137; and retreat to Gazala, 145, 148-9, 151
Turkey: threat of attack through, 2, 126; aid for, 124; conference with, 124n

U.73: 318
U.74: 192

*U.*75: 90
*U.*79: 90
*U.*81: 108
*U.*133: 157
*U.*205: 313
*U.*331: 22n, 109
*U.*372: 315, 329
*U.*557: 110
*U.*565: 163
*U.*568: 192
*U.*573: 192
*U.*652: 328
Una, H.M.S.: 328
United States Army Forces in Middle East: 374
United States Army Middle East Air Force: *see also* Halverson Detachment; reinforcements for, 283; operations of, 311; integration of, 374-5; and Battle of Alam el Halfa, 385
United States Chiefs of Staff: and conduct of War, 122; and Halverson Detachment, 309
United States Military Iranian Mission: 373-4
United States Military North African Mission: 373-4
United States of America: flow of munitions from, 3-4; entry into war of, 96, 121, 200; and operation 'Gymnast', 120; and operation 'Torch', 361; increasingly active in Middle East, 373-5
United States Persian Gulf Service Command: 374, 426
Unwin, Brigadier E. S.: 2
Upham, Captain C. H.: 293, 350
Upholder, H.M.S.: 104, 171, 192-3
Urge, H.M.S.: 110, 171, 192-3
Utmost, H.M.S.: 105

Vaerst, Lieut.-General Gustav von: 227, 383, 386
Valiant, H.M.S.: and enemy convoys, 109; and human torpedo attacks, 115, 192, 329; mentioned, 117; leaves for Durban, 192
Vallentin, Brigadier C. M.: 138, 144
'Venezia': 223
Veniero: 328
Vian, Rear-Admiral Sir Philip: commands 15th Cruiser Squadron, 110; and enemy convoys, 110, 163; in convoy operations, 111-13, 157, 159-60, 164-72, 180, 183n, 307-8, 310-13, 316; mentioned, 117, 158; leaves 15th Cruiser Squadron, 328
Vice-Admiral, Malta: *see* Ford *and* Leatham
Vice-Chief of the Air Staff: *see* Freeman
Vice-Chief of the Imperial General Staff: *see* Nye
Vichy Government: 121
Victoria: 159
Victorious, H.M.S.: 182, 316, 319
'Vigorous': mentioned, 245, 251, 255-6, 315-6, 324, 328; plan for, 299-300, 307-9; description of operation, 307-13
Vittorio Veneto: 110, 310
Vivaldi: 304-6
Volo, m.v.: 90
Volturno: 106
Voroshilov, Marshal: 366
Wachtfels: 326
Wafd Party: 130
Waimarama, m.v.: 320-1
Wairangi, m.v.: 320
Wakenshaw, Private A.: 289
Waldau. Lieut.-General Otto Hoffmann von: reinforcements for, 193; forces of, 212; on lack of army/air co-operation, 227, 336; on misuse of air forces, 235; on R.A.F. performance, 337; on shortage of fighters and fuel, 339; commands Fliegerkorps X, 381
Waller, Brigadier R. B.: 348n
'Wall Group': 348
Walter, Captain P. N.: 262, 270
Wanklyn, Lieut.-Commander M. D.: 193
War Cabinet: *see also* Defence Committee; and Tobruk, 23; should be represented in Middle East, 129; mentioned, 130; and Dobbie, 186; and timing of a resumed offensive, 198, 201, 203-4; on Middle East Command, 368; and Persia and Iraq Command, 375-6
War Office: 23, 362, 391
Ward Gunn, 2nd Lieutenant G.: 44
Warspite, H.M.S.: 184, 308
Warszawa, m.v.: 90
Wasp, U.S.S.: carries fighters for Malta, 155, 182, 187, 300, 318
Watkins, Brigadier H. R. B.: 37, 95
Wavell, General Sir Archibald: mentioned, 2-3, 10, 368; and 17th Indian Division, 123; and Iraq and Persia Command, 128, 375; in Cairo with Churchill, 362, 364, 366; appointed Viceroy of India, 376
Welshman, H.M.S.: carries supplies to Malta, 155, 187-9, 300, 306, 314, 324-5
Western Cyrenaica: air attacks on enemy airfields in, 51; maintenance of forces in, 94; air superiority in, 99; threat to, 141; British reoccupation of, 161; effect of loss of airfields in, 197
Western Desert Air Force: strength and state of, 12, 18, 31, 139-40, 205, 210, 220, 230, 282-3, 385, 392, 420-3; mobility of, 13; training of, 13, 207, 373; and air support, 14, 35, 208, 256, 352; and operation 'Crusader', 14, 17, 35, 38, 41, 51, 55, 57, 60, 74-6, 83, 86-7, 92-3, 96, 98, 205; losses of, 51, 60, 76, 79, 99, 213, 227, 237, 241-2, 258, 288; and Tobruk, 90, 275; co-operates with 8th Army, 98, 294, 296, 370; and retreat to Gazala, 148-9; reorganization of, 205-9; and defence of airfields, 208; operations during the lull, 210-13; and Battle of Gazala, 224-5, 227, 230, 234-5, 237, 239, 241, 255-6, 258-9; and 'Vigorous' convoy, 251; reinforcements for, 282, 372, 375, 393; and a withdrawal to Matruh, 283, 287-8; and withdrawal to El Alamein, 293-6, 335, 373; based on Egypt, 335; and fighting at El Alamein, 343, 346, 352, 358, 361; and Battle of Alam el Halfa, 383, 385
Western Desert Escort Force: 24n, 90
Western Desert Force: becomes 13th Corps, 1
Westphal, Colonel Siegfried: and operation 'Crusader', 58; and advance to Gazala, 139; and Battle of Gazala, 226; wounded, 229

Weygand, General Maxime: 120-1
Wheeler, Brigadier General Raymond A.: 373-4
Whiteley, Brigadier J. F. M.: 272
Whyte, Lieut.-Colonel I. B.: 271
Willison, Brigadier A. C.: commands 32nd Army Tank Brigade, 38; and operation 'Crusader', 43, 61-2; at Tobruk, 261, 263, 267-8, 271
Wilson, General Sir Henry Maitland: 1, 376
Wishart, H.M.S.: 192
Wolverine, H.M.S.: 318
Wrestler, H.M.S.: 192

Yarra, H.M.A.S.: 124

Zaffiro: 115, 328
Zulu, H.M.S.: 165

Wt. 2466 9/59 K24 C.B.&S.Ltd. Gp. 1246 S.O. Code No. 63-111-23-3*

HISTORY OF THE SECOND WORLD WAR

UNITED KINGDOM MILITARY SERIES

Reprinted by the Naval & Military Press in twenty two volumes with the permission of the Controller of HMSO and Queen's Printer for Scotland.

THE DEFENCE OF THE UNITED KINGDOM

Basil Collier

Official history of Britain's home front in the Second World War, from the Phoney War, through the Battle of Britain and the Blitz to victory in Europe.
ISBN: 1845740556
Price £22.00

THE CAMPAIGN IN NORWAY

T. H. Derry

The catastrophic 1940 campaign which caused the downfall of Neville Chamberlain and brought Winston Churchill to power.
ISBN: 1845740572
Price: £22.00

THE WAR IN FRANCE AND FLANDERS 1939-1940

Major L. F. Ellis

The role of the BEF in the fall of France and the retreat to Dunkirk.
ISBN: 1845740564
Price £22.00

VICTORY IN THE WEST

Volume I: The Battle of Normandy

Major L. F. Ellis

The build-up, execution and consequences of D-Day in 1944.
ISBN: 1845740580
Price: £22.00

Volume II: The Defeat of Germany

Major L. F. Ellis

The final stages of the liberation of western Europe in 1944-45.
ISBN: 1845740599
Price £22.00

www.naval-military-press.com

THE MEDITERRANEAN AND MIDDLE EAST

Volume I: The Early Successes against Italy [to May 1941]

Major-General I. S. O. Playfair

Britain defeats Italy on land and sea in Africa and the Mediterranean in 1940.
ISBN: 1845740653
Price: £22.00

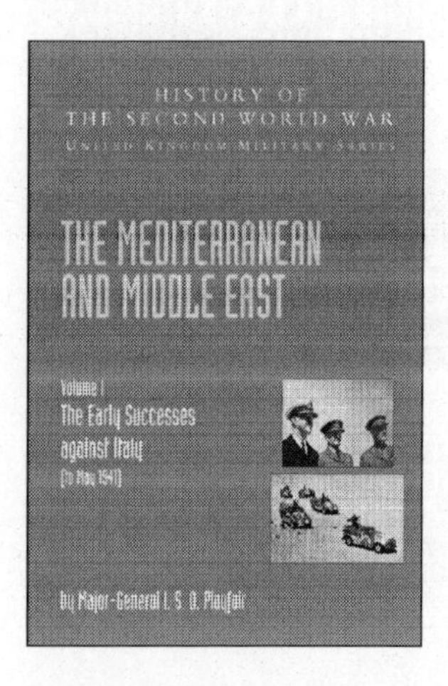

Volume II: The Germans Come to the Help of their Ally (1941)

Major-General I. S. O. Playfair

Rommel rides to Italy's rescue, Malta is bombarded, Yugoslavia, Greece and Crete are lost, and Iraq and Syria are secured for the Allies.
ISBN: 1845740661
Price: £22.00

Volume III: (September 1941 to September 1942) British Fortunes reach their Lowest Ebb

Major-General I. S. O. Playfair

Britain's darkest hour in North Africa and the Mediterranean, 1941-42.
ISBN: 184574067X
Price: £22.00

Volume IV: The Destruction of the Axis Forces in Africa

Major-General I. S. O. Playfair

The battle of El Alamein and 'Operation Torch' bring the Allies victory in North Africa, 1942-43.
ISBN: 1845740688
Price: £22.00

Volume V: The Campaign in Sicily 1943 and the Campaign in Italy — 3rd Sepember 1943 to 31st March 1944

Major-General I. S. O. Playfair

The Allies invade Sicily and Italy, but encounter determined German defence in 1943-44.
ISBN: 1845740696
Price: £22.00

Volume VI: Victory in the Mediterranean Part I: 1st April to 4th June 1944

Brigadier C. J. C. Molony

The Allies breach the Gustav, Hitler and Caesar Lines and occupy Rome.
ISBN: 184574070X
Price: £22.00

Volume VI: Victory in the Mediterranean Part II: June to October 1944

General Sir William Jackson

The 1944 Italian summer campaign breaches the Gothic Line but then bogs down again.
ISBN: 1845740718
Price: £22.00

Volume VI: Victory in the Mediterranean Part III: November 1944 to May 1945

General Sir William Jackson

The messy end of the war in Italy, Greece, and Yugoslavia.
ISBN: 1845740726
Price: £22.00

THE WAR AGAINST JAPAN

Volume I: The Loss of Singapore

Major-General S. Woodburn Kirby

The fall of Hong Kong, Malaya and Singapore in 1941-42.
ISBN: 1845740602
Price: £22.00

Volume II: India's Most Dangerous Hour

Major-General S. Woodburn Kirby

The loss of Burma and Japan's threat to India in 1941-42.
ISBN: 1845740610
Price: £22.00

Volume III: The Decisive Battles

Major-General S. Woodburn Kirby

Turning the tide in the war against Japan at the battles of Kohima, Imphal and the Chindit campaigns.
ISBN: 1845740629
Price: £22.00

Volume IV: The Reconquest of Burma

Major-General S. Woodburn Kirby

The reconquest of Burma by Bill Slim's 'forgotten' 14th Army.
ISBN: 1845740637
Price: £22.00

Volume V: The Surrender of Japan

Major-General S. Woodburn Kirby

Victory in South-East Asia in 1945 - from Rangoon to Nagasaki.
ISBN: 1845740645
Price: £22.00

www.naval-military-press.com

THE WAR AT SEA - 1939—1945

Captain Roskill has long been recognised as the leading authority on The Royal Navy's part in the Second World War. His official History is unlikely ever to be superceded. His narrative is highly readable and the analysis is clear. Roskill describes sea battles, convoy actions and the contribution made by technology in the shape of Asdic & Radar.

Volume I: The Defensive

Captain S. W. Roskill, D.S.C., R.N.

2004 N&MP reprint (original pub 1954).
SB. xxii + 664pp with 43 maps and numerous contemporary photos.
ISBN: 1843428032
Price: £32.00

Volume II: The Period of Balance

Captain S. W. Roskill, D.S.C., R.N.

2004 N&MP reprint (original pub 1956).
SB. xvi + 523pp with 42 maps and numerous contemporary photos.
ISBN: 1843428040
Price: £32.00

Volume III: Part I The Offensive 1st June 1943-31 May 1944

Captain S. W. Roskill, D.S.C., R.N.

2004 N&MP reprint (original pub 1960).
SB. xv + 413pp with 21 maps and numerous contemporary photos.
ISBN: 1843428059
Price: £32.00

Volume III: Part 2 The Offensive 1st June 1944-14th August 1945

Captain S. W. Roskill, D.S.C., R.N.

2004 N&MP reprint (original pub 1961).
SB. xvi + 502pp with 46 maps and numerous contemporary photos.
ISBN: 1843428067
Price: £32.00

www.naval-military-press.com

1378267R0

Printed in Great Britain by
Amazon.co.uk, Ltd.,
Marston Gate.